Successful Strategies
Triumphing in War and Peace from Antiquity to the Present

Successful Strategies is a fascinating new study of the key factors that have contributed to the development and execution of successful strategies throughout history. With a team of leading historians, Williamson Murray and Richard Hart Sinnreich examine how, and to what effect, states, individuals, and military organizations have found a solution to complex and seemingly insoluble strategic problems to reach success. Bringing together grand, political and military strategy, the book features thirteen essays each of which explores a unique case or aspect of strategy. The focus ranges from individuals such as Themistocles, Bismarck, and Roosevelt to organizations and bureaucratic responses. Whether discussing grand strategy in peacetime or that of war or politics, these case studies are unified by their common goal of identifying in each case the key factors that contributed to success as well as providing insights essential to any understanding of the strategic challenges of the future.

WILLIAMSON MURRAY is Adjunct Professor at the US Marine Corps University and Emeritus Professor at The Ohio State University.

RICHARD HART SINNREICH is President of Carrick Communications, Inc.

D1592806

Successful Strategies

Triumphing in War and Peace from Antiquity to the Present

Edited by

Williamson Murray and Richard Hart Sinnreich

CAMBRIDGE
UNIVERSITY PRESS

CAMBRIDGE
UNIVERSITY PRESS

University Printing House, Cambridge CB2 8BS, United Kingdom

Cambridge University Press is part of the University of Cambridge.

It furthers the University's mission by disseminating knowledge in the pursuit of education, learning and research at the highest international levels of excellence.

www.cambridge.org
Information on this title: www.cambridge.org/9781107633599

© Williamson Murray and Richard Hart Sinnreich 2014

First published 2014

A catalogue record for this publication is available from the British Library

Library of Congress Cataloguing in Publication data
Successful strategies : triumphing in war and peace from antiquity to the present / edited by Williamson Murray and Richard Hart Sinnreich.
    pages   cm
Includes bibliographical references.
ISBN 978-1-107-63359-9 (Paperback) – ISBN 978-1-107-06273-3 (Hardback)
1. Strategy–History. 2. Strategy–Case studies. 3. Military history.
4. War–History. 5. Peace–History. I. Murray, Williamson. II. Sinnreich, Richard Hart.
U162.S872 2014
355.02–dc23   2013040414

ISBN 978-1-107-06273-3 Hardback
ISBN 978-1-107-63359-9 Paperback

To Lee Murray and Carol Sinnreich,
whose patience with two old troglodytes
knows no bounds

Contents

Tables and map

Contributors

WILLIAMSON MURRAY, Adjunct Professor at the US Marine Corps University and Emeritus Professor, The Ohio State University

RICHARD HART SINNREICH, Carrick Communications, Inc.

VICTOR DAVIS HANSON, Hoover Institute

JAMES LACEY, Marine Corps University

CLIFFORD J. ROGERS, United States Military Academy

JAMEL OSTWALD, Eastern Connecticut State University

DENNIS SHOWALTER, Colorado College

WAYNE HSIEH, United States Naval Academy

MARCUS JONES, United States Naval Academy

COLIN GRAY, University of Reading

PETER R. MANSOOR, The Ohio State University

BRADFORD A. LEE, Naval War College

THOMAS G. MAHNKEN, Naval War College

Acknowledgments

The project from which this book emerged was the inspiration of one of America's foremost strategic thinkers. Dr. Andrew Marshall, Director of the Pentagon's Office of Net Assessment, provided the intellectual guidance for the questions that the book attempts to answer, made available the resources that allowed us to recruit our superlative contributors, then helped guide our work through both an initial framing meeting and a second critical conference to discuss, debate, and refine the draft chapters. Throughout, his incisive questions and thoughtful suggestions merely confirmed his unique stature as a defense intellectual. He was ably seconded by his capable and incisive assistant, Dr. Andrew May, who not only helped move administration of the project though the Pentagon's bureaucracy, but also participated actively in designing and managing the two conferences.

We also owe a debt to Washington's Potomac Institute for Policy Studies for hosting the conferences and making sure the T's were crossed and the I's dotted. General (Retired) Al Gray, USMC, and Colonel (Retired) Tom O'Leary, USMC, were especially helpful in insuring that the project received the logistical support it needed. Finally, our thanks to our contributors for their timeliness in submitting their outstanding essays.

Central to Dr. Marshall's motives in launching and supporting this effort were his conviction that effective strategy remains essential to the success of future US foreign and defense policy, and that history remains a vital source of strategic insight. With both beliefs, we can only gratefully agree.

Williamson Murray
Fairfax, VA

Richard Hart Sinnreich
Oklahoma City, OK

Introduction

Williamson Murray

> Everything in strategy is very simple, but that does not mean that
> everything is very easy. Once it has been determined ... it is easy to chart
> its course. But great strength of character, as well as great lucidity and
> firmness of mind, is required in order to follow through steadily, to carry
> out the plan, and not to be thrown off course by thousands of diversions.[1]

In my career as a military historian, the subject of strategy has come to play
an increasingly important role in the topics that I have examined.[2] This has to
a considerable extent been the result of the realization expressed by my
colleague Allan Millett and myself in an article dealing with the lessons from
our study on military effectiveness in the first half of the twentieth century:

> Whether policy shaped strategy or strategic imperatives drove policy was irrelevant.
> Miscalculations in both led to defeat, and any combination of politico-strategic error
> had disastrous results even for some nations that ended the war as members of the
> victorious coalition ... This is because it is more important to make correct decisions
> at the political and strategic level than it is at the operational and tactical level.
> Mistakes in operations and tactics can be corrected, but political and strategic
> mistakes live forever.[3]

Not surprisingly, then, this is a book about strategy. Unlike its most recent
predecessor, *The Shaping of Grand Strategy*, it addresses strategy in the widest
sense: grand strategy in peacetime as well as in war, theater strategy, military
strategy, and political strategy. In most of these case studies, the key players
in success have been the statesmen and military leaders at the center of
events, who not only crafted and guided the approach to a knotty and inevitably complex environment but also had the strength of character to pursue
their perceptions through to successful conclusion. But this study is more

---

[1] Carl von Clausewitz, *On War*, ed. and trans. by Michael Howard and Peter Paret (Princeton,
NJ, 1976), p. 178.

[2] For two of the works that have resulted from this interest, see Williamson Murray,
MacGregor Knox, and Alvin Bernstein, eds., *The Making of Strategy, Rulers, States, and
War* (Cambridge, 1992); and Williamson Murray, Richard Hart Sinnreich, and James
Lacey, eds., *The Shaping of Grand Strategy, Policy, Diplomacy, and War* (Cambridge, 2011).

[3] Allan R. Millett and Williamson Murray, "Lessons of War," *The National Interest*, Winter
1988–1989.

than just an examination of how a few exceptional individuals shaped and molded strategy. There are also several examples of how organizational culture or groups succeeded in setting the parameters for strategic success. Since statesmen and military leaders will make strategy in the future, the authors of these essays believe it is of crucial importance that America's political and military leaders understand how their historical predecessors have developed and executed approaches to successful strategy.

In particular, these essays do not confine themselves to examinations of the employment of military forces in war to achieve political aims, although any volume that discusses strategic performance in the realm of relations between states must devote much of its space to the use of military power in achieving political aims, the only reason for waging war. Inevitably, the conduct of strategy in the international environment is intertwined with force and the threat of its employment. As that much quoted, but little understood statement of Clausewitz underlines: "we see, therefore, that war is not merely an act of policy but a true political instrument, a continuation of political intercourse, carried on with other means."[4]

This collection is about approaches to the guiding of polities and military organizations into the future. Its case studies focus on individuals or corporate bodies that have developed, then prosecuted successful strategies. It does not examine strategies that have failed. Why not? Largely because history is replete with examples of states, statesmen, and military leaders who failed ignominiously in pursuit of flawed strategy or strategies or who possessed no discernible strategy. In fact, the failures throughout history in strategic decision making have been legion. They litter the landscape with broken armies, collapsed economic systems, and the wreckage of states and empires. The simple truth is that statesmen and military leaders throughout history have embarked on military ventures or attempted to manipulate the international arena with an enthusiastic disregard for reality. Clausewitz, with enormous irony, notes that "no one starts a war – or rather, no one in his senses ought to do so – without first being clear in his mind what he intends to achieve by that war and how he intends to conduct it."[5] But, of course, too many have done so in the past and will continue to do so in the future.[6]

---

[4] Clausewitz, *On War*, p. 87. For the obdurate, and disastrous unwillingness of Germany's military leaders to recognize the wisdom of Clausewitz's observation, see particularly Isabel V. Hull, *Absolute Destruction: Military Culture and the Practices of War in Imperial Germany* (Ithaca, NY, 2006).
[5] Clausewitz, *On War*, p. 579.
[6] One might cynically note that in the case of the invasion of Iraq in 2003, the senior policy makers simply wished away the possibility that there might be an insurgent conflict after the conventional conflict in spite of everything that history suggested about the political and religious milieu of Mesopotamia. They might even have read the memoirs of the British general who put down the uprising of the Iraqi tribes against British rule in 1920, but they did not. See Lieutenant General Aylmer L. Haldane, *The Insurrection in Mesopotamia, 1920* (London, 1922). Not surprisingly it was reissued in 2005 – a bit late in the game.

Monday-morning quarterbacking of this wreckage, of course, has provided royalties for innumerable historians, some with useful insights, but most without.[7] The reasons and factors that have produced successful strategies, however, have received either less attention than they deserve or overly critical analysis that set standards of strategic behavior that would have been impossible to meet in the past, and probably so in the future.[8] Much of the inadequacy of such accounts reflects the fact that most historians have never had the opportunity to serve in the highest levels of government, where they could observe how strategy is made or not made as the case may be.[9] Nevertheless, experience does have its limits.[10]

Thus, this volume focuses specifically on those few areas where states, or military organizations, or individuals crafted strategies that led to success in the international arena in peacetime, the conduct of complex military operations, or the projection of military forces to achieve a successful end state. The purpose has been to suggest those attributes that might be of use to those charged with thinking about, developing, articulating, and then conducting strategy for the United States in the twenty-first century.[11] Under-lying our effort has also been a belief that history can provide insights and perceptions that are germane to any understanding of the strategic challenges that will confront the nation in the future.

Moreover, it is our sense that simply achieving success in the short term, a period of say five to ten years, represents a considerable success at the strategic level, while successes that last for several decades represent strategic genius. Beyond several decades, it is almost impossible for statesmen and military leaders to plan, and those who believe that leaders can articulate strategies that will reach out far into the future are naïve and disregard the complexities that human interactions inevitably involve.[12] The proof lies in the fact that

---

[7] For some of the factors that have lain behind and contributed to strategic and military disasters, see Eliot A. Cohen and John Gooch, *Military Misfortunes: The Anatomy of Failure in War* (New York, 1990).

[8] Moreover, historians have a tendency to minimize the difficulties and uncertainties that are intimately intertwined with the development, articulation, and execution of successful strategic approaches.

[9] Maurice Ashley, one of the great historians of Oliver Cromwell and who served Winston Churchill as a research assistant on the writing of the great man's biography of the Duke of Marlborough, noted that Churchill's work would stand as a great work of history well into the future particularly because he knew how great men interacted and talked with each other. See Maurice Ashley, *Churchill as Historian* (London, 1966).

[10] One is reminded of Frederick the Great's comment that the most experienced individual in his army was a mule who had participated in every campaign, but was none the wiser for that experience.

[11] There is, of course, a caveat. One could argue that in some of the cases in this volume, strategic success largely resulted from the incompetence of the losers.

[12] There are exceptions. The policy of containment that was developed in the late 1940s (see the chapters by Brad Lee and Thomas Mahnken later in this collection) certainly formed the basis for American strategy for most of the remainder of the Cold War, but it is doubtful that George Kennan and Paul Nitze foresaw a strategy that would have to last for over 40 years,

successful strategies that last for a decade or more are so extraordinarily rare. Their rarity suggests the extent of the fog that enshrouds decision making in human affairs. Uncertainty and ambiguity as well as incomplete information dominate the strategist's world.

So what is strategy? Simply put, one can argue that it is a matter of connecting available means to a political goal or goals. But, of course, it is much more. As Sun Tzu suggests, not only a deep understanding of oneself, but an equally sophisticated understanding of one's opponents distinguish the great strategist from the herd. Moreover, strategy demands constant adaptation to ever changing political and military environments. And that is where history proves to be the crucial enabler. Those who have developed and conducted successful strategic approaches have in almost every case possessed a sophisticated understanding of history and historical precedents. Moreover, the most sophisticated theorists of war and strategy, namely Thucydides and Clausewitz, immersed their examination of those topics in a deep under-standing of history. As the ancient Greek historian explained, his reason for writing his history lay in his hope that "these words of mine [will be] judged useful by those who want to understand clearly the events which happened in the past and which (human nature being what it is) will, at some time or other and in much the same ways be repeated in the future."[13]

For the Prussian theorist of war, the value of history lay in its ability to educate the mind of the future strategist or commander, not to provide answers. As he suggests, in a comment about war, but which is equally applicable to strategy:

[A theory] is an analytical investigation leading to a close *acquaintance* with the subject; applied to experience – in our case, to history – it leads to thorough *familiarity* with it. The closer it comes to that goal, the more it proceeds from the objective form of a science to the subjective form of a skill, the more effective it will prove in areas where the nature of the case admits no arbiter but talent.[14]

Historical knowledge provides the opening through which one can frame the right question or questions, and if strategists ask the right question, they have the chance of discovering answers of some utility. On the other hand, the wrong question, no matter how brilliantly articulated or phrased, will always provide an irrelevant answer.

In the Washington of the first decade of the twenty-first century, the concept of strategy has generated considerable interest with innumerable

---

or which would have to wind its way through so many twists and turns, in some cases involving even major limited wars, before reaching its end in the late 1980s and early 1990s – that end which virtually no one saw until after the Soviet collapse came. For the best overall summary of the Cold War, the reader might want to consult John Gaddis, *Now We Know: Rethinking Cold War History* (Oxford, 1998).

[13] Thucydides, *History of the Peloponnesian War*, trans. Rex Warner (London, 1956), p. 48.
[14] Clausewitz, *On War*, p. 141.

"strategic" products. Proliferating like tasteless mushrooms in an overheated dark room, they include the "National Strategy for Maritime Security," the "National Strategy for Homeland Security," the "National Strategy for Combating Terrorism," and the "National Military Strategy," among others. The list seems to stretch on forever, but these efforts are useless. A perceptive examination of the military balance in Asia has noted: "Recent national security strategies – as well as the Obama administration's recent defense guidance white paper – tend to speak in general terms. Rather than outlining a limited and prioritized set of objectives, they often contain undifferentiated lists of desirable ends … [T]hey tend to speak of challenges in only the vaguest terms."[15]

A senior officer once commented to this author about a draft of the "National Military Strategy" that, if one were to take every place where US or American or United States appeared and replace those adjectives and nouns with Icelandic and Iceland, the document would be equably applicable to that tiny island nation. The problem lies in the fact that these so-called strategic documents are the products of bureaucratic processes that aim to remove contentious issues, while insuring that those issues near and dear to the hearts of the participants receive the highlighting.[16] Written by groups of the unimaginative, they pass up the chain of command to insure there is nothing daring or controversial that might upset the conventional wisdom with its comfortable assumptions.

In his own day Clausewitz accurately portrayed a similar array of theories about the nature of war:

It is only analytically that these attempts at theory can be called advances in the realm of truth; synthetically in the rules and regulations they offer, they are absolutely useless.

They aim at fixed values; but in war everything is uncertain, and calculations have to be made with variable quantities.

They direct the inquiry exclusively towards physical quantities, whereas all military action is intertwined with psychological forces and effects.

They consider only unilateral action, whereas war consists of a continuous interaction of opponents.[17]

Each statement applies equally to strategy. Thus, as in so many human endeavors, "*plus ça change, plus c'est la même chose* [the more things change, the more they stay the same]."[18]

---

[15] Thomas G. Mahnken with Dan Blumenthal, Thomas Donnelly, Michael Mazza, Gary J. Schmitt, and Andrew Shearer, "Asia in the Balance, Transforming US Military Strategy in Asia," American Enterprise Institute, June 2012.

[16] This is true of virtually all government documents, the one exception being the *9/11 Report*, a report much of bureaucratic Washington attempted to strangle before it even got started.

[17] Clausewitz, *On War*, p. 136.

[18] A French proverb – one that goes well with the comment about the Bourbons on their return to France in 1815 – "they have learned nothing, and forgotten everything" is equally applicable to those most responsible for making strategy.

Paralleling the search in Washington for the elixir of strategic success has been an equal effort by so-called business strategists to unlock strategy, or more specifically strategic concepts to repair and guide corporations to success. Virtually all of those efforts over which business consultants spend endless hours – at great cost, one might add, to those who employ them – are useless. As one of the few perceptive theorists of business strategy has noted: "Bad strategy is long on goals and short on policy or action." Like most of those interested in strategy in Washington, "It puts forward strategic objectives that are incoherent and, sometimes, totally impracticable. It uses high sounding words and phrases to hide these failings."[19]

The same must be said of most of what passes for strategy in the policy and military realms – as well as in the academic world. Again, Clausewitz's analysis is equally applicable to our current world of governmental and business strategy making: "Thus, it has come about that our theoretical and critical literature, instead of giving plain, straightforward arguments in which the author at least always knows what he is saying and the reader what he is reading, is crammed with jargon, ending at obscure crossroads where the author loses his reader."[20]

The importance of history to strategic success

From the enemy's character, from his institutions, the state of his affairs and his general situation, each side, using the *laws of probability*, forms an estimate of its opponent's likely course and acts accordingly.[21]

Why then is history so important to the strategist? Just as laying a course to a destination requires a point of departure, in thinking about the future the strategist must understand the present. But the only way to understand our own circumstances, as well as those of our allies and opponents, demands an understanding of how we and they have reached the present. And that demands historical knowledge. Absent such knowledge, we are like the English tourists who, having asked an Irish farmer how they might get to Dublin, were told: "If I were going to Dublin, I would not start from here."[22] With no knowledge of the past, any road into the future will do, and it will inevitably prove the wrong road. Simply put, "a perceptive understanding of the present based on historical knowledge is the essential first step for thinking about the future."[23]

---

[19] Richard P. Rumelt, *Good Strategy, Bad Strategy: The Difference and Why It Matters* (New York, 2011), pp. 36–37.

[20] Clausewitz, *On War*, p. 169.   [21] Ibid., p. 80.

[22] I am indebted to Sir Michael Howard for this story. Unfortunately most of those who have practiced strategy throughout history have had little or no understanding of where they stand.

[23] Williamson Murray, "History and the Future," in Williamson Murray, *War, Strategy, and Military Effectiveness* (Cambridge, 2011), p. 16.

The question then arises as to why so few statesmen, diplomats, and military leaders have been willing to examine strategic problems and issues through the lens of historical analysis. The unfortunate answer is that complexities of history demand time, effort, and guidance to grasp to the point where they are useful to the strategist. To be of any real utility in dealing with the complex problems and uncertainty of strategy, their study must be a lifetime avocation involving real commitment, not just an occasional reading or briefing.[24] As Henry Kissinger notes, "the convictions that leaders have formed before reaching high office are the intellectual capital they will consume as they continue in office."[25] Without that commitment, history becomes no more than a dumping ground from which one can salvage irrelevant ideas to justify preconceived notions. Where the statesman has prepared herself or himself by lifelong study, history becomes an important tool to compare, contrast, and evaluate the present against the past. As Bismarck once noted, he preferred to learn from the mistakes of others.[26]

What then might history suggest about the fundamental requirements involved in the developing and conduct of successful strategy? First, it might suggest that even when a strategic course of action has some connection with reality and the means available, more often than not it will involve complex and difficult choices, annoying setbacks, and constant surprises. Those choices in turn will demand adaptation to a constantly shifting environment that changes in response to one's actions. Those who make strategy confront the fact that the world is in constant flux. Not only are their opponents making every effort to frustrate their moves, but unexpected and unpredictable events buffet strategists like waves pounding on a shore.

Constant change and adaptation must be ... the companions of grand strategy if it is to succeed. Not only does it find itself under the pressures and strains of the politics and processes of decision making, but the fact that the external environment can and often does adapt will inevitably affect the calculations of those who attempt to chart its course. The goals may be clear, but the means available and the paths are uncertain. Exacerbating such difficulties is the reality that ... strategy demands intuitive as much as calculated judgment.[27]

---

[24] I addressed this problem in an earlier essay: See Williamson Murray, "Thoughts on Military History and the Profession of Arms," in Williamson Murray and Richard Hart Sinnreich, eds., *The Past as Prologue: The Importance of History to the Military Profession* (Cambridge, 2006).

[25] Henry Kissinger, *The White House Years* (New York, 1979), p. 561.

[26] One must also underline that great literature as well as history can be of enormous utility in preparing the statesman or military leader to grapple with the strategic and political problems of the present. Bismarck, not surprisingly, was a great fan of Shakespeare.

[27] Murray, Sinnreich, and Lacey, *The Shaping of Grand Strategy*, p. 11.

A table in *The Joint Operational Environment* of 2008 suggests the extent of the political, diplomatic, economic, and ideological changes over the course of the last century:

1900: If you are a strategic analyst for the world's leading power, you are British, looking warily at Britain's age-old enemy France.

1910: You are allied with France [and Russia], and your enemy is Germany. [Nevertheless, Britain's chief trading partner is Germany. The world's first period of globalization is reaching its peak.]

1920: Britain and its allies have won World War I, but now the British find themselves engaged in a naval race with their former allies, the United States and Japan. [The Great War has ended the first period of globalization, while the United States has emerged as the world's dominant economic and industrial power.]

1930: For the British, the naval limitation treaties are in place, the Great Depression has started, and defense planning for the next five years assumes a ten-year rule with no war in ten years. British planners posit the main threats to the Empire as the Soviet Union and Japan, while Germany and Italy are either friendly or no threat.

1935: A British planner now posits three great threats: Italy, Japan, and the worst a resurgent Germany, while little help can be expected from the United States.

1940: The collapse of France in June leaves Britain alone in a seemingly hopeless war with Germany and Italy, with a Japanese threat looming in the Pacific. The United States has only recently begun to rearm its military forces.

1950: The United States is now the world's greatest power, the atomic age has dawned, and a "police action" begins in June in Korea that will kill over 30,000 Americans, 58,000 South Koreans, nearly 3,000 allied soldiers, 215,000 North Koreans, 400,000 Chinese, and 2,000,000 Korean civilians before a cease-fire brings an end to the fighting in 1953. The main [American] opponent is China, America's ally in the war against Japan.

1960: Politicians in the United States are focusing on a missile gap that does not genuinely exist; [the policy of] massive retaliation will soon give way to flexible response, while a small insurgency in South Vietnam hardly draws American attention.

1970: The United States is beginning to withdraw from Vietnam, its military forces in shambles. The Soviet Union has just crushed incipient rebellion in the Warsaw Pact. Détente between the Soviets and the Americans has begun, while the Chinese are waiting in the wings to create an informal alliance with the United States.

1980: The Soviets have just invaded Afghanistan, while a theocratic revolution in Iran has overthrown the Shah's regime. "Desert One" – an attempt to free American hostages in Iran – ends in a humiliating failure, another indication of what pundits were calling the "hollow force." America is the greatest creditor nation the world has ever seen.

1990: The Soviet Union collapses. The once hollow force shreds the vaunted Iraqi Army in less than 100 hours. The United States has become the world's greatest debtor nation. Few outside of the Department of Defense and the academic community use the internet.

2000: Warsaw is the capital of a North Atlantic Treaty Organization (NATO) member. Terrorism is emerging as America's greatest threat. Biotechnology, robotics, nanotechnology, HD energy, etc. are advancing so fast they are beyond forecasting.[28]

Perhaps the most difficult problems that any strategist confronts are those involved in securing the peace after a war.[29] What many now call conflict termination represents a host of intractable problems. In some cases, the making of peace confronts a "wicked problem," one where there are no satisfactory solutions. Historians and pundits often criticize the Treaty of Versailles as not only unfair, but also an incompetent treaty that made the Second World War inevitable.[30] Yet, what other avenues were open to peace makers at Versailles? A harsher peace would have made a future conflict impossible, but that path required the continuation of military operations, as the American General John J. Pershing urged, and the imposition of peace terms in Berlin. However, there was no willingness among the French and British after four years of slaughter to continue the fighting. The other option would have been to grant the Germans an easy peace, but such a peace would have made Germany the dominant power in Europe – in other words the victor, a conclusion that was absolutely unacceptable, given the atrocities the Germans had committed in France and Belgium throughout the war.[31]

---

[28] Joint Forces Command, *The Joint Operational Environment* (Norfolk, 2008). Jim Lacey and the author of this essay were the authors of this document.

[29] For a wider discussion of the issues involved in the aftermath of war, see Williamson Murray and James Lacey, eds., *The Making of Peace: Rulers, States, and the Aftermath of War* (Cambridge, 2008).

[30] The magazine, *The Economist*, commented in January 2000 the "The final crime [was] the Treaty of Versailles, whose harsh terms would ensure a second [world] war." For an examination of the complexities of peace making in 1919 see my piece, "Versailles: the Peace without a Chance," in *The Making of Peace*.

[31] Not only had the Germans slaughtered approximately 6,000 civilians as hostages in response to supposed guerilla activities (most of which had not occurred), but thereafter they had come close to starving the Belgians and French in the areas they had occupied, and then during their retreat back toward the German frontier in the war's last months they had destroyed everything that could be destroyed. Among the more recent examinations of the

Similarly, the great strategist Otto von Bismarck confronted the wicked problem of war termination in making peace with France in 1871. In Prussia's victory over Austria in the Seven Weeks' War in 1866, the Iron Chancellor had finessed the problem of making peace by imposing a peace in which the Austrians lost nothing, while the Prussians made their gains entirely at the expense of the other German states. However, in the case of France, Bismarck confronted the difficulty that the French empire of Napoleon III had collapsed to be replaced by an intransigent republic that had declared a *levée en masse*. Moreover, having let loose German nationalism to cement the south German states to his new creation, Bismarck discovered he was now leading an aroused populace that demanded its pound of flesh, while the army leaders were urging an extension of the new German Empire to the west for purposes of strategic security.

As a result Bismarck imposed a peace treaty on the French that saw the inclusion of the provinces of Alsace and Lorraine within the borders of the new German Empire – an inclusion that poisoned Franco-German relations for the next 43 years. Bismarck recognized that the French Republic would never have reconciled to the appearance of a powerful German state on its western frontier. Thus, whatever the nature of the peace, it contained the seeds of future conflict. In every respect the peace of 1871 represented an unsatisfactory alternative to the war, but in the real world of politics and rabid nationalism was there a viable alternative?

The problems involved in the making of peace reflect the inherent difficulties in all strategic decision making. Inevitably, unpredictable and unforeseen second and third order effects arise to plague strategic decisions. The problem that confronts most flawed strategies is that in a non-linear world of complexity and uncertainty, most policy makers and military leaders follow a linear course which fails to consider three fundamental drivers in international relations. The first is the nature of the human condition. No matter how clever and sophisticated the policy, it will in the end be executed by individuals who are often less than competent as well as those who obstruct clear thinking with obfuscations.[32] The second lies in the fact that chance and the unforeseen will inevitably interfere with whatever path is chosen. And the third lies in the fact that one's opponent always has a vote and will more often than not choose the unexpected.[33]

---

extent of German atrocities in 1914, see John Horne and Alan Kramer, *German Atrocities, 1914: A History of Denial* (New Haven, CT, 2001).

[32] For the role of incompetence in human affairs, see the concluding chapter in Williamson Murray, *The Change in the European Balance of Power, 1938–1939: The Path to Ruin* (Princeton, NJ, 1984).

[33] This is particularly the case because estimates of how an opponent might react are so often cast with little knowledge of his history, his culture, and his Weltanschauung that he is fundamentally at odds with what we would like to believe.

Nevertheless, no matter how rare, sophisticated strategic thinking has been around since the beginning of recorded history. In his brilliant account of the Peloponnesian War, one that is both historical and theoretical in its examination of war, Thucydides imbedded in his history a deep appreciation of strategy, along with the difficulties involved in its implementation. There have been a number of recent classical historians who have cast doubt on the idea that the Greeks and the Romans had a conscious understanding of strategy in the modern sense, but a simple reading of the first book in the Peloponnesian War suggests otherwise.[34]

The Spartan king, Archidamnus in addressing the Spartan assembly as to whether Sparta should declare war on Athens, laid out the strategic issues in exquisite and all too accurate terms. It is a speech driven by a keen sense of the strategic environment and the difficulties Sparta might – and did – confront in the war on which it embarked in 431 BC.

Spartans, in the course of my life I have taken part in many wars, and I see among you people of the same age I am. They and I have had experience, and so are not likely to share in what may be a general enthusiasm for war, nor to think that war is a good thing or a safe thing. And you will find, if you look carefully into the matter, that this present war which you are now discussing is not likely to be anything on a small scale ... [Against the Athenians] we shall be engaged with people who live far off, people who also have the widest experience of the sea and who are extremely well equipped in all other directions, very wealthy both as individuals and as a state, with ships and cavalry and hoplites, with a population bigger than that of any other place in Hellas, and then, too, with numbers of allies who pay tribute to them. How then can we irresponsibly start a war with such a people? What have we to rely upon if we rush into it unprepared? ... What sort of war, then, are we going to fight? If we can neither defeat them at sea nor take away from them the resources on which their navy depends, we shall do ourselves more harm than good.[35]

Archidamnus' opponent in the debate was the Spartan *ephor*, Sthenelaidas, whose speech at first glance appears a simple-minded strategic approach: march into Attica and destroy the countryside and the Athenian shrines, and the Athenians will march out to face the hopeless task of defeating the Spartan phalanx.[36] Yet, in fact, the *ephor*'s strategic vision came close to realization in the war's first year. Only by preventing the Athenian assembly from meeting was Pericles able to prevent the Athenians from voting to march out and meet the Spartans, in what would have probably resulted in a disastrous Athenian defeat.

---

[34] The publication of Edward Luttwak's *Grand Strategy of the Roman Empire: From the First Century to the Third* (Baltimore, MD, 1979) set off efforts by a number of Roman historians to dismiss Luttwak's thesis entirely on the basis that the ancients had no understanding of strategy. See the discussion of this phenomenon in the Lacey chapter of this collection.
[35] Thucydides, *History of the Peloponnesian War*, pp. 82–83.
[36] Given the secretive nature of Spartan society, it is not entirely clear where the position of *ephor* fits within the political framework of the Spartan constitution. Nevertheless, the position appears to have been similar to that of tribune in the Roman Republic.

Nevertheless, the question inevitably must arise: if, in the end, Archidamnus' strategy was so wise, why did the Spartan assembly reject it out of hand? Here Clausewitz provides the most cogent answer: "Everything in strategy is very simple, but that does not mean that everything is very easy. Once it has been determined, from the political conditions, what a war is meant to achieve and what it can achieve, it is easy to chart its course." But there is a stumbling block. "But great strength of character, as well as great lucidity and firmness of mind, is required..."[37] For the Spartans, a major contributor to the vote against Archidamnus' strategic approach was the fact that not only did it postpone the settlement of the Athenian problem to some later date, but also it posited a difficult and uncertain strategic course of action that had as its sub-text great difficulties and challenges in military terms, as well as to the Spartan way of life.[38] Nevertheless, Archidamnus' alternative may seem both reasonable and perceptive to us in the twenty-first century, especially given the fact that we know how the war will turn out, but to the Spartans nothing was clear or certain, as the debate in the assembly of warriors unfolded.

Thus, when it turned out that Sthenelaidas was wrong, and the Athenians did not come out to fight, the Spartans ended up following the advice of their king, but only because the circumstances forced them to follow that hard strategic path. But it was to prove an extraordinarily difficult course of action that saw the Spartans confronted with defeats not only at sea, but even on land. And at the Battle of Mantinea against the Argives and Athenians, they came close to losing the war. In the end they won, but even Archidamnus could not have conceived of a struggle that would last for 27 years, exhaust all the contestants, and in the long-run undermine the political and demographic basis on which Spartan society had rested for nearly three centuries. Indeed, even successful strategy can have a darker downside. Success in the present may well carry the seeds of future unpredictable and negative results. Moreover, the unintended effects of success can have serious consequences, as American policy makers discovered in the aftermath of the invasion of Iraq in April 2003.

Any attempt to draw lessons from the past demands close attention to the context within which past events have occurred. Not to do so is to court a faulty approach to the problems of the present. In understanding the lessons of strategic history, the context matters. Basil H. Liddell Hart, one of the great strategic pundits of the first half of the twentieth century, developed a theory of what he termed "the British way in war." Repelled by the horror of the First World War, Liddell Hart argued that in the eighteenth and early part of the nineteenth century, Britain, employing a strategy of indirect approach, had committed relatively few troops to the great wars that had erupted on the

---

[37] Clausewitz, *On War*, p. 178.
[38] Which is why, of course, no one listened to the Trojan princess Cassandra – she demanded that her countrymen address the realities that challenged their comfortable assumptions.

continent, but had instead attacked its main enemies, France and Spain, on the periphery. Thereby, the British had seized a great colonial empire. Thus, he posited that Britain's decision to create a great army in the First World War and commit it against the Germans in northern France and Belgium represented a serious strategic mistake.

All in all, the theory of the "British way in war" seemed to make great sense in the aftermath of the Great War. It certainly influenced British political leaders like Neville Chamberlain to minimize the British Army's preparation for a war on the continent until too late.[39] However, there was a major flaw in Liddell Hart's strategic theory. It entirely ignored the contextual differences between the First World War and the great global conflicts of the eighteenth century. As Michael Howard has suggested: "It was ... precisely the failure of German power to find an outlet and its consequent concentration in Europe, its lack of any significant possessions overseas, that made it so particularly menacing to the sprawling British empire in two world wars and which make so misleading all arguments about 'traditional' British strategy drawn from earlier conflicts against the Spanish and French Empires, with all the colonial hostages they had offered to fortune and the Royal Navy."[40]

But even in the war against the French at the turn between the eighteenth and nineteenth centuries, the British had discovered that what had worked for them in earlier wars was no longer applicable. At the start of the war against Revolutionary France, the strategy of attacking the French colonies again came into play. As Henry Dundas, in charge of Britain's conduct of the war against Revolutionary France, commented, "This country [Britain] having captured the French West India islands and destroyed their existing fleet, may long rest in peace."[41] Dundas was wrong. Napoleon put paid to the British minister's assumptions, because in his destruction of the other major powers, the emperor could not have cared less about what the British did or did not do in the Caribbean. Thus, as Richard Sinnreich points out in his essay in this volume, British governments that attempted to cobble together a strategy that looked much like what Liddell Hart suggested discovered that such a strategy was irrelevant. Not until the British could confront the power of France on the continent with allies capable of staying the course and with a major military effort in Spain could they finally overthrow Napoleon.

In addressing the strategic problems of the present, one must remember that history always suggests that unexpected third and fourth order effects will plague our steps and that the unintended impact of such results will inevitably affect strategy. Nor should we forget that strategic surprises will haunt

---

[39] For a discussion of these issues see Murray, *The Change in the European Balance of Power*, chp. 2.

[40] Michael Howard, *The Continental Commitment* (London, 1989), p. 32.

[41] Quoted in N. A. M. Rodger, *The Command of the Ocean: A Naval History of Britain, 1649–1845* (London, 2004), p. 426.

the decisions that we make. Indeed as Saint Paul's letter to the Corinthians suggests about our understanding of the future. "We see through a glass darkly."[42]

History can suggest possibilities about the future, but it can never remove the fact that chance, ambiguity, and uncertainty will always haunt our decisions about the future.

Conclusion

It has always been a shortcoming of the Germans to seek all or nothing, and to focus exclusively on a particular method. In contrast I was always pleased if I managed to come three steps closer to German unification, by whatever means. I would have grasped at any solution that led to the expansion of Prussia and German unity without war. Many paths led to my goals, and I had to arrange them one after the next, with the most dangerous last. Uniformity in business is not my way.[43] (Bismarck)

During the twentieth century, the United States confronted three great challenges: the First World War, the Second World War, and the Cold War. In each, it found itself engaged in existential struggles in which values it regarded as fundamental to its conception of civilization were in danger of collapse, at least in the outside world, if not within its borders. The strategic approaches cast by America's political and military leaders proved essential in the defeat of Wilhelmine Germany, the Axis coalition, and the Soviet Union.

In those three contests, one of the major advantages the Americans enjoyed was the fact they understood their opponents far better than their opponents understood the United States.[44] That understanding was informed by historical knowledge that allowed American statesmen and military leaders to recognize the fundamental nature of their opponents, their strengths as well as their weaknesses. Many American leaders were deeply informed about the course of human events, reaching far afield, even into ancient history. Thus, it is not surprising that George C. Marshall, in an address at Princeton in February 1947, commented that he doubted "whether a man can think with full wisdom and with conviction regarding certain of the basic

---

[42] 1st Corinthians, 13–12, King James Version of the Bible.

[43] Quoted in Marcus Jones, "Strategy as Character: Bismarck and the Prusso-German Question," in Murray, Sinnreich, and Lacey, *The Shaping of Grand Strategy*, p. 86.

[44] In the late 1970s and early 1980s, American military historians became intrigued with the tactical and operational virtuosity of the German Army. What they missed was the extraordinarily flawed approach to strategy that drove the Germans to defeat in both the great world wars. And at the heart of that misshapened strategy lay the German ignorance not only of America's political strengths and capabilities, but also of its extraordinary economic strengths that in the Second World War would allow it to fight a two front war in the Atlantic and the Pacific as well as supporting the military efforts of its allies, Britain and the Soviet Union.

international issues today who has not reviewed in his mind the period of the Peloponnesian War and the fall of Athens."[45]

Unfortunately for the prospects of US strategy in the twenty-first century, most of those who today lead America's military institutions reflect the society from which they spring. One doubts that many if any of the generals or admirals on active duty have read Thucydides, much less others of the great books that inform and educate their readers about the complexity, ambiguities, and uncertainties of history.[46] As for America's political leaders, given what has occurred in major universities with the destruction of the serious study of history, one can doubt whether senior policy makers in Washington have any better understanding of history.[47] What makes this particularly worrisome is the fact that a sophisticated knowledge of history is necessary to understand who we Americans are: our strengths, our weaknesses, and the perspectives of potential opponents in the twenty-first century. Over the past several decades we have come to mirror image, distort, and misunderstand not only the nature of our allies, but our opponents as well.

In Thucydides' history of the Peloponnesian War, Corinth's ambassadors to Sparta describe the Athenians in the following terms:

An Athenian is always an innovator, quick to form a resolution and quick at carrying it out. You [Spartans] on the other hand are good at keeping things as they are; you never originate an idea, and your action tends to stop short of its aim ... Think of this too; while you are hanging back, they never hesitate ... [E]ach man cultivates his own intelligence, again with a view to doing something notable. If they aim at something and do not get it, they think they have been deprived of what belongs to them already; whereas, if their enterprise is successful, they regard the success as nothing compared to what they will do next ... Of them alone it may be said that they possess a thing almost as soon as they have begun to desire it, so quickly with them does action follow upon decision. And so they go working away in hardship and danger all the days of their lives, seldom enjoying their possessions because they are always adding to them.[48]

The Corinthians' description of the Athenians was not intended to be complimentary, but rather to awaken Sparta to the magnitude of the Athenian threat.

---

[45] Quoted in W. Robert Conner, *Thucydides* (Princeton, NJ, 1984), p. 3. It is clear that Marshall had read Thucydides, because there was no other source for an understanding of that conflict that provides the richness of that history by the greatest of all military and strategic historians.
[46] There is one exception in that the Strategy and Policy course at the Naval War College has at its centerpiece a week-long study of Thucydides and the course of the Peloponnesian War. But then, the navy sends few of its most outstanding officers to study at its own war college.
[47] In the early 1990s the US Postal Service printed a series of stamps to commemorate the fiftieth anniversary of the major events that involved US military forces. One of those stamps was to commemorate the dropping of the atomic bomb on Japan in early August 1945, but on 7 December 1994, considering the vociferous objections of the Japanese government, the Clinton administration canceled the issuing of the stamp.
[48] Thucydides, *History of the Peloponnesian War*, p. 76.

Yet, should someone describe today's Americans in similar terms, it is likely that many Americans would take such words as a favorable description of who we are and how we act on the world's stage. It is equally likely that most outside the United States would believe such words were complimentary. That alone underscores the extent of our inability to understand the "other." And in the twenty-first century the "other" will matter to an extent never before true in the history of the United States.

In the end, the development and articulation of a successful strategy in a world of constant political and economic turmoil demands that the right questions be asked. Such questions must address not only the possibilities that rest on an understanding of our potential opponents, but of ourselves as well. Moreover, the examination of critical strategic decisions must also address the possibility of unintended effects on the other complex issues that confront policy makers and military leaders. It is our hope that these case studies may illuminate the complexities of the past as a means to further the education of the strategists of the future.

1   The strategic thought of Themistocles

Victor Davis Hanson

The ancient world generally regarded the Athenian statesman and general Themistocles (524–459 BC) as the architect of fifth-century Athenian naval power and visionary who put in place the foundations of the Athenian Empire that came to fruition under the subsequent leadership of Pericles (ca. 461–429 BC). Contemporaries were quick to note that his strategic forethought (*pronoia*) was neither ad hoc nor piecemeal, but carefully planned and systematic in its implementation. Most famous of later encomia of the foresight of Themistocles was the in-depth assessment of the historian Thucydides, who concluded: "To sum up, whether we consider the extent of his natural powers, or the slightness of his application, this extraordinary man must be allowed *to have surpassed all others in the faculty of intuitively meeting an emergency*" (κράτιστος δὴ οὗτος αὐτοσχεδιάζειν τὰ δέοντα ἐγένετο).[1]

We can divide that faculty of "intuitively meeting an emergency" into three areas that also follow chronologically: (a) the construction of the Athenian navy (482); (b) the decision to privilege naval power during the invasion of Xerxes (480–479) as the chief arm of Athenian defense; and (c) the subsequent policy of Athenian fortification, military and civilian evacuation, and the creation of a maritime empire (479). None of these policies would have followed without Themistocles' leadership, and most faced strong opposition from rivals at the time. At the same time, while Themistoclean foresight helped defeat the Persians and found the Athenian Empire, it also led to a radicalization of the Athenian state that contributed to its eventual defeat by Sparta.

From Marathon to the construction of the Athenian fleet

The Persian interest in at first punishing, and later annexing, mainland Greece ostensibly originated in the breakaway attempt of the subjugated Greek city-states on the coast of Asia Minor. After the failure of the Ionian

---

[1] Thucydides (1.138.3–4, Crawley translation; emphasis in the original). Cf. the contemporary appreciation of Themistocles as the father of the Athenian navy and the architect of Athenian maritime hegemony, in J. R. Hale, *Lords of the Sea: The Epic Story of the Athenian Navy and the Birth of Democracy* (New York, 2009), pp. 3–14.

Greeks to end their half-century of Persian occupation and to win their freedom from King Darius (494), the Persians sought to punish the Athenians, who had sent aid to their rebellious Ionian cousins across the Aegean. The Persians expected such retribution to be an easy matter given the absence of a credible Athenian fleet. Despite an initial failure in northern Greece, Darius struck back directly against Athens in 490. The king dispatched his generals Datis and Artaphernes with a second expeditionary force of some 25,000–30,000 sailors and infantry. This time the expedition headed on a beeline across the Aegean to the Greek mainland; the king's force was not large enough to conquer Greece, but was sufficient to occupy and punish the Athenians for their interference in Persian affairs.

After easily conquering the island of Naxos in mid-route, the Persians captured the key city of Eretria on the large island of Euboea across from the Attic mainland. Next, sometime in mid August 490 BC, the generals landed on the eastern coast of Attica itself at the plain of Marathon, just 26 miles from Athens, in hopes of defeating Athens' outnumbered infantry, marching overland to the city, and installing a pro-Persian government. Given the absence of Athenian ships, the Persians felt that they could land in Attica almost anywhere they pleased.

Yet in a set-piece infantry battle, the outnumbered but more heavily armed Athenian and Plataean hoplites won a crushing victory over the lighter-clad Persians. The invaders had foolishly advanced into the enclosed plain of Marathon apparently without cavalry support. Though enjoying numerical superiority, the Persians nonetheless found themselves trapped by an Athenian double envelopment that turned a defeat into a rout. Although the Persians may have outnumbered the defenders by three to one, the combined Greek forces still killed over 6,400 of the enemy for a loss of only 192 Athenians and Plataeans. Heavy armor and columnar tactics had smashed apart the more loosely deployed and lighter-clad invaders. Then, almost immediately, the Athenians sent the majority of their infantry back over the mountains to the harbor at Phaleron to prevent the surviving Persian fleet from circling back to land at a relatively undefended Athens. Most Greeks, Spartans especially, who had stayed away, could not quite fathom how the two Greek city-states had turned back a massive Persian invasion.[2]

Themistocles was in his mid thirties and probably fought as a hoplite at Marathon. Indeed, he had been elected magistrate, or archon, of the young democracy just three years prior to the battle (493). Yet, credit for the victory properly belonged to the more conservative leader Miltiades, commander-in-chief of the Greek infantry on the day of battle. Even before the fighting began, Miltiades proved the architect of the winning strategy of weakening

---

[2] For the campaign and battle, especially the date, strategy, and the numbers of combatants involved, see the controversies in J. Lazenby, *The Defence of Greece, 490–479 B.C.* (Warminster, 1993), pp. 46–64.

the Greek center to draw in and envelop the wings of the charging Persians. In a tactical sense, Miltiades had foreseen that Greek hoplites, in a pitched battle on their rather narrow terms and if the numerical odds were not too lopsided, were nearly invincible, given their superior armament, shock tactics, cohesion, and discipline.

The clear consensus of the times, then, was that an entire Persian invasion had been thwarted by a single glorious battle of better men in bronze. For each Athenian or Plataean hoplite that fell, 33 Persians perished. Both the infantry victory and the subsequent famous 26-mile march to beat the Persian fleet back to Athens were immortalized as the proper way to defend the city. No walls or ships, or poor people, had been necessary to save Athens from the Persian hordes. Courage, more than mere numbers, mattered. That Athenian hoplites had won without the crack troops of Sparta made the victory all the more reassuring. Such iconic status made it difficult over the next decade to second-guess the supremacy of the Athenian hoplite.[3]

Yet despite the contemporary Athenian ebullition, Marathon under closer examination soon proved not quite the final victory it had appeared. A worried young Themistocles, almost alone among Athenian leaders, seems to have drawn quite different lessons from Marathon. He saw no grand Athenian strategy involved in the infantry victory, in which Persian negligence played an unappreciated role. Instead, to his mind, Marathon signaled a "beginning of far greater struggles," given the superior resources of Persia that were still uncommitted to the war against the Greeks, and that had hardly been attrited by the humiliating defeat at Marathon. Themistocles immediately tried to warn his fellow Athenians that, unfortunately, there would be no future Marathons in the face of "events still to come." Yet few Athenians wished to hear that ominous message – perhaps the ancient equivalent of someone admonishing the Americans in January 1991 that their four-day brilliant victory over Saddam Hussein was the beginning, not the end, of a far longer rivalry with a determined foe, one that might last for 12 more years.[4]

Themistocles rightly saw that the superior Persian forces had arrived in Attica in 490 BC after conquering both the islands of Naxos and Euboea without much Greek interference. No Athenian naval forces had intercepted the Persians when their transports were most vulnerable at sea. The Persian choice of battle at Marathon was in retrospect unwise, but nevertheless theirs alone. The Persian admirals under their general Datis – without worry about their Greek counterparts – alone had chosen when and where to fight.

---

[3] Agrarian conservatives always claimed exclusive credit for Marathon; see V. D. Hanson, *The Other Greeks: The Family Farm and the Agrarian Roots of Western Civilization* (Berkeley, CA, 1999), pp. 323–327. For the "Marathon men," cf. Aristophanes, *Clouds*, 986.

[4] On Themistocles' foresight, see Plutarch, *Themistocles* 3.3–4. Most generals tried to best use the resources their societies put at their disposal; Themistocles, in contrast, insured that his society would have the wisdom and capability to put the right resources at his disposal.

The Greeks had been reactive, given limited options, and apparently lucky that the Persians unwisely fought when and how they did.

Despite the Greek victory and the high enemy losses, as much as three-fourths of the defeated invaders, or more, had simply sailed away unscathed. Sea-power, Themistocles would soon argue, had enabled the Persians to arrive when and where they wished and had also allowed thousands of survivors a chance to leave unscathed. In contrast, Athens by 490 still had only a small fleet and thus no comparable capability of maritime lift. Only a far-seeing, perhaps even contrarian, mind along with a willingness to endure ridicule might appreciate that fundamental strategic Athenian vulnerability at a time of infantry triumphalism.

Themistocles apparently came to a second conclusion. Despite the brilliant Greek victory, the defeated Persians forces, utilizing their control of the sea, had almost outpaced the victorious Athenians back to a nearly defenseless city. In the future, if an Athenian army had to march up and down the coast each time a Persian armada in the Aegean threatened an amphibious attack on the Attic coast, how could the city itself ever be truly safe without fortifications?

Third, the young democracy at Athens was only 17 years old. Most citizens, despite the radical notion of "power to the people," remained poor. At least half did not own land. Current Athenian infantry dominance, based on the property wealth of the hoplite class, did not reflect the demography of the young democracy. To the mind of the radical Themistocles, such a new Athenian experiment in egalitarian politics would never work if the defense, and with it the prestige and wealth, of the city rested only with a minority of conservative property owners, who would judge their own interests as the same as those of Athens at large. Was not there a way that Athens still might survive, even should its farmland be overrun? How could the city remain safe against the Persian hordes when the city failed to mobilize thousands of landless Athenians?

Military strategy, in other words, also had to reflect class realities. Wars could be as much about internal politics as they were strictly a matter of national defense. Accordingly, using public money to pay thousands of the poor to row in the fleet or build fortifications would in addition strengthen the new democracy, both militarily and politically. With a navy and walled city, the poor would have wages in silver coin and share in the prestige of protecting the city. But most importantly, given the vast resources of the Persian Empire, the expeditionary force under Datis and Artaphernes in 490, while large in comparison to the Greek resistance, was actually somewhat small. The Persian strike was intended to be merely punitive, concerned more with Euboea and Attica than the whole of the Greek main-land. Yet certainly Darius' empire of some 20 million possessed the means not merely to punish Athens, but also, and more likely, to destroy it outright.

If Athens were to be safe, Themistocles further reasoned, the young democracy needed to reinvent itself, and almost immediately, given the imminent threat of another Persian strike. Athens required a large navy. A fleet in turn demanded a protected port and urban fortifications to secure the naval population. In symbiotic fashion, such investments gave work to the poor *thetes* and taxed the wealthy to pay for civic investment. We do not know the degree to which Themistocles grasped the ramifications of such a complex departure from Athenian hoplite protocol, only that he had deeply embedded his military agenda within his popular politics.

Yet the implementation of these radical ideas demanded rare political skills to convince his countrymen that Marathon was an anomaly rather than a blueprint. Of course, even before Marathon, as archon in 493 BC, Themistocles had sought to change the course of Athenian defense policy. In part, he remembered the lessons of the failed Athenian intervention in Asia Minor during the Ionian revolt; in part, he worried about a future amphibious Persian attack. The result was that, even by the time of Marathon, the Athenians had already adopted some of Themistocles' proposals in beginning to build walls around their small harbor at Phaleron.[5]

However, to fulfill his strategic vision, Themistocles would have to eliminate his conservative opponents and win the Athenian assembly over to the cause of naval construction and more extensive urban fortifications. As a result, after Marathon, each major traditional political figure who might have challenged Themistocles' new strategic vision – Megacles, Miltiades, Xanthippus, and Aristides – found himself fined, ostracized, or under public suspicion. This growing infantry and naval divide between Themistocles and his more conservative rivals came to a head in 483 BC, just three years before the arrival of the Persians at Salamis, when an unusually rich vein of silver ore was discovered at the state-controlled mines at Laurium in southern Attica. The strike offered an opening for the impatient Themistocles to see his strategic thinking at last become state policy.[6]

Themistocles prevented the distribution of the windfall to the citizens on an equitable basis; instead, the assembly voted to build enough ships to produce an Athenian fleet of some 200 triremes. Ostensibly, the expressed threat was the nearby rival island power of Aegina, although Themistocles understood the real danger was a return of the Persians.[7] The rivalry with Aegina, and the chance strike at Laurium, now gave Themistocles the pretext, public support,

---

[5] Almost everything connected with Themistocles archonship – date, actuality, and achievement – is under scholarly dispute. For an introduction to the controversy see, A. Podlecki, *The Life of Themistocles: A Critical Survey of the Literary and Archaeological Evidence* (Montreal, 1975), pp. 45–66.

[6] On the new silver find at Laurium and the disbursement, see Hale, *Lords of the Sea*, pp. 8–14. Apparently, wealthy private citizens were allotted much of the newly minted silver; they, in turn, would use such public funds to oversee the building of a ship.

[7] See Podlecki, *Life of Themistocles*, p. 11: "Themistocles' purpose in eliminating his opponents one by one was the realization of a scheme he had cherished at least since his archonship, the transformation of Athens from a second-rate land power to the leading maritime state in Greece."

and money to prepare for that existential Persian threat. By late summer 480 BC, the Athenians may have completed as many as 170 triremes. Somewhere around 30,000 trained seamen were ready to protect the city from invasion, which inevitably would come by both land and sea.[8]

Naval strategy against Xerxes

King Xerxes (somewhere in his late thirties) assumed power on the death of his father Darius in 486/5. As a young and untried king, he almost immediately determined to draw on the empire's entire resources to avenge his father's failure. He aimed to annex Southern Europe across the Aegean as the westernmost province of Persia and end entirely the idea of an independent Greece. Accordingly, by fall 481 BC, the Greeks had received word that Persian mobilization was in full swing, mostly from its westward base at Sardis. Xerxes might well cross the Hellespont into Europe within a year. Themistocles and his supporters at Athens immediately tried to prepare the Athenians for the existential danger. Under his leadership, the democracy passed various resolutions recalling political exiles and preparing to mobilize the fleet to join a combined Hellenic defense on land and at sea.[9]

Once it was known to the Greek city-states that Xerxes' forces were gathering in the western Persian provinces, their leaders hastily agreed to meet at their own Panhellenic congress at the Isthmus of Corinth. When the generals arrived, the usual bickering and delay characterized the debate. Athens and Aegina needed to end their internecine war, while Athens found itself forced to grant supreme command of the allied resistance to the more esteemed Spartans, despite the latter having far fewer ships. Spies were to be sent out to obtain more accurate intelligence. The Greeks also extended invitations to distant Greek states to contribute resources for a common defense. Yet no concrete action followed.

---

[8] The so-called Naval Bill of Themistocles rests on good ancient authority (cf. Aristotle, *Constitution of Athens*, 22.7; Herodotus 7.143–44; Plutarch, *Themistocles* 4.1–2; and especially Thucydides 1.14.3). We are not sure whether 100 ships were built in 482 to augment an existing 70–100, or whether up to 200 were ordered from the revenues – only that the Athenian fleet that was ready at Salamis two years later numbered some 180–200 triremes. See Hale, *Lords of the Sea*, pp. 10–15.

[9] See Herodotus 8.79–82. The nature of these various decrees and their relationship to the texts of Herodotus and Plutarch are under dispute. These earlier resolutions probably concerned general contingency efforts and the recall of exiles, while the famous, subsequent "Themistocles' Decree" belonged to late summer 480 BC, and in more precise detail outlined the nature of the evacuation of Attica in August or September. We still do not know whether the decree accurately reflects a preemptory and long-planned Athenian decision to leave the city to fight at Salamis *before* the loss of Thermopylae, or was simply a later compilation of several authentic decrees, and thus is at odds with a more accurate Herodotean account that the evacuation of Athens was an ad hoc, last-ditch effort after Thermopylae was unexpectedly breached.

In early spring of 480 BC, the squabbling Greek states again met. This time, they finally agreed to organize a combined land and sea force to fight as far to the north as possible. The apparent strategy was to keep Xerxes and the Persians as far away from the Greek heartland as possible. Nevertheless, for the next six months, all attempts at Panhellenic resistance resulted in utter failure. Sometime in April 480 BC, Xerxes crossed the Hellespont into Europe with a combined force of hundreds of thousands of infantry and seamen. The exact numbers of the Persian muster are unknown and remain hotly debated. But merely to man a fleet of over 1,200 triremes required nearly a quarter-million sailors, quite apart from cavalry and infantry. Most modern estimates place his land forces alone at somewhere between 100,000 to 200,000 combatants and support troops, making Xerxes' grand expedition the largest amphibious invasion of Europe until the Normandy invasion more than 2,400 years later. Scholars still do not quite understand how the Persian quartermasters solved the enormous logistical problems of feeding and caring for such a horde.

The allied congress earlier had assembled a force of almost 10,000 Greek hoplites and a large enough naval contingent to transport them up to Thessaly. Themistocles was co-commander of this initial Panhellenic expeditionary force. Upon arrival, the position of the Greeks almost immediately became untenable, even before they marshaled their forces for battle. At this early date, the mostly central and southern Greek states had little idea of the geography of Macedon, the planned routes of the Persian invasion, or the huge size of Xerxes' forces.

The generals had even less inkling that the proposed line of defense in the Vale of Tempe between Mt. Olympus and Ossa was topographically indefensible in the face of a large invasion. They had also come north unprepared, without sufficient supplies, and too early, and still under the impression that land forces alone might stop Xerxes in the manner that Marathon had ended Darius' efforts. In utter dejection, the humiliated Greek expeditionary force returned to the isthmus well before the Persians even arrived, ostensibly to plot a second fallback strategy. But time was running out and morale eroding. By late summer, the Persians had swept through the north and were ready to enter central Greece itself through the narrow pass at Thermopylae, with an apparently unstoppable strategy of picking off northern Greek city-states, one by one, as those to the south found themselves more isolated day by day. As panic set in, all eyes looked to the Spartans to stop the massive Persian descent.[10]

---

[10] For discussion of the contradictory numbers in ancient sources, see B. Strauss, *The Battle of Salamis: The Naval Encounter That Saved Greece – and Western Civilization* (New York, 2004), p. 42. C. Hignett, *Xerxes' Invasion of Greece* (Oxford, 1963), pp. 345–355, in detailed fashion, reviews the literary evidence, arriving at a low estimate of a Persian Army of some 80,000, and naval force of about 600 ships (that would require some 120,000 seamen).

Somehow the usually conservative Spartan leadership galvanized the Greek resistance and marshaled an ad hoc second land force of at least 7,000 infantrymen under the Spartan King Leonidas, a little over half the force mustered from the city-states of the Peloponnese. A combined fleet of nearly 300 ships under the command of his fellow Spartan Eurybiades was to accompany and supply the land forces. Themistocles enjoyed a quasi-autonomous command of the fleet of almost 200 Athenian triremes. He apparently insisted that his Athenians would only serve at sea and not augment the hoplite defense at Thermopylae.

Amid the gripping drama of the heroism at Thermopylae and the gallant sacrifice of Leonidas and the Spartan 300 (along with nearly 1,100 Thespians and Thebans, and several hundred others) on the last day of the battle, we may forget that Thermopylae was a terrible defeat. The loss of the pass allowed the victorious Persian Army a wide-open path of descent southwards into the wealthiest of the Greek city-states.[11]

Three subsequent naval engagements at nearby Artemisium proved only a nominal Greek victory. Themistocles' aggressive tactics to draw the much larger Persian fleet into the Straits of Artemisium, his choice to engage in the unaccustomed late afternoon, and his reliance on speed, maneuver, and ramming, all continued to confound enemy triremes before they could deploy in proper order. By the naval battle's end, the allies had destroyed more Persian ships than they lost. Posterity usually has forgotten that the sea-battle did far more harm to the Persian cause than did the far more dramatic last stand at Thermopylae. In addition, sudden storms caught the retiring Persian fleet without adequate harborage, and wrecked dozens more. Yet for all the damage to the huge Persian armada, in battle and in the rough seas at Artemisium – perhaps 600 triremes lost altogether – it was the Greek fleet that retreated southward. Xerxes' ships followed closely at their rear. How might the Greeks save Athens and the Peloponnese when even a naval victory and providential storm proved inadequate to stop the Persian advance, given the enemy's vast numbers and constant resupply?[12] That was the dark question that haunted the weary Greeks.

The fighting thus far had now damaged or destroyed half the Greek fleet. As many as a hundred triremes needed repair. More ominously, most of the Greek city-states north of Athens joined the Persians or were making arrangements to do so. Xerxes' forces were growing again, the allies shrinking,

---

[11] Herodotus (8.25.2) believed that there were 4,000 Greek dead left on the battlefield, which, *if* true, would mean that almost 60 percent of Leonidas' original force perished in the pass. Apparently that figure would have to include large numbers of dead on the first two days of battle from the original force of 7,000, together with all of those (the 400 Thebans, 700 Thespians, 300 Spartans, and some Phocians and helots) left behind to be wiped out with Leonidas.

[12] Themistocles at Artemisium, see Diodorus 11.12.5–6. There is a good account of the battle and its aftermath in Hale, *Lords of the Sea*, pp. 46–54.

as the king supplied his forces from the "earth and water" of his northern Greek hosts. The Athenians' desperate appeal to field another Panhellenic army to stop the Persians on Athens' borders with Boeotia was ignored by the Peloponnesian infantry, who streamed all the way back to the isthmus, wanting no more part of any plan to fight north of the isthmus. Any Greek state not defended by the retreating alliance either was obliterated or joined the Persians. The polyglot forces of imperial Persia were now more united than the Greeks, who ostensibly shared the same religion, language, and culture.[13]

During the Persian descent into Greece, the Athenians had customarily consulted the oracle at Delphi. Their envoys received various responses from the always politically astute Pythia. The last and most famous reply from the priestess offered cryptic advice: first, retreat before the enemy; second, trust in a mysterious "wooden wall," and, third, put hope in a "Holy Salamis" and thereby achieve the promise that the Greeks would at some date "destroy" the Persians. Dispute broke out over the oracle's deliberately ambiguous meaning. For those Athenians who did not wish to fight here at sea, or were too poor to flee the city, the prophecy was read either as gibberish or as recommending a defense on the Athenian Acropolis behind wooden walls of old doors, cast-off furnishing, and logs.

Instead, Themistocles persuaded his fellow generals that Delphi's "wooden wall" could only refer to their own fleet of pine- and fir-planked triremes. After all, why would the oracle at Delphi call Athenian-held Salamis "holy" if she did not mean victory was ensured there for the Greeks, if they would only dare fight by sea? Whether Themistocles' agents had something to do with cooking up the prophecy or twisting its interpretation, we do not know. But Themistocles was not going to let the superstitious or pusillanimous thwart his plans to gamble all at Salamis, plans based on a decade of reason, not hocus-pocus. Having pulled off a stalemate at Artemisium, perhaps the Greeks could now defeat a weaker and wounded Persian fleet as it sailed south to Athens and away from its original bases of support in northern Greece.[14]

The real divide now arose over the proper last-ditch strategy to defend the Athenians from hundreds of thousands of Persians. The enemy infantry and marine forces had not suffered a single defeat in the five months since their arrival in Europe. Two diametrically opposed defensive strategies now were debated, one among Athenians themselves, whether to protect the city proper or evacuate the population, and a second between the remaining city-states of the alliance over whether to fight by sea in the Bay of Salamis, or to fall back even further.

---

[13] Cf. Plutarch, *Themistocles* 9.3. Herodotus 7.33–4.
[14] Cf. Herodotus 49–50. J. R. Lenardon, *The Saga of Themistocles* (London, 1978), pp. 64–65, discusses the various interpretations of the famous oracular reply.

At least some of these deliberations were cut short when Xerxes arrived in Attica and quickly stormed Athens, killing its defenders. The doomed Athenians on the Acropolis proved that the oracle's "wooden wall" apparently did not mean their futile timber barricade. Themistocles had just introduced a decree to evacuate the city.[15] The surviving Athenians hastily scattered among the nearby islands and the northern Argolid. In panic, the city-state's defense was now reduced to those who manned 180 triremes in the Bay of Salamis, along with the contingents of hoplites who guarded the refugees or helped to man the ships.

The renegade Spartan ex-King Demaratus, now a Persian court advisor, had urged Xerxes to avoid the Greeks. Instead, according to Herodotus, he advised Xerxes to sail around the Peloponnese to occupy the island of Cythera off Sparta. That way, Demaratus argued, the Persians could avoid losses, tie down the Spartan Army and raise a helot revolt, perhaps putting Demaratus himself back in power as a puppet king. But with Athens in flames and the Greek fleet trapped in the Straits of Salamis, such cautious advice seemed passé. Once they had swamped the outnumbered Greeks at Salamis, the Persians could land wherever they pleased in the Peloponnese. Then they could pick off the city-states south of the isthmus one by one.[16]

Other Greek leaders had proposed several complicated alternative strategies before and after the retreat from Thermopylae. Many conservative Athenians, for example, still wished to fight on the Attic plain, not at sea – perhaps in some sort of decisive infantry confrontation that might repeat the verdict of Marathon – and save their city while restoring the prestige of the hoplite class. But that dream quickly died after the disaster at Thermopylae. The rapidity of the Persian descent, the absence of willing allies, and the fact that Xerxes this time had ten times the number of land forces that his father Darius had sent ten years earlier all made another Marathon unthinkable. Athenians at Marathon had been outnumbered three to one. But now the Persian land forces were at least ten times larger than the Athenian hoplite force. Only a few isolated pockets of Athenians remained in the Attic countryside.[17]

Another choice was simply for Athenians and the remaining allies to quit and join the Persians. This option was not so far-fetched. There were plenty of Athenians furious at the Peloponnesian city-states for abandoning them to

[15] A later interpolated version of it on stone came to light in 1959, and was published the following year.
[16] On Demaratus' advice, see Herodotus 7.235.3. For the evacuation and the circumstances around the decree, see Lenardon, *Saga of Themistocles*, pp. 69–72. Demaratus' proposal may be telescoped backwards from Herodotus' own time, when in the initial years of the Peloponnesian War, there was much talk of the Athenians using helot revolts as a tool against the Spartans.
[17] On the few who stayed behind either in the Attic countryside or at Athens, see P. Green, *The Greco-Persian Wars* (Berkeley, 1996), pp. 156–160. A year after Salamis the Greeks would win a glorious infantry victory at Plataea over Mardonius. But that battle came after careful preparation, was prompted in part by the shameful retreat of King Xerxes and his fleet back to Asia after their defeat at Salamis, and was waged with near equal numbers on both sides.

the Persians without an infantry fight somewhere to the immediate north in Boeotia that might have prevented the fall of the city. Many now felt their cause was hopeless, and that the northern Greek city-states such as Thebes offered a possible model of accommodation. Still, most at Salamis stayed firm. As long as the surviving Greeks had nearly 400 ships, the Athenian population was still safe, and the soil of the Peloponnese was still Greek, such surrender seemed premature, even if that now meant camping in the countryside for thousands of Athenians without guaranteed shelter and food.

Most of the remaining allies, in fact, initially preferred yet another option: to retreat south to fight on land behind makeshift ramparts along the 6-mile isthmus, saving what was left of Greece, while engaging the Persian fleet somewhere off the coast of the Peloponnese. The maritime Athenians, remember, earlier had not offered their 10,000 hoplites to fight at Thermopylae. In similar fashion, the land-powers of the Peloponnese preferred not to risk their own ships in the defense of the evacuated Athenians. Perhaps a second Thermopylae at the isthmus might turn out differently.

Still, Themistocles, as we learn from Herodotus, wondered whether the Spartans who advocated further retreat were acting even in their own best interests. In theory, what would prevent a Persian amphibious landing in the Peloponnese behind an isthmus wall (as the turncoat Demaratus had, in fact, advised Xerxes to do)? Fighting in more open seas off the Peloponnese only gave more advantages to the far larger enemy fleet. And why would the Athenians sacrifice any hope of recovering their city in order to fight on behalf of Peloponnesians who clearly all along cared only for their own defense? Ceding more land was no strategy for a defense of Greece.

More immediately, what would the assembled Greeks do about thousands of hungry refugees on Salamis, whose safety depended entirely on the Greek ships in the harbors of the island? Who could restore morale after four successive withdrawals from the Vale of Tempe in Thessaly, Thermopylae, Artemisium, and now Salamis? An alliance that either loses battles or does not fight them finds it almost impossible to turn on its aggressor and cede no more ground. The squabbling Greeks before Salamis heard yet another alternative – a most bizarre, but apparently serious, threat from Themistocles himself. He warned that the Athenians might pull up stakes entirely. If the Athenians were to be abandoned by their Peloponnesian and island allies, and a general retreat ordered to the south, then Themistocles would round up the city's refugees, sail to distant Sicily and settle perhaps 200,000 of the evacuated Athenian residents near their old colony at Siris – rebirthing Athenian culture in safety 800 miles to the west.[18] "If you do not do these things [fight at

---

[18] On the Greeks' desire to vacate Salamis, see the synopsis in Diodorus 11.15.4–5. Even if the Athenians had 200 triremes, and an unknown number of merchant ships, it is hard to see how they would have the lift capacity to move their women, children, and slaves to Italy across the Mediterranean in fall and winter.

Salamis]," Themistocles threatened the Peloponnesians, "then we quite soon will take up our households and sail over to Siris in Italy, a place which has been ours from ancient times, and at which the oracles inform us that we should plant a colony. And the rest of you without allies such as ourselves will have reason to remember my words." One wonders how Themistocles planned to transport tens of thousands of Athenians during the fall and winter storm season, across treacherous waters some 800 miles to the west, while leaving behind thousands of Athenians who were still scattered and in hiding throughout Attica.[19]

The final poor choice from among the far worse alternatives was for the remaining allies to fight a last-ditch, sea-battle at Salamis. That way, the Greeks would cede no more territory. Instead, the admirals would preserve Greek unity and hope to cripple the Persian fleet – and with it any chance of escape for many of the massive army of Xerxes. Because there were finite supplies at Salamis, and thousands of refugees to feed, there was simply no time left for talk. The battle had to be joined almost immediately, even if that meant that most of the assembled admirals would have to both concede to Themistocles' threats and override their original directives from political authorities at home to retreat to a Panhellenic defense at the isthmus. While the Greeks had been beaten by land, they had not yet lost at sea, where the numbers were not so lopsided.[20]

Our ancient sources, the historian Herodotus and the contemporary playwright Aeschylus, along with later accounts in Plutarch, Diodorus, and Nepos, believed the Persians outnumbered the reconstituted Greek fleet by three or four to one. In fact, it may have been little more than two to one. There is no information on how many ships joined the respective fleets after the retreat from Artemisium as reinforcements. But ancient accounts suggest that between Persian replacements and the growing number of "Medizing" Greeks, the enemy might have been at least as large as when it had left Persia months earlier.

If some Greeks quietly slipped away from Salamis and headed south, most triremes stayed. Even after wear and tear on the fleet and losses at Artemisium, there may have somewhere between 300 and 370 Greek vessels at Salamis to take on a Persian armada of at least 600 warships, although both Herodotus and Aeschylus record that the enemy fleet had been reinforced to over 1,200 enemies ships, a figure that cannot be entirely discounted. The Greek fleet, still under the nominal overall command of the Spartan Eurybiades, was less experienced than the imperial Persian flotilla. Moreover, Greek triremes were heavier and less maneuverable.

---

[19] Herodotus, 8.62; cf. Plutarch, *Themistocles* 11. We have no reason to doubt this strange threat, given that it seems to be accepted by most ancient authorities.

[20] See, Green, *Greco-Persian Wars*, pp. 159–160, on the degree of operational authority among the Greek generals at Salamis.

In contrast, the king's armada comprised various veteran contingents from Phoenicia, Egypt, Asia Minor, Cyprus, and Greece itself. Most had patrolled the Aegean and Mediterranean for years enforcing the edicts of the Persian Empire. And more Greek ships at Salamis would fight on the Persian than on the Hellenic side.[21]

The alliance's best hope, according to Themistocles, was to draw the Persians into the narrows between Salamis and the Attic mainland. There the more numerous but also lighter enemy triremes would be vulnerable to the heavier and presumably slower Greek ships. Themistocles reasoned that, in confined waters, the invaders might not have sufficient room to maneuver all their fleet and would lose some of the advantages of their numbers and superior nautical skill. Surprise – and greater Greek knowledge of currents and contrary winds inside the straits – would also aid the defenders. The unity of the Greeks versus the motley nature of the subject Persian armada, the psychological advantages defenders enjoy over aggressors, the hope that free peoples would fight for their own destiny more stoutly than subjects would amid their subservience: in Themistocles' mind, all these advantages might trump Persian numbers.[22]

Various sources also refer to a ruse on the part of Themistocles on the eve of the battle. He secretly sent his own slave Sicinnus to Xerxes with a purported warning of a Greek withdrawal. The Persians might well have swallowed that story of Themistocles' treachery, given the rumors of Greek infighting and the well-reported Peloponnesian desire to go home. Themistocles' intention with the trick must have been multifold: he wanted to incite the Persians hastily to deploy and prematurely man their ships in the night. Second, he sought to fool them into splitting their larger enemy fleet by persuading them to cover all the potential exits from the Straits of Salamis. Third, Persian preemption would force his reluctant Greek allies to commit to the sea-battle by forcing them to mobilize immediately in the face of the advancing Persian enemy. Apparently, the agreement to stay at Salamis had strengthened the position of Themistocles. In the few hours before battle, he began to exercise de facto tactical authority despite the nominal overall command of the Spartan Eurybiades.

[21] On the numbers of Greek and Persian ships at both Artemisium and Salamis, see again the review of the sources in Hignett, *Xerxes' Invasion of Greece*, pp. 345–350; cf. Green, *Greco-Persian Wars*, pp. 162–163, who conjectures an allied fleet of about 311 triremes, corrected for probable losses from the retreat from Artemisium. Herodotus (8.66) implies that the Persian land and sea forces had made up all the prior losses at Thermopylae and Artemisium and were about the same size as when they had crossed into Europe the prior spring.

[22] Herodotus – writing two generations after the battle – believed that the Greek ships were the "heavier." Scholars usually interpret that he meant that they were water-logged, built of unseasoned, heavier timber, or simply larger and less elegant – and thus less maneuverable – than the Persians' triremes. Whatever the true case, it was clearly in the Greeks' interest not to sail too far out to sea where they would be both outnumbered and outmaneuvered, but to stay inside the straits where their ramming would have far greater effect.

In response, the Persians without careful planning rushed out into the Straits of Salamis, as Themistocles hoped, but not before dispatching parts of their Egyptian squadrons to block the southern and western entrances to the straits. As expected, the Persians could not make full use of their numerical superiority inside the narrows of the Salamis Straits where the Greek fleet was moored. Instead, they had now sent some of their best contingents on a wild goose chase to ambush a Greek retreat that never came.[23]

Xerxes probably was forced to attack just before dawn. The Persian fleet rowed forward in three lines against the Greeks' two. The king's captains worried that they "would lose their heads" should the enemy fleet escape. Quickly the attackers became disorganized due to the Greek ramming and the confusion of having so many ships in confined waters. Themistocles himself was at the van of the advancing Greek triremes. Xerxes, in contrast, watched his Persians from afar, purportedly perched on his throne atop nearby Mt. Aigelaos on the Attic shore. In the words of the dramatist Aeschylus, "The mass of ships was crowded into the narrows, and none was able to offer help to another."[24]

The sea-battle was fought all day – most likely sometime between 20 and 30 September 480 BC – perhaps on the morning of 25 September. By nightfall the Greeks had sunk half the Persian fleet. The rest scattered. Defeat shattered the morale of the survivors despite their collective fear of the outraged king. The Persians suffered "utter and complete ruin." In theory the surviving Persian triremes still outnumbered the Greeks, but the Persian armada was no longer battle-worthy or eager to reengage. Over 100,000 imperial sailors were killed, wounded, or missing, making Salamis perhaps the largest and most lethal one-day naval battle in history, far bloodier than Lepanto, Trafalgar, Jutland, or Midway. Ancient accounts record the macabre scene of the human carnage where Persian corpses were "battered by the surf, lifeless, tossed here and there in their cloaks." Given that most of the Persians could not swim, we should assume the Greeks speared survivors clinging to the flotsam and jetsam, knocking them beneath the waves – "hitting and hacking them with broken oars and the wreckage of the ships."[25]

---

[23] Plutarch, *Themistocles* 12.3–5; and cf. Diodorus 11.19. Many scholars doubt the veracity of the Sicinnus ruse, and the idea that the Persians ever diverted a portion of their fleet to cover possible escapes from the Bay of Salamis. But the Sicinnus incident is a mainstay in nearly all ancient descriptions of the battle. See the lively account of the trick in T. Holland, *Persian Fire: The First World Empire and the Battle for the West* (New York, 2005), pp. 312–316.

[24] Aeschylus, *Persians* 371, 412–3, 425–6. Aeschylus, a veteran of the battle, may have meant as well that dozens of Persian ships in the middle of the fleet simply never came in contact with the Greeks attacking at the periphery, a sort of naval Cannae in which thousands of combatants remained outside the battle for quite some time, if at all.

[25] Aeschylus, *Persians* 274–6, 282–3. As at Lepanto, there is a likelihood that few prisoners were taken, the Greek idea being that any killed in the waters of Salamis would not fight again the next year. See V. Hanson, *Carnage and Culture: Landmark Battles in the Rise of Western Power* (New York, 2001), pp. 46–51, for the motif of *eleutheria* (freedom) at Salamis and the role it played in galvanizing the Greeks.

Within weeks of the defeat, a panicky Xerxes left a ruined Athens and sailed home with survivors of the imperial fleet to the Hellespont, accompanied by a guard of 60,000 infantry. The king left behind his surrogate commander Mardonius, with a considerable infantry and cavalry force, to resume the struggle the next spring. The remaining Persian land forces quickly retreated northward to winter in the pastures of Boeotia. The Athenian refugees – for a time – got back their burned out city.

Although the Greeks had immediately declared victory after Salamis, Mardonius returned within a few months over the pass from Boeotia to reoccupy Athens. The population again fled, the Persians torching the city a second time. Then Mardonius retreated back into Boeotia yet a third time in late summer 479 BC to prepare for the expected Greek counterattack. After the victory and flight of Xerxes, some 70,000 reenergized Greeks now flocked to Plataea near the mountainous Attic border to finish off Mardonius. In a small plain along the Asopos River on the lower slopes of Mt. Kithairon, the Greeks crushed the Persians, killed Mardonius, and watched the survivors scatter to the north. Themistocles apparently did not take part in the land-battle, but was still at sea pursuing enemy vessels along the coast of Asia Minor – or, more likely, had suffered some sort of falling out with the Greek high command tired of his constant boasting.

After the storm and losses at Artemisium and the subsequent naval defeat at Salamis, Xerxes may have lost over 900 triremes. Now, with Mardonius' annihilation in Boeotia, perhaps as many as a quarter-million Persian imperial infantry and sailors had perished or were scattered in Greece in little over a year. Rarely in the ancient world had so few killed so many. The cultural result was exultation in Greek freedom: "No longer was there a bridle on the speech of mortals, for the people were set free to say what they wished, once the yoke of power was broken."[26]

The postwar foundations of the Athenian Empire

The victory at Salamis, however, was not the capstone of Themistocles' strategic career, who was still only in his mid forties. Rather, it marked the beginning of an even more radical subsequent agenda that involved transforming Athens itself – and offending most of the city's most powerful landed families. From 479 BC until his exile from Athens in 463, Themistocles, who would die in Persian-held Asia Minor under mysterious circumstances in 459, systematically attempted to transform a once largely agrarian city-state into a trans-Aegean mercantile empire, based on a standing navy of well over 200 triremes.

---

[26] Aeschylus, *Persians* 591–4. Aeschylus records (402–5) that the Greeks rowed into battle chanting cries of "Free your children, your wives, the images of your fathers' gods and the tombs of your ancestors."

Following the Persians' defeat at Plataea and Mycale, the Greek postwar alliance against the common enemy, Persia, proved no more lasting than did the Soviet–American pact following the common defeat of Nazi Germany. Themistocles' immediate postwar efforts to expand the city's fortifications and enlarge its fleet immediately provoked the parochial Spartans and their sympathizers in Athens. Especially galling to Themistocles' rich and pro-Spartan countrymen was his ruse of visiting Sparta to agree to a utopian desire for an unwalled Greece. Then, while Themistocles assured the gullible Spartans of Athens' shared wish for Panhellenic cooperation in the postwar era, the democrats feverishly fortified both the city and harbor. With new walls, the urban core of Athens was now mostly immune from traditional infantry attack; and a far better harbor at Piraeus meant the fleet could be more easily and safely moored. That trickery at once challenged Spartan hoplite preeminence, at least to the extent that potentially besieged Athenians might stay inside their walls longer than an invading Spartan army could camp outside the city's wall in Attica.[27]

But the city's new defenses also reduced the political and economic clout of the traditionally powerful in Attica, who held farmland outside the walls, and were recovering from the devastations of the Persian invasion and the loss of their property. Themistocles' advocacy of postwar fortifications might even mean in conflicts to come that the Athenians might perennially sacrifice the extramural farmland of the wealthy to the enemy, as the landless poor – now the more valuable citizens as rowers in the growing fleet – remained safe inside ramparts.

Fortifications certainly were a better way of meeting a formidable invasion than evacuating and abandoning the city in panic as had happened before Salamis. What formerly had been ad hoc now would be institutionalized. Urban walls also required larger government expenditure and their construction tended to spread wealth. Fortifications helped to transfer the burden of national defense to the fleet, and with it the empowerment of the poorer and more numerous rowers. Sea-defense at Salamis had been the right choice at the time. But in the aftermath of the Persian retreat, Themistocles saw that he could improve on his strategy by abandoning the countryside of its richer landowners and hoplite class – not, as in 480 BC, sending the poor of the city into makeshift hovels on the surrounding islands.

Conservatives understandably resented Themistocles' decade-long divisive democratic agenda that soon after Salamis insidiously weakened the power of the hoplite landowning heavy infantrymen. In their eyes, he had turned

---

[27] On the famous Themistoclean ruse of deceiving the Spartans while his countrymen fortified the city, see Diodorus 11.40. While it might take a week to reach Athens and another to return home, it seems incredible that the Spartans had no intelligence concerning Athens' sudden massive wall building, while Themistocles conducted his deceptive diplomacy.

the city from one of "steadfast hoplites into sea-tossed mariners."[28]
The conservative philosopher Plato – looking back over a century of radical
Athenian history – later wrote that the Athenians would have been better off
to have lost sea-fights like those at Salamis even if they had saved Greece,
rather than have such Themistoclean victories lead to the establishment of
an extremist and unsustainable democracy and the rise of the uncouth to
unbridled power. It was Themistocles, Plato also scoffed, who had first
"stripped the citizens of their spear and shield, and brought the Athenian
people down to the rowing-pad and oar."[29]

As was the fate of many Greek visionaries, novel ideas – that instantly
branded Themistocles a dangerous radical and earned him exile – would be
institutionalized by Pericles and others as official policy within decades. But
that acceptance came only after Themistocles' exile and with little acknowledgment of his role of the creator of maritime empire. Themistocles, Plutarch
concluded, "increased the power of the common people against the aristocracy,
filling them with recklessness, once the control of the state came into the hands
of the sailors, boatswains, and captains." Equally important, the fortification
of both the city and the new harbor at Piraeus encouraged the successors of
Themistocles – by 457 BC three years after his death – to finish two parallel
Long Walls that ran the 4.5 miles between city and the new harbor, and
thus to complete the Themistoclean dream of a maritime city immune from
being cut off from the sea. Athens *in extremis* could now become an island.[30]

The strategic achievement of Themistocles

In four general areas, the strategy of Themistocles proved critical to the
salvation of the Greeks and the future of Athens as an unrivaled power,
and it seems to have been recognized as such by his contemporaries. Themistocles' strategic achievements hinged on singular diplomacy, political
partisanship, grand strategy, battle tactics, and unabashed cunning. That
"foresight" separated Themistocles from most successful Greek military
thinkers, who either had no comprehensive strategic view, or claimed
foreordained knowledge only after success.

---

[28] Plato, *Laws* 4.706; cf. Plutarch, *Themistocles* 4. To conservatives, Marathon was the last time
that Athenian infantrymen fought gloriously for their own land – thanks to radicals like
Themistocles.

[29] Plato, *Laws* 4.706. Much of Plato's criticism of democracy was predicated on the efforts of
low-born demagogues to emasculate the well-born militarily, economically, and politically.
In Plato's eyes, the defeat of Athens in the Peloponnesian War was the logical result of an
unfortunate decision to invest in sea-power and the poor largely attributed to Themistocles.

[30] Plutarch, *Themistocles* 19.3–4. Almost all extant Greek literature is anti-democratic
(reflecting the class, learning, and privileges of most authors), at least in the sense of
emphasizing the dangers of allowing a majority of citizens to set policy on any given day
by simple majority vote, without either constitutional restraints or the checks and balances of
parallel, but more oligarchical bodies.

(1) *A fleet.* Had Themistocles earlier (483 BC) not urged the Athenians to build their fleet with the sudden revenues from the silver mines at Laurium, there would probably have been no chance for a credible Greek defense at Salamis. We sometimes forget that Themistocles plowed ahead against the advice of most Athenians, contrary to the received infantry wisdom from the recent victory at Marathon. In early Athenian democracy, most popular leaders would have divvied up the money and distributed it to the people, while their conservative opponents would have never allowed state funds to establish an enormous navy. Themistocles alone saw a third way, at a time when all others were still building monuments to the valor of Marathon.

(2) *Evacuating Athens.* But even the new fleet was not enough to offer Athens a chance of victory. Had Themistocles not convinced the Athenians in September 480 BC to evacuate the Attic countryside, the Persians would have wiped out their hoplite army in a glorious Thermopylae-like last stand in Attica, as the fleet retreated south or westward. Nor earlier did he try to rally the Greek allies to march northward to stop the Persians on the Boeotian plains. Themistocles had fought at Marathon, and co-commanded the failed defense at Tempe in summer 480. He knew by September that hoplites could not overcome ten to one numerical odds. The infantry fight the next year at Plataea was a close-run thing – even after tens of thousands of Persians had died at Salamis or retreated home, and only with a massive muster of over 50,000 Greek soldiers and the rise in morale after the great sea victory the year before.

Themistocles' later postwar efforts to fortify Athens, followed by the subsequent measures of Pericles after his death to build two extensive Long Walls connecting the city to the Piraeus, emphasized how determined later generations were *never* to repeat the horror of 480 BC in abandoning the city. The subsequent imperial leader Pericles was a Themistoclean at heart. He argued that the only way to defeat Sparta in the Peloponnesian War (431–404) was, as at Salamis, to fight at sea after abandoning the defense of the Athenian countryside against Spartan ravagers. But unlike Themistocles, Pericles advocated such strategy only with the reassurance that the city itself and its port at Piraeus were safe behind walls. Yet ironically there would be problems of disease in cramming citizens into a small municipality rather than dispersing them across the surrounding countryside and islands. The subsequent plague of 429 BC and the chronic inability to expel the Spartans from Attica reminded the Athenians of the dangers inherent in Themistocles' legacy of focusing on the fleet and fortifications without a credible land deterrent that might persuade infantry enemies that it was unwise to invade Attica.

(3) *The Tactical Plan at Salamis.* Later Greek tradition credited Themistocles with the decision to "fight in the strait." Although most southern Greeks apparently came to understand at the eleventh hour that Themistocles'

logic was in their own interests in providing a forward defense for the Peloponnese, and in keeping the Athenian fleet engaged in the Greek defense, there was still no guarantee that the Peloponnesians would fight at Salamis, given their near completion of a massive wall at the Isthmus. To read Plutarch's *Life of Themistocles* is to collate a list of ancient attacks on both the character and wisdom of Themistocles on the eve of battle. So two further actions of Themistocles were required to guarantee a fight at Salamis and then to achieve victory.[31] The ruse of Sicinnus persuaded the Persians immediately to embark and thereby to force the wavering non-Athenian Greeks to stay and fight. Scholars are divided over the authenticity of the tale. But there is little reason to doubt the general truth of the ancient account, inasmuch as at the point when the alliance was about to break up, the news was announced to the Greek admirals that the Persians were at sea and the approaches in the Salamis channel were now blocked. Only then did the Greeks discover that they could now no longer retreat to the Isthmus. The choice was either to fight immediately or surrender – or attempt flight amid the Persian fleet.[32]

Because Themistocles had in effect persuaded the Persians into committing their ships into the narrow channels, it is probable that the actual plan of the Greek deployment was also his as well, as later Greeks surmised. The secret to the Greek success was to draw the cumbersome enemy fleet further into the narrows, and to insure it could not utilize its overwhelming numerical advantage. Thus Themistocles had the Greek ships initially backwater. That made the Persians row further into the channel, on the assumption that the Greeks were in fact trying to flee as their fifth-column "intelligence" had indicated. When the two fleets collided, the Persians, again as Themistocles had planned, found themselves disordered, and thus incapable of bringing their full strength against the ordered Greek armada.

Controversy surrounds yet another Themistoclean stratagem – the purported postwar second secret message to the defeated Xerxes urging him to sail home while Themistocles magnanimously prevented the Greeks from reaching his bridges at the Hellespont first, and destroying easy entry back into Asia. If this second effort at deception was also true – Xerxes, after all, could always ferry his retreating and reduced forces across the Hellespont – then it had the added effect of encouraging another split in Persian forces after the battle. That meant at the subsequent battle of Plataea the following August, the enemy forces under Mardonius were not all that much more numerous than the assembled Panhellenic Greek Army.

[31] The "straits": Thucydides 1.74.1–2; cf. Plutarch, *Themistocles* 2–6.
[32] On the assessment of the role of Themistocles, the value of his deceptions, and the tactics at Salamis, see Diodorus 11.18–19.

Such machinations, however, also came at a cost. When a coalition leader must mislead his own allies, suspicion follows even in victory. After Salamis it was no surprise that Themistocles both repeated his efforts to delude the Spartans, and they in turn became ever more suspicious of his leadership.[33]

(4) *Fortifications.* As archon before Marathon, Themistocles had advocated building municipal fortifications around the city and the harbor at Phaleron. Even after the victory at Marathon, when such infantry excellence suggested the proper way to defend Athens lay in the shields of its hoplites, Themistocles pressed on to complete the urban fortifications. After the defeat of Xerxes' armada, he continued to advocate for more wall building and finished the urban ramparts and walls around the new, better port at the Piraeus. His successor Pericles brought his vision to fruition shortly after his death with the completion of the Long Walls. Note that, as in the case of his tactics at Salamis, intrigue and deception were keys to the leadership style of Themistocles.

The strategic implications of Themistocles' insistence on fortifications were multifold and symbiotic: (a) the city could be assured that a maritime strategy no longer necessitated the upheaval of urban evacuation; (b) Athens would not have to predicate its defense choices on the protection of farmland outside the walls that might entail unwise hoplite battles against superior land forces, foreign or Greek; (c) the democracy would be strengthened by offering employment for the rowing poor who could be assured of wages, the prestige of shouldering the primary defense of the city, and protection of their homes inside the city; (d) with a protected port, and later uninterrupted access to the city proper, Athens was not so dependent on its own agricultural production, farmers, or hoplites, in comparison to a navy and its crews who kept the imperial sea-lanes open and food imported into the Piraeus.

Such autonomy gave the city strategic options entirely lacking before the career of Themistocles – and also sharpened class differences between rich and poor. Later Athenian literature, ranging from the anonymous "Old Oligarch" to the *Acharnians* of Aristophanes, attests to rich/poor, oligarchic/democratic, urban/rural, and hoplite/*thete* divides that sharpened before and during the Peloponnesian War, and were a logical result of Themistoclean strategy – and would eventually tear Athens apart. That said, we must remember that almost all ancient Greek literature that deals with Themistocles, from the history of Thucydides to Plato's dialogues, is written from an aristocratic point of view.

---

[33] Herodotus 8.109–111; Diodorus 11.19. Salamis also ensured that Plataea was an existential battle: without a fleet to allow a maritime retreat, a defeated Persian Army would be trapped deep within Greek territory with the only avenue of escape a march through hundreds of miles of suddenly hostile Greek territory.

The Themistoclean legacy

Themistocles was the strategic architect of fifth-century Athens. He saved his city-state from the Persians and his vision became the foundation of the Athenian Empire and the city's later strategy against Sparta during the Peloponnesian War. Yet just as Themistocles must be credited with making Athens great, so too some ramifications of his strategy led to many of the city's later dilemmas. He was largely responsible for the growing divide between landowner and landless. Athens under Themistocles abandoned the old centrality of the hoplite-citizen and the idea that a property qualification was as essential to constitutional government as the phalanx had been for the practical and moral defense of the *polis*. In addition, evacuating thousands inside the walls would lead to the great plague, and the greatest loss of Athenian manpower in the history of the city-state. Finally, a maritime alliance that had started out as a pragmatic way to prevent the return of the Persians, by 454 BC, with the transfer of the Delian League treasury to Athens, became a de facto Athenian imperial empire, fulfilling Themistocles' original vision.

In short, ancient assessments of the greatness of Themistocles reflected his singular genius in fostering great power and danger all at once, while dividing Athenians for his visions of the greater common good. No one had done more to save Greece, and none more to insure an eventual showdown between Athens – the ascendant maritime and radically democratic empire – and Sparta, the champion of the traditional Greek landed *polis* and the primacy of hoplite infantry.

2   The grand strategy of the Roman Empire

James Lacey

If nothing else, the Roman Empire had a good run. From Octavian's victory at Actium (31 BC) to the date traditionally assigned to the empire's demise in 476, it lasted a solid 500 years – an impressive number by any standard. In fact, the decline and final collapse of the Roman Empire took longer than most other empires even existed. Any historian trying to unearth the grand strategy of the empire must, therefore, always remain cognizant of the fact that he or she is dealing with a period that covers nearly a fifth of recorded history.

Although the pace of change in the Roman era never approached that of the past 500 years, Rome was not an empire in stasis. While the visible trappings may have changed little, there were vast differences between the empire of Augustus and those of his successors. Over the centuries, the empire's underlying economy, political arrangements, military affairs, and, most importantly, the external challenges the empire faced were constantly changing. In truth, all of the factors that influence grand strategy were in a continuous state of flux, making adaptation as important to Roman strategists as to those of the modern era.

Tackling a subject as complex as Roman grand strategy involves another factor. If one defines grand strategy as including politics, diplomacy and economics along with military power, then there are currently no works on the totality of Roman grand strategy. In fact, the very idea of a Roman grand strategy did not concern historians until Edward Luttwak wrote his study on Roman grand strategy.[1] But even that work only concerned itself with the military aspects of grand strategy, while classical historians have assailed Luttwak's work since its publication.

Did Rome have a grand strategy?

Most historians of the Roman era question whether the Romans possessed a grand strategy, or whether their leaders were even capable of thinking in

---

[1] Edward Luttwak, *The Grand Strategy of the Roman Empire: From the First Century A.D. to the Third* (Baltimore, MD, 1976).

such terms. The most recent edition of *The Cambridge Ancient History* clearly captures the general consensus:

It is probably incorrect to define Roman military policy in terms of long-term strategical objectives, which saw the emergence of various systems designed to achieve "scientific" defensible frontiers. For one thing, the Romans lacked a high command or government office capable of giving coherent direction to overall strategy, which was therefore left to the decision of individual emperors and their advisers ... Military decisions were probably ad hoc, as emperors were forced into temporary defensive measures to limit damage ... In any case, the Romans lacked the kind of intelligence information necessary to make far-reaching, empire-wide decisions. Indeed they probably did not have a clear-cut view of frontiers, and came slowly to the idea that they should constitute a permanent barrier and a formal delineation of Roman territory.[2]

The above passage is not an original proposition of its author. Rather, it is a condensation of the theories of several prominent historians of the Roman era, particularly of frontier studies. These historians in their haste to decimate Luttwak's scholarship have made a hash of any reasonable attempts to understand Roman grand strategy.[3] While their scholarship on the Roman frontiers may be without parallel, many of their interpretations of the strategic and military rationale for the frontier defy reason.

For instance, at one point, C. R. Whittaker shows a picture of Qasr Bshir in Jordan, and asks, "as there is evidence this building had a civil function, are we too quick to think all frontier buildings were for defense?"[4] It takes a peculiar way of thinking to look at the pictures of what is obviously a fort, with combat towers and crenelated battlements along the walls, and then dismiss its military purpose. Just as with any medieval castle, a Roman fort had both civil as well as military purposes. This inability to see that Roman military installations, and even the legions themselves, had multiple uses plagues current scholarly analysis of Roman strategy.[5]

---

[2] Brian Campbell, "The Army," in Alan K Bowman, ed., *The Cambridge Ancient History: The Crisis of Empire*, vol. XII (Cambridge, 2009), p. 114.

[3] See: J. C. Mann, "The Frontiers of the Principate," ANRW 2 (1974), pp. 13–35; J. C. Mann, "Power and the Frontiers of the Empire," *The Journal of Roman Studies*, vol. 69, 1979, pp. 175–183; C. R. Whittaker, *Frontiers of the Roman Empire: A Social and Economic Study* (Baltimore, MD, 1994); Benjamin Isaac, *The Limits of Empire: The Roman Army in the East* (Oxford, 1990), and Arthur Ferrill, *The Fall of the Roman Empire: The Military Explanation* (London, 1986). For a more recent and better reasoned view of Roman strategy, as it pertained to the frontiers, see David J. Breeze, *The Frontiers of Imperial Rome* (Barnsley, UK, 2011).

[4] Whittaker, *Frontiers of the Roman Empire*.

[5] My criticism of Roman historians, in their commentary on Roman strategy, echoes Everett Wheeler's similar critique. See: Everett L. Wheeler, "Methodological Limits and the Mirage of Roman Strategy: Part I," *The Journal of Military History*, vol. 57, no. 1, January 1993, pp. 7–41; and, Everett L. Wheeler, "Methodological Limits and the Mirage of Roman Strategy: Part II," *The Journal of Military History*, vol. 57, no. 2, April 1993, pp. 215–240.

Simply put, according to historians of ancient Rome, the Romans had no conception of frontiers as boundaries requiring defense.[6] Following this logic, one must therefore assume that Roman emperors somehow managed to station their legions along these frontiers by some act of supreme serendipity. At least one noted Roman historian neatly disposes of the problem of the legions' apparent "strategic" positioning, by declaring that conclusions about Rome's ability to think strategically based on the dispositions of the army are nothing but the rankest speculation.[7]

If one takes modern historians at their word, Rome had no true idea of the geography of its empire or the world beyond its borders.[8] Given that the Romans conducted trade, built roads, and ran what appears to be an efficient postal service (much used by Pliny to pester the emperor with his missives), the evidence is clear that they understood the geography within the empire's boundaries. Likewise, numerous examples of Roman plans to assault enemies beyond the frontier with coordinated columns launched from widely divergent points suggest they had a solid grasp of what lay beyond their borders for several hundred miles.[9] In fact, a historian who looked deeply into the subject deduced that one of the main duties of the *mensores militum* was the production of military maps.[10] Interestingly, Herodotus tells of an Ionian named Aristogoras trying to induce Sparta into a war with Persia in 499 BC by producing "a bronze tablet, whereupon the whole circuit of the earth was engraved, with all its seas and rivers."[11] Apparently, according to today's Roman historians, in the intervening 500 years, Roman governments discontinued the use of maps. Yet, as one historian points out, "Such territory [the Eastern Empire and beyond] was hardly *terra incognita* and a vast store of geographical information and campaign experience probably circulated within the Roman officer corps."[12] In fact, given the geographical ignorance many current ancient historians attribute to the Romans, it is remarkable that barring disaster, every Roman army ever dispatched to attack the Persian capital of Ctesiphon seemed to unerringly find its way to the objective.

There is one further element that supposedly made it impossible for Rome to think strategically – the lack of a general staff or its ancient equivalent.

---

[6] See Isaac, *Limits of Empire*, pp. 397–401; and, Whittaker, *Frontiers of the Roman Empire*, pp. 60–70.

[7] Isaac, *Limits of Empire*, p. 33.

[8] See particularly Susan P. Mattern, *Rome and the Enemy: Imperial Strategy in the Principate* (Berkley, CA, 1999), pp. 24–80; and Whittaker, *Frontiers of the Roman Empire*, pp. 401–408; and, Isaac, *Limits of Empire*, pp. 10–30.

[9] For example, Roman plans to overwhelm the Marcomanni in AD 6, when 12 legions were set to march from Rhaetia, Germany, and Illyricum, all along separate routes converging in Bohemia (see: Velleius: 2.108–111).

[10] R. K. Sherk, Roman Geographical Exploration and Military Maps II.1 (ANWR, 1974), pp. 534–562.

[11] Herodotus 5.49.

[12] Wheeler, "Methodological Limits and the Mirage of Roman Strategy: Part II," p. 237.

Of course, no nation had a general staff or its equivalent until the Prussians invented such an entity in the nineteenth century. Does that mean that Alexander, Gustavus Adolphus, or Napoleon were incapable of strategic thinking? As one historian notes: "Should we accept the view that the institution consuming, even on a conservative estimate, 40 to 50 percent of the state's revenues and the most bureaucratized and best documented aspect of Roman government lacked administrative oversight and planning?" In fact, the Romans maintained a vast administrative apparatus for the military in both the republic and empire.[13] How could it have been otherwise? Without such an administrative and planning function, it would have been impossible to arm, pay, and feed a far-flung army. Without some degree of strategic forethought, Rome could not have fought wars on multiple fronts, as it often did.

Roman capability in maintaining its army, as well as an emperor's ability to transfer units from one frontier to another and assemble expeditionary forces for major wars, clearly indicates general staff work was done, even if the specific mechanisms of higher command and control remain one of the arcana of Roman government.[14]

In fact, there is clear evidence the Romans kept excellent military records throughout the centuries. Tacitus relates how one such document was read to the Roman Senate soon after Augustus' death (AD 14):

This contained a description of the resources of the State, of the number of citizens and allies under arms, of the fleets, subject kingdoms, provinces, taxes, direct and indirect, necessary expenses and customary bounties. All these details Augustus had written with his own hand, and had added a counsel, that the empire should be confined to its present limits, either from fear or out of jealousy.[15]

That such records existed is clear from Tacitus. Considering that nearly 100 years had passed before he wrote his account, he must have had extensive records to consult when he outlined the dispositions of the empire's military forces for the year AD 23. Tacitus not only knew the exact location of the legions and fleets, but he was also keenly aware of their purpose.

It certainly appears that the Romans of AD 23 were thinking in strategic terms and laid out such notions with enough clarity that Tacitus could reiterate them almost a century later:

Italy on both seas was guarded by fleets, at Misenum and at Ravenna, and the contiguous coast of Gaul by ships of war captured in the victory of Actium, and sent by Augustus powerfully manned to the town of Forojulium. But chief strength was on the Rhine, as a defense alike against Germans and Gauls, and numbered

---

[13] See ibid., part II, pp. 231–234 for a brief but pointed detailing of the evidence for such an apparatus.
[14] Ibid., p. 232.
[15] Tacitus, *Annals*, 1.11.7. An earlier version of this inventory was known to exist in 23 BC; see: Suetonius, *Augustus* 28.1: "when he went so far as to summon the magistrates and the senate to his house, and submit an account of the general condition of the empire."

eight legions. Spain, lately subjugated, was held by three. Mauretania was King Juba's, who had received it as a gift from the Roman people. The rest of Africa was garrisoned by two legions, and Egypt by the same number. Next, beginning with Syria, all within the entire tract of country stretching as far as the Euphrates, was kept in restraint by four legions, and on this frontier were Iberian, Albanian, and other kings, to whom our greatness was a protection ... Thrace was held by Rhoemetalces ... the bank of the Danube by two legions in Pannonia, two in Moesia, and two also were stationed in Dalmatia, which, from the situation of the country, were in the rear of the other four, and, should Italy suddenly require aid, not too distant to be summoned. But the capital was garrisoned by its own special soldiery, three city, nine praetorian cohorts, levied for the most part in Etruria and Umbria, or ancient Latium and the old Roman colonies. There were besides, in commanding positions in the provinces, allied fleets, cavalry and light infantry, of but little inferior strength. But any detailed account of them would be misleading, since they moved from place to place as circumstances required, and had their numbers increased and sometimes diminished.[16]

This passage by Tacitus also demolishes another claim, that if the Romans had any conception of modern strategic principles "they kept quiet about it."[17] But here is clear evidence of a Roman specifically thinking in terms of a mobile defense at the strategic level. As Tacitus states, the eight legions on the Rhine were responsible for two crucial missions: to defend against the Germans and handle any trouble that might arise in recently pacified Gaul, while the Dalmatian Legions were to support the four legions on the Danube, or, if required to aid Italy. "This is a strategy of mobile defense, if anything is."[18]

Almost 400 years later, there is the *Notitia Dignitatum*. This remarkable work, one of the few documents from the Roman chanceries to survive into the modern era, contains a complete accounting of the Western Roman Empire in the 420s and the Eastern Roman Empire in the 400s. It lists all court officials, as well as vicars and provincial governors, arranged by praetorian prefecture, and diocese. Moreover, it lists by name all military commanders (*magistri militum, comites rei militaris,* and *duces*), along with their stations and the military units under their control. In short, it is a complete record of the empire's military formations along with their locations.[19] In between these periods there are numerous references to censuses and other strategic assessments. "If emperors kept detailed records on military strengths and location of troops, did they then fail to ponder their use?"[20]

---

[16] *Annals* 4.5.   [17] Isaac, *Limits of Empire*, p. 376.
[18] James Thorne, "Battle, Tactics, and the Limites in the West," in Paul Erdkamp, ed., *The Companion to the Roman Army* (London, 2007), p. 229.
[19] The *Notitia Dignitatum* records a number of forts as in barbarian territory. This is rather clear evidence that the Romans possessed an excellent idea of where their frontiers ended and where barbarism began.
[20] Wheeler, "Methodological Limits and the Mirage of Roman Strategy: Part I," *The Journal of Military History*, Jan. 1993, pp. 7–41.

A recent work captures these beliefs in all of their inanity: "It is unclear, however, whether the Romans themselves ever understood the frontiers to have behaved, militarily or administratively, as zones, or indeed as any other kind of territorially defined unit."[21] If this were the case, it is a true wonder to find that Rome invested so much time and treasure constructing a line of fortifications, watchtowers, and administrative posts, the *limes* or *limitanei*, along the frontiers they supposedly did not know existed. The writer continues: "There is also little reason to believe that the Romans believed it to be their duty to protect provincial populations against those who lived beyond the frontiers."[22] To believe this, one has to ignore a truly overwhelming amount of evidence. Why else place the legions along the frontier or within frontier provinces? Since there were few clamoring to escape the empire for the barbarian hinterlands, one can assume that the Romans placed the legions along the frontier to keep someone out. And yet our "expert" continues: "And even if the imperial government had wanted to develop a coherent system of defensive barriers and fortifications, it is unlikely that it could have overcome the delay in communications and transportation that were a necessary consequence which separated the frontiers from the capital, and from each other."[23]

Of course, overcoming such distances was a primary factor in the selection of frontier zones. The Rhine and Danube greatly eased transport and communication. Moreover, where the seas and rivers ended, Roman roads began. For centuries, Rome constructed and improved upon a system that appears to have been designed primarily for military purposes. If the roads had been primarily for trade, the Romans would have made them sufficiently wide for two carts to pass each other in opposite directions. Why go through the effort of extending the road system from the capital to the edge of the frontier, if not to conquer the tyranny of distance? Furthermore, as many recent archeological finds show (the Vindolanda Tablets) that even soldiers on Hadrian's Wall were accustomed to a significant degree of specialized Mediterranean foodstuffs and certain other Roman luxuries. If the transport system was capable of delivering these comfort goods from the center, to the edge of the empire, it could certainly handle the transport of military necessities. As for communications, Pliny's unceasing prattle in his numerous letters to the emperor stands in testament to the efficiency of the imperial communication system.

If much of the above appears too harsh a critique of historians, one must remember that, in their haste to undermine Luttwak's overly schematized construction of Roman grand strategy, they put forth conclusions unsupported by evidence. It is therefore important to stipulate certain points up front: (1) Roman leaders had a strong understanding of the geography of the empire

---

[21] David Cherry, "The Frontier Zones," in Walter Schiedel, et al., eds., *The Cambridge Economic History of the Greco-Roman World* (Cambridge, 2007), p. 721.
[22] Ibid.   [23] Ibid.

and possibly 500 miles or more beyond the empire's borders. (2) There was an organized body serving the emperor, which was responsible for military administration, and capable of forward planning. (3) The purpose of the legions was to defend the empire, either through holding the border or through launching offensives against Rome's enemies (often moving the border). When not involved in their primary duty, the legions were available to help maintain internal stability, or to help make one of their generals emperor of Rome. (4) Rome's leaders had a solid mental conception of the frontier zones, primarily consisting of the Rhine and Danube Rivers in Europe, the Saharan Desert in North Africa, and the barren wastes of Mesopotamia in the East between Syria and the Euphrates; and (5) they took war seriously and devoted a substantial portion of their mental energies to pondering conflict. In short, they were capable of strategic thought and used it in planning the empire's defenses.

Roman grand strategy – an overview

Admittedly, the lack of surviving records that allude to strategic issues hampers the study of Roman grand strategy. Ammianus, who provides almost the only contemporary history of the late empire, explains why he and other ancient historians failed to cover the ideas behind Roman actions: "Such details are beneath the dignity of history."[24] Still, a historian can glean sufficient information from various histories and the archeological record to demonstrate that Rome possessed and adhered to a grand strategy, even if never articulated as such. If one were to examine first principles, any emperor's foremost concern had to be the empire's security and stability. In practice, this meant securing the frontiers against external enemies while limiting the causes of and presenting as few opportunities as possible for internal revolt. To accomplish these overarching tasks, the emperors and their advisors adapted their strategies and methods, as they confronted a dynamic and changing threat. Along the way there were failures and setbacks, as not every emperor was mindful of the fact that his first duty was the empire's security.

Moreover, many of the emperors who acknowledged that responsibility adopted policies that risked more than any possible gain. Others were so beset by internal challenges that they were precluded from adopting a strategy that did not have personal survival at its core. Strategic failures cannot, therefore, be interpreted as proof that the Romans were devoid of strategic design. In fact, examination of the deployment of the legions underlines that Roman leaders never lost sight of where the permanent threats to the empire resided, or what it took to keep those threats at bay.[25] In fact, whenever Rome

---

[24] Breeze, *The Frontiers of Imperial Rome*, p. 27. See Ammianus 26.1.1.
[25] For an excellent history of the legions and their movements over the centuries, see Stephen Dando-Collins: *The Legions of Rome* (London, 2010).

denuded the frontiers of troops (usually to participate in a civil war or an invasion of Parthia), emperors returned those legions to the frontier as quickly as they could. Unfortunately, there were often gaps of several years between the legions' departure and their return, time for an ambitious chieftain to gather warriors for a destructive raid or lengthy invasion of the empire's interior.

The economics of empire

At the center there was Rome, which maintained itself through taxes drawn from the wealth and productive capacity of the rest of the empire.[26] As one historian has pointed out, the empire had three distinct segments: (1) The outer ring of the frontier provinces in which the defensive armies were stationed. (2) An inner ring of rich, tax exporting provinces (Gaul, Spain, Egypt, North Africa, Asia Minor, and Syria); and (3) the center, Rome, later joined by Constantinople.[27]

The crucial element of Rome's long-term survival, therefore, rested on keeping the tax exporting provinces secure and stable. Only by doing so could the Roman elites maintain themselves, while still feeding approximately one-quarter million Roman citizens free of charge. Moreover, by the first century AD, neither Rome nor the Italian Peninsula produced sufficient excess wealth to sustain themselves, and neither could pay even a small fraction of the cost of a large professional army. Therefore, it fell to the provinces to fund the frontier armies, on which their safety and prosperity depended. Even at the time, however, Rome recognized that the frontier provinces or zones could not produce sufficient wealth to sustain the troops stationed there. Cicero, who never confronted the expense of empire, complained that the republic's many provinces could barely pay anything in their own defense.[28] Strabo did not believe that future provinces would be able to support the cost of a single legion.[29] And yet, throughout much of the empire's existence, at least four legions remained stationed on the British Isles.

In the end, the process of building the empire paid for itself:

conquest by the Romans disrupted established patterns even in economically advanced regions: Romans plundered the stored reserves of generations, from towns, temples and from rich individuals' treasure chests. They siphoned off skilled and

---

[26] The evidence used for determining the size, structure, and development of the Roman economy is rather thin and patchy. What is presented here is the best analysis possible condensed from a number of scholars who have spent decades piecing together Roman economic history from scant original source material.

[27] Keith Hopkins, "Taxes and Trade in the Roman Empire (200 BC–AD 400)," *The Journal of Roman Studies*, vol. 70, 1980, pp. 101–125.

[28] Richard Duncan-Jones, *Structure and Scale of the Roman Economy* (Cambridge, 2002), p. 30.

[29] Ibid., p. 30. Here Duncan-Jones is relying on Appian, 5:7 and Dio 75.3.3.

unskilled labor as slaves; they gave loans to oppressed landowners and then distrained upon their estates, when they were unable to pay extortionate rates of interest.[30]

As Rome ceased its expansion, this source of funding dried up, and the empire had to rely on internal resources to support its strategic policies.[31] Anyone trying to grasp the full range of strategic options available to Rome must first comprehend the extent of this resource base. Using recent estimates, one historian places the Roman government's expenditures during the Augustan era at between 600 million and 825 million sesterces.[32] This amounted to between 3 and 4 percent of the empire's total national product. While Rome might have been able to raise that total a few percent points during times of crisis or civil war, it could not have sustained such spending for long.[33] Given the practical economic limits on Roman expenditures, how much of a military force could the empire bear? Through the first three centuries of the empire, Rome, on average, spent approximately 450 million (perhaps as high as 500 million) sesterces annually on the maintenance of its military forces. This represents about half of total imperial expenditures during the early empire.[34] For this, the empire received a military establishment of 150,000 legionnaires, 150,000 auxiliaries, a Praetorian Guard, transport, and a navy.[35] Interestingly, the amount Rome spent on its military represented only a fraction of the revenues and expenditures of the Roman elite, which were several times higher than the revenues received each year by the empire's treasury. This disparity likely increased in the later empire, as private fortunes grew while the empire was having trouble maintaining its tax base. Rome's inability, or unwillingness, to tax the accumulated wealth of its elites was a crucial handicap when the funds necessary to secure the empire ran short.

[30] Hopkins, "Taxes and Trade in the Roman Empire," pp. 101–125.

[31] The author recognizes that the offensive impulse toward conquest was not extinguished for at least several centuries. Still, it is clear that the great conquests were over by the time Tiberius assumed the purple.

[32] R. W. Goldsmith, *Premodern Financial Systems* (Cambridge, 1987), p. 48. For an analysis of Goldsmith's conclusions that led to further adjustments to Roman GDP and expenditures, see Angus Maddison, *Contours of the World Economy 1–2030 AD: Essays in Macro-Economic History* (Oxford, 2007), pp. 11–62. Maddison places the average per capita GDP within the empire at $540 (1990 G–K dollars), as compared to England during the Glorious Revolution (1688) of $1,411.

[33] See, Hopkins, "Taxes and Trade in the Roman Empire" for a discussion of Rome's capability to raise taxes by installing a much larger administrative infrastructure, akin to that of China at the time, within the empire. Whether such an infrastructure could have been installed or tolerated among the empire's diverse populations is doubtful.

[34] Willem M. Jongman, "The Early Roman Empire: Consumption," p. 611 in Walter Scheidel, Ian Morris, and Richard P. Saller, editors, *The Cambridge Economic History of the Greco-Roman World* (Cambridge, 2007), pp. 592–618.

[35] In an appendix to "Taxes and Trade in the Roman Empire," Hopkins presents calculations for the size of the Roman military establishment that are accepted here. However, Hopkins only accounts for the cost of pay. He leaves out the costs of such things as supplies, armaments, military fortifications, ships, ports, and many other necessary items. These costs are unquantifiable, at present, but they were certainly substantial.

Table 2.1 *Roman per capita GDP as given by the main references for this section*

GDP Per Capita In	Goldsmith	Hopkins	Scheidel	Lo Cascio	Maddison
	(AD 14)	(AD 14)	(AD 150)	(AD 150)	(AD 14)
Sesterces	380	225	260	380	380
Wheat	843 kg	491 kg	680 kg	855 kg	843 kg
1990 International Dollars			$620	$940	$570

Table 2.1 is built from a paper by Elio Lo Cascio and Paolo Malanima, which provides an excellent summary of the various estimates for Roman GDP and the methodologies used to achieve them. See: Elio Lo Cascio and Paolo Malanima, "Ancient and Pre-Modern Economies: GDP in the Roman Empire and Early Modern Europe" (Venice, 2011). A copy can be found at: www.paolomalanima.it/default_file/Papers/ANCIENT-PRE-MODERN-ECONOMIES.pdf (accessed 5 March 2012).

Evidence suggests that Roman policy makers were aware of these limits. As one historian notes: "What we know of the *ratonarium*, which was published regularly by Augustus and his successors, and the *breviarium totius imperii* left by Augustus at his death, shows that state authorities kept track of the various elements of income and expenditure."[36] The pains Augustus took to reorganize the taxation system of the Principate further attest to this knowledge.

During the empire's early years, "uniform, if not universal, criteria for counting subjects and assessing their wealth were extended first of all to the *provinciae Caesaris*, the provinces under the direct control of the emperor, and later to the *provinciae populi* as well."[37] Numerous documents found in Egypt, as well as a fragment from the Severan jurist and praetorian prefect Ulpian, verify that this system remained in place for at least the empire's first two centuries, and demonstrate that formal censuses (*forma censualis*) remained a regular feature of provincial administration. Rome may have been what most historians call a "low tax state," and most of the evidence does indicate that the Roman yoke was not particularly harsh. Still, these historians are examining Roman tax rates from a modern standpoint, where collecting under 5 percent of GDP in annual taxes does indeed appear miniscule. In relation to other pre-industrial subsistence economies, however, the Romans were as good as any and better than most when it came to revenue collection. Only Egypt and the Persian Empire, where wealth was more concentrated on a per capita basis, did better. In later centuries, Western European rulers did not approach Roman levels of revenue collection until the early modern era. By creating a tax infrastructure capable of drawing substantial revenue

[36] Elio Lo Casico, "The Early Roman Empire: The State and the Economy," in Scheidel, et al., *Cambridge Economic History of the Greco-Roman World*, p. 623.

[37] Ibid., p. 631.

Table 2.2 *Population and tax revenues 350 BC to AD 1221*

	Population (Millions)	Revenues (Tons of Silver)	Revenues Per Head (Grams of Silver)
Persia (350 BC)	17	697	41
Egypt (250 BC)	7	384	55
Rome (AD 1)	50	825	17
Rome (AD 150)	50	1,050	21
Byzantium (850 BC)	10	150	15
Abbasids (AD 800)	26	1,260	48
Tang (AD 850)	50	2,145	43
France (AD 1221)	8.5	20.3	2.4
England (AD 1203)	2.5	11.5	4.6

Table 2.2 can be found in James MacDonald. *A Free Nation Deep in Debt* (New York, 2003), pp. 65 and 109.

toward the center, Rome made up for a GDP per capita that was probably only half that of Western Europe in the late medieval era.

However, when it comes to military power, the amount of national wealth is secondary to a nation's ability to mobilize that wealth. For this reason, a strategist cannot examine Roman revenues in isolation. Wealth and the ability to draw on such wealth for military purposes must always be weighed against enemy capabilities. In this regard, Rome had a distinct advantage through the first few centuries of the empire, particularly in Western Europe. Estimates indicate that the barbarian region in the early empire was only half as populous as the Roman Empire and had a per capita GDP of $400.[38] Such a level was just barely enough for survival and left little excess for a centralized authority to build the structures of a functioning state. This alone accounts for the fragmentation of the barbarian tribes through the empire's first two centuries, a situation that changed as the tribes grew richer in succeeding centuries.

On Rome's eastern front, the Parthian Empire was much richer and had the infrastructure to collect substantial funds and deploy them for military purposes. In fact, Parthia proved quite capable of defending itself against Roman incursions despite periodic setbacks, such as those inflicted by the emperors Trajan and Severus. When facing Rome, however, Parthia was almost always on the defensive. Pressed by barbarians on its own northern and eastern borders, along with continuous upheavals within the ruling dynasty, Parthia could never mount a formidable challenge to Roman power. This dramatically changed, however, when the Sassanid Persians overthrew the Parthian Empire in AD 226. The new Persian dynasty was highly

[38] Maddison, *Contours of the World Economy*, p. 54.

centralized and determined to reconquer the lands that formerly made up the Achaemenid Empire, which included the bulk of the Eastern Roman Empire. For the next several centuries, until the Arab invasions in the early seventh century, the Sassanids remained a mortal threat.

In summary, the Roman Empire possessed vast, but not unlimited, riches. Given the character of the economy and the low growth rate in its early centuries followed by a declining economic situation from at least the Antonine Plague (AD 165–180) forward, the size of the Roman military establishment likely represented the greatest possible sustained effort the empire was capable of maintaining. As long as its enemies remained fragmented and/or weak, this was sufficient to guard the frontiers and maintain internal stability. However, as Rome's economic fortunes declined and its enemies grew in wealth and strength, the empire found itself hard pressed to maintain frontier integrity. Compounding this was a corrupted political order, particularly after the period of the "good emperors," that increasingly damaged the empire's internal stability and denuded the frontier of legionary protection just when most needed. *Still, as long as Rome was able to protect and make use of its core central tax base, it had the wherewithal to survive, counterattack, and restore its fortunes.* Nowhere is this better displayed than by Rome's recovery from the crisis of the third century.

Grand strategy – its practical application

Throughout its five centuries of existence, the Roman Empire had the same singular fixed purpose of any other state – survival. During the early years of the Principate, when the expansionary impulse of the Republic was still a driving political and intellectual force, Romans considered that they could best achieve the empire's continued survival and integrity through conquest. The destruction of Varus' three legions at Teutoburger Wald (AD 9) and the near mortal threat presented by the Pannonian revolt (AD 6–9) established in Roman minds that the Rhine and the Danube were the practical limits of empire. Although the embers of this "impulse to conquest" would flare-up repeatedly during next few centuries, these events brought with them the realization that Rome had reached the limits of empire, where the cost of further conquests was beyond the empire's fiscal capacity. Significantly, these rivers did not demarcate a specific linear border. Rather, they are best thought of as zones under Roman control and always under the wary eye of its legions. There is no doubt, however, that for most Romans, true civilization ended at the edges of the Rhine and the Danube, and beyond was barbarism.

The situation was different on Rome's eastern borders. Here, advanced and thriving civilizations had existed for two millennia before the Romans arrived. Rome also had to contend with a Parthian state potentially as militarily powerful as itself. On this frontier, what played out was typical of any two great powers in close geographical contact with one another. There was a constant push-and-pull as each side sought local advantages. On the long African frontier, the threats were all relatively "low-intensity." Berbers and other such nomadic tribes could conduct raids, but there was no serious danger of their allying and forming a force large enough to seriously threaten Roman control. Moreover, the expanses of desert, with their concomitant lack of water, tended to canalize any movement or raid along predictable routes. This frontier, therefore, never required a large force of legionnaires, as small numbers of legionnaires could control wide swathes of territory just by garrisoning water points and patrolling the routes between them.

Some historians examining the multiple defensive methods Rome employed on its various frontiers view this as proof there was no existing concept of grand strategy:

One of the main difficulties about the "grand strategy" thesis is, as its opponents have demonstrated, that the Roman frontiers seem to lack any kind of uniformity, even where there were visual similarities. Hadrian's Wall in Britain, for example, was manned by thousands of forward troops, always auxiliaries; the African *clausurae* in Tripolitania were apparently maintained by small detachments drawn from a single legion and not before the late second century; Mauretania Tingitana never seems to have possessed a linear structure of frontier at all; in Arabia the frontier was a trunk road.[39]

This entirely misses the point that the strategy is always and everywhere the matching of ends, ways, and means to a specific threat or objective. By this measure, what some see as randomness in the Roman defensive scheme is, in reality, a demonstration of Roman understanding of the various threats surrounding the empire, as well as a clear demonstration of the imperial administration's ability to implement the most cost efficient way of handling each.

Geography is only one part of building a coherent grand strategy. A more important element, obvious to the Romans, is the requirement for a thorough threat assessment, as well as a calculation of available resources to underpin strategic and operational decisions. Where the Romans determined that the threat was great enough to build a wall, they built a wall. Where they judged that a zone needed only an access road to allow rapid reinforcement, they built a road. Such discrimination is the essence of strategy. Moreover, as conditions changed, both outside and within the empire, Rome's strategic approach changed.

At the root of any Roman defensive strategy was the legion. As noted, Roman means were always limited to 5 percent of GDP, out of which all of the expenses of government had to be paid, including the army. Fiscal limits, therefore, placed an almost inviolable constraint on the number of legions. Augustus set the number at 28, and it changed little until the reign

[39] C. R. Whittaker, "Frontiers," in Alan Bowman, et al., *The Cambridge Ancient History: The High Empire, A.D. 70–192* (Cambridge, 2000), p. 312.

of Diocletian almost 300 years later. The fact that the Romans did not replace the three legions lost at Teutoburger Wald until Nero's reign 50 years later demonstrates the challenge of raising new legions. In AD 215, Rome had 33 legions, a minimal increase considering the expansion into Dacia and the British Isles.

No emperor could ever lose track of the harsh reality: his rule and the defense of the empire rested on only 150,000 legionnaires along with a similar number of auxiliaries. In other words, less than 0.5 percent of the empire's total population was responsible for the security of the remaining 99.5 percent. This represents a surprisingly small number considering the size and ferocity of external, and occasionally internal, threats. The success of Roman strategy rested on the professionalism and military capacity of the legions. As Gibbon stated in his magisterial history, "The empire of Rome comprehended the fairest part of the earth, and the most civilized portion of mankind. The frontiers of that extensive monarchy were guarded by ancient renown and disciplined valor."[40] For more than 250 years, the legions met the challenge. Still, no large military organization is ever disciplined or valorous unless it benefits from a training program to instill military character and ingrain the habit of obedience even under the brutal conditions of the ancient battlefield. As Flavius Josephus, historian of the Roman–Jewish War, related:

For it is not actual war that gives them the first lesson in arms; nor at the call of necessity alone do they move their hands, having ceased to use them in time of peace: but, as if they had grown with their weapons they have no truce with exercises, no waiting for occasions. These trainings differ in nothing from the veritable efforts of combat; every soldier kept in daily practice and acting with energy of those really engaged in war. Hence the perfect ease with which they sustain the conflict. For no confusion displaces them from their accustomed order: no panic disturbs; no labor exhausts ... [nor] would he err, who would style *their exercises bloodless conflicts and their conflicts bloody exercises.*[41]

The Romans well knew the character of their enemies and the advantages their training and discipline brought in battle. The future emperor Titus commented to his troops before battle:

I fear lest any of you should be inspired with secret alarm by the multitude of our foes. Let such a one reflect who he is against, and against whom he is arrayed; and that the Jews though undaunted, and reckless in life, are nevertheless ill disciplined and unskilled in war, and may rather be styled a rabble than an army ... Again, it is not the multitude of men, however soldier-like they may be, that ensures victory in the field; but fortitude, though only a few. For such, indeed, are easily marshaled and brought up to each other's support; whilst unwieldy masses are more injured by

[40] Edward Gibbon, *The Decline and Fall of the Roman Empire* (New York, 1995), p. 1.
[41] Josephus 3.5.1 (emphasis added). Flavius Josephus, trans. Robert Traill, *The Jewish War: A New Translation* (Boston, 1958), p. 282. Another translation is available, see: Flavius Josephus, trans. William Winston, *Josephus: The Complete Works* (New York, 1998), p. 770.

themselves than by the enemy. The Jews are led on by temerity and self-confidence, affections of mere madness, and, though highly efficient in success, extinguished by the slightest mischance.[42]

Nowhere was this Roman military superiority over barbarian hordes better displayed than when the reinforced XIV Gemina Legion, approximately 10,000 strong, annihilated upwards of 70,000 Britons at the Battle of Watling Street.[43] Before going into battle, their commander, Suetonius Paulinus, encouraged his men:

"There," he said, "you see more women than warriors. Unwarlike, unarmed, they will give way the moment they have recognized that sword and courage of their conquerors, which have so often routed them ... Only close up the ranks, and having discharged your javelins, then with shields and swords continue the work of bloodshed and destruction, without a thought of plunder. When once the victory has been won, everything will be in your power."[44]

As long as the legions were capable of delivering victories, everything was within Rome's power – at least within the empire's frontiers. Beyond the frontiers, things rapidly became more problematic, for Rome was pushing the edge of what any pre-modern state was capable. The farther an army moves from the center of empire, the less force it can muster.[45] On all fronts, Rome reached the limits of empire. Any further expansion could only be attained by one of two ways. The first was to expand the military establishment, so as to provide additional legions. As already suggested, however, Rome's subsistence economy had already reached the brink and was incapable of sustaining larger military forces for long.

The second method was to denude portions of the frontier, so as to assemble a mass of legionnaires for an offensive. During the early years of empire, this could be accomplished without serious risk, such as during the Claudian invasion of Britain and Trajan's invasions of Mesopotamia and Dacia. However, even these conquests put great strain on the empire's resources. Although other emperors (Severus and Julian) repeated the Mesopotamian invasion, the legions were soon recalled and more-or-less restored to their positions along the original border. As for Dacia, when troubles mounted, it was the first province abandoned, as there were better uses elsewhere for the troops and the resources their maintenance required.

---

[42] Josephus 3.10.3. Trail, trans., *The Jewish War*, p. 315.
[43] This is a modern estimate for the forces engaged. Tacitus claims 100,000 and Dio a spectacular 230,000 barbarians, see Cassius Dio, *Roman History* 62.8.2.
[44] Tacitus, *Annals*, XIV, 36.
[45] At Marathon, a Persian army at least as large as Rome's was capable of mustering a mere 30,000 troops. When Xerxes led a larger force into Greece ten years later he required years of preparation and silent borders on all of Persia's other fronts. Even then he was unable to sustain more than a fraction for more than a single fighting season.

One historian makes the case that Rome reached the limits of empire because of the lack of any economic wealth on the other side of the frontiers. In this he is half right, although his thesis is difficult to maintain when one considers the riches of the Parthian Empire. Moreover, during its long history, Rome never failed to launch a war of conquest just because the territory in dispute was economically marginal. If this were sufficient cause to halt the march of Roman arms, much of Gaul, at least half of Spain, and much of Britain should have remained outside the empire. There must have been something else in the equation. And that something was also economic: Rome's inability to sustain forces financially or logistically sizeable enough to pacify new regions far from the center of the empire.

Rome possessed one other major strategic advantage – domination of the Mediterranean. What the Romans referred to as *mare nostrum* had been a Roman lake since Pompey finished the conquest of its eastern littoral and defeated the pirate menace. Rome's Mediterranean dominance, along with the resulting economic benefits, provided the Romans interior lines that sped up communications and military movements. As long as Rome maintained this dominance, it could move troops rapidly from one threatened point to another. Even when the troops moved overland, naval superiority eased the logistic burdens. When the Romans temporarily lost their naval dominance of the eastern Mediterranean in the third century, the result was a catastrophe, as the Goths took to the sea to raid deep into the empire. In short, naval dominance was a critical element of Roman strategic superiority. Once lost, the defeat undermined Rome's ability to confront the threats closing in on its borders.

Strategy through the centuries: the first and second centuries

One of the most remarkable elements of the Roman Empire was the sheer duration of its existence. In comparison to the modern era, there was an undeniable degree of stasis in the ancient world. Still, even relatively glacial rates of change will, over the course of centuries, create major shifts in the strategic environment. The empire could not have survived five centuries without a capacity to recognize and adapt to those changes. Therefore, to comprehend Roman strategic conceptions, one must appreciate that, while maintaining a single grand strategic aim, *the security of the empire's core tax producing provinces*, Rome developed multiple strategies to adapt to the changing threats.

There are no indications that the expansionary impulses of the Republic had yet run their course in the early years of the first century AD, while Augustus was still alive. On the contrary, after waging prolonged campaigns to secure the empire's internal stability, Augustus attempted to expand the empire farther. Despite the historical evidence and his own writings – the *Res Gestae* – many historians still argue that Augustus did not favor expansion of the empire. This outlook rests on his supposed final testament to his successors, advising them to "be satisfied with present possessions and in no way seek to increase the area of empire."[46] Whether or not Augustus actually bequeathed such advice remains a matter of historical debate.[47]

What is certain is that Augustus himself never followed such a policy.[48] One look at *Res Gestae* makes it clear that Augustus saw himself as a conqueror in the same mold as his uncle and adopted father, Julius Caesar.[49] He dedicated eight of *Res Gestae*'s 35 pages to his conquests and military accomplishments. In fact, some historians believe that Augustus, based on a mistaken notion of geographic distance, was intent on conquering the entire world.[50] After all, if Caesar could conquer Gaul in ten years with only a fraction of Rome's resources behind him, what could Augustus do with the entire might of the empire behind him?[51]

There seems little doubt that Augustus saw that the security of the empire demanded above all the conquest of Germany. The Elbe would only have formed a temporary frontier. Was the further aim to envelop the lands beyond the Danube, and even beyond the Black Sea, thus securing the vulnerable left flank for an ultimate advance into Iran? Such plans need not have seemed wildly unrealistic to the Rome of Augustus. At the foundation of the republic, who could have foreseen that one day Rome would control all Italy? Even with all of Italy under Roman control, who would have forecast that one day she would control the whole Mediterranean basin? It is necessary to try to imagine the state of mind of the Roman of the Augustan period. With such a history of unparalleled divine benevolence, how could he fail to conclude that it was Rome's destiny to conquer? The preamble to the Res Gestae makes the view plain.[52]

Thus, supposedly the Roman frontier was an accident, drawn at the limits of Rome's ability to project power any farther. In this interpretation, Rome did not halt its expansion as a matter of policy, but as a result of exhaustion.

---

[46] Dio 56.33.

[47] See Josiah Ober, "Historia: Zeitschrift für Alte Geschichte," vol. 31, no. 3, 3rd qtr., 1982, pp. 306–328. It is more recently discussed in David J. Breeze's *The Frontiers of Imperial Rome*, pp. 14–19.

[48] Modern historians have followed P. A. Brunt's lead, and it is now generally accepted that Dio created a fiction that Augustus was always oriented toward peaceful solutions. Dio, who was always opposed to expansion, was perfectly willing to create a pacific Augustus as an exemplar for future emperors. See P. A. Brunt, *Roman Imperial Themes* (Oxford, 1990), pp. 96–109.

[49] Alison Cooley, *Res Gestae divi Augusti, edition with introduction, translation, and commentary* (Cambridge, 2009).

[50] Brunt, *Roman Imperial Themes*. The author has argued that the Romans had a clear idea of the geography of the empire and beyond the frontier for several hundred miles (much farther in the east). They certainly did not, however, have any idea how much farther the world extended beyond that zone, making it feasible that Augustus, and others, believed that with one great push beyond the existing frontiers they could occupy the world.

[51] C. M. Wells, *The German Policy of Augustus: An Examination of the Archaeological Evidence* (Oxford, 1972).

[52] J. C. Mann, "Power, Force, and the Frontiers of the Empire," p. 179.

Unfortunately, too many historians still cling to the idea that Augustus fought wars of necessity, allowing them to overlook the simple fact that, for the Romans during the early decades of empire, expansion and conquest were a necessity, politically and strategically. Still, for the most part, the path established by Gibbon on the first page of his great history has remained a dominant historical theme:

The principal conquests of the Romans were achieved under the Republic: and the emperors, for the most part, were satisfied with preserving those dominions which had been acquired by policy of the senate, the active emulation of the consuls, and the martial enthusiasm of the people. The seven first centuries were filled with a rapid succession of triumphs; but it was reserved for Augustus to relinquish the ambitious design of subduing the whole earth, and to introduce a spirit of moderation into public councils.[53]

Although this interpretation of Augustan policy was waning by the mid twentieth century, particularly in regards to Germany, it has never entirely disappeared. The reality is that the Roman Empire of the Julio-Claudian era did not hunker down behind a series of fortified lines (the *limes*) or look for protection through the creation of buffer states surrounding the empire. Whatever truth this position may hold for the later empire, it is certainly without validity for the early Principate. "There is no trace at this period of *limes* such as developed under the Flavians. The Augustan commanders did not have the Maginot Line mentality. They were not thinking about keeping the barbarians out, but of going out themselves to conquer the barbarians."[54] Augustus never viewed either the Rhine or the Danube as settled frontiers. It was always his intention to conquer Germany, at least as far as the Elbe. While various interpretations of ancient writers might appear to make this arguable, the actual actions of Roman armies during the period make Rome's intent clear. From 12 BC and for several years after the Varian disaster in the Teutoburger Wald, Roman armies campaigned across the Rhine, and at least until AD 9 they were building the infrastructure of empire. For Rome, the words of Virgil were part of the ingrained national consciousness: *Romane, memento (hae tibi erunt artes) pacique imponere morem, parcere subiectis et debellare superbos* (Remember, Roman, you rule nations with your power (these will be your talents) and impose law and order, spare the conquered, and beat down the arrogant).

During the first century AD, such a strategy made sense with no external enemies capable of reaching deep into the empire's core areas. This was particularly true after the legions crushed the Pannonian revolt in AD 9. Moreover, given the economic conditions within the empire, a limited penetration of the frontier was unlikely to strike anything of significance. There were agricultural settlements along the frontiers, but these were of

---

[53] Edward Gibbon (author) and David P. Womersley (ed.), *The History of the Decline and Fall of the Roman Empire*, vol. I (New York, 1996), pp. 1–2.
[54] Wells, *The German Policy of Augustus*, p. 246.

limited economic consequence. Moreover, the Romans could quickly repair damage in these areas. Finally, since barbarian bands were rarely able to move fast, there was time to concentrate the legions and auxiliaries to crush the barbarians before they could reach the empire's heart.

Conditions were somewhat different in the east. Here, the Parthians loomed. In the first century, however, this threat was manageable. Client states in Cappadocia and Armenia provided buffers, as well as substantial forces, to counter Parthian incursions. Still, if, as occasionally happened, a client state switched allegiance, the result would open up the heart of the empire to attack. Similarly, if the Parthians approached Syria out of Mesopotamia, they could attack some of the empire's richest provinces. To counter the threat, many of the eastern cities were walled and capable of resistance until help arrived.

Not surprisingly, Roman legionary dispositions reflected strategic realities. The preclusive defense seen in the next century is rarely noticeable in the Julio-Claudian era. Rather, the legions concentrated in crucial areas. In Gaul, this translated into deployments along the major invasion routes from Germany. From their camps the legions could march to contain an incursion, while also maintaining their ability to launch preemptive or punitive attacks into Germany. On the Danube, the legions maintained much the same stance, with the added element of being in a position to watch hostile tribes in the Balkans. In the east, Rome concentrated the legions well back from the frontier. This made them easier to supply and also kept them available for major military operations. Such operations could range from internal stability, that is, crushing the Jewish revolts, to annexing client states (Cappadocia, Judea, and later Armenia), to fighting wars (e.g., with Parthia in AD 54–63 over the Armenian succession).

Thus, Rome's enemies presented only sporadic threats along the frontier. Moreover, these fragmented enemies were incapable of coordinating their activities. Hence it was always possible for Rome to concentrate much of its army whenever needed and still defend the empire from internal or external enemies. In the first century, the Romans also possessed an advantage in strategic mobility (on land and particularly by sea) that insured the empire's integrity and left open the option for expansion. At no time was this better exemplified than in AD 6, when 12 of Rome's 28 legions massed along three fronts to invade Bohemia and destroy the power of the Marcomanni. The assault was barely underway when the Pannonian revolt erupted. Augustus immediately called off the offensive and marched the 12 legions, plus a like number of auxiliaries, into Illyricum. The destruction of the rebels took three years and required reinforcements from throughout the empire. It did, however, display the basic element of Roman grand strategy: the ability to move superior forces rapidly to threatened points on the frontier with the near certain knowledge that no major threats would develop elsewhere.

The speed with which the disposition of the legions returned to their previous pattern immediately after the disruptive exigencies of the moment underlines the Romans were aware of the strategic realities. During his war of conquest in Britain, Claudius, despite needing several legions for its completion, altered frontier arrangements in only minimal fashion. Even more tellingly, in AD 69, after the turmoil of civil war and four emperors in a single year, the victor, Vespasian, immediately ordered the legions back to their original frontier positions.

At the beginning of the second century, Rome's impulse toward expansion was still in evidence. Trajan, a true soldier-emperor, led the legions into Dacia, adding this gold-rich region to the empire in AD 106. A decade later, when the Armenian settlement with Parthia collapsed, Trajan launched an invasion of Armenia and Mesopotamia. By 117 the legions had taken Parthia's richest provinces and sacked its capital, Ctesiphon. For Rome, this represented a high-water mark.[55] A revolt within the empire, coupled with a spirited Parthian counterattack, led Trajan and most of his army to return home. He did not survive the march. His successor, Hadrian, held on to Dacia, but rapidly divested the empire of Mesopotamia.

After Trajan's reign, much of the expansionary drive, marking Roman strategic culture since the conquest of Latium, disappeared. The Ionian Greek Aelius Aristides lectured Antoninus Pius that the army protected the empire's frontiers, allowing the demilitarization of the core provinces.[56] Continuing, he suggested:

To place the walls around the city itself as if you were hiding or fleeing from your subjects you considered ignoble and inconsistent with the rest of your concept, as if the master were to show fear of his slaves. Nevertheless, you did not forget walls, but these you placed around the Empire, not the city. And you erected walls, splendid and worthy of you, as far away as possible, visible to those within the circuit, but, for one starting from the city, an outward journey of months and years if he wished to see them. Beyond the outermost ring of the civilized world, you drew a second line, quite as one does in walling a town, another circle, more widely curved and more easily guarded. Here you built walls to defend you ... An encamped army, like a rampart, encloses the civilized world in a ring ... Such are the parallel harmonies or systems of defense which curve around you, the circle of fortifications at individual points, and that ring of those who keep watch over the whole world.[57]

Appian of Alexandria, a Roman historian and tutor for Marcus Aurelius, seconded Aristides observations:

The emperors ... in general possessing the best part of the earth and sea they have, on the whole, aimed to preserve their Empire by the exercise of prudence, rather

[55] Future emperors would gain as much, but they too soon found empire's resources overextended and were forced to abandon hard-won gains.
[56] Breeze, *The Frontiers of Imperial Rome*, p. 19.
[57] Ibid., pp. 19–20. See Aristides, *Roman Orations* 26, 80–4. Translation by J.-H. Oliver.

than to extend their sway indefinitely over the poverty stricken and profitless tribes
of the barbarians ... They surround the empire with a great circle of camps and
guard so great an area of land and sea like an estate.[58]

Such statements from Greek writers may not have reflected the sentiments
of the emperors or the Roman elite, but they most certainly described the
reality of most of the second century. On all fronts, Rome had ceased
expanding. Moreover, most of the legions now were dispersed along the
frontiers. Only in the east, where the Parthian threat persisted, did they
remain concentrated. But even here, there was substantially more dispersion
than in the previous century, while the Romans established numerous forts
deep in the frontier zone. However, it is along the Rhine and Danube where
one sees the biggest shifts. During this period the *limes* became more than a
road network designed to enhance army mobility. In the second century, the
Romans developed fortified zones, as the physical definition of frontiers that
had remained fluid through the Julio-Claudian era. The frontiers still, for the
most part, remained more a zone than an established line, but there is no
mistaking where fortifications ended and barbarism began.

Establishing and maintaining such a preclusive strategy occurred only
at great expense. Even where there was not an extensive wall to equal what
Hadrian constructed in northern Britain, the *limes* were extensive. The army
built new road networks along with forts large and small, and in between
hundreds of signaling towers, and palisaded ditches, sometimes running over
200 miles. This activity and expense were born out of the necessity to adapt to
a changing strategic situation. The barbarians on the other side of the Rhine
and Danube were becoming more powerful and concentrated. Moreover,
on the Roman side of the frontier, development had been steady. The conquered territories up to the frontier had made good use of the prolonged
Roman peace to cultivate substantially more land than was the case during the
early empire. At the same time, other investments in the frontier provinces
significantly altered the economic character of the empire, particularly in the
areas adjacent to the frontier, previously of marginal value. As regions became
richer, they naturally demanded greater security, and as their political power
grew in lock-step with their increased wealth, Rome met their demands.
In summary, there were now stronger enemies on the barbarian side of the
frontier, and they were threatening provinces that had much more to lose.

The changing nature of the threat, coupled with Roman economic growth
and expansion, meant that Julio-Claudian strategy, which had allowed small
enemy forces to penetrate the border, was no longer feasible. In the second
century, it became necessary to stop attackers before they penetrated the
frontier. As Rome could not recruit or maintain much more than the 30 legions
in existence, the only remaining option was fortifying the frontier. This change

[58] Ibid., p. 20. See Appian, *History of Rome*, Preface 7.0. Translation by H. White.

in strategy did not involve the adoption of a "Maginot Line" mentality. Thus, forts were often pushed far beyond the frontier zone, and the Romans always maintained a constant diplomatic and economic focus beyond the frontiers. Moreover, they were rarely hesitant to send the legions deep into barbarian territory to smash dangerous concentrations, or punish tribes that failed to toe the Roman line. Although pressure occurred on several occasions, the line held until stressed beyond endurance beginning in approximately AD 160.

The third century – crisis and recovery

In AD 160 the empire suffered its first major assault on the frontiers by the Marcomanni along the Danube. The legions of Marcus Aurelius repulsed the attack with considerable difficulty. Close upon the repulse of this invasion, a strategic wild card struck the empire, the Antonine Plague. By the time the plague had run its course, some areas of the empire had lost a third of their population. Even worse, the army was among the groups hardest hit, with some legions decimated.[59] Among the casualties was the emperor himself.

His death also broke a succession tradition that had served the empire well. Rather than adopt a qualified successor, Marcus had allowed Commodus, his vicious son, to succeed to the purple. A dozen years later, Commodus' murder initiated a period of instability. At one point, the Praetorian Guard sold the empire to the highest bidder, who did not last a year. The longest-serving emperor of the period, Septimius Severus, took the throne by force, and then spent five years fighting civil wars to hold it. After his death in 211, there followed 24 emperors, the so-called barracks emperors, and as many, if not more usurpers, over the next 70 years. As Luttwak noted of the period:

Most were short-lived, but some usurpers ruled substantial parts of the empire for several years. In fact the longest reign of the period was that of a usurper, Postumus, who controlled Gaul for nine years. The average reign of the "legitimate" emperors was only three years. One emperor, Decius (249–251) died in battle fighting the Goths; another, Valerian (253–260), was captured by the Persians and died in captivity; Claudius II (268–270) died of the plague. All other emperors and most usurpers were murdered or perished in civil war.[60]

Such turmoil could not have come at a worse time. The federation of tribes, already apparent in the previous century, grew throughout this period. Where Roman diplomacy, threats, and minimal military action once sufficed to manage the fragmented tribes beyond the Rhine and Danube, such

---

[59] Other plagues during the third century were almost as destructive, and particularly damaging to the army. These include a plague that broke out in Egypt in AD 251 and was still raging in AD 270, when it killed the emperor Claudius Gothicus. See: 21 Zosimus, *New History* I, 26, 37 and 46.

[60] Luttwak, *The Grand Strategy of the Roman Empire*, p. 128.

efforts were less effective against these larger federations of the third century. Moreover, new, more powerful, and less Romanized tribes, such as the Goths, were pressing up against the Roman frontier. As if this were not enough, in 224, the Persian Sassanids toppled and replaced the weak Arsacid Parthian Empire. From this point forward, Rome, and later Byzantium, would confront a fierce struggle against the Sassanid Empire.

During the third century crisis, the empire verged on collapse. Although Rome still possessed a workable strategy, conditions rarely permitted Roman leaders to stay on the strategically sensible course. Emperors were too concerned with survival to focus on strategy. Moreover, incessant civil wars and the need to crush usurpers exhausted and undermined the army's morale and discipline. As discipline declined, so, inevitably, did training. The crucial element underpinning Roman strategy, the battlefield superiority of the legions, slowly withered.

Rome's enemies, sensing weakness, attacked. Throughout the middle decades of the third century, barbarians launched devastating raids. Many reached deep into the empire's core, while wrecking provinces that had not felt the cruel hand of war in over two centuries. In one such raid, the Goths and Heruli attacked Byzantium with 500 ships. After the Romans repelled them, the raiders moved on into the Aegean and sacked Athens, Sparta, Corinth, and Argos. The emperor Gallienus eventually halted that invasion, but was assassinated soon thereafter. His death opened the door to a larger Gothic seaborne invasion. Ancient sources give various sizes for this fleet, ranging from 2,000 to an incredible 6,000. Whatever the number, this represented a massive invasion, and as moving by sea, it struck the empire's unguarded inner core. The Goths sacked Crete, Rhodes, and Cyprus and retreated only after receiving news of the approach of a large Roman army. Plundering as they withdrew, the Goths left the empire and took with them a huge amount of booty.

As these seaborne assaults reached their height, the Rhine and Danubian frontiers crumbled. Worse, the Sassanids also took the offensive. After invading Goths killed the Emperor Decius and destroyed his army, the floodgates opened. As Luttwak relates:

In the next four years came the deluge: Dacia was submerged by invaders, the Goths reached Salonika, sea raiders ravaged the coasts, and Shapur's [the Sassanid ruler] armies conquered territory as far away as Antioch, while in the West, Franks and Alamanni were subjecting the entire Rhine frontiers and upper Danube to almost constant pressure. The attacks in the West culminated in 260 – the year of Valerian's disaster, when Shapur's advance threatened even Cilicia and Cappadocia.[61]

Under relentless pressure the empire began to disintegrate. At one point, it split into three major parts. In 258, Britain, Gaul, and Hispania broke off to

---

[61] Ibid., p. 153.

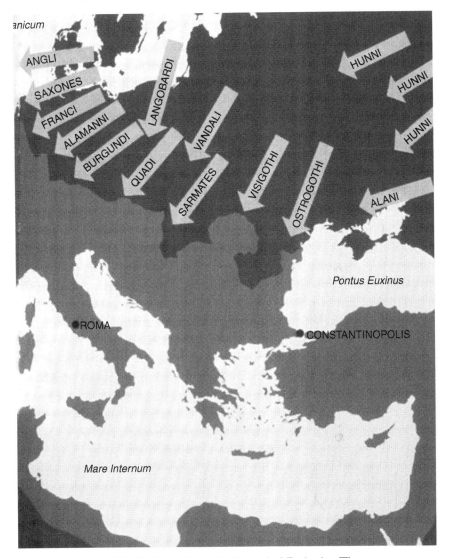

Map 2.1 The Third and Fourth Centuries' Barbarian Threat

form the Gallic Empire under the former governor of Germania Superior and Inferior, Postumus. Two years later, the eastern governor, Septimius Old-aenathus, created his own Palmyrene Empire out of Syria, Palestine, and Egypt. However, he died soon thereafter, leaving his son Vaballathus, a weakling controlled by his mother Zenobia, to lead the eastern legions in a war of conquest into Syria, Egypt, and Lebanon.

As bad as this fragmentation was, the true damage to the empire's prospects was the economic changes that were occurring unnoticed against the backdrop of military crisis. As widespread unrest made safe travel for merchants impossible, the vast Roman trading network broke down. This breakdown disastrously exacerbated a financial crisis just when Rome needed to find new funds to defend the empire, and that grew worse as various provinces were devastated or broke away. As a result, cities and large landowners began establishing autarkic economic zones. Wide swathes of the empire stopped exporting or importing goods. From this point, these regions looked only to themselves for subsistence crops, as well as manufacture. At the same time, cities, no longer confident that legions could hold the frontier lines, looked to their own defenses. Such changes to the empire's basic fabric made themselves felt in the following century. By then local leaders, despairing of support from Rome, rather than fight, began finding it advisable to come to terms with the invading barbarians.[62]

A leading historian argues "that the survival of the Empire, in the face of intolerable odds, is something of a miracle, and one of the most remarkable phenomena in human history."[63] While saving the empire was remarkable, it was not a miracle, for the empire, even in this dark hour, still possessed formidable strength. As a result of invasions and revolts, its leaders found themselves forced back on the core provinces, and here they found salvation. Despite all the empire's travails, its core of the empire (Anatolia, Italy, Spain, and, most importantly, North Africa) remained sufficiently wealthy for one great effort. All that was required was leadership, which, when most needed, the emperors Gallienus, Aurelian (the self-declared restorer of the empire), and Diocletian provided. In a series of lightning campaigns, these emperors reunited the empire, restored the borders (except for Dacia, which they abandoned), and damaged the Sassanids sufficiently to negotiate a 30-year peace.

Restoration of the empire allowed Rome to reinstate the strategy that had served it for three centuries. From the start of his reign, Diocletian's main priority was to strengthen the frontiers and rebuild structural underpinnings of the empire's military security.

If Diocletian had a policy, it was to hold the limits of Roman territory, prevent barbarian incursions, and attack where appropriate. This looked back to the days of Hadrian and the Antonines. The differences between Diocletian and his

[62] Over the past two decades, a number of scholars have fundamentally redefined our knowledge of these events and the era. For the best summaries of this recent scholarship see Peter Heather, *The Fall of the Roman Empire: A New History of Rome and the Barbarians* (Oxford, 2006); Peter Heather, *Empires and Barbarians* (Oxford, 2010); Chris Wickham, *The Inheritance of Rome: Illuminating the Dark Ages 400–1000* (New York, 2009); Adrian Goldsworthy, *How Rome Fell* (New Haven, CT, 2009); and Bryan War-Perkins, *The Fall of Rome: And the End of Civilization* (Oxford, 2006).
[63] Michael Grant, *The Collapse and Recovery of the Roman Empire* (London, 1999), p. 67.

predecessors of the mid-third century should not be exaggerated. What he achieved was doubtless the ambition of all emperors, but circumstances, not policy or doctrine prevented them. Diocletian was in control of the whole empire, and the creation of the tetrarchy temporarily ended the disruption of civil war and ensured responsibility for the military affairs of the empire was shared.[64]

After the breakdown of Diocletian's political arrangements and another period of instability, Constantine, through force of arms, seized control in the early fourth century. He kept many of Diocletian's military arrangements, but made one important change. He reduced the status of the frontier troops, the *limitanei*, to enhance the empire's field army, the *comitatenses*, which still existed after the campaigns that restored the empire. Zosimus, writing a century later, strongly disapproved of Constantine's actions:

Constantine likewise took another measure, which gave the barbarians unhindered access into the lands subject to the Romans. For the Roman Empire was, by the foresight of Diocletian, everywhere protected on its frontiers ... by towns and fortresses and towers, in which the entire army was stationed; it was thus impossible for the barbarians to cross over, there being everywhere sufficient opposing force to repel their inroads. But Constantine destroyed that security by removing the greater part of the soldiers from the frontiers and stationing them in cities that did not require protection; thus he stripped those of protection who were harassed by the barbarians and brought ruin to peaceful cities at the hands of the soldiers ... He likewise softened the soldiers by exposing them to shows and luxuries. To speak plainly, he was the first to sow the seeds of the ruinous state of affairs that has lasted up to the present time.[65]

Zosimus, a witness to the devastation of the Western Roman Empire, may have been too harsh in his judgment. "Diocletian may have renewed the frontiers, but he did not create them, nor did Constantine remove all the soldiers; rather, he built on Diocletian's creations, including the field armies." The fact of the matter is that the empire was facing enemies far more dangerous than ever before. On no front, except Africa, were the *limes* sufficiently strong to hold a determined assault. Moreover, once a large force did penetrate the *limes*, the troops stationed along these thousands of miles of frontiers became useless. The larger forces Rome's enemies could throw against the empire in the fourth century could wreck several entire provinces before the *limitanei* could concentrate in sufficient numbers. The need to gather sufficient legions to attack large enemy forces had erased Rome's earlier advantage of strategic mobility. Moreover, constant duty along the *limes* eroded much of the soldiers' ability to fight set-piece battles as part of a trained and disciplined legion.

In fact, in the decades after Constantine's death, the new permanent field armies performed well. Constantine II used one to defeat the Alemanni

---

[64] Campbell, *The Cambridge Ancient History*, vol XII, p. 125.
[65] Quoted in Breeze, *The Frontiers of Imperial Rome*, p. 23. See; Zosimus 2.34. Translation by N. Lewis and M. Reinhold.

in 338, and then the Persians at the Battle of Singara a decade later. Later, in 357, the Emperor Julian used a field army to inflict a severe defeat on Franks at the Battle of Strasbourg. It was only after Julian's defeat by the Sassanids in 363, coupled with the loss of the eastern field army to a Gothic force at Adrianople in 378, that the Roman world began its final collapse.

For four centuries, the overarching Roman strategy, built around precluding enemies from penetrating the core economic zones of the empire, was remarkably successful. Constructed around the matchless capabilities of the legions, Rome's strategy of adaptive-preclusion allowed the empire to prosper. In turn, prosperity underwrote the expenses of the large military establishment. Despite periodic setbacks, usually the result of an unstable internal political system, Rome remained a successful enterprise as long as its energies focused on the frontier. In fact, Rome's relentless defense of its frontiers produced the singularly most successful strategy in global history. To date, no other empire or nation has come close to matching the longevity and effectiveness of Rome's grand strategic conceptions.

3   Giraldus Cambrensis, Edward I, and the conquest of Wales

Clifford J. Rogers

In 1063, Harold Godwineson, heir to the English throne, launched a major invasion of Wales. His forces spread fire and slaughter through the rough Welsh terrain, killing so many men, Gerald of Wales tells us, that he "left not one that pisseth against a wall."[1] Such large-scale campaigns of devastation were typical of medieval warfare, and the result was also typical, at least for the early and high Middle Ages: the numerous Welsh "princes," who independently governed their own mini-states, "submitted" to the English and acknowledged their over-lordship in a loose way. Harold and his men then went home with their booty (mostly cattle, no doubt), confident they had both weakened the Welsh and taught them a lesson, so that they would make little trouble for years to come. Harold did not, so far as our limited sources indicate, annex any territory, or depose and replace any Welsh ruler, or hold and garrison outposts within Wales.

Having succeeded by the standards of the day, Harold found himself on the defensive in England three years later against two foreign attackers, first Norway's Harald Hardrada, then William of Normandy. Against the Norwegians, who fought in the same style as the English, he won a decisive battle, but the Normans defeated him at Hastings. The result was the Norman Conquest of England, an extremely thorough occupation and domination vastly different from the loose subordination Harold had imposed on Wales. A French-speaking aristocracy of knights, barons, and counts supplanted the thegns and ealdormen who had been the principal landholders and political elite of the Anglo-Saxon realm. French replaced English as the language of the royal court and of law-courts, and as the second language (after Latin) for writing history or literary works. Although William retained some elements of the old system, broad aspects of Norman military and political organization arrived with the conquerors. For more than two centuries, the dominant form of Anglo-Norman armies was the armored cavalry rather than heavy infantry.[2]

---

[1] Gerald of Wales, *Description of Wales*, in *The Journey through Wales and The Description of Wales*, trans. Lewis Thorpe (London, 1978), p. 266. Further citations to the *Description* are to this translation unless noted otherwise.

[2] This assertion is not one that all scholars would accept, because of a fundamental disagreement about the importance of cavalry in medieval warfare generally. For the degree of divergence, contrast J. F. Verbruggen, "The Role of the Cavalry in Medieval Warfare," *Journal of*

Throughout that period, the Anglo-Norman kings of England fought intermittently with the Welsh, but the patterns of these conflicts resembled Harold's expeditions rather than William the Conqueror's conquest of England. This is in some ways surprising, for in this period the Normans showed an astounding capacity for conquest, with Norman warlords seizing control over substantial portions of Ireland, the southern half of the Italian Peninsula, the island of Sicily, and even far-flung Antioch. Anglo-Norman "Marcher" barons, whose English estates bordered on Wales, did make their own conquests within Wales, mainly along the southern coast, where they built towns and brought in English and Flemish settlers to populate the conquests. Yet, William and his successors, with the huge resources of England, Normandy, Maine, and later Aquitaine at their disposal, failed to push beyond the negligible barrier of Offa's Dyke to bring the 200,000 to 300,000 inhabitants of Wales under their direct rule. Not until the wars of 1277 and 1282–1283 did Edward I achieve just that, with consequences for the Welsh comparable to the effect of 1066 on the English.[3]

A principal reason for this is simply that the Welsh, for all their relative poverty and small numbers, were not easy to defeat. William managed to impose fealty and tribute on the Welsh princes by invading the country in 1081, but his son William Rufus accomplished nothing by his costly invasions of 1095 and 1097.[4] Henry I, by spending liberally in his invasions of 1114 and 1121, extracted hostages and submission from the Welsh generally and imposed heavy indemnities on the princes of Gwynedd and Powys, but left the native rulers in possession of their lands.[5] In the troubled reign of King Stephen, the Welsh largely threw off even nominal subordination to the English crown.[6] In his first major expedition into Wales, Edward I's great-grandfather

---

Medieval Military History, vol. 3, 2005, with Bernard Bachrach, "Verbruggen's 'Cavalry' and the Lyon-Thesis," *Journal of Medieval Military History*, vol. 4, 2006.

[3] A Scotsman of the next century referred to Edward I as having "reduced [Wales] to such serfdom." John Barbour, *The Bruce*, ed. A. A. M. Duncan (Edinburgh, 1997), p. 50. Since this chapter is intended mainly for an audience of military historians and strategists rather than medievalists, it generally cites English translations of source material rather than the Latin originals, when such translations exist. It also cites older public domain editions (available on the internet) in preference to more accurate recent editions unless the older edition is problematic at the point referenced. An exception is the text of Gerald's *Description of Wales*, for which I have generally cited the Penguin edition rather than the public domain Forester translation.

[4] Frederick C. Suppe, *Military Institutions on the Welsh Marches: Shropshire, A.D. 1066–1300* (Woodbridge, 1994), pp. 13–14; *Anglo-Saxon Chronicle* [s.a. 1097]; *The Chronicle of Florence of Worcester*, trans. Thomas Forester (London, 1854), pp. 198, 201 ("he was scarcely able to take or kill one of them, while he lost some of his own troops and many horses"); *History of Gruffydd ap Cynan*, ed. and trans. Arthur Jones (Manchester, 1910), pp. 141–143 ("He did not take with him any kind of profit or gain except one cow. He lost a great part of the knights and esquires and servants and horses and many other possessions....").

[5] *History of Gruffydd ap Cynan*, pp. 86–87, 151–153.

[6] The *Acts of King Stephen* notes that Stephen's first effort to restore his lordship in the area after a widespread rebellion involved great expense for horsemen and archers, but

Henry II (whom Jordan Fantosme flatteringly described as the greatest conqueror since Charlemagne) restored English over-lordship. However, his second campaign, reportedly aimed at actual conquest, failed completely.[7]

The offensives of Henry II

In 1157, Prince Owain of Gwynedd, whose principality in north and north-west Wales was one of the three main native-ruled regions, along with Deheubarth in the south and Powys in between, drove out his brothers, occupied their territories, and attacked the English royal castle of Tegeingl in northeast Wales. In response, Henry II collected a substantial army and fleet and advanced into Powys by the Dee Valley.[8] About a dozen miles into Welsh territory, Owain blocked Henry's advance with an entrenched position and offered battle, an unusual choice for a Welsh ruler. The English king ordered his main force toward the Welsh lines, but meanwhile led a detachment through the woods in an outflanking maneuver. His men, who seem to have been mostly light troops, stumbled into an ambush led by Owain's sons, resulting in an "extremely sharp fight," in which the Welsh killed the constable (the leading military officer) of the great Marcher earldom of Chester. Henry himself barely escaped.[9]

Quitting while he was ahead, Owain withdrew and returned to traditional Welsh guerilla tactics. Henry turned north, toward the coast, and proceeded to Rhuddlan, where he began the construction of a castle and sent his fleet to attack the large island of Anglesey. Here too the Welsh chose to stand and fight, and here too they won, inflicting a "great slaughter" on the disembarked English, killing among others Henry FitzHenry, Henry II's own half-Welsh uncle.[10] If he ever had ambitions of significant conquests, the king abandoned

---

nonetheless his paid troops, "after many of their number were slain fighting gloriously, the rest, shrinking to encounter the ferocious enemy, retreated in disgrace after fruitless toil and expense." He then sent a second force which was checked by the Welsh and ultimately "withdrew in poverty and disgrace." Stephen then concluded "that he was struggling in vain, and throwing away his money in attempting to reduce them." *Acts of King Stephen*, in Thomas Forester, ed. and trans., *The Chronicle of Henry of Huntington ... also, the Acts of Stephen* (London, 1853), pp. 329–333.

[7] Jordan Fantosme, *Chronicle of the War between the English and the Scots in 1173 and 1174*, ed. and trans. Francisque Michel (London, 1840), vol. II, pp. 112–114. For the following paragraph, see John D. Hosler, "Henry II's Military Campaigns in Wales, 1157 and 1165," *Journal of Medieval Military History*, vol. 2, 1994, pp. 53–71.

[8] This was described by Robert of Torigni as "an extremely large invasion force," including one-third of all the knights in England. *The Chronicle of Robert of Torigni*, in Richard Howlett, ed., *Chronicles of the Reigns of Stephen, Henry II, and Richard I*, vol. IV (London, 1889), p. 193.

[9] Hosler, "Military Campaigns," p. 64; quotation from John Williams ab Ithel, ed., *Annales Cambriae* (London, 1860), p. 46 (*acerrimo certamine*).

[10] Ibid., p. 47 (where FitzHenry is given the name FitzGerald after his stepfather, Gerald FitzWalter). FitzHenry's mother was Nest, daughter of the last king of Deheubarth, Rhys ap Tewdwr, and thus he was an uncle of both Gerald of Wales, who was 12 years old at the time of FitzHenry's death, and of Henry II (Henry I's grandson).

them after this second setback. Instead, he accepted Owain's offer of fealty, backed up by the provision of hostages. Owain also restored the lands he had confiscated from his brother, whose call for assistance had prompted the campaign. Henry could thus count the campaign a success, but not an easy, inexpensive, or one-sided victory. Indeed, less than a decade later, apparently in response to Henry's efforts to convert his acknowledged over-lordship into a more strictly defined feudal homage, Owain's son Dafydd led the Welsh in a bid to "throw off the rule of the French." In return, Henry launched another major invasion in 1165. The Welsh, at least, believed that this time the English, frustrated by the pattern of nominal Welsh submission, followed by "rebellion," intended to destroy their nation, or at least drive them from their homeland.[11]

Once again, a Welsh army, relying on a strong defensive position in a wooded valley where Henry could not use his cavalry effectively, blocked the English advance. After a period of stalemate, the invaders tried chopping down the trees to clear their way against the Welsh, but the latter made a brash attack on Henry's men. Welsh sources indicate the fighting was a tactical draw, with heavy casualties on both sides. From a strategic perspective, the combat was a clear defeat for the English, who had failed to advance and who took a serious blow to their martial prestige when they failed to beat the Welshmen in an open fight. Subsequent events compounded the failure: Henry turned onto a different route, which took him into even more difficult terrain, where his troops suffered heavily from bad weather and lack of supplies. "Seeing that he could not at all arrange things according to his will," wrote the author of the *Annales Cambriae*, Henry killed or mutilated the Welsh hostages he held, then dismissed his army and "returned in shame into England."[12]

Giraldus Cambrensis (Gerald of Wales) and the strategic problem

It was after and with full cognizance of these events, but also with a detailed knowledge of the successful conquest of much of Ireland by his FitzGerald cousins, that the distinguished cleric Gerald of Wales – Archdeacon of Brecknock, the youngest son of a powerful Marcher lord and the grandson of a Welsh princess – wrote his famous *Description of Wales* (1194). This text culminates with a chapter entitled "How This Nation May Be Conquered": the earliest prospective strategic document (that is, a written plan for how

[11] Hosler, "Military Campaigns," 68n; *Annales Cambriae*, p. 50 ("planning the overthrow or destruction [*excidium*] of all the Welsh"); R. R. Davies, *Domination and Conquest: The Experience of Ireland, Scotland and Wales, 1100–1300* (Cambridge, 1990), pp. 76–77.
[12] *Annales Cambriae*, p. 50. According to Hoveden, Henry blinded the boys and cut off the noses and ears of the girls. Roger of Hoveden, *The Annals*, trans. Henry T. Riley, 2 vols. (London, 1853), p. 278.

to win a war, prepared in advance) still extant in any medieval source.[13] Remarkably, considering its originality, Gerald's text is highly sophisticated in its approach.

Gerald was one of the most significant thinkers and writers of a period of remarkable intellectual efflorescence, often referred to as the "Renaissance of the twelfth century." Like most of the other important men of letters of his day, he studied at the undisputed center of advanced education in Latin Christendom, the University of Paris. This was the home of "scholastic" education, which focused on honing students' logical thinking and rhetorical skills through competitive, public debates. In these battles of the mind, it was crucial to see both sides of a question, for it was difficult to dispute an argument one had not anticipated and reflected on. This training was excellent preparation for the study of the law, which Gerald also learned and taught in Paris. It was equally good preparation for the formulation of strategy. Gerald also mastered the discipline of rhetoric, the core of which was the ability to form a coherent, logical argument and express it clearly, so well that he lectured on the subject to packed halls.[14]

Having come from a warlike knightly family, Gerald was both interested in and well informed about military affairs. As the "kinsman of all the princes and great men in Wales," and one of the chief ecclesiastical officers of the region, he had free access to the best sources of information.[15] All of these elements of his background contributed to the high quality of his *Description of Wales*, which historian Robert Bartlett describes not only as "the high point of twelfth-century ethnography," but also extremely innovative in conception.[16] Bartlett emphasizes the exceptional quality of Gerald's work as a cohesive anthropological study, but he neglects the equally extraordinary and well-conceived nature of its strategic plan within the same work.

In devising his plan for the conquest of Wales, Gerald expressly takes into account the lessons of history. He wisely notes that anyone "who is really prudent and provident must find out what pitfalls are to be avoided by taking note of the disasters which have befallen others in the same position. It costs nothing to learn from other people's experience."[17] He also draws on his own deep knowledge of Wales and contemporary events elsewhere. He considers

---

[13] Gerald's slightly earlier *The History of the Conquest of Ireland* does include a short prospective chapter entitled "In What Manner Ireland is to Be Completely Conquered," but its contents are almost entirely about what sort of troops should be used, rather than what they should do. See *The Historical Works of Giraldus Cambrensis*, trans. Thomas Forester and Sir Richard Cold Hoare, ed. Thomas Wright (London 1894), pp. 320–322.

[14] Gerald of Wales, *The Autobiography of Giraldus Cambrensis*, ed. and trans. H. E. Butler (London, 1937), p. 37. He also taught the other two elements of the *trivium*: Latin grammar and, significantly, logic.

[15] Ibid., p. 60.

[16] Robert Bartlett, *Gerald of Wales, 1146–1223* (Oxford, 1982), pp. 175–182.

[17] *Description*, p. 272. Gerald's remark is reminiscent of the *bon mot* attributed to Bismarck, that "fools say that to learn, one must pay with mistakes … I, however, have always striven to

English strengths and weaknesses, Welsh advantages and disadvantages, and situational factors. Moreover, Gerald takes into account military, political, cultural, topographical, and economic considerations. Rather than taking force structure as a given, he reflects on the troops best suited to accomplish the mission, and implicitly recommends changes in recruitment, tactics, and equipment. Perhaps most impressively, after describing how to conquer Wales, he adds a second chapter on how to rule it after its conquest. He then concludes with yet another strategic chapter, this one on how the Welsh might best resist English conquest. This he pitches as being for the benefit of the Welsh, a sort of testimony to his own intellectual impartiality.[18] Whether intended so or not, it rounds out his strategic analysis for an English audience, since any competent planner must reflect on and appreciate the enemy's most effective parry and riposte.

Gerald was something of a celebrity; he premiered his *Topography of Ireland* with a three-day public reading at the University of Oxford in 1188, and he was an important figure in the courts of Henry II, Richard I, and John. It is entirely likely that Edward I, whose military career began with fighting in Wales a quarter-century after Gerald's death, was familiar with the *Description of Wales* and indeed studied it with great care. He was far from averse to learning about warfare from books: before his coronation, while on crusade in the Holy Land, he had commissioned the first known translation of Vegetius' *De re militari* into the vernacular.[19] If he did not himself study Gerald's work, it seems his advisors had. In any case, when Edward decided to undertake the complete conquest of Wales, he followed Gerald's strategic prescriptions quite exactly. The king clearly understood the strategic problems involved in a conquest of Wales, as Gerald had described them.

An invader "can never hope," Gerald wrote, "to conquer in one single battle a people [who] will never draw up its forces to engage an enemy army in the field, and will never allow itself to be besieged inside fortified strongpoints."[20] The Welsh had no major towns, no fixed economic hubs the English could threaten to force them to fight. Even if an invader did somehow come to grips with and crush a Welsh army, the Welsh "do not lose heart

learn from the mistakes of others," Comte Emile Kérartry, *Le Dernier des Napoléon* (Paris, 1872), p. 240.

[18] It would be natural to think this was part of his program of portraying himself as someone favorable to Welsh interests, as part of his campaign to become bishop of St. David's, the chief primate of Wales. However, the timing does not fit that interpretation, as the *Description of Wales* was written at a time when he seems to have been interested only in a rich English bishopric and not a Welsh see. Bartlett, *Gerald*, p. 48.

[19] The miniature embellishing the manuscript "shows Vegetius, the philosopher, inviting a group of young knights to come to him with the words... 'come to me, lord knights who wish to have the honor of chivalry.'" Christopher Allmand, "The *De re militari* of Vegetius in the Middle Ages and the Renaissance," in Corinne Saunders, Françoise le Saux, and Neil Thomas, eds., *Writing War: Medieval Literary Responses to Warfare* (Cambridge, 2004).

[20] *Description*, p. 267.

when things go wrong, and after one defeat they are always ready to fight again."[21] That meant it was practically impossible to beat them quickly. But in a long war too "they are difficult to conquer ... for they are not troubled by hunger or cold, [and] fighting does not seem to tire them." It is not easy to employ a strategy of exhaustion against foes who are fierce, agile, courageous, highly mobile, "passionately devoted to their freedom and to the defense of their country," and who, far from dreading conflict, "in peace ... dream of war, and prepare themselves for battle" by exercising constantly with their weapons and by hunting and mountain-climbing.[22]

Three principal synergistic advantages enjoyed by the Welsh redoubled the inherent difficulty of conquering them. First, their countryside was covered with woods, marshes, and mountains, terrain "where foot-soldiers have the advantage over cavalry" and where the standard Norman battle tactics were "no good at all."[23] Second, they had large numbers of soldiers relative to their small population, because (unlike in England) "the entire nation, both leaders and the common people, are trained in the use of arms."[24] Thanks to constant internecine fighting – like contemporary Irish warfare, focused on cattle-raiding – the Welsh were skilled in ambushes, night attacks, and hit-and-run raids. Thus, on their home ground, they were ideal troops for executing a defensive strategy aimed at defeating an invading army by harassing it, depriving it of forage and profit, both relatively scarce in Wales anyway, and ultimately exhausting it. Third, while the Welsh could hardly have more pressing concerns than dealing with an invasion of their homeland (a cause for which they would "willingly sacrifice, suffer, or die"), England was a power with significant strategic interests in Scotland, Normandy, and Aquitaine, each more important than Wales. Each frequently required English attention and military resources.[25]

The roster of difficulties facing an English strategist planning to conqueror Wales would not have required too much modification to apply to a British commander in the American Revolution, while some of the principal English advantages would fit with analogies to innumerable wars: larger numbers of well-equipped, paid soldiers; general superiority in open battle; and far greater economic and fiscal resources. However, that match-up of advantages against disadvantages did not suffice to guarantee success for the English against Wales, as Gerald recognized.[26] Gerald did think England's superior wealth and manpower could bring victory, but only if used properly for a sustained effort. A king who wanted to conquer Wales, he insisted, "must be determined to apply a diligent and constant attention to this purpose for at least one year" without distractions by other business in England, France, or

[21] Ibid., p. 260.   [22] Ibid., pp. 233–234, 236.   [23] Ibid., p. 269.
[24] *Description*, trans. Forester, p. 490.   [25] *Description*, pp. 233, 267.
[26] R. R. Davies refers to the war of 1276–1277 as a struggle between David and Goliath, seemingly forgetting who won that Biblical combat. *Age of Conquest* (Oxford, 1987), p. 335.

elsewhere. The king would also have to face heavy losses of men and large expenditures, equal to many times the annual revenues expected from the province.[27] And he would have to follow a sound strategic plan to make the best use of his superior resources.

Gerald's plan for the conquest of Wales

Well before the start of an invasion, Gerald suggested, the English should employ economic sanctions to prepare the way: they should prevent the Welsh from importing the grain, cloth, and salt (for preserving meat and fish) they usually imported from England. Garrison forces patrolling the land border and ships patrolling the coast should enforce a blockade. Next, an army should invade the coastal lowlands, where the English could take advantage of their naval superiority and receive supplies by sea, forcing the Welsh to take refuge in the highlands of Snowdonia. Third, the invaders should ring this area with infantry, drawn as much as possible from the Anglo-Welsh border zone known as the Marches and equipped with light armor, so that they would be better protected than the normally unarmored Welsh, but agile enough for fighting in difficult terrain. These men should prevent the Welsh from collecting additional supplies. Once winter set in and the trees had lost their leaves, English troops should push into the forests to probe and harass the Welsh. Reinforcements should replace casualties and allow exhausted troops to pull back and recuperate. Thus, the English, drawing from their larger population, would keep their forces up to strength, while the Welsh would have difficulty replacing losses.

All this military action, in Gerald's scheme, was to be accompanied by a culturally sensitive political offensive. Three long-standing customs of the Welsh aristocracy, Gerald argued, severely weakened their nation. First, their inheritance customs involved dividing patrimonial lands among brothers, including illegitimate ones, instead of conferring them on the eldest son. Second, Welsh noble youths were generally raised by foster families, with parents sending each of their sons to a different lord to establish bonds between families – which, however, weakened the bonds of affection between brothers who later had to agree on the division of the family lands, or to fight over them. Third, the Welsh princes refused to subordinate themselves to a single king (who, had he existed, might have resolved many inheritance disputes by law rather than force).

These three factors contributed to constant family feuds over inheritances, in which there were winners and losers; the losers often went looking for someone to help recover what they saw as their rights. This meant there were always opportunities for the English to divide and conquer. Gerald's exact

---

[27] *Description*, p. 270.

advice was to "stir the Welsh up to internecine feuds by bribery and by granting away each man's land to someone else." "They will quarrel bitterly with each other," he predicted, "and assassinations will become an everyday occurrence." Although Gerald did not quite say so, he suggested that these bloody internal struggles would not only deprive the Welsh of the unity and strength necessary for effective resistance; they would also leave them disheartened and, in some cases, eager for the return of law and order, even if imposed by a foreign power. "In a short time," he concluded, "they will be forced to surrender."[28]

Between Gerald and Edward

In the 82 years between the writing of Gerald's plan and its execution, there was no lack of warfare between Wales and England. A review of the history of the conflicts of this period both reveals the soundness of his judgment and supports the conclusion that the ultimate defeat of the Welsh was indeed the result of implementation of a sound strategic conception, and not simply the inexorable consequence of England's superior resources.

In Henry II's day, the principality of Gwynedd in North Wales had been the rock on which his two invasions had broken, and it long remained the seat of Welsh ambitions for some degree of autonomy. When Edward I launched his conquest of "Wales," it was principally a conquest of Gwynedd, the ruler of which had recently acquired the more sweeping title of "Prince of Wales." In South Wales, the Norman Marcher lords and creation of English and Flemish towns on the coast had begun the process of undermining the power of the native rulers, but it was the death of Lord Rhys of Deheubarth in 1197 that left South Wales incapable of mounting independent resistance to English domination. The basic reason was one Gerald had emphasized: the Welsh practice of partible inheritance. With 15 of Rhys' sons competing for their shares of his estates, fragmentation and weakness were inevitable. In Powys, the main principality of central Wales, the same problem emerged, though not so dramatically. In 1160 it was split between two heirs; the chances of heredity thereafter allowed the southern half to remain united under the dynasty that later became English earls as De la Poles, but in 1236 northern Powys was divided among five brothers, with each receiving no more than the equivalent of a minor barony.[29]

If the English had left the Welsh to their own devices, the centripetal tendencies of the inheritance system might have been counteracted by the power of warfare to unite; it was this possibility, after all, that led to much of the internecine warfare that Gerald noted. But the English did not want that to happen, and Welsh law, along with their status as suzerains of the Welsh princes, enabled English kings to wrap themselves in the mantle of justice as

[28] Ibid., p. 272.   [29] David Walker, *Medieval Wales* (Cambridge, 1990), pp. 90–92.

they stepped in to support the weak against the strong, thereby perpetuating disunity. Thus, after Llywelyn ap Iorwerth had led his cousins against his uncles to gain power in Gwynedd, the natural tendency of English policy would have been to undermine him, but in 1205 he made an astute marriage to Joan, the illegitimate eldest daughter of King John. For once, the Welsh tradition of treating natural-born children as equal to those born in wedlock proved advantageous, since Llywelyn could give John the benefit of a princely marriage for his favorite daughter without shaming himself.

Nonetheless, when Llywelyn, having consolidated his power in Gwynedd, occupied the former kingdom of Ceredigion in western Wales and took control of southern Powys, John recognized the threat. If Llywelyn could solidify his control of those regions, he would be so superior to the other Welsh princes that, even with English support, they could not serve as effective foils to the power of Gwynedd. Llywelyn would be in a position to become de facto prince of Wales, rather than merely of North Wales (a title he actually used). In 1209 John aided the attempts by several Welsh lords to recover lands and lordships which had fallen to Llywelyn, most importantly southern Powys. The Prince of Gwynedd, unwilling to accept this, struck back. John, according to the *Brut y Tywysogion*, "became enraged, and formed a design of entirely divesting Llywelyn of his dominion." For the purpose he led a "vast army," including six Welsh *tywysogion* ("princes," or "leaders"), against Gwynedd.[30]

The result, however, was almost a replay of 1165. By the time the English Army reached Deganwy, "the army was in so great a want of provisions, that an egg was sold for [three-quarters of an English foot soldier's daily wage]; and it was a delicious feast to them to get horse flesh." John returned to England in shame.[31] This was an intolerable result, and he quickly raised an even larger army. With better logistical preparations, he was more successful, capturing Bangor and building 14 or more castles (doubtless of timber, not stone) to secure his gains. Llywelyn sued for peace, agreeing to give up significant portions of his lands, secure the capitulation of the other Welsh lords, and pay a large indemnity.[32] This was accounted a great success for John, and modern historians have generally seen it that way. Nevertheless, the effort to actually conquer Gwynedd, rather than simply securing the subordination of its leader, had once again failed.[33]

---

[30] *Brut y Tywysogion*, ed. and trans. John Williams ab Ithel (London, 1860) (hereafter *ByT*), p. 267.

[31] Ibid., pp. 267–269; *Annales Cambriae*, p. 67. The whole expedition seems to have taken place during May. John Edward Lloyd, *A History of Wales from the Earliest Times to the Edwardian Conquest*, 2nd edn. (London, 1912), vol. II, pp. 634–635.

[32] *Annales Cambriae*, pp. 67–68; 67n. This was from July to August. Lloyd, *History of Wales*, vol. II, p. 635.

[33] R. R. Davies overstates the situation when he characterizes the campaign as bringing Llywelyn to "the most abject surrender," and showing that conquest "was well within the king of England's reach." *Domination and Conquest*, p. 79. The fact that John planned another campaign in 1212 and failed to launch it for causes that at least partly resulted

The extent of the difference was made clear in the following year, when John, evidently intending to secure his gains, ordered the construction of numerous castles inside Wales. From the new castle at Aberconwy, the king's men pushed their authority to the point that Llywelyn "could not brook the many insults done to him." Once again he rallied the other Welsh lords against the English, and within two years captured all the castles just ceded to John.[34] Llywelyn then cooperated with the English barons who had risen in rebellion against John's tyrannical rule, gaining even more territory in the ensuing conflict, occupying southern Powys again and greatly strengthening his position in western and southern Wales with the capture of Cardigan, Carmarthen, and even Swansea. He even carried the war into England, seizing Shrewsbury and joining the rebels at the Battle of Lincoln. However, the royalist victory in that battle, along with the death of John and the accession of the young Henry III, led many English magnates to make peace with the crown, and Llywelyn followed suit. The Treaty of Worcester in 1218 left him far stronger than he had been before John attacked him in 1211, and Wales more united that it had ever been. The Welsh princes still did homage to Henry III but did so only with Llywelyn's permission.[35]

This settlement endured until 1223, when the Earl of Pembroke led an offensive to regain his and the crown's lost lands in southwest Wales. He regained Cardigan and Carmarthen, as well as Montgomery in the middle March. Henry's government tried to follow up this success with a more ambitious royal expedition in 1228. Yet, again the crown aimed "to subjugate Llywelyn, son of Iorwerth, and all the Welsh princes." But the English offensive, which began only in late September, ground to a halt in Ceri, near the border, where Llywelyn seems to have won a small battlefield victory. The Welsh captured the great Marcher baron William de Braose, later exchanged for the important castle of Builth.[36] The normal result followed: the English king returned to England without any success more concrete than receiving the fealty of the Welsh *tywysogion*. Neither Llywelyn nor Wales was "subjugated" except in the loosest sense, which is much less than Henry seems to have intended. Another spate of conflict broke out from 1231 to 1234, with Llywelyn again coming out on top.[37]

"If their princes could come to an agreement and unite to defend their country," Gerald had warned, "or better still, if they had only one prince and

from the strain the 1211 campaign had placed on relations with his magnates suggests that a complete conquest of Wales was more difficult than Davies implies.

[34] *ByT*, pp. 271–279.   [35] Davies, *Age of Conquest*, pp. 242–243.

[36] *ByT*, p. 317; *Calendar of Close Rolls, 1227–31* (hereafter *CCR*), p. 115 (military summons issued on 3 September).

[37] In 1231 an English army advanced to Painscastle and covered the reconstruction of the fortification in mortared stone. In 1233 Llwelyn sided with various Marcher barons against the king and destroyed the town of Brecon. In 1234 he and his allies secured a peace which left him in secure control of all his territories. Lloyd, *History of Wales*, vol. II, pp. 675–681.

he a good one ... no one could ever beat them."[38] The career of Llywelyn ap
Iorwerth, later known as Llywelyn Fawr (Llywelyn the Great) bears out his
prediction. Llywelyn himself appreciated the importance of Welsh unity
under a single strong leader and went to great effort to insure that his
principality would pass intact to his legitimate son Dafydd, rather than being
split with Dafydd's elder brother Gruffydd, as Welsh tradition demanded.
Henry's government, however, issued letters forbidding Dafydd to receive the
homages of the nobles of Gwynedd and Powys, thereby sabotaging Llywelyn's
effort.[39] The Welsh prince apparently could not bring himself to take the only
step that would have prevented Henry III from playing the two brothers off
against each other to weaken Wales – executing Gruffydd for treason, which
he had opportunities to do. The result was that, after the prince's death in
1240, Gruffydd became a pawn of the English, and Dafydd's position was
consequently weak.[40] This, combined with Dafydd's lack of Welsh allies and
sheer bad luck – an extraordinarily dry summer made the marshes and rivers
that usually played such a large role in defending the region easily passable –
made Henry's invasion of Gwynedd in 1241 unusually successful. To buy
peace, Dafydd had to give up all his father's gains since 1216, pay an indemnity to cover the costs of Henry's offensive (a debt subsequently discharged by
the surrender of Deganwy), and, most gallingly, accept the judgment of the
English court as to what share of Llywelyn's inheritance his brother Gruffydd
should receive.[41] Nonetheless, this was still part of the usual pattern of Anglo-
Welsh warfare and a long way from the "conquest" of Gwynedd.

The death of Gruffydd in 1244 freed Dafydd to launch a counterstroke
against the English, which he immediately did. Most of the leading men of
Wales joined, and by year's end he had forced the three hold-outs to do the
same. Within Wales, the countryside was his; the power of the English hardly
extended beyond the walls of the castles they garrisoned.[42] Welsh raiders
came "swarming from their lurking places, like bees," carrying fire and sword
into England and ambushing English forces sent to check their incursions.[43]
Henry III's counterattack of 1245 followed the path of 1165 and the first
campaign of 1211. As the Welsh chronicle summarizes it:

Henry assembled the power of England and Ireland, with the intention of subjecting
all Wales to him, and came to Deganwy. And after fortifying the castle, and leaving
knights in it, he returned to England, having left an immense number of his army
dead and unburied, some having been slain and others drowned.[44]

---

[38] *Description*, p. 273.
[39] Thomas Rymer, ed., *Foedera, conventions, literae*, etc. (Hague edition), I:1:132.
[40] Matthew Paris, *English History, From the Year 1235–1273*, trans. J. A. Giles, 3 vols. (London, 1852–1854), vol. I, p. 372.
[41] Lloyd, *History of Wales*, vol. II: 697–8; *Foedera*, I:1:138–9.   [42] *ByT*, p. 331.
[43] Paris, *English History*, vol. II, pp. 27–28, 45–47.
[44] This is not simply Welsh propaganda. A newsletter from a noble in the English Army notes four "knights" (including a Gascon crossbowman) and about a hundred of their retainers

This was hardly a favorable result for the English monarch, but the campaign had also been hard on Gwynedd. The Welsh had destroyed crops within reach of the English as part of their logistical strategy, and troops from Ireland had ravaged the island of Anglesey, the bread-basket of Wales.[45] This step was particularly effective because the agrarian sector of the Welsh economy was increasing markedly in this period.[46] In addition, the English cut off the livestock-for-grain trade that was important for feeding the Welsh even when their own crops were left intact.[47]

The following spring, moreover, Dafydd died of natural causes. Two of his four nephews, Llywelyn and Owain ap Gruffydd, divided the portions of his lands still under native control. Without a single dominant figure, Welsh unity fractured further, with two minor *tywysogion* siding with the English to dispossess two others. The English drove Llywelyn and Owain and their allies temporarily into the mountains and the wilderness. But Henry faced serious troubles in France and England, so the English chose to accept Dafydd's nephews' proffers of peace. By the Treaty of Woodstock in 1247, they ceded the portion of Gwynedd east of the Conwy – nearly half the principality – to Henry, marking a new low-point for the fortunes of native Wales.[48] It has rarely been appreciated, however, that this was a compromise peace. By the terms of the agreement of 1241, Henry had a double right to take all of Gwynedd into his own hands, since Dafydd had not left an heir of his body, and because of his rebellion.[49] Instead, the majority of the principality, including its most valuable parts (Anglesey and Snowdonia), remained under native Welsh rule.

Prince Edward and Prince Llywelyn ap Gruffydd

A decade later events drove home the great difference between a humbled principality of Gwynedd and a completely conquered one. Once again, the Welsh were able to make an effective counterattack when they united behind a single heir of Llywelyn the Great – in this case Llywelyn ap Gruffydd, Dafydd's nephew, who in 1255 defeated two of his brothers in battle,

had been killed, aside from an uncertain number who drowned, during just one skirmish over a supply ship that grounded on the wrong side of the river separating English and Welsh forces. Paris, *English History*, vol. II, pp. 109–110. Henry entered Wales on 21 August, reached Deganwy on the 26th, and stayed there, fortifying the position, for two months. Ibid., and Lloyd, *History of Wales*, vol. II, pp. 703–705.

[45] Gerald notes an old proverb that Anglesey "is the mother of Wales" and could provide enough grain to feed all the Welsh. *Description*, p. 230; *Journey through Wales*, trans. Thorpe, p. 187.

[46] Suppe, *Military Institutions*, p. 15.

[47] *Foedera*, I:1:155; Paris, *English History*, vol. II, pp. 114–115, 244.

[48] Davies, *Age of Conquest*, pp. 302–304; *Foedera*, I:1:156.

[49] *Littere Wallie, Preserved in Liber A in the Public Record Office*, ed. J. Goronwy Edwards (Aberystwyth, UK, 1940), no. 8.

imprisoned them, and thereby gained control of all the principality except the portion that had been ceded to England in 1247.

King Henry III's son and heir, the future Edward I, had recently received the border earldom of Chester and the royal lands in Wales as part of his appanage. In 1256, perhaps anticipating trouble as a result of Llywelyn's victory over his brothers, 15-year-old Edward paid an unusual visit to his new lordship of eastern Gwynedd. Gerald's strategic plan, as noted above, had included a section on how to occupy and govern Wales once conquered. He advised that a firm and just official who would obey the laws and exercise moderation toward those who accepted royal rule, and in particular flatter the Welsh lords with honors, which they craved, should govern the land.[50] Henry III had not heeded this sage counsel; on the contrary, he sold the right to extract revenue from his Welsh lands to the highest bidder, first to John de Grey and then Alan de la Zouche. Since the latter paid 1,100 marks for the fee-farm, more than double the amount offered by the former, it should have been obvious to the king that his tax gatherers would have to squeeze the Welsh population immoderately and bend or break their laws to recoup his costs.[51] Moreover, de la Zouche publicly boasted how he had brought the Welsh to submit to *English* laws, in place of their traditional codes.[52] When Edward received the area from his father, rather than ameliorate the situation, he turned the administration over to Sir Geoffrey Langley, a *parvenu* royal official already infamous for his rapacity and oppression of the king's English subjects, who was working to extend the English structure of government into occupied Gwynedd.[53]

Moreover, far from being honored, the Welsh under Edward's control were treated in what they considered high-handed and demeaning ways. Such indignities would have been bad enough coming from Henry III, whom they had however unwillingly accepted as their lord, but the Welsh perceived them as much worse coming from young Edward. For men who viewed their status as deriving principally from their distinguished lineages rather than land or wealth,[54] slights coming from a mere *officer* of relatively low birth (such as Geoffrey Langley) were doubly humiliating.[55] The English did little better with regard to another of Gerald's suggestions, to reward those Welsh who

---

[50] *Description*, vol. II, p. 21.

[51] *Roger of Wendover's Flowers of History: Comprising the History of England from the Descent of the Saxons to A.D. 1235*, trans. J. A. Giles (London, 1849), vol. II, pp. 435, 486.

[52] Roger of Wendover, *Flowers of History*, vol. II, p. 486.

[53] Paris, *English History*, vol. II, p. 200; *Annales monastici*, vol. III, pp. 200–201.

[54] *Description*, trans. Forester, p. 505.

[55] Though he had become wealthy and powerful in the service of Henry III, Langley was the son of a "modestly endowed Gloucestershire knight," who had inherited only one manor, and gained one more by marriage. P. R. Coss, "Sir Geoffrey de Langley and the Crisis of the Knightly Class in Thirteenth-Century England," in T. H. Aston, ed., *Landlords, Peasants and Politics in Medieval England* (Cambridge, 1987), pp. 167, 168n10.

had assisted in the king's conquest.[56] The princes of Deheubarth had hoped to use England's might to throw off the loose subordination to Gwynedd they had experienced under Llywelyn the Great. However, they were disappointed to find themselves under the stricter tutelage of a lord who made no pretense of respecting their independence.

It was a sign of the dissatisfaction with the crown's management of Welsh affairs that by 1251 Owain and Llywelyn of Gwynedd had brought three of the other main Welsh princes into a secret sworn brotherhood aimed at resisting further erosion of native Welsh power.[57] The greater part of Wales then united behind Llywelyn ap Gruffydd when, in late 1256, his former subjects in eastern Gwynedd came before him to announce "that they would rather be killed in war for their liberty, than suffer themselves to be trodden down by strangers in bondage."[58] Within a short time, eastern Gwynedd, Deheubarth, Ceredigion, and Builth were all under the control of Llywelyn and his allies.

Despite his extensive possessions, Edward had neither the cash nor the men to put up effective resistance. He went to his father for aid. Henry dismissed him, saying his coffers were empty and he had more pressing business. Edward's uncle loaned him 4,000 marks, but that was a drop against the tide. The Marches suffered heavily from raiders, and the Welsh routed a substantial English force led by John Lestrange, Rhys Fychan, and Gruffydd ap Gwenwynwyn, marching under Prince Edward's banner, near Montgomery. They crushed an even larger army at Cymerau, reportedly inflicting a loss of 3,000 men, and captured and destroyed numerous castles held by the English or their allies.[59] Anticipating that this would provoke a large-scale response, the Welsh took precautions: they

prudently sent away their wives, children, and flocks into the interior of the country, about Snowdon and other mountainous places inaccessible to the English, ploughed up their fields, destroyed the mills in the road which the English would take, carried away all kinds of provisions, broke down the bridges, and rendered the fords impassable by digging holes, in order that, if the enemy attempted to cross, they might be drowned.[60]

---

[56] For Henry III's mistreatment of his Welsh supporters see *ByT*, p. 333; Davies, *Age of Conquest*, pp. 225, 228; and Lloyd, *History of Wales*, vol. II, pp. 710–711.

[57] *Littere Wallie*, nos. 261 (between Llywelyn and Gruffydd of North Powys) and 284 (between Llywelyn and Owain on the one hand and the two Rhyses on the other: *in conseruando ius suum et acquirendo quod iniuste ablatum est pro loco et tempore iuuabit alium et manutenebit contra omnes viuentes ac si essemus fratres conterini*). Technically Gruffydd was not bound to the Rhyses, but by transitivity he was, in effect.

[58] Maredudd ap Rhys Gryg, Rhys Fychan, and the prince of northern Powys. *ByT*, pp. 341, 343. By this point, however, Maredudd ap Owain had replaced Rhys Fychan in the alliance; they could not both be accommodated because their territorial claims were incompatible.

[59] In addition, two smaller defeats elsewhere cost the English 194 and 130 soldiers, respectively. *Annales Cambriae*, pp. 92–95; Lloyd, *History of Wales*, vol. II, p. 720. Two more minor Welsh victories followed in 1258. *Annales Cambriae*, pp. 95–96.

[60] Paris, *English History*, vol. II, p. 238.

Because a large portion of the Welsh economy rested on animal husbandry rather than farming, and the slopes of Snowdon offered excellent pasturage, these steps were not as painful as the equivalent would have been for the English. Moreover, the war allowed the Welsh to recoup some of their losses by plundering their neighbors over the border.[61] The rainy season made any English reprisals difficult, since it rendered the roads through the wetlands impassable for the invaders, though the locals could still make their way through.[62] According to Matthew Paris, though Edward threatened to "crush them like a clay pot," the Welsh "only laughed at ... and ridiculed" his efforts, until the English prince, seeing how little he could accomplish, was tempted to give up Wales and the Welsh as untameable, while Henry was "overcome with grief ... at the slaughter of so many of his liege subjects."[63]

Eventually rallying, the king summoned troops from all his lands, and meanwhile took the drastic step of destroying the harvests in the fields of the border-lands to prevent the Welsh from gaining access to the crops by force or by commerce. This caused serious shortages in his army, as well as for the population. Between his actions, the Welsh raids, and the end of normal cross-border trade, the economy of the Marches collapsed to the point of causing a serious famine. Henry's army, once assembled, advanced as far as Diserth and Deganwy, the only two fortresses within Gwynedd still under his control, to break Llywelyn's sieges and resupply them. But without accomplishing anything else, Henry dismissed his forces and returned to London, with Welsh warriors nipping at his heels and killing any stragglers.[64] By year's end, the three main Welsh *tywysogion* who had not immediately joined the rebellion had either fallen in line or (in the case of Gruffydd ap Gwenwynwyn) gone into exile in England.

When Henry began to prepare a new war, his knights protested at the prospect of another costly and useless campaign, and parliament took the extremely unusual step of refusing a grant of taxation.[65] Many Englishmen were in some respects sympathetic toward the Welsh cause, since they too felt abused and oppressed by royal ill-government and the greed of the king's officials and foreign relatives. Henry's inability to wage effective military operations combined with many other grievances to provoke what soon turned into a full-scale rebellion led by the Earl of Leicester, Simon de Montfort. The disunity that had so often plagued Wales now struck England in full measure, and Llywelyn quickly seized the opportunity. He allied with the earl and barons, just as his grandfather had done with the opposition to John, and ultimately with greater success. The Treaty of Montgomery in

---

[61] *Description*, p. 233; Paris, *English History*, vol. II, pp. 243, 267, 269.
[62] Paris, *English History*, vol. II, pp. 204, 217.   [63] Ibid., pp. 238 (trans. modified), 241.
[64] Ibid., pp. 245–247, 269, 291; Lloyd, *History of Wales*, pp. 721–722. The army left Chester on 19 August, and seems to have begun the march back to England as soon as 4 September.
[65] Ibid., pp. 267–269, 273.

1267 conceded to Llywelyn both the title of "Prince of Wales" and the feudal status that it implied: henceforth the other leading men of Wales, and not just Gwynedd, would do homage to him, rather than directly to the king of England.[66] Llywelyn, in turn, would do homage to Henry.

The importance of strategy

Perhaps influenced too much by the outcome, historians have tended to view the eventual English conquest of Wales as inevitable, or nearly so.[67] The argument is essentially that the general path of development of European concepts of monarchy and sovereignty insured that the English crown would seek a more thoroughgoing control of Wales; that the disparity of resources between the two countries provided England the strength needed; and that the loss of most of England's continental possessions led the English to focus those resources on military efforts within Britain. In this view, John's campaigns of 1211–1212 "had laid the ground-plans of a military conquest and settlement of the country which it only remained for Edward I to copy and put fully into operation." John had failed because of political miscalculations and lack of patience, but nonetheless had demonstrated "that the native Welsh kingdoms had little chance of withstanding the military might of the English state."[68] The author of those words was the greatest historian of medieval Wales of his generation, but he was not a military historian, and had a somewhat exaggerated view of what the simple application of resources and conventional military power can accomplish.

In reality, the humiliations of Gwynedd in 1211–1212, 1241, and 1247 no more show that Wales was ultimately doomed than the English disasters of 1218, 1256, and 1257 prove the opposite. When the Welsh were divided, the English had the advantage; when the English were distracted by civil strife or foreign wars, the Welsh made gains. Even when a king of England applied his realm's military strength fully toward the conquest of Wales, he could be stymied entirely, or limited to minor gains such as the construction of a single new castle (all that was accomplished in 1157, 1165, 1228, and 1245). It would take a large number of such campaigns to subdue Wales, and each expedition involved "heavy and quite alarming expenses."[69]

---

[66] Davies, *Age of Conquest*, pp. 314–315; *Littere Wallie*, no. 1. Llywelyn's possession of various lands he had conquered was also confirmed. One lone Welsh prince, Maredudd ap Rhys, remained a tenant in chief of the crown, but these were minor considerations compared to the creation of a real principality of Wales. This was a reversal of the agreement of 1241, by which Dafydd conceded to Henry III the homage of all the nobles of Wales. *Littere Wallie*, no. 4.

[67] E.g. Davies, *Age of Conquest*, p. 330.   [68] Ibid., pp. 292–293, 297, 295.

[69] *Description*, p. 270 ("as much as is levied in taxes from the Welsh over a whole series of years").

Indeed, since the Welsh could capture or destroy several castles in a single campaigning season with less effort and expense than it took the English to build a new one, this sort of offensive could lead to regression rather than advance in English territorial control. In 1231, for example, the Dunstaple annals record that Llywelyn Fawr destroyed ten castles of the March, while Henry III's army remained immobilized in order to rebuild just one.[70] Moreover, even when feudal service (and the shield-tax levied on knights who chose not to muster) paid for much of the manpower, extracting the soldiers needed for an unpleasant and unprofitable campaign drained the king's political capital. Henry III's campaign of 1245 best illustrates this point. "His majesty the king is staying with his army at Gannock [Deganwy]," wrote a nobleman:

for the purpose of fortifying a castle which is now built in a most strong position there; and we are dwelling round it in tents, employed in watchings, fastings, and prayers, and amidst cold and nakedness. In watchings, through fear of the Welsh suddenly attacking us by night; in fastings, on account of a deficiency of provisions, for a farthing loaf now costs five pence; in prayers, that we may soon return home safe and uninjured; and we are oppressed by cold ... because our houses are of canvas, and we are without winter clothing ... Whilst we have continued here with the army, being in need of many things, we have often sallied forth armed, and exposed ourselves to many and great dangers, in order to procure necessaries, encountering many and various ambuscades and attacks from the Welsh, suffering much ... There was such a scarcity of all provisions, and such want of all necessaries, that we incurred an irremediable loss both of men and horses. There was a time, indeed, when there was no wine ... amongst the whole army, except one cask only; a measure of corn cost twenty shillings [four months of wages for a foot soldier], a pasture ox three or four marks [160 or 240 days' wages], and a hen was sold for eight pence [four days' wages]. Men and horses consequently pined away, and numbers perished from want.[71]

When the army returned to England after ten weeks, the king's coffers were empty – indeed, he had to impose on his brother for a loan of 3,000 marks, which the latter secured by pawning his jewels. The army had suffered substantial losses, the soldiers had gained no plunder or glory, and, as one chronicler notes, Henry was *"unable,* as well as unwilling, to make any longer stay."[72] He nonetheless claimed that the king returned "crowned with good fortune," convinced that the devastation wrought by his forces had brought the Welsh to the edge of ruin, and planning to return in the spring to finish the job. This, however, seems to be a distortion of hindsight, since the king's subsequent actions bespeak more desperation than confidence:

in order that the Welsh might not obtain provisions from the neighbouring [English] provinces ... he caused the inhabitants of that country, and those in subjection to him, to be impoverished, and especially deprived of food, so much so, that, in

[70] *Annales monastici*, vol. IV, p. 127.   [71] Paris, *English History*, vol. II, p. 113.
[72] Ibid., p. 114 (emphasis added).

Cheshire and other neighbouring provinces, famine prevailed to such a degree, that the inhabitants had scarcely sufficient means left to prolong a wretched existence.[73]

This action fits better with the perspective of the Welsh chronicle, which depicts Henry's campaign as a costly failure, and by implication attributes the subsequent collapse of Gwynedd's fortunes instead to the death of Dafydd and the consequent defection of Maredudd ap Rhys Gryg and other Welsh princes.[74]

The resources of the English crown were large, but the king's territories were much smaller at the start of Edward I's reign than in Henry II's day, due to the loss of most of the wealthy Angevin lands in France. Llywelyn ap Gruffydd, on the other hand, controlled a larger portion of Wales than Owain had in 1157 or 1165, and the Welsh had in the meantime adopted elements of the Anglo-Norman style of war. They had added barded cavalry to their forces, developed sophisticated siege methods for attacking castles, and built their own castles in substantial numbers to strengthen their defensive capabilities, without losing their native martial tradition.[75] For Edward to achieve greater success than his predecessors against a stronger foe, he would have to conduct his war not just with greater determination, but also with a better plan.

As Clausewitz points out, an offensive that culminates and halts before it renders the enemy incapable of counterattack leaves the initial attacker in a dangerous position. Until he fully consolidated his gains, he would continue to suffer the disadvantages of being on the offensive (logistical difficulties, long lines of communication, the disadvantage in information that comes from operating in the midst of a hostile populace) without benefitting from its advantages (concentration and initiative).[76] Moreover, an invader seeking

---

[73] Ibid.   [74] *ByT*, pp. 331, 333.

[75] Gerald says one of the things that would contribute to making the Welsh nation unconquerable would be if they "were more commonly accustomed to the Gallic mode of arming, and depended more on steady fighting than on their agility." By his time the nobles had become good horsemen, but were still not numerous and remained light-armored, typically with small coats of mail (*loricis minoribus*). *Description*, trans. Forester, pp. 521, 491; *Opera*, ed. James F. Dimock, vol. VI (London, 1868), p. 190. By 1245, according to Matthew Paris' probably exaggerated report, the Welsh fielded 500 well-armed knights on iron-clad horses (along with 30,000 footmen). *English History*, vol. III, p. 217. Although the sources give little tactical detail, Welsh victories in six consecutive clashes of 1257–1258 indicate a high level of tactical proficiency had been achieved. *Annales Cambriae*, pp. 92–96. The Welsh had also made progress in siege warfare. The *Brut y Tywysogion* has an isolated (and possibly anachronistic) mention of the use of "engines" for breaching castles by the Welsh as early as 1113, but common reference to the use of "engines" in siege warfare begins in 1196. *ByT*, pp. 113, 243, 253, 277, 321 (in 1231 an army led by Llywelyn ap Iorwerth, among others, "broke the castle" of Cardigan [Aberteivi] with engines). Miners are noted as used against the Welsh in 1196, and by a mixed Anglo-Welsh army in 1214. Ibid., pp. 243, 277.

[76] This is a major and under-appreciated theme in Carl von Clausewitz, *On War*, ed. and trans. by Michael Howard and Peter Paret (Princeton, NJ, 1976). See particularly Books VII.5 and VIII.4, and cf. VIII.7.

to hold on to any substantial territory suffers from the principal disadvantage of the operational-level defense: if he wants to control the countryside and exploit its resources, he must disperse his forces, but scattered troops are vulnerable to defeat in detail. Therefore, an effective offensive strategic plan aimed at the defeat of the enemy has two requirements. First, it must identify physical targets that, if captured or destroyed, will either break the enemy's *will* to continue, or eliminate his *ability* to do so. Second, it should insure the attacker has sufficient strength and staying power to reach those centers of gravity before the campaign drains his ability to continue the offensive.

In most cases, a defender should consider the attacker's situation as well as his own: if the defender can see that the attacker has reached the point of exhaustion, he has a favorable negotiating position and is likely to limit the concessions he is willing to make accordingly. Until the reign of Edward I, some English invasions of Wales were so ineffective that they failed to impel the defenders to offer any concessions at all for peace; others gained the English a forward position or induced Welsh leaders to renew the homage that they in any case generally acknowledged they owed to the English king; only in a few cases had the princes of Gwynedd surrendered any territory. Indeed, since the capitulation of 1247 followed the death of Dafydd rather than being a direct result of the prior campaign, only the invasions of 1211 and 1241 clearly had that last result, and only briefly. In any case, not one of the English attacks left the Welsh so badly defeated in military terms that they would not have been *able* to continue the war. In no case had the invaders succeeded in engaging and destroying the army of Gwynedd or occupying Snowdonia.

Until 1276, the strategies the English had employed to attempt the conquest of Wales reflected too much concern with how best to use what they *had*, rather than how to get what they *needed*. To force the complete surrender of Gwynedd, as Gerald had made clear, required pushing the Welsh into their mountain refuges and keeping the pressure on them for a full year to wear them away by attrition and ultimately hunger. Anything less allowed the defenders to wait out the offensive and then counterattack to recover territory and destroy castles held by the English, or at least launch raids on enemy territory to resupply themselves and encourage the enemy to accept a compromise peace. Yet, English king after king had begun a campaign in the summer or even the fall and returned home before winter. John, unusually, had begun his campaign early and returned for a second attack in the same year, and that was a major reason for his greater success. In most cases, however, not only had the English failed to sustain the offensive in winter, but they had also declined or failed to mount a new attack the following spring.

The basic reason was simple: because it was *difficult and expensive* to do what Gerald's plan required, namely to sustain an offensive effort to the point where the Welsh had to choose among starvation, complete surrender, or an attempt to restore their situation with a near hopeless effort to crush the invaders in a direct battle.[77] In the thirteenth century, the English had geared their military system, like that of all contemporary Western powers, toward mounting major campaigns over the summer, spearheaded by armored cavalry who owed service at their own expense for relatively short periods – 40 days, in England. It was possible to bring feudal contingents into operation in rotation, but even England's resources were not so disproportionately great that one-eleventh of her strength could be counted upon to defeat a counterattack by the concentrated forces of the princes of Gwynedd and their allies. The latter could draw on the martial ardor and skill of much of their population, not just its upper stratum. In any case, English knights had little enthusiasm for the rigors of camping in the cold and rain of a Welsh winter under constant harassment. Knights and footmen willing to do what was needed could nonetheless be found in sufficient numbers, provided that the king had the money and was willing to pay them, but that required straining the fiscal system to its limits, as only a strong king could do, and then only if he could avoid dividing the proceeds between the conquest of Wales and other conflicts.

Even a king who raised great sums and was willing to devote them to Welsh matters would likely not have had much success, had he spent the money to keep twice as many armored horsemen in his employ from July through October and insure they had adequate supplies. In fact, although there are no specific figures from the earlier campaigns to compare them to, by later standards Edward I's highly successful campaign of 1276–1277 was not exorbitantly expensive; the expenditures he made would have been within the reach of Henry I, John, or Henry II, for example.[78] The success of Edward's conquest of Wales between 1276 and 1282 did owe something to favorable circumstances as well as his military competence, but it was also the result of his application of a better strategy, which, in all key respects, was the one that Gerald of Wales had outlined almost a century earlier, but that none of his predecessors had implemented.

---

[77] Modern historians have tended to downplay these issues, emphasizing instead that the English kings were generally satisfied to leave their Welsh vassals in power, provided they offered due fealty. This was doubtless true in some instances, but especially given the chroniclers' frequent assertions of more ambitious aims, and indeed common sense, it seems likely that in some other years, the English monarchs would happily have dismembered the principality of Gwynedd entirely, or indeed depopulated it entirely, if they thought it could be done easily or cheaply. It may be true – though the chronicles say otherwise – that, as R. R. Davies puts it, "for much of the twelfth and thirteenth centuries the kings of England seemed neither capable nor anxious to deliver the *coup de grâce*," but then, there is little point in being anxious to do what one is not capable of doing. *Domination and Conquest*, p. 24.

[78] The total cost of the war was somewhere around £23,000 – well less than the amount raised by the war-tax granted by parliament to pay for it. John E. Morris, *The Welsh Wars of Edward I* (Oxford, 1901), pp. 140–142. The war of 1282, by comparison, cost £120,000 or more. Michael Prestwich, *Edward I* (Berkeley, CA, 1988), p. 200.

The war of 1276–1277

Gerald's principal recommendations, as already noted, were: (1) divide the Welsh, especially taking advantage of the family feuds that arose from the practice of partible inheritance, promising some lords the lands of others; (2) use economic warfare, preparing the ground for conquest by cutting off all imports; (3) invade by the coastal lowlands, insuring supply by sea; (4) employ light-armed troops drawn from the Marches and within Wales, led by locals who knew the terrain and Welsh tactics and were hardier and more accustomed to campaigning in wilderness areas than most Anglo-Norman soldiers. Use them to ring Snowdonia, apply "patient and unremitting pressure," and wear down the Welsh with probes, raids, and skirmishes, and by denying them food. Bring up fresh troops as necessary; and (5) keep the king's attention focused on Wales for a full year, without becoming distracted by strife elsewhere.

It was part of England's standard repertoire for Welsh wars to execute steps 1 and 3, and in Henry III's reign the value of step 2 had been well appreciated, though in 1245 the English had taken the most stringent measures along these lines only after the end of the main army's campaign. English kings had also made substantial use at times of Marcher troops and Welsh allies, though not in the ways Gerald called for. However, most military offensives against Wales were begun in late summer and finished by early fall. In John's two-stage invasion of 1211, the second phase was merely an ad hoc response to the embarrassment of the first. Even so, the two campaigns lasted only from May to August. By contrast, Edward I opened his first war as king in November of 1276, and finished it in November of 1277, requiring just three days less than Gerald's estimate of one year.[79]

Most historians see the war of 1276–1277 as arising from arrogance and intransigence on both sides: Edward had sheltered Llywelyn's younger brother Dafydd and Gruffydd ap Gwenwynwyn of southern Powys after the two had plotted to assassinate Llywelyn, had made difficulties about Llywelyn's rights to certain disputed lands, and had supported the Bishop of St. Asaph against Llywelyn over the latter's encroachments on the bishopric's revenues. Llywelyn, feeling that Edward was acting in bad faith, tried to bring diplomatic pressure to bear by declining to give the new king the homage he was due, as well as withholding installments of the large sum he owed to the crown by the terms of the Treaty of Montgomery.[80] This was poor policy, however. Although Llywelyn had reason to be dissatisfied, nothing Edward

---

[79] Thus, even if we consider only the operations of King Edward's own army, from July through November, the campaign was not "brief" compared to previous efforts. Certainly the war as a whole should not be interpreted as a mere "military promenade, followed by successful negotiations." See Prestwich, *Edward I*, p. 182.

[80] See Davies, *Age of Conquest*, pp. 320–330 for a clear discussion.

did should have been an unbearable affront, or as painful as what war could bring, whereas Llywelyn's refusal to do homage was a challenge Edward simply could not ignore.

In 1275, both parties could see war coming. A group of Irish "kings" asked Edward to aid them in suppressing a rebellion against his authority in Ulster, while the King of Castile requested help in the war against the Saracens, but Edward refused to allow himself to be distracted. He relied on peaceful diplomacy to pursue his stepmother's claim to the county of Agen and to resolve other tensions between England and France.[81] At the end of the year, Edward discovered that Llywelyn had, by proxy, married Eleanor de Montfort, daughter of the Earl of Leicester, who had so severely challenged royal authority in the reign of Henry III, and sister of Simon and Guy de Montfort, who had recently murdered Edward's own cousin, Henry of Almain, whom Edward had sent to the de Montforts as a peace envoy. Under the circumstances, Edward interpreted the betrothal as a provocation, even a threat. After capturing Eleanor as she sailed to Wales, he imprisoned her, which Llywelyn naturally considered a hostile act.[82] In spring and summer of 1276, both sides complained of raids and border skirmishes.[83] In October, Edward ordered defensive preparations in Montgomery and Oswestry on the Welsh border.[84]

The next month, Edward decided that Llywelyn had already received sufficient opportunities to deliver his homage, declared him a rebel, and began hostilities.[85] Llywelyn would gladly have continued to put off the conflict or avoid it altogether, so it was Edward's choice to begin the conflict in late fall.[86] The English king initially set the date for the feudal muster as midsummer 1277.[87] He could have done the same even if he had allowed the diplomatic process to continue through mid-spring. The declaration of war in November, however, gave him the opportunity to begin the war over the winter, something none of his predecessors had ever shown the slightest inclination to do, but an action that made good sense in terms of Gerald's strategic plan. By opening hostilities at an unexpected time, Edward fore-stalled the Welsh from laying in supplies in anticipation of the war. Already

[81] *Foedera*, I:4:76–77; I:2:147–153.

[82] Edward seems to have been convinced, as he wrote at the time, that Eleanor was inspired by the desire to use her new husband's power to revive the Montfortian program of resistance to royal tyranny. J. Beverley Smith, *Llywelyn ap Gruffudd, Prince of Wales* (Cardiff, 1998), pp. 391–399, 402.

[83] Ibid., pp. 402–406.   [84] *CCR, 1272–9*, p. 315.   [85] Ibid., pp. 359–361.

[86] In early 1277 Llywelyn was pleading to be given the king's grace and proclaiming his willingness to do homage and to pay a substantial cash indemnity in exchange for a peace of goodwill (including the release of Eleanor). Smith, *Llywelyn*, pp. 410–411.

[87] Ibid., p. 360. The writs of summons were issued 12 December. *CCR*, p. 410. On 24 January, several dozen men received letters of protection for service through midsummer as they were "going" on service in Wales; from 3 March additional letters were mostly for those who had "gone." *Calendar of Patent Rolls, 1272–81* (hereafter *CPR*), pp. 189–192.

in the declaration of war itself, the king forbade all communication between his subjects and Llywelyn's men, and ordered "that no one shall take into [Llywelyn's] land, or permit to be taken thither through their land or power, by land or by sea, victuals, horses, or other things that may be useful to men in any way."[88]

Within a week of the declaration of war, the king appointed three magnates as his lieutenants for the conduct of the war, each based in a royal fortress: the Earl of Warwick in Chester in the north, closest to Gwynedd; Roger Mortimer at Montgomery in the middle March, opposite southern Powys; and Pain de Chaworth in the south, at Carmarthen. Each was a Lord Marcher, who well understood the land and the enemy, just as Gerald had advised.[89] The king provided them with moderate-sized strike forces of cavalry at royal wages and gave them direction over the feudal contingents and arrayed infantry of regional landholders as needed. Each captain, in pursuance of the divide-and-conquer strategy advocated by Gerald, received authority to receive into the king's peace any Welshmen willing to submit.[90] All sorts of other preparations were initiated: collecting a tax granted by parliament, taking loans from Italian bankers, purchasing and stockpiling grain, importing warhorses, summoning Gascon crossbowmen, repairing border fortresses, purchasing large numbers of crossbow quarrels, and so on.[91] On 10 February, the Archbishop of Canterbury excommunicated Llywelyn on the basis of his failure to fulfill his oaths to his lord. The archbishop subjected his followers to the same sanction, if they did not leave his service within a month. This made it possible for the war against the Welsh prince to be presented as a holy war and gave any Welshman who considered defecting to the English a convenient excuse for doing so.[92]

Edward did not allow winter weather to delay the initiation of active campaigning against the outer ring of Llywelyn's dominions. Each of

---

[88] *CCR*, p. 361. Cf. the orders of 12 December 1276 and 3 January 1277 to prevent "corn [grain], wine, honey, salt, iron, arms," or other goods from moving into Wales. Ibid., pp. 410, 366.

[89] John E. Morris untangles the narrative in *Welsh Wars*, an outstanding book, especially considering its age. However, especially since his approach is mainly from the English perspective, his work should be read in conjunction with Smith, *Llywelyn*. Chaworth had under royal pay both infantry and 100 cavalry under John de Beauchamp, custodian of Carmarthen and Cardigan castles. Smith, *Llywelyn*, p. 419n. He also had substantial contingents of cavalry provided by the Marcher lords, who did not receive royal pay.

[90] *CPR*, p. 186 (Mortimer); *Foedera*, I:2:158 (Chaworth); it is scarcely conceivable that Warwick was not given the same authority. Dafydd ap Gruffydd and the justiciar of Chester were given similar but more limited powers. *CPR*; see also pp. 201, 219. A petition of Trahaern ap Madog from this period refers to his coming into the peace of Bohun (the Earl of Hereford) and the king. *Calendar of Ancient Petitions Relating to Wales*, ed. W. Rees (Cardiff, 1975), p. 468; Smith, *Llywelyn*, p. 417n.

[91] Morris, *Welsh Wars*, p. 115; *CPR*, pp. 193, 195–196.

[92] Smith, *Llywelyn*, pp. 407–409, 412–413, 428 (*expediccione votiva*). It is interesting to note that Gerald did not mention this step in his strategic plan, perhaps because he was unwilling to advocate the use of the Church as a tool of the crown.

Edward's three field forces was sufficiently strong to be secure against anything but a full-scale attack by Llywelyn, and that was not much of a threat, since the requirement of mobilizing for a major counterattack would have ruined any real chance of surprise. In any case, the English could afford whatever losses fighting might entail, whereas the Welsh could not, so Llywelyn ordered his men to avoid major clashes. The force operating from Chester, which included Llywelyn's brother Dafydd, seems to have occupied the neighboring district of Maelor or Bromfield in northern Powys before the end of the year.[93] The lord of that region turned against his brother, Madog ap Gruffydd, who then also surrendered to avoid losing all his lands. Dinas Brân, one of the strongest castles in Wales, had fallen to the English by early May.[94] In December Llywelyn in person opposed Mortimer's detachment in the middle March, but before 5 February 1277 the English had driven the prince out of the region with the help of the Earl of Lincoln and the men of Shropshire and Hereford. Moreover, southern Powys was largely under control by the English and the most loyal of the Welsh *tywysogion*, Gruffydd ap Gwenwynwyn.[95] Dolforwyn castle, recently constructed by Llywelyn to block the route up the Severn, fell to Mortimer's men on 8 April after a short siege. The same force quickly asserted control over Cydewain, Ceri, and Gwertheyrnion. Before the month's end they occupied the ruins of Builth castle and dominated that district as well.[96]

Pain de Chaworth, meanwhile, employed a combination of military pressure and negotiations to secure submission of Llywelyn's ally-by-compulsion, Rhys ap Maredudd. Rhys had a claim to the castle of Dinefwr, traditional capital of Deheubarth, and the surrounding district, then held by his cousin Rhys Wyndod, Prince Llywelyn's nephew. In accordance with Gerald's advice to divide the Welsh by promising one man another's lands, Chaworth promised, or at least strongly implied, that once Edward conquered Dinefwr and the surrounding area, he would insure Rhys ap Maredudd received his due rights to those lands, or if Edward chose to keep them as royal lands, he would compensate Rhys ap Maredudd for his losses.

In exchange, Rhys put his castles and men at Chaworth's disposal.[97] Gruffydd ap Maredudd, the principal Welsh lord in Ceredigion, also entered

[93] The power given on 26 December to Dafydd and to the justiciar of Chester to receive the submission of Llywelyn ap Gruffydd of Maelor and all his men seems clearly to have been the result of a negotiation with the *tywysog*, not merely an anticipatory tool. *CPR*, p. 186.
[94] Smith, *Llywelyn*, pp. 423–434 [*CAC*, p. 83]; *CCR*, pp. 398–399.
[95] Morris, *Welsh Wars*, pp. 120–121; *CPR*, p. 192.
[96] *ByT*, p. 365. Refortification of the castle of Builth had begun by 3 May. Smith, *Llywelyn*, p. 418.
[97] Smith, *Llywelyn*, pp. 419–421; *Foedera*, 1:2:158. The language is a bit ambiguous: it could be interpreted to leave the king room to decide that Rhys did not have the right to Dinefwr in the first place, in which case Edwards' retention of the castle would not involve his "demanding" Rhys' rights (*ius suum deposcet*), and therefore would not require "restitution." Rhys agreed to do homage to Edward, and Edward agreed that he would never alienate Rhys' homage to another, except by the latter's free will – i.e., Rhys would not be subjected again to Llywelyn.

the king's peace.[98] The three *tywysigion* combined might have been a fair match for royal forces in the Tywi Valley, but with two in English service and Llywelyn in no position to lend effective assistance, Rhys Wyndod had little choice but to surrender. By the first week of June, his castles of Dinefwr, Llandovery, and Caercynan were in Chaworth's hands as royal property, and the British immediately began strengthening their fortifications.[99] The remaining Welsh nobles of Deheubarth soon came into the king's peace, generally losing some of their lands and keeping others, just as Llywelyn ultimately would.[100] Meanwhile, the Earl of Hereford used a combination of his resources and royal assistance to make good his claim on the three cantrefs of Brycheiniog (Brecknock), thus securing the rear of Mortimer's and Chaworth's advances.[101]

The bill for wages for the winter and spring operations of the three advance forces amounted to nearly £3,000 sterling – a far from trivial sum, but nonetheless an excellent bargain, considering the extent to which they had weakened Llywelyn and prepared the ground for the summer's main push.[102] Not only had Llywelyn lost lands and access to their men, money, and supplies, but he had also been compelled to commit his forces to the field in winter, which, despite the legendary disdain of the Welsh for difficult conditions, began the process of wearing his men down. The same was true, no doubt, for those of the king's men in these preliminary actions, but unlike the Welsh, large contingents of fresh troops were about to join them.

Edward had summoned the feudal host for 1 July. Most joined at Chester, from whence the English Army would follow the traditional invasion route along the northern coast, while a few hundred more troopers, now under the king's brother Edmund, advanced on Aberystwyth and began a large new castle at Llanbadarn, from which they could control the country right up to the southern border of Gwynedd, at the River Dyfi. The main army at Chester, under Edward himself, had approximately 1,000 heavy cavalry – more than enough to insure superiority in open battle, but only one-third of what the kingdom could have supplied.[103] However, Edward had provided for a much larger force of foot soldiers, as well as carters, craftsmen, and laborers

---

[98] Smith, *Llywelyn*, p. 421 [*CAC*, pp. 55–56, 71–72].
[99] *CPR*, p. 212. Pain de Chaworth was in charge of all three castles. £285 10s. were disbursed for the strengthening of the "king's castles" of Dinefwr and Caercynan. The National Archives, Kew, UK (hereafter TNA), E101/3/20.
[100] Smith, *Llywelyn*, pp. 421–422.
[101] *ByT*, p. 365; Morris, *Welsh Wars*, p. 123; Smith, *Llywelyn*, pp. 416–418.
[102] Morris, *Welsh Wars*, pp. 118, 141.
[103] Ibid., p. 127. Edward III mustered some 3,000 men-at-arms for the 1346 campaign, and a similar number for 1359–1360, even though these were overseas campaigns and, in the latter instance, after the Black Death. Clifford J. Rogers, *War Cruel and Sharp: English Strategy under Edward III, 1327–1360* (Woodbridge, 2000), Appendix 1.

by the thousands.[104] Gerald had called for the English to hold Wales after its conquest by building castles and insuring access to them by clearing wide paths through the woods to hinder ambushes. Edward decided to begin the process during the campaign itself, but (unlike most English kings before him) neither to settle for construction a short distance into Wales, nor to drive in deep without a secure line of communications to the rear.[105]

Instead, during his advance, he would stop each 15 miles or so, begin construction of a fortress, and start by digging large ditches to protect a camp. As soon as the defensive works were sufficient to prevent the camp from being overrun by a sudden assault, he would garrison it with infantry and cavalry. Meanwhile, the main strength of the army would keep Llywelyn at bay and provide cover for a large force of axe-men – over 1,500 men during August – as they burned and cut down the forests to create an "extremely broad" open way to the next destination, advancing at a rate of something like half a mile per day.[106]

Once the way was clear, the army advanced to Flint. In addition to the quantities of wood made available by the forest-clearing, Edward had a great deal of prepared timber brought in by sea, allowing for construction of more lasting works and, probably more importantly, speeding up the process. With over 500 skilled carpenters and masons on hand, the labor went quickly.[107] Still, it took until 26 July for the army to reach Flint. Moreover, the 40 days' unpaid service owed by the feudal cavalry had ended before the army was ready to advance from Flint to Rhuddlan on 20 August. The earls, most of whom still brought their retinues at their own expense, remained with Edward nonetheless. With their men, approximately 125 volunteers from the feudal contingents retained at pay, and the king's own household, the strength of the cavalry was approximately 500 men, probably at least double what Llywelyn (deprived of his allies) could muster, and better equipped as well.

The mass of Edward's army at Rhuddlan, however, consisted of infantry (bowmen, spearmen, and a few crossbowmen), whom he had recruited in

---

[104] Morris, *Welsh Wars*, pp. 127–132, 139. The abbot of St. Werburg's in Chester sent 100 laborers for the construction at Flint at his own expense; if others of the king's men did similarly, the total of workmen may have been substantially larger even than the pay records indicate. *CPR*, p. 226.

[105] Though on the scanty evidence available, John may have done the same in 1211.

[106] Morris, *Welsh Wars*, pp. 131–135. Wykes' chronicle, in *Annales monastici*, vol. IV, p. 273 (quotation); Osney annals, in *Annales monastici*, vol. IV, p. 272 (burning).

[107] Morris, *Welsh Wars*, pp. 130, 138–139. This required substantial advance planning. At the start of May, a knight of the royal household was sent to supervise the taking of oaks from the forest of Chester for the construction at Flint (which the king would not reach until July). TNA E101/3/15. Royal officials had been sent to diverse parts of England as early as mid June, specifically to collect masons and carpenters, "as many as [they] can get, and in whosesoever works or service they may be." When the clerks brought in one contingent, they were sent back out to gather more workers. *CPR*, p. 213; TNA E101/3/16. Thomas Wykes' chronicle says both Flint and Rhuddlan were strengthened so well they became impregnable. *Annales monastici*, vol. IV, p. 273.

unprecedented numbers. Of these, approximately 3,000 came from Lanca-
shire, Derbyshire, and Rutland, but the great majority, as Gerald had recommended, were from Wales (9,000) and the English Marches (3,500).[108]
A good portion of the English infantry would have had light or medium armor
(a quilted gambeson or short mail shirt and metal helmet), as Gerald had also
called for.[109] Another 2,000 or so, perhaps 10 percent cavalry and the rest
infantry, patrolled the roads from bases at Chester and Flint. In addition, over
700 sailors manning 26 ships were on station to support the campaign.[110] In
later wars, Edward used the royal right of purveyance (forced purchase of
goods at fixed, moderate prices) to acquire supplies for his armies.[111] But
in 1277 he seems to have used it only for his own household troops and relied
on profit-seeking merchants to keep the rest fed.[112] This served the purpose
well enough: there are no reports of shortages, starving soldiers, or the
butchering of prized horses for food.[113]

While the work of fortification and road-clearing proceeded, Edward's
soldiers made frequent raids into Welsh territory. This was doubtless done
partly to collect supplies and partly to keep the troops occupied. Nevertheless,
Thomas Wykes' chronicle notes that Edward's purpose was to leave the Welsh
destitute and use hunger to push them into their final refuge on Snowdonia,
until they gave up all thought of resistance.[114]

Edward did not ignore the political aspects of the war during military
operations. Llywelyn's brother Dafydd was in Edward's army with 20 horsemen and 200 infantry at English pay.[115] In a document sealed at Flint on

[108] Morris, *Welsh Wars*, pp. 131–133.
[109] The Assize of Arms promulgated by Henry III in 1252 required lesser gentry with
freeholders with 5 to 10 pounds of land revenues to own a purpoint and iron helmet;
those with 10 to 15 pounds were to have a mail haubergeon and a helmet; but only those
with more than 15 pounds had to maintain a horse. William Stubbs, *Select Charters*, 8th
edn. (Oxford, 1905), pp. 371–372. Even earlier, in 1231, a levy of infantry from
Gloucestershire for a Welsh campaign was limited to those with metal armor. Michael
Prestwich, *Armies and Warfare in the Middle Ages. The English Experience* (New Haven, CT,
1996), p. 122.
[110] Morris, *Welsh Wars*, pp. 128, 132–133.   [111] Ibid., pp. 84, 197.
[112] This is indicated by the relatively small expenditures recorded on the relevant account roll –
just £416 17s. 10d. ob., including the clerks' expenses – even though the heading of the
document says the sums were spent on supplies to sustain the king's *army* (*exercitus*) in the
Welsh War. TNA E101/3/16. Numerous letters of protection were issued to merchants
bringing food to the army. *CPR*, pp. 224, 226, 227, 230.
[113] In September the king was prepared to order that any goods taken from the priory of
Daventry should be restored to the monks, and a whole group of similar orders was made as
late as 16 October, which shows that the supply situation was still far from desperate, ibid.,
pp. 228–229, 232 (note also the various protections "notwithstanding the need of the king
and the others in the army of Wales," ibid.). Cf. Prestwich, *Edward I*, p. 181. That a
messenger was sent in September to hasten the collection of supplies by royal purveyance
does indicate some concern, but not necessarily actual "difficulties," of which there are no
mentions in the chronicles or letters (in sharp contrast to most previous expeditions).
[114] *Annales monastici*, vol. 4, p. 274; cf. Gerald, *Description*, p. 268.
[115] Morris, *Welsh Wars*, p. 128.

23 August, Edward promised to provide him and his brother Owain (imprisoned by Llywelyn) with the share of Gwynedd they were due under Welsh law. This was a clear example of Gerald's recommendation to divide the Welsh by promising to one man what another held. However, the document also laid the groundwork for the post-combat occupation policy; it made clear that all Wales was forfeited to the crown, so that Dafydd and Owain would hold their lands as fiefs graciously provided by the king and carrying the same obligations connected to English fiefs, including attendance at Edward's parliaments, rather than as inherited properties. Moreover, the agreement included the proviso that Edward could retain for himself Anglesey and parts of Snowdonia, thus making future rebellions impossible, or at least impractical.[116] Gruffydd ap Gwenwynwyn of southern Powys and Madog ap Llywelyn ap Maredudd, exiled claimant to the lordship of Meirionydd (held by Prince Llywelyn since 1256), were also in Edward's service.[117]

At the end of August, the army advanced to Deganwy on the Conwy River, the border between western and eastern Gwynedd. The English had tightened the ring around Snowdonia from both the east and south. The Conwy was a difficult barrier, but Llywelyn could not both defend it and protect the Isle of Anglesey in his rear. After reducing his logistical burdens by dismissing the troops in surplus of his needs (mainly Welsh infantry), Edward sent roughly half his remaining force by sea to Anglesey. Along with the soldiers went 360 harvesters with scythes and sickles to collect the island's grain. The wheat Llywelyn was surely counting on to sustain his people through the winter would instead feed the English garrisons occupying eastern Gwynedd and Ceredigion.[118]

Normally, if they succeeded in continuing resistance until the hungry invaders retreated for the winter, the Welsh would "burst out like rats from their holes" to raid the marches or otherwise obtain provisions "as they would commonly do, even in time of war, either by purchase, or by robbery, through friendship, relationship, or kindred."[119] With all Wales except Gwynedd under English control, and Edward's men holding Deganwy, Rhuddlan, Flint, Ruthin, and Llanbadarn, and also Anglesey, it would be practically impossible for the Welsh to bring in significant quantities of food. Rhuddlan and Flint, moreover, were being fortified on a scale that "outshadow[ed] anything that had gone before," and on the water so that they could be supplied and reinforced by sea.[120] The principal route toward England would, thus, be blocked securely.

---

[116] *Littere Wallie*, pp. 103–104 (*pro securitate nostra et pacis populi seruande*).
[117] Smith, *Llywelyn*, pp. 425–426. So also, it would appear from the letters of protection they received in October on departing the army, were Rhys Fychan and Cynan ap Mareduddd. *CPR*, p. 229.
[118] Morris, *Welsh Wars*, pp. 134–135.
[119] Roger of Wendover, *Flowers of History*, vol. II, p. 539; Paris, *English History*, vol. II, p. 114; translation modified.
[120] Norman J. G. Pounds, *The Medieval Castle in England and Wales: A Political and Social History* (Cambridge, 1993), p. 169. At Rhuddlan a canal was dug to facilitate supply by water.

So far, Edward had followed Gerald's strategy practically to the letter. The next phase in the archdeacon's plan was to wait for the leaves to fall and then send detachments of Marchers and friendly Welsh to harry the refugees in the hills until they surrendered. For the first time in the Anglo-Norman wars against Wales, the English were in a position to do just that. By 20 September, the king had decided against further major field operations in winter,[121] but even after Edward had disbanded much of his army, he kept sufficient troops in the castles encircling Llywelyn's remaining dominions to "besiege Snowdon," as the contemporary chronicler Bartholomew Cotton put it, and harry the Welsh with continued raids.[122] Edward was even bringing in relays of fresh troops to replace worn-out soldiers, as Gerald had advised: 1,930 infantry joined the army as late as 23 September.[123] A few days before that, two merchants were given letters of protection to bring food in to the army, lasting until Christmas.[124] An extension of the campaign into winter proved unnecessary, however, since by early November Llywelyn was ready to capitulate.

The settlement of 1277

The Treaty of Aberconwy, sealed on 9 November 1277, represented a disastrous defeat for Llywelyn and a clear victory for Edward. Nevertheless, the prevailing view is that it represented a "negotiated settlement" rather than a "total submission" by the Welsh prince, and that Edward made concessions to Llywelyn due to his difficulties and to avoid the costs and dangers of continuing the war until the English had completely overrun Gwynedd.[125] The evidence is not sufficient to determine if this is correct, but it appears to this author that the treaty did indeed represent a "total submission": perhaps a negotiated *surrender*, but not a mere negotiated *settlement*.[126] Indeed, Edward

---

[121] He sent his tents back to the Tower of London on 20 September. *CPR*, p. 229.

[122] Bartholomew Cotton, *Historia Anglicana*, ed. Henry Richards Luard (London, 1859), p. 155. Another contemporary similarly described "Wales encircled and besieged." *Opus chronicorum*, in *Chronica monasterii S. Albani. Johannis de Trokelowe*, etc., ed. Henry Thomas Riley (London, 1866), p. 38.

[123] Morris, *Welsh Wars*, p. 136. These troops only stayed one week, probably because they were deemed unnecessary and a logistical burden.

[124] *CPR*, p. 230; see also p. 222 for protections from September and October to last until Easter.

[125] Smith, *Llywelyn*, p. 434; Prestwich, *Edward I*, pp. 181–182.

[126] I thus disagree with the view that Wales was "not conquered" in 1277. Prestwich, *Edward I*, p. 182. In evaluating the Treaty of Aberconwy, it should be remembered that during the course of the war of 1276–1277, Edward gave similar terms to lesser Welsh *tywysigion* who sought to enter his peace, even when he clearly had the ability to dispossess them completely if he chose. A lord who had learned the price of rebellion through defeat and partial confiscation, but who on the other hand still retained enough land to be a useful servant, and one with something to lose if he rebelled again, could be an ideal vassal. Llywelyn had argued, in his last-ditch effort to avoid the war of 1276–1277, that "he would

seems to have designed the treaty's terms specifically to make clear that it was *not* the result of a compromise imposed on him by Llywelyn's continued resistance. Rather, Edward intended the Treaty of Aberconwy to reflect the status of Wales as a conquered land, his to dispose of however he wished.

By its terms, Llywelyn retained possession of the lands he still controlled, and even regained Anglesey, but he held the island only as a life grant, for which he would pay an annual fee to the royal treasury.[127] On the prince's death, if he had legitimate children, they were to receive part of Anglesey (the rest falling to Edward) and part of western Gwynedd (the rest going to Dafydd). If, as seemed likely, Llywelyn died without heirs of his body, all his lands would revert to the crown, rather than to his next of kin. Llywelyn's elder brother Owain Goch was to be freed from prison and settled on suitable lands, which were to come out of Llywelyn's remaining possessions. Eastern Gwynedd and Ceredigion were to be retained by the king, as were Builth, Cydewain, Ceri, and Dinefwr and the other castles of the Tywi Valley, and whatever else he or his men had occupied. Although the Welsh were to retain their own law, Edward and his judges were to be supreme in the interpretation of that law, with even cases arising inside Gwynedd subject to appeal to the king. The homages of all the major Welsh princes, which under the Treaty of Montgomery had been due to Llywelyn as Prince of Wales, were now to be rendered directly to Edward.[128]

On the other hand, Edward allowed Llywelyn to retain the title of "Prince of Wales" and the homages of five minor *tywysogion* of distinguished lineages but little territory, "since," as a contemporary summary of the text explains, "he could not call himself 'prince' if he had no barons under him."[129] These concessions, however, were personal and would lapse with Llywelyn's death. The king also allowed the prince to complete his already contracted marriage to Edward's first cousin, Eleanor de Montfort, granddaughter of Henry II. In evaluating the significance of these sops to the prince's dignity, one should remember Gerald's admonitions that their conqueror should treat the Welsh magnanimously after their surrender, since they

---

be of greater service to the king than those who, even though they waged the king's war, sought their own advantage rather than the king's honour," Smith's paraphrase, *Llywelyn*, p. 410. This did not carry much weight when the prince was unwilling to do homage, but once he had fully admitted his subordination to the English crown, it might well be persuasive.

[127] This was to make a point that they were held by the king's grace; once the point was made by inclusion in the treaty, Edward immediately granted that the sum need not be paid. *Calendar of the Welsh Rolls* (hereafter *CWR*), in *Calendar of Various Chancery Rolls: Supplementary Close Rolls, Welsh Rolls, Scutage Rolls* (London, 1912), p. 158.

[128] *Littere Wallie*, pp. 118–122 for the Latin; *Annales monastici*, vol. IV, pp. 272–274, for an interesting summary in French. Related documents are summarized in *CWR*, pp. 158–159.

[129] From the French summary of the agreement, *Annales monastici*, vol. IV, p. 273. For the small practical value of this concession, see Smith, *Llywelyn*, p. 443.

valued honors above all else, and especially treasured the opportunity to marry into illustrious bloodlines.[130]

Nevertheless, apparently to insure that neither Llywelyn nor anyone else would conclude that these concessions reflected the strength of the Welsh negotiating position, or any weakness on Edward's part, Llywelyn also had to agree to pay the immense sum of £50,000 as a fine for his "disobedience." Since he could not possibly pay such an amount, he could only ask for the king's "grace and pity" regarding it. Edward promptly forgave the debt, but he had made the point: he had the right to take for himself everything Llywelyn possessed. If he did not do so, it was only by choice, his "grace and mercy" to a prostrate foe.[131]

Even within the portion of Gwynedd retained by Llywelyn, moreover, his lordship over his own men would be expressly subordinated to the loyalty they owed the English crown. Ten of the most noble of Llywelyn's followers, delivered to Edward as hostages, arrived at Chester to swear fealty to Edward on the fragment of the True Cross – a relic for which the Welsh were known to have particular veneration. They had to promise they would never bear arms against the king or in any way oppose him, and that if Llywelyn or other Welsh leaders should again rebel, they would serve the king with all their strength to crush the rebellion.[132] Even more gallingly, 20 leading men from each cantref remaining to Llywelyn had to swear a similar oath *every year*, for an indefinite period.[133] These provisions only reinforced the point already implicit in the treaty's territorial terms: everything Llywelyn retained, he owed to Edward I's munificence, not his hereditary rights or power of continued resistance. He was not to be allowed to doubt that the English had indeed conquered Wales, and that his dream of a semi-autonomous native state under a Welsh prince had been broken "like a clay pot," as young Edward had once threatened. Except for privileged areas held by English Marcher Lords, all Wales was subject to the crown's authority just as thoroughly and directly as the counties of England were, and moreover a much larger portion of Wales than of England was under the immediate lordship of the king, rather than his vassals.[134]

---

[130] *Description*, pp. 271, 251 ("The Welsh value distinguished birth and noble descent more than anything else in the world. They would rather marry into a noble family than a rich one"), p. 263.

[131] "En la grace e la pite del rey" in the French summary of the treaty, *Annales monastici*, vol. IV, pp. 272–273); *graciam et misericordiam* in the Latin (*Littere Wallie*, 119).

[132] *CWR*, p. 169; *Littere Wallie*, p. 121. In 1279, the bailiff of Ruthin was ordered by Edward to allow four Welsh lords to remain in Llywelyn's service "for so long as it shall please the king, saving the king's faith," *CCR*, p. 564.

[133] *Littere Wallie*, p. 121.

[134] Especially after Edward in November 1279 acquired Carmarthenshire and Cardiganshire from his brother Edmund, who was given English estates in compensation.

Epilogue

Edward had subdued Wales by following the strategic plan laid out long before by Gerald of Wales, but he was somewhat less attentive to the archdeacon's advice for post-combat occupation. Admittedly, he did, by his own lights if not by those of the conquered, take into account Gerald's observation that the Welsh "want more than anything else to be honoured," and his advice that "once they have paid the penalty for their wrongdoing and are at peace again, their revolt should be forgotten as long as they behave properly, and they should be restored to their former position of security and respect, for 'The quarrel over, it is wrong to bear a grudge.'"[135] In addition to allowing Llywelyn to marry into the royal family, Edward himself gave away the bride and, what is more, paid for the wedding. He also almost immediately allowed Llywelyn's hostages to return home once they had sworn fealty to him, explicitly as an expression of Edward's faith that Llywelyn would remain faithful to his obligations – probably not at all what they had expected when delivered to English custody![136]

Even before the end of the war, Edward had begun to implement Gerald's recommendation to "build castles, [and] widen the trackways through the woodlands," and indeed he did more in these respects than Gerald could probably have imagined. He vigorously continued to build up Flint, Rhuddlan, Builth, and Llanbadarn outside Aberystwyth, creating royal boroughs attached to each, and retaining and strengthening Dinefwr, Carreg Cennen, and Llanymddyfri (Landovery) in Deheubarth. Edward spent more on these massive works, over five years, than on the conduct of the war itself.[137] Although he did make use of some Welsh officers, the castles, as Gerald had recommended, remained under the control of English captains and garrisons.[138] In addition to clearing the road from Chester to the Conwy during the war, after the peace treaty Edward ordered Marcher barons and native rulers alike "that the passes through the woods in diverse places in Wales should be enlarged and widened, so that access might be more open to those travelling through." Commissioners were sent to insure that this was done, and all royal subjects ordered to assist them.[139]

However, though Edward himself might have disagreed, a modern historian cannot say that the conquered lands kept under royal control were ruled "with

---

[135] *Description*, p. 271.

[136] *CWR*, p. 169. Remember the Welsh hostages executed or mutilated by John and Henry II when their lords or family member rebelled.

[137] Rhuddlan alone ultimately cost some £11,000, almost half the cost of the 1276–1277 war. Morris, *Welsh Wars*, p. 145. Edward's expenditures on his Welsh castles over the course of his reign amounted to around £80,000. Very full details can be found in *The History of the King's Works*; the relevant sections have been published separately as Arnold Taylor, *The Welsh Castles of Edward I* (London, 1986).

[138] *Description*, p. 271.   [139] *CWR*, pp. 164, 168, 171, 173, 188.

great moderation," Gerald had emphasized the importance of dealing justly with the subject population. "The governor appointed must be a man of firm and uncompromising character," he wrote. "In times of peace he will observe the laws, and never refuse to obey them; he will respect his terms of appointment and do all in his power to keep his government firm and stable." Gerald noted how easy it was for officers in such situations to "turn a blind eye to lawlessness, allow themselves to be influenced by flattery ... rob the civilian population in time of peace, [and] despoil those who can offer no resistance."[140] The problem started at the top. Although Edward presented himself as the fount of justice and is remembered in history as "the English Justinian," in the case of his first major dispute with Llywelyn over lordship of the district of Arwystli, he "made a mockery of justice by turning the law into an instrument of his own power."[141] As historian R. R. Davies notes, "high-handed and tyrannical officials" in the newly occupied royal territories received "too free a hand to bully native society into submission." All too often, even where the Treaty of Aberconwy had guaranteed the natives their ancient liberties and customs, the English failed to uphold these promises.[142]

The result was a great rebellion, launched in March 1282 by Dafydd ap Gruffydd and several other Welsh princes, but soon enough coming under Llywelyn's leadership.[143] This required a second conquest of Wales, employing the same methods as the first, but on an even larger scale, and pressed to the bitter end. Once again Edward created three military commands to begin operations in the north, the middle March, and the southwest. These forces restored royal control in Ceredigion and the Tywi Valley, and kept the Welsh in check in Powys. An even larger force of infantry than in 1277, supported by an even greater fleet, deployed for the main operations in the north. Dafydd's castles of Ruthin and Denbigh were captured and eastern Gwynedd secured. The English again subdued Anglesey with a large amphibious force. This detachment suffered a minor disaster when the Welsh attacked and defeated the head of the column crossing the Menai Straits by a pontoon bridge, but the English retained control of the island. Warm clothing was provided for the troops, and the war continued into the winter without remission.

It was December when Llywelyn himself was killed in a skirmish near Builth. Dafydd continued the struggle in his place, but in January Edward's main force crossed the Conwy and moved into Snowdonia to capture Dolwyddelan. The troops on Anglesey crossed over and moved into the mountains from the west. By April all of Snowdonia had fallen, and the fortress of Castell-y-Bere in Merionydd, Dafydd's last stronghold, surrendered to the

[140] *Description*, p. 271.   [141] Davies, *Age of Conquest*, pp. 345–347, quotation at p. 346.
[142] Ibid., p. 348.
[143] As with the war of 1276–1277, this war can best be understood by reading Morris' *Welsh Wars* in conjunction with Smith's *Llywelyn*.

king's mercy. In June, Dafydd and his entire family were captured. Edward had Dafydd hanged, drawn, and quartered and refused his niece (Llywelyn's daughter) and children permission to marry, which practically extinguished the line of Llywelyn Fawr. Anglesey, Meriontheshire, and western Gwynedd (renamed Caernarfonshire) became direct royal lordships, secured by massive and architecturally state-of-the-art castles at Beaumaris, Cricieth, Harlech, and Castell-y-Bere. Edward largely dispossessed the Welsh rulers of Powys, the middle March, and Deheubarth, except for two *tywysogion* who had remained loyal to the crown. "For the native dynasties of Wales, the disinheritance of 1282–83 ... was as traumatic as were the events of 1066–70 for the Anglo-Saxon aristocracy."[144]

There would be other revolts, under Llywelyn ap Gruffydd's distant cousin Madog ap Llywelyn in 1294–1295, and Owain Glyndwr in 1400–1412, but they had no chance from the start. The experiences of 1276–1277 and 1282–1283 had demonstrated that the crown's resources, when mobilized by a determined ruler and *applied in accordance with a sound strategy*, were sufficient to overcome even the difficult problems posed by a warlike people skilled in guerilla tactics, fighting to defend a region fortified by nature with formidable swamps, great forests, and rugged hills, and inspired by "the sheer joy of being free."[145]

---

[144] Davies, *Age of Conquest*, p. 361.   [145] *Description*, p. 270.

4 Creating the British way of war: English strategy in the War of the Spanish Succession

Jamel Ostwald

Over the course of the seventeenth century, England had emerged from its position as a peripheral second-rate power to become a core partner in a European-wide coalition united against Louis XIV's France. Its participation in the War of the Spanish Succession (1702–1712) cemented the country's status as a great power.[1] Its military victories were critical to this transition, and the strategic approaches that directed its forces led to a peace shaped largely by English concerns. Unlike the rest of Europe, England was in the fortunate position of possessing real strategic options. Its geographical location allowed it to draw on two distinct schools of strategic thought: a focus on its foe in Europe (a continental strategy), or on the unfolding vista of overseas territories and the trade they brought back to Europe (a "blue water" strategy).[2]

The conduct of the Nine Years' War (1688–1697) inaugurated an uneasy amalgamation of these two traditions, but it required the War of Spanish Succession to turn England's strategy into a fully 'English' one. The decision to enter the war as a major participant of a grand coalition, wage a full-scale war against France's armies and navies in multiple theaters while simultaneously targeting the French economy, sustain such a massive effort by mobilizing the resources of a broad coalition, and end the war on its own terms help to explain England's ultimate success. In addition to providing the stepping stones for future British success, the strategic decisions of the

---

[1] Any investigation of England's efforts during the Spanish Succession must start with John Hattendorf, *England in the War of the Spanish Succession: A Study of the English View and Conduct of Grand Strategy* (New York, 1987). The most balanced account of the war in English remains A. J. Veenendaal, Sr., "The War of the Spanish Succession in Europe," in J. S. Bromley, ed., *The New Cambridge Modern History*, vol. VI: *The Rise of Great Britain and Russia 1688–1725* (Cambridge, 1970). John Lynn, *The Wars of Louis XIV, 1667–1714* (New York, 1999) remains the only modern overview in English from a French perspective.

[2] England and Scotland were united in the person of the joint monarch from 1603, the two countries formally uniting with the 1707 Act of Union. Since English and Scottish interests differed significantly even after the Union, and since English interests always dominated, I will retain this distinction by referring to "English" strategy throughout, reserving "British" for later in the eighteenth century.

War of the Spanish Succession also helped establish a model for future British strategy: a distinctive way of war.[3]

The Williamite strategic revolution

As for any country, geography shaped England's strategic choices. The dominant power on an island on Western Europe's periphery, England enjoyed the Channel's protection from land-borne invasion, while its isolation from the center of Europe fed a maritime culture. Thus, while earlier Tudor and Stuart monarchs had dabbled in continental land wars, it was William III's invasion of England that forced the country into an unprecedented commitment against Louis XIV's France, which in turn required the English to pursue war both on land and at sea on a geographical scale and with a level of commitment not seen since the Hundred Years' War.[4] Several English monarchs had launched haphazard naval descents along the continental littoral. Britain exported mercenary swordsmen for service abroad throughout the seventeenth century. Yet these engagements with the continent were decidedly tepid. England could, and did, quickly retreat back behind its moat. As a result, strategic discussions in England repeated classical adages on battle versus siege, while explicit discussion of English grand strategy tended to focus on the main strategic challenge for an isolationist island nation: how to defend against invasion.

Forcing England to abandon its isolationist tendencies, William was the first monarch to incorporate fully the country into a massive coalition, a sustained war against Louis XIV waged on land and at sea across Europe.[5] The Dutch-born king invaded England in 1688, forced it into the war, and then made the most important strategic decisions.[6] As a result, his defense of his home country led to widespread resentment that the king was sacrificing English interests for allied benefit. But opposition required formulating an alternative strategy, one that conceived of England as a coalition partner, as well as balancing national and allied objectives while coordinating operations in multiple theaters. Over the course of William's war, a blue water

---

[3] For the modern debate, see B. H. Liddell Hart, *The British Way in Warfare* (New York, 1933); Michael Howard's response in "The British Way in Warfare: A Reappraisal," in Howard, *The Causes of War and Other Essays* (Cambridge, MA, 1983); and David French, *The British Way in Warfare, 1688–2000* (New York, 1990).

[4] William Maltby, "The Origins of a Global Strategy: England from 1559 to 1713," in Williamson Murray, MacGregor Knox, and Alvin Bernstein, eds., *The Making of Strategy: Rules, States, and War* (New York, 1994), pp. 151–177.

[5] Roger B. Manning, *An Apprenticeship in Arms: The Origins of the British Army 1585–1702* (Oxford, 2006); John Childs, *The Nine Years' War and the British Army, 1688–1697: The Operations in the Low Countries* (Manchester, 1991).

[6] Stephen Baxter, *William III and the Defense of European Liberty, 1650–1702* (New York, 1966); Wout Troost, *William III, The Stadholder-king: A Political Biography* (Sussex, 2005).

alternative to massive land commitments developed.[7] Both strategies rested on England's ability to develop an adequate fiscal apparatus, another step in the gradual development of a British fiscal-military state.[8] Taxes increased, including the introduction of a four-shilling-to-the-pound land tax. William further strengthened the royal treasury by establishing the Bank of England in 1694, an instrument largely patterned on the Bank of Amsterdam, which allowed the crown to mobilize the resources of investors through the financing of a public debt – some £6.8 million during the war. Yet, despite such innovations, the war's attritional campaigns pushed the treasury's finances to the limit. The system almost collapsed in 1696, and it was only through an emergency recoinage that royal finances stabilized. By 1697 exhaustion on all sides led to the peace of Rijswijk (Ryswick).

Interwar: 1698–1700

Even with the war concluded, a vigorous debate over the management of the 'foreign-run' war raged on. The increasing costs of the war and the indecisiveness of the Flanders campaigns became a key political issue. The Tories, defenders of rural landed interests, complained of the burden imposed by the land tax and the concomitant enrichment of London's financial interests at the expense of country squires. Many Tories and some Whigs were also uneasy with the army's expansion and the corrupting influence of William's foreign advisors in both the army and at court. According to ancient and contemporary experience, large standing armies were associated with tyranny – not only for the heavy taxes they required, but also for the despots they defended. Rome's praetorians and Cromwell's New Model Army, as well as James II's more recent attempt to 'Catholicize' the army, all highlighted the dangers. Moreover, the Tories accused their commanders of intentionally extending the wars, the better to line their pockets with taxpayer gold. As a result, parliament forced William to reduce his requested 30,000-man peacetime army to a mere 7,000 men. His most experienced regiments were either shifted to the Scottish and Irish establishments or sent into Dutch service.[9]

With a weakened hand, the Stadholder-King turned to diplomacy to prevent a future conflict over the looming issue of the Spanish Succession. The inbred and feeble Spanish Habsburg king, Carlos II, had failed to

---

[7] Required reading is T. J. Denman, "The Political Debate Over War Strategy 1689–1712," Ph.D. dissertation, University of Cambridge, 1984. Various pamphlets, particularly those by Edward Littleton, served to provide a public justification for a naval war.

[8] D. W. Jones, *War and the Economy in the Age of William III and Marlborough* (New York, 1988); John Brewer, *The Sinews of Power: War, Money and the English State, 1688–1783* (New York, 1989).

[9] L. G. Schwoerer, *"No Standing Armies": The Anti-Army Ideology in Seventeenth Century England* (Baltimore, MD, 1974), pp. 155–187; John Childs, *The British Army of William III, 1689–1702* (Manchester, 1987), pp. 184–208.

produce an heir, leaving European rulers to decide how to deal with the succession on his death. In the first Grand Alliance of 1689, William had pledged to support the Austrian claim to the Spanish throne upon Carlos II's demise; by the end of the Nine Years' War William had abandoned this avenue and sought rather to divide the Spanish inheritance peacefully between Austria and France.[10] William agreed to a partition treaty in 1698, although this quickly collapsed, when the Bavarian compromise candidate for the Spanish throne died. A second partition treaty was signed by early 1700, but its implementation was always in doubt: not only were the English and Dutch worried that Louis would not honor the terms, but Louis was equally skeptical the Austrians would accept partition.[11]

Principal or auxiliary?

Contemporaries did not have long to wait. Carlos II died in November 1700, and in a blow to moderation, his will insisted on an intact Spanish Empire. The will offered the entirety of Spain first to Louis' grandson Philippe, Duke of Anjou. If the French declined to agree to the terms of the will, it instructed the Spanish ambassador to offer the crown of the Spanish Empire to Archduke Charles of Austria instead. After a day's deliberation, Louis accepted the will on the behalf of his grandson. Thus, Philippe of Anjou was crowned Felipe V of Spain. Louis moved quickly to occupy Spanish territories along his border to secure them for his grandson. The apparent union of France and Spain in the hands of two Bourbon kings plunged Europe into another war, Austria and France coming to blows in June 1701 over lands in northern Italy included in Carlos II's will.

Yet, England's role in the conflict remained unclear, as the Nine Years' War had left English strategists still confronting three fundamental and interrelated questions: How involved should England be in a new war against France? In which theaters would England best utilize its military? What military strategies should they use to defeat Bourbon France? William's first war had not ended in a convincing victory, leaving these questions unresolved. As the issue of the Spanish Succession forced itself to the fore, English leaders had first to address the broadest strategic question of whether to limit their efforts to the sea, or wage war on land as well. William desired a forceful response to this Bourbon challenge. But most of his subjects – with the Channel for a moat, the Royal Navy its "wooden walls," and a quiescent northern border – felt England could afford to deliberate as to whether or not to go to war and

---

[10] A. D. Francis, "The Grand Alliance in 1698," *The Historical Journal*, vol. 10, 1967, pp. 352–360.
[11] David Onnekink, "Anglo-French Negotiations on the Spanish Partition Treaties (1698–1700): A Re-evaluation," in G. Richardson, ed., *The Contending Kingdoms: France and England, 1430–1700* (Burlington, VT, 2008).

what that commitment, if made, should look like. Technically, declaring war was a royal prerogative. Yet, the Glorious Revolution settlement had illustrated the need for parliamentary acquiescence in foreign affairs. While the monarch could declare war, the crown could only fight with the funds granted by parliament's consent.[12] William had accepted this constraint in order to mobilize English resources, and it would remain one throughout the eighteenth century.

Even so, growing English concern over French actions enabled William to begin rearmament. By 1701 a public relations campaign was in full swing, reminding the English of Louis' treachery and deceit, his hegemonic aspirations, and his desire to enslave England by placing a Catholic tyrant on the throne.[13] A series of poorly timed French decisions removed any doubt. In February 1701 French forces occupied the Spanish Netherlands on behalf of Philippe, placing French troops uncomfortably close to the English coast. Louis then proceeded to pour salt onto the issue of England's Protestant succession by recognizing James 'III' as king of England on his father's death.[14]

The timing could not have been worse, since a successional void had recently led parliament to pass a controversial Act of Settlement, which would bring in a Hanoverian Protestant to continue the line of monarchs after the future Queen Anne's demise. Louis' willingness to interfere yet again with the English succession confirmed William's anti-French propaganda. Nor would Louis allow Philippe to renounce his claim to the French throne, reinforcing fears of a united Franco-Spanish monarchy. Finally, Louis alienated another pacifistic English interest group when he declared a French monopoly on trade with Spain's colonies, including the *asiento* (the right to trade slaves). In the span of a year, he had managed to menace England's political, religious, and commercial interests; these measures eliminated the anti-war sentiment of all but the most isolationist.[15] In September 1701 representatives of the Holy Roman Empire (led by the Austrian

---

[12] On 1688 from a continental perspective, see Jonathan Israel, *The Anglo-Dutch Moment: Essays on the Glorious Revolution and its World Impact* (Cambridge, 1991); and Mordechai Feingold and Dale Hoak, eds., *The World of William and Mary: Anglo-Dutch Perspectives on the Revolution of 1688–89* (Stanford, CA, 1996). A recent Anglocentric perspective can be found in Steven Pincus, *1688: The First Modern Revolution* (New Haven, 2009).

[13] William had relied heavily on Protestantism to consolidate his legitimacy in the wake of the Glorious Revolution and buttress the war against France. Tony Claydon, *William III and the Godly Revolution* (Cambridge, 1996).

[14] Mark Thomas, "The Safeguarding of the Protestant Succession, 1702–18," in J. S. Bromley, ed., *William III and Louis XIV: Essays 1680–1720 by and for Mark A. Thomson* (Liverpool, 1968).

[15] Earlier anti-French explanations for the war have been challenged in Mark Thomson, "Louis XIV and the Origins of the War of the Spanish Succession," in J. S. Bromley, ed., *William III and Louis XIV*.

Habsburg emperor), the Netherlands, and England formed a second Grand Alliance.[16] Its members formally declared war in May 1702.

A heated debate occurred among English policy makers over the nature of a future war effort.[17] Whigs, who had been the continental strategy's strongest supporters in the previous war, naturally supported a rapid, vigorous response. But Tories and country Whigs hesitated to abandon diplomacy and cautioned restraint toward Louis' provocations. Behind this was a shared distrust of William and his foreign advisors, as well as the London financiers and court Whigs who profited from the land campaigns. This mistrust of their political foes combined with a deep cynicism toward their potential allies, whether Dutch or Imperial. As a result, war skeptics argued for a limited role with England serving as only an "auxiliary."

Such a distinction rested on the land–sea dichotomy debated in the prior war: let the allies bear the costs of the land war while the English waged war against French trade at sea. These same naval vessels could protect and expand English commerce in peacetime as well as in times of war, and posed little threat to parliamentary rule, unlike a standing army. William and his Whig supporters argued that a blue water strategy could never by itself defeat France, while the Tories interpreted a continental war of sieges and maneuver as a waste of English treasure and lives. In their minds, the resulting blood and expenses benefitted allied rather than English interests.[18]

To the extent that land campaigns were necessary to neutralize naval power, the Tories resurrected the traditional amphibious strategy of naval descents to attack French coastal ports.[19] This alternative to a major land commitment had served as a rallying point around which Tory opposition to William had coalesced in the Nine Years' War and would continue to be urged as an alternative to campaigning in the Low Countries in the War of the Spanish Succession. Nor were coastal descents a uniquely Tory contrivance.

---

[16] The treaty has been reprinted various times. Charles Jenkinson, *A Collection of all the Treaties of Peace, Alliance and Commerce between Great-Britain and Other Powers: from the Treaty Signed at Munster in 1648, to the Treaties Signed at Paris in 1783...* (London, 1785), vol. I, pp. 326–331.

[17] Denman, "The Political Debate," pp. 128ff.

[18] Edward Littleton, *The Management of the Present War against France Consider'd. In a Letter to a Noble Lord. By a Person of Quality* (London, 1690). See also Craig Rose, *England in the 1690's: Revolution, Religion and War* (Oxford, 1999), pp. 117ff.

[19] On the English love affair with descents, see Denman, "The Political Debate," pp. 16–17, 61–76; John Childs, "Secondary Operations of the British Army during the Nine Years' War, 1688–1697," *The Journal of the Society for Army Historical Research*, vol. 73, 1995, pp. 73–98; Keith A. J. McLay, "Combined Operations and the European Theatre during the Nine Years War, 1688–1697," *Historical Research*, vol. 78, 2005, pp. 506–539; John Stapleton, "The Blue-Water Dimension of King William's War: Amphibious Operations and Allied Strategy during the Nine Years' War, 1688–1697," in M. C. Fissell, ed., *Amphibious Warfare 1000–1700: Commerce, State Formation and European Expansion* (Leiden, 2006), pp. 315–356; and Robert McJimsey, "England's 'Descent' on France and the Origins of Blue-water Strategy," in Michael S. Neiberg, ed., *Arms and the Man: Military History Essays in Honor of Dennis Showalter* (Leiden, 2011), pp. 243–257.

Even continentalist Whigs would occasionally propose or support such descents, as William had done previously, although he saw such operations as secondary in importance to Flanders.[20] This tension over where to direct English resources would persist throughout the war.

England's expanding strategic commitments and the making of strategy

The decision to enter into a second Grand Alliance and declare war on France in early 1702 required a concerted effort to convince the English public and overcome Tory opposition in the Commons. Even more controversial were the related strategic questions of how and when to fight, as well as determining England's (and the alliance's) strategic objectives. The English consensus that emerged over the course of the war drew from the Williamite experience and became the basis for a British way of war. Fundamentally, it consisted of a strategic compromise necessitated by political divisions and facilitated by fiscal strength. In each theater of operations, English strategic choices led to specific challenges. The extent to which England overcame these challenges helped in determining the war's outcome.

The second Grand Alliance treaty itself kept the participants' goals vague. The overarching objective was to prevent the union of France and Spain lest they "easily assume ... dominion over all Europe" (preamble). For the English, the agreement specified protecting and expanding its free trade within the Spanish dominions. A later addendum would add recognition of the Protestant English succession. The Dutch were promised similar access to Spanish markets as well as a barrier of fortresses in the Spanish Netherlands, garrisoned by Dutch troops and paid for by the southern Netherlands.[21] For his part, the emperor was to receive an "equitable and reasonable" satisfaction of his claim to the Spanish throne. After William died in March 1702, Anne quickly sent her Captain-General John Churchill, the Earl of Marlborough, to assure her allies of England's intent to abide by the treaty's terms.

The grand strategy to achieve these objectives would develop over the next several years, and the English played a major role in defining the contours left amorphous by the treaty itself. Spain's territories ranged across Europe from Spain to the Spanish Netherlands, Milan, and the Kingdom of Naples and Sicily. The king of Spain also claimed sovereignty over the Mediterranean islands of Sardinia and the Balearics and a vast empire overseas, especially in the New World but also in the Philippines. Conducting operations across

---

[20] Stapleton, "The Blue-Water Dimension of King William's War," pp. 337ff; McJimsey, "England's 'Descent' on France," p. 247.

[21] A recent accessible overview is Olaf van Nimwegen, "The Dutch Barrier: Its Origins, Creation, and Importance for the Dutch Republic, 1697–1718," in J. A. F. de Jongste, ed., *Anthonie Heinsius and the Dutch Republic 1688–1720: Politics, Finance and War* (The Hague, 2002), pp. 147–175.

the entirety of the Spanish empire potentially represented a worldwide-ranging affair. Emperor Leopold of Austria had a predictable commitment to his border areas first and foremost – Italy, and Hungary once a Hungarian rebellion under Ferenc Rákóczi ignited. The German states of the Holy Roman Empire provided a buffer between Austria and France, but the princes of the empire could do little more than provide mercenaries to the allied powers and campaign ineffectively along the Rhine, while keeping a wary eye on the contemporaneous Great Northern War being waged by Sweden, Saxony-Poland-Lithuania, Russia, and Denmark. The maritime powers coordinated their naval efforts at sea, with England taking the lead. On land, the only specific Dutch objective in the treaty was combating Louis in the Low Countries, as French troops were encamped menacingly on its southern border. On the periphery, England alone enjoyed the ability to choose where to fight.

As the principal–auxiliary debate suggests, the choice of theaters was neither a simple decision made by one or two figures nor one determined at a single point in time. The common claim that England's Spanish Succession strategy was a product of the singular genius of Marlborough ignores the broader, collective process of English strategy making.[22] The crown made most strategic decisions directly through the monarch and his or her ministers, as well as the generals and diplomats operating in distant theaters. Anne's predecessor had been a true warrior-king, manipulating parliament to acquire the necessary funds, while personally leading his armies in the field and on parade until his death in March 1702. Yet, the new queen hesitated to take an active lead in the war effort, while her inept husband, Prince George of Denmark, held the empty title of Generalissimo and was only nominally in charge of the navy as Lord High Admiral.

Although the queen attended most council meetings and ultimately assented to all decisions, the war's detailed management fell to her ministers in the cabinet, the "Lords of the Committee."[23] From 1702 to 1710, this meant foremost the duumvirs: Lord Treasurer Sidney Godolphin and Captain-General Marlborough. Yet, these two were not all-powerful, for they had to coordinate their plans and actions with the rest of the cabinet. The broader Privy Council left most details to the inner cabinet.[24] Diplomatically,

---

[22] Hattendorf, *England in the War of the Spanish Succession*, pp. 21–51. Hattendorf provides an informative overview of the dispersed British decision making leading to the attack on Port Mahon (1708) in "The Machinery for the Planning and Execution of English Grand Strategy in the War of the Spanish Succession, 1702–1713," in R. Love, ed., *Changing Interpretations and New Sources in Naval History: Papers from the Third United States Naval Academy History Symposium* (New York, 1980), pp. 89–91.

[23] Detailed analysis of the debates can be found in Denman, "The Political Debate," pp. 152–305.

[24] Henry Snyder, "The Formulation of Foreign and Domestic Policy in the Reign of Queen Anne," *The Historical Journal*, vol. 11, 1968, pp. 144–160.

the secretaries of state for the southern and northern departments controlled their respective spheres of influence, while English diplomats often possessed unprecedented independence of action.[25] The southern secretaries of state in particular had significant leeway. Marlborough had little control beyond the Low Countries and Germany more generally and was abroad for seven or more months out of every year in any case. There was further input from the various administrative departments, such as the Admiralty, as well as advice and proposals from England's allies. In short, no one person designed and implemented English strategy, although Godolphin came closest, given his long tenure.[26]

The queen's reliance on her cabinet further opened the formulation of strategy to the political process, since the Lords of the Committee, the speaker of the house, and the crown's officers relied not only on her good graces but on parliamentary support as well – in some cases formally, and in every case through the influence of patronage networks. Even in the monarch's purview of foreign policy, funding levels determined by the House of Commons could hamstring strategic choices, as William had experienced.[27] The composition of Anne's cabinet shifted, therefore, depending on a combination of her assertiveness and which party held sway in parliament. Ministers ultimately served at the monarch's behest, but every ruler had to be sensitive to the direction of the political winds. Frequent shifts in the parliamentary majority presented the crown with an increasingly difficult situation, given the charged political atmosphere of the partisan struggle between Whig and Tory, a rivalry enhanced by the legal requirement to hold parliamentary elections every three years.[28]

Anne's personal preference for Tory ministers competed with her desire to have a mixed ministry that would put her above the control of either party. The moderate Godolphin retained his position as lord treasurer until late 1710, whereas the secretaries of state followed the partisan alternations in the House of Commons more closely. In Anne's early cabinets Tory politicians such as the earls of Rochester and Nottingham (as secretary of state for the south) outnumbered the Whigs, but as the latter gained political strength, she found herself forced to jettison her Tory minsters. Marlborough's centrality to the English war effort also gave him leverage, for example, when he pressured the queen to bring his son-in-law, the Earl of Sunderland, an extreme Whig, into her cabinet in 1706. By 1708 a new Whig majority in parliament and the death

[25] Onnekink, "Anglo-French Negotiations on the Spanish Partition Treaties (1698–1700)."

[26] William Calvin Dickinson, *Sidney Godolphin, Lord Treasurer, 1702–1710* (Lewiston, NY, 1990); Roy Sundstrom, *Sidney Godolphin: Servant of the State* (Newark, DE, 1992).

[27] David Onnekink, "Anglo-French Negotiations on the Spanish Partition Treaties (1698–1700)" argues that parliament's demobilization emboldened Louis to dismiss any threat from England when deciding for war.

[28] The politics of the period are best approached in Geoffrey Holmes, *British Politics in the Age of Anne* (London, 1987) and W. A. Speck, *Birth of Britain: A New Nation, 1700–1710* (Cambridge, MA, 1994).

of Anne's beloved consort allowed the Whigs to dominate her cabinet and adopt an uncompromising position in peace negotiations. Anne's increasing weariness of Whig stridency, facilitated by a Tory landslide in the parliamentary election of 1710, would, in turn, upend the Whig ascendancy.

Parliament pressed its own strategic conceptions in various forums: in debates over wartime funding bills, when investigating English defeats, when giving thanks to a successful general, or even when 134 Tories attempted to 'tack' a controversial religious proposal onto a war funding bill.[29] These discussions indirectly influenced those who formulated and implemented the royal will. A politically active public influenced both crown and parliament. By 1700 England's public sphere had grown to be one of the most sophisticated in Europe, fed by an explosion of information on current affairs debated in dozens of newspapers and pamphlets and in innumerable coffeehouses. While the initiative remained with the queen, her cabinet, her commanders, and her diplomats, political considerations necessarily influenced the options available, as well as how long they could continue particular strategies. The longer the war lasted, the more influence public expectations had on the broad outlines of English strategy.

Italy

The commencement of hostilities between Austria and France in 1701 allowed England little input over how these operations were fought.[30] At the same time, the first region to see fighting was also the least relevant to English interests, beyond a desire to "encircle" France and pressure Louis on multiple fronts.[31] London traders, including those invested in the Levant Company, were interested in northern Italy and the Mediterranean more generally. For Tories such as the Southern Secretary of State Nottingham, Savoy offered an opportunity to enhance English commerce while drawing attention away from Flanders, where he expected to see fighting similar to that conducted by William. Starting in late 1702, English diplomacy seconded Habsburg discussions to turn Louis' ally the Duke of Savoy Victor Amadeus II.[32]

---

[29] D. H. Wollman, "Parliament and Foreign Affairs, 1697–1714," Ph.D. dissertation, University of Wisconsin, 1970.

[30] As with the Flanders and German theaters, details on the Italian operations can be found in Vault, *Mémoires militaires relatifs à la succession d'Espagne sous Louis XIV*, 12 vols. (Paris, 1836–1842); Kriegsarchiv, *Feldzüge des Prinzen Eugen von Savoyen: nach den Feldacten und anderen authentischen Quellen*, vols. 3–15 (Vienna, 1876–1891); and J. W. Wijn, *Het Staatsche Leger: Het Tijdperk van de Spaanse Successieoorlog, 1702–1715*, 3 vols. (The Hague, 1956–1964).

[31] In addition to Hattendorf's monograph, English grand strategy is summarized in his "Alliance, Encirclement, and Attrition: British Grand Strategy in the War of the Spanish Succession, 1702–1713," in Paul Kennedy, ed., *Grand Strategies in War and Peace* (New Haven, CT, 1992), pp. 11–28.

[32] W. Blackley, ed., *The Diplomatic Correspondance of the Right Hon. Richard Hill... Envoy Extraordinary from the Court of St. James to the Duke of Savoy in the Reign of Queen Anne:*

Yet the 1703 addition of Savoy to the Grand Alliance was less crucial than English leaders had hoped; ironically, it placed new burdens on the allies. Inauspiciously, Louis' intelligence on Victor Amadeus' betrayal led him to imprison most of the veteran Savoyard troops. The next several years witnessed French armies reconquering Piedmont fortress after fortress while the Imperial–Savoyard Army looked on. Regardless of the results, England contributed the same £640,000 to subsidize Savoy's efforts each year. By mid 1706 Victor Amadeus' capital of Turin was under siege. But Prince Eugene's relief of the fortresses smashed the French Army and reversed the situation entirely: the French evacuated all of northern Italy.

Even in victory, however, allied actions did not meet English expectations. The Austrians allowed the remaining French garrisons to evacuate freely rather than attempt to imprison them. Nor was the relief of Turin the beginning of a major offensive into southeastern France. Many Englishmen had envisioned a killing stroke into the heart of France accompanied by an uprising of the Huguenots. Instead, the last major operation in the region was the failed siege of Toulon in 1707, an operation that required a drawdown of allied troops in the Low Countries and the deflection of the Royal Navy from other tasks in the Mediterranean.[33] The year 1708 was the last to see operations of any note. Savoy and Eugene had fallen out over Toulon, and Victor Amadeus felt little need to push his campaigning further now that allied armies had eliminated the French threat. Austria used the lull to secure Naples. The result was Austrian domination of Italy, but Louis reinforced his troops in the remaining theaters, inflating the strength of French armies confronting the allies elsewhere. England found that its diplomacy could entice an enemy to switch sides, but that it was harder to direct their behavior toward English goals.[34]

Low Countries

Unlike Italy, the Low Countries were central to English interests on the continent. The proximity of Flanders necessitated cooperating with the Dutch: it served as a potential jumping off point for any invader, while

From July 1703 to May 1706, 2 vols. (London, 1845). For modern discussions: Geoffrey Symcox, *Victor Amadeus II: Absolutism in the Savoyard State, 1675–1730* (London, 1983); Christopher Storrs, *War, Diplomacy and the Rise of Savoy 1690–1720* (Cambridge, 1999); Onnekink, "Anglo-Dutch Diplomatic Cooperation during the Opening Years of the War of the Spanish Succession, 1702–1704," p. 57 in J. A. F. de Jongste and A. J. Veenendaal, Jr., eds., *Anthonie Heinsius and the Dutch Republic 1688–1720: Politics, Finance and War* (The Hague, 2002), pp. 45–63.
[33] Ciro Paoletti, "Prince Eugene of Savoy, the Toulon Expedition of 1707, and the English Historians – A Dissenting View," *The Journal of Military History*, vol. 70, 2006, pp. 939–962.
[34] Geoffrey Symcox, "Britain and Victor Amadeus II: or, The Use and Abuse of Allies," in Stephen Baxter, ed., *England's Rise to Greatness, 1660–1763* (Berkeley, 1983), pp. 151–184.

its ports served as profitable entrées into the mainland's trade networks, and its population served as a potential market. The extent of England's military commitment to the theater, however, was reopened after William's death. The Earl of Rochester's proposal to limit England's troop contribution to 10,000 men failed in Anne's Privy Council, which authorized a 40,000-man army for service alongside the Dutch. Led by Marlborough, in the first five years of the war, it achieved what William's campaigns had failed to: the conquest of almost the entirety of the Spanish Netherlands, by siege and maneuver in 1702–1703 and 1705, and by battle and siege in 1706.[35] Yet, this was hardly a succession of triumphs: the first several years of the war passed uncomfortably, as the more cautious Dutch opposed English designs to force the French into a decisive battle. For Tories, this reinforced their distrust of the Dutch and encouraged them to push for more vigorous military operations elsewhere. Even the Whigs and Marlborough's supporters grew impatient, pressuring the United Provinces' Grand Pensionary Anthonie Heinsius and the States-General to give Marlborough the freedom to fight at will. The result of this pressure was the battlefield victory at Ramillies in 1706. A two-week pursuit followed with four successive sieges that secured the Spanish Netherlands, the latter subsequently administered by a joint Anglo-Dutch condominium.

This would be the high point of the Flanders War. By 1708, Vauban's fortified *pré carré* had halted Marlborough's advance, and English strategists were unable to avoid the expensive, time-consuming war of sieges they had railed against for the previous 20 years. Fully 60 percent of Marlborough's last four campaigns (1708–1711) was spent in the trenches. Just as disconcerting were battle's diminishing returns. The 1708 encounter engagement at Oudenaarde completely routed one-half of the French Army, but the other half escaped, leaving the allies little to do but turn to the siege of Lille. Desperate to avoid further sieges, Marlborough hoped to turn the French flank, relying on the Royal Navy to supply his forces as they skirted along the coast. With his allies unwilling to attempt such a risky maneuver, Marlborough pushed for an augmentation of the Anglo-Dutch forces by another 20,000 men. Consequently, 100,000-man armies faced off against each other the following year, operating in the confined and heavily fortified space along the French border. The bloodbath of Malplaquet was the result: some 10,000–12,000 French losses bought at the price of 20,000–24,000 allied casualties. Immediately after this slaughter, English believers in decisive battle predicted a rapid French collapse, but objective observers could see even before Malplaquet that Marlborough's battle-seeking strategy had

---

[35] Jamel Ostwald, "The 'Decisive' Battle of Ramillies, 1706: Prerequisites for Decisiveness in Early Modern Warfare," *Journal of Military History*, vol. 64, 2000, pp. 649–677; Jamel Ostwald, *Vauban under Siege: Engineering Efficiency and Martial Vigor in the War of the Spanish Succession* (Leiden, 2007), pp. 92ff.

achieved all the results it could hope to. However, Louis refused to submit to the allies' escalating terms and the war of attrition continued. The Whigs, now in control of both the cabinet and parliament, insisted on continuing the war until Spain was in Charles' hands. By late 1711, the English public was exhausted with both the war and Whig policies. A backlash enabled a new Tory ministry to end the war, illustrating the limitations of a battle-seeking strategy.

Germany

Like Italy, Germany was initially of secondary importance to English strategy. Although William had pressured Leopold to campaign along the Rhine, the region served primarily as a recruiting ground for England.[36] The theater became directly relevant when the two Wittelsbach siblings, Maximilian Emmanuel (Duke and Elector of Bavaria) and Joseph-Clement (Elector of Cologne and Archbishop of Liège), declared for Louis in late 1702. Max Emmanuel went on to capture a number of towns in southern Germany, which risked intimidating several Imperial Circles into neutrality.[37] At the same time, French reinforcements sought to link up with the Italian theater, transferring the war into the heart of the empire. This pressure within the empire was heightened by the outbreak of the Rákóczi rebellion in 1703; Hungarian kuruc raiders burned the suburbs of Vienna and Austria consequently withdrew forces from Italy to counter the Bavarian threat and pacify their recently acquired Hungarian lands.[38]

Pressed on two sides, the Viennese court appealed to the maritime allies for assistance. The English encouraged the Austrians to resolve the Bavarian matter peacefully (as was their hope for Hungary), for they desired greater pressure on France in Italy, and perhaps even to bring Bavarian troops into the Grand Alliance. The emperor, however, dismissed English suggestions that he cede some of his Italian territories to the Elector, and the Habsburg insistence on a military resolution carried the day. For many, it was a relief to abandon the Low Countries, since the two campaigns in Flanders had been spent arguing with the Dutch over the need for a field engagement. The resulting campaign of 1704 included storming the Schellenberg Heights,

[36] Susan Spens, *George Stepney, 1663–1707: Diplomat and Poet* (Cambridge, 1997).
[37] John Hattendorf, "English Grand Strategy and the Blenheim Campaign of 1704," *International History Review*, vol. 5, 1983, pp. 3–19.
[38] John Hattendorf, "The Rákóczi Insurrection in English War Policy, 1703–1711," *Canadian-American Review of Hungarian Studies*, vol. 7, 1980, pp. 91–102; William Slottman, *Ferenc II Rákóczi and the Great Powers* (Boulder, CO, 1997); Lothar Höbelt, "The Impact of the Rákóczi Rebellion on Habsburg Strategy: Incentives and Opportunity Costs," *War in History*, vol. 13, 2006, pp. 2–15. See also the various chapters in Béla Király and János Bak, eds., *War and Society in Eastern Central Europe*, vol. III: *From Hunyadi to Rákóczi: War and Society in Late Medieval and Early Modern Hungary* (Brooklyn, NY, 1982).

negotiations interspersed with the devastation of Bavaria, and Marlborough and Eugene's victory at Blenheim in August. Several sieges followed the battle, eliminating Bavaria from the war.

The year 1704 saw a French army destroyed, a French ally neutralized, and a theater eliminated from contention. Yet, the result was the same as would occur in Italy in 1706: Louis would rebuild his armies, and French forces would be ever more concentrated on their fortified frontiers. The next year reinforced Blenheim's lesson and reminded the allies once again that there was a reason Louis had spent so much effort fortifying his open northern border. The inability of the German princes to support an attack into "undefended" Lorraine forced Marlborough to abandon his campaign on the Moselle and return to the Meuse to forestall a French offensive. The year 1705 dashed English hopes of an alternate route to penetrate deep into France just as 1707 would do in Provence. Smashing successes in one year were quickly followed by the inevitability of further Flanders campaigns. Predictably, the fortified Rhine theater saw back-and-forth campaigning for the rest of the war. England's limited German experience had shown that battlefield success was possible, but also that its Imperial allies were unable or unwilling to follow them up with constant pressure on France's border.

Iberia

Although the war revolved around the question of who would become the next king of Spain, the Iberian Peninsula was not an obvious theater of operations.[39] Philippe had established himself in Spain in 1701, while Louis' diplomats signed a treaty of friendship with Portugal's King Pedro II. With no base from which to operate, William had found it expedient to recognize Philippe's claim to the throne. Even the Grand Alliance treaty made no reference to Charles ascending the Spanish throne; in fact, Article Five only identified Imperial pretensions to Spain's Italian and Netherlands possessions. The Habsburg court focused on the Italian holdings, and although the Dutch were interested in Mediterranean trade, they were more concerned about other theaters diverting attention from the defense of their southern border.

The allied decision to commit to a 'No Peace without Spain' policy was, therefore, made by the English, a decision encouraged by naval strength. England's goals in the Mediterranean and Iberia were numerous: to protect its Levant trade, threaten Spain's incoming trade from the Americas, neutralize France's fleet based at Toulon, buttress Austria in Italy, encourage the defection of France's allies (Portugal and Savoy), and support uprisings

---

[39] David Francis, *The First Peninsular War, 1701–1713* (London, 1975); J. A. C. Hugill, *No Peace without Spain* (Oxford, 1991); Henry Kamen, *The War of Succession in Spain, 1700–1715* (Bloomington, IN, 1969).

in Bourbon-held territories (Naples, Catalonia, the Balearics and the Cevennes in particular). The Whig Lords had already concluded in 1701 that the only acceptable peace was one that saw Charles sitting on the throne in Madrid.[40]

This maximalist goal would be implicitly accepted for much of the war by both parties. The first attempt to open the theater was a repeat of previous English strategy: an Anglo-Dutch fleet landed forces to capture the Andalusian port of Cadiz in September 1702, hoping to establish a naval base and threaten the colonial trade off-loaded at Seville. Repulsed, they attacked a Spanish bullion fleet that had anchored at Vigo on the Galician coast. The capture of several French men-of-war excited the public back home and illustrated the Royal Navy's strategic flexibility. The victory, nonetheless, had less effect on the Bourbon war effort, at least in direct attritional terms.[41] More important was the encouragement it gave Pedro to join the Grand Alliance. The resulting Methuen Treaty of 1703 inaugurated an Iberian war, committing the English and Dutch, as well as their Austrian ally, to a land campaign to capture Spain.[42] The English diplomatic team negotiated with Portugal in secret and intentionally excluded the Dutch envoy until the details had already been decided, terms which obligated the English and Dutch to a far larger Iberian commitment than the Dutch had envisioned.[43] A few months after the treaty of alliance was completed, an Anglo-Portuguese commercial treaty was signed which promised the English preferential trade with Portugal.

The Portuguese were, however, an unreliable ally. Most towns along the Hispano-Portuguese border were difficult to besiege, while foreign witnesses expressed their amazement at the heat and barrenness of the region. The Spanish nevertheless captured several Portuguese fortresses in 1704, while command disputes and undermanned regiments hindered the allied response. The allies would take several fortresses back in 1705 and even march to Madrid in 1706, but for the rest of the war, the Portuguese front degenerated into inconclusive operations. These early setbacks encouraged the English to look for other fronts from which to attack Philippe, a strategy perfectly suited against a Spanish enemy who in 1703 boasted a negligible navy and a mere 20,000 troops to defend a territory 16 times the size of the

[40] Denman, "The Political Debate," pp. 126–127ff. A few Whig pamphleteers did express their concerns about the impact of such terms on the balance of power.
[41] On Vigo's results: Francis, *The First Peninsular War*, pp. 53–55; Hugill, *No Peace without Spain*, p. 46.
[42] For a general view, see A. D. Francis, *The Methuens and Portugal 1691–1708* (Cambridge, 1966). One of the terms of the Methuen Treaty was the Portuguese insistence that Charles personally campaign in Iberia, leading the English to pressure Austria to send troops to the theater.
[43] Onnekink, "Anglo-Dutch Diplomatic Cooperation during the Opening Years of the War of the Spanish Succession, 1702–1704," pp. 55–56. A secret article promised Spanish territory to Portugal, presumably at the expense of Charles.

Spanish Netherlands with 3,000 miles of coastline.[44] As a result, an August 1704 attack on the poorly prepared town of Gibraltar captured the port within three days. The newly installed garrison, with the support of the Anglo-Dutch fleet, then resisted a subsequent eight-month siege and blockade. The English pillaging of both Port St. Mary (near Cadiz) and Gibraltar, however, poisoned relations with the Andalusians and made it impossible for the allies to support an offensive from Gibraltar.[45]

The year 1704 thus saw a further allied naval attempt to open yet another front by landing 1,600 marines at Barcelona, an area once governed by the allied commander (Prince George of Hesse-Darmstadt) and conveniently situated close to both hard-pressed Savoy and rebellious Camisards in south-eastern France. That first effort miscarried, but the next year 10,000 troops captured the Catalonian capital after a siege. Now Charles controlled an independent Spanish base supported by Catalans, and this reinvigorated English hopes for an alternative to operations in the Low Countries.[46] By the end of 1705, the uprising against Philippe had spread to Aragon and Valencia, allowing the allies to garrison fortresses along Spain's eastern coast.

In April 1706 the Bourbons returned to the offensive, besieging Barcelona and drawing supplies from their fleet. After Admiral Leake's flotilla chased off the French, Philippe withdrew with Charles slowly pursuing him to Madrid. The lack of fortresses and logistical difficulties in Aragon and Castile meant that possession of Madrid was left to those who could gain the support of the Castilian people. Madrid was briefly held by an allied army, but the popular resistance to the presence of heretical northerners, Portuguese foes, Catalan separatists, and plundering troops soon forced the allied army from Castile. In the aftermath, the Duke of Berwick's army began the slow reconquest of Valencia and Murcia. In early 1707 the battlefield victory at Almansa magnified the Bourbon advantage. This forced the allied field army back to Catalonia, and inaugurated the reconquest of Valencia and Aragon, successes facilitated by the absence of allied fleets which were transporting troops or making new conquests.

By the beginning of 1710, Charles and his polyglot forces found themselves holed up in Catalonia. But two allied victories, precipitated by Louis' withdrawal of French troops from the peninsula, allowed the allies to march again on Madrid and occupy it. Once again, however, the Castilian populace resisted the foreign claimant, and on the retreat back to Catalonia, the entire English contingent was captured at Brihuega. Suffering from whiplash, the new Tory ministry would gradually abandon its commitment to the theater, seeking to secure its bases at Gibraltar and Port Mahon. The Iberian theater,

---

[44] Spanish Army sizes: Kamen, *The War of Succession in Spain*, pp. 59–61.
[45] Francis, *The First Peninsular War*, pp. 49, 115.
[46] Denman, "The Political Debate," p. 188.

expected to deliver a quick victory in contrast with the Low Countries, turned into almost as deep a quagmire as Flanders, with worse results.

Naval commitments

England's natural maritime orientation necessitated a strong naval component in its wartime strategy.[47] The island straddled the main European trade routes into and out of Europe and was replete with both private and royal shipyards and spacious ports, all closely linked to London. The major ports of London, Bristol, Liverpool, Dover, and a host of others provided a ready supply of sailors available for impressment, as well as the facilities with which to unload England's sprawling overseas trade. No surprise, then, that the English spent almost as much on their navy as on their land forces. The average estimated naval war expenditures hovered around £2 million per year, although the actual costs were much higher.[48] Even without significant growth, such funds far outstripped what France could afford to spend on its fleet. In the middle of the Nine Years' War, Louis had recognized his inability to sustain a major land war against half of Europe and still maintain a large French fleet capable of defeating allied flotillas at sea.[49] He consequently slashed naval funding and shifted to a *guerre de course*, a strategy of attacking allied merchant shipping with a mixture of royal and privateer ships.[50]

The de facto union of French and Spanish forces in 1701 further stretched Louis' navy throughout the Atlantic, Mediterranean, and Spain's sprawling colonial empire.[51] After the indecisive naval battle off Málaga in 1704, it once again became evident that France could not afford to fight a major land war in four theaters against a European-wide coalition. Offensive operations again became dependent on privateers, while Louis' warships focused on defending French and Spanish merchantmen. The sea power of

[47] The standard works on naval aspects of the period are Jan Glete, *Navies and Nations: Warships, Navies and State-Building in Europe and America, 1500–1860* (Stockholm, 1993); Richard Harding, *Seapower and Naval Warfare, 1650–1830* (New York, 1999); and N. A. M. Rodger, *The Command of the Ocean: A Naval History of Britain, 1649–1815* (London, 2004). Works focusing on the Royal Navy during the Spanish Succession include J. H. Owen, *War at Sea under Queen Anne, 1702–1708* (Cambridge, 2010 reprint of 1938 orig.); R. D. Merriman, *Queen Anne's Navy: Documents Concerning the Administration of the Navy of Queen Anne, 1702–1714* (London 1961); and significant portions of Hattendorf's *England in the War of the Spanish Succession*. For a contemporary view, see Josiah Burchett, *A Complete History of the Most Remarkable Transactions at Sea: From the Earliest Accounts of Time to the Conclusion of the Last War with France...* (London, 1720), pp. 575–800.
[48] Hattendorf, *England in the War of the Spanish Succession*, pp. 130–133, 138–141, and Appendix B, including its many caveats. The year was reckoned from 30 September to 29 September; 1711–1712 was an exceptional year.
[49] On the many French naval disadvantages, see Daniel Dessert, *La Royale: Vaisseaux et marins du Roi Soleil* (Paris, 1996), pp. 103ff.
[50] The classic work is Geoffrey Symcox, *The Crisis of French Naval Power, 1688–1697* (The Hague, 1974).
[51] There is little detail on the Spanish navy of the period.

England's Dutch allies also dwindled. They found it increasingly difficult to conduct an expensive land war along their border and also outfit the increasing number of vessels the English demanded, setting the stage for even greater English domination at sea.[52]

Descents

The Iberian theater highlighted the importance of descents to the Royal Navy. Almost a third of the English fleet operated in the western Mediterranean, exposing Spain's entire coastline to attack. But this strategic flexibility also tempted English strategists to disperse their efforts. The number of vessels in the Royal Navy remained constant at approximately 225 vessels, while the Dutch contribution declined by half. Yet England's Mediterranean fleet, peaking at 73 ships in 1706, found itself stretched from Gibraltar to Valencia to the Balearics to Barcelona to Toulon to Genoa to Naples. Moreover, it had to sail back home every winter until the capture of Port Mahon in 1708. English ships patrolled sea-lanes and escorted convoys, supplied troops in coastal garrisons, escorted allied contingents from Italy to Spain and supported various offensive landings. Such constant activity, combined with a halving of vessels sent to the theater from 1708 onward, made it impossible to support besieged garrisons on the Iberian coast, much less project power inland to hold Madrid. Naval power's amphibious capacity was best used offensively and was less suited to the support of defending land forces.

The strategy of descents was also resurrected elsewhere. A dozen projects proposed landing troops along the French littoral from Normandy to Bordeaux to Provence, all in the hopes of establishing a base for Protestant rebellion, landing an invading army to march to Paris, or at least diverting troops from other theaters.[53] For most Tories, these early projects served as an alternative to Flanders. Godolphin, Nottingham, and St. John were particularly enthusiastic about their use, but even Marlborough approved of several ventures when his own operations bogged down among the Flanders fortresses. Only one of these descents was actually carried through to successful conclusion: the inconsequentially brief occupation of the two Languedoc towns of Sète and Adge in 1710.[54] Article Six of the Grand Alliance treaty also allowed England to keep any West Indies colonies it

[52] Hattendorf, *England in the War of the Spanish Succession*, pp. 156–160; John Hattendorf, "'To Aid and Assist the Other': Anglo-Dutch Cooperation in Coalition Warfare at Sea, 1689–1714," in Jan de Jongste, ed., *Anthonie Heinsius and the Dutch Republic 1688–1720: Politics, Finance and War* (The Hague, 2002), pp. 178ff.

[53] Owen, *War at Sea under Queen Anne*, pp. 50–54; Denman, "The Political Debate," pp. 162ff; Hattendorf, *England in the War of the Spanish Succession*, pp. 150–155. For a typology of amphibious tactics (landings, raids, and bombardments), see Stapleton, "The Blue-Water Dimension of King William's War," pp. 319–320.

[54] British Library, Additional Manuscripts, vol. 61, pp. 79ff, 314ff.

captured. Reflecting the English maritime mindset, early pro-war pamphlets proposed various Caribbean schemes, and such projects would appear throughout the war.[55] Attempted landings occurred in the Caribbean (San Domingo 1706) and in Canada (Port Royal 1707 and 1710, Quebec 1711). There were some successes, but the overall results were disappointing.

Naval commerce

In contrast with the Nine Years' War, the War of Spanish Succession would see no major fleet actions: the largest was an indecisive engagement between 50 Bourbon ships and 53 allied vessels off of Gibraltar at Málaga. The Royal Navy's most significant setbacks stemmed rather from accidents inherent in the maritime environment. The damage caused by the Great Storm of 1703, and the wreck of a fleet off the Scilly Islands in 1707, each cost the lives of more than 1,000 sailors; the 1711 foundering of Walker's flotilla in the St. Lawrence River similarly drowned 900.[56] The Royal Navy overcame such disasters to maintain its dominance; it had little difficulty defending the homeland or protecting communication with the continent. The only threat to English soil was the 1708 aborted Jacobite landing at the Firth of Forth.[57]

The English dedicated a little over half of the Royal Navy to their final naval strategy: attacking Franco-Spanish trade and protecting their own.[58] Particularly enticing were the silver fleets transporting bullion from South America to Iberia. The Royal Navy devoted dozens of ships to capturing these specie-laden prizes, but there were only two significant successes. The most notable was Wager's action in June 1708 off Cartagena in modern-day Colombia, where the Spanish merchantmen escaped but their flagship the *San José* blew up, taking several million pesos to the bottom of the sea.[59] Such incidents, however, were exceptional. More often, convoys escaped while their escorts battled with the raiders.

Smaller-scale English privateering was also encouraged from the conflict's outset.[60] Opportunistic merchantmen received letters of marque authorizing

[55] For one example, see *Europa Libera: Or, a Probable Expedient (the Like Scarce Ever to Be Hop'd for Again) to Restore and Secure the Publick Peace of Europe, for this and Future Ages. Humbly Submitted to the Consideration of the Queen's Most Excellent Majesty; and Both the Honourable Houses of Parliament* (London, 1703).

[56] Gerald Graham, ed., *The Walker Expedition to Quebec, 1711* (London, 1953).

[57] John Gibson, *Playing the Scottish Card: The Franco-Jacobite Invasion of 1708* (Edinburgh, 1988).

[58] See Jones, *War and Economy in the Age of William and Marlborough*; Brewer, *Sinews of Power*.

[59] Carla Rahn Phillips, *The Treasure of the San José: Death at Sea in the War of the Spanish Succession* (Baltimore, MD, 2007).

[60] G. N. Clark, "War Trade and Trade War, 1701–1713," *Economic History Review*, vol. 1, 1928, pp. 262–280; W. Meyer, "English Privateering in the War of the Spanish Succession, 1702–1713," *Mariner's Mirror*, vol. 69, 1983, pp. 435–446; and Hattendorf, *England in the War of the Spanish Succession*, pp. 161–166 for a summary discussion, as well as Appendix F.

attack on enemy shipping in exchange for a small cut of the spoils. Sallying from London, Bristol, and particularly the Channel Islands of Guernsey and Jersey, some 1,380 ships were granted such letters, although only a few hundred managed to capture prizes.[61] Yet, all these English privateering ravages (some 2,239 prizes) were less significant than many English contemporaries hoped. Early dreams of cutting off France's maritime commerce and forcing Louis to peace in a year or two failed to recognize that French trade consisted mostly of luxury items that contributed little to French strength.[62]

More critical to England's war effort was protecting its own sea trade. Newspapers and reports to the secretaries of state noted every report of vessels taken by privateers, applying steady pressure on decision makers to attend to trade protection. As the French shifted to a less expensive *guerre de course,* English losses mounted. By 1708 public pressure prompted parliament to pass a Cruisers and Convoy Act earmarking the construction of 43 new vessels designed for trade protection.[63] As the waters around Britain became more crowded with patrols, French privateers increasingly targeted less-well-protected Dutch and Portuguese merchants in the North Sea and Atlantic.[64] By late in the war, this retasking, along with construction of faster vessels, allowed the English to withstand French commerce raiding.

Overall, the Royal Navy served two primary purposes in the War of Spanish Succession. Its flexibility allowed the allies to expand the war into the Mediterranean, even if it could not project that power far inland or maintain forces there indefinitely. More importantly, the many naval activities kept England in the war by protecting its maritime trade and by illustrating to those unenthusiastic Englishmen that there was an alternative to the war in Flanders.

Economic warfare

England's final strategy dovetailed with its commerce raiding: an attempt to weaken the French economy by enforcing an embargo on enemy goods. Yet, this effort to damage French trade was only half-hearted. At the time,

---

[61] J. S. Bromley, "The Channel Island Privateers in the War of the Spanish Succession," in Bromley, ed., *Corsairs and Navies, 1660–1706* (London, 1986), pp. 339–388.

[62] Meyer, "English Privateering," pp. 436, 445; Jean Meyer, "Stratégies navales et terrestres: domaines complémentaires ou indépendants? Le cas de l'Ancien Régime," in Pierre Chaunu, ed., *Le Soldat, la stratégie, la mort: mélanges André Corvisier* (Paris, 1989), p. 74.

[63] On convoys, see Merriman, *Queen Anne's Navy,* pp. 338–353; and Rodger, *The Command of the Ocean,* pp. 159–160. The act itself is excerpted in Owen, *War at Sea under Queen Anne,* Appendix F.

[64] J. S. Bromley, "The Importance of Dunkirk Reconsidered, 1688–1713," p. 84; Bromley, "The French Privateering War," p. 220; Bromley, "The North Sea in Wartime," p. 77, all in Bromley, ed., *Corsairs and Navies.* Also Clark, "War, Trade, and Trade War, 1701–1713," in Bromley, ed., p. 264.

any close blockade of French ports was out of the question, and the trade ban was challenged not only by smugglers, but also by legal exceptions for privateer prizes, Scottish, and neutral merchants, and all trade with Spain.[65] France and Spain reciprocated the trade bans, and since no power had a monopoly on critical resources, the effects on the belligerents' economies appear to have been a wash. The strategy of economic attrition also extended to pressuring England's allies to cut their own trade with Louis. This was most contentious with regard to the Dutch, a commercial competitor with the English.[66] Any embargo would hurt the Netherlands as much as the French, for the Dutch war effort largely rested on its taxes from trade and its financial industry. In 1703 the English forced the United Provinces to cut off all their trade with France by linking any augmentation of troops to the issue, including even postal communication, since this was the medium by which Paris could order bills of exchange from Amsterdam to pay French troops in other theaters.[67]

The one-year embargo appears to have been so financially painful (to the Dutch, at least) that even Marlborough, who had earlier insisted on Dutch compliance, argued against renewal.[68] Not only was an already weakened Dutch economy losing money needed to support the war effort, but both maritime powers were seeing their market share of French trade eroded by neutral merchants. Hence the governments reverted to reliance on tariffs and prohibitions filled with loopholes, while merchant communities continued their time-tested strategies of bribery, smuggling, and collusion with foreign merchants. Economic warfare was popular with the English public and fitted England's strategic objectives, but its impact was necessarily limited by its effect on its allies, and by England's own stated goal of increasing trade with Spain.

Resource mobilization

To wage war across multiple theaters required an unprecedented mobilization of allied resources, with England bearing close to a majority share in the allied war effort. This nation of five million managed this by efficiently mobilizing its own economic resources, as well as drawing on the wealth, manpower, and expertise of its allies. In 1701 pro-war pamphlets naïvely promised a quick victory over Louis, but as the war dragged on, England's wartime

---

[65] Generally, see Clark, "War Trade and Trade War," pp. 268ff; and G. N. Clark, "Neutral Commerce in the War of the Spanish Succession and the Treaty of Utrecht," *British Yearbook of International Law*, vol. 9, 1928/9, pp. 69–83.

[66] Jonathan Israel, *The Dutch Republic: Its Rise, Greatness, and Fall, 1477–1806* (Oxford, 1995).

[67] For a contemporary explanation of financial transactions, see *A General Treatise of Monies and Exchanges in Which Those of all Trading Nations are Particularly Describ'd and Consider'd* (London, 1707).

[68] Clark, "War Trade and Trade War," pp. 270–273.

expenditures grew.[69] The first wartime budget year (October 1702–September 1703) saw parliament voting £3 million for the overall war effort; by 1710/11, as new theaters and allies were added and army sizes increased, costs doubled to £7 million.[70] The need to refinance past military debt and make good on naval arrears led expenditures to skyrocket to £12.6 million in 1711/12, before returning back down to £4.7 million as the Tory government wound down the war effort. In total, the 11 years of warfare cost the crown and its taxpayers £55–62 million, a many-fold increase over their expenses in the previous Nine Years' War. Compiling from various estimates, of the £25 million spent in the four main theaters of war, 90 percent went to the Low Countries (£13.6 million, 54 percent) or Iberia (£8.9 million, 36 percent). Half of English expenditures (£26 million) were spent on the army, with the other half (£27.1 million) dedicated to the navy.[71] Although estimates differ, all agree that England spent a fortune combating Louis XIV's France.

England's ability to raise such vast amounts was predicated on its efficient tax base and its creditworthiness. From an estimated net national income of £50 million per year, parliament approved the crown's efforts to raise £1.8 to 2.6 million in taxes every year, £21 million over Anne's reign.[72] Even so, military expenditures exceeded England's ordinary tax income by £29 million.[73] Making war feed war through contributions in theater could provide some relief, but with occupied territories simply unable to supply the advance funds necessary to sustain campaigning by military establishments numbering 100,000 men or more, every belligerent had to borrow. England was in the privileged position of being able to use its large economic base as collateral for loans at advantageous terms. The man most responsible for maintaining England's creditworthiness was Anne's experienced Lord Treasurer Godolphin. Through his efforts, England's growing economy sold annuities and lotteries backed by its future tax revenues, an astounding £28.8 million between 1704 and 1712, or £3.2 million per year on average. This compares favorably with England's borrowing during the previous war, which totaled only £6.8 million at much higher interest rates. England achieved this feat in part by balancing its import and export of specie through

[69] The standard work on English finances is P. G. M. Dickson, *The Financial Revolution in England: A Study in the Development of Public Credit, 1688–1756* (London, 1967). The detailed financial records are found in William Shaw and Joseph Reddington, eds., *Calendar of Treasury Books and Papers 1702–1712, Preserved in Her Majesty's Public Record Office* (London, 1871–1947), vols. II–IV.
[70] These figures come from Hattendorf, *England in the War of the Spanish Succession*, Appendix B. Dickson, "Sword of Gold," in *Financial Revolution*, provides slightly different numbers.
[71] Theater expenditures from Hattendorf, *England in the War of the Spanish Succession*, Appendix C; Army–Navy expenses from Appendix B. The various groups of figures do not necessarily correspond with one another, for reasons mentioned by Hattendorf.
[72] These figures come from Dickson, "Sword of Gold."
[73] Dickson, *Financial Revolution*, p. 10.

growing economic trade.[74] Its growing empire and naval preeminence fueled its wars, while the concessions gained from the war expanded its markets.

The government further benefitted from its close relationship with several important economic players. Godolphin not only attended to the creditworthiness of the English crown by deftly prioritizing payments, but as one of the Bank of England's early supporters and an important shareholder, he also used his personal connections to call directly on wealthy corporations to loan additional money.[75] This close relationship, along with the crown's power to extend the bank's charter (scheduled to expire in 1708), facilitated close cooperation between the government and the bank. As the war dragged on, the Lord Treasurer returned again and again to the bank, acquiring £6.5 million in loans over the span of just four years. By 1709 the treasury even began to refinance its higher-interest debt at lower, longer-term rates. Godolphin could also call upon other corporations when necessary: in 1708 the crown negotiated a similar £1.2 million loan with the East India Company.

After Godolphin and the Whigs fell from power in 1710, the Whig-leaning directors of the Bank of England refused to loan additional funds to the new Tory ministry – no surprise, given that Tories had attacked the Whigs for more than two decades for redistributing wealth via the land tax from the landed gentry to the London merchant/financier class represented by the bank.[76] The new Lord Treasurer Harley resolved the crisis by creating an entirely new South Sea Company, whose goal was to establish English colonies near South American gold and silver mines.[77] Holders of government debt received stock in the new company, which resulted in a budgetary windfall of over £9 million in 1711. Much of this amount was used to refinance previous government debt. The next year, the bank shed its partisan stance, running a lottery to raise additional funds for the crown. The combination of commercial wealth, willingness among investors to purchase government-backed debt, public–private partnerships cemented by personal connections between ministers and investor elites, and the government's ability to revise charters reinforced patriotic motivations and the self-interest directors had to assist the war effort.

Combined with other ordinary sources of revenue which facilitated this public debt, these resources not only gave England an ability to tap directly the country's growing commercial wealth, but also allowed the government to help finance its allies. Together, the English and Dutch subsidized eight allied countries to the tune of some £8 million during the war, with England paying

[74] Jones, *War and the Economy in the Age of William III and Marlborough*.
[75] Dickson, "Sword of Gold."
[76] Dickson, *Financial Revolution*, pp. 62–75 on the transition from Godolphin to Harley.
[77] Brian W. Hill, *Robert Harley, Speaker, Secretary of State, and Premier Minister* (New Haven, CT, 1988).

two-thirds of the amount.[78] In addition to such subsidies, allies were occasionally allowed to acquire their own loans from the London credit markets, Austria, for example, acquiring £340,000 late in the war.[79] England was better at raising more credit, more quickly, and more cheaply than the other combatants, including its allies.[80] The fiscal instruments described above gave England enough money to support a whole range of strategies to combat France.[81] English gold fed English credit, which in turn fed allied success, and by the end of the conflict England had risen to become the most powerful commercial power in Europe.

Mobilizing allied resources

Yet, England did not win the war by itself. Without the Grand Alliance, there would have been no victory for the English. This too was an important part of the evolving British way of war, the ability to marshal the resources of a European-wide coalition and manipulate them as needed. Most important was England's ability to open up multiple fronts against a common foe and its ability to acquire foreign soldiers who would fight with the support of English gold.

The number and composition of the armies in which English troops fought illustrate the importance of this coalition context. Even in the theaters most important to the English, their contributions were subsumed within larger allied efforts. The original September 1701 agreement determining troop contributions stipulated 90,000 to be fielded by the emperor, a 40,000-man English army, and a 102,000-man States (i.e., Dutch) Army.[82] In the case of the Low Countries theater, the Anglo-Dutch contingents in what became Marlborough's army were set at two-fifths English and three-fifths Dutch. The Dutch provided almost 80,000 of their own men, with another 34,000 German mercenaries in Dutch pay. With Dutch coaxing, the maritime nations agreed to an augmentation of 20,000 troops in 1703, with the costs of almost all of the regiments split equally.[83] Another Anglo-Dutch

[78] Hattendorf, *England in the War of the Spanish Succession*, pp. 132–133; for the amount, see Dickson, "War Finance, 1688–1714," in *Financial Revolution*, p. 285.
[79] Dickson, *Financial Revolution*, p. 333.
[80] J. Aalbers, "Holland's Financial Problems (1713–1733) and the Wars against Louis XIV," in A. C. Duke, ed., *Britain and the Netherlands*, vol. IV: *War and Society. Papers delivered to the Sixth Anglo-Dutch Historical Conference* (The Hague, 1977), pp. 79–93. For a general comparison between English, Dutch, French, and Austrian finances, see Dickson, "War Finance, 1688–1714."
[81] Maltby, "The Origins of a Global Strategy."
[82] Godfrey Davies, "Recruiting in the Reign of Queen Anne," *The Journal of the Society for Army Historical Research*, vol. 28, 1950, pp. 146–159. Also Childs, *The British Army of William III, 1689–1702*, pp. 102–103.
[83] Wijn, *Het Staatsche Leger*, vol. III, p. 338 lists the costs and number of regiments. See also vol. I, pp. 678–682, which goes from 1707 to 1709, and vol. III, pp. 339–343. Douglas Coombs shows the Dutch initiation of this troop increase, and how it was hijacked by

augmentation in 1709 added an additional 20,000 troops, this time two-thirds in British pay and one-third in Dutch.[84] Neither maritime power could fill the increasing demand for troops from native reserves, and therefore both relied heavily on German mercenaries, employing 97,000 at their peak in 1711.[85] The 1703 Methuen Treaty committed the Portuguese to provide a regular army of 15,000 and another 13,000 auxiliaries, supported by the maritime allies, while the Anglo-Dutch troops were to number some 12,000. A similar number of British troops served under Charles in Catalonia. Overall, the English sent 60,000–80,000 men to Iberia, with the Dutch contributing a third of that number.[86]

A less recognized but equally important contributor to English success was the expertise that their Dutch allies provided Marlborough's armies.[87] The States-General, in addition to providing the majority of troops and experienced officers for the duke's armies, also provided the necessary logistical and engineering expertise.[88] English troops in the Low Countries relied on the efficient Dutch supply system built from William's connections with a cosmopolitan network of Jewish merchants and financiers and civilian contractors who used their financial networks and business connections with local merchants to provide bread and fodder.[89] The hated Dutch field deputies played a pivotal role providing bread for Marlborough's armies, not only in the Low Countries, but even on the allied march to the Danube.[90] It was also the Dutch who facilitated Marlborough's advances after his Flanders battles by providing the personnel, expertise, and supplies needed for siege craft.[91] The chief engineer at each of "Marlborough's" sieges was in Dutch

English politicians, in "The Augmentation of 1709: A Study in the Workings of the Anglo-Dutch Alliance," *English Historical Review*, vol. 72, 1957, pp. 643–646 for the 1703 augmentation.

[84] Coombs, "The Augmentation of 1709."

[85] Peter H. Wilson, *German Armies: War and German Society, 1648–1806* (London, 1998), pp. 105–109. Davies, "Recruiting," esp. p. 157 for England's recruiting problems starting in 1708 – over 11,000 were needed to replace the losses from the Spanish loss at Almanza.

[86] Davies, "Recruiting," p. 153. Wijn, *Het Staatsche Leger*, 3, pp. 364–367 – including 15,000 Portuguese, 33,400 Imperials, 5,000 Italians, and 6,000 Spanish. See also vol. III, pp. 356–358; vol. II, p. 791; as well as a comparison of the scattered figures presented in Francis, *The First Peninsular War* and Hugill, *No Peace without Spain*.

[87] Douglas Coombs, *The Conduct of the Dutch: British Opinion and the Dutch Alliance during the War of the Spanish Succession* (The Hague, 1958).

[88] For a discussion of Marlborough's early inexperience in Flanders campaigning, see John Stapleton, "'By thes difficultys you may see the great disadvantage a confederat army has': Marlborough, the Allies, and the Campaigns in the Low Countries, 1702–1706," in John Hattendorf, ed., *Marlborough: Soldier and Diplomat* (Rotterdam, 2012).

[89] Jones, *War and Economy in the Age of William and Marlborough*.

[90] Olaf van Nimwegen, *De subsitentie van het leger: Logistiek en strategie van het Geallieerde en met name het Staatse leger tijdens de Spaanse Successieoorlog in de Nederlanden en het Heilige Roomse Rijk (1701–1712)* (Amsterdam, 1995), pp. 132ff. and 369 n8 for the Dutch supply of Marlborough's march to the Danube.

[91] Jamel Ostwald, "Marlborough and Siege Warfare," in Hattendorf, ed., *Marlborough: Soldier and Diplomat*.

pay, either Menno van Coehoorn or one of several Huguenots who found employment in the States' service. Similarly, the Dutch provided the siege trains, while the onerous duty of siege service was similarly borne on the backs of Dutch soldiers: English regiments provided 14 percent of the average siege army's manpower, and no more than 20 percent for the larger sieges later in the war. Since the main Dutch objective was to gain their barrier fortresses and the English detested siege craft, the English were more than willing to have the Dutch pay the extraordinary costs of sieges. English strategists could retain their battle-centric outlook only because they relied on their allies to perform other necessary tasks.

War exhaustion and a separate peace

Even with English gold and battlefield success, the war lasted longer than its proponents had expected. The most controversial English decision by far was the decision to end it. Allied military successes from 1702 to 1706, along with constant English pressure, enabled the allies to present a united front against Louis. The increasingly desperate Sun King began to send out private peace feelers to the Dutch as early as August 1705, and offered at least nine different concrete proposals for terms over the period 1705–1710, each one more advantageous to the allies than the last, and each dismissed by the English as insincere.[92] Through all his proposals, Louis attempted to split off the Dutch and achieve a partition of Spain, while giving both maritime powers something they wanted, a barrier for the Dutch and recognition of Anne (but only at the signing of the final peace), and commercial concessions. Concerned about alienating a powerful English ally, Heinsius was careful to include Marlborough and Godolphin in all such discussions; in the end the Dutch paid heavily for their unreciprocated loyalty to the alliance.

The allies summarily rejected Louis' earliest proposals. The military reverses of 1706 added urgency to Louis' discussions: two more French proposals to partition Spain were rejected that year. The result was a defeat for the war-ending decisive battle ideal: three considerable battlefield victories (Blenheim, Ramillies, and Turin) had failed to force Louis to his knees after seven years of war, at least on terms acceptable to the allies. Two more offers were rejected the next year as Louis stiffened his terms after the multiple allied disappointments of 1707.

By 1709 Louis' France was clearly in decline. Allied advances from battle and siege pressed Louis on all sides, and the French treasury was in a

---

[92] With the exception of 1707. Mark Thomson, "Louis XIV and the Grand Alliance, 1705–10," in R. Hatton, ed., *William III and Louis XIV: Essays 1680–1720* (Liverpool, 1968), pp. 190–212. A Dutch perspective is in Stork-Penning, "The Ordeal of the States: Some Remarks on Dutch Politics during the War of the Spanish Succession," *Acta Historiae Neerlandica*, vol. 2, 1967, pp. 120–121.

shambles.[93] On top of all this, January 1709 saw the beginning of one of the worst winters and attendant famines France had seen in a generation.[94] While these setbacks made peace more critical for France, they also made the allies even more obdurate. In early 1709 they rejected the most serious French offer yet, in part because the French negotiators could not assure the allies that Philippe would abide by the terms.[95] The three allies then crafted a unified peace proposal for Louis to accept, the 40 articles of the Preliminaries of The Hague, demanding that within two months France raze and evacuate its Rhine fortifications as well as Dunkirk, evacuate French troops from Spain, force Philippe to abandon the Spanish throne without any guarantee of compensation, and turn over additional places of surety for a Dutch barrier. Most insulting was Article 37: that Louis contribute French troops to evict his own grandson from Spain, if Philippe refused to abdicate. Only after accepting these terms would the allies allow Louis to negotiate the terms of the peace. Pushed into a corner, Louis rejected the Preliminaries and appealed directly to the French people to defend their country from these outrageous demands. As his diplomatic advisor Polignac noted, Louis would agree to a peace, but not one that required him to "[part] with fortresses, [abandon a] kingdom, [dismantle] Dunkirk . . . only to gain a truce for two or three months."[96]

Unaware of how much they had overestimated their strategic advantage, most Englishmen judged the rejection yet another example of Ludovician duplicity, even as a few privately reconsidered the severity of the terms.[97] In March 1710, Louis once again sent representatives to meet with Dutch envoys at the town of Geertruijdenberg in the hopes of compromising on Article 37. However, the British refused to make any concessions, and the Dutch had no territory to offer Philippe in exchange for Spain, since the Austrians were unwilling to abandon any of their Italian possessions. Many Whigs believed France would have to accept even these terms, but the 1710 Castilian uprising against the Habsburg candidate illustrated how poorly their demands fit the Spanish reality. As outraged as Louis might be by Article 37, he was so desperate for peace that, as a last concession, he offered as a compromise to subsidize the allied war in Spain at 500,000 *livres* per month. The allies rejected even this. Thus, the war carried on into its tenth year as

---

[93] The Sun King was reduced to replacing his Controller-General of Finances Chamillart with Nicolas Desmaretz in June 1708 to try to replenish his empty coffers: Gary McCollim, *Louis XIV's Assault on Privilege: Nicolas Desmaretz and the Tax on Wealth* (Rochester, NY, 2012).

[94] M. Lachiver, *Les Années de misère: La famine au temps du Grand Roi* (Paris, 1991).

[95] John Rule, "France and the Preliminaries to the Gertruydenberg Conference, September 1709 to March 1710," in M. S. Anderson, ed., *Studies in Diplomatic History: Essays in Memory of David Bayne Horn* (London, 1970), pp. 97–115; John Rule, "King and Minister: Louis XIV and Colbert de Torcy," in R. Hatton, ed., *William III and Louis XIV*; Thomson, "Louis XIV and the Grand Alliance, 1705–10"; Stork-Penning, "Ordeal of the States," pp. 120ff.

[96] Quote in Rule, "France and the Preliminaries to the Gertruydenberg Conference," p. 106.

[97] Thomson, "Louis XIV and the Grand Alliance, 1705–10," pp. 207–208.

the allies continued their slow advance in the Low Countries, while Philippe resolutely chipped away at the remaining Habsburg possessions in Catalonia, thus insuring a partitioned Spanish Empire.

Just as England had played a key role in preventing peace in 1709–1710, it also played the pivotal part in ending the war. Anne began abandoning her extreme Whig ministers in 1710 and soon after, a new peace-seeking Tory ministry took power, leading to the possibility of a separate peace with France. In 1711 while Marlborough conducted his last campaign under partisan attack, a few months of London negotiations led to the outline of an agreement.[98] The new ministry had finally recognized that a strategy of decisive battle would deliver neither Spain nor the rest of Vauban's *pré carré*, and continuation of the war to achieve "No Peace without Spain" was not worth the cost, particularly after Charles inherited the mantle of Holy Roman Emperor.

In the end it was easier for the two linchpin countries to present a fait accompli peace to the rest than to coordinate terms among four or more different parties. Harley's minimal territorial demands were easy for France to accept once England recognized Philippe's position in Spain, while Dutch participation would only hamper England's efforts to maximize its commercial advantages. The resulting London Preliminaries gave most Englishmen what they had wanted from Spain: trade. They received the *asiento* as well as a limited trade status within the Spanish Empire, the promised destruction of Dunkirk's fortifications, and confirmation of their holdings in Gibraltar, Minorca, and Newfoundland. With this outline, the English and French had only to convince the other allies to attend a peace congress, which was not difficult. The Dutch had always tied their terms to England's, hence their decision to agree to the rejection of Louis' 1709 terms even when they found them acceptable.[99] No amount of concessions appeared likely to placate the Austrians; however, they feared being left out of any talks.

The Congress of Utrecht thus opened on 29 January 1712, with representatives from 18 belligerents and 12 neutrals. Neither the betrayed Dutch nor the stubborn Austrian participants were initially willing to accept the Anglo-French terms, but the Dutch hand was forced in the field after British troops abandoned them in July and Villars halted the Austro-Dutch advance and went over to the offensive. On 11–12 April 1713, all parties signed the final peace treaties with the exception of the Habsburgs, who would fight on until the Treaties of Rastatt (with Austria, signed 7 March 1714) and Baden

---

[98] On Harley's management of these negotiations, see A. D. MacLachlan, "The Road to Peace 1710–1713," in Geoffrey Holmes, ed., *Britain after the Glorious Revolution, 1689–1714* (London, 1969), pp. 206–208.

[99] The one non-negotiable position for the Dutch was that there be a joint peace agreed to by the two Maritime powers; since they were unable to convince the English to accept a partition, they stuck to England's 'entire Spanish monarchy' position. Stork-Penning, "The Ordeal of the States," pp. 114, 122.

(with the empire, signed 7 September 1714) officially ended their conflict with France. Even at Rastatt, Charles refused to accept Philippe's claim to the Spanish throne. By the end of the war, England had adopted a variety of strategies in its attempts to defeat France. Their proponents all promised a quick victory, but whether by battle, by siege, by descent, or by fleet, England won the attritional war only when the electoral system placed English policy makers into office who were willing to abandon past demands and satisfy themselves with the original terms in the second Grand Alliance treaty.

The Treaties of Utrecht and Baden–Rastatt, like England's wartime strategy, represented a compromise. As often happened in the early modern period, every participant received something. If one strictly measures success by the name of the war, it was a Bourbon victory, with Philippe V retaining the Spanish throne. Spain lost to the extent that it failed to maintain its territorial integrity beyond Iberia. The Austrian House of Habsburg gained Spain's other European territories: the southern (now Austrian) Netherlands, Milan, Sardinia, and Naples. The Dutch received the barrier fortresses as a buffer against future French aggression. Victor Amadeus maintained his independence and would eventually (in 1720) expand his holdings to include Sardinia and Naples. Frederick III of Brandenburg-Prussia had already received the title of "King *in* Prussia" in exchange for his participation, and temporarily gained possession of Gelderland. Maximilian Emmanuel of Bavaria regained his electorate.

England gained little territory, but was careful to insist on retaining those lands that furthered its commercial interests: Gibraltar and Minorca in the Mediterranean, as well as Newfoundland and St. Kitts in the Americas. The *asiento* provided the English with a monopoly on the slave trade to the Spanish colonies, and they negotiated preferential commercial terms at the expense of their allies. The expensive war had weakened England's commercial competitors on the mainland, while reestablishing a balance of power by partitioning Spain's European holdings. These successes were significant, but their worth would depend on the extent to which later British strategists took advantage of them. The maximalist Whigs judged the terms an outrageous sell-out, impeaching Harley and St. John for their treasonous peace when they returned to power in 1715. In retrospect it would gradually become clear that the Utrecht settlement launched Britain's ascent to world power. But a decidedly Whiggish view of the war's strategy would also come to dominate, an interpretation that emphasized the possibility that Marlborough's battles might have ended the war, a potential unrealized due to obstructionist allies and the 1710 Tory stab-in-the-back.[100] The politicized

---

[100] This is the tone taken by almost all of the dozen biographies of Marlborough. Notable examples include Winston Churchill, *Marlborough: His Life and Times*, 2 vols. (Chicago, 2002 reprint of 1933 orig.) and David Chandler, *Marlborough as Military Commander* (New York, 2000 reprint of 1973 orig.).

strategic debates of the age became ossified in the historical literature, with the continental battle-seeking strategy declared the victor.

Conclusion

William's 1688 invasion ushered in a sea change in English grand strategy. No longer able to sit on the sidelines, England found itself increasingly drawn into Europe's continental wars to maintain a balance of power while defending and expanding its overseas commerce and territories. The War of the Spanish Succession created a native version of William's continental strategy, Marlborough's "English" battlefield victories leading his supporters to laud the return of English courage. The duke's striking successes placed serious strains on Louis, but too often they have blinded historians to the wide-ranging strategies that beleaguered France. Tory and Whig, court and country politicians promoted competing continental and naval strategies in multiple theaters which, thanks to England's ability to fund them all, ended up complementing one another. English policy makers clearly made significant strategic mistakes: initial English expectations of a quick war – whether by economic strangulation or decisive battle – were frustrated by 1707, and persistent expectations of an imminent French collapse extended the war, ironically increasing the likelihood of a negotiated peace.

English acquisitions at Utrecht laid the groundwork for later British success, but were even more successful in providing a model of British expeditionary warfare. England was able to create a successful formula for mobilizing its growing financial power to harness continental allies and manpower to its own goals – the "British way in warfare." The legacy of the great duke and the disgust with his "obstructionist" allies lasts to this day, as does British possession of Gibraltar. But the real success in the War of the Spanish Succession was to create a formula of grand strategy that would allow it to win the future wars of the eighteenth century even more decisively.

5   Failed, broken, or galvanized?
Prussia and 1806

Dennis Showalter

Prussia's experience is *sui generis* in the context of this project. The other contributions feature discussions of strategies with positive starting points. Prussia's strategy of recovery involved the reconstitution of, if not a "failed state" in the contemporary sense, then arguably a broken state. A military system considered formidable even after the French Revolution's innovations found itself overthrown in a single campaign. Its disintegration in the aftermath of the Battle of Jena-Auerstädt was comprehensive and immediate, almost literally a matter of the marching speeds of French armies. As Joachim Murat allegedly reported to Napoleon, the fighting was over because there was no enemy left.

Prussia's collapse was humiliating. Fifty-one of the 60 infantry regiments, the army's backbone, many with over a century of victory to their names, disappeared. Strongly garrisoned, well-provisioned fortresses surrendered at the first challenge. With no hope of relief from a broken field army, resistance appeared futile and pointless. The few last stands and hold-outs only highlighted a wasteland of senescence and incompetence. The familiar jest that Prussia was an army with its own country became grim reality as the state's social and political fabric unraveled. The royal family fled Berlin, leaving their capital open to French occupation and looting. The Berliners for their part greeted their French conquerors with applause, while other Prussian cities greeted the French with wine and flowers. What remained of the army attached itself to a Russian ally more embarrassed than gratified by the connection.[1] King Frederick William III focused on the surrenders when denouncing humiliations "without precedent" in his public pronouncement after the collapse. He concluded by declaring that, in the future, any soldier who distinguished himself was to be made an officer regardless of social standing. On one hand this represented a revolutionary announcement; on

---

[1] As perceptive as it is concise is Peter Paret, *The Cognitive Challenge of War: Prussia 1806* (Princeton, 2009). See Robert M. Citino, *The German Way of War* (Lawrence, KS, 2009), pp. 109–122 and Ludger Hermann, "Die Schlachten von Jena und Auerstedt und die Genese der politischen Oeffentlichkeit in Preussen," in G. Fesser and R. Jonscher, eds., *Umbruch im Schatten Napoleons, Die Schlachten von Jena und Auerstedt und ihre Folge* (Jena, 1998), pp. 39–52.

the other, it carried forward ideas current in both state and army well before 1806.[2] From either perspective, the king's words highlighted what came to be called the Prussian Reform Movement.

Origins of the recovery

Prussia's recovery was not a matter of adjustment, but of reconstruction, the projected scope of which was as comprehensive as the catastrophe that focused it. The reform movement's genesis, purpose, and method were to strengthen the Prussian state, but not merely in the context of enhancing its military power and diplomatic influence. Reform in its developed version was grand strategy in the highest sense: a synergy of approaches designed to transform not merely policy but also mentality. Nor was reform a specific response to a particular catastrophe. Its taproot was a German *Aufklaerung* (enlightenment) that fostered development of a common culture and advocated the creation of a public sphere affirming unity in diversity. Formal philosophy also addressed questions of identity in the context of community. G. W. F. Hegel further developed Immanuel Kant's emphasis on individual consciousness as the fulcrum for universal principles into a process that synthesized the individual and collective, the particular and the general. The *Aufklaerung* rejected what it considered the limited, artificial values of the French Enlightenment. Literature, philosophy, and art were provinces of reason and domains of human endeavor.[3] That held true for law as well. The *Allgemeines Landrecht fuer die Preussischen Staaten*, completed in 1794, was the product of four decades of discussion among lawyers and bureaucrats. In more than 19,000 sections, it addressed what seemed every possible permutation of interaction among Prussians that might involve a matter of law. Its complexity simultaneously acknowledged tradition and innovation. The *Allgemeines Landrecht*, in short, epitomized the relation between *Aufklaerung* and state.[4]

One historian has described Prussia's version of the German *Aufklaerung* as being "about conversation," open, public, civil dialogue among subjects of a

[2] See generally Georg Hebbelmann, "Das preussische 'offizierkorps' im 18. Jahrhundeert: Analyse der Sozialstruktur einer Funktionselite," dissertation, Muenster, 1999.
[3] See H. B. Nisbet, "'Was ist Aufklaerung?' The Concept of Enlightenment in 18th Century Germany," *Journal of European Studies*, vol. 12, 1982, pp. 77–95; Horst Moeller, *Vernunft und Kritik. Deutsche Aufklaerung im 17. und 18. Jahrhundert* (Frankfurt, 1986); Thomas Saine, *The Problem of Being Modern: or, The German Pursuit of Enlightenment from Leibniz to the French Revolution* (Detroit, 1997); Hans Erich Boedeker, "Aufklaerung und Kommunikationsprozess," *Aufklaerung*, vol. 2, 1987, pp. 89–112; and T. Yasukata, *Lessing's Philosophy of Religion and the German Enlightenment* (New York, 2002).
[4] See Hermann Conrad, *Die geistigen Grundlagen des Allgemeinen Landrechts fuer die preussischen Staaten von 1794* (Koeln, 1956); and more comprehensively Reinhard Koselleck, *Preussen zwischen Reform und Revolution: Allgemeines Landrecht, Vverwaltung und soziale Bewegungne von 1791 bis 1848* (Stuttgart, 1976).

state of laws and a state of rights.[5] That identity with the state reflected Frederick the Great's championship of enlightened values and practices. It reflected the dominance of public servants, broadly defined, in *Aufklaerung*'s ranks. Officials, attorneys, pastors, teachers, even officers, held their posts because of educational qualifications. From 1770, for example, all higher government positions required a state examination. The result was a heterogeneous mix of backgrounds and personalities that had to work together to accomplish anything worthwhile. That development reflected and reinforced a strong consultative element in Prussian government at all levels, from the collegial structure of the General Directory to the unofficial interactions among government officials and men of affairs who underwrote and shaped local policy. *Aufklaerung* as a concept was closely linked in Prussia to established social interests and political patterns. For progressives, the state was not merely acceptable but desirable as a participant in the process of change, in a practical sense.[6]

Kant argued eloquently for the synergy between public power as vested in the monarchy and the refinement of civil rights and broadly defined liberties.[7] The ideas of enlightened activists, developed through observation and analysis, could be worked through on personal levels, incorporated into government institutions, and translated into public policy. The process was hardly linear. It involved a spectrum of events from the status of Jews to censorship of the press to the issue of religious tolerance. More fundamental questions, such as land reform and serfdom, developed as sub-texts. A new generation of officials was making its mark, combining persuasion, coercion, and an ability to stimulate efficiency by challenging traditional practices and privileges. A few were non-Prussians, attracted by the prospect of not merely careers open to talent, but also the opportunity to make significant contributions on a larger scale.

Among these were men like Nassau's Baron Karl Friedrich vom und zu Stein and Hanoverian Karl August von Hardenberg. Both had studied at Goettingen, Germany's leading training ground for aspiring public administrators. Even before the French Revolution, they and their counterparts were beginning to establish institutional matrices for change. Moreover, Frederick William III, who succeeded to the throne in 1797, systematically addressed controversial questions, including taxation of the nobles, prison reform, and servile labor on crown lands from the beginning of his reign. The result of this push toward progress was a "two-headed state" with polarity between tradition

---

[5] Christopher Clark, *Iron Kingdom: The Rise and Downfall of Prussia 1600–1947* (Cambridge, MA, 2008), p. 247.

[6] Rolf Straubel, *Beamte und Personenpolitik im altpreussischen Staat: sozial Rekrutierung, Karrierenverlauef, Entscheidungsprozesse) 1763–1806* (Potsdam, 1998) is a valuable overview. See also Isabel Hull, *Sexuality, State, and Civil Society in Germany* (Ithaca, NY, 1999).

[7] Immanuel Kant, "Beantwortung der Frage 'Was ist Aufklaerung?'" originally published in *Berliner Monatsschrift*, Sept. 10, 1784, reprinted in *Derliner Monatsschrift (1783–1796)* (Leipzig, 1986), pp. 89–96.

and innovation. Participants were more likely to perceive an affirmative dialectic between status and change – a dialectic taking Prussia in a positive direction.[8] In that context, to speak of the primacy of either foreign or domestic policy is to apply a neologism. Prussia's hard-won position in Europe and Germany was as a rational actor whose pursuit of limited goals its credible armed force backed. That credibility in turn depended on the state's effectiveness and the support of society for systems for financing and recruitment, traits generally accepted as essential elements of the Prussian social contract.[9]

The Prussian variant of the German *Aufklaerung* had a significant impact on military thought between the Rhine and Vistula. Carl von Clausewitz was anything but exceptional in considering it natural and necessary to incorporate emotional factors into the analysis of war. Aesthetics influenced and shaped the contents and the forms of his theories. Much like their counterparts in cultural and intellectual spheres, Clausewitz and his mentors were less concerned with establishing abstract scientific systems than with broadening and disseminating practical knowledge.[10] In Prussia Frederick the Great's death opened a window of opportunity. His successors banned the more extreme forms of physical punishment unofficially introduced in Frederick's later years. Regimental schools with state-of-the-art curricula emerged, encouraging fathers to remain with their families and with the colors. Family allowances were introduced for children under 13. Soldiers' homes offered superannuated veterans a respectable alternative to the begging bowl or state sinecures like school mastering not always available.[11]

Limited as they were, these innovations kept desertion rates moderate even during the 1790s, despite the appeal of French propaganda stressing the advantages of desertion in the name of liberty, equality, and fraternity. French Revolutionary armies, especially their attitudes and behavior in the Rhineland, gave the lie to claims of universal fraternity. Nevertheless, it grew increasingly clear to Prussia's military professionals that the French had now set the standards of war and that French human and material resources exponentially exceeded anything Prussia could match. The fundamental problem confronting the Prussians was how best to confront such an adversary. It is a common cliché that the French military system was a direct product of the social and political changes generated by the revolution.[12] If, as critics like Gneisenau

---

[8] Clark, *Iron Kingdom*, pp. 267–283.
[9] Dennis Showalter, "Hubertusberg to Auerstaedt: The Prussian Army in Decline?" *German History*, vol. 12, 1994.
[10] See the contributions to E. Kramer and P. A. Simpson, eds., *Enlightened War: German Theories and Cultures of War from Frederick the Great to Clausewitz* (Rochester, NY, 2011).
[11] John E. Stine, "King Frederick William II and the Decline of the Prussian Army, 1786–1797," dissertation, University of South Carolina, 1980.
[12] Michael Sikora, " Die Franzoezische Revolution der Heeresverfassung," in P. Baumgart, B. Koerner, and H. Sruebig, eds., *Die preussische Armee zwisschen Ancien Regime und Reichsgruendung* (Paderborn, 2008), pp. 135–163 provides a good overview.

posited, armies were inseparable from their social values, then logic suggested comprehensively remodeling Prussia on French lines. But if this path were taken, why bother to fight France?

That question had particular resonance in a Prussia where war and *Aufklaerung* combined to reinforce an increasingly defined, comprehensive sense of Prussian patriotism. Since the era of the Great Elector, a social contract of protection and security in exchange for loyalty and service had permeated Prussian identity. It reached perihelion during the Seven Years' War, when it was stressed to the limit on both sides and not found wanting. A major part of Frederick the Great's mystique reflected, not his heroic mastery of the battlefield, but the fatigues and hardships he shared with his soldiers: the aging man in the snuff-spotted coat who could crack a dialect joke on the march or reward a regiment's performance with uniform braid from his own pocket.

An aristocracy which bled itself white in the king's service had come to understand and value the men it led as well as commanded, less in a sentimental, pre-Romantic sense than as sharing a common enterprise and sacrifice. Spilled blood and torn flesh were the same colors, while the rank and file had proven anything but driven automata more frightened of their officers than their enemies. Religion-based sense of duty combined with pride in unit and craft to produce soldiers who could think and act as well as endure. Structured by obedience to authority, the army nevertheless offered a basis for identity with the state.[13]

As early as 1763, Lessing's *Minna von Barnhelm* depicted the bonds of honor existing between an officer and his sergeant and provided the king a central role in resolving the drama's crisis. In 1781 Schiller's *The Robbers* put a civilian spin on male bonding in an atmosphere of violence: the outlawed Karl Moor is loyal to the honorable commoners who follow him. The dawn of 1798 saw the first public performance of *Wallenstein's Camp*, with Goethe directing. The bulk of the play deals with high-level intrigue. *Camp*, the most familiar and the best read in German or translation, brings to center stage common soldiers who come from everywhere in Europe to serve Wallenstein. Their multicultural affirmation of freedom offered a counterpoint and challenge to contemporary events across the Rhine – and highlighted a changing image of the peasant "from pariah to patriot."[14]

The modified Prussian Army's performance in limited contexts during the early 1790s had on the whole been satisfactory. Valmy represented a specific problem of command rather than an indication of institutional decline.

[13] See Dennis Showalter, "Roi-Connetable und Feldherr: Frederick the Great and His Times," unpublished paper; and Sascha Moebius, *Mehr Angst vor dem Offizier als vor dem Feind? Ein mentalitaetsgeschichtliche Studien zur preussischen Taktik im Siebenjaehrigeen Krieg* (Saarbruecken, 2007).

[14] John Gagliardo, *From Pariah to Patriot: The Changing Image of the German Peasant, 1770–1840* (Lexington, KY, 1960).

Inexperienced troops facing strong positions in bad weather seldom achieve glory, and Brunswick himself showed to better advantage in the next campaign. Prussian line battalions committed against the French combined well-controlled volleys and well-regulated local counterattacks that matched, if not always surpassed, French *élan* and *cran*. Prussian light infantry proved formidable opponents against French raiders and foragers and taught their enemies sharp lessons in skirmishing and marksmanship.[15] Applied *Aufklaerung* offered a matrix for further changes. The answer, articulated by military intellectuals like Friedrich von der Decken, was that Prussia required a "quality army," able to counter French mass and skill with even greater fighting power. Prussia could replicate the military qualities admired in the French Army by institutional reform, underpinned by social changes well short of revolution.[16]

Gerhard von Scharnhorst, another high-profile immigrant, had emerged as a leading German military theorist during his years in Hanoverian service before transferring to the Prussian Army in 1801. Initially working through the newly established Berlin *Militaerische Gesellschaft*, Scharnhorst proposed to introduce, a few at a time, a new generation of leaders with a common background. These new leaders would advise their official superiors in commanding the kind of army Scharnhorst saw necessary for Prussia's survival.[17] In essence this was the Prussian general staff system. It also represented a long-term project.

In the years immediately prior to Jena, officers and administrators favoring change concentrated on three specific reforms. The first was administration. Regulations were simplified. Baggage, supply, and ammunition trains were reduced. The logistical system was overhauled. The Prussian Army that took the field for the Jena campaign was a good deal leaner than it had been since the Seven Years' War.[18] It was also better articulated – at least on paper. Scharnhorst had argued since his arrival for introducing the French divisional system into the Prussian Army. Not until the 1806 campaign was actually under way, however, did the army establish a divisional system. At that late date, it is not surprising that, apart from the normal problems inherent in improvised formations with inexperienced commanders, the divisions were badly balanced, deficient alike in fire power and shock power.

---

[15] Dennis Showalter, "Instrument of Policy: The Prussian Army in the French Revolutionary Wars" – forthcoming in an anthology on military effectiveness in the French Revolutionary period, edited by Frederick Schneid.

[16] Friedrich von der Decken, *Betrachtungen ueber das Verhaeltniss der Kriegstand zu dem Zwecke der Staaten* (Hanover, 1800).

[17] Charles White, *The Enlightened Soldier: Scharnhorst and the Militaerische Gesellschaft in Berlin, 1801–1805* (New York, 1989).

[18] Hans Heifritz, *Geschichte der Preussischen Heeresverwaltung* (Berlin, 1938), pp. 173ff.; W. O. Shanahan, *Prussian Military Reforms 1786–1813* (New York, 1945) p. 84.

[18] E. von Conrady, *Leben und Werken des Generals der Infanterie... Carl von Grolman*, 3 vols. (Berlin, 1894), vol. I, pp. 45–46, and Max Lehmann, *Scharnhorst*, 2 vols. (Leipzig, 1886–7), vol. II, pp. 412–413.

The third subject of reform, tactical doctrine, remained a matter of debate. Enthusiasts like Adam Heinrich von Buelow advocated the infusion of formal training with appeals to the goodwill and natural enthusiasm of the individual soldier, supplemented when necessary by issues of alcohol.[19] Scharnhorst, Gneisenau, and a junior officer beginning to make his mark, Carl von Clausewitz, favored synthesizing the French open-order tactics with the linear formations that continued to prove their worth when appropriately handled. The declaration of war made the argument temporarily moot. Jena-Auerstädt made it temporarily irrelevant.[20]

One can reasonably describe the Prussian Army of 1806 as well into the process of adapting to the new ways of war-making developed in the previous decade. In comparative terms, it was about where the Austrians would be three years later at Wagram. Not until at least 1810 would Britain's principal field army reach the structural and administrative levels at which the Prussian Army stood immediately before Jena-Auerstädt. Nor did the army disgrace itself at the sharp end. For all their shortcomings in planning, command, and tactics, the Prussians gave the French more than a few bad quarters of an hour at Jena. At Auerstedt, however, a single French corps shattered more than twice its numbers in a single long day. But that was also probably the finest tactical performance of the entire Napoleonic era, by one of the finest fighting formations ever to take the field: Marshal Louis Nicolas Davout's III Corps.[21]

Since 1763 the Prussian Army had developed as a deterrent force in the context of a multipolar state system. By 1805 it was required to wage all-out war against a hegemonic empire with an army possessing extraordinary combat effectiveness, commanded by one of history's greatest captains. For over a decade, however, the Prussians had designed their strategy to avoid exactly that contingency. Opportunistic neutrality had served the state well since the Peace of Basel in 1795. When asked in 1805 to join the Third Coalition forming against France, Frederick William and his advisors reasoned that the prospective adversaries seemed evenly enough matched. Instead, the Austerlitz campaign left Prussia confronting an imperium that suddenly abandoned any pretenses of conciliation. Prussia went to war in September 1806, not unilaterally, but as a necessary gesture of good faith to an embryonic Fourth Coalition that would include Russia, Britain, and Sweden. Sufficient time seemed available in the normal campaigning season for one major battle. And even there, the Prussian Army had to do no more than bloody Napoleon's nose, buying time for British guineas and Russian bayonets to influence the balance. This did not represent an optimal situation,

---

[19] S. D. H von Buelow, *Neue Taktik der Neueren, wiie sie seyn sollte* (Leipzig, 1805).

[20] Heinz Sruwbig, "Berenhorst, Buelow und Scharnhorst als Kritiker der Preussischen Heeeres der nachffriderizianisch Epoche," in *Die preussische Armee zwisschen Ancien Regime und Reichsgruendung*, pp. 96–120.

[21] See the analysis in Pierre Charrier, *Le Marechal Davout* (Paris, 2005), pp. 165–208.

but neither did it seem obviously beyond the capacities of Prussia's army. The war hawks of 1806 included men of the caliber of Gneisenau, Scharnhorst, and Clausewitz, who did not see themselves as engaging in a forlorn hope.[22]

The campaign of 1806 and its aftermath, culminating in the Peace of Tilsit, cost Prussia its great power status and concentrated its official mind. Prussia's immediate fate much resembled what Austria had sought to impose on it during the Seven Years' War. Napoleon's aims in Germany were as concrete as his grand strategy was boundless. He wanted men and money. He wanted Austria kept out and discontent kept down.[23] To those ends, massive territorial losses and a huge indemnity accompanied the limiting of the Prussian Army to 42,000 without reserve or militia systems with the requirement of its presence when summoned by Napoleon. That Vienna retained its place at the head diplomatic table, albeit for the emperor's convenience, only salted wounds in Berlin.

Prussia's response to this new German order differed significantly from that of the medizing elites elsewhere in middle Germany.[24] The multiple disasters of 1806 did not discredit the mentality that for two decades previously had sought to strengthen both the state and society. The initial emphasis of what developed from individual policies into a synergized movement was not, however, directly preparing for a second round with the French. Prussia's immediate challenge was to reestablish the state as an effective part of the European order. Above all, that involved restoring the army as a force effective but non-threatening. The first steps in that process involved escaping clientage by the conquerors and establishing Prussia as an intermediate power, if only in a Central European context. After that, much would depend on events beyond Prussia's control.[25]

In July 1807 Frederick William established a reorganization commission with the following brief: determine the structure of the new Prussian Army. This was a committee in fact as well as name. Scharnhorst was its head, but it included a spectrum of positions, from committed reformers like Gneisenau and Clausewitz to more measured types like Christian von Massenbach and Hans David Yorck. In composition and behavior, it embodied the essence of the reform movement. It developed a strategy not based on emergency responses, or emergency recovery. Nor was it guided by a small cabal or

---

[22] Frederick R. Kagan, *The End of the Old Order: Napoleon and Europe, 1801–1805* (New York, 2006); and Brendan Simms, *The Impact of Napoleon: Prussian High Politics and the Creation of the Executive* (Cambridge, 1997).

[23] See the excellent contributions to *The Bee and the Eagle: Napoleonic France and the End of the Holy Roman Empire 1806*, eds. A. Forrest and P. Wilson (New York, 2009).

[24] See P. Nolte, *Staatsbildung als Gesellschaftsreform. Politische Reformen in Preussen und den sueddeutschen Staaten 1800–1820* (Frankfurt, 1990); and Matthew Leviunger, *Enlightened Nationalism: The Transformation of Prussian Political Culture, 1806–1848* (New York, 2000).

[25] Still useful in this context is Heinz Stuebig, *Armee und Nation. Die Paedagogisch-politischen Motive der preussischen Heeresreform, 1807–1814* (Frankfurt, 1971).

a single dominant figure. Instead, it built on over a quarter-century of *Aufklaerung*, of rational discourse bringing together divergent, often sharply conflicting opinions. The resulting synergy was in practice a negative consensus, based as much on defeating a common enemy as on planning for a reconfigured Prussia. The resulting compromises would not endure much past the emergency that generated them. But they lasted long enough to accomplish their initial goal.

Civil and military reform

The September 1808 Convention of Paris rigidly defined the army's post-Jena institutional framework. According to its terms, the Prussian Army was to be recruited by conscription, but limited to 42,000 soldiers. It prohibited any reserve or second-line force. Foreign enlistment had been abolished in November 1807, as much from a shortage of candidates as from principled determination to rely on Prussia's own *Landeskinder*. The historic canton system, with its elaborate structure of exemptions and limited annual periods of service, gave way to universal liability, with those conscripted serving officially for three or four years. The often cited Kruemper system of creating a reserve by more or less clandestinely replacing trained men with recruits, though never systematically implemented, was another significant element in changing Prussia's historic pattern of long service.

No less important was an emphasis on structural and institutional flexibility, initially reflected by an organization of six combined-arms brigades, eventually to be embodied in a new set of drill regulations. More important still was the abolition of social qualifications for an officer's commission. After August 1808 every man in Prussian uniform had "the same duties and the same rights"– at least in principle. The army also abolished corporal punishment except under extreme circumstances on active service. The ultimate intention of these and related innovations was less to inculcate military skill than to strengthen commitment and confidence. The military reform commission called for nurturing of a sense of involvement to actualize the latent loyalty Prussians felt for state and crown. Since the days of Frederick the Great, its members agreed, patriotism had been strong among the native peasants and townsmen who filled the army's ranks, and who perceived Prussia as more than the faceless authority behind tax collectors and conscription officials. For conservatives the new-model Prussian soldier must become an active subject of a revitalized state. For reformers the effective soldier had to be a citizen whose military service epitomized his membership in a political community. The difference between those positions, eventually significant after Napoleon's fall, seemed sufficiently abstract in the months after Jena to be tabled.[26]

---

[26] Dierk Walter, *Preussische Heeresreformen 1807–1870. Militaerische Innovation und der Mythos der Roonschen Reformen* (Paderborn, 2003), pp. 235–324, and Michael Sykora, "Militaerung

More significant for the construction of even the system permitted by the Convention of Paris was its financing. Paying the draconian indemnity levied by the Treaty of Tilsit was even more urgent. Nothing like sufficient ready cash was available for initial installments, and the treaty's terms put Prussia's sovereignty at stake if the state failed to meet the payments. The indemnity itself was 120 million francs. The real cost of defeat, however, lay in paying the expenses of a French occupation that lasted from August 1807 to December 1808 – over 200 million thalers for a state the income of which was not to exceed 30 million until 1816.

The king's senior financial advisors saw two alternatives. One involved mortgaging and selling Prussian crown land. The other was to institute a comprehensive income tax. Implementing either required agreement of the provincial estates. For one man, at least, the situation offered opportunity. Frederick William had dismissed Baron vom Stein in spring 1807, as "refractory, insolent, obstinate, and disobedient." In October the king recalled him in spite of these qualities – or perhaps because of them.[27] Stein's first aim was to use the existing financial crisis as leverage to reform the estates as a first step toward a Prussian representative institution.

In January 1808 the East Prussian Diet was summoned as a trial balloon. With its structure and functions expanded from strictly financial matters to general consultation on public affairs, it even approved an income tax. But attempts to extend the tax to other provinces foundered. To civil administrators formed by the theories of mercantilism, Prussia's economy was at best a fragile thing, requiring comprehensive state management and efficient participation by its subjects. Bringing the truncated kingdom's finances into order and under control left little room for drastically overhauling the social and economic distinctions under which the state had previously prospered.[28]

The government's policy of "flight forward" loosened what might have become a Gordian knot by the implementation of land reform. The developing British blockade of the continent now further affected Prussia's commercial and industrial capacities, limited as they were before 1806. On an intellectual level, the French physiocracy's support for government intervention in an agricultural sector that was the ultimate source of surplus wealth interacted with Adam Smith's application of free market principles to agricultural development. Prussia's rural order was unraveling. Rapid population

---

und Zivilizierung. Die Preussische Heeresreform und ihre Ambivalenzen," in *Preussische Armee zwischen Ancien Regime und Reichsgruending*, pp. 164–175, combine the most up-to-date perception of the military reforms.

[27] Hans Duchwardt, *Stein. Eine Biographie* (Muenster, 2007) is the most recent and comprehensive work on the great reformer.

[28] Bernd Muenchenow-Pohl, *Zwischen Reform und Krieg. Untersuchungen zur Bewusstseinslage in Preussen, 1807–1812* (Goettingen, 1987), pp. 3ff. See also the documents in *Preussische Finanzpolitik 1806–1810: Quellen zur Verwaltung die Ministerien Stein und Altenstein*, eds. E. Kehr, H. Schissler, and H.-U. Wehler (Goettingen, 1984).

growth after the Seven Years' War had significantly increased both the supply of labor and the demand for grain. Landowners were finding it easier to hire workers than to maintain increasingly complex systems of labor service. Well-off rural communities, even individuals, were acquiring enough surplus cash either to fight feudal obligations in court, or simply to hire substitutes.

Comprehensive dissatisfaction thus underwrote the edict of 9 October 1807. It included a number of specific provisions. By ending restrictions on the sale of noble-owned land, it created a de facto free market on land. The act created a similar free market in labor, opening occupations to all social classes and abolishing serfdom. In many ways the edict was a preliminary document. It did not address the question of who owned peasant land, or settle the issue of whether labor services as a form of rent remained enforceable. It took almost a decade to iron out these and similar details in the debates characteristic of the bureaucratic *Aufklaerung*.[29] The free market in labor also addressed a military question. Official figures had listed over 2.3 million cantonists available in 1805. Even where the existing legal exemptions continued, over 300,000 could be conscripted in a given year without summoning the unfit, middle-aged, and the less physically capable. Under universal service, the number would double, and no one in the Prussian government seriously expected the artificially truncated post-Jena force structure to endure.[30]

Stein's eventual successor as chancellor, Karl von Hardenberg, had no better success when he sought to get landowners and bankers to cooperate informally in liquidating the state's debts through a national bank. His finance edict of October 1810 was a statist response, proclaiming the goals of equalizing tax burdens and creating freedom of occupation. A second edict a month later allowed anyone to practice any enterprise by paying an annual tax. Like Stein, Hardenberg reasoned that financial engagement would encourage political participation, which in turn would lead to the ultimate goal of parliamentary institutions encouraging public harmony through institutionalized patriotism. Like Stein, however, he encountered a Prussia that at its roots remained more of a geographical expression than the state-level innovators were willing to recognize. Jena and Tilsit by themselves were not sufficient to

---

[29] The best contextualization of land reform in any language is William W. Hagen, *Ordinary Prussians: Brandenburg Junkers and Villagers, 1500–1840* (Cambridge, 2002). More specific is Hartmut Harnisch, "Vom Oktoberedikt des Jahres 1807 zur Deklaration von 1816: Problematik und charackter der preussische Agrarreformgesetzgebung zwischen 1807 und 1816," *Jahrbuch fuer Wirtschaftsgeschcihte*, Special Issue, 1978, pp. 231–293.

[30] See J. Kloosterhuis, ed., *Bauern, Buerger und Soldaten: Quellen zur Sozialisation des Militärsystems im preußischen Westfalen 1713–1803*, 2 vols. (Muenster, 1992); Dierk Walter, "Meeting the French Challenge: Conscription in Prussia, 1807–1815," in D. Stoker, F. Schneid, and H. Blanton, eds., *Conscription in the Naopleonic Era: A Revolution in Military Affairs?* (London, 2009), pp. 24–45; Ute Frevert, "Das jakobinische Modell: Allgemeine Wehrpflicht und Nationsbildung in preussen-deutschland," in U. Frevert, ed., *Militaer und Gesellschaft im 19. und 20. Jahrhundetrs* (Stuttgart, 1997), pp. 18–27.

disturb a network of local and regional traditions and behaviors, where informal behavior shaped formal structures, and where law and custom interfaced.[31]

State authority offered a possible shortcut. Historians have widely blamed the efflorescently collegial nature of the Prussian cabinet system as a major factor in the disaster of 1806. Two centuries of ad hoc adaptations had created a structure where government through influence had largely replaced diffused and confused responsibility. Frederick William III had not only consistently failed to impose his will on his advisors; he had ascribed his own indecision to the conflicting pressures of grayer, presumably wiser, heads. It was a position sufficiently comfortable that it took much persuasion, some of it spousal, before the king approved a streamlined structure in November 1808. As finally reorganized, the Prussian cabinet included five ministries, each with a defined set of functions, each with the right of direct access to the monarch. Expected to encourage direct discussion of policy issues at the expense of behind the scenes manipulation and to facilitate rapid, coherent decision making, the new system represented an improvement over its predecessor. Nevertheless, it remained essentially collegial rather than authoritarian.[32]

Thus, Prussia's post-Jena, post-Tilsit state strategy rested on the synergistic reform of four secondary structures: military, financial, occupational, and administrative. All four reforms generated widespread, bitter opposition based on other powerful synergies of principle and interest. Patrimonial powers and jurisdictions generated legal protests and civil disobedience from nobility and peasantry alike. The reformers themselves, moreover, were significantly divided on questions of details on one hand, implications on the other. An *Aufklaerung* dominated by intellectuals and officials had not generated a mentality of urgency. There had always seemed time for discussion and persuasion, time for ideas to churn and settle, time for opponents to find a middle ground. In any case, Prussia's ability to apply direct force to domestic opposition was sorely limited. Forty thousand men could not maintain armed control indefinitely. Prussia's only chance to recover its status under the conditions prevailing involved presenting a united front that at the same time seemed non-threatening.

Evaluating the initial achievements of Prussia's institutional reforms is in good part a question of perspective. Are they best judged by what was done, or by what remained to do? One historian of the period describes the reforms as

---

[31] See Ernst Klein, *Von der Reform zur Restauration. Finanzreform und Reformgesetzgebung des preussischen Staatskanzlers Karl August von Harfenberg* (Berlin, 1967); and Barbara Vogel, *Allgemeine Gewerrbefreiheit: die Reformpolitik des preussischen StaatskanzlersHardenberg (1810–1820)* (Goettingen, 1983).

[32] Hans Rosenberg, *Bureaucracy, Aristocracy, and Autocracy: The Prussian Experience, 1669–1815* (Cambridge, MA, 1958) and Thomas Stamm-Kuhlmann, *Koenig in Preussens grosser Zeit. Friedrich William III, der Melancholiker auf dem Thron* (Berlin, 1992), pp. 340ff.

"acts of communication" presented in "plebescitary rhetoric."[33] To take effect, such rhetoric could not be presented in a vacuum. A comprehensive program of educational reform initiated in 1808, structured and guided by Wilhelm von Humboldt, promised wonders: "new Prussian men," developed in schools that taught their students how to think for themselves. As early as 18, he had begun designing a comprehensive system ranging from state-run elementary schools, through secondary gymnasiums for the classical and practical education of the elite, to the new University of Berlin. Results, however, were decades away.[34]

In immediate and emotional contexts, reformers and conservatives found particular common ground in a sense of unique victimization. After 1806 an increasing body of emotion insisted that Prussia was suffering tribulations meriting special recognition. Conservatives developed systematic depictions and defenses of the "old Prussian" virtues threatened by Napoleon and those Germans who believed the best way to beat the French was to become like them.[35] Reformers made no secret of their conviction that a revitalized Prussia would become a lodestone and magnet for Germany. The legends that grew up around Frederick the Great had already generated a sense – at least among Protestants – that Prussia was special, different from both the universalist Austrian Empire and the parish-pump principalities of the west and south.[36]

The German "nation of the self," based on individual consciousness, was a product of the late eighteenth century. Before its existence there was an external "Germany of the senses": sight, space, and sound, a physical way of understanding the world.[37] In that latter context, post-Jena Prussia emerged as a monarchical nation, integrating its ethnic and religious communities into a wider community that epitomized a German nation whose unity rested on a shared history, language, and culture.[38] Popular nationalism was essentially an urban, Protestant, literate, bourgeois phenomenon. At a time of social and

---

[33] Clark, *Iron Kingdom*, p. 342.

[34] Clemens Menze, *Die Bildungsreform Wilhelm von Humboldts* (Dortmund, 1975); and Tillman Bosche, *Wilhelm von Humboldt* (Munich, 1990).

[35] See particularly Robert Berdahl, *The Politics of the Prussian Nobility: The Development of a Conservative Ideology 1770–1848* (Princeton, 1988).

[36] See in particular Thomas Stamm-Kuhlmann, "'Man vertraue doch der Administration!' Staatsverstaendnis und Regierungshandeln des preussiscnen Staatskanzlers Karl von Hardenberg," *Historische Zeitschrift*, vol. 264, 1997, pp. 613–654; Joerg Echterkamp, *Der Aufstieg der deutschen Nationalismus* (Frankfurt, 1997); and Levinger, *Enlightened Nationalism* (New York, 2000).

[37] Helga Schultz, "Mythos und Aufklaerung: Fruehformen des Nationalaismus in Deutschland," *Historische Zeitschrift*, vol. 263, 1996, pp. 31–67. Cf. Hagen Schulze, *Der Weg zum Nationalstaat: Die deutsche Nationalbewegung vom 18. Jahrhundert bis zur Reichsgruendung* (Munich, 1985); and Hans-Maartin Blitz, *Aus Liebe zum Vaterland. Die deutsche Nation im 18. Jahrhundert* (Hamburg, 2000).

[38] Manfred Harnisch, "Nationalisierung der Dynastie oder Monarchisierung der Nation? Zum Verhaeltnis von Monarchie und Nation in Deutschland im 19. Jahrhundert," in A. Birke et al., eds., *Buergertum, Adel und Monarchie. Zum Wandlr der Lebensform im Zeitalter der buerglichen Nationalstaat* (Munich, 1989), pp. 71–92.

economic uncertainty, geographic mobility was increasingly common among soldiers, officials, and clergymen. Degrees from Halle, Goettingen, and Berlin were universal currency between the Rhine and the Vistula. Expanding public employment attracted the underemployed and marginally employed willing to seek opportunities anywhere their linguistic and educational profiles offered. Wanderers between worlds, they were simultaneously engaged by the concepts of meritocratic egalitarianism and community solidarity.

A German intelligentsia that had increasingly discovered the appeals of political community and as yet possessed little immunity to its negatives reinforced this mindset. After 1800 "nation," "people" and "fatherland" were used interchangeably, in Prussian and in German contexts. Fichte's *Reden an die Deutsche Nation* (Speeches to the German Nation) were delivered in Berlin. From Berlin Friedrich Schleiermacher issued his call for a Germany combining cultural identity and political patriotism. Professors and clergymen extolled the German fatherland from lecture halls and pulpits. That did not mean unreflecting endorsement of the Prussian model. Fichte, for example, eloquently denounced the contributions of Frederick William III to the catastrophe of 1806. Not for the last time, however, advocates of a vision transcending state boundaries and state loyalties saw Prussia as a fulcrum in spite of itself.[39]

The cultural and intellectual mobilization nurtured by the reform movement fostered significant changes in gender identity as well. Middle-class males needed encouragement to accept military service which their community largely rejected. *Aufklaerung*/Pietist/bourgeois ideals of family-oriented "gentle masculinity" attached little value to physical courage or prowess. Abstract promises of political rights in return for military service likely generated abstract responses among men who on an everyday basis had more obviously appealing things to do with their lives than risk them in war. The process of modification involved a redefinition of masculinity. Its previous foci had been intellectual, religious, and cultural, increasingly in domestic environments: "hearth and home." Friedrich Wilhelm Jahn, "the Father of Gymnastics," began by asserting that only a reassertion of physicality in broad public contexts, from "power walking" to competitive games, could recover Germany's language and culture.[40]

The concept had its clearest resonance among the bourgeoisie, but its popularity with young men transcended social class. Physicality's relationship to military service developed quickly in the years prior to the Wars of Liberation in the context of the development of a general ideology of revenge.

[39] Karen Hagemann, "Federkrieg. Patriotische Meinungsmobilisierung im Preussen in der Zeit der Antinapoleonischen Krieges," in B. Soesemann, ed., *Kommunikation und Medien in Preussen vom 16. bis 19. Jahrhunderts* (Stuttgart, 2002), pp. 281–302; and Otto W. Johnson, *The Myth of a Nation: Literature and Politics in Prussia Under Napoleon* (Columbia, SC, 1989).

[40] Gerhard Stoecker, *Volkserziehung ind Turnen: Wuntersuchung der Grundlagen des Turnen von Fr. L. Jahn* (Schondorf, 1971).

Male courage and male duty were expressed in terms of service under arms.[41] This pattern permeated the Jewish community where numbers of urban young men volunteered for service despite a persistent hostility depicting them as "outsiders" to the Prussian and German national communities. For the next 60 years, Prussian Jews furnished sons to the draft as proof of acculturation in a society where normality was a moving target.[42]

The connection of masculinity with soldiering found literary expression as well. For a quarter-century, Goethe's Werther had been the archetype of the labile male who defines himself by his paralyzingly exquisite sensitivity, to the point where suicide is preferable to action. That model was increasingly challenged and displaced by action-focused prototypes, best illustrated in the works of Theodor Koerner. Born in Dresden, his literary achievements secured him a place as court poet in Austria. In 1813, he joined the war against Napoleon in a volunteer unit, the Luetzow Freikorps, the soldiers of which swore allegiance to Germany.[43] His patriotic poetry depicted war as a means of self-realization and self-fulfillment through sacrifice for a great cause – "the soldier not as citizen but as artist." Koerner's own heroism, culminating in his death in combat, made him a model for the "heroic youth" of the middle classes, the archetype of the *Befreiungskrieg* (war of liberty).[44]

Its expression in familial contexts further refined the archetype. In France the soldier's familial role was an aspect of defending *la patrie*, whether republic or empire. Its popular portrayals emphasized collective contexts: recruits leaving home as a preliminary to their integration into the army. In Prussia that imagery was reversed. German popular representations were domestic and patriarchal, centering on the father blessing his son or sons as they depart for war. The mother wears an expression of mixed pride and concern. In various backgrounds younger brothers look on admiringly. Teenage sisters busy themselves with presumably supportive needlework. The Bible is on the table; patriotic artifacts ordain the walls. Unlike their French counterparts, these young men will not be entering a community of arms. They will create that community by their service and sacrifice.[45]

The image is strongly gendered, but not gender exclusive. In particular, it assigned aristocratic and middle-class women proactive, public roles

---

[41] See Karen Hagemann, *"Mannlicher Muth und Teutsche Ehre." Nation, Militaer und Geschlecht zur Zeit der Antinapoleonischen Kriege Preussens* (Paderborn, 2002), pp. 255ff.; and Anne Charlott-Trepp, *Sanfte Maennlichkeit und selbststaendige Weiblichkeit* (Goettingen, 1996).
[42] Horst Fischer, *Judentum, Staat und Heer. In Preussen im fruehen 19. Jahrhundert* (Tuebingen, 1968).
[43] Peter Brandt, "Einstellungen, Motiven und Ziele von Kriegsfreiwilligen 1813/14: Das Freikorps Luetzow," in J. Duelffer, ed., *Kriegsbererritschaft und Friedensordnung in Deutscakand: 1800–1814* (Muenster, 1995), pp. 21–33.
[44] Eric C. Kollman, *Theodor Korener. Militaer u. Politik* (Munich, 1973).
[45] Karen Hagemann, "The Military and Masculinity: Gendering the History of the Revolutionary and Napoleonic Wars," in R. Chickering and S. Foerster, eds., *War in an Age of Revolution, 1775–1816* (Cambridge, 2010), pp. 331–352.

heretofore discouraged by religion and culture. In general these were exten-
sions of maternal, supportive functions: knitting items of personal clothing;
cutting back domestic expenses; donating jewelry; collecting money; perform-
ing auxiliary nursing duties; seeing to the welfare of the families left behind
by mobilized artisans and peasants. The general emphasis was maternal:
Prussian womanhood collectively nurturing its sons. But public support of
men marching to war was also a major element, especially in towns with
garrisons and located on marching routes. A flower or a kiss freely given did
not mean automatic social derogation.[46]

The makings of revolt

Political or cultural, the reform initiatives did not take place in a vacuum.
Though formal French occupation ended with the Treaty of Tilsit, the actual
withdrawal of the troops took time. Even then, French clients and satellites,
including the particularly unwelcome Grand Duchy of Warsaw, created at
Tilsit, surrounded Prussia. Nor was the concept of recovering status by
cooperating with France an obviously forlorn hope. For at least a decade
before 1806, the dominant French position had been that Prussia was better
conciliated than fought. Prussian leaders for their part remained cool. Napoleon rewarded their neutrality in 1802 at the Peace of Lunéville with extensive
territorial gains in northern Germany. When French troops overran the
Electorate of Hanover in 1803, French diplomats followed established precedent in suggesting that Prussian patience would be well rewarded. And in fact
Prussian troops occupied Hanover in October 1805 as the French withdrew.[47]

From its beginning, the nature of the French occupation wrecked Prussian
hopes of at least moving toward something approximating the pre-Jena relationship. French behavior and attitude from the emperor to unit quartermasters were those of long-term conquerors, not potential allies. The views of the
rank and file were summarized in the aphorism "want-take-have," a pattern
exacerbated as Prussia even after Tilsit remained a highway for soldiers moving
across the empire. Any remaining optimists considering a French connection
had only to consult statistics. Tilsit reduced Prussia's territory by half, its
population from 10 million to a little over 4.5 million. In an era when land and
people were the touchstones of prosperity and power, Napoleon's intentions
could hardly have been more obvious. The growing numbers of officials
unpaid or dismissed as well as growing numbers of bankrupt businesses and
estates suggested not temporary crisis but permanent catastrophe.[48]

---

[46] Karen Hagemann, "Female Patriots: Women, War and the Nation in the Period of the
Prussian–German Anti-Napoleonic Wars," *Gender & History*, vol. 16, 2004.

[47] Philip G. Dwyer, "Politics of Prussian Neutrality," *German History*, vol. 12, 1994, pp. 251–272.

[48] Karen Hagemann, 'Occupation, Mobilization, and Politics: The Anti-Napoleonic Wars in
Prussian Experience, Memory, and Historiography,' *Central European History*, vol. 39,
2006, pp. 589–592. For the growing antagonism generated in Baden, Wuerttemberg, and

The reforms initiated in 1807–1808 did little either to allay French suspicion or to alleviate public malaise. Anti-French sentiment was high, but essentially verbal and increasingly routine in the minds of the French agents omnipresent in what remained of Prussia. State-initiated changes, by adding financial burdens and challenging traditional values, only enhanced popular angst and alienation. In such contexts any thought of a general uprising in the short term was a pure abstraction.[49]

In spring 1809, Austrian Foreign Minister Philipp Stadion transformed his long-nurtured project of a vengeance war against France into military action. From Stein and Scharnhorst downwards, influential ministers and generals coalesced into an active war party. But Frederick William's dry observation that "a political existence, be it ever so small, is better than none" outweighed Stein's exhortation that "it is more glorious ... to fall with weapons in hand than patiently to allow ourselves to be clapped in chains." The fact that Stein delivered his rhetoric from exile in Austria, where he had fled after being declared an enemy of France by Napoleon, further diminished its effect. At the time the emperor, completing what seemed the conquest of Spain, barely considered Prussia as a potential nuisance.[50] Not surprisingly, Frederick William concluded that to sit tight was the best option. Prussia remained neutral. A few unofficial outbursts culminated when Major Ferdinand von Schill took his hussars on a "long ride" from history into myth and legend in a vain attempt to incite a rebellion. Schill died fighting. Eleven of the officers who followed him faced firing squads. For reformers and resisters, Schill's expedition to nowhere was a warning and an encouragement: systematic, comprehensive preparation was necessary. The conciliators, for their part, could only derive the negative comfort that things could always get worse.[51]

That prospect came true as Napoleon prepared his apocalyptic invasion of Russia.[52] Well before the campaign began, Prussia became a concentration zone for an army whose collective behavior reflected the worst of a hardened *soldateska* on one hand and poorly trained, ill-disciplined levies on the other. Seed grain disappeared into *Grande Armée* haversacks. Where horses were not

---

Bavaria by Napoleon's state of permanent occupation see Uthe Planert, *Der Mythos vom Befreiungskrieg. Frankreichs Kriege und der deutschenSueden: Alltag-Wahrnehmung-Deutung 1792–1841* (Paderborn, 2007).

[49] Echterkamp, *Aufstieg der deutschen Nationalismus*, pp. 167ff.

[50] Allen Vann, "Habsburg Policy and the Austrian War of 1809," *Central European History*, vol. 7, 1974, pp. 219–310; Stamm-Kuhlmann, *Melancholiker auf dem Thron*, p. 304.

[51] Sam A. Mustafa, *The Long Ride of Major von Schill: A Journey Through German History and Memory* (New York, 2008).

[52] The following narrative is based on Hagemann, "Occupation," pp. 593–694; Bernd von Muenchenow-Poehl, *Preussen Zwischen Reform und Krieg*, pp. 94ff.; and Rudolf Ibbeken, *Preussen 1807–1813; Staat und Volk als Idee und in Wirklichkeit.* (Koeln, 1970), pp. 376ff. Cf. Peter Paret, *Yorck and the Era of Prussian Reform, 1807–1815* (Princeton, 1966), pp. 155 *passim*; and Theodor Schiemann, "Die Wuerdigung der Konvention von Tauroggen," *Historische Zeitschrift*, vol. 84, 1900, pp. 210–243.

forthcoming, peasants were harnessed in their place. On 24 February 1812, Frederick William concluded, at diplomatic pistol point, one of history's more one-sided alliances. Napoleon required Prussia to furnish 30,000 men, and that was only the beginning. Over 700,000 tons of flour, well over 1 million tons of forage, 6 million bushels of oats, 15,000 horses, 44,000 oxen, and not least 2 million bottles of beer and the same amount of brandy was the material price. The moral and political price was whatever shreds of credibility and honor remained to a Prussia, the title of which had become a joke and a reproach.

The Prussian people received the reports of French defeats with great delight. When the remnants of Napoleon's Grand Army straggled back into East Prussia, a peasantry left with "nothing but eyes to weep" took revenge with flails and scythes. Tavern brawls spread into the streets as fists and clubs gave way to knives. Napoleon's response was to request more men and supplies from Prussia. Despite increasing pressure to denounce the alliance, Frederick William favored great power negotiations at least as an interim approach. Yorck, the commander of the Prussian auxiliary corps serving under French colors, forced the king's hand. The general negotiated an armistice allowing Russian troops to enter Prussian territory. The go-between was none other than Clausewitz, who like a number of other Prussian officers, had chosen Russia over Prussia, a decision the king never forgave. The Prussian contingent had fought well on the northern flank of Napoleon's drive on Moscow, but had also distinguished itself by refusing to cheer the emperor when he inspected them. Disaffection among the officers was rife, and it metastasized among the rank and file when a French retreat left the Prussians isolated. Yorck was identified with the reform movement as a tactical progressive. He was also socially conservative to his fingertips and correspondingly loyal to the concept of the monarchy. In the waning days of December 1812, he faced a choice: seek to break through to the west, or negotiate with the Russians for the sake of his men – and for a wider cause as well.

The Convention of Tauroggen was an act of mutiny and treason, justified by appealing, cautiously and in circumlocutions, to the authority of the Prussian "nation," and by challenging Frederick William to "breathe life and enthusiasm back into everything." It allowed Yorck to engage "the true enemy."[53] Frederick William reacted by relieving Yorck of his command, but the Russians blocked the missive's delivery. Yorck remained a central figure in Tauroggen's aftermath as East Prussia slipped into de facto insurrection. This time, words were underwritten with the raising of a local militia based on universal service, Jews included.

Despite his enduring fear of Napoleon as well as his visceral desire to remain on good terms with France, Frederick William began moving in the

---

[53] The letter is reprinted in Schiemann, ibid, pp. 229–232.

direction of resistance. He left Potsdam for Breslau in response to rumors that the French intended to arrest him. He recalled Scharnhorst from retirement and authorized raising volunteer "free corps." Not until the end of February, however, did Prussia's king finally commit to changing sides, in return for Russian guarantees of the approximate restoration of the 1806 frontiers and compensation for territory to be included in Russia's new client Kingdom of Poland. Prussia declared war on Napoleon on 16 March. The royal address "To My People" the next day simultaneously defended the previous policies of caution and called for a general uprising against the French. Frederick William went even further in his 25 March Proclamation of Kalisch, in which he joined Czar Alexander of Russia in proclaiming support for a united Germany.

These and similar gestures reflected the king's growing fear of Russia, whose troops were flowing into East Prussia in ever greater numbers. They were also a response to Frederick William's no less significant fear of being swamped by an irresistible tide of enthusiasm from below. But how was the general uprising proclaimed with such apparent boldness to be conducted and constructed? The "Order on the Organization of the *Landwehr*," also issued on 17 March, made service in this new force obligatory for every male between 17 and 40. A month later, a second edict established a home guard, the *Landsturm*, the officers of which were to be elected, albeit from selected social and professional groups. Put together, the two documents offered at least the potential matrix for a movement that might, in the pattern of Revolutionary France, sweep away what remained of Prussia's old order and its still-embryonic structure of reforms. A "war of books" began as a tide of patriotic, nationalist, warmongering publications flooded Prussia with the full support of the authorities. Poems, songs, and sermons underwrote the call to arms.[54]

Prussia's actual strategy was more measured. Its essence, as the Sixth Coalition against Napoleon emerged and the campaigning season approached in spring 1813, aimed at positioning Prussia to best advantage. This in turn involved striking a balance on two levels: the first required reconciling the rhetoric and reality of Prussia as the focal point of a war of liberation and as a participant in an alliance of monarchies committed ideologically to quenching such popular enthusiasm. The second involved establishing Prussia as a fulcrum between the coalition's principal players: a Russia the ruler of which had his own semi-hegemonic ambitions and who considered Prussia a junior partner; an Austria that came on side slowly and reluctantly and trusted Prussia not at all; and a collection of small German states, recent allies of Napoleon, who trusted Prussia even less, because the compensation Russia offered Prussia for

---

[54] See Dorothea Schmidt, *Die preussische Landwehr. Ein Beitrag zur Geschichte der Allgemeine Wehrpflicht in Preussen, zweischen 1813 and 1830* (Berlin [DDR], 1981); Hagemann, *Maennlicher Muth*, pp. 396ff.

its lost Polish territory was the Kingdom of Saxony. And if one of Napoleon's erstwhile German allies were thus to be sacrificed to Czar Alexander's new European order, what might the rest expect?[55]

Key to the policy aspects of this conundrum was Karl von Hardenberg, Prussia's chancellor since 1810. His initial focus had been on domestic issues, but he had retained his connection to the reform movement and played a significant behind-the-scenes role in Frederick William's decision to switch sides. For the next two years, he proved a no less astute diplomat. Austria's formal accession to the coalition in August 1813 represented a welcome reinforcement of troops and funds, albeit still a potential one. It also established a counterweight to Alexander in the person of Austria's foreign minister, Clemens Metternich. As the two worked to outmaneuver each other in differences as much personal as political, Hardenberg feared becoming either a Russian client or an Austrian catspaw. Thus, he brokered, shifted, and juggled to secure Prussia's role as makeweight, albeit a suitably compensated one. The prize of Saxony never left his mind. Achieving that at minimal diplomatic cost was the rub.

Frederick William, whose congenital caution reasserted itself, was even less willing to be caught between Russia and Austria, even at the price of a negotiated peace. The king and chancellor, however, agreed on Prussia's best card in the diplomatic game. That was the army. Throughout the campaign of 1813–1814, it proved both a formidable instrument of war and sufficiently institutionally flexible to keep from bursting at the seams. The concept of a "people's rising," a *Volkserhebung*, had never been popular among Prussia's leaders. After Schill's fiasco, it seemed mere fustian and bombast. A people's army, a *Volksheer*, was another matter. The images of the new-model Prussian soldier developed in 1807–1808 had been increasingly translated into realities. Half of each Prussian infantry regiment was trained as light infantry – the highest proportion of any European army. As embodied in the new 1812 drill regulations, Prussian tactics now rested on the coordination of skirmishers to wear an enemy down by extended fire-fights and small, flexible columns that sought out weak spots for a final combined-arms thrust.[56]

---

[55] The literature on the military and diplomatic aspects of the campaigns of 1813–1814 is vast and still growing. Best in English among the new overviews are Dominic Lieven, *Russia against Napoleon* (New York, 2009), pp. 285–520; and Charles Esdaile, *Napoleon's Wars: An International History, 1803–1815* (New York, 2007), pp. 490–530. Paul W. Schroeder, *The Transformation of European Politics, 1763–1848* (Oxford, 1994) is superb in presenting and contextualizing the diplomacy of the period. Enno E. Krahe, *Metternich's German Policy,* vol. I: *The Contest With Napoleon, 1799–1814* (Princeton, 1963) is solid for details from its protagonist's perspective.

[56] Walter, *Preussische Heeresreformen 1807–1870*, pp. 143–166, 235–324, is state of the art in scholarship and reasoning. Dennis E. Showalter, "The Prussian *Landwehr* and its Critics, 1813–1819," *Central European History*, vol. 4, 1971, remains useful. Underlying the academic analysis is the mine of detailed institutional information in Grosser Generalstab, *Der preussische Armee der Befreiungskrieg*, 2 vols. (Berlin, 1912–1920).

These were tactics ill-suited for striking decisive, independent blows in the context of the increasingly massive forces that marched and fought across Germany and into France. Leipzig, "the Battle of the Nations" on 16–19 October 1813, involved over 600,000 soldiers. Not until the First World War would a single battle exceed that number. Army corps increasingly gave way to field armies as the basic unit of combat and maneuver.[57] Only first-rate troops, moreover, could display the shaping tactics evoked by the reformers: to deploy as skirmishers, withdraw, rally, and return now in line and now in column, as the tactical situation changed. Partial mobilizations beginning in January 1813 brought Prussia's active army to approximately 65,000 in March: serving soldiers, reservists of all kinds, and some volunteers. These were Prussia's main contribution to the spring campaign that ended in an armistice on 4 June. They made a favorable impression on friend and foe alike with their skill in skirmishing and marksmanship, particularly in the hard-fought early engagements of Luetzen and Bautzen.[58] But they were relatively few, and thus a wasting asset.

When hostilities resumed in the fall, each regiment had formed a duplicate reserve regiment. The bulk of Prussia's contribution, however, came from the 113,000 *Landwehr* more or less ready. In the "core provinces" of Old Prussia, Neumark, Kurmark, Pomerania, and East Prussia, enrolling *Landwehr* had faced few difficulties. Between the Vistula River and the Russian border, where the French presence had been most oppressive, almost half of those between 16 and 45 entered service in the first ten months. Elsewhere enthusiasm was less marked. Ethnic and religious differences in Silesia and West Prussia made willingness to serve so low that it was frequently inspired at bayonet point. The regional differences were sufficient that most *Landwehr* recruits were chosen by lot. That method had been the basis of recruiting in the cantonal system and was correspondingly familiar and acceptable. Particularly in rural areas, moreover, enough behind the scenes finagling took place to insure that high proportions of those selected were socially expendable: young, poor, and restless enough to see the army as, if not a means of liberty, at least a new form of servitude.

Once sworn in, Prussia's new defenders accepted their situation with a minimum of overt complaint despite a general lack of everything from boots to muskets. A system of local recruiting that as far as possible kept men with friends, neighbors, and relatives together and placed local officials, landowners, and professional men in immediate command facilitated

---

[57] On this point see Robert M, Epstein, "Patterns of Change and Continuity in Nineteenth-Century Warfare," *The Journal of Military History*, vol. 56, 1992, pp. 375–388.

[58] See George Naaziger, *Luetzen and Bautzen: Napoleon's Spring Campaign of 1813* (Chicago, 1992); and Peter Hofsschroer, *Luetzzen and Bautzen 1813: The Turning Point* (Oxford, 2001).

acculturation. One may reasonably suggest that the propaganda intended for the bourgeoisie had some secondary effect among the *Landwehr*'s peasants and artisans. Even more likely is that the religious sentiments noted as present in the Seven Years' War served to support endurance and to inspire blood-thirstiness.[59] Certainly the evidence indicates that, despite a lack of training, the *Landwehr* demonstrated in the war's early fighting a ferocity that at times shocked the professional officers who exercised its company and battalion commands.

The numerical expansion after the summer Armistice of Plaeswitz nevertheless diminished operational effectiveness. Units themselves, often newly raised, found themselves milked for cadres for even less experienced formations, then brought back to strength by officers and men untrained in the new methods, and often in no methods at all. The tendency toward mass that characterized Prussian tactics in the Wars of Liberation progressed in part because of limited ability at brigade and battalion levels to execute the sophisticated punches of tactical concepts originally designed to maximize the effectiveness of numerically limited forces.[60] Nor was the command structure exactly a band of brothers. There had been neither time nor opportunity to produce a new cadre of general officers. Soldiers in the post-Frederician mold, such as Friedrich von Buelow, Boguslav von Tauentzien, and Yorck himself led the corps, divisions, and brigades. Fundamentally, they saw the cause of Prussia's defeat in 1806 as the result less of structural problems than of specific defects and were increasingly critical of the reformers' ideas of recreating state and society from the ground up. The stresses of campaign and battle periodically transformed tensions to flash points, and absorbed will and thought better focused on Napoleon.[61]

Considered in a comparative perspective, however, the picture looks different. Austria was consistently unwilling to commit its forces to high-risk operations. The Russian contingent was tough and willing, but was far from home, short of replacements and supplies, and on the edge of being fought out. Troops from German states recently part of the French imperium were

[59] Cf. Sascha Moebius, *Mehr Angst vor dem Offizier als vor dem Feind?* (Saarbruecken, 2007), pp. 106ff.; Hagemann, *Mannlicher Muth*, pp. 271ff.
[60] Andrew Uffindell and Andrew Roberts, *The Eagle's Last Triumph: Napoleon's Victory at Ligny, June 1815*, new edn. (London, 2006) is an excellent case study of the Prussian Army in action from an opponent's perspective and demonstrates the point. It should be noted that the *Landwehr* veterans of 1813–1814 were not required to serve in 1815.
[61] Michael Leggiere, *Napoleon and Berlin: The Franco-Prussian War in North Germany* (Norman, OK, 2002) and *The Fall of Napoleon, 1813–1814*, vol. I: *The Invasion of France* (Cambridge, 2007) contextualize the Prussian Army's operational effectiveness. I gratefully acknowledge Prof. Leggiere's courtesy in allowing me to read a pre-publication draft of the forthcoming second volume, *The Eagle and the Cross: Napoleon and Prussia: The Struggle for Germay in 1813*, an outstanding work focusing on the Prussian Army's structure and performance during the 1813 campaign.

uncertain just where best to point their guns. In operational matters the allied high command remained consistently divided and indecisive.[62]

The Prussian Army might not have been as formidable as its Frederician predecessor. Operating within a coalition held together by the lowest common denominator of defeating Napoleon, however, it was at the cutting edge of effectiveness and fighting spirit. Marshal Gebhard von Bluecher, a fierce old soldier whose character and behavior harked back to the Thirty Years' War and prefigured the Erwin Rommels and Walther Models of a later century, set the army's tone in allied councils.[63] No one ever accused Bluecher of having any more social polish or strategic insight than he actually needed, but he led from the front. "Marshal Forward's" rough tongue, his unfailing courage, and his straightforward sense of honor inspired the inexperienced conscripts in the ranks of the army's line regiments and the *Landwehr*.

Bluecher knew only one way of making war: fight without letup. This mindset was shared by Gneisenau, his chief of staff, an early and defining example of the kind of intergenerational collaboration Scharnhorst had sought to generate. Neither was popular with his allied counterpart. The Austrian chief of staff, the future Field Marshal Joseph von Radetzky, described Gneisenau as being in the pay of foreign powers.[64] Even Frederick William considered him dangerously reckless. But by the turn of the year, with allied troops poised to strike into France, the army's performance had sufficiently impressed both the king and Hardenberg that they agreed on it as Prussia's trump card. That Hardenberg was more willing than his monarch to play it was a matter of detail. Even though at times by default, it was the Prussians who took a consistent lead in demanding action as well as negotiation. It was Prussia that reminded its coalition partners that peace was contingent on victory, and that victory depended on preserving unity. Ultimately, even Frederick William agreed that the coalition must depose Napoleon.[65] And during the coda of the Hundred Days, it was Prussia, personified once more by Bluecher, that fulfilled the spirit as well as the letter of alliance to pull the Duke of Wellington's chestnuts from the fire of Waterloo and transform "a damned near-run thing" into a decisive victory.[66]

In these contexts, the smooth and rapid integration of Prussia into the new German Confederation stands among the least logical consequences of the

---

[62] See Robert M. Epstein, "Aspects of Military and Operational Effectiveness of the Armies of France, Austria, Russia and Prussia in 1813," in F. C. Schneid, ed., *The Projection and Limitations of Imperial Powers, 1618–1850* (Leiden, 2012), pp. 122–148.

[63] Roger Parkinson, *The Hussar General: Life of Bluecher, Man of Waterloo* (London, 1975) has no scholarly pretensions but compensates by generally reliable data.

[64] Leggiere, *Fall of Napoleon*, vol. I, p. 29.

[65] See ibid., vol. I; and Andrew Uffindell, *Napoleon 1814: The Invasion of France* (Barnsley, 2009).

[66] Peter Hofschroer overstates the case – but not by much – in *1815, The Waterloo Campaign*, 2 vols. (London, 1998–1999).

Vienna settlement. The common thread of policy recommendations across the political and ideological spectrum during the Wars of Liberation had involved Prussia developing as a European power in a German context. In other words, it recovered the status won by Frederick the Great, only with a new foundation. After 1815, however, Prussia depended on an army of short-service conscripts brought to war strength by mobilized reservists. This was not a force well suited to policies of limited intimidation. Its similarity to the French *levée en masse*, combined initially with Prussia's image as a focal point for "progressive" forces, including nationalism, generated the risk of Prussia becoming Europe's designated successor to Napoleon's France: an objective military threat combined with a destabilizing and unpredictable ideology.

Reform and state strategy in the age of Metternich

Such a position, Prussia was neither able nor willing to sustain. If Hardenberg favored the expansion of Prussian rule and Prussian control in northwest Germany, he also understood that expansion to require a general context of cooperation, first with the small and middle-sized states, and later with Austria, for the sake of strengthening the "German center" against both a resurgent France and a Russia, the messianic emperor of which seemed to have no more sense of boundaries and limitations than Napoleon had possessed. For the sake of that objective, Hardenberg settled for only part of Saxony and followed Metternich's lead in the aftermath of the Congress despite harsh criticism from disgruntled reformers and Prussian nationalists alike.[67] For a decade after Waterloo, Prussia correspondingly and consciously assumed a facilitator's role in the Concert of Europe, the Holy Alliance of the three eastern empires, and the German Confederation.[68]

On the level of events, the key points of Prussia's state strategy in the aftermath of 1806 are relatively clear. Comprehensive military reforms were underwritten and sustained by wider social and political ones. When Napoleon's disaster in Russia forced the state's hand, the army became the fulcrum of a policy of opportunism: maximizing Prussia's position in Germany and Europe, but at limited risks and costs. This dichotomy, producing limited but acceptable results, reflected domestic disagreements about Prussia's identity and future. Initially mediated more or less successfully by the reasoned discourse of *Aufklaerung*, these tensions nevertheless brought

---

[67] Philip Dwyer, "The Two Faces of Prussian Foreign Policy: Karl August von Hardenberg as Minister for Foreign Affairs, 1804–1815," in T. Stamm-Kuhlmann, ed., *"Freier Gebrauch der Kraefte." Eine Bestandsaufnahme der Hardenberg-Forschung* (Munich, 2001), pp. 75–91.

[68] See Lawrence J. Baack, *Christian Bernstorff and Prussia: Diplomacy and Reform Conservatism, 1818–1832* (New Brunswick, NJ, 1980) and from a more general perspective Helmut Rumpler, *Deutscher Bund und deutsche Frage 1815–1866: Europaeischer Ordnung, deutsche Politik, und gesellschaftlicher Wandel im Zeitalter der buergerlich-nationalen Emanzipation* (Munich, 1990).

power to center stage in Prussia's state and society, first as reason's counter-point, eventually as its supplanter.[69]

In consequence, the decisiveness of the events of 1806 for Prussia, Germany, and Central Europe remain unquestioned at least among academicians. The 200th anniversary of Jena-Auerstädt witnessed an explosion of scholarly publication, broadly defined.[70] Running through Prussia's specific experience like a red thread, however, is the question of whether the "Napoleonic shock" was cause or catalyst of the reform movement that carried Prussia toward its fateful role in Europe.[71] The appropriate answer is "both." The Prussia that went to war in 1806 was not a failed state. The occupation and the Peace of Tilsit made it a defeated one. Prussia's internal resources and internal dynamics were, however, sufficiently developed to withstand Napoleon's efforts at state-breaking – efforts that in turn limited the effects of his wider ambitions.

The result was a galvanic effect, a salutary shock inviting some comparison to the US military/diplomatic recovery after Vietnam. That recovery also focused on the armed forces' reconfiguration, albeit in the opposite institutional direction – professionalization rather than nationalization. It involved addressing and overcoming, at least to a degree, domestic malaise. It involved resuming an unapologetic place in international relations' executive game. The major difference, of course, is fundamental. Vietnam was a limited defeat in a limited war. The United States endured occupation and exploitation only in apocalyptic fictions like the film *Red Dawn*. Yet the kinds of fundamental disagreements on state and society that shaped Prussia's response to 1806 were – and are – significantly present in America as well. That story remains unfinished. And Clio has a well-cultivated sense of irony.

---

[69] Lothar Kittstein, *Politik im Zeitalter derRrevolution: Untersuchungen sur preussischen Staatlichkeit, 1792–1897* (Stuttgart, 2003) offers a similar perspective in far greater depth.
[70] Katherine Alestad and Karen Hagemann, "1806 and its Aftermath: Revisiting the Period of the Napoleonic Wars in Central European German Historiography," *Central European History*, vol. 29, 2006, pp. 547–579.
[71] Clark, *Iron Kingdom*, p. 527.

6   Victory by trial and error: Britain's struggle against Napoleon

Richard Hart Sinnreich

On 15 July 1815, wearing the uniform of a chasseur of the Imperial Guard, Napoleon Bonaparte surrendered to Captain Frederick Maitland, commanding the British ship-of-the-line *Bellerophon*, blockading the French Atlantic port of La Rochelle. His surrender concluded a war that, with one brief interruption, had consumed Britain for 22 years, and that ended by propelling her to a position of preeminence among the world's great powers that she would retain for more than a century.

There was no reason for British leaders to expect that happy result when, on 1 February 1793, France's Revolutionary government declared war on Britain and Holland. On the contrary, the evidence suggests that the British government went to war against France with considerable reluctance.[1] Politically, the French Revolution had divided the country, fracturing even the reformist Whigs. Economically, Britain was still recovering from the injurious effects of her unsuccessful effort to suppress the American rebellion. Nor was there any great feeling of obligation toward France's deposed Louis XVI, the same Louis XVI who had helped defeat that effort. Conservatives such as Edmund Burke might rail against the revolution's excesses, and Britons like most other Europeans were shocked by Louis' execution and that of his queen. But few were interested in fighting to restore what even many British conservatives recognized as a corrupt and despotic Bourbon monarchy. All in all, as one writer put it, "So far as Britain was concerned, every consideration of national self-interest warned her away from involvement in French affairs."[2] As the context of the war, the character of the enemy, and the interests at stake mutated during the conflict, however, so also did British war aims and her approach to achieving them. The struggle against Napoleonic France thus offers a useful context in which to examine the wartime evolution of military strategy.

Any such examination, however, confronts the awkward problem that the term "strategy," with its connotation of a deliberately chosen scheme to

---

[1] For a detailed albeit heavily editorial discussion of the political context preceding Britain's commitment to war, see Robert Harvey, *The War of Wars* (New York, 2006), chs. 11–14.

[2] John M. Sherwig, *Guineas and Gunpowder: British Foreign Aid in the Wars with France, 1793–1815* (Cambridge, MA, 1969), p. 1.

achieve well-defined aims, did not even appear in English until nearly the end of the struggle. Nor was the deficit merely lexicographic. As one distinguished commentator insists, "there was never, in all the twenty-two years of war, any real attempt to think out the [strategic] implications of Britain's position."[3] That may be too harsh a judgment. But it certainly is true that the absence in turn-of-the-nineteenth century Britain of anything resembling the elaborate analysis and decision processes upon which modern states rely for the formulation and regulation of defense policy complicates the task, never easy in any case, of linking action retrospectively to strategic intention. Moreover, one must be wary of the historian's fallacy, which imputes contemporary reasoning to policy makers operating in an earlier and much different cultural and political milieu.[4]

There is also the challenge of defining just what constitutes an effective military strategy. Of course, any victorious belligerent may claim to have pursued such a strategy based on success alone. But that definition surely begs the question. For starters, a sufficient power imbalance tends to render it trivial. Not many would attribute the Nazi's conquest of Poland in 1939 or the US overthrow of Panamanian dictator Manuel Noriega 50 years later to strategic cleverness on the part of the victors. Similarly, as the latter suggests, a conflict so limited that it begins and ends with a single engagement offers little scope for the sequential shaping of action to intention that the word strategy connotes. That does not mean that such a contest has no strategic content, only that one must look for that content in the decision to fight and its consequences rather than in the manner in which the war itself was prosecuted.

Finally, there is the question whether the appraisal of strategic performance turns at all on how often and extensively a nation at war, or even at peace, finds itself compelled to amend or abandon a chosen course of action. However prudent, every such alteration invites a penalty, if only by deferring achievement of the strategic aim. In many cases, of course – perhaps most – the developments prompting strategic adaptation may have been unforeseeable and/or unavoidable. Enemies may prove stronger than expected, allies weaker. Moreover, even the cleverest strategy may find itself undone by battlefield defeat. During Britain's struggle against Napoleon, that unhappy event occurred more than once, for the British all the more frustrating inasmuch as the prompting defeats often were not their own. Indeed, the real measure of strategic competence may be precisely the willingness and ability to adapt with minimal cost and loss of strategic momentum to unforeseen setbacks.[5]

---

[3] A. D. Harvey, *Collision of Empires: Britain in Three World Wars, 1793–1945* (London, 1992), p. 114.

[4] David Hackett Fischer, *Historians' Fallacies: Toward a Logic of Historical Thought* (New York, 1970), pp. 209–213.

[5] Discussing the achievements of Prince Otto von Bismarck, Prussia's "Iron Chancellor," ranked by many historians among history's supreme strategists, Marcus Jones contends

However, even if effective strategy rarely permits, let alone requires, rigid adherence to a preconceived roadmap, neither can one sensibly define it by choices made randomly or solely in reaction to events. Instead, one can consider a nation's behavior strategic only to the extent that it is guided by reasonably explicit and enduring aims and reflects some more or less systematic approach to achieving them.[6] Accepting as inevitable the need for strategy to adapt, therefore, the observer still has some obligation to determine to what extent avoidable errors of appraisal or choice impelled that adaptation. That the resulting adjustment may successfully have redeemed those errors does not excuse ignoring the factors that produced them. On the contrary, especially where one can show the errors in question to have reflected recurring institutional or political proclivities, they are at the core of the examination to which this study is directed.

Such an examination thus confronts several key questions: Who made what we would today call strategic decisions, and toward what end? How did they define their problem?[7] What alternative solutions, if any, did they consider? What induced them to adopt the courses of action they actually chose? And finally, with what result? Attempting to answer these questions with respect to every strategically relevant undertaking during the two decades of Britain's war against Napoleon would require more space than this essay permits.[8] During those two decades, British and French military and naval forces collided in engagements large and small from the Baltic Sea to the Bay of Bengal. Instead, it examines only three such episodes, each the product of a different British government at a different stage in the war and transpiring in a different geographic theater. Thus individually distinguishable, collectively they illustrate some of the recurring impulses and difficulties influencing Britain's strategic behavior in its prolonged struggle with Napoleon.

---

that "Bismarck's great genius . . . lay not in his adherence to a systematic program or plan, but in his expert navigation of uncertain events through intuition and broad experience." Marcus Jones, "Strategy as Character: Bismarck and the Prusso-German Question, 1862–1878," in Williamson Murray, Richard Hart Sinnreich, James Lacey, eds., *The Shaping of Grand Strategy, Policy, Diplomacy, and War* (Cambridge, 2011), pp. 80–81.

[6] Eliot Cohen has defined strategy as "the art of choice that binds means with objectives," requiring that priorities be established and actions sequenced in accord with a theory of victory, a view shared by this author. Eliot A. Cohen, "In Afghanistan We Have a Plan – But That's Not the Same as a Strategy," *The Washington Post*, 6 December 2009.

[7] Here understood to include, *inter alia*, the context, capabilities, and constraints limiting strategic choice.

[8] Two contemporary scholars who have attempted with considerable success to describe Britain's strategic behavior throughout the war are Christopher D. Hall, *British Strategy in the Napoleonic War, 1803–15* (Manchester, 1992) and Rory Muir, *Britain and the Defeat of Napoleon, 1807–1815* (New Haven, 1996). Hall's work is more focused, Muir's more comprehensive. This essay relies heavily on both, together with J. W. Fortescue's dated but nevertheless indispensable *A History Of The British Army* (London, 1915) (hereafter Fortescue).

Prelude

The first year of the nineteenth century found Britain weary of nearly a decade of war against Revolutionary France. Having originally joined a contest in which Europe's other major powers already were engaged, with the limited aim of immunizing Britain against France's efforts to export its revolutionary zeal and preventing its domination of the Low Countries, British leaders had expected the war to be brief and inexpensive. Instead, apart from a string of British naval victories and mixed success in expeditions against French and later Dutch colonies in the East and West Indies, it proved a prolonged and expensive failure.[9] Accordingly, early in 1801, over the objections of his foreign secretary William Grenville, Prime Minister William Pitt the Younger began exploring the possibilities of a settlement with Napoleon, now France's First Consul and effective dictator. Following Pitt's resignation in February, his successor Henry Addington continued those negotiations, and after reaching preliminary agreement with Napoleon's agents in September, signed the Treaty of Amiens on 25 March 1802.[10]

Most historians doubt the treaty ever had any real chance of enduring.[11] Notes one, "the peace must be put into context. It was never imagined to be a permanent peace."[12] Few attentive Britons expected it to last, and some hoped it would not.[13] Writing to his brother a month before the signing of the treaty, Grenville complained that "It is a curious thing to hear him [Pitt] confess that our peace system is to cost as much as Defensive War – which is in other words that our peace is to be war, only without the power of defending ourselves or annoying our enemies."[14] Napoleon's subsequent correspondence suggests he also expected war to resume, although apparently not as quickly as it did.[15]

---

[9] As Fortescue comments with respect to the campaign in the West Indies,

> If the losses of the Army, Navy, and transports be added together, it is probably beneath the mark to say that twelve thousand Englishmen were buried in the West Indies in 1794 … [British leaders] poured their troops into these pestilent islands, in the expectation that thereby they would destroy the power of France, only to discover, when it was too late, that they had practically destroyed the British Army.

Fortescue, vol. IV, p. 385.

[10] For reasons unrelated to the war Pitt resigned over George III's refusal to endorse Catholic emancipation in Ireland. Grenville and other Pittite ministers followed suit.

[11] For the most negative view, holding that Napoleon agreed to the treaty in the first place merely to recover French colonial possessions and buy time to reconstitute French naval power, see Harvey, *The War of Wars*, chp. 42. Robert Markley offers a more nuanced appraisal in "Peace of Amiens 1801," www.napoleon-series.org/research/government/ diplomatic/c_peace.html.

[12] Markley, "Peace of Amiens 1801."

[13] George III, for one, considered the treaty no more than an "experiment." Stanley Ayling, *George the Third* (London, 1972), p. 423.

[14] *Correspondence of Thomas Grenville with his Brother William Wyndham Grenville*, vol. II (ff. 373), 23 Nov. 1790–30 Dec. 1808, British Library Ref. 41852.

[15] Fortescue, vol. V, p. 193. See also Hall, *British Strategy in the Napoleonic War*, p. 103.

In the meantime, both signatories played fast and loose with their treaty obligations. Napoleon refused to repeal France's wartime ban on British trade or return property confiscated during the revolution. Meanwhile, he continued to gobble up additional territory by annexing Elba, Piedmont, and Parma, and in September 1802 reinvaded Switzerland. For their part, the British refused to evacuate Malta, which the treaty required them to return to the Knights of St. John. At the same time, reformist angst at Napoleon's reinstitution of slavery in Haiti compounded British indignation over the reinvasion of Switzerland, both sentiments reflected in increasingly inflammatory editorials and cartoons.[16]

However one chooses to apportion responsibility, by spring 1803 matters had reached a head, and on 2 May, Britain's ambassador asked for his passport. Two weeks later, after scarcely a year of peace, Britain and France were again at war. This time, however, British leaders had no illusions about the difficulty of the challenge they were undertaking. Although, given Pitt's continuing parliamentary support, the decision to resume hostilities secured an overwhelming vote of confidence in the Commons, Whig leader Charles Fox, whose opposition to Britain's original commitment to war with France had split his party, unleashed a scathing criticism of the government. Even longtime Pitt ally William Wilberforce complained that "we have been too apt to make ourselves principals in continental quarrels ... and above all we have continued them too long."[17] Comments one historian, "To modern eyes the most immediate and wide-ranging shortcoming [of the renewal of war] was the absence of any formal, wide-ranging political unity with which to face the French threat."[18] Compounded by the clash of personalities, royal stubbornness, the deaths in office of two prime ministers, one of natural causes, the other by assassination, and a duel between two of Britain's ablest politicians, forcing both from office, that disunity would produce six successive governments during the next 12 years, not one enduring more than three years and several considerably less.[19]

But if political unity left much to be desired, popular commitment to the war during the years that followed rarely wavered. For that, British leaders largely could thank Napoleon himself, who, unlike Revolutionary France's relatively faceless Directory, furnished a visible focus for public antipathy. The average Briton might not follow the twists and turns of a foreign policy that saw other European nations allies one year, enemies the next, and allies again the year after. But he or she could readily fear and loathe the man believed responsible for making it necessary, especially one openly

---

[16] Markley, "The Peace of Amiens, 1801."   [17] Harvey, *Collision of Empires*, p. 19.
[18] Hall, *British Strategy in the Napoleonic War*, p. 53.
[19] Addington's, one year after the resumption of war; Pitt's, on his return to office, two years; Grenville's, one year; Portland's and Perceval's, two-and-a-half years each. Liverpool's ministry governed from June 1812 until 1827, but, excluding the interval between the first Treaty of Paris and the "Hundred Days," barely three wartime years.

contemptuous of what he publicly disparaged as "a nation of shopkeepers."[20] In the British press after 1803, "cartoons and prints converged on a single portrait of Napoleon ... diminutive, autocratic, haunted by his misdeeds and assassination threats and aspiring to power beyond measure."[21]

That antipathy only increased immediately following the renewal of hostilities, during which Napoleon seized George III's Electorate of Hanover, declared continental ports closed to British produce, and assembled men and ships to launch an invasion across the Channel. Britain had endured invasion threats before, in 1796 and 1798, but the first had aimed at Ireland, and Bonaparte himself had aborted the second in favor of invading Egypt. In any case, both were relatively small in scale. The massive force assembling at Boulogne and other French and Belgian ports in 1803 and 1804 was quite another matter, especially inasmuch as regular British troops based at home when hostilities resumed numbered fewer than 70,000, of whom nearly 20,000 were stationed in Ireland.[22]

The Addington government's response was one of the most significant of the war, but less from a strategic than from a sociopolitical perspective. In addition to undertaking what one account describes as the most extensive fortification of the British coastline since the reign of Henry VIII,[23] in July 1803, the government introduced a bill amending the Defence of the Realm Act to permit recruiting volunteers for a territorial auxiliary for employment in the event of invasion to harass and disrupt the invading force. In thus proposing to arm large numbers of ordinary citizens, British leaders were compelled to rise above the conservative dread of radicalism that had prevailed since Cromwell, and that the French Revolution had only intensified. As Addington argued, "in these times, it is better to run the hazard even of the people making a bad use of their arms, than that they should be actually left in a state of entire ignorance of the use of them."[24] For once, both Pitt and Fox agreed, the king made no objection, and the proposed amendment passed without difficulty.

---

[20] Plagiarizing Adam Smith. See *An Inquiry into the Nature and Causes of the Wealth of Nations* (New York, 1937), p. 579.
[21] Alexandra Franklin and Mark Philip, *Napoleon and the Invasion of Britain* (Oxford, 2003), p. 14.
[22] Another 50,000-odd local militia, conscripted by ballot unless paying a substitute, were usable only for home defense.
[23] Franklin and Philip, *Napoleon and the Invasion of Britain*, p. 11. The program resulted in construction of more than a hundred "Martello" towers along Britain's southeast coast. Still others were built in Scotland, Ireland, and the Channel islands, and eventually in British possessions as distant as Canada, South Africa, and Australia. Not all approved, Pitt's former acolyte George Canning versifying derisorily, "If blocks can a nation deliver, two places are safe from the French: The one is the mouth of the river [Thames], the other the Treasury Bench." Harvey, *The War of Wars*, p. 422.
[24] Addington to parliament, *The Times*, 19 July 1803, p. 1, http://archive.timesonline.co.uk/tol/archive/.

The public reaction was as overwhelming as it was unanticipated. "The government was faced with a tide of volunteering that they could neither ignore nor, seemingly, control."[25] By 1804, more than 400,000 volunteers had enrolled. Together with the addition of a second battalion to each regular regiment and improvements of the militia, by the end of the year Britain arguably was in better condition to defend itself against invasion than at any time since joining the war against France more than a decade earlier. In the event neither fortifications nor volunteers were needed. In summer 1805, facing renewed war with Russia and Austria, Napoleon shifted his attention and his army eastward. Then, on 21 October, off Spain's Cape Trafalgar, Admiral Horatio Nelson annihilated the combined French and Spanish fleets.[26] In the process, he effectively removed any future threat of cross-Channel invasion.[27]

But while the immediate threat subsided, the passions that it had aroused did not, nor did the antagonism toward its author. Even radical reformers no longer could pretend that the war was merely an excuse to enlarge Britain's commercial reach, or Napoleon the standard-bearer of a popular revolution, especially after he crowned himself emperor in December 1804, then King of Italy in May 1805. Nor could arcane diplomatic objectives such as the restoration of a balance of power pacify the fear and anger excited by the threat of invasion. The invasion threat of 1804–1805 thus transformed the war in a profound way; and although there would be additional efforts to seek a negotiated peace, a growing number of ordinary Britons were coming to share the conviction of many of their leaders that no settlement was conceivable that left Napoleon in power.

There remained the problem of how to defeat a military genius owning Europe's most powerful army and who had contemptuously swatted down every continental power daring to oppose him. In the end, Britain's central strategic problem was that of any maritime power confronting a continental adversary. As long as Britain maintained naval supremacy, she could count herself nearly immune from outright invasion. But without allies, she remained correspondingly helpless to confront Napoleon on the European mainland. From 1803 to 1814, six successive British governments sought to answer that dilemma, in the process enduring the disappointing collapse of three more British-subsidized coalitions, until at last, with Bonaparte's vital help, hitting on a successful military formula. Along the way, British troops found themselves fighting in overseas expeditions large and small from Copenhagen to Cape Town. It is on three of those expeditions that this

---

[25] Franklin and Philip, *Napoleon and the Invasion of Britain*, p. 13.

[26] Spain declared war on Britain in December 1804, in response to the Royal Navy's seizure of its annual treasure flotilla homeward bound from Spanish America, Pitt & Co. having judged an impoverished actual enemy to be less dangerous than a wealthy probable one.

[27] Although, as will be seen, fear of one would continue to afflict successive British governments until 1812.

chapter will focus. Two resulted in embarrassing and expensive failures. The third ended with a British-led army on French soil, helping earn Britain a seat at the top table when, following Napoleon's abdication, the victorious allies met in Vienna to reconstruct a war-ravaged Europe.

British strategic decision making

Before examining those expeditions and their results, a few words may help to frame the decision-making context from which they emerged. Early nineteenth century British strategic policies resulted from a complex interaction among elected politicians, primarily but by no means exclusively members of the government charged with ministerial responsibilities; appointed bureaucrats; senior diplomatic officials, some resident in foreign capitals and others dispatched on special assignment; and military and naval commanders at home and abroad. In several ways, however, that interplay differed significantly from its modern successor.

The first such difference reflected the influence of the monarch. By 1803 George III had worn the crown for more than 40 years. For all his obsession with maintaining his royal prerogatives, he was widely popular and, within the limits imposed by Britain's still-evolving unwritten constitution, very much a hands-on ruler until 1811, when the mental illness that had afflicted him episodically since 1788 finally overcame him.[28] His influence was especially marked in the appointment of ministers – his contempt of Fox, for example, debarred the latter from ministerial office until the Grenville government of 1806. Above all, treating as literal the word "royal" in the formal titles of the army and navy, he insisted on active personal involvement in their administration and employment, involvement that not infrequently demonstrated a good deal more thoughtfulness than that of his ministers.

A second and closely related difference lay in the character of turn-of-the-nineteenth century parliaments. Acceptance of rigid party discipline was still to come and intra-party schisms were common, especially when the views of party leaders and monarch collided. The Whigs in particular split outright over Britain's response to the French Revolution, with Fox and younger reformers such as Charles Grey sympathetic to the revolutionaries, while conservatives such as Burke strongly opposed them. Hence, when Britain went to war with France in 1793, many of the party's luminaries defected, including the Duke of Portland and William Windham, soon to be secretary at war. While Grenville's short-lived ministry reunited them, its collapse in 1807 revived the old divisions, helping no little to exclude Whigs from power for the next quarter-century.

---

[28] Modern medical research now believes George's "madness" actually to have been a result of the blood disorder porphyria, probably hereditary, and possibly aggravated in its later stages by arsenic-infused medication.

Compared with today, in short, the effect of parliamentary indiscipline was less to moderate inter-party tensions than to magnify personal and policy disagreements within the government itself, making it that much more difficult to develop and pursue anything resembling a consistent strategy. Beholden more to their own parliamentary factions than to their ministerial colleagues, cabinet members were not loathe to agitate against each other, a practice only encouraged by a succession of relatively weak prime ministers. Perhaps most egregious was the backdoor campaign waged in early 1809 by Foreign Secretary George Canning to engineer the removal of his war office colleague, Robert Stewart Viscount Castlereagh, an effort culminating in a duel that brought down the Portland government as well as the combatants.

The third major difference between strategic policy making then and now reflected the tyranny of time and distance. Hostage to horse-mounted couriers and sail-powered ships, governments at the turn of the nineteenth century exercised only the most fragile oversight of distant events. To receive a report or dispatch an order between London and Lisbon, a distance of scarcely 1,000 miles, took weeks. Two-way communication with more distant stations such as the Cape of Good Hope could take months.

In the circumstances, close political oversight of remotely stationed soldiers and diplomats was impossible, and both perforce enjoyed a discretion that would astonish their modern successors. That broad discretion offered advantages and imposed penalties. Among the advantages were a certain, though far from complete, insulation of overseas officials from London's periodic political scandals, and an understanding that policy directives must be formulated to allow some looseness in interpretation and execution. More than once, that understanding permitted officials distant from London to ignore policy directives that events during the interval between dispatch and receipt had rendered infeasible or imprudent. The principal penalty, of course, was London's utter inability to know for certain what its distant subordinates were up to until well after they were up to it, with the result that the cabinet occasionally found itself committed to a course of action into which it had had little or no input. Just such an episode prompted the first of our three cases.

A most astonishing plan: Buenos Aires, 1806

The first decade of war had demonstrated conclusively that, while blockading the French coast and depriving France of her overseas colonies and their revenues could annoy Bonaparte and diminish the privateer threat to Britain's carrying trade, it could not threaten a French economy increasingly financed by Napoleon's continental conquests.[29] Indeed, soon after taking office in

---

[29] Austerlitz alone earned Napoleon the equivalent of £4 million in Austrian reparations. Ironically, a quarter of that probably was contributed – involuntarily – by Britain. Sherwig, *Guineas and Gunpowder*, p. 170.

1806, the new First Lord of Admiralty, Viscount Howick, complained to the cabinet that "while we are acquiring colonies, the enemy is subjugating the Continent."[30] At the same time, however, for Grenville, appointed prime minister after Pitt's death, direct military engagement on the continent seemed no more promising.[31] Disillusioned by the defeat and collapse of three successive anti-French coalitions and exasperated by allies who, in Grenville's view, expected Britain to contribute more, in financial terms at least, than they themselves were willing to invest, the government mocked by its detractors as a "ministry of all the talents" (or simply "the Talents") first attempted to make peace with Napoleon, then, when that failed, chose to disregard past experience and expend Britain's limited military resources on strategically ancillary enterprises.

In June 1806 occurred one of the more bizarre such expeditions, the origins of which, still more its subsequent evolution, tell a good deal about the impulses driving and frictions afflicting British strategic behavior.[32] The story begins at the Cape of Good Hope, seized by Britain in 1795 after the French conquest of Holland to prevent its use to interdict Britain's maritime lifeline to India. Pursuant to the Peace of Amiens, the British returned the colony to the Dutch, only to reinvade it in January 1806 following the resumption of war.[33] The easily achieved reoccupation left some 6,000 troops under Lieutenant General David Baird unemployed, upon which his supporting naval commander, Commodore Sir Home Popham, persuaded him to release some 1,500 soldiers under Brigadier-General William Beresford for an attack on the Spanish colonies along the Rio de la Plata in today's Argentina and Uruguay.

The origins of this ambitious project were peculiar, to say the least. According to Fortescue, it began as the brainchild of a Venezuela-born expatriate Spanish officer named Miranda, who apparently was in equal parts revolutionary, promoter, and rogue. In October 1804, he and Popham, whom he had met previously and who was both politically and commercially well connected, attempted to persuade Pitt, recently returned to office after a three-year hiatus, to authorize an expedition to liberate Spanish America.[34] Their aim was to deprive Spain (and by extension Napoleon) of its revenues and offer British merchants long-coveted access to its resources and markets.[35]

---

[30] Harvey, *Collision of Empires*, p. 25.
[31] Pitt had returned as prime minister in May 1804, but without Grenville, who refused to serve without Fox, to whom the king remained adamantly hostile. He died in office in January 1806.
[32] The definitive account is Ian Fletcher, *The Waters of Oblivion: The British Invasion of the Rio de la Plata, 1806–07* (Stroud, Gloucester, 2006).
[33] The Anglo-Dutch Treaty of 1814 would award it permanently to Britain.
[34] In fact, he was elected to parliament from the Isle of Wight in 1804, and again in 1806 and 1807, by no means the only serving officer of the day to enjoy such dual political and military status (Wellington was another).
[35] According to Fortescue, Miranda had tried three times earlier to sell the idea of fomenting revolution in Spanish America, in 1783, 1790, and 1796, but without success. Fortescue, vol. V, p. 311.

Despite its authors' entreaties, the proposal went nowhere, Pitt at the time hoping that Russia might succeed in detaching Spain from its French alliance. However, in spring 1806 Pitt having died, and learning of the allied disasters at Ulm and Austerlitz, Popham convinced Baird that invading Spanish America would be a monument to Pitt's memory and an easy and inexpensive way to "add lustre to his Majesty's arms, distress our enemies and open a most beneficial trade for Britain."[36] Persuaded by Popham's argument (or, as critics later claimed, by his promise of two-thirds of whatever prize money might accrue from the enterprise), Baird agreed to release the troops. After stopping briefly at St. Helena to embark a few hundred more men, the small expedition of six warships and five transports reached the mouth of the Plata in June. On 25 June, following a brief debate between the commanders about where to land, the first British soldiers disembarked at Quilmes, some 10 miles south of Buenos Aires.[37]

The subsequent defeat of the city's exiguous defenders was as quick and inexpensive as Popham had promised, not least because wealthy *Porteños* initially welcomed the British as liberators. That happy condition proved short-lived. Seizing the city's treasury following the flight of Spain's viceroy, Popham and Beresford promptly dispatched it to London.[38] Its arrival, paraded through the streets with great fanfare, caused a sensation; but most of Buenos Aires' citizens were infuriated by what Fletcher describes as an "act of almost Elizabethan buccaneering."[39] Their resentment only mounted with the repeal of the locals' monopoly on overseas trade and a growing suspicion of Britain's political intentions. The invading force's initial welcome thus soon gave way to passive and active resistance. Meanwhile, Spanish troops which had escaped the city's surrender and others garrisoned elsewhere began assembling under the leadership of an enterprising Spanish naval captain, Santiago de Liniers, eventually reaching a strength of nearly 10,000. With his 1,600 British soldiers already overstretched to maintain control of an increasingly hostile population of 40,000, Beresford found himself in an untenable position. On 12 August, he surrendered the city to Liniers on condition that the Spanish repatriate his troops.

Meanwhile, however, news of his original success had set commercial London afire. Perhaps anticipating official displeasure at his unsanctioned initiative, Popham had written to merchants in the City of London describing in glowing terms the new markets that soon would be opened to British

---

[36] Thomas Byrne, "British Army, Irish Soldiers: The 1806 Invasion of Buenos Aires," www.irlandeses.org/1003byrne.htm#1.

[37] The original plan called for landing at Montevideo. Popham insisted instead on going straight for Buenos Aires.

[38] Fletcher estimates the total take at 1.5 million Spanish dollars, or roughly £7 million. Baird was awarded nearly £24,000 in prize money, Beresford nearly £12,000. Popham had to settle for £6,000. Fletcher, *The Waters of Oblivion*, p. 18.

[39] Ibid., p. 4.

commerce.[40] On 17 September, still unaware of Beresford's capitulation, the London *Times* editorialized rhapsodically, "We know not how to express ourselves in terms adequate to our ideas of the national advantages which will be derived from this conquest."[41] Given the general euphoria, the government had little choice but to make the best of Popham's fait accompli, and after ordering Popham home to explain himself,[42] dispatched Brigadier-General Samuel Auchmuty with 2,000 men to reinforce Beresford.

With the government's negotiations with Napoleon going nowhere,[43] even Grenville, previously no enthusiast for colonial expeditions, found himself caught up in the popular excitement, encouraged no little by William Windham, his secretary of state for war and the colonies.[44] Accordingly, with Grenville's approval, Windham ordered Admiral Sir George Murray to convey still another force of 4,000 men under Brigadier-General Robert Craufurd to seize Valparaiso, Chile, with a view ultimately to linking British conquests on the Atlantic and Pacific seaboards. Not invariably generous to politicians, Fortescue declared this "one of the most astonishing plans that ever emanated from the brain even of a British Minister of War," adding caustically, "How it was to be effected, and how at the same time Valparaiso, Buenos Ayres [*sic*], and Monte Video were to be occupied by a total force of six thousand men, the Minister did not explain."[45]

In the event, before Craufurd could link up with Murray at the Cape of Good Hope, word reached London of Beresford's surrender. By that time, however, the government had publicly committed itself, a commitment reinforced by Popham's grandiloquent promises to Britain's trading houses. Accordingly, the cabinet dispatched new instructions by fast ship directing Murray and Craufurd to link up with Auchmuty, retake Buenos Aires, and rescue Beresford. With Craufurd and Auchmuty considered too junior to command the combined force, in March 1807 Windham dispatched

---

[40] Richard Gott, "Bad Day for the Empire," www.guardian.co.uk, Friday, 13 July 2007.

[41] Hall, *British Strategy in the Napoleonic War*, p. 145.

[42] Tried for leaving his station (at the Cape of Good Hope) without authority, Popham claimed at his court-martial that he had been authorized to act on his own initiative should Spain remain a belligerent, a claim that Fortescue does not entirely dismiss, noting that both Pitt and Melville at the Admiralty might have been "guilty of some indiscretion in their frequent conversations with Popham, for the enterprise was exactly of a nature to captivate their unmilitary minds." Fortescue, vol. V, p. 312. In the end, Popham was admonished but not cashiered, remained on active service, and in 1814 was promoted to rear admiral.

[43] Begun in April, almost immediately after Grenville took office, they would break down altogether in October.

[44] A. D. Harvey points out that Grenville did consult his elder brother, the Marquis of Buckingham, who lacked any military experience, however; and Buckingham's protégé, then Major-General Sir Arthur Wellesley, who, though a veteran, was still very junior. Grenville notably forbore consulting his other brother Thomas, who just happened to be First Lord of the Admiralty. Harvey, *Collision of Empires*, pp. 116–117.

[45] Fortescue, vol. V, pp. 375–376.

Lieutenant General John Whitelocke to the Plata with 1,500 additional reinforcements to command a force that now exceeded 10,000 men.

Meanwhile, arriving at Rio de Janiero in December 1806, and learning of Beresford's surrender, Auchmuty wisely decided to land at Maldonado, 70 miles east of Montevideo, where reinforcements sent independently by Baird, arriving too late to save Beresford, had established themselves. Concluding he was too weak to recapture Buenos Aires, Auchmuty instead attacked Montevideo and carried the city in a costly assault on 3 February 1807. There matters remained until Whitelocke's arrival on 10 May. Taking command, the latter thereupon mounted an attack on Buenos Aires remarkable chiefly for its ineptitude. After incurring more than 2,500 casualties, the campaign concluded ignominiously on 7 July with Whitelocke's virtual surrender, the British general agreeing in exchange for the return of captured British personnel to evacuate Buenos Aires altogether within ten days and Montevideo within two months.

So ended in humiliating failure one of the stranger episodes of a war that witnessed more than a few. News of the defeat, to say nothing of the speculative losses incurred by those who had invested on the strength of Popham's promises, produced a storm of public criticism. By that time, however, the Grenville government was history. At the end of March 1807, with Fox dead, Windham discredited, Grenville himself worn out, and the administration condemned for what many justifiably considered its failure either to make peace or effectually make war, Grenville used the excuse of George III's continuing stubbornness on Irish Catholic emancipation to resign. The Talents thus were spared the direct fall-out of the Buenos Aires debacle.[46] In the end, of those who played major roles, including the two military commanders who had instigated it, only the hapless Whitelocke, who returned home to public humiliation, court-martial, and cashierment, paid personally for a failure for which he alone scarcely was responsible.[47]

---

[46] Although it would continue to haunt them in opposition throughout the remainder of the war.

[47] The verbatim record of his court-martial, published in London in 1808 by S. Tipper, has been digitized and can be read online at www.archive.org/details/trialoflieutenan00whit. The cover page notes pointedly that "This is not the Case of an Officer on his Trial by Court-Martial for any one particular fact alledged [sic] against him, but it is the *first* Trial by Court-Martial, instituted to investigate into the Conduct of a General Officer, having the command of an Expedition against a foreign province." That disclaimer notwithstanding, it is hard to read the transcript without some sympathy for Whitelocke as a man both out of his depth and ill-served by superiors and subordinates alike. Comments Fortescue with uncharacteristic generosity,

If the indignant shade of Whitelocke still broods over the fortune of many British Generals who, though no less deserving of disgrace than himself, have escaped court-martial and cashierment, it may at least find consolation in the thought that the evacuation of South America after his defeat was a wise, true, and courageous service to his country.

Fortescue, vol. V, pp. 435–436.

So much for the sequence of events. What insight, if any, does it offer concerning British strategic decision making? As for who made the vital decisions, the answer depends no little on the breadth of the aperture through which one examines them. In the narrowest sense, of course, the Buenos Aires expedition resulted from the venturesome initiative of two distant military commanders whose freedom from political supervision enabled them to commit their government to an enterprise that their superiors had not even contemplated, much less approved, for purposes in which their nation's interests and their personal aims are difficult to separate. Similarly, viewed narrowly, one can explain the government's decision, once advised of the expedition, to reinforce and even enlarge it, as the product of commercial greed coupled with a desire to avoid political embarrassment, both magnified by the excitement aroused initially by Popham's report and subsequently by the arrival of Buenos Aires' purloined treasure.

More than anything else, however, the Buenos Aires expedition was a reflection of strategic drift. To operate on the continent without powerful allies was out of the question, but given the collapse of three previous such coalitions, the Talents were profoundly reluctant to reengage with – and perforce subsidize – Europe's other major powers. Thus, unable to make peace with Napoleon, but unwilling to confront him on the only battlefield on which he could be decisively defeated, the Grenville government found itself reaching for any strategically plausible military alternative.

It remains to ask whether the expedition ever had any real hope of succeeding, and, if it did, whether success was likely to contribute in any significant way to Napoleon's defeat. Concerning the first question, the evidence is compelling that, even had Whitelocke succeeded in retaking Buenos Aires, his prospects for hanging on to it were poor. Notes one historian of the episode, "At no moment did the Talents ever seem to grasp that the British in Spanish America were regarded not as liberators but rather as another unwelcome set of outside rulers like the Spanish, and ones, moreover, seen as godless Protestants out for loot."[48] Even had that not been true, "it is questionable whether the commercial benefits would ever have been on the scale anticipated."[49] Nor, regarding the second question, would liberating Spanish America have done much more in any case to deprive Spain and its French ally of its shrinking revenues than Britain's naval dominance after Trafalgar already had assured. Instead, in the end, Buenos Aires simply reconfirmed what previous British colonial operations already had demonstrated: that to defeat Bonaparte, means must be found to confront him on his own ground. The next case began as an effort to do precisely that.

[48] Hall, *British Strategy in the Napoleonic War*, p. 147. The comment seems unfortunately all too contemporary.
[49] Ibid., p. 148.

A long agony: Walcheren, 1809

Grenville's successor was the Duke of Portland, the same Portland whose defection from Fox's Whig opposition to become home secretary at the beginning of the war had led Pitt to establish the position of war secretary in order to keep Henry Dundas in the cabinet. Sixty-nine years old, in ill-health, and succeeding such commanding figures as Pitt and Grenville, Portland was bound to suffer by comparison. "Portland," wrote Fortescue, "presided over a Cabinet he did not lead."[50] Critics characterized his administration as a "government of departments," in which ambitious young ministers drove strategic direction with little adult supervision.[51] Accordingly, in contrast with the Talents' South American adventure, launched without prior political approval by two remotely stationed commanders on their own initiative, a single minister, Robert Stewart, Viscount Castlereagh, Portland's secretary of state for war, largely devised and directed the Walcheren expedition of July 1809.

The roots of the expedition lay in Britain's on-again, off-again alliance with Austria. Notes another historian, "The Austrian government had never been reconciled to its defeat in 1805, but it had felt too weak to join Prussia and Russia against France in 1806–7."[52] Then, in 1808, Napoleon invaded Spain, deposing its ruler in favor of his brother Joseph and inciting a nation-wide rebellion. By early 1809, the French having been ejected by the British from Portugal and having more than 200,000 troops tied down in Spain, the Austrians were ready once more to try conclusions with Bonaparte, but desired Britain to subsidize the effort and fix French reserves that otherwise might be sent east by mounting a diversionary effort in the west, preferably in north Germany.

Conveyed to the Portland government in spring 1809, the Austrian request arrived at a peculiar juncture, both strategically and politically. In January, in a preview of Dunkirk, General Sir John Moore's brief foray from Portugal into Spain had ended in a narrow escape at Corunna. A subsequent plan to reinforce Cadiz, still held by the Spanish, fell afoul of Spanish suspicions only aggravated by an attempt in February, at the behest of a diplomatically obtuse British military agent, to land British troops without the approval of Spain's

---

[50] Fortescue, vol. VII, p. xx.
[51] A criticism to which Spencer Perceval, Portland's chancellor of the exchequer, replied, not entirely unreasonably, that "It is not because the Duke of Portland is at our head that the Government is a Government of Departments, but it is because the Government is and must be essentially a Government of Departments that the Duke of Portland is at our head." Sherwig, *Guineas and Gunpowder*, p. 184. Muir likewise claims that, at least where war policy was concerned, "Important decisions were usually made by the cabinet as a whole, not by individual ministers, and on a number of occasions ... the relevant minister's own views were overruled." Instead, he argues, the most troublesome result of Portland's weak leadership was that "disputes could drag on for months before being decided." Muir, *Britain and the Defeat of Napoleon*, p. 9.
[52] Muir, *Britain and the Defeat of Napoleon*, p. 81.

Supreme Junta. Together, the two debacles materially dampened the government's enthusiasm for operations in Spain that had been aroused by the uprising of 1808. Instead, "In the wake of the rebuff at Cadiz, it was by no means clear where in or beyond the Peninsula Britain would concentrate her military effort."[53]

Meanwhile, throughout the first few months of 1809, the Portland government was consumed less by strategy than by scandal. In January, accusations were leveled against the Duke of York, George III's second son and the army's highly regarded commander-in-chief, that he had allowed his mistress to peddle military commissions and appointments. Subsequent parliamentary investigation cleared the duke of personal involvement in the scheme, but the public embarrassment nevertheless prompted his resignation. The resulting political turmoil together with the bureaucratic confusion engendered by York's abrupt replacement at Horse Guards further dampened interest in strategic discussion. In Fortescue's words, "The petty sordid details of the scandal – such is human nature – excluded all other considerations from the minds of the Commons, the press, and the public."[54]

It was into this nexus of military irresolution and political preoccupation that, at the end of March, Count Ludwig Walmoden, Austria's special envoy, returned to London to report that war with France was imminent.[55] He renewed Emperor Francis II's request for both a substantial financial subsidy and a diversionary British military commitment on the continent.[56] Walmoden proposed three possible targets of such a diversionary effort: the Peninsula, where a British army already was deployed; Italy, from which the French earlier had evicted the Austrians; or northern Germany between the Ems and Elbe Rivers.

None appealed to the cabinet. With respect to the Peninsula, while the Austrian plea doubtless contributed to the cabinet's continued, albeit nervous, support of Sir Arthur Wellesley's operations in Portugal, ministers were not eager to increase Britain's troop investment, particularly given the impact of the requested Austrian subsidy on an already troublesome shortage of hard money.[57] As Fortescue explains,

---

[53] Ibid., p. 82.   [54] Fortescue, vol. VII, p. 31.
[55] It actually began on 12 April with Austria's reinvasion of Italy.
[56] As Sherwig notes, the requested subsidy presented a serious problem for a government chronically short of hard money and already having difficulty meeting Wellesley's requirements. Nevertheless, through a variety of means, Britain eventually managed to pony up more than £1 million, the most yet contributed to an ally, though far less than the £5 million demanded. Sherwig, *Guineas and Gunpowder*, pp. 208–213.
[57] Absolved of responsibility for the widely unpopular August 1808 Cintra Convention, by which French troops in Portugal were repatriated unmolested, arms, loot, and all, and by British ships at that, Wellesley was reappointed to command of British peninsular forces following Moore's death at Corunna.

the question ... arose whether Wellesley's army should not be still further increased; whether, in fact, the whole strength of England should not be turned against that single point, for there could be no doubt of the effectiveness of such a diversion. In opposition to such a policy, however, stood the insuperable difficulty of finding specie to pay the expenses of the campaign.[58]

Italy presented a different problem. While British forces in Sicily were adequate to its defense, they were not nearly sufficient to invade Italy with any prospect of success, and with Austria proposing to go to war momentarily, the cabinet concluded that reinforcing them early enough to influence French dispositions on the Danube simply was infeasible. Instead, ministers contented themselves with urging British commanders in Sicily and the Mediterranean to cooperate with the Austrians with the means at hand.

That left northwest Europe. The Austrians' suggestion of north Germany had its attractions, not least the possibility of liberating Hanover, and certainly would have had the most immediate impact on French operations against Austria. But the objections were even stronger. As recently as 1805, an expedition intended for a similar purpose had sailed to Bremen only to be greeted by news of Austerlitz. Moreover, compelled to operate without the immediate support of a continental ally, any British force sufficient to divert the French would need to be logistically self-sufficient, once again requiring hard currency. In the end, the government was unwilling to recommit a British army to northern Germany unless Prussia also reengaged against France, an unlikely event given King Frederick William's refusal to confront Bonaparte again despite pressure from his military leaders.

Instead, the ministers cast their eyes on the Low Countries' Scheldt Estuary, French seizure of which had played a major role in Britain's decision to go to war in 1793, and that, since Napoleon's construction of a major naval base at Antwerp, constituted what the Admiralty feared could become a potential invasion platform. In fact, Castlereagh had proposed invading the estuary shortly after taking office in April 1807 and had revived the suggestion a year later. However, events on the Peninsula had overtaken both proposals. Now, two years later, he circulated a detailed memorandum once again urging such an expedition and describing its supposed benefits. On 18 April, without troubling to consult anyone but Portland, he went so far as to proffer command of the expedition to the Earl of Chatham.[59]

The cabinet, however, were indisposed to approve out of hand an expedition that even Castlereagh conceded would denude the homeland of active

---

[58] Fortescue, vol. VII, p. 44. Moreover, were Wellesley's command enlarged to any significant extent, the king almost certainly would require appointment of a more senior commander, which, in addition to superseding Britain's most successful soldier, would embarrass a government with which the Wellesley faction in parliament was closely associated.

[59] Lt-Gen. the Earl of Chatham, Pitt's elder brother and Master-General of the Ordnance, had been offered but had declined command in Portugal in 1808, claiming an inability for personal reasons to respond on the notice given.

army strength outside of Ireland, and insisted on first consulting several military authorities, few of whom were sanguine. As one objected, "Against the destruction of the enemy's fleet at Antwerp, must be put the risk of the loss of the whole disposable force of the empire, and, with this addition to the comparison, that the risk may be suffered and the object not attained."[60] Perhaps reflecting that concern, George III's order appointing Chatham had a distinctly ambivalent ring:

You will consider that this conjoint expedition has for its object the capture or destruction of the Enemy's ships either building at Antwerp and Flushing, or afloat in the Scheldt; the destruction of the arsenals and Dockyards at Antwerp, Terneuse, and Flushing; the Reduction of the Island of Walcheren; and the rendering if possible the Scheldt no longer navigable for ships of war.

If the attainment of all the above mentioned objects should be rendered infeasible by the enemy collecting in such strength as to render perseverance inconsistent with the Security of the Army, you are in that case to use your utmost endeavor in concert with the officer commanding the Naval Force to secure as many of the objects as circumstances will permit; and so soon as the Service should be completed, or such part thereof as is attainable, you will take immediate measures for reembarking the Army and returning with it to England, leaving a sufficient force to maintain possession of the Island of Walcheren till our further pleasure should be signified.[61]

In other words, Chatham's orders urged him to be bold, but not too bold, and above all not to hazard the army. In a separate note, Castlereagh added, "His Majesty feels assured that his Army and Navy will vie with each other in giving effect to an enterprise than which none has been confided of greater importance to their united efforts [and] that the utmost spirit of concert and harmony will prevail throughout the whole of their operations."[62] Given the conflicting personalities of Chatham and his senior naval commander, Admiral Sir Richard Strachan, that was more prayer than prediction. All in all, it is little wonder that caution prevailed over audacity from the outset of the exercise.

In the event, between political scandal and the logistical challenge of assembling a joint army–navy force described by Fortescue as "incomparably the greatest armament that had ever left the shores of England,"[63] it was 28 July before the expedition was ready to depart.[64] By then, defeated at Wagram three weeks earlier, Austria was already petitioning Bonaparte for

---

[60] Lieutenant Colonel Alexander Gordon, "Memorandum Upon the Supposed Practicability of Destroying the French Ships and Vessels in the Scheldt, and in the Arsenals at Antwerp" 31 May 1809, in Charles William Vane (ed.), *Correspondence, Despatches, and Other Papers of Viscount Castlereagh*, vol. VI (London, 1851), p. 260 (hereafter *Castlereagh Correspondence*).

[61] George III to the Earl of Chatham, 16 July 1809 (National Archives, WO1 – 191).

[62] Castlereagh to Chatham, 16 July 1809 (National Archives, WO1 – 191).

[63] Fortescue, vol. VII, p. 56. By the time it finally sailed, the expedition comprised more than 200 warships and some 40,000 troops. Ironically, it set out on the very day that Wellesley and Questa were meeting Victor at Talavera.

[64] Noted one writer, "It needs something more than 'the invincible loitering habit,' to which, in public affairs, at least, the British temper so easily leads itself, to explain this delay."

an armistice, nullifying the principal objective of the expedition even before it began. Nevertheless, it went forward, at least in part because, as with the Buenos Aires expedition, the government had invested so much public and political capital in it.[65]

About the actual conduct of the expedition itself, little need be said.[66] As with Buenos Aires, initial success soon gave way to embarrassing failure. On 30 July, troops finally began landing on Walcheren, seizing several interior towns and the fort of Batz on the adjacent island of South Beveland. But the vital port city of Flushing, guarding the entrance to the Scheldt, held out against investment by land and bombardment by sea until 16 August, by which time, having been afforded more than enough warning, the French had withdrawn their naval squadron in the Scheldt to the protection of Antwerp's fortifications and had sufficiently reinforced the latter to make any successful attack on the city itself infeasible.

Meanwhile, Chatham's cautious advance on land coupled with the navy's inability to penetrate upriver in the teeth of worsening weather and French artillery soon shattered the army–navy harmony on which Castlereagh had counted so optimistically. By late August, with more than a quarter of the British force stricken with "Walcheren fever,"[67] it was apparent that seizure of Antwerp was out of reach. A council of war having reached the same conclusion,[68] on 27 August, Chatham advised London that the expedition must be abandoned and began withdrawing, leaving behind some 19,000 troops to garrison Walcheren in accordance with his orders.

But the abandonment of offensive operations was only the beginning of Walcheren's "long agony."[69] Hoping that Austria might yet reenter the war, the government delayed for nearly three months evacuating the forces that

William Henry Fitchett, *How England Saved Europe*, vol. III (New York, 1900), p. 104 (hereafter Fitchett).

[65] There was also a political undercurrent: openly critical of Castlereagh's management of military affairs on the peninsula, especially Moore's abortive venture into Spain, which Canning had bitterly opposed, the latter had surreptitiously been pressing Portland to replace Castlereagh. Doing so in the prevailing political climate threatened to split the cabinet, however. Since the Walcheren expedition was largely Castlereagh's project, allowing it to go forward offered Portland a perfect excuse to put Canning off. But the latter's machinations contributed their own quantum of confusion to the expedition's preparations. As one critic comments, "The plot in the Cabinet, and the public scandal which drove the British commander-in-chief from his office, left the Walcheren expedition drifting like a derelict ship on stagnant waters where no tide stirred and no wind blew." Fitchett, vol. III, p. 105.

[66] For a comprehensive description, see Gordon C. Bond, *The Grand Expedition: The British Invasion of Holland in 1809* (Athens, GA, 1979).

[67] Believed by modern medical researchers to have combined malaria, typhus, and typhoid fever. See John Lynch, "The Lessons of Walcheren Fever, 1809," *Military Medicine*, vol. 174, no. 3, March 2009, pp. 315–319.

[68] A conclusion to which only Strachan among Chatham's subordinates objected, possibly to protect himself against future recriminations. Muir, *Britain and the Defeat of Napoleon*, p. 103.

[69] Fortescue, vol. VII, p. 91.

Chatham had left behind. By the time it finally conceded failure and withdrew the last contingent from the island, more than 4,000 men had perished and thousands more were ill, some never to recover.[70] Of those who did, many suffered permanent weakness or periodic relapses that rendered them effectively unfit for further duty, degrading the army's ability to replace peninsular casualties well into 1812.[71]

At home, outrage over the debacle and its human costs culminated in a bitterly divisive parliamentary inquiry, which, however, ended by whitewashing the whole affair.[72] Not so public opinion, from which neither the government nor the expedition's two principal commanders emerged unscathed. As one caustic ditty proclaimed:

> Great Chatham, with his sabre drawn
> Stood waiting for Sir Richard Strachan
> Sir Richard, longing to be at 'em,
> Stood waiting for the Earl of Chatham.[73]

In October, 1809, in failing health, and embarrassed not only by Walcheren but also by Castlereagh's subsequent duel with Canning, forcing both from office, Portland resigned, dying shortly thereafter. The final melancholy withdrawal from Walcheren thus fell to their successors, Spencer Perceval, Liverpool, and Bathurst respectively.

The real question, of course, is why the British squandered so much effort on an objective that, even had they attained it, promised so little return. Part of the answer certainly lay in the Admiralty's persistent fear that Antwerp might enable Bonaparte to rebuild warships undisturbed, then to use them to break the blockade, a fear that Trafalgar had by no means entirely allayed. Contrariwise, supported by warships in the protected waters of the Scheldt, a British garrison at Antwerp might similarly have troubled Napoleon, at least to the extent of requiring him to maintain a significant covering force, and might conceivably have helped prompt rebellion in the Netherlands or convince a wavering Prussia to rejoin the fight.[74] In that case, Fortescue's claim

---

[70] Peace between Austria and France having been formalized on October 14th in the Treaty of Schönbrunn.

[71] Wellington eventually requested that no more units that had served on Walcheren be sent to him.

[72] Its initial and all too accurate conclusions – "That the expedition to the Scheldt was undertaken under circumstances which afforded no rational hope of adequate success … and that the advisers of this ill-judged enterprise are, in the opinion of this House, deeply responsible for the heavy calamities with which its failure has been attended" – failed on a division of the House by only 48 votes. See Robert Walsh, ed., *Select Speeches of The Right Honourable William Windham and The Right Honourable William Huskisson* (Philadelphia, 1837), p. 231.

[73] Believed to have appeared first in London's *Morning Chronicle* sometime in late 1809.

[74] Although, as Robert Harvey points out, "There was no real sign of disaffection in the Low Countries, which the highly strung King Louis, through his moderate policies, had effectively won over." Harvey, *The War of Wars*, p.673.

that "the expedition gave him [Bonaparte] some of the most anxious and unpleasant moments of his life" might actually have been correct.[75]

As we have seen, however, Chatham's orders envisioned no such permanent lodgment. Instead, the largest amphibious expedition until then mounted by Britain, not equaled until Gallipoli more than a century later, in effect represented nothing more than a raid. Executed as originally intended, to fix French forces otherwise available for redeployment against Austria, such an exercise might conceivably have been justifiable, although in contrast with the rejected north German alternative, it is far from clear that it would have achieved such a result. Deprived even of that rationale by the Franco-Austrian armistice, the expedition utterly lacked a convincing strategic aim; nevertheless, British leaders never contemplated abandoning it.

There remains the argument, advanced by Clausewitz among others, that the exercise could "be justified by the fact that the British troops could not be used in any other way."[76] That argument might have been valid in April, when Castlereagh proposed the expedition, and when there was no assurance that Wellesley would be successful even in recovering Oporto, let alone in ejecting the French from Portugal. By July, however, he had achieved both objectives and was about to go on the offensive against Victor. The Battle of Talavera, which coincidentally took place on the very day that Chatham sailed, was touch-and-go. It is hard to believe that Wellesley would have found an additional 10,000 troops superfluous. Moreover, Walcheren's deleterious effects on the army lingered long after the final evacuation, depriving Wellington of reinforcements for which he might well have found employment the following year, when French Marshal André Masséna invaded Portugal with 65,000 troops.

Instead, argues one critic,

It was not because no way could be found of employing her troops that Great Britain undertook the expedition to Walcheren, it was because the Government took more pains to help her continental allies than in giving to the general already in the field the number of troops that he needed for conducting his operations with credit.[77]

---

[75] Fortescue, vol. VII, p. 96. "Could British Ministers have seen the Emperor's letters to Clarke during the month of August?" He comments later,

his reiterated statements that Flushing was impregnable, the violent reproaches over his subordinate's slowness in enrolling troops, and his pungent criticism of his generals in Spain, they would have perceived that their perseverance was beginning to tell ... These things, however, were of course almost entirely hidden from the Cabinet and were totally invisible to the nation. The people could see nothing but armies squandered by generals, and Ministers, who tried to dress up defeat as victory.

Ibid., pp. 329–330.

[76] Carl von Clausewitz, *On War*, ed. and trans. by Michael Howard and Peter Paret (Princeton, 1976), p. 563.

[77] Colonel George Armand Furse, *Military Expeditions Beyond the Seas* (London, 1897), p. 24. Not all agree with this criticism, Fortescue in particular arguing that, as late as 1812,

Whether or not that was true, that the Walcheren debacle abundantly illustrated the government's continued inability and/or unwillingness to concentrate its military efforts is difficult to refute.

Although there is no doubt that Castlereagh was the mover and shaker of the original plan, assigning responsibility for the final decision, and especially for the failure to evacuate more promptly when the expedition clearly had failed, is much harder. Chatham himself was a significant proponent; he had been agitating for a field command ever since declining command in Portugal – and through him, although less enthusiastically, the king. Nor can one wholly absolve Canning of responsibility, although his motives appear to have owed less to strategic than to domestic political objectives. Meanwhile, the cabinet shared responsibility with Castlereagh for the delayed evacuation, and while the subsequent investigation prompted various excuses for the delay, it is hard to avoid concluding that the dominant motive was the government's desire to minimize its own embarrassment.

In the end, perhaps the most telling comment on the strategic decision making (or lack thereof) leading to Walcheren once again is Fortescue's, who argues that "From the beginning to the end of this war Ministers, when they chanced to have troops at their disposal, could never be easy until they employed them somewhere, doubtless because factious politicians were always demanding with clamor and contumely for what purpose, if not for foreign service, an army was maintained."[78]

One supreme blow: Spain, 1813

Between 1808 and 1812, British forces on the Iberian Peninsula, alone or with Spanish and Portuguese allies, invaded French-occupied Spain three times, only to be forced each time to withdraw. Frustratingly, defeat in the field prompted none of those withdrawals. Even the Battle of Corunna in January 1809 could be claimed a tactical success, although its only strategic result, like Dunkirk's a century later, was to enable the British Army to evacuate Spain in one piece. Talavera and Salamanca both were outright allied victories, the latter ending in the virtual rout of a larger French Army.

That even Salamanca produced no enduring strategic advantage supports Rory Muir's argument that British operations on the Iberian

---

Wellington lacked the logistics to support more British troops even had they been made available. Fortescue, vol. IX, p. 18. As will be seen, Wellington himself complained more frequently of an insufficiency of money than of troops.

[78] Fortescue, vol. VII, p. 53. He thus anticipated a more recent episode: UN ambassador Madeleine Albright's notorious challenge to then Joint Chiefs chairman Gen. Colin Powell during the 1990s Bosnian crisis – "What's the point of having this superb military you're always talking about if we can't use it?" – which Powell claims nearly gave him an aneurysm. See Colin Powell, *My American Journey* (New York, 2003), p. 561.

Peninsula were "made in isolation, not as part of a wider strategic plan."[79]
Several factors combined to discourage successive British governments before
1813 from concentrating sufficient military resources on the Peninsula.
The first was persistent fear of losing the forces committed. As Canning had
warned Moore prior to the latter's initial incursion into northern Spain,
"the army which has been appropriated by His Majesty to the defence of
Spain and Portugal is not merely a considerable part of the dispensable force
of this country. It is, in fact, the British army."[80]

Perhaps pardonably, Canning exaggerated. The 40,000 troops subsequently
committed to the Walcheren expedition did not materially reduce British
strength in the Peninsula, and Britain committed additional forces during
the same period to smaller peripheral expeditions. But the sub-text reflected
a genuine concern. With a volunteer army small to begin with compared with
continental armies, more than half of it stationed in Ireland or deployed to
secure Britain's expanding colonial seizures, British leaders could visualize no
way of confronting the more than 200,000 French troops in Spain on their own
with any hope of success.[81] The ease with which French armies shattered one
continental opponent after another did nothing to alleviate that concern, a
concern compounded by the lingering fear that outright destruction of any
significant expeditionary force would lay the British Isles open to invasion. The
army's narrow escape from Corunna in January 1809 helped not at all.
Together with Napoleon's concurrent defeat of Spain's regular forces, it
largely dispelled the public and political euphoria prompted initially by Spain's
1808 rebellion and brief military success.[82] "Gone forever was the dream of a
quick and victorious union in arms with the Spanish patriots, its place now
taken by an equally uncritical condemnation of all things Spanish."[83]

Indeed, as French Marshal Nicholas Soult's forces moved south from
Corunna, the government briefly despaired even of retaining Britain's foothold in Portugal. In a lengthy memorandum in April 1809, however, Castlereagh insisted that a relatively modest British troop commitment could defend
Portugal with the support of a reconstituted Portuguese Army equipped and
trained to British standards.[84] Similarly exhorted by Canning, who warned

---

[79] Muir, *Britain and the Defeat of Napoleon*, p. 104.
[80] David Gates, *The Spanish Ulcer* (Cambridge, MA, 1986), pp. 114–115.
[81] According to Fortescue, "The Army at the end of January 1809 numbered, as nearly as can
be calculated, about two hundred thousand effective rank and file, of whom at the moment
rather more than one half were abroad, and rather fewer than one half at home." Fortescue,
vol. VII, p. 33.
[82] Initial French operations in Spain were humiliatingly unsuccessful, culminating in July
1808 in the surrender of an entire French *corps d'armée* at Bailén in Andalusia. Furious,
Napoleon took personal command of a reinforced French commitment, routed three
Spanish armies in short order, and recaptured Madrid in December.
[83] Sherwig, *Guineas and Gunpowder*, p. 203.
[84] *Castlereagh Correspondence*, vol. VII, p. 39. His arguments reflected a March 7th
memorandum from Wellesley making the same case.

that, absent British assistance, Portugal certainly would be lost, the cabinet reluctantly agreed to dispatch Beresford, now a major-general, to rebuild Portugal's shattered army.[85] In the meantime, the French were moving south, brushing aside Portugal's exiguous defenders as they came. By the end of March, they had taken Oporto. Accordingly, with Mackenzie's troops denied entry to Cadiz and returned to Lisbon, Castlereagh dispatched Wellesley with an additional 10,000 troops to command them, under orders, however, explicitly prohibiting operations in Spain without prior ministerial authorization.

In the event, Wellesley soon sought relief from that prohibition. After recapturing Oporto and ejecting an overextended Soult from northern Portugal, he proposed to combine with the Spanish to defeat French forces in Estremadura. Buoyed by his success against Soult, the cabinet agreed. "Nevertheless, reluctance breathes through every word of the Cabinet's permission ... The ministers, including Canning, remained disillusioned with Spain, and were unwilling to look beyond the immediate defence of Portugal." Hence, "the foundation of Britain's future strategy throughout the war was laid, not as the keystone of a master plan, but as an ad hoc decision to try to preserve an existing asset."[86] His modified instructions permitted Wellesley to enter Spain only for tactical purposes, and only provided that doing so would incur no significant risk to the defense of Portugal or the preservation of his army. The crucial language is worth quoting at some length:

The Government of Spain not having thought fit to accede to this preliminary and indispensable condition [reinforcement of Cadiz], and having actually declined to permit the British troops, under Major-Generals Sherbrooke and Mackenzie, who were sent as the advanced guard of the British Army, to land at Cadiz, his Majesty does not feel that he can, in justice to the safety of his own troops, again employ an auxiliary army in Spain, till the Spanish Government and nation shall cease to entertain those feelings of jealousy, which are equally inconsistent with their own interest and the effectual prosecution of the war.

You will therefore understand that it is not his Majesty's intention, in authorizing you to co-operate with the Spanish armies in the defence of Portugal and of the adjacent Spanish provinces, that you should enter upon a campaign in Spain without the express authority of your Government; and, in any concert you may form with the armies of Spain, you will cause it to be understood that it is to be confined to the specific object in view; and that the service of your arm (under the orders you

[85] A task he carried out so effectively as to earn praise even from Wellington, who was not given to complimenting other generals. "To [Beresford] exclusively, under the Portuguese Government," Wellington wrote to the secretary of state for war on 30 September 1810, "is due the merit of having raised, formed, disciplined, and equipped the Portuguese army, which has now shown itself capable of engaging and defeating the enemy." Wellington to Liverpool, "Dispatches, September 21st–24th, 1810," www.wtj.com/archives/Wellington.
[86] Muir, *Britain and the Defeat of Napoleon*, p. 86.

have received) cannot be employed in general operations in Spain, as the force under Sir John Moore was intended to have been, without a previous arrangement being settled to that effect between the two Governments.[87]

The Battle of Talavera that followed earned Wellesley his peerage, but also vindicated the government's caution. The Spanish proved stubbornly uncooperative, the British did most of the fighting and suffered most of the casualties, promised Spanish logistical support failed to materialize, and Wellington was compelled to retreat back to Portugal. Responding to criticism of that decision, he wrote to Lord Burghersh, "I lament as much as any man can the necessity for separating from the Spaniards, but I was compelled to go and I believe there was not an officer in the army who did not think I stayed too long."[88]

That Spanish failure to cooperate was the second major factor inhibiting an unreserved British commitment to operations in Spain, and would continue to plague Anglo-Spanish relations for the next three years. In part, it reflected persistent (and not entirely unjustified) Spanish suspicion of British motives and reliability. Only four years had elapsed since Trafalgar, after all, and only two since Britain's failed attack on Spanish America. For many Spaniards, alliance with Britain was at best the lesser of two evils, a sentiment in no way allayed by their detestation of the Portuguese, a problem of which Wellington himself was forced to take note.[89]

But Spanish intractability also reflected the persistent internal disunity of the Spanish government and military. While the establishment of a Supreme Junta in September 1808 supposedly furnished unified politico-military direction, the Spanish Army was less one army than several separate and autonomous armies under commanders each jealous of his own authority. Not until mid 1812, over their bitter objections, were Spanish commanders subordinated even nominally to unified military direction under Wellington, and even that subordination proved to be honored mostly in the breach. Wellington's retreat from Spain in the wake of his great victory at Salamanca, for example, owed no little to Spanish General Francisco Ballesteros' mutinous refusal to obey his orders.[90]

What rescued the Spanish from themselves were the activities of the *guerrilleros* who sprang up in every province, and who year by year inflicted a

---

[87] *Castlereagh Correspondence*, vol. VII, pp. 49–50.
[88] Michael Glover, *The Peninsular War, 1807–1814: A Concise Military History* (London, 2001), p. 115.
[89] "To the Earl of Liverpool, 30 March 1810": "I am fully aware of the mutual hatred of the Spanish and Portuguese people toward each other…" Walter Wood (ed.), *The Despatches of Field Marshall the Duke of Wellington* (London, 1902), p. 206 (hereafter *Wellington's Despatches*).
[90] For which he subsequently was arrested, replaced, and imprisoned. Gates, *The Spanish Ulcer*, pp. 371–372.

progressively greater drain on the French military.[91] As Wellington wrote to Lord Liverpool in April, 1810:

My opinion is that, as long as we shall remain in a state of activity in Portugal, the contest must continue in Spain; that the French are most desirous that we should withdraw from the country, but know that they must employ a very large force indeed in the operations which will render it necessary for us to go away; and I doubt whether they can bring that force to bear upon Portugal without abandoning other objects and exposing their whole fabric in Spain to great risk. If they should be able to invade it, and should not succeed in obliging us to evacuate the country, they will be in a very dangerous situation; and the longer we can oppose them, and delay their success, the more likely are they to suffer materially in Spain.[92]

Wellington's subsequent defense of Lisbon's "Lines of Torres Vedras" against Masséna's invasion wholly justified his confidence and went far toward reconciling the government to a continued peninsular commitment. Even so, while such defensive efforts preserved Britain's foothold, they offered little prospect of ejecting the French from Spain unless Britain's peninsular allies could be made effective. Thanks to Beresford's efforts, Portuguese regulars had so improved by 1812 that British commanders considered them virtually the equal of their British counterparts, but their limited numbers and the need to safeguard Portugal's frontiers restricted their employment in Spain. Hence, as Wellington himself acknowledged, "It is obvious that we cannot expect to save the Peninsula by military efforts unless we can bring forward the Spaniards in some shape or other."[93]

Apart from Spanish fecklessness, the major obstacle to that ambition, and the third major deterrent to concentrating Britain's military effort on the Peninsula, was lack of money. "During the early days of the Spanish uprising in 1808, London had flooded the Peninsula with more than £2.5 million in silver. Having spent their majority like gentlemen, the ministers were now hard-pressed to lay their hands on more."[94] To some extent, gifts of the military materiel – uniforms, weapons, ammunition, and so on – that British industry was turning out in growing quantity could compensate for lack of hard currency with which to satisfy the allies' incessant demand for British subsidies. But soldiers' pay and the purchase of subsistence still required specie, and by 1812 it had become hard to find.[95] As Wellington wrote to Bathurst in July,

---

[91] René Chartrand's *Spanish Guerrillas in the Peninsular War, 1808–1814* (London, 2004) offers an agreeably readable description of the character and operations of the irregulars. A more detailed analysis, albeit limited to a single province, is John Lawrence Tone's *The Fatal Knot* (Chapel Hill, NC, 1994), which examines partisan warfare in Navarre.

[92] "To the Earl of Liverpool, 2 April 1810," *Wellington's Despatches*, pp. 208–209.

[93] Quoted in Charles Esdaile, *The Peninsular War* (New York, 2002), p. 421.

[94] Sherwig, *Guineas and Gunpowder*, p. 224. With respect to financing the war in general, Sherwig's is the definitive treatment.

[95] As Fortescue points out, "the difficulties arising from the dearth of specie reached their climax in 1812 ... The Bank [of England] had exhausted its store of foreign gold

"We are absolutely bankrupt. The troops are now five months in arrears, instead of being one month in advance. The staff have not been paid since February; the muleteers not since June 1811; and we are in debt in all parts of the country."[96]

After pay for Wellington's soldiers, the principal effect of this dearth of money was logistical. As early as August 1809, in the aftermath of Talavera, Wellington had complained that "We are miserably supplied with provisions, and I do not know how to remedy this evil. The Spanish armies are now so numerous that they eat up the whole country. They have no magazines, nor have we, nor can we collect any; and there is a scramble for everything."[97] Three more years of armies marching back and forth across a Spain economically depressed even before the war did little to improve the situation. There could be no question of a strategically decisive offensive unless and until means could be found to keep British and allied forces resupplied on the march without having to rely on a Spanish countryside denuded of surplus food.[98] Accumulating such means, needless to say, was above all a question of money.

No single problem prompted more persistent and occasionally bitter correspondence from Wellington to his political masters, the general at one point writing the secretary to the treasury, "It will be better for Government in every view of the subject to relinquish their operations in Portugal and Spain, if the country cannot afford to carry them on."[99] On this issue, however, Fortescue uncharacteristically sides with the politicians.

Liverpool had wisely and rightly abjured Pitt's system of great spasmodic effort, followed by helpless collapse, in favour of a policy of steady, even and sustained endeavour. When the right moment should arrive, Ministers were ready to concentrate the whole of England's military resources for the striking of one supreme blow.[100]

In 1813, thanks to several related developments, that moment finally arrived. By the beginning of 1813, with the lingering after effects of Walcheren at last overcome, British troop strength in Iberia exceeded 60,000. To these could be added another 15,000 Portuguese troops, bringing the total manpower available to Wellington to nearly 80,000. The money problem likewise

---

and of bar-gold, and had nothing left but guineas, which it was illegal either to export or to exchange for more than their nominal value." Fortescue, vol. IX, pp. 12–13.

[96] *Wellington's Despatches*, p. 324.

[97] "To Viscount Castlereagh, August 1809," *Wellington's Despatches*, p. 176.

[98] As George Murray, one of Wellington's quartermaster-generals, commented not altogether facetiously at one point, "Historians will say that the British army ... carried on war in Spain & Portugal until they had eaten all the beef and mutton in the country, and were then compelled to withdraw." Elizabeth Longford, *Wellington: The Years of the Sword* (New York, 1969), p. 305.

[99] "Wellington to Huskisson, 28 March 1810," in Fortescue, vol. VII, pp. 435–436.

[100] Fortescue, vol. IX, p. 18.

having eased,[101] Wellington was at last enabled to accumulate sufficient supply and transport to sustain a prolonged offensive campaign. Finally, the lull in operations during fall and winter 1812 enabled him to realize significant improvements in the army's health and tactical proficiency.[102] As he reported to the secretary of state for war on 11 May, "I shall never be stronger or more efficient than I am now."[103]

Improvement of Spanish forces paralleled, if it did not equal, that of the British and Portuguese. Furious at Ballesteros' insubordination in the aftermath of Salamanca, Wellington demanded and the Cortes reluctantly approved a significant enlargement of his authority over Spanish commanders. While the tactical proficiency of Spanish units continued to lag behind that of their allies, the willingness of their commanders to cooperate improved measurably. So also did their relations with the irregulars, some units of which had by now become so large and successful that they were integrated formally into the regular Spanish Army, their commanders awarded rank and privileges commensurate with their professional counterparts.

Meanwhile, even as the allies' condition improved during the winter and spring, that of their adversaries eroded. Units withdrawn from Spain the year before to feed Napoleon's disastrous invasion of Russia were not replaced, and with a new threat facing him in Central Europe, still more would be withdrawn. Those remaining in Spain were overstretched and under mounting pressure from both regular Spanish forces and *guerrilleros*, the latter by now so numerous and self-confident as to make unhindered French movement in less than battalion strength nearly impossible. Couriers and supply columns were especially favored targets, to the point where French commanders effectively were blind outside their immediate garrisons and had to enlarge the escorts of every foraging party and convoy.

It was Napoleon's own intemperate reaction to that problem that unlocked the last door to a decisive allied offensive. In April, furious at mounting insurgent depredations in the northern provinces (Asturias, Cantabria, Navarre, and northern Aragon) and convinced Wellington lacked the stomach to mount another offensive campaign, he ordered Joseph to reassign a significant portion of Reille's Army of Portugal to Clausel's harried Army of the North, leaving his hapless brother fewer than 40,000 troops to bar any allied advance into central Spain.

---

[101] By, among other means, the grudging but economically providential shift within Great Britain proper to paper currency at a guaranteed rate of exchange, freeing specie for use abroad.

[102] "The army after the retreat from Burgos enjoyed, as it sorely needed, the longest period of repose vouchsafed to it in the whole course of the war." Fortescue, vol. IX, p. 107.

[103] Gates, *The Spanish Ulcer*, p. 383. It should be noted that, although Britain and the US went to war in June 1812, no significant reinforcement of British forces in North America occurred before the summer of 1814. The War of 1812 thus had little direct impact on Wellington's operations.

On 22 May 1813, Wellington charged through the door thus opened, feinting toward Salamanca as Joseph frantically sought to concentrate his scattered forces, while the main allied effort sliced north toward Valladolid and Burgos. Repeatedly turned out of position, the French withdrew hastily toward the Ebro, until at last on 21 June, fearing to be hustled out of Spain altogether, Joseph finally stood to fight at Vitoria. The defeat that followed spared most of his army, but left it little choice but to recoil back to the Pyrenees, whence, over the following two months, the allies drove it back into France, followed not long thereafter by French forces in eastern Spain. Meanwhile, announced triumphantly by London, the allied victory at Vitoria encouraged Austria to join Britain, Russia, Prussia, and Sweden in a Sixth Coalition. On 6 April 1814, invaded from north, east, and south, and pressured by his own generals, Napoleon finally abdicated.

Napoleon's abdication and subsequent exile on Elba failed to end the struggle. Minor military actions continued throughout spring 1814 in Italy, Spain, and Holland. Then, on 26 February 1815, with the allies at loggerheads in Vienna over how to carve up post-Napoleonic Europe, and Louis XVIII making himself nearly as unloved by the French people as his late brother, Bonaparte slipped away from Elba with 600 of his personal guard and landed in southern France on 1 March. Three weeks later, without a shot fired to prevent it, he triumphantly reentered Paris. His return inaugurated what became known as the Hundred Days, culminating in his decisive defeat by Wellington and Prussia's Marshal Gebhard von Blücher at Waterloo on 15 June, followed on 8 July by Louis XVIII's (second) restoration and a week later by Napoleon's surrender to Maitland and final exile to St. Helena.

From a strategic perspective, the principal effect of these events was to shake the delegates at the Congress of Vienna out of their torpor.[104] While one can argue in retrospect that Napoleon had no real chance of retaining power as long as Britain and Russia remained committed to his removal,[105] that reality was less apparent to the representatives of the great powers that had expended so much blood and treasure to bring him down and had endured so many disappointments. The allied victory at Waterloo thus came as an enormous relief, its swiftness and conclusiveness helping to avert a prolonged struggle that, even though eventually won by the allies, almost certainly would have reopened questions settled painfully in Vienna, and imposed on France a significantly more punitive and fragile peace. That it took place in Belgium was appropriate, given that French intervention in Belgium had largely prompted Britain's war with France in the first place,

---

[104] Famously derided by Austria's Prince de Ligne with the quip, "Le congrès danse, mais il ne marche pas." (The congress dances, but doesn't walk – i.e., makes no progress.)

[105] An argument that the writer has made elsewhere. See Richard Hart Sinnreich, "In Search of Military Repose: The Congress of Vienna and the Making of Peace," in Williamson Murray and James Lacey, eds., *The Making of Peace: Rulers, States, and the Aftermath of War* (Cambridge, 2009), p. 148.

just as there was a certain poetic justice in a final contest pitting Napoleon himself against the one adversary who had beaten every other French general against whom he had fought. At any rate, the war thus ended with a drama shared with few other such military-historical events.

Conclusion

In the wake of the terrible bloodletting of 1914 to 1918, a scholarly debate arose about British military strategy that persists to this day, for which Britain's victory over Napoleon more than any other single experience furnished the core evidence in contention. The instigator of the debate was British military commentator Sir Basil Liddell Hart, who argued that in the Great War, Britain had abandoned what he conceived to be a preferred British "way of war" dictated by both its geopolitical circumstances and history. Central to that way of war, in his view, was the deliberate avoidance of decisive land operations on the European mainland in favor of an "indirect approach" designed to exploit British seapower and focused on the continental periphery. Just such a strategy, he insisted, had underwritten Britain's intervention on the Iberian Peninsula from 1808 through 1813 in support of Portuguese and Spanish resistance.[106]

Liddell Hart's viewpoint resonated with many in the years after the First World War and resurfaced during the Second World War, albeit in somewhat different form, in Winston Churchill's "soft underbelly" arguments. In the end, though, the latter failed to deter Britain's involvement in land operations in the European interior. Since then, several military historians have refuted Liddell Hart's assertion of a historically validated British way of war, notably Sir Michael Howard. Not least of the grounds for Howard's objection was a very different interpretation of Britain's strategy in the war against Napoleonic France. For Howard, Britain's decision ultimately to engage Napoleon decisively only on the Iberian Peninsula reflected less a considered strategic preference than a dearth of realistic military alternatives.[107] When Napoleon's escape from Elba and his subsequent invasion of Belgium in spring 1815 presented a renewed threat to the peace, Howard points out, Britain did not hesitate to commit British troops to operations on the European mainland.[108]

---

[106] B. H. Liddell Hart, *The British Way in Warfare* (London, 1932), pp. 35–37.

[107] Hall agrees, arguing that "the politicians whose responsibility it was to formulate policy did so in circumstances of very limited strategic choice." Hall, *British Strategy in the Napoleonic War*, p. xi.

[108] Michael Howard, "The British Way in Warfare: A Reappraisal," in Michael Howard, *The Causes of War and Other Essays* (Cambridge, MA, 1983), pp. 178–180. Indeed, as he noted in another context,

It was ... precisely the failure of German power to find an outlet and its consequent concentration in Europe, its lack of any significant possessions overseas, that made it so particularly menacing to the sprawling British Empire in two world wars and which make so

Although mutually contradictory, both arguments similarly attribute to deliberate strategic intention what the episodes described in the preceding pages strongly suggest resulted instead from a prolonged and circuitous process of trial and error. That strong-willed ministers such as Pitt, Grenville, Canning, and Castlereagh held and sought to impose views about how Britain should employ its military and naval power cannot be doubted. But not until after years of false starts and disappointments did the British government finally settle on an agreed set of strategic priorities. Until then, disagreement recurred repeatedly with respect to definitions of strategic success, the mechanism by which it should be achieved, in particular the role of the British Army, and finally the theater in which that army's effort should focus.

Those debates rarely resembled the formal deliberative processes that we have come to associate with strategic decision making, but instead manifested themselves in the exchange and circulation of contending letters, notes, and memoranda. Even these tended to focus on immediate military issues. Secondary sources are replete with references to "the cabinet felt," "the cabinet decided," and "the cabinet directed." But even a cursory examination of ministerial minutes reveals much of that as convenient shorthand. One searches in vain for meetings comparable, say, to those of Presidents Bush's and Obama's National Security Councils concerning Iraq and Afghanistan, during which they and their principal political and military advisors examined and debated explicitly competing policy options. Cabinet meetings at the turn of the nineteenth century tended to be informal and participation often limited. Opposition leaders did not participate at all, some declining even to remain in London.[109]

Reviewing the circumstances surrounding cabinet decisions of the time, it is apparent that, as continues to be true today, views concerning what strategic aims Britain should pursue and by what means reflected differences ranging from genuine economic and military conviction to political factionalism and personal ambition. And yet in retrospect, though perhaps only in retrospect, the strategic problem confronting successive British governments really involved only three interdependent but distinguishable questions: (1) how to convert maritime supremacy into continental advantage; (2) how heavily to rely on allies who repeatedly had proved either incompetent or inconstant; and (3) given answers to the first two questions, when and where to employ Britain's limited ground combat power.[110]

---

misleading all arguments about "traditional" British strategy drawn from earlier conflicts against the Spanish and French Empires, with all the colonial hostages they offered to fortune and the Royal Navy.

Howard, *The Continental Commitment* (Oxford, 1971), p. 32.

[109] Hall, *British Strategy in the Napoleonic War*, p. 61.

[110] A fourth question might be added – whether to settle for a negotiated peace aimed at containing Napoleon rather than seeking to remove him altogether at whatever cost. But despite post-Amiens efforts by both the Grenville and Perceval governments to engineer a

Each of the episodes in this essay sought to answer all three questions, but in different ways. Thus, though launched without prior political approval by two overaggressive military commanders, the Buenos Aires expedition was consistent with earlier British efforts to exploit naval supremacy to deprive France and its allies of colonial resources and with the Grenville government's disaffection with continental allies. But, apart from commercial inducements, it was above all the seductive opportunity to pursue the first and avoid the second with a limited commitment of troops that convinced the government to honor its brash subordinates' unsanctioned initiative. That what began as a limited commitment soon grew into one much more extensive (and expensive) reflected the political concern to avoid embarrassment and amortize sunk costs more than any considered strategic decision.

In contrast, while the Walcheren expedition originated at the behest of an ally, compounded by the Admiralty's lingering fear that Antwerp might resurrect the French naval threat, the target largely reflected the government's reluctance to commit a large land force where it could not count even on allied logistical support, let alone additional forces, hence where large expenditures would be necessary merely to sustain the expedition. Just such considerations ruled out northern Germany of unhappy memory, while the impossibility of mounting a timely assault ruled out Italy. The final plan envisioned what amounted to a raid, not a decisive confrontation with Napoleon. That the expedition went forward even after Austria's defeat at Wagram had nullified its original purpose reflected political inertia, compounded, as in the Buenos Aires debacle, by the desire to avoid political embarrassment.

As for the Iberian commitment, the British largely could thank Bonaparte himself for furnishing a strategically convincing answer to all three questions as well as for the allies' eventual success. By seeking to conquer a nation that he might easily have ruled without reigning, by imposing on his brother and the latter's generals a troop-to-task mismatch only compounded by French mistreatment of the Portuguese and Spanish people, and, finally, by first diverting already insufficient forces to his disastrous invasion of Russia, then interfering with the employment of those remaining, Napoleon furnished the very conditions that a decisive British land commitment required. These included a geography allowing optimal exploitation of the Royal Navy's freedom of action; allies who, if occasionally troublesome, were for the most part steadfast, and whose military manpower, both regular and irregular, represented an essential force multiplier for a British peninsular army that never reached a third of its antagonist's numerical strength; and an aroused civil population that forced the French to dissipate that strength even as it eroded. As Fortescue scathingly notes, "let the worshippers of the great Emperor say what they will, there is among the manifold blunders that ruined

settlement, the reality, eventually perceived by most Britons both in and out of government, was that no attempt to contain Bonaparte by treaty promised to endure.

the French cause in the Peninsula not one that may not be traced directly to the orders of the Emperor himself."[111]

In short, examined in hindsight, Britain's crucial achievement was to preserve intact its physical safety, maritime freedom of action, and economic and military resources until presented with an opportunity to act decisively, then recognize and exploit that opportunity. But that achievement reflected no preconceived or enduring strategic design. If the problem confronting successive British governments was a dearth of attractive strategic alternatives, much as Howard characterized it, their solutions throughout most of the war seem largely to have been extemporaneous.[112]

One hesitates to extrapolate from so brief an examination of so lengthy and remote a history definitive lessons about the ingredients of successful strategy. Nevertheless, one scarcely can review that history without concluding that Britain's ultimate triumph against Napoleon owed less to strategy than to other factors: to a geostrategic position that afforded it the luxury, provided the Royal Navy remained supreme, of choosing when and where to engage its enemy; to an economy able not only to satisfy its own military needs but also repeatedly to subsidize those of its allies; to a political system sufficiently robust to transcend scandals and embarrassments; and above all, to a public self-confidence and resolve that enabled the British people, as they would again a century later, to endure and recover from repeated military disappointments without ever losing faith in eventual victory.

All this tends to suggest that, in the end, strategic success is likely to result less from preconceived planning than from continuous and often contentious adaptation underwritten by effective diagnosis of changes in the operating environment. The latter, moreover, is much more than just a matter of collating and evaluating information. Instead, it is above all about recognizing the evolving *Gestalt* of the strategic problem – about answering Ferdinand Foch's famous rhetorical question, "De quoi s'agit-il?" From a strategic standpoint, the vital task of assessment is not gathering details, but rather abstracting their larger meaning. In Britain's war against Napoleonic France, the crucial assessment was that, while Britain remained secure from invasion and its people committed, Napoleon could not prevail; and that, given his own strategic imperatives and the demons driving him, not to prevail sooner

---

[111] Fortescue, vol. VIII, p. 625.

[112] One might argue that, given Britain's long history of struggles with France, its strategy was so deeply imbedded in the minds of British leaders that no explicit discussion of strategic alternatives was necessary. A case can be made that just such an implicit strategic understanding informed Britain's initial commitment in 1793. If so, however, it certainly no longer prevailed after the collapse of three successive continental coalitions. Indeed, following Austria's defeat at Austerlitz on 2 December 1805, Pitt is famously alleged to have remarked, "Roll up that map of Europe. It will not be wanted these ten years." James L. Stokesbury, *Navy and Empire: A Short History of Four Centuries of British Sea Power and its Influence upon Our World* (New York, 1983), p. 202.

or later meant losing. Britain's central military and political challenge was to sustain the struggle long enough to reach that painfully prolonged but ultimately successful outcome, and that challenge, successive British governments met successfully.

In contrast, as long as the strategic problem is misdiagnosed, no amount of effort and sacrifice will produce success.[113] In famously arguing that "No one starts a war – or rather, no one in his senses ought to do so – without first being clear in his mind what he intends to achieve by that war and how he intends to conduct it,"[114] Clausewitz describes an ideal, but on the evidence, one rarely achieved in practice. Instead, in Britain's case at least, both judgments occurred, not as ingredients of a coherent strategic design carefully devised before going to war, but instead in successive course corrections after doing so: first accepting that naval and colonial successes alone could not restrain Napoleon's ambitions, then acknowledging that only his outright removal could do so and would require defeating him on his own ground, and finally, settling on where to focus Britain's limited land combat power to help bring that about.

At each stage, British statesmen arrived at the necessary conclusion reluctantly, contentiously, and only after trying other alternatives. That the outcome nevertheless laid the foundation for a century of British supremacy is, or should be, a humbling lesson to those convinced that preconceived strategy is either prerequisite to or a guarantor of victory. Instead, success is more likely to crown belligerents willing and able to jettison their own strategic preconceptions when the latter are falsified, as they often will be, by the painful but rarely disputable evidence furnished by war itself.

---

[113] In Afghanistan, for example, NATO's core strategic appraisal has been that "the center of gravity is the Afghan people." If that appraisal is incorrect, the likelihood that NATO will succeed in defeating the Taliban is slim. For a more refined argument, see David E. Johnson, "What Are You Prepared to Do? NATO and the Strategic Mismatch Between Ends, Ways, and Means in Afghanistan – and in the Future," *Studies in Conflict & Terrorism*, vol. 34. no. 5, pp. 383–401.

[114] Clausewitz, *On War*, p. 579.

7   The strategy of Lincoln and Grant

Wayne Hsieh

Abraham Lincoln's primary grand strategic aim during the Civil War, to preserve the Union, contained within itself a deceptive simplicity. On the one hand, it meant preserving the Federal Union of 1860 and the results of the 1860 presidential election, which had elected a Republican Party committed not to abolishing slavery, but to restricting it to the states where it existed. On the other hand, the outbreak of war in 1861 raised questions within the states loyal to the Union as to whether or not the Republican Party's ante-bellum goals could provide a lasting political and military solution to the rebellion. Some Republicans hoped to strike at what they saw as the root cause of Confederate treason – a social system dominated by slaveholding planters – with punitive measures most would have disavowed during the 1860 election, while many Democrats and even some conservative Republicans feared the consequences of harsh measures for both domestic liberty in the free soil states and the prospects of long-term reunion.

Lincoln eventually determined that only "hard war" measures could break Confederate resistance, but he had to manage a divided Northern public opinion even as his own views evolved. In 1864, in accordance with his commander-in-chief's political ends, Ulysses Grant selected a military strategy of coordinated and simultaneous military movements against Confederate military power that had the virtues of simplicity and inherent flexibility. Grant adapted his military methods to Lincoln's need to manage his political coalition, even when it required overriding Grant's own professional preferences as to military priorities and personnel. Above all, Lincoln had to prevent political support for the war from collapsing under the stress of increasing losses in blood and treasure, even when the North's political system's own misplaced priorities helped bring about the very losses that came so close to demoralizing it.

By winter 1863/4, Lincoln and Grant had developed the grand strategy that eventually won the war. Coordinated pressure on every front attacked the South's ability to feed its armies when Northern armies could not destroy its military forces more directly, and Union armies facilitated emancipation by either freeing slaves directly or serving as magnets that attracted the most intrepid slaves in areas under nominal Confederate control but in the vicinity of Federal forces. Emancipation weakened the South's economic basis and foreclosed intervention by anti-slavery Britain, while adding badly needed recruits to the Union Army. Union naval power at the same time enforced a tightening blockade that hastened the decline of the Confederacy's crucial but vulnerable railroads.[1] Finally, the Lincoln administration recognized that, because former Confederates would have to acquiesce to Federal supremacy and the end of slavery, Federal forces could not embark on a scorched-earth campaign of punitive retribution after the surrender and demobilization of Confederate military forces. Given unlimited time, this strategy would almost certainly have succeeded in any plausible scenario, but the looming 1864 presidential election insured that the Lincoln administration would have so little time from the Northern electorate to show progress that failure became a real possibility.

Historians have paid ample attention to the merits of the Union's final victorious strategy, and whatever controversies persist over Lincoln's leadership center on either a libertarian fear of his supposedly statist policies or left-wing disappointment with Lincoln's policies and views on race. Few modern historians question Lincoln's consummate political skill.[2] While Grant's military reputation has oscillated between different poles in the 150 years since the war, few competent historians since J. F. C. Fuller subscribe to the view of Grant as a "butcher" who blundered his way to victory via clumsy and sanguinary methods of attrition.[3]

However, academic historians have not examined the experiences of Lincoln and Grant in light of the problems and challenges that early twenty-first-century strategic planners face in formulating American foreign policy and grand strategy.[4] Historians should avoid glib comparisons, but neither

---

[1] Since the focus of this essay is on Lincoln and Grant, the Union blockade will not receive extensive coverage. While historians have argued over the blockade's effectiveness, the most recent scholarship judges the blockade's most serious military effects to have been in how the Federal suppression of coastal domestic shipping in the Confederacy further overburdened an inadequate, deteriorating, and irreparable Confederate railroad network. See Lance E. Davis and Stanley L. Engerman, *Naval Blockades in Peace and War: An Economic History since 1750* (Cambridge, 2006), p. 158, and David G. Surdam, *Northern Naval Superiority and the Economics of the American Civil War* (Columbia, SC, 2001), pp. 83–84, 207.

[2] For two recent and relevant scholarly studies of Lincoln, see David Herbert Donald, *Lincoln* (London, 1995); Philip Paludan, *The Presidency of Abraham Lincoln* (Lawrence, KS, 1994).

[3] Joan Waugh, *U.S. Grant: American Hero, American Myth* (Chapel Hill, NC, 2009), pp. 304, 307; J. F. C. Fuller, *The Generalship of Ulysses S. Grant* (London, 1929). The current standard scholarly biography is Brooks D. Simpson, *Ulysses S. Grant: Triumph over Adversity, 1822–1865* (Boston, 2000).

[4] The strictly historical literature on Union strategy and the American Civil War cannot be summarized here, but the two most important recent books are James M. McPherson, *Tried by War: Abraham Lincoln as Commander in Chief* (New York, 2008), and Donald Stoker, *The Grand Design: Strategy and the U.S. Civil War* (New York, 2010). McPherson's work is the sounder history, and while Stoker is more engaged with modern discussions of strategy, his book is weaker in its grasp of both the history itself and the larger literature. Herman Hattaway and Archer Jones, *How the North Won: A Military History of the Civil War* (Urbana, IL, 1991) remains the standard one-volume military history of the Union war

should they cede the field of policy formulation to political scientists, and the American Civil War highlights to a modern audience the importance of public opinion and democratic coalition building in the formulation of grand strategy. In an era of instantaneous communication, social media, public opinion polling, and relentless media coverage, the American Civil War underlines that current policy makers should recognize that past American leaders have had to reconcile their ends with a political system designed to respond more readily to changes in public sentiment, rather than to the exigencies of long-term strategic realities.

In the context of mid-nineteenth-century American politics, Lincoln as party leader had to manage the diverse factions within the Republican Party while retaining sufficient support from the Democratic minority in the North to prosecute the war to its successful conclusion. While the Republicans had swept the North in the election of 1860, in the words of one historian, "though divided between two candidates and forced to defend one of the most unpopular and corrupt administrations in American history, the Democrats still won almost 44 percent of the popular vote in the free states in 1860," compared to almost 54 percent for Lincoln.[5] The Democratic Party remained the "Democracy," which had risen to prominence under Andrew Jackson during the 1820s and 1830s and which historians still call the Jacksonian period.

As a young man, Lincoln had grown up a Whig, the party which had opposed the Democracy, but which had later collapsed as a coherent political force in the 1850s. Various political parties, including the Republicans, competed with one another to rally opposition to a Democratic Party increasingly dominated by slaveholders. The fractured political landscape of the free states in the election of 1860 showed that, even then, the Republican Party still only held a fragile political position in the North, never mind slaveholding border states such as Missouri, Kentucky, Maryland, and Delaware which had remained in the Union.[6] As the war dragged on, Lincoln never lost sight of Northern Democrats' potential political power at the polls and through widespread acts of civil disobedience. While the vast majority of Northern Democrats supported the war to restore the Union, many did not want victory at the cost of what they viewed to be excessive restrictions on liberty at home and overly punitive measures against former Confederates, which in their view would compromise the long-term goal of reunion.

---

effort. This chapter attempts to take a more systemic approach to the role of political influences on Union strategy during the Civil War by focusing on Lincoln and Grant.

[5] Michael Holt, *Political Parties and American Political Development from the Age of Jackson to the Age of Lincoln* (Baton Rouge, LA, 1992), pp. 325–326; James M. McPherson and James K. Hogue, *Ordeal by Fire: The Civil War and Reconstruction*, 4th edn. (New York, 2000), p. 138.

[6] Holt, *Political Parties*, pp. 333–334. For a concise treatment of American political history and the coming of the Civil War, see Michael F. Holt, *The Fate of Their Country: Politicians, Slavery Extension, and the Coming of the Civil War* (New York, 2004).

Even Civil War specialists have not always paid sufficient attention to the scale of Northern dissent against the mobilization measures that became necessary to prosecute the war to a victorious conclusion. Conscription proved to be the most vexatious issue, and the New York City draft riots of 1863 proved only the most spectacular and violent manifestation of Northern opposition to the draft. Casualties from these riots included approximately 119 dead and over 300 injured. The working-class white rioters reserved special fury for African-Americans, whom they saw as dangerous competitors at the lowest end of the economic scale. They incinerated a black orphanage and murdered African-Americans they found on the streets. After the initial suppression of the rioters by troops from the Army of the Potomac, the Lincoln administration acquiesced to a long-term solution that allowed New York City authorities to fund commutation fees or obtain substitutes to excuse their constituents from military service. Utica, Brooklyn, Albany, Troy, Syracuse, and Auburn followed New York City's lead in subsidizing draft avoidance.[7] In the run-up to the election, various episodes of draft resistance bubbled up, the most serious in central Pennsylvania, where 1,200 to 1,800 deserters, defiant draftees, and Copperheads killed the colonel sent to round up deserters before being eventually suppressed.[8]

During the war, draft resisters murdered 38 conscription officials and wounded 60 others.[9] Serious draft-related disturbances occurred across the North in communities as diverse as Chicago's Third Ward, Boston, Portsmouth, Troy, Milwaukee, St. Paul, and among Irish-American miners in Pennsylvania's Tenth Congressional district.[10] Different localities had different reasons for disorder, including corrupt or inept district provost marshals, but one modern historian has generalized that "depending on the area, the basis for their objections emanated mainly from racial animosity, general dissatisfaction with the Lincoln administration, and discontent with employers who sought to employ federal authority against their interests."[11] Indeed, the authorities relied so much on partisan political machinery that the crucial provost marshal's office in charge of the draft relied on the Republican political apparatus for officials, described by one historian as "narrow-minded partisans totally lacking in tact or judgment."[12]

---

[7] Iver Bernstein, *The New York City Draft Riots: Their Significance for American Society and Politics in the Age of the Civil War* (New York, 1990), p. 5; Philip Paludan, *People's Contest: The Union and Civil War, 1861–1865* (Lawrence, KS, 1988), pp. 191, 193.

[8] Jennifer L. Weber, *Copperheads: The Rise and Fall of Lincoln's Opponents in the North* (New York, 2006), p. 195.

[9] Hattaway and Jones, *How the North Won*, p. 438.

[10] Paludan, *People's Contest*, pp. 191–192.

[11] James W. Geary, *We Need Men: The Union Draft in the Civil War* (DeKalb, IL, 1991), pp. 71, 107–108.

[12] Paludan, *People's Contest*, p. 236.

For all its political controversy, the conscription law still only produced 46,347 direct conscripts, or 3.67 percent of the soldiers in Union armies, although it did produce 118,010 substitutes and served as the bedrock of a complicated system of bounties that helped keep the armies in the field.[13] Nevertheless, while the draft squeezed the loyal white population as severely as circumstances would allow, by itself it could not have sustained the Union armies. Emancipation and the enrollment of African-American troops played such a large part in the Union war effort for precisely this reason: just as Northern white commitment weakened, the Federal government could draw on a body of manpower fiercely committed to the destruction of the Confederacy.[14] African-Americans numbering 186,017 (out of roughly 2.3 million) served in the Union armies, and of those, 93,346 came from Confederate states.[15]

The Lincoln administration's claims to war powers allowed it to enforce the draft and various other restrictions on civil liberties in the loyal states of the Union, but the farther one moved from the front, the weaker those wartime powers became. In the hostile territories of the South, Union forces confiscated property, demanded loyalty oaths, expelled civilians, and even executed guerillas without due process, but constitutional scruples hemmed in executive power in the loyal states. While the loyal states made concessions to Federal power, especially with regard to questions of supply, they served as crucial conduits for much of the Union's military mobilization. For example, the states retained control over recruiting and, despite complaints by generals such as Major General William T. Sherman, continued to raise new regiments rather than fill out veteran regiments depleted by losses, which Sherman described in his memoirs as "the greatest mistake made in our civil war."[16] Governors preferred to raise new regiments because they offered a regiment's worth of officers to distribute as patronage.

The dispersed nature of the American political system also hindered the Union's ability to mobilize the loyal states' enormous advantages in industrial capacity and economic potential. Few modern historians subscribe to the sort of demographic determinism claimed by historian Richard N. Current in 1960, that "in view of the disparity of resources, it would have taken a miracle, a direct intervention of the Lord on the other side, to enable the South to win. As usual, God was on the side of the heaviest battalions."[17]

[13] Geary, *We Need Men*, pp. 168, 173–74.
[14] Joseph T. Glatthaar, "Black Glory: The African-American Role in Union Victory," in Gabor S. Boritt, ed., *Why the Confederacy Lost* (New York, 1992), p. 161.
[15] Marvin A. Kreidberg, *History of Military Mobilization in the United States Army, 1775–1945*, DA Pamphlet 20–21, Department of the Army, November 1955, pp.114, 94.
[16] William T. Sherman, *Memoirs of General W. T. Sherman*, Library of America Edn. (New York, 1875; New York, 1990), p. 879. Also see Wayne Wei-siang Hsieh, *West Pointers and the Civil War: The Old Army in War and Peace* (Chapel Hill, NC, 2009), p. 161.
[17] Richard N. Current, "God and the Strongest Battalions," in David Herbert Donald, ed., *Why the North Won the Civil War* (New York, 1996), p. 37.

Nevertheless, few would deny the North's advantages in material resources. In 1860 the last year before the outbreak of war, the free states produced 97 percent of American firearms, 93 percent of American pig iron, almost 96 percent of American locomotives, and possessed double the Confederacy's railroad mileage measured on a per square mile basis.[18] The Union also possessed roughly two-and-a-half times more white men of military age than the Confederacy, even adjusting for manpower unavailable to the Union and white men made available to Confederate armies by slave labor.[19]

Nevertheless, despite all this raw economic potential, Union institutions struggled early on to translate material strength into military power. It was not until early 1862 that the professional logisticians of the US Army's Quartermaster Bureau solidified their control over procurement and purchasing, in opposition to state governments dominated by political machines, despite the fact that it was by far the most qualified American institution to manage the mammoth administrative and logistical problems faced by the Union Army.[20] Nevertheless, even the well-resourced Union would struggle to feed, clothe, and pay soldiers in the Army of the Potomac as late as winter 1862/3, due in large part to Ambrose Burnside's weaknesses as an administrator.[21] Furthermore, while the Civil War certainly saw a massive expansion in Federal authority, the Union effort retained much of the decentralized apparatus of antebellum American politics with its reliance on partisan machines at the local and state levels of government.[22]

Despite the concessions made by his administration to local prerogatives, and the boost in manpower provided by freedmen, Lincoln believed that he would have lost the 1864 elections had it not been for Sherman's capture of Atlanta in September 1864. Even after Atlanta's fall, and positive results for Republicans in the October elections in Pennsylvania, Ohio, and Indiana, Lincoln still believed as late as mid-October 1864 that he would only defeat George B. McClellan by the bare margin of 120 to 114 votes in the Electoral College.[23] Lincoln eventually won the election by a virtual landslide thanks to the rapidly improving military outlook and the Democratic Party's own missteps. Nevertheless, despite the taint of their prewar associations with

---

[18] James M. McPherson, *Battle Cry of Freedom: The Civil War Era* (New York, 1988), pp. 318–319.
[19] Ibid., p. 322.
[20] Mark Wilson, *The Business of Civil War: Military Mobilization and the State, 1861–1865* (Baltimore, 2006), pp. 65–68.
[21] Hsieh, *West Pointers and the Civil War*, p. 170.
[22] For example, one political scientist who studies American state formation has argued that "many features of the Confederate war mobilization were far more statist and modern than their counterparts in the Union." Richard Franklin Bensel, *Yankee Leviathan: The Origins of Central State Authority in America, 1859–1877* (Cambridge, 1990), p. 6.
[23] Andre M. Fleche, "Uncivilized War: The Shenandoah Valley Campaign, the Northern Democratic Press, and the Election of 1864," in Gary W. Gallagher, ed., *The Shenandoah Valley Campaign of 1864* (Chapel Hill, NC, 2006), p. 200.

Southerners, aggressive Republican efforts to turn out the pro-Lincoln soldiers' vote, and the glow of an impending Union victory, the Democrats still secured 45 percent of the popular vote in the 1864 canvas.[24] Even had he wanted to do so, no successful Union leader could afford to take for granted Republican political dominance.

Not only did Lincoln have to contend with the resistance of state governors, legislatures, and the Democratic Party, he also had to manage the Republican Party's internal divisions. In addition to conscription, emancipation served as the other yoke fellow of political controversy during the war. Even among Republicans, the question of emancipation raised much debate, especially at the war's opening. In its origins the Republican Party had been a polyglot assemblage of former Whigs (like Lincoln), disaffected Northern Democrats, and nativist Know-Nothings fearful of the Democracy's friendliness toward Irish Catholic immigrants. Although unified by opposition to the "slave power," as Lincoln put it in his first inaugural address, before the war many Republicans had no objection to a proposed constitutional amendment designed to placate slaveholders by explicitly declaring that "the federal government, shall never interfere with the domestic institutions of the States, including that of persons held to service [i.e., slavery]," because they held "such a provision to now be implied by constitutional law."[25]

The outbreak of war transformed the political environment and sharply increased sentiment in favor of coerced emancipation at bayonet point. Furthermore, as the casualty rolls lengthened, more and more Republicans saw emancipation as a way to strike at the heart of the rebellion and punish Confederate treason. In August of 1862 the influential newspaper editor and "radical" Horace Greeley published a famous letter in which he declared, "there is not one disinterested, determined, intelligent champion of the Union cause who does not feel that all attempts to put down the Rebellion and at the same time uphold its inciting cause are preposterous and futile."[26]

Lincoln's deft if necessarily circuitous – and perhaps even duplicitous – handling of Greeley's famous letter exemplifies the president's approach to managing party politics. While Lincoln had already decided to issue a preliminary Emancipation Proclamation in response to the increasingly pro-emancipation sentiment of many Republicans, his own anti-slavery sentiments, and reasons of military necessity, Lincoln wrote Greeley a cautionary missive, declaring that

My paramount object in this struggle *is* to save the Union, and is *not* either to save or destroy slavery. If I could save the Union without freeing *any* slave I would do it, and if I could save it by freeing *all* the slaves I would do it; and if I could save it by freeing

---

[24] William Frank Zornow, *Lincoln & the Party Divided* (Norman, OK, 1954), p. 215.
[25] Roy P. Basler, ed., *The Collected Works of Abraham Lincoln* (New Brunswick, NJ, 1953), vol. IV, p. 270.
[26] Ibid., vol. V, p. 389.

some and leaving others alone I would also do that. What I do about slavery, and the colored race, I do because I believe it helps to save the Union; and what I forbear, I forbear because I do *not* believe it would help save the Union.[27]

At that point, the president was awaiting a military victory to issue the proclamation, which he would do after Antietam; but until then, he could not afford to alienate Republican conservatives such as Secretary of State William Seward and the influential Blair family, who not only held positions inside his cabinet but also served as generals in the field.[28]

Lincoln positioned himself as a consummate moderate who realized that only the immensely powerful but much debated concept of "Union" fully unified Northern public support behind the war's prosecution. For many Northern Democrats, even as emancipation's military advantages looked all the more impressive, to make emancipation a war aim in those parts of the Union where slavery existed in 1861 not only represented an unconstitutional expansion of Federal power, but also a revolutionary attack on Southern white society that would make postwar reconciliation impossible. As Horatio Seymour, the influential Democratic governor of New York, put it at the 1864 Democratic convention, the Republicans "will not have Union except upon conditions unknown to our constitution; they will not let the shedding of blood cease, even for a little time, to see if Christian charity, or the wisdom of statesmanship may work out a method to save our country."[29] While Lincoln's position in American political thought derives from his eloquent expression and interpretation of freedom's meaning during the war, of which emancipation became an important component, he also needed to build support for emancipation as a *war measure*. Lincoln in effect demonstrated his conservative bona fides to reluctant Republicans and suspicious Democrats with the Greeley letter, while at the same time preparing the ground for his eventual legal and political argument that military necessity required emancipation as a means to suppress the rebellion.

While Lincoln both guided and managed loyal public opinion's increased enthusiasm for emancipation as a war measure, he also shared the public's desire for decisive battlefield victories. Like many other Northerners, Lincoln began the war under the impression that widespread Unionism existed in the Confederacy, which could be exploited with a few military victories and moderate political measures. While Lincoln later embraced emancipation and other aggressive military measures directed at Confederate civilians, including confiscation of property, expulsions, and the use of martial law, he remained fixated on set-piece battles, as opposed to the sorts of operations Sherman made famous with his March to the Sea in 1864.

---

[27] Donald, *Lincoln*, p. 368; Basler, *Collected Works of Abraham Lincoln*, vol. V, p. 388.
[28] Paludan, *The Presidency of Abraham Lincoln*, pp. 262, 288.
[29] Quotation in Weber, *Copperheads*, p. 169.

Federal political leaders, including Lincoln himself, demanded hard-fought battles, both because their voting constituents demanded such measures, and because they themselves shared the same assumptions about war as their constituents. Both the Union and Confederate armies sprang forth as manifestations of Jacksonian political culture; the volunteers of 1861 formed locally raised units, officered by the same elites that held political sway in the rough-and-tumble world of American partisan politics, and closely linked to their home communities through both letter-writing and the vibrant newspaper culture of nineteenth-century America. The same self-organizing voluntarism that Alexis de Tocqueville had seen as the hallmark of American democracy in the 1830s also drove the recruitment and organizing of early Civil War regiments. Seeking the suppression of a rebellion, Northerners obviously could not draw on the American tradition of irregular warfare, from the Revolutionary exploits of Saratoga and Francis Marion to the Fabian tactics of George Washington. Instead, they focused on the prospect of crushing the Confederacy in a decisive battle reminiscent of Napoleon's exploits.[30]

While historians have tended to praise Lincoln's focus on destroying Confederate armies, contrasting it to the seemingly pusillanimous activities of Major General George B. McClellan, one should discard an unnecessary fixation on the virtues of battlefield decisions as the most effective means of crushing Confederate military power. Indeed, as one historian has pointed out, for all its famous and sanguinary battles, the pattern in the Eastern Theater was that "both sides would seek battle, but battle would achieve little, in part because it proved so hard to follow up on any advantage gained in the field."[31] Even the Overland Campaign only set the stage for the grinding siege of Petersburg that finally broke the back of the Army of Northern Virginia. The Union commander who supervised that campaign, U. S. Grant, compiled the most impressive military record of any American commander during the war, destroying multiple Confederate field armies while fighting on the offensive: first during the Fort Henry and Fort Donelson campaign, again at Vicksburg, and finally at the war's end. However, his more impressive and less costly achievements in the Western Theater were produced by deft maneuver leading to Confederate defeat via siege, as opposed to a climactic battlefield decision.

Nevertheless, from the war's outset, a thirst for battle drove American military strategy at the highest levels. In 1861, it drowned out the strategic preferences of the greatest American military leader between Washington and Grant, Major General Winfield Scott. Scott had commanded the Vera Cruz

---

[30] Marcus Cunliffe, *Soldiers and Civilians: The Martial Spirit in America, 1775–1865* (Boston, 1968), pp. 4–5; Hattaway and Jones, *How the North Won*, pp. 19, 85; Hsieh, *West Pointers and the Civil War*, pp. 117–118, 161.

[31] Brooks D. Simpson, *The Civil War in the East: Struggle, Stalemate and Victory* (Santa Barbara, CA, 2011), p. 6.

campaign in 1847 that captured Mexico City – perhaps the single most successful military campaign in American history. With an army of approximately 11,000 men, Scott had defeated every Mexican field army sent against him and, more importantly, laid down the political preconditions necessary for the postwar settlement. He had managed the occupation of Mexican territory, including short-term pacification efforts against Mexican guerillas, and facilitated the search for Mexican leaders willing to acquiesce to a peace treaty fulfilling with consummate skill American war aims.

Scott now called for a military plan that combined a naval blockade with an expedition down the Mississippi "to clear out and keep open this great line of communication in connection with the strict blockade of the seaboard, so as to envelop the insurgent States and bring them to terms with less bloodshed than by any other plan."[32] Scott hoped to use Federal naval power to turn Confederate military positions, with New Orleans as the southern anchor of the Federal envelopment. The plan aimed at eroding Confederate will gradually, and at avoiding the losses that would make the war a remorseless revolutionary struggle.

Northern public opinion believed Scott's ideas, derisively called the "Anaconda Plan," far too passive, and to use Scott's own words, "they will urge instant and vigorous action, regardless, I fear, of consequences."[33] Greeley's *New York Tribune*, reflecting much of Northern public opinion, famously declared in early July 1861, "*Forward to Richmond! Forward to Richmond! The Rebel Congress must not be allowed to meet there on the 20th of July!*"[34] The Lincoln administration thus placed great pressure on Major General Irwin McDowell for such an advance. While a decisive Union victory at Bull Run might have strangled the Confederacy in its cradle, Scott had good reason to warn one of his subordinates in early June that "we must sustain no reverse ... a check or a drawn battle would be a victory to the enemy, filling his heart with joy, his ranks with men, and his magazines with voluntary contributions."[35] McDowell moved forward, and the Confederates won a major victory at First Bull Run.

Realistically, a Federal victory at First Bull Run would not have been sufficiently decisive to prevent surviving Confederate forces from retreating to Richmond, where they could have rallied stragglers and defended the city in the same way that the broken Federal Army after the actual battle had retained its hold on Washington. With the possible exception of the Battle of Nashville in December 1864, no Civil War field army ever annihilated its opponent in an open battle. The long-brewing sectional crisis, and the

---

[32] United States War Department, *The War of the Rebellion: A Compilation of the Official Records of the Union and Confederate Armies*, 128 vols. (Washington, 1880–1901), Series 1, vol. 51, pt. 1, p. 369 (henceforth cited as *OR*).
[33] Timothy D. Johnson, *Winfield Scott: The Quest for Military Glory* (Lawrence, KS, 1998), pp. 227–228; *OR*, Series 1, vol. 51, pt. 1, p. 370.
[34] *New York Daily Tribune*, 2 July 1862.   [35] *OR*, Series 1, vol. 2, p. 671.

obvious commitment to Confederate nationalism – during the course of the war, roughly one out of five Southern white men of military age perished – meant that only the complete destruction of the Confederate Army (extremely unlikely) at First Bull Run would have resulted in an immediate Confederate collapse.[36] In short, by moving quickly, the Federals risked a defeat that substantially improved Confederate prospects for the sake of gains that did not outweigh the risks involved.

The stinging defeat at First Bull Run chastened Northern public opinion, and Northern leaders proved willing to give Scott's successor, McClellan, time to train and reorganize his army. The newspapers quickly rediscovered their impatience, however, as did the Republican leaders who closely tracked the public pulse. Lincoln shielded his most important general from the criticism, but he also urged McClellan to pay heed to public opinion.[37] The general, who combined the twin vices of egotism and political ignorance, squandered the reservoir of public patience produced by Bull Run and Lincoln's conditional support.[38] Nevertheless, McClellan's strategic ideas deserve a fair hearing, and in the words of his most recent biographer,

McClellan especially looked to impose a military paradigm that limited the number of battles and, by relying on maneuver and siege-craft, insured that any fighting that took place would result in decisive Union victories. Fighting battles, he understood, meant accepting casualties, too many of which would exacerbate sectional enmity and jeopardize the effort to restrain passions on both sides.[39]

McClellan's strategic ideas, like Scott's, also integrated judicious military movements with a cautious and conservative political strategy. As he later argued famously in his Harrison's Landing letter, the Union effort "should not be a war looking to the subjugation of the people of any state ... but against armed forces and political organizations." In McClellan's view, attacking slavery would have disastrous effects on the morale of the Union armies and unnecessarily alienate Southern white opinion.[40] According to one historian, McClellan believed "it was essential ... that the task of restoring the Union be guided by reason, moderation, and enlightened statesmanship. The success of that endeavor would be as much dependent on the ability of Northern statesmen to restrain the passions of the people, and the irresponsible politicians who stirred them up, as it would be upon the tactical skill of Billy Yank and his commanders."[41] Such a policy casting scorn on the

---

[36] Gary W. Gallagher, *The Confederate War* (Cambridge, MA, 1997), pp. 28–29; Drew Gilpin Faust, *This Republic of Suffering: Death and the American Civil War* (New York, 2008), p. xi.
[37] Donald, *Lincoln*, pp. 318–319.   [38] Hsieh, *West Pointers and the Civil War*, pp. 156–157.
[39] Ethan S. Rafuse, *McClellan's War: The Failure of Moderation in the Struggle for the Union* (Bloomington, IN, 2005), p. 388.
[40] Stephen W. Sears, ed., *The Civil War Papers of George B. McClellan: Selected Correspondence, 1860–1865* (New York, 1989), p. 344.
[41] Rafuse, *McClellan's War*, pp. 5–6.

democratic habits of Americans would face difficult political challenges, and McClellan also paired his strategy with the erroneous assumption that large reservoirs of Unionism continued to exist in the Confederacy.

Paradoxically, even while the more aggressive measures McClellan despised ultimately became part of the Union's winning strategy, Lincoln and much of the Northern electorate, especially Democrats, shared McClellan's concern to pave the way for postwar reconciliation. How Lincoln's reconstruction policy would have evolved in light of postwar Southern white intransigence will always be uncertain, but we do know that he preferred, if circumstances allowed it, a reconciliationist policy.[42] Andrew Johnson, his slaveholder-hating vice president, who had been a Democrat from Tennessee before the war, embarked on just such a lenient policy; and while that approach failed due to former Confederates' intransigence, subsequent Northern outrage, and Johnson's own political ineptitude, most Northerners hoped that former Confederates eventually would recognize the legitimacy of the Federal government.[43]

In the context of the American political system, for most loyal citizens in the free states, ex-Confederates would eventually have to give a measure of real democratic consent to rule by Washington. Northern whites, including many Republicans, thus proved willing at the end of Reconstruction to abandon political and military support for African-American civil and political rights to obtain that consent. In the end, restoration of the Union and the destruction of slavery served as the most important and permanent war aims for the North, but it would take a hundred years before Federal power would support the achievement of full political equality by African-Americans.

Both McClellan and Scott understood that a harshly punitive military strategy had serious political drawbacks for a war that aimed at reunion. Scott in particular had ample experience with complex environments that required as much political as strictly military skill. McClellan had participated in Scott's Vera Cruz campaign, and like many other regulars, he found the behavior of volunteer citizen-soldiers toward Mexican civilians at times "shameful and disgraceful."[44] Scott shared such humanitarian sympathies, which reflected the paternalistic ethos of much of the regular army's officer corps, but he had a deeper reason to demand decent treatment of Mexicans from his troops – military necessity. As the commander of a small expeditionary force in hostile territory, Scott recognized the danger of unnecessarily inflaming local opinion against his soldiers, both during the campaign to capture Mexico City and during its occupation.[45]

---

[42] Brooks D. Simpson, *The Reconstruction Presidents*, (Lawrence, KS, 1998), pp. 37, 63.
[43] Ibid., pp. 99, 129–130.
[44] Thomas W. Cutrer, ed., *The Mexican War Diary and Correspondence of George B. McClellan* (Baton Rouge, LA, 2009), p. 39.
[45] Timothy D. Johnson, *A Gallant Little Army: The Mexico City Campaign* (Lawrence, KS, 2007), p. 269.

In addition to his deft handling of the local population in Mexico, which McClellan himself witnessed, Scott had also managed civil disturbances that involved the antebellum "Old Army." Success in these circumstances always involved a cautious and judicious use of military force. On the Canadian border in the late 1830s, he had helped suppress private American support for Canadian rebels with minimal forces and maximum political delicacy, while assuaging British concerns. More directly related to the Civil War, Jackson sent Scott to South Carolina during the Nullification Crisis of 1832–1833 to show Federal resolve in the face of South Carolina's threat to nullify the Federal tariff (a proxy for increasing sectional animosities over slavery), while not unnecessarily inflaming a tense situation.[46] In Scott's memoirs, written during the Civil War, he recalled that he had told his men that

these nullifiers, have no doubt, become exceedingly wrong-headed, and are in the road to treason; but still they are our countrymen, and may be saved from that great crime by respect and kindness on our part. We must keep our bosoms open to receive them back as brothers in the Union.[47]

The regular army had struggled to manage the sectional guerilla war over slavery that plagued "Bleeding Kansas," and it had the most success when it acted with restraint and sensitivity toward local tensions. After the passage of the Kansas–Nebraska Act of 1854 stipulated that the local population would determine Kansas' status as a slave or free state, free soil and pro-slavery settlers clashed over the territory's future. Successive Democratic administrations favored the pro-slavery settlers from Missouri, while regular army units in the state attempted to maintain a semblance of law and order while sustaining Federal authority. In general, regular army officers proved effective and relatively impartial under the circumstances, in spite of the sometimes blatantly pro-slavery policies of political authorities in Washington.[48] They understood the limits of their authority as soldiers and the importance of civil authority. When one pro-slavery acting governor demanded that Colonel Philip St. George Cooke use the army to capture free soil Topeka, he refused and explained that "if the army be useless in the present unhappy crisis, it is because in our constitution and law civil war was not foreseen, nor the contingency [of] a systematic resistance by the people to governments of their own creation, and which, at short intervals, they may either correct or change."[49]

Indeed, even advocates of stringent anti-Confederate policies frequently brought a patience and prudence to civil order questions that came out of

---

[46] Hsieh, *West Pointers and the Civil War*, pp. 94–95.
[47] Winfield Scott, *Memoirs of Lieut.-General Winfield Scott, LL.D* (New York, 1864), vol. I, p. 248.
[48] Hsieh, *West Pointers and the Civil War*, pp. 97–99.
[49] Philip St. George Cooke to Daniel Woodson, 2 September 1856, reprinted in United States, War Department, *Report of the Secretary of War*, Senate Executive Document No. 5, Serial Set No. 876, vol. 3, pt. 2, 34th Congress, 3rd Session (Washington, D.C., 1857), pp. 91–92.

the Old Army's long tradition of constabulary duty on the frontier. Major General John Pope, who introduced more aggressive policies in the Eastern Theater after McClellan's failure during the Seven Days, would grumble in Milwaukee after his post-Second Bull Run exile that, in enforcing the draft, "federal officers should learn to hold their tongues and do their duty without making counter threats of blustering about the use of military force, which probably would not be required if they did their duty quietly and discreetly."[50] The Old Army in which McClellan and Scott had served had extensive experience with what we would now call stability operations, and it should not be a surprise that some regulars carried those then judicious habits into the Civil War.

Modern historians too frequently dismiss McClellan's ideas about conciliation and restraint as naïve and anachronistic for a conflict they characterize as a "total war" similar to the world wars of the twentieth century. Others have argued that the Civil War did not see the widespread violence against non-combatants associated with the rise of total war, and that, at least in the North, political divisions limited the Lincoln administration's power to mobilize the population in support of the war effort.[51] However, most historians agree that the Civil War was a "people's war," and that public opinion in both sections could not be ignored.[52] Surely McClellan deserves some credit for not wanting to wage the war in a manner that would make every white Southerner an "irreconcilable," to use the term used by General David Petraeus in current American counterinsurgency practice.

Ironically enough, McClellan's own moral collapse during the Seven Days in early summer 1862 made impossible his political goal of conciliation. Lincoln did not make the decision to adopt emancipation as an explicit Union war aim until after McClellan's defeat in July, and McClellan's Harrison's Landing letter to Lincoln fell on deaf ears.[53] Lincoln now recognized that he had to strike directly at the institution of slavery to win the war. Northern advocates of "hard war" saw attacking slavery as only one of a whole constellation of more stringent measures to suppress the rebellion, including forced confiscation of supplies from areas loyal to the Confederacy, expelling individuals who refused to swear loyalty oaths in recaptured parts of the South, summary executions of pro-Confederate guerillas, and other similar

---

[50] Pope quoted in Paludan, *People's Contest*, p. 236; Clay Mountcastle, *Punitive War: Confederate Guerrillas and Union Reprisals* (Lawrence, KS, 2009), p. 54.

[51] Mark Grimsley, *The Hard Hand of War: Union Military Policy toward Southern Civilians, 1861–1865* (Cambridge, 1995); Mark E. Neely, Jr., *The Civil War and the Limits of Destruction* (Cambridge, 2007); Wayne Wei-siang Hsieh, "Total War and the American Civil War Reconsidered: The End of an Outdated 'Master Narrative,'" *Journal of the Civil War Era*, vol. 1, Sept. 2011, pp. 394–408.

[52] Stig Förster and Jörg Nagler, eds., *On the Road to Total War: The American Civil War and the German Wars of Unification, 1861–1871* (Cambridge, 1997), p. 4.

[53] Donald, *Lincoln*, pp. 360–364.

devices.[54] None inspired as much controversy as did emancipation, however, because of the institution's importance to the Southern social order. The bondsmen and women of the Confederate home front made possible the direct military mobilization of roughly 80 percent of Confederate white men of military age, but they also formed a potential dagger pointed at the heart of the Confederacy.[55] Advancing Union armies made it possible for freedmen and women to aid the Federal cause, most directly in the form of black regiments.

Emancipation also served an important grand strategic purpose in forestalling British recognition. Historians should not overstate the importance of British recognition, because, as George Cornewall Lewis, Britain's secretary for war during the American Civil War, informed his cabinet colleagues, the vast distances of the Atlantic Ocean, the vulnerability of Canada, and the vulnerability of the ships of the Royal Navy to Union ironclads all presented significant military obstacles to direct British military intervention. At most, the British government seriously considered an attempt to mediate the sectional conflict, as opposed to providing direct military aid to the Confederacy.[56] However, even without such aid, British recognition of the Confederacy would have boosted Confederate morale considerably, and, more importantly, it would have further eroded support for the war in the free states.

Nevertheless, even after he had decided to issue the Emancipation Proclamation, Lincoln remained attuned to Unionist Northerners who remained skeptical of abolition. Not wanting to make the proclamation appear as a sign of weakness, Lincoln waited for a victory, and McClellan achieved an ambiguous triumph at Antietam in September 1862. Even then, Lincoln remained sensitive to some Northerners' skepticism of abolition and hard war measures in general, and he delayed the proclamation's enactment until 1 January 1863. McClellan's repulse of Lee's invasion of Maryland won the general only a brief extension at the head of his beloved Army of the Potomac. His conduct on the Peninsula, exacerbated by his unwillingness to support Pope during the Second Bull Run campaign, had fatally compromised his position.

McClellan's victory at Antietam, however, combined with his well-known opposition to hard war measures, made him a popular figure among Northern Democrats. Despite Lincoln's disappointment with the general's post-Antietam movements, he forbore to relieve him until after the 1862 elections in order to postpone the unavoidable political criticism from Democrats. Nevertheless, for all of McClellan's missteps and the obsolescence of his political strategy after the Seven Days, his aversion to fighting pitched battles remained reasonable and compatible with the goal of destroying Confederate military power. McClellan realized that the defeat of Confederate armies did not require set-piece battles, but could in fact be achieved by the encirclement

---

[54] Grimsley, *Hard Hand of War*, pp. 4–5.   [55] Gallagher, *Confederate War*, p. 28.
[56] Howard Jones, *Blue and Gray Diplomacy: A History of Union and Confederate Foreign Relations* (Chapel Hill, NC, 2010), pp. 277–280, 243, 269, 218–219, 240–241, 323.

of Confederate forces through superior Union mobility, especially via naval power. Until the Seven Days, McClellan had in fact placed the primary Confederate field army at peril with relatively little loss in moving the Army of the Potomac via water transport to the Peninsula. McClellan thus avoided the vexations of an overland route, which posed challenges of resupply and provided ready-made barriers to Federal advance due to the east–west flow of the Rapidan and Rappahannock Rivers. Even after McClellan's gross mishandling of the Seven Days, he remained entrenched in a base on the James River – the same strongpoint from which Grant would conduct the decisive siege that finally doomed the Army of Northern Virginia.[57] From there, had McClellan had more resolve and the confidence of the Lincoln administration, he could have pushed the campaign to a victorious conclusion over Lee's battered forces. He thus might have saved his own strategy of conciliation. Neither of these sufficient conditions existed, however, and McClellan's failures during the Seven Days would forever tarnish the Peninsula as a line of operations.

Instead, in order to reach a similar position on James in summer 1864, Grant had to fight his way from Washington to Richmond via the almost catastrophically costly Overland Campaign, during which the Army of the Potomac suffered roughly 55,000 combat casualties, losses that nearly broke Northern morale.[58] Grant himself had originally hoped for a strategy focused on maneuver rather than on pitched battle. In early 1864 Major General Henry Halleck, still the army's general in chief and Lincoln's chief military counselor, asked Grant for ideas about the coming spring campaigns. Grant, yet to be named the commander of Union armies, replied as too "whether an abandonment of all previously attempted lines to Richmond is not advisable, and in lieu of these one be taken further south." Instead, he suggested a movement by 60,000 troops from Suffolk in southeastern Virginia to Raleigh, NC, to

destroy first all the roads about Weldon ... From Weldon to Raleigh they would scarcely meet with serious opposition. Once there the most interior line of rail way still left to the enemy, in fact the only one they would then have, would be so threatened as to force him to use a large portion of his army in guarding it. This would virtually force an evacuation of Virginia and indirectly of East Tennessee.[59]

The Weldon railroad connected the Army of Northern Virginia to North Carolina, and Robert E. Lee would fight long and hard during the siege of Petersburg in summer 1864 to maintain that crucial supply line. Had Grant

---

[57] Hsieh, *West Pointers and the Civil War*, p. 155; Rafuse, *McClellan's War*, p. 161.
[58] Hsieh, *West Pointers and the Civil War*, p. 191; Gordon Rhea, *Cold Harbor: Grant and Lee, May 26–June 3, 1864* (Baton Rouge, LA, 2002), p. 393. Rhea counts about 33,000 casualties for Lee during the Overland Campaign.
[59] Ulysses S. Grant to H. W. Halleck, 19 Jan. 1864, John Y. Simon, *The Papers of Ulysses S. Grant* (Carbondale, IL, 1982), vol. X, pp. 39–40 (henceforth cited as *PUSG*).

been able to execute this campaign, he would have had an opportunity to threaten Lee's logistics and force a battle on his own terms.[60]

Halleck contemptuously rejected Grant's campaign plan. He wrote his more creative subordinate that

I have never considered Richmond as the necessary objective point of the army of the Potomac; that point is *Lee's army* ... The overthrow of Lee's army being the object of operations here, the questions arises how can we best attain it? If we fight that army with our communications open to Washington, so as to cover this place and Maryland, we can concentrate upon it nearly all of our forces on this frontier; but if we operate by North Carolina or the peninsula, we must act with a divided army, and on exterior lines, while Lee, with a short interior line can concentrate his force upon either fragment.

Furthermore, Halleck remained wary of Lee's aggressiveness; he asked Grant,

Suppose we were to send thirty thousand men from that army [the Army of the Potomac] to North Carolina; would not Lee be able to make another invasion of Maryland and Pennsylvania? But it may be said that by operating in North Carolina we could compel Lee to move his army there. I do not think so. Uncover Washington and the Potomac River, and all the forces which Lee can collect will be moved north, and the popular sentiment will compel the Government to *bring back* the army in North Carolina to defend Washington, Baltimore, Harrisburg and Philadelphia. I think Lee would tomorrow exchange Richmond, Raleigh and Wilmington for the possession of either of the aforementioned cities.[61]

Nevertheless, even if Lee had captured a major Northern city and accepted the trade Halleck proposed, he would not have been able to hold the city for any length of time, if his source of ammunition and ordnance fell to Union forces. Perhaps the political blow of such a Confederate triumph on Northern soil would have ended the war in one fell swoop, but surely such an event would have been canceled out by Richmond's fall. Furthermore, the actual course of events would show that Lee himself highly valued Richmond and Petersburg and would accept a siege to defend it, as fatal as he knew it to be, simply because he felt he had no other choice. Halleck's "headquarters doctrine," to use the terminology of several historians, overstated Washington's vulnerability (by 1864 ringed by powerful fortifications) and understated the possibilities of striking the Army of Northern Virginia's crucial logistics network based in Richmond and Petersburg.[62]

For the lay reader, however, "doctrine" overstates the ad hoc nature of Union strategic planning, which involved letters written between Halleck and Grant. For better or for worse, Civil War Washington possessed none of

---

[60] Historians have generally treated Grant's plan with respect. See Simpson, *Triumph over Adversity*, pp. 251–252; Hattaway and Jones, *How the North Won*, pp. 512–516.
[61] *PUSG*, pp. 110–112. [62] Hattaway and Jones, *How the North Won*, pp. 335, 513–514.

the strategy making apparatus created during and after the Second World War. Before Grant's elevation, Halleck had served as Lincoln's primary military aide, providing advice to the president and transmitting his views to field commanders, but providing little direct guidance.[63] Halleck's exchange showed him at his worst, as he stifled creative strategic thinking and encouraged the administration's worst military prejudices with pedantic references to interior and exterior lines.

While Halleck justified the overland route to Grant in part by referring to Jominian principles of strategy, McClellan's failures during the Seven Days, his dubious conduct during the Second Bull Run campaign that contributed to Pope's defeat, and his failure to exploit fully his opportunities during the Antietam campaign made strategy a dirty word for many Union political leaders. Lee's successes, in contrast, seemed to vindicate Northerners' strong cultural preference for offensive operations, and the latter tarnished the Army of the Potomac's single victory between McClellan's relief and Grant's arrival – Major General George Meade's defensive victory at Gettysburg. Even the usually sagacious Lincoln proved impatient with Meade, but he could not allow Meade to depart – he remained the only commander of the Army of the Potomac who had ever won a clear-cut victory.

However, Lincoln did not have sufficient confidence in Meade to allow another reprise of McClellan's advance on Richmond via the peninsula. Meade thus attempted an overland offensive during the Mine Run campaign in the late fall following Gettysburg, but declined to assault Lee in his works when he failed to outmaneuver the Confederates. While Meade lacked Grant's dogged determination to find a way to push through, making the latter's move east necessary, the fearsome losses of the 1864 campaigns show Meade's reluctance to have been hardly unreasonable. One historian has gone as far as to argue that "an exaggerated aggressiveness that was part of what might be called the cult of manliness" encouraged excessive aggressiveness among Union political and military leaders.[64]

In spite of Halleck's interference, Grant's strategic ideas still had the supreme virtue of clarity and simplicity. As he described it to one of his subordinates on 2 April 1864,

it is proposed to have co-operative action of all the armies in the field as far as this object can be accomplished. It will not be possible to unite our armies into two or three large ones, to act as so many units, owing to the absolute necessity of holding on to the territory already taken from the enemy. But, generally speaking, concentration can be practically effected by armies moving to the interior of the enemy's country from the territory they have to guard. By such movement they interpose

[63] John F. Marszalek, *Commander of All Lincoln's Armies: A Life of General Henry W. Halleck* (Cambridge, 2004), pp. 1–3, 226; Simpson, *Triumph over Adversity*, p. 277.
[64] Mark Neely, "Wilderness and the Cult of Manliness: Hooker, Lincoln, and Defeat," in Gabor S. Boritt, ed., *Lincoln's Generals* (New York, 1994), pp. 67–74.

themselves between the enemy and the country to be guarded, thereby reducing the numbers necessary to garrison important points and at least occupy the attention of a part of the enemy's force if no greater object is gained.[65]

Or, as Grant put it later in his report summing up the campaigns of 1864–1865,

From the first I was firm in the conviction that no peace could be had that would be stable and conducive to the happiness of the people, both North and South, until the military power of the rebellion was entirely broken. I therefore determined, first, to use the greatest number of troops practicable against the armed force of the enemy, preventing him from using the same force at different seasons against first one and then another of our armies, and the possibility of repose for refitting and producing necessary supplies for carrying on resistance; second, to hammer continuously against the armed force of the enemy and his resources until, by mere attrition, if in no other way, there should be nothing left to him but an equal submission with the loyal section of our common country to the constitution and laws of the land.[66]

In order to execute this strategy, Grant himself would take the field against Lee with the Army of the Potomac, in coordination with a series of other military movements that would place simultaneous pressure on the Confederacy. Sherman would move against the important railroad junction and logistical hub at Atlanta, Major General Nathaniel P. Banks would strike at Mobile, Major General Franz Sigel would interdict supplies coming from the Shenandoah Valley, and Major General Benjamin Butler would advance from Fort Monroe up the James River and strike at Richmond from the south.[67] Grant adapted his own planning to Washington's concerns, and he explained to Butler on 2 April that

Lee's Army, and Richmond, being the greater objects towards which our attention must be directed in the next campaign it is desirable to unite all the force we can against them. The necessity for covering Washington, with the Army of the Potomac, and of covering your Dept. with your Army, makes it impossible to unite these forces at the beginning of any move.[68]

Grant then laid out to Butler his simultaneous advance on Richmond from the South while the Army of the Potomac used the overland route as the next best alternative to Halleck's Jominian obsession with concentration.

Grant's instructions to his field commanders emphasized that all these movements should be part of a larger design. On 4 April, he wrote Sherman, his most talented and capable subordinate,

it is my design, if the enemy keep quiet and allow me to take the initiative in the Spring Campaign to work all parts of the Army together, and, somewhat, towards a common center ... You I propose to move against Johnston's Army, to break it

[65] *PUSG*, pp. 245–246.   [66] *OR*, Ser. 1, vol. 38, pt. 1, 2.
[67] Simpson, *Triumph over Adversity*, pp. 268–271.   [68] *PUSG*, p. 246.

up and to get into the interior of the enemy's country as far as you can, inflicting all the damage you can against their War resources.[69]

Sherman intuitively understood Grant's idea of coordinated action, and he wrote one of Grant's aides on 5 April that "concurrent action is the thing ... We saw the beauty of time in the Battle of Chattanooga, and there is no reason why the same harmony of action should not pervade a continent."[70]

Grant's orders to Butler also emphasized coordination: "Richmond is to be your objective point, and that there is to be co-operation between your force and the Army of the Potomac must be your guide."[71] Grant built flexibility into his plan for the Army of the Potomac, and as he put it to Butler later on 19 April, "with the forces here I shall aim to fight Lee between here and Richmond if he will stand. Should Lee however fall back into Richmond I will follow up and make a junction with your Army on the James River."[72]

On 31 March Grant had also ordered Banks to wrap up operations on the Red River and prepare for the more important campaign against Mobile, telling him "it is intended that your movements shall be co-operative with movements of armies elswhere [sic] and you cannot now start too soon."[73] While Grant had acquiesced to the administration's desire to mount an expedition via the Red River to support Louisiana Unionists' attempt to establish a loyal state government and signal Federal resistance to French designs on Mexico, Grant had earlier impressed on Banks the need to prioritize Sherman's operations. He also directed Banks to act aggressively, telling his subordinate that "I look upon the conquering of the organized armies of the enemy as being of vastly more importance than the mere acquisition of their territory."[74] Finally, Grant reminded Sigel in the Valley on 15 April that "you must occupy the attention of a large force (and thereby hold them from reinforcing elsewhere) or must inflict a blow upon the enemies [sic] resources, which will materially aid us."[75] Or, as he put it to Sherman, reflecting a comment Lincoln had made to him, "if Sigel can't skin himself he can hold a leg whilst some one else skins."[76]

Unfortunately, Sigel proved incapable of holding a leg, nor were Banks and Butler any more successful. While Sherman rightly described Grant's strategic design as "Enlightened War," Grant could never escape the demands of partisan politics in the North.[77] In addition to the overland route, as opposed to his early ideas about raiding from southeast Virginia, Grant also accepted

---

[69] *PUSG*, pp. 251–252. Lincoln himself had suggested to Halleck and Buell in January 1862 a strategy of coordinated movements by Federal armies on exterior lines, with little effect. See McPherson, *Tried by War*, pp. 70–71, 214.
[70] Ibid., p. 219.   [71] Ibid., p. 246. See also, p. 292.   [72] Ibid., p. 327.
[73] Ibid., p. 243.   [74] Simpson, *Triumph over Adversity*, p. 275; *PUSG*, p. 201.
[75] *PUSG*, p. 287.
[76] Ibid., p. 253. Lincoln had actually inspired this turn of phrase about skinning. See Simpson, *Triumph over Adversity*, p. 273.
[77] *PUSG*, p. 253.

the political necessity of assigning important field commands to marginal, but politically important, commanders. While Grant himself in the initial phases of the campaign misperceived Butler's abilities, he had always recognized his appointments of Sigel and Banks as necessary evils. As Grant and Lee grappled in the Wilderness and Spotsylvania, Sigel and Banks proved unable even to prevent Confederate reinforcements from being sent to Lee from their areas of responsibility, much less force Lee to weaken his own forces in order to respond to threats elsewhere.[78] In the highly politicized environment of an election year, in which McClellan eventually stood against Lincoln as the Democratic nominee, Lincoln had good reason to respect the important political constituencies represented by these generals. Due to these factors, only two of Grant's planned five coordinated campaigns for 1864 actually played their projected role in pressuring the Confederacy strategically.

Sigel represented an important German constituency, especially since roughly 8 percent of the Union Army had been born in Germany.[79] Many of those Germans had immigrated due to the failed Revolution of 1848, and Sigel had commanded revolutionary forces in Baden before his defeat by a Prussian army. During the war Sigel became the favorite of German immigrants and Unionist state legislators in West Virginia who, in an election year, represented important political constituencies Lincoln had to placate. The president especially worried about losing the states of Missouri, Wisconsin, and Illinois if he alienated the German vote, and German Radicals did attempt to back John Frémont as a third party alternative to Lincoln.[80] McClellan's nomination on a platform that declared the war a virtual failure, promptly followed by Atlanta's fall in September, eventually allowed Lincoln to suppress a Radical Republican revolt, but during the previous spring, he had had to heed Radical sympathies. Butler, in contrast, had been a Democrat before the war, and early in his career he represented the War Democrats whom Lincoln needed to cultivate. He eventually became a Radical, and like Sigel, he represented an important political constituency. Furthermore, Butler had support among Radical Republicans for the nomination, and had Lincoln discarded the general, he might have mounted a presidential bid himself. Lincoln may even have offered Butler the vice presidency, which, according to one historical account, the general refused from fear that the office would only stifle his ambitions.[81]

Banks, like Butler, had been a Democrat earlier in his political career, but he remained more moderate in his political views. More importantly, he helped superintend Lincoln's early attempt at reestablishing a loyal civil

[78] Simpson, *Triumph over Adversity*, pp. 270, 274–277, 314.
[79] Ella Lonn, *Foreigners in the Union Army and Navy* (Baton Rouge, LA, 1951), pp. 576–578.
[80] Thomas J. Goss, *The War within the Union High Command: Politics and Generalship during the Civil War* (Lawrence, KS, 2003), pp. 177–178; Zornow, *Lincoln & the Party Divided*, pp. 74, 84–85, 211.
[81] Zornow, *Lincoln & the Party Divided*, pp. 66–67.

government in Louisiana, which Lincoln saw as an important experiment for Reconstruction policy in general. Lincoln announced his "10 percent" plan for Reconstruction in December 1863, which envisioned Southern state governments reforming when the number of qualified voters with pardons matched 10 percent of the ballots cast in the 1860 election. Voters (excluding certain groups such as Confederate officials) could only obtain pardons by swearing future loyalty to the Union and acceptance of emancipation. Lincoln backed Banks' decision to placate conservatives in Louisiana, despite some grumbling from Radicals, and the administration had hoped that the Red River campaign would help consolidate control over Louisiana as Unionists in the state attempted to reestablish a civil government. Banks' political duties further delayed his campaign and helped lead to the military fiasco that resulted when the Red River's water level dropped, depriving Grant of the coordinated move on Mobile he desired.[82] Grant understood these complexities, and he moved to relieve Banks only when the latter proved completely ineffective in the field.

Few historians would dispute the idea that military methods should correspond with political objectives. But how does any individual polity determine and establish political objectives? The mid-nineteenth-century American state had a decentralized political system that dispersed authority among mass political parties working at multiple levels of government – local, state, and Federal. While Lincoln stood at the head of this system, he still had to channel even his most ambitious and aggressive wartime powers through this diffuse system, where most officials (including himself) still had to answer at the polls in a mass participatory democracy. While the popular basis of the system provided great latent strength, it also demanded concessions to military measures more related to popular prejudice than to any coherent conception of military strategy. Indeed, when Northern public opinion found in Grant a general willing to give it the hard fighting it claimed it desired, it had a severe case of buyer's remorse after seeing the consequences.

Nevertheless, at the level of grand strategy, for all its military inefficiencies, Lincoln rightly focused on aligning domestic politics with the larger goal of restoring the Union. As a veteran and consummate player in the partisan politics of this era, Lincoln intuitively understood this truth, and he probably could not have acted otherwise even had he desired to do so. Indeed, even the haughty McClellan played the partisan game by cultivating contacts in the Democratic press during his tenure at the head of the Army of the Potomac, which helped lead to friction with Republican party leaders.[83] Grant self-consciously stayed aloof from partisan ambitions related directly to his own person, which helped him win Lincoln's confidence, but he recognized the political imperatives Lincoln confronted and adjusted his own military

---

[82] Simpson, *Triumph over Adversity*, pp. 274–277; Simpson, *Reconstruction Presidents*, pp. 39–44.
[83] Stephen W. Sears, *George B. McClellan: The Young Napoleon* (New York, 1988), pp. 117–118.

measures accordingly.[84] The Jacksonian period had bequeathed to Civil War Americans a political system that dealt with social conflict by channeling it through adversarial political parties. That system had allowed and perhaps even encouraged civil war; it could not help but reflect, and perhaps even exacerbated, divisions within the loyal states. Union civil and military leaders could not escape that structural reality, even had they desired to do so.

If Carl von Clausewitz's dictum that "war is merely the continuation of policy by other means" should guide our understanding of grand strategy, then it should serve as the lodestar for all the subordinate levels of military activity, that is, strategy, operations, and tactics, to use the standard formulation.[85] A recent study on military effectiveness demonstrates the importance of this insight, declaring that "no amount of operational virtuosity ... redeemed fundamental flaws in political judgment ... Mistakes in operations and tactics can be corrected, but political and strategic mistakes live forever."[86] The American Civil War, however, saw a reversal of this paradigm. The Union's responsive and vigorous two party system produced grand strategies so responsive to political concerns that they actually compromised operational and tactical effectiveness, which in turn threatened the most important grand strategic imperative of preserving the Union and dismantling the Confederacy. Nevertheless, Lincoln's political acumen and Confederate missteps (some taken due to the Confederate leadership's own needs to answer political imperatives) still made possible the emergence of Grant, who formulated a military strategy capable of achieving the Union's preservation. Both Lincoln and Grant kept the primary long-term objective of restoring the Union in mind, but in line with one group of historians' metric for successful strategy, "at the same time that they have maintained a vision focused on the possibilities of the future, they have adapted to the realities of the present."[87]

When historians judge the grand strategy of Lincoln and Grant, they should first understand that the political aspects of Union grand strategy went beyond managing civilian manifestations of power, "soft power" to use the current terminology, involving economics, diplomacy, and the shaping of international public opinion. Those factors played a role during the Civil War, but none more so than managing political support for the war effort *within* the loyal states of the Union. Even though Lincoln and Grant had put in place by late spring 1864 a grand strategy for victory, integrating all the outward-looking military, naval, diplomatic, and political measures necessary to defeat the Confederacy, their obligations to respect domestic political

---

[84] McPherson, *Tried by War*, pp. 211–212.
[85] Carl von Clausewitz, *On War*, ed. and trans. by Michael Howard and Peter Paret (Princeton, 1976), p. 87.
[86] Quoted in Williamson Murray, Richard Hart Sinnreich, and James Lacey, eds., *The Shaping of Grand Strategy: Policy, Diplomacy, and War* (Cambridge, 2011), p. 4.
[87] Ibid., p. 3.

concerns nearly sabotaged their success in every other line of effort. Grant's decision to face Lee directly, combined with the Army of the Potomac's institutional shortcomings, resulted in the mind-numbing casualties of the Overland campaign which, coming after three long years of war, threatened to exhaust Northern political will.[88] Nevertheless, while in retrospect the Overland campaign represented a terrible error and one of the last lamentable legacies of McClellan's disastrous relationship with Lincoln, how could one have expected Lincoln and Grant to have acted differently?

Writers on strategy too frequently assume that states and polities have centralized decision-making systems that promulgate coherent strategies, with explicitly declared ends and measured means necessary to achieve those ends at a reasonable cost. Lincoln and Grant could promulgate clear ends, but the political structure of their republic allowed countless points of influence, ranging from the violent resistance of immigrants hostile to the draft to demands by Radical Republicans that politically sound generals receive significant military responsibilities. As the most able politician of his era, Lincoln owed his success in large part to the natural sympathy he felt for the currents of Northern public opinion, and he himself famously claimed "not to have controlled events, but confess plainly that events have controlled me."[89] Lincoln's stated fatalism had much to do with his religious views on Providence, and he understated his own historical influence on the course of events, but Lincoln himself would have found a portrayal of him as some sort of far-seeing philosopher-statesman guiding history as both inaccurate and contrary to the republic's sacred principle of self-government.

Indeed, according to Gideon Welles' diary, when Lincoln presented his decision to issue the Emancipation Proclamation to his cabinet after Antietam, he told them that before the battle, he had "made a vow, a covenant, that if God gave us the victory in the approaching battle, he would consider it an indication of Divine will, and that it was his duty to move forward in the cause of emancipation."[90] Lincoln's attempt to divine the will of God reflected his own unwillingness to play the part of the Promethean statesman, or the Clausewitzian genius who overcomes friction through force of will and *coup d'oeil*. The Clausewitzian general or statesmen combined both the discerning intellect of an Enlightenment philosopher and the force of will of a Romantic hero. In contrast, if Lincoln had genius, it was a democratic version that allowed him to perceive and guide Northern sentiment to victory. Lincoln thus served less as a dictator endowed with absolute power and called from the plough to guide the republic through an existential crisis, and more

---

[88] Hsieh, *West Pointers and the Civil War*, pp. 186–187.

[89] This served as the controversial epigraph to David Donald's biography of Lincoln.

[90] Howard K. Beale, ed., *Diary of Gideon Welles: Secretary of the Navy under Lincoln and Johnson* (New York, 1960), vol. I, p. 143; Allen C. Guelzo, *Abraham Lincoln: Redeemer President* (Grand Rapids, MI, 1999), pp. 341–42. Salmon P. Chase's diary also confirms Welles' account in its broad outlines.

as a tribune of the people, leading public opinion while never departing too far from it. When he flexed his most impressive wartime executive power – the Emancipation Proclamation – it is little wonder that Lincoln would search for God's will in that act, and he would later declare that "in *giving* freedom to the *slave*, we *assure* freedom to the *free* – honorable alike in what we give, and what we preserve. We shall nobly save, or meanly lose, the last best, hope of earth."[91]

In the small world of those who think about, write about, and hope to determine American grand strategy in the present day and in the near future, the democratic habits of the American people and its elected representatives might seem hostile and threatening to the rational formulation and development of true grand strategy. Lincoln and Grant, however, show that strategy can still exist in a world in which democratic political processes intersect at every level of policy formulation and execution. The "people" may have made mistakes and rued their own impetuousness, without really acknowledging their own portion of responsibility for mistakes and errors, as they did after the Overland Campaign, but their deep involvement with the war also gave great strength and resilience to Northern public opinion. When Atlanta gave them hope again that their sons' sacrifices in the Wilderness and Cold Harbor were not in vain, they returned Lincoln to the presidency and gave Grant his due, eventually rewarding the general with the presidency and a spectacular equestrian monument facing Washington's outside the Capitol. In an era of social media and radically decentralized information technology, perhaps the institutions of the national security state should find a way to embrace the natural democratic genius of the American people.

---

[91] Basler, *Collected Works of Abraham Lincoln*, vol. V, p. 537 (emphasis in original).

8   Bismarckian strategic policy, 1871–1890

Marcus Jones

This phenomenon of a political genius of German stock, who in three bloody wars created the Prussian-German realm of power and for decades secured for it the hegemony in Europe – a hysterical colossus with a high voice, brutal, sentimental, and given to nervous spasms of weeping ... a giant of fathomless cunning and ... cynical frankness of speech ... contemptuous of people and overwhelming them with charm or force, careerist, realist, absolute anti-ideologist, a personality of excessive and almost superhuman format who, filled with himself, reduced everything about him to adulation or trembling ...

At the mere mention of a political opponent, his look was that of an angry lion. Gargantuan in his appetites, he devoured half a henturkey at dinner, drank half a bottle of cognac and three bottles of Apollinaris with it, and smoked five pipes afterwards ... Like Luther, he took a passionate joy in hating, and with all of the European polish of the aristocratic diplomat he was, like him, Germanic and anti-European ... Revolutionary and at the same time the product of the enormous powers of reaction, he left liberal Europe, thanks to the success of his seasoned Machiavellianism, in the most complete disarray and in Germany strengthened the servile worship of power to the same degree as he weakened faith in tenderer, nobler human ideas and values.[1]

If one accepts Thomas Mann's extravagant characterization of Otto von Bismarck, there seems little for the historian to do. But who can resist the temptation to relate such an outsized historical figure to the circumstances of his age and to understand his policies in the context that they did so much to create? No other individual in European history between Metternich and the First World War approaches the stature of Bismarck. Between 1866 and 1890, he guided the German-speaking lands of Central Europe to a destiny that many wished for, but few could clearly envision and no other could bring to pass. His own evolution as a statesman paralleled that of his country: if he railed against the forces of revolutionary change, nationalism, and liberalism

---

[1] Thomas Mann, "Die Drei Gewaltigen," *Reden und Aufsätze*, vol. I (Oldenburg, 1965), pp. 62–63; from Gordon A. Craig, "The Reich Stuff," *The New York Review of Books*, 31 January 1991, p. 26.

early in his career, he later harnessed them skillfully to the cause of Prussian dominance over northern Germany and the growth of German power. In a lecture commemorating the anniversary of his death, the conservative German historian Arnold Oskar Meyer recounted how the great statesman had embodied the passage through the modern age of the Hegelian historical spirit, albeit with a distinctively Prusso-German character: "What [Bismarck] accomplished for his people is greater than that for which any other people in Europe can be thankful to a single man."[2] After 1871, like a sorcerer's apprentice, he struggled with increasing futility to control the forces he had helped to release and save the new German Empire from the strategic circumstances of its birth.

The past century has seen innumerable attempts by historians to come to terms with Bismarck's foreign and strategic policies.[3] To greater or lesser degrees and irrespective of the political orientation of the scholars in question, almost all focus intently on the towering personality of Bismarck, particularly on his intentions, expectations, decisions, and miscalculations. To be sure, historians have not neglected the international context in which he operated, a transformative era in which high cabinet diplomacy gradually gave way to populist nationalism and legitimacy, with a correspondent emphasis on social and economic affairs. But one cannot gainsay the imprint that Bismarck left on his age, or the extent to which he shaped, as opposed to having been shaped by, the trends and forces that defined the strategic landscape. In terms of Morton White's model of historical explanation, Bismarck was the "abnormal" factor, whose presence in the historical process meant the difference between war and peace.[4]

Narrowly seen, Bismarck determined almost every facet of German foreign policy during the first two decades of the empire's existence, a period which, like the preceding half-century, one can view as a discrete era in strategic terms. So comprehensive was his command of almost all questions that bore on the external posture of the Reich, that contemporaries and historians alike have sometimes described him unfairly as a dictator, or at least of governing Germany as a dictator might. Such accusations miss the true complexion of Bismarck's long term in power. His policy bore the hallmarks of the limited but meaningful constitutional constraints that he had a decisive role in crafting in the late 1860s, when Prussia consolidated its power over Germany through the North German Confederation. Most importantly, one cannot overlook the fact that, throughout his tenure after 1862 as minister-president

---

[2] Günther Wollstein, "Bismarck Heute," in Jürgen Elvert, ed., *Ein deutsches Jahrhundert 1848–1945: Hoffnung und Hubris. Aufsätze und Vorträge* (Stuttgart, 2010), p. 164.

[3] Most notably in the recent past by Andreas Hillgruber, Konrad Canis, Wolfgang Mommsen, and Klaus Hildebrand.

[4] Morton White, *Foundations of Historical Knowledge* (New York, 1965), p. 126; from Otto Pflanze, *Bismarck and the Development of Germany*, vol. III, *The Period of Fortification* (Princeton, 1990), p. 433.

of Prussia and after 1871 as chancellor of the *Kaiserreich*, Bismarck was directly subordinate to the Prussian king, who was at the same time emperor of Germany after 1871. Moreover, nobody could have anticipated – his chancellor least of all – that Wilhelm I would live 92 years before his death in 1888, and that Bismarck would not have to serve under another monarch with whom he was to enjoy a less tolerant and accommodating relationship until 1888, or, as was more probable in a regime of Friedrich III, not serve as chief minister at all.[5]

Much scholarship on Bismarck over the past few decades has tended to interpret his foreign and strategic policies in light of the *Primat der Innenpolitik* (primacy of domestic politics).[6] According to this notion, Bismarck's decision making in almost every meaningful sense aimed at the consolidation of the power of German, and particularly Prussian agrarian, financial, and industrial elites against the rising social and economic power of other, marginal groups and classes. Such approaches to the vexing problems of Bismarckian strategic policy, however elegant and gratifying to certain ideological perspectives, find virtually no basis in the documentary record.[7] Indeed, Bismarck was extraordinarily sensitive to the inherent tension between domestic and foreign affairs and pointedly, perhaps self-servingly, rejected the idea that a responsible statesman made decisions about the latter in light of the former. "Foreign policy and economic affairs must never be combined with one another," he avowed in the 1890s. "Each is balanced within itself. If one of them is burdened by the other, the equilibrium is lost."[8]

Moreover, there is much to commend the view that a conscientious statesman is well enough absorbed by the secular attributes of an outwardly directed strategic policy. Perhaps the greatest historian of Bismarckian Germany has characterized the Iron Chancellor's preoccupations as "the attitudes of rulers and foreign ministers, changing alignments and

---

[5] Andreas Hillgruber, *Otto von Bismarck: Grunder der europäischen Großmacht Deutsches Reich* (Göttingen, 1978), pp. 71–72.

[6] This historiographical concept most plausibly originated in the pathbreaking scholarship of Eckart Kehr in the 1960s; see Eckart Kehr, *Der Primat der Innenpolitik: Gesammelte Aufsätze zur preussisch-deutschen Sozialgeschichte im 19. und 20. Jahrhundert*, Hans-Ulrich Wehler, ed. (Berlin, 1965); for a mature expression of the trend, perhaps the most powerful in modern German historiography, see Hans-Ulrich Wehler, *Deutsche Gesellschaftsgeschichte*, vol. III: *Von der Deutschen Doppelrevolution bis zum Beginn des Ersten Weltkrieges, 1849–1914*, 2nd edn. (Munich, 2007); see the appraisal by Winfried Baumgart, "Eine neue Imperialismustheorie? Bermerkungen zu dem Buche von Hans-Ulrich Wehler über Bismarcks Imperialismus," *Militärgeschichtliche Mitteilungen*, vol. 10, 1971, pp. 197–208.

[7] See especially the published lecture by Otto Pflanze, "Bismarcks Herrschaftstechnik als Problem der gegenwärtigen Historiographie," Elisabeth Müller-Luckner, ed. (Munich, 1982).

[8] To Hermann Hoffmann, editor of the *Hamburger Nachrichten*, in the 1890s: in Hermann von Petersdorff, ed., *Bismarck: Die gesammelten Werke*, vol. IX (Berlin, 1924–1935), p. 400; from Pflanze, *Bismarck and the Development of Germany*, vol. II: *The Period of Consolidation, 1871–1880* (Princeton, 1990), p. 246, see especially p. 246n2, wherein Pflanze cites numerous similar references from Bismarck's collected writings.

realignments among states, alternating fears of isolation and entanglement, shifts in the balance of power engendered by those fears, and the changed margins of safety and danger those shifts produce."[9] So complex and dangerous a collection of factors would fully absorb even the most capable leader and serves to underscore that Bismarck's policy is best understood, in the words of still another historian, as the "pragmatic security policy of a state understood as internally coherent," and not a form of "outwardly directed social policy."[10]

Historians consider him perhaps the greatest practitioner of *Realpolitik* in history, a nebulous concept that, depending on how it is applied, takes on alternately sinister and praiseworthy overtones. At the least, it refers to a political understanding of international and strategic affairs based on the imperatives of power instead of some notion of legalism, idealism, or morality. Neither legal niceties nor selfless altruism lay at the root of prudent strategy, Bismarck held, but rather the "rational determination of legitimate interests, the careful assessment of the risks involved in their fulfillment, and the measuring of the power available to that end."[11] Friedrich Meinecke called attention in 1906 to Bismarck's scant regard for the great intellectual and nationalist bellwethers of his age – thinkers like Kant, Hegel, or Ranke and soldiers like Scharnhorst, Gneisenau, or Boyen – who considered the German nation to be nothing less than the earthly instantiation of a moral and spiritual ideal.[12]

For Bismarck, the German nation was nothing more than a *Machtstaat*, an expression of the power that it aggrandized to itself and which permitted it to flourish in the self-help environment of international politics.[13] From this flowed his measured appreciation of the place of the military in the life of the nation. As a young man, he had observed how the loyalty of the army had permitted the Prussian crown to retain its prerogatives against revolutionary reform in 1848, and he later made his political reputation in defending those prerogatives, and the military itself, against liberal parliamentarians in the Prussian constitutional crisis of the early 1860s. At root, it was brute force that reinsured the Prussian state. "It is not by speeches and majority resolutions that the great questions of the time are decided," Bismarck proclaimed

---

[9] Pflanze, *Bismarck and the Development of Germany*, vol. II, pp. 246–247.

[10] Theodor Schieder, *Staatensystem als Vormacht der Welt 1848–1918* (Frankfurt a.M., 1977), p. 42; other leading exponents of a view that champions the *Primat der Aussenpolitik* (primacy of foreign policy) include Gerhard Ritter, *Staatskunst und Kriegshandwerk: das Problem des Militarismus in Deutschland*, 4 vols. (Munich 1954–1968); Andreas Hillgruber, *Bismarcks Außenpolitik* (Freiburg, 1972); and Klaus Hildebrand, *Deutsche Außenpolitik 1871–1918* (Munich, 1989).

[11] Otto Pflanze, "Bismarck's 'Realpolitik,'" *The Review of Politics*, vol. 20, 1958, p. 495.

[12] Friedrich Meinecke, "Bismarcks Eintritt in den christlich-germanischen Kreis," in idem, *Preussen und Deutschland im 19. und 20. Jahrhundert; historische und politische Aufsätze* (Munich/Berlin, 1918), pp. 296ff.; from Hajo Holborn, "Bismarck's Realpolitik," *Journal of the History of Ideas*, vol. 21, 1960, p. 85n4.

[13] Hans Mombauer, *Bismarcks Realpolitik als Ausdruck seiner Weltanschauung* (Berlin, 1936).

to the liberal Max von Forckenbeck in 1862, "but by iron and blood."[14] Until the end of his career, he never fully abandoned the possibility that, in the event of a parliamentary challenge to the executive authority of the crown, a *coup d'état* against the constitution by the Prussian Army was wholly justified.[15] Force, prudently applied, was the final arbiter of political disagreement: regardless of any other means by which the German power was understood, the naked power of the military would underpin Germany's standing in Europe, just as it had his beloved Prussia in 1866.

In 1862, the new Prussian king, Wilhelm I, called Bismarck to serve as minister-president of Prussia, the foremost political officer in the crown's administration, at the height of a protracted constitutional crisis. Key military advisors to the Prussian king had sought to expand and modernize the army based on the exclusive right of royal command, a process for which the elected Prussian legislative chambers refused to pay. A military *coup d'état* from above was judged to be too risky. Wilhelm's appointment of Bismarck, considered a reactionary even by Prussian standards as well as a political cipher with little experience in the practical administration of domestic affairs, offered a less obvious version of the same. The new minister-president simply sidestepped the legislature to all intents and purposes by openly flouting the constitution, collecting tax receipts, disbursing revenues, and reforming the army without legislative approval.[16] The memory of his defiance never quite left him: throughout the remainder of his long political career, whenever his frustrations with the challenges of policy mounted, he flirted with the possibility of another *coup d'état* from above, however implausible such a course seemed by the 1880s.

Bismarck's first major foreign policy initiative as Prussia's minister-president laid the foundation for Germany's later rise to great power status. In January 1863, he authorized General Gustav von Alvensleben to negotiate a draft convention with czarist Russia providing for joint military action against Polish rebels who crossed into the Polish territories of Prussia.[17] The immediate purpose was to persuade Russia not to abandon her Polish territories as a reaction to the last Polish revolt of 1863; it also served

---

[14] Otto von Bismarck, *Reden 1847–1869*, Wilhelm Schüßler, ed., vol. X: *Bismarck: Die gesammelten Werke*, Hermann von Petersdorff, ed. (Berlin, 1924–1935), pp. 139–140.
[15] Egmont Zechlin, *Die Staatsstreichpläne Bismarcks und Wilhelms II, 1890–1894* (Berlin and Stuttgart, 1929).
[16] See the collection by Jürgen Schlumbohm, *Der Verfassungskonflikt in Preußen 1862 bis 1866* (Göttingen, 1970); on Bismarck's approach to the crisis, see Kurt Promnitz, *Bismarcks Eintritt in das Ministerium* (Vaduz, 1965); reprinted from *Historische Studien*, vol. 60, 1908, pp. 67–99.
[17] On Bismarck's intentions, see Stéphanie Burgaud, "Février 1863: la Convention Alvensleben, 'coup de poker' ou erreur stratégique pour la diplomatie bismarckienne?" *Etudes Danubiennes*, 1er semestre, vol. XVII, no. 1, Strasbourg, 2001; Helmuth Scheidt, *Konvention Alvensleben und Interventionspolitik der Mächte in der polnischen Frage 1863* (Munich, 1937).

Bismarck's cynical determination to keep those territories divided and preserve the solidarity of the three conservative monarchies of Eastern Europe, Prussia, Russia, and Austria-Hungary, against the creation of an independent Poland. The convention triggered a storm of protest in London, Paris, and Vienna and threw Bismarck abruptly onto the defensive. In the end, he disowned it and rather weakly proposed to Vienna and St. Petersburg a restoration of the Holy Alliance of 1815 in its place. But the larger result of the Alvensleben Convention was to purchase a substantial measure of Russian goodwill in the struggle against Austria for primacy in the German Confederation.[18]

In the 1860s Bismarck engineered a series of three short, sharp, and opportunistic wars on his way to unifying northern Germany under Prussian auspices.[19] He derived immediate advantages from the Prussian and Austrian war against Denmark in 1864, which gained Schleswig for Prussia but also provided a source of leverage against Austria. By embroiling the Habsburg monarchy in Schleswig-Holstein's labyrinthine problem and forcing Austria's hand in the process of reforming the German Confederation, Bismarck found a convenient pretext for war in 1866 against Austria and most of the rest of the major German states. The Battle of Königgrätz on 3 July decided Prussian hegemony over Germany north of the Main River and allowed Bismarck a free hand to enlarge Prussia by annexing Hanover, Northern Hesse, and Frankfurt.[20] While the southern Catholic German states remained outside of the new polity and Bismarck was circumspect in crafting a settlement that excluded Austria from northern German affairs without humiliating her, the strategic foundation for the Second Empire had been laid.

It was left to overcome the French, historically the underwriter of southern German autonomy and a spoiling factor in any German plans for greater cohesion. By cynically manipulating the liberal movement in Germany and savvy diplomacy abroad, Bismarck succeeded between 1868 and 1870 in isolating France and portraying the regime of Napoleon III in European popular media as both an illegitimate aggressor and the last obstacle to the liberal unification of Germany. Greater German manpower only partially determined the Franco-Prussian War itself; far more important was superior German operational planning and a brilliant execution of the military

---

[18] A key argument in Egmont Zechlin, *Bismarck und die Grundlegung der deutschen Großmacht* (Stuttgart, 1960).

[19] For background, see Andreas Kaernbach, *Bismarcks Konzepte zur Reform des Deutschen Bundes: zur Kontinuität der Politik Bismarcks und Preußens in der deutschen Frage* (Göttingen, 1991).

[20] As historians have made clear, what saved Bismarck was not so much Prussian military brilliance as Austria's terrible mistakes: see especially Gordon A. Craig, *The Battle of Königgrätz: Prussia's Victory over Austria, 1866* (Philadelphia, 2003); Frank Zimmer, *Bismarcks Kampf gegen Kaiser Franz Joseph: Königgratz und seine Folgen* (Graz, 1996); and Gerd Fesser, *1866 – Königgratz-Sadowa: Bismarcks Sieg über Österreich* (Berlin, 1994).

campaign in the war's opening months. German forces prevailed over the French at Sedan and captured Napoleon III – disastrously for Bismarck, who had desired a viable partner for a quick settlement. Instead the Prusso-Germans found themselves in a vicious and taxing hybrid war against the forces of the nascent French republic with the aim of annexing Alsace and Lorraine.[21] The German Empire was officially proclaimed on 18 January 1871 at Versailles in a ceremony pregnant with symbolism, precisely 170 years after the coronation of the first King of Prussia at Königsberg.[22]

The new Reich suffered from major strategic handicaps, all of which were in evidence in Bismarck's strategic policy after 1871.[23] As a latecomer among the great powers, it lacked not only the legitimacy born of tradition and experience, but also a persuasive civilizing idea, in contrast to the liberalism or republicanism of the Western European nations and pan-Slavism of Russia. Particularly by the 1880s, as the Bismarckian era wore on, the lack of a compelling civic ideology in an increasingly populist age made Bismarck's creation seem distinctly antediluvian, based as it was on balancing the "necessities of states" more than on shaping a bolder future.[24] More concretely, the creation of the Reich unhinged a balance of power that had rested since the Metternichian settlement, however precariously, on a weak European center.[25] Germany, often referred to as the "Germanies," had traditionally served as the locus of decision, the landscape over which the strategic contests among other powers were resolved. Henceforth it would exert a strong and sovereign influence on European affairs.

Finally, in part because of its geographic centrality and vulnerable frontiers, the new Reich had to cultivate a powerful military establishment, balanced on a knife's edge against a host of possible threats, any one of which could

---

[21] On Bismarck's policy throughout this period, see Marcus Jones, "Strategy as Character: Bismarck and the Prusso-German Question, 1862–1878," in Williamson Murray, Richard Hart Sinnreich, and James Lacey, eds., *The Shaping of Grand Strategy: Policy, Diplomacy, and War* (Cambridge, 2011); and idem, *"Vae Victoribus*: Bismarck's Quest for Peace in the Franco-Prussian War, 1870–1871," in Williamson Murray and Jim Lacey, eds., *The Making of Peace: Rulers, States, and the Aftermath of War* (Cambridge, 2009).

[22] See Theodore Schieder and Ernst Deuerlein, eds., *Reichsgründung 1870–71: Tatsachen, Kontroversen, Interpretationen* (Stuttgart, 1970); from Imanuel Geiss, *German Foreign Policy 1971–1914* (London, 1976), pp. 5–6, n9.

[23] A useful introduction to scholarly approaches to the Prussian dilemma is Michael Stürmer, "Das zerbrochene Haus – Preußen als Problem der Forschung," *Militärgeschichtliche Mitteilungen*, vol. 10, 1971, pp. 175–196.

[24] Siegfried A. Kaehler, "Bemerkungen zu einem Marginal Bismarcks von 1887," in idem, *Studien zur deutschen Geschichte des 19. Und 20. Jahrhunderts. Aufsätze und Vorträge* (Göttingen, 1961), p. 182; from Klaus Hildebrand, "Opportunities and Limits of German Foreign Policy in the Bismarckian Era, 1871–1890: 'A System of Stopgaps?'" in Gregor Schöllgen, ed., *Escape Into War? The Foreign Policy of Imperial Germany* (Oxford and New York, 1990), p. 76n17.

[25] See Theodor Schieder, "Europäisches Staatensystem und Gleichgewicht nach der Reichsgründung," in Karl Ottmar Freiherr von Aretin, ed., *Bismarcks Aussenpolitik und der Berliner Kongress* (Wiesbaden, 1978), pp. 17–40.

unwind Bismarck's new creation.[26] By necessity, the Prussian Army had long focused more on the offense than defense and had excelled at waging short, decisive wars for limited objectives. By radically expanding the scope of threats and interests, the unification of Germany expanded the importance of the military, not only in Germany but throughout Europe.[27] The allure of a decisive military campaign to solve the country's problems was greater than any lasting solution it offered to the strategic dilemmas of the Reich, a fact no less true in every other European capital.[28] Julius Andrassy, the Austro-Hungarian foreign minister, lamented that "The consequence of the recent wars is that 'might dominates over right' ... that foreign policy is only correct, when it is also [military-]strategically correct."[29] Bismarck correctly grasped that the problematic scale of the German Empire, easily the most powerful single piece on the European chessboard but vulnerable to any coalition against it, made far-reaching military entanglements inevitable.

How to minimize the likelihood of a general European war that Germany could not win became an enduring strategic problem after 1871, as was the domestic political problem of diminishing a military alternative that seemed to offer an easy escape from the country's dilemmas. Bismarck understood the problem as early as 1871 and thereafter embraced the idea that German security depended on peace and stability in Europe.[30] As the post-Franco-Prussian War strategic landscape gradually came into focus, he foresaw that military conflict involving any two other continental powers would inevitably involve the new Reich. "Whatever the origins, whoever the combatants, wherever the battlefield, Germany was likely to become involved. In such a war she would find herself trapped into fighting for someone else's interests. *Realpolitik* dictated that Germany strive to preserve the peace of Europe."[31] Bismarck's strategic policy had to manage the transition from a power striving militarily for its zenith to a "satisfied power," but one that at the same time

[26] Josef Joffe, "'Bismarck' or 'Britain:' Toward an American Grand Strategy after Bipolarity," *International Security*, vol. 19, 1995, pp. 105–106.

[27] A perspective on the Prusso-German civil-military dilemma is offered by Michael Schmid, *Der Eiserne Kanzler und die Generäle: Deutsche Rüstungpolitik in der Ära Bismarck, 1871–1890* (Paderborn, 2003); also the provocative argument about the last half of Bismarck's tenure in office in Konrad Canis, *Bismarck und Waldersee: die aussenpolitischen Krisenerscheinungen und das Verhalten des Generalstabes 1882 bis 1890* (Berlin, 1980).

[28] See the classic treatment by Stig Förster, "Der deutsche Generalstab und die Illusion des kurzen Krieges, 1871–1914: Metakritik eines Mythos," *Militärgeschichtliche Mitteilungen*, vol. 54, 1995, pp. 61–96.

[29] Heinrich Lutz, *Österreich-Ungarn und die Gründung des Deutschen Reiches: europäische Entscheidungen, 1867–1871* (Frankfurt a.M., 1979) pp. 488ff.; from Hildebrand, "Opportunities and Limits," p. 76n15.

[30] Heinz Wolter, "Bismarck als 'Realpolitiker:' Das Problem des europäischen Friedens," in Helmut Bock and Marianne Thoms, eds., *Krieg oder Frieden im Wandel der Geschichte: von 1500 bis zur Gegenwart* (Berlin, 1989), pp. 166–173.

[31] Pflanze, *Bismarck and the Development of Germany*, pp. 252–253.

provoked fear and suspicion among its neighbors and that could not expand without provoking a balancing coalition against it.

Especially after 1875, Bismarck cast himself as an impartial arbiter in international disputes, most notably at the Congress of Berlin on the Near Eastern question. Then, and during other crises too, he correctly calculated that Germany had little to gain and everything to lose in a general European war, particularly a two front war. Given the hostility of France, he focused much of his diplomacy on Russia to prevent one. In the late 1880s, some of his critics urged a preventive war against what they saw as a growing Russian threat, a course of action he famously dismissed as "committing suicide for fear of death." Nevertheless, the chancellor never embraced the abstract principle of European peace as an end in itself and never ruled out the ultimate need for war to safeguard Germany.[32] Indeed, he reasoned that in all probability, Germany would eventually have to go to war with France again, and better sooner than later.

But Bismarck opposed war for the sake of any objective apart from cold state interest. As early as the famous Olmetz speech in December 1855, he fulminated against wars waged on "principled" grounds, such as honor, glory, or the partisan domestic political advantage.[33] For Bismarck, the sledgehammer of the military was almost always a poor substitute for the scalpel of diplomacy, and wars represented the least attractive strategic instrument in most cases: difficult to contain, uncertain in their outcome, and prone to slippage in their aims and justifications. Wars frequently destroyed more than they created, and Bismarck preferred throughout his career to exhaust almost every other option before resorting to the armed conflict.

The strategic dilemmas created by Bismarck's unification of Germany converged after 1871 in the central question of how the great powers would react to the new and destabilizing presence at the heart of the European continent represented by the German Empire. France was Bismarck's most urgent problem. The greater part of German popular opinion regarded the annexation of Alsace and Lorraine, once part of the Holy Roman Empire, but since the seventeenth century France's eastern frontier, as the legitimate fruits of a victorious war. But the inhabitants of both regions thought of themselves as Frenchmen and displayed little enthusiasm for becoming subjects of the Prusso-German monarch. Further complicating the matter was the fact that the Prussians reached well into French-speaking areas to satisfy the great general staff, which insisted on control of the western invasion routes

[32] Karina Urbach, "Bismarck: Ein Amateur in Uniform?" in Brendan Simms and Karina Urbach, eds., *Die Rückkehr der "grossen Männer": Staatsmänner im Krieg. Ein Deutsche-Britischer Vergleich* (Berlin and New York, 2010), pp. 87–96.
[33] Bismarck, *Werke in Auswahl*, vol. 1, *Das Werden des Staatsmannes 1815–1854* (Stuttgart, 1962), pp. 333–344; from Jost Dülffer, "Bismarck und das Problem des europäischen Friedens," in Jost Dülffer and Hans Hübner with Konrad Breitenborn and Jürgen Laubner, *Otto von Bismarck: Person – Politik – Mythos* (Berlin, 1993), p. 109.

into Central Europe. Although conceding that it was militarily useful, Bismarck felt the policy of annexation excessive and agreed grudgingly to the military's position. As he understood, if Alsace and Lorraine enhanced Germany's western defenses, they also tied a strategic albatross around the new empire's neck.

He also recognized the long-term consequences of that annexation of territory. The French – rich, powerful, and influential even after defeat in 1871 – would not forgive the loss and would contrive to recover the two provinces. France's abiding animosity became a constant in Bismarck's strategic calculus. "Nobody ought to harbor any illusions; peace will end once France is again strong enough to break it," he remarked in 1874.[34] Fortunately for Bismarck, the other powers regarded France, as the one republican government among the major powers, with suspicion. For his part, Bismarck focused on keeping France isolated, in part by fanning the flames of a militant republicanism that the other powers detested and in part by encouraging the French to become involved in colonial ventures and rivalries with other powers, thus deflecting them from Alsace and Lorraine.

Nor did Bismarck balk at sowing dissension among the other European powers. Such conflicts, especially on the periphery of Europe and overseas, were not engineered by Bismarck exclusively, of course. But he understood how he might turn them to Germany's advantage. He could also count on greater or lesser degrees of indulgence from the other major powers of Europe. A prominent strain of British thinking had viewed German strivings for a unified nation as praiseworthy and potentially consistent with British interests on the continent, at least when unification seemed synonymous with democratization.[35] But the new and muscularly Prussian character of Germany after 1871 made even the normally unflappable British apprehensive. Speaking in the House of Commons, Sir Robert Peel said,

I must say that I look on the unification of Germany as a great peril to Europe ... We have at this moment the unification of Germany as a military despotism. It cannot be for the good of Europe that there should be a great military despotism in Germany built on the ruin and destruction of France.[36]

Disraeli expressed British misgivings in darker terms. "This war [of 1871] represents the German Revolution, a greater political event than the French Revolution of the last century," he said, describing the uncertain pall it cast over European affairs. He went on to lament that "There is not a diplomatic

---

[34] Dispatch to the German ambassador in St. Petersburg, dated 28 Feburary 1874, in Johannes Lepsius, et al. eds., *Die Grosse Politik der europäischen Kabinette*, vol. I: *Der Frankfurter Friede und seine Nachwirkungen, 1871–1877* (Berlin, 1924), p. 240; from Joffe, "'Bismarck' or 'Britain,'" p. 106.

[35] See Klaus Hildebrand, *"No Intervention": Die Pax Britannica und Preußen 1865/66–1869/70: eine Untersuchung zur englischen Weltpolitik im 19. Jahrhundert* (Oldenbourg, 1997).

[36] *Hansard's Parliamentary Debates*, 3rd Series, vol. CCIV (London, 1871), pp. 404–405.

tradition which has not been swept away. You have a new world, new influences at work, new and unknown objects and dangers with which to cope, at present involved in that obscurity incident to novelty in such affairs."[37] Disraeli grasped that the *Pax Britannica* rested on a careful European balance of power, a fact that had been clear six decades earlier to Metternich, who had worked with Lord Castlereagh in 1814–1815 to insure that no state gained too much from the defeat of Napoleon.

Bismarck labored for years to allay British fears and remove pretexts for disagreement or conflict, but never fully dispelled British concerns over the rapid growth of the German population and economic power in the decades after unification, nor stopped them from coming to see that affairs on the European continent had a growing potential to destabilize their empire.[38] For the British, this meant paying greater attention to potential threats to their lines of communication, especially in the Middle East, the Persian Gulf, and Central Asia, where the Russians had spread their influence with alarming implications for the British Empire.

Even as they noted British influence in those areas where their own imperial designs were moving them, the Russians fixated closely on Austrian intentions in Southeastern Europe. The czarist empire had earlier viewed Prussia's domination of Germany as the best among several unappealing possibilities and done much to midwife the new German Reich into existence, seeing it as another conservative bulwark against Western liberalism and republicanism.[39] In return for their passivity during the wars of 1866 and 1870–1871, the Russians felt they could count on the support of the new German nation for their policies. They also fell into the comfortable mindset of regarding Prussia as a strategic junior partner, and were not shy about conveying their opinion to Bismarck, who was no less prickly about Prussia's status against Russia than he had been with Austria some 20 years earlier.[40]

The most urgent aspects of Russia's strategic posture in the new European landscape had to do with Turkey. As Turkish power gradually waned, the Russians cultivated aggressive plans to expand their influence in the Slavic areas of that decrepit empire and were sensitive to the intentions of other

---

[37] William Flavelle Moneypenny and George Earle Buckle, *The Life of Benjamin Disraeli, Earl of Beaconsfield*, rev. edn., vol. II: *1860–1881* (London, 1929), pp. 473–474.

[38] Scholarship on the long and conflicted relationship between Germany and Britain in this era, so important for world history, is broad and deep. See especially Raymond James Sontag, *Germany and England: Background of Conflict, 1848–1894* (New York, 1969) and especially Paul M. Kennedy, *The Rise of the Anglo-German Antagonism, 1860–1914* (London, 1980).

[39] Barbara Jelavich, "Russland und die Einigung Deutschlands unter preussischer Führung," *Geschichte in Wissenschaft und Unterricht*, vol. 19, 1968, pp. 521–538; also Eberhard Kolb, "Russland und die Gründung des Norddeutschen Bundes," in R. Dietrich, ed., *Europa und der Norddeutsche Bund* (Berlin, 1968), pp. 183–219.

[40] This emerges unmistakenly from Ulrich Lappenküper, *Die Mission Radowitz: Untersuchungen zur Russlandpolitik Otto von Bismarcks, 1871–1875* (Göttingen, 1990).

powers, especially Austria-Hungary, to contain them.[41] While Austro-Hungarian designs were not as insidious as the Russians supposed, the imperial government in Vienna had indeed come to view its center of strategic gravity after 1866 as residing more in the Balkans than in the German-speaking parts of Central Europe. The Austrians looked with increasing indulgence on the new German nation, a fact which had as much to do with Bismarck's careful cultivation of that relationship as it did with any secular strategic gain to be had.[42] The Austrians also kept a weather eye on the newly united Italian nation, particularly in light of its strong interest in the Brenner provinces (the Trentino) and the port of Trieste. The puckish Italians seemed eager throughout this period to assert themselves and make up for centuries of fractiousness and strategic irrelevance.[43]

For Bismarck, the essence of strategic policy, particularly when it involved the potential for war, consisted not in military success alone but in a stable and enduring settlement. On behalf of a nation with much to lose in any realignment of the European strategic balance, Bismarck rightly foresaw complications for the new Germany in each of the relationships described above and struggled in the first years after unification to chart a course between them. The period between 1871 and 1875 was a phase of consider-able flexibility and uncertainty in his policy. He tested the constraints of the international system and clarified which squares on the chessboard of international politics were covered and which open. He never wavered in his broad focus on mitigating disturbances to the delicate equilibrium established by the consequences of the wars of unification, but he explored, at times indelicately, the full extent of his strategic *Handlungsspielraum*, or room for maneuver.

To prevent France from exploiting the insecurities of either Russia or the Habsburg monarchy for its purposes, Bismarck struck quickly after the War of 1871 to forge an accommodation between them. Through artful press policy and gentle suasion, he engineered a meeting between his mon-arch and Emperor Franz Joseph of Austria-Hungary at Bad Gastein in August 1871, reassuring the czar that a warming of German–Austrian relations need not diminish Germany's reliance on Russia. The apprehen-sions raised in St. Petersburg persuaded Alexander to join Franz Joseph on a visit to Berlin in September 1872. The occasion resulted in the so-called *Dreikaiserabkommen*, or Three Emperors' League of 22 October 1873,

---

[41] On the strategic dimensions of Russian concerns in the Balkans, see Barbara Jelavich, *Russia's Balkan Entanglements, 1806–1914* (Cambridge, 1991).

[42] Nicholas Der Bagdasarian, *The Austro-German Rapprochement, 1870–1879: From the Battle of Sedan to the Dual Alliance* (Rutherford, 1976).

[43] For the place of Italy in Bismarck's calculations, see Joachim Scholtyseck, *Alliierter oder Vasall? Italien und Deutschland in der Zeit des Kulturkampfes und der "Krieg-in-Sicht" Krise 1875* (Cologne, 1994).

the basic concept behind which remained the strategic constant in Bismarck's thinking until 1890.[44]

In the short term, the agreement served to lessen tensions in the Balkans between Austria-Hungary and Russia and stave off a rift between the two, thereby papering over one of the gravest threats to European peace. But the dynamics of the continent's strategic landscape even at this early point highlight the enduring difficulties of Bismarck's program. As successful as his attempts over the next two decades seemed, the writing was already on the wall dooming any program to bind the Austro-Hungarian and Russian Empires. The decline of the Ottoman Empire drew both into an inescapable competitive rivalry over the Balkans, leading directly to the First World War. The Three Emperors' League was little more than a temporary stopgap to the need to choose between Russia and Austria-Hungary, while keeping France marginalized. It did nothing to ameliorate the underlying conditions that fueled the strategic rivalry, as Bismarck himself understood. Despite the fact that France was a republic and Russia a reactionary autocracy, the cold and hard facts of *Realpolitik* pointed to France as Russia's natural ally against an increasingly powerful and thereby threatening Germany. As time wore on, Bismarck found it harder to remain on the side of three great powers against two.

If Bismarck had succeeded in papering over the latent conflict between the eastern empires, he could not quite master the shifting circumstances of European diplomacy more generally. Two developments in 1873 – the rise of the conservative administration of Marshal MacMahon in France and a decrease in Hungarian influence over the dual monarchy in Austria – called into question key components of his postwar strategy. By early 1875, events pointed to a growing isolation of Germany.[45] Bismarck had supported the republican government of Adolphe Thiers in France against the forces of monarchical reaction, reasoning that it made the country a less attractive alliance partner to the conservative monarchies of Eastern Europe.[46]

---

[44] Volker Ullrich, *Die nervöse Grossmacht: Aufstieg und Untergang des deutschen Kaiserreichs 1871–1918* (Frankfurt a.M., 1997), pp. 77ff.; most generally, William N. Medlicott, *Bismarck and the Three Emperors' Alliance* (London, 1945).

[45] For so discrete a diplomatic event, the historiography on the War-in-Sight crisis is imposing. The basis for the present interpretation is Johannes Janorschke, "Die 'Krieg-in-Sicht' Krise von 1875: Eine Neubetrachtung," *Historische Mitteilungen*, vol. 20, 2007, pp. 116–139; see also idem, *Bismarck, Europa und die "Krieg-in-Sicht"-Krise von 1875* (Paderborn, 2010); James Stone, *The War Scare of 1875: Bismarck and Europe in the mid-1870s* (Stuttgart, 2010); Andreas Hillgruber, "Die 'Krieg-in-Sicht' Krise 1875: Wegscheide der Politik der europäischen Großmächte," in Ernst Schulin, ed., *Gedenkschrift Martin Göhring: Studien zur europäischen Geschichte* (Munich, 1968), pp. 239–253.

[46] See Allan Mitchell, *The German Influence in France after 1870: The Formation of the French Republic* (Chapel Hill, 1979); the French perspective is handled by Bert Böhmer, *Frankreich zwischen Republik und Monarchie in der Bismarckzeit: Bismarcks Antilegitimismus in französischer Sicht 1870–1877* (Kallmünz, 1966); the diplomatic corollary to this policy is detailed skillfully in James Stone, "Bismarck and the Containment of France, 1873–1877," *Canadian Journal of History*, vol. 29, 1994, pp. 281–304.

By 1875 forces led by MacMahon were contemplating a *coup d'état* to put an Orleans prince on a restored throne and seeking the support of the Russian czar for their plans. There were further indications that Léon Gambetta, the republican firebrand and hero of the French resistance in 1871, would bridge the ideological divide and support the Orleanist candidacy.[47]

In Austria-Hungary, Bismarck had supported the appointment of Julius Andrassy as foreign minister of the dual state in Austria in 1871, which diluted the power of Austro-German centralism and a revanchist foreign policy against Germany. Within a couple of years, however, the financial insolvency of Hungary threatened to unwind the dual state constitution, and the conservative forces of centralism in Vienna rallied. A strong Austro-German regime was bound to pursue a revanchist policy against Germany. Matters with Italy, a new factor in Bismarck's calculations, were scarcely better.[48] Most alarmingly, perhaps, relations with Russia had chilled considerably by 1875.

To shore up that crucial connection, Bismarck appointed Joseph Maria von Radowitz, a privy councilor in the Foreign Office, as special envoy to St. Petersburg in February 1875.[49] Much speculation surrounded the special mission, at the time and since. Rumors circulated of potential German toleration of Russian expansion in the Balkans at the expense of Austria-Hungary, in exchange for benevolent neutrality in the event of a German preemptive strike against France.[50] Dark mutterings followed of German, French, and Russian troop movements. Informed opinion, both diplomatic and military, held that neither France nor Germany could risk war; both militaries, it was widely known, were rearming and reorganizing after the war of 1870–1871, a process Germany expected to complete in 1876 and France in 1877. The militaries of Austria-Hungary and Russia were even less prepared. At the center of these swirling currents stood Bismarck, whose assessment of the situation remained unclear to contemporaries.

Historians too have struggled mightily to divine Bismarck's reasons for igniting the crisis of 1875.[51] In the first decades of the twentieth century, they focused on whether he anticipated a general European war, similar to the First World War, 30 years before the fact, and whether they could thus write

[47] James Stone, "The War Scare of 1875 Revisited," *Militärgeschichtliche Mitteilungen*, vol. 53, 1994, p. 312.

[48] The difficulties are well detailed in Scholtyseck, *Alliierter oder Vasall?*

[49] Hajo Holborn, *Bismarcks Europäischer Politik zu Beginn der siebziger Jahre und die Mission Radowitz* (Berlin, 1925).

[50] See Janorschke, "Krieg-in-Sicht," p. 117n4, who points out that the documentary record does not support this interpretation of the Radowitz Mission, which was almost axiomatic in older scholarship on the crisis; find a good survey of the matter in James Stone, "The Radowitz Mission: A Study in Bismarckian Foreign Policy," *Militärgeschichtliche Mitteilungen*, vol. 51, 1992, pp. 47–71; the interpretation dismissed by Janorschke is that of Ulrich Lappenküper, *Die Mission Radowitz: Untersuchungen zur Russlandpolitik Otto von Bismarcks, 1871–1875* (Göttingen, 1990).

[51] See especially Janorschke, "Krieg-in-Sicht," p. 119.

him into the interpretative archaeology of that tragedy. A major study on Bismarck's understanding of preventive war in 1957 has demolished that suggestion resoundingly, sending historians back to the sources for an entire generation of fresh insights.[52] The absence of documentation directly attesting to his objectives and strategic calculations makes any interpretation unstable, and compels historians to consider the crisis within the broad sweep of Bismarck's strategic policy. Regardless of where one falls, however, there can be no question that Bismarck badly misjudged the support of the other major powers for a strong French counterweight to Germany in 1875. His role in what quickly came to be called the *Krieg-in-Sicht* (War-in-Sight) crisis of 1875 had its origins in rumors of a massive French effort to purchase military mounts in Germany, presumably to mobilize for war. Moreover, a French decision on 12 March to add a fourth battalion to each regiment and fourth company to each battalion of the army further exacerbated tensions. According to estimates of the German general staff that leaked to the press, the reform implied a massive and ready superiority over the German Army in a war.

Bismarck turned to the press to discipline the French temper. In early April the *Kölnische Zeitung* carried an article accusing the French of plotting a revanchist war against Germany in league with Italy and Austria, a revival of Bismarck's abiding fear of a so-called *Kaunitzian* coalition of Catholic powers against Prussia to undo the results of 1866 and 1871.[53] More seriously, the Berlin *Post* ran a piece on 8 April by a journalist known to be close to Bismarck entitled "Is War in Sight?" The article argued that, while clouds had indeed gathered, they could yet disperse. The articles sent shock waves throughout Europe; even the Kaiser expressed dismay over the alarmist mood, precipitating a three-week campaign by both Bismarck and the French foreign minister, Louis Decazes, to score diplomatic points.

At an official dinner in Berlin on 21 April, a tipsy Radowitz declared to the French ambassador, Elias de Gontaut-Biron, that a preventive war would be entirely justified "politically, philosophically and even in Christian terms," if France continued to rearm with the intention of overturning the results of 1871.[54] Only the British ambassador, Odo Russell, remained unruffled by the unfolding drama, writing to Lord Derby that

Bismarck is at his old tricks again alarming the Germans through the officious press and intimating that the French are going to attack them and that Austria and Italy

---

[52] Karl Ernst Jeismann, *Das Problem des Präventivkrieges im europäischen Staatensystem, mit besonderem Blick auf die Bismarckzeit* (Freiburg, 1957); Janorscke, "Krieg-in-Sicht," p. 119 points to further confirmation in Robert Ziegs, *Die "Krieg-in-Sicht-Krise" von 1875 und ihr militärpolitische Hintergrund* (Hamburg, 2000).

[53] A point made by Bagdasarian, *The Austro-German Rapprochement*, who argues that Bismarck's war scare was directed as much against Austria as France.

[54] Andreas Hillgruber, *Bismarcks Außenpolitik* (Freiburg, 1972), p. 141.

are conspiring in favour of the Pope ... This crisis will blow over like so many others but Bismarck's sensational policy is very wearisome at times ... I do not, as you know, believe in another war with France.[55]

By insinuating that Germany would declare war against France, Bismarck had overreached and provoked swift British and Russian reaction. Disraeli persuaded the Russians to intervene jointly in Berlin to tamp down tensions and preserve peace, while Russell was instructed to support a Russian peace initiative during the czar's scheduled visit in May. The visit provided a prime opportunity for the Russian state chancellor, Alexander Gorchakov, to chasten Bismarck before his monarch, informing him bluntly and directly that the European powers would not tolerate the subordination of France.[56] Bismarck "never forgave Gorchakov for what he believed to have been a deliberate attempt by the Russian to portray himself as an 'angel of peace'. ... If Gorchakov enjoyed putting his German 'pupil' in his place, Bismarck was the chief cause of his own humiliation."[57]

The War-in-Sight crisis marked the greatest setback of his career. If Bismarck's strategic policies over the preceding 11 years had set a standard for cultivating multiple alternatives, managing risk, and achieving great outcomes at minimal cost, his ill-conceived bluff in 1875 – inflating a half-baked war scare – seemed more like the haphazard bungling of a second-rate statesman. To be sure, the crisis arose at a time of great personal stress for Bismarck. The extraordinary pace and intensity of the events leading to German unification had exacted a high price on his health and psychological disposition, which in turn contributed to his general crankiness and adversarial disposition. His personal papers and letters list innumerable complaints about his dreadful physical health and declining energy in the years after unification. "My energy is all used up," he complained in May 1872. "I can't go on."[58]

Restless and in a constant state of discomfort, he spent only half of his time in the 1870s in Berlin, passing the remainder at his estates in Varzin and Friedrichsruh and at several spa retreats. Much of Bismarck's suffering was probably psychosomatic and characteristic of a massively self-absorbed personality, which detracts in no way from his statecraft.[59] A good bit also undoubtedly derived from his grossly unhealthy lifestyle, which involved, not least among its features, astonishing gluttony. During a visit to Bismarck's retreat at Friedrichsruh, Christoph von Tiedemann, the chief of the Reich Chancellery, recounted that "as before, one eats here until the walls

---

[55] Karina Urbach, *Bismarck's Favourite Englishman: Lord Odo Russell's Mission to Berlin* (London and New York, 1999), p. 138.

[56] Reinhard Wittram, "Bismarck und Gorchakov im Mai 1875," *Nachrichten der Akademie der Wissenschaften in Göttingen*, 1955, pp. 221–244.

[57] Pflanze, *Bismarck and the Development of Germany*, vol. II, p. 271.

[58] Volker Ulrich, *Otto von Bismarck* (Reinbek, 1998), p. 111.

[59] Eberhard Kolb, *Bismarck* (Munich, 2009), pp. 94–95.

crack."[60] Breakfast consisted of roast beef and beefsteak with potatoes, cold roast venison, game birds, dessert puddings, and "so forth," all washed down with copious amounts of red wine, champagne, and beer. Bismarck, who had been slim in his youth, gained weight steadily in the 1870s and had broken the scales at 273 pounds by the end of the decade. Only with the appointment of Dr. Ernst Schweninger as his personal physician and the imposition of a strict diet did his weight fall and his overall health improve.

But one cannot overlook Bismarck's continual stream of complaints and references to his health and state of mind throughout his tenure as chancellor, all of which contributed to lengthy periods away from Berlin and innumerable threats to resign. It also contributed to a disposition that was sometimes nothing short of nasty: political associates, friendly and hostile alike, struggled to compensate for his adversarial streak. "[His] inclination to seize on every triviality as a pretext for conflict is pathological and leads to unending friction," argued Robert Lucius von Ballhausen, a Prussian politician. "With such shaky nerves he'll only hold the Reich and state together if he abandons a good part of his responsibilities and cedes some leeway to other actors. In quiet moments he recognizes that and sets himself to it."[61]

But even if Bismarck's travails in 1875 had a personal dimension, they had important lessons for his strategic policy he could not afford to overlook. Nurturing alternatives as a strategic device has utility only when the alternatives are plausible. The crisis revealed the fault lines among the great powers and the limits to Germany's discretion that the other powers were willing to enforce. Bismarck had little choice after 1875 but to face the implications of Germany's strangely "half-hegemonial" position in Central Europe; the empire's political isolation; the ad hoc willingness of France, England, and Russia to counteract German initiatives if pushed too far; and the dependence of core German interests on Austro-Hungary.

But if the emphasis in the preceding analysis is on Bismarck's policies, the real justification for it lies in what the War-in-Sight crisis reveals of the European strategic landscape in the prelude to the First World War. The record of the crisis and its aftermath marks it as the basis of Bismarck's program after 1875 to secure the German Empire through a policy of stabilization and peace across the continent. It shaped his sense that a reordering of the strategic landscape in Central Europe was impossible after 1871 without a major war, and that such a war threatened to undermine Germany as much as help it. The British and Russians seized upon the opportunity to temper German ambitions, and the Russian foreign minister, Gorchakov, reveled in the chance to cast himself as an honest broker on behalf of European peace, a role that Germany's strategic dilemmas demanded it fulfill. The War-in-Sight

---

[60] Volker Ullrich, *Das erhabene Ungeheuer: Napoleon und andere historische Reportagen* (Munich, 2008), p. 42.
[61] Freiherrn Lucius von Ballhausen, *Bismarck Erinnerungen* (Stuttgart, 1920), p. 134.

crisis of 1875 points to the broader view historians of grand strategy take of Bismarck's approach to German security and European peace after 1875. Clearly, gone were the days when Bismarck could boast that Europe's fate could "always be made ready, combed and brushed in ten to fifteen minutes over breakfast" by him.[62]

In the aftermath of the War-in-Sight crisis, tensions in the Balkans flared and the long-simmering 'Eastern Question' again pushed to the forefront of European affairs. Bismarck observed the situation warily, if not with outright relief. Initially, he hived to a policy designed to reassert the central role in the European balance of power that he had enjoyed in the late 1860s: "a total political situation, in which all powers, except France, need us and are kept from coalitions against us as much as possible by their relations with each other."[63] A chain of events beginning in July 1875 with uprisings against Turkish rule in Bosnia and Herzegovina challenged the stability of all Southeastern Europe.

The gradual collapse of Turkish power threatened to create a vacuum that Austria-Hungary and Russia, circling like vultures around a dying animal, would compete to fill. In the worst case, the crisis would lead to a war in which each power sought direct German assistance against the other. The best possible outcome, an international conference in which each would likewise seek German support, if only diplomatically, was scarcely better. Bismarck could not afford to find himself in a position in which he would have to choose; indeed, a decision one way or the other would cut against the grain of a strategy of alternatives. The rebuffed party would almost certainly turn to France and strategic fault lines across the continent would harden to Germany's detriment. Initially, Russia and Austria-Hungary were able to cooperate sufficiently to agree in July 1876 on a plan to partition the Balkans peacefully.

However, unexpected Turkish military success against Serbia and Montenegro soon forced the hand of the czar, who was under immense pressure by a radical pan-Slavic faction in his retinue to step forth as the protector of Balkan Slavs. In October, he pointedly asked Bismarck whether Germany would remain neutral in the event of war with Austria. Bismarck's reply, while exhibiting rare candor, exasperated the Russians. He emphasized that Germany could ill afford a weakening of either eastern power and hoped still for an accord that would resolve the matter without a firm German

---

[62] Letter to his daughter Marie, 23 June 1872, in *GW*, in Hermann von Petersdorff, ed., *Bismarck: Die gesammelten Werke*, vol. XIV (Berlin, 1924–1935) p. 834 (hereafter *GW*); from Klaus Hildebrand, "Primat der Sicherheit. Saturierte Kontinentalpolitik," in Lothar Gall, ed., *Otto von Bismarck und Wilhelm II. Repräsentanten eines Epochenwechsels?* (Paderborn, 2000), p. 15n7.

[63] Johannes Lepsius, Albrecht Mendelssohn Bartholdy, and Friedrich Thimme, eds., *Die grosse Politik der europäischen Kabinette 1871–1914*, vol. II (Berlin, 1922–1927), pp. 153–154; from Pflanze, *Bismarck and the Development of Germany*, vol. II, p. 418.

commitment in either direction. Unable to wait, Russia declared war on Turkey in April 1877. The Russian Army broke the resistance of the Turks and forced the capitulation of the fortress at Plevna before dictating peace at the gates of Constantinople. The Treaty of San Stefano on 3 March 1878 restricted Turkey's European territory to a small region around the Ottoman capital. Russian intentions of establishing a greater Bulgarian duchy as a satellite, however, challenged British interests in the Mediterranean as well as those of Austro-Hungary in the Balkans. Neither was prepared to allow so large an increase in Russian power, and Bismarck called a general conference to head off a major war.

The challenges of his relationships with Austria-Hungary and Russia, as well as the war scare of 1875, spurred Bismarck to step back from international affairs in 1877 and recover his energies by an extended leave. While taking a cure at Bad Kissingen in June, he had occasion to ruminate on his strategic policy and dictated the so-called 'Kissingen Diktat,' wherein he described his "nightmare of coalitions" and enumerated the vision that guided his thinking on the developing strategic landscape:

A French newspaper said recently about me that I have a "le cauchemar des coalitions"; a nightmare of this kind lasts for a long time, maybe forever, an entirely justified worry for a German minister. Western coalitions against us can be formed if Austria joins one. More dangerous, perhaps, would be a Russian–Austrian–French combination; a greater intimacy among two of the above would give the third means to exercise a not inconsiderable pressure on us. In my concern about such eventualities, not suddenly but over years, I would see the following as a desirable outcome of the Oriental crisis: 1) a gravitation of Russian and Austrian interests and rivalry towards the east; 2) a pretext for Russia, in order to achieve a strong defensive position in the Orient and on its coasts, to seek an alliance with us; 3) for England and Russia a satisfactory status quo that gives them the same interest in maintaining it as we have; 4) division of England from France, which remains hostile to us, as a result of Egypt and the Mediterranean; 5) relations between Russia and Austria that make it hard for both to create the kind of anti-German coalition which centralizing or clerical forces in Austria are somewhat inclined to pursue.

Were I capable of work, I would complete and refine the picture that I have in mind: not that of the acquisition of territory, but a total political situation, in which all powers, except France, need us and are kept from coalitions against us as much as possible by their relations with each other.[64]

Energized by his vacation, Bismarck successfully defused the immediate tensions for war through his masterly administration of the Congress of Berlin, which convened under his chairmanship on 13 July 1878 in the Reich Chancellery. The congress drew the most important European statesmen together for the first time since the Crimean War to overcome the Balkan

[64] Michael Stürmer, ed., *Bismarck und die preußisch-deutsche Politik, 1871–1890*, text no. 40 (Munich, 1973), pp. 100f.

crisis and remove the strongest pretext for conflict in a generation.[65] That it was held in Berlin reflected the enormous importance that Germany now had for international politics, particularly as viewed through Bismarck's strategic policy over the preceding 15 years. His careful course between Austria-Hungary and Russia left him as the only statesman with the stature and impartiality necessary to oversee a diplomatic settlement to the problem.[66] He resolved to act as "an honest broker, who really wants to get the business settled," ameliorating tensions and generating compromise among the major stakeholders.[67] Even before the congress met, broad consensus emerged on the most controversial potential points – most importantly, the unwillingness of the Russians to fight both the British and Austrians in defense of the Treaty of San Stefano – which contributed as much to its successful outcome as Bismarck's evenhanded administration of its proceedings.

Nevertheless, his task was far from simple in practical terms:

Quite apart from the importance of the negotiations, it is extremely tiring to express one's self in a foreign tongue [French] – even though one speaks it fluently – so correctly that the words can be transcribed without delay in the protocol. Seldom did I sleep before six o'clock, often not before eight in the morning for a few hours. Before twelve o'clock I could not speak to anyone, and you can imagine what condition I was in at the sessions. My brain was like a gelatinous, disjointed mass. Before I entered the congress I drank two or three beer glasses filled with the strongest port wine ... in order to bring my blood into circulation. Otherwise I would have been incapable of presiding.[68]

Bismarck dominated the congress in three languages, nearly driving the delegates to exhaustion. ("No one has ever died from work," he told them.) He established the agenda, directed the deliberations, and husbanded the resulting consensus through the ratification process, which he accomplished with speed and aplomb. Ultimately, Russia relinquished a sizeable proportion of its gains, although Serbia, Montenegro, and Romania became fully autonomous and Bulgaria a semi-autonomous, tribute-paying possession of the Ottoman Empire. Apart from Germany and France, every major European power profited in some manner from the settlement – with the British gaining the most.

Nevertheless, the autonomy of Bulgaria and enhanced sovereignty of the Slavic territories were not enough to dissuade the Russians that the congress

---

[65] Ralph Melville und Hans-Jürgen Schröder, eds., *Der Berliner Kongress von 1878: die Politik der Grossmächte und die Probleme der Modernisierung in Südosteuropa in der zweiten Hälfte des 19. Jahrhunderts* (Wiesbaden, 1982).

[66] William L. Langer, *European Alliances and Alignments, 1871–1890* (New York, 1931), pp. 140–142.

[67] Horst Kohl, ed., *Die politischen Reden des Fürsten Bismarck: Historisch-kritische Gesammtausgabe*, vol. VII (Stuttgart, 1892–1905), p. 92.

[68] *GW*, vol. 8, p. 280, also pp. 265–266; from Pflanze, *Bismarck and the Development of Germany*, vol. II, p. 438.

had shortchanged them.[69] Gorchakov, who headed the Russian delegation, directed his ire at the deputy Russian plenipotentiary, Peter Shuvalov, and at Bismarck, whom he accused of giving scant support to Russian initiatives; a poor reward, in his estimation, for the sturdy backing that Russia had lent Prussia in its most vulnerable years. If Bismarck had succeeded in convincing the Reich's doubters that Germany was a stabilizing element in the European balance, then he did so at the cost of Russian distrust and hostility. But the net effect was to allay the still-simmering apprehensions of the new German Empire and Bismarck's policies among most statesmen in Europe, so much so that historians see the Congress of Berlin, only three years removed from the War-in-Sight crisis, as the high point of his public stature, if not his actual influence.

Tensions between Germany and Russia worsened with the so-called *Ohrfeigenbrief* of 15 August 1879, wherein Czar Alexander II demanded, in the form of a virtual ultimatum, that Kaiser Wilhelm issue a binding declaration on the future course of German strategic policy. The czar criticized Bismarck in undiplomatically sharp terms. In a cabinet meeting, Bismarck declaimed that "Russia has comported herself toward her sole friend like an Asiatic despot ... the behavior and letter are like those of a master to his vassal." He resolved to pursue a policy from which he had long shied, namely, a compact between the Habsburg monarchy in Austro-Hungary and the German Empire. He found a reliable negotiating partner in Graf Andrassy, the Austrian foreign minister, and, during a sojourn in Vienna at the end of September 1879, brokered a secret treaty. For this diplomatic coup to take effect, Bismarck had to overcome the formidable opposition of his sovereign, who viewed any closer relationship with Austria as a personal betrayal of his nephew, the czar. Because the chancellor and his monarch were in widely separated locations at the time, they engaged in the most serious disagreement to plague their long and productive relationship by letters. Bismarck employed every device – from unanimous cabinet resolutions to the threat of resignation – to persuade Wilhelm to ratify the document on 16 October 1879.

The Dual Alliance was a strictly defensive treaty, renewable every five years and containing secret language that obliged both parties to come to the defense of the other in the event that Russia attacked either. Bismarck's purpose in negotiating the alliance with Austria was not to close off the possibility of further accommodation with Russia; rather, he intended the reorientation to lever the Russians into a more intensive relationship with the German Empire, an outcome served with the renewal of the Three Emperors' League in June 1881. The terms of the treaty, renewed in 1884, were secret and offered Bismarck the most important source of ongoing

---

[69] Manfred Müller, *Die Bedeutung des Berliner Kongresses für die deutsch-russischen Beziehungen* (Leipzig, 1927).

leverage he possessed, however modest, over the potentially disastrous Austro-Russian rivalry in the Balkans.

The outcome of Bismarck's efforts in the 1880s was a complicated web of alliances designed to prevent the outbreak of a general European war; and failing that, to guarantee that Germany faced such an unfortunate eventuality on the side of a sturdy alliance. In May 1882 the Italians, who felt duped and isolated by French annexation of Tunis in 1881, transformed the Austro-German coalition into the Triple Alliance; Romania, Spain, and Turkey followed them in short order, propelling Bismarck to the height of his international influence. "At St. Petersburg," wrote Odo Russell in 1880, "his word is Gospel, as well as at Paris and Rome, where his sayings inspire respect, and his silence apprehension."[70] To be sure, the fact that the German Empire confronted no great strategic challenges in the early 1880s aided Bismarck considerably.

During these years in which he enjoyed a comparatively free hand, he embarked on a short-lived and misbegotten flirtation with colonialism, placing southwest Africa, Togo, Cameroon, East Africa as well as New Guinea and a slew of other Pacific Islands under German protection after German merchants and colonial enthusiasts ran up the Reich's flag. Historians have long agonized over what Bismarck might have intended in pursuing a policy that so badly contradicted core tenets of his strategic doctrine and incurred needless liabilities while providing few meaningful advantages.[71] For a time, popular historical wisdom focused on the putative domestic-political agenda, namely the reinforcement of the Reich's legitimacy through social-imperialistic manipulation of popular opinion. The influence of this interpretation has waned as much as suggestions that Bismarck, anticipating a monarchical succession in the near term, intended his colonial policy to antagonize the British and hence the domestic position of the Anglophilic crown prince and his English wife.

Another explanation for Bismarck's colonial policy, which he himself continually reiterated, was straightforward and simple. As he put the matter in the Reichstag on 10 January 1885, German colonialism aimed at the "protection of oversees settlements which our trade has brought forth."[72] In another connection, he argued that "we follow no foreign example, rather we follow our merchants with our protection. That is the principle." Of course, no single explanation captures so multifaceted a phenomenon, and historians like

---

[70] Lord Odo Russell to Lord Granville, 27 November 1880; from Edmond Fitzmaurice, *The Life of Granville George Leveson Gower, Second Earl Granville, K. G., 1815–1891* (London, 1905), p. 207.

[71] As seen in Henry Ashby Turner, Jr., "Bismarck's Imperialist Venture: Anti-British in Origin?" in Prosser Gifford and William Roger Louis, eds., *Britain and Germany in Africa* (New Haven, 1967), pp. 47–82.

[72] Rudolf Hafeneder, "Deutsche Kolonialkartographie 1884–1919," dissertation, Universität der Bundeswehr, Munich, 23 January 2008, p. 5.

A. J. P. Taylor are correct to point to Bismarck's flirtation with colonialism as "the accidental by-product of an abortive Franco-German entente," or a brief campaign to cooperate with the republican government of France in the colonial sphere to dissipate revanchist passions.[73]

In fact, Bismarck's efforts indeed resulted in a momentary relaxation of tension with France during a period of relative calm in European strategic affairs. But with the fall of Jules Ferry in late March 1885, tensions again grew. General Boulanger, minister of war in 1886 and a rabid anti-German, fostered a populist and blatantly revanchist policy against the Reich's protectorates over Alsace and Lorraine. Aggressive agitation for war complemented the French push for a Russian alliance, a clear prerequisite to any potential conflict with Germany. Although tensions again slackened with the departure of Boulanger in May 1887, the ground was laid for major challenges to Bismarck's policy of stabilization.

Once again, the problems arose in Southeastern Europe. In September 1885 Bulgaria united under Prince Alexander of Battenberg, the pro-British and pro-German interloper who had married the granddaughter of Queen Victoria. That action resulted in a Serbian attack on the country to enforce a new partition. Even the Serbian defeat at the Battle of Slivnitza would have little mattered, had it not moved the Russians to pressure Alexander, who fortunately for them was kidnapped and ultimately resigned his shaky throne. Increasingly alarmed by these muscular Russian initiatives on their borders, the Austrians informed them in November 1886 that an occupation of Bulgaria was unacceptable. For his part, Bismarck was willing to tolerate a Russian occupation for the sake of salvaging his accommodation with the czarist empire and was at pains to temper both of his allies, whom he compared to "two savage dogs."

But Germany stood to lose as much as either Russia or Austria in the event of a war between the two. Bismarck clung to his basic view that Germany could perhaps tolerate a war in which one or the other side lost a battle, but could not afford to have either mauled so badly that it endangered its position as a great power. In the meantime, he had to work feverishly to keep them bound in the alliance: "We must spin out the Three Emperors' League as long as a strand of it remains."[74] Bismarck understood this to be especially important with the Boulanger threat then percolating in France and the possibility of a Franco-Russian alliance. Bismarck's efforts in this period reflected increasingly desperate maneuverings to maintain an open channel to the Russians, while strengthening Austro-Hungarian resolve and building a Mediterranean

[73] A. J. P. Taylor, *Germany's First Bid for Colonies, 1884–1885* (London, 1938), p. 6.
[74] Johannes Lepsius et al., eds., *Die Grosse Politik der europäischen Kabinette*, vol. V: *Neue Verwickelungen im Osten 1885–1887* (Berlin, 1926), pp. 78n96, 123–153 (hereafter *GP*); from Pflanze, *Bismarck and the Development of Germany*, vol. III, p. 225.

coalition of Britain, Italy, and Austro-Hungary to contain the Russians on the southwestern flank.[75]

The czar ultimately refused to renew the Three Emperors' League, but assented to direct and secret negotiations with Germany over what became the Reinsurance Treaty of 18 June 1887. Bismarck conceded much to Russia's discretion by acknowledging its right to exert a dominant influence over Bulgaria and acquiescing to the closure of the straits to foreign warships. To uphold the Dual Alliance with Austria, he further agreed to a Russian proposal binding Germany and Russia to neutrality in the event of a war fought by either against a third power, except in the event that Germany attacked France or Russia attacked Austria. With this expedient, Bismarck may have fulfilled his ultimate strategic objective of heading off a Franco-Russian alliance, but he effectively committed Germany to support Russia in Bulgaria, a contradiction of his commitments to Austria-Hungary. He consequently ran the risk of igniting the very war in Southeastern Europe that his policies had done so much to avert. The provisions of the treaty – quite apart from its advantages or disadvantages – point to the fact that Bismarck had run out of space to maneuver. Almost all of the squares on the chessboard of European politics were now blocked off, and he had precious few alternatives remaining to head off aggressive French efforts to insinuate themselves into the Austro-Russian rivalry. As he well understood, any benefits to Germany's strategic position on the continent rested on conditions that were changing fast, and Russian expansionism could not be contained for long.

Throughout fall 1887, Russia agitated aggressively against developments in Bulgaria that it viewed as evidence of an Austrian conspiracy against its interests. Although Bismarck was initially sympathetic, his irritation with Russian initiatives mounted, and he began to apply financial pressure to head off an increasingly likely Russian occupation of Bulgaria. In November 1887 the German government effectively vetoed a major loan to Russia when it ordered the Reichsbank not to accept Russian bonds as collateral. Bismarck's moves may have restrained the Russians from overt military action, but also drove them into the welcoming arms of the French, where a Russian loan was so oversubscribed in March 1890 that the czarist regime was able to finance its new military programs on a grand scale. Perhaps paradoxically, the accession of Wilhelm II, who favored a British alliance, and the vehemently anti-Russian counsels of senior military and diplomatic advisors (in stark contrast to Bismarck, who consistently felt that "the Russian shirt [was] preferable to the English jacket"), alarmed the Russians into reopening negotiations to

---

[75] The complexities of Bismarck's policy toward Russia are detailed in Hans-Ulrich Wehler, "Bismarcks späte Russlandpolitik 1879–1890," in idem, *Krisenherde des Kaiserreichs 1871–1918: Studien zur deutschen Sozial- und Verfassungsgeschichte* (Göttingen, 1970), pp. 163–180; Andreas Hillgruber, "Deutsch-Russland Politik 1871–1918: Grundlagen – Grundmuster – Grundprobleme," *Saeculum*, vol. 1, 1976, pp. 94–108.

renew the Reinsurance Treaty.[76] But Wilhelm dismissed Bismarck in March 1890, and his successor as chancellor, General Leo von Caprivi, convinced the young Kaiser to let the treaty lapse, knocking out the most pivotal single strut supporting Bismarck's alliance system.[77] With that, the "conjuring trick," as one skeptical historian referred to Bismarck's complex and contradictory alliance system, collapsed against the basic causes of European insecurity: the spiraling fragmentation of the Austro-Hungarian Empire, the disintegration of Ottoman authority in Southeastern Europe, and increasingly strident Russian expansionism.[78]

Conclusion

In a poignant comment on one of his favorite historical actors, A. J. P. Taylor once remarked that historians who wrote about Bismarck always had "some political axe to grind, they were all concerned to show that he had failed or succeeded."[79] It is striking that Bismarck himself took pains to forswear any explicit responsibility for the outcome of his decisions and policies. "One cannot possibly make history," he was fond of repeating, apparently without irony, to many of the admirers who sought out the great man after his retirement. At most, he would add, one might guide affairs more prudently on the basis of it. To a university delegation, he declared that "One can always learn from [history] how one should lead the political life of a great people in accordance with their development and their historical destiny." In Bismarck's cautious outlook, the constantly shifting currents of strategic affairs and the changing terms in which power is expressed render even the greatest strategic accomplishments transitory. Success in the near term may well translate into failure later, as the circumstances that contributed to the former are apt to change in ways nobody can anticipate. In a lengthy series of post-retirement interviews with Hermann Hofmann, editor of the *Hamburger Nachrichten*, Bismarck summed up his strategic career with characteristic modesty:

My entire life was spent gambling for high stakes with other people's money. I could never foresee with certainty whether my plans would succeed ... Politics is a thankless job, chiefly because everything depends on chance and conjecture.

[76] Karl Messerschmidt, *Bismarcks russische Politik vom Berliner Kongreß bis zu seiner Entlassung* (Thesis/Hamburg, Würzburg, 1936), p. 87; from Hildebrand, *German Foreign Policy* (London, 1989), p. 87n47; the running conflict between Bismarck and senior military officials over policy toward Russia is detailed in Konrad Canis, *Bismarck und Waldersee: die außenpolitischen Krisenerscheinungen und das Verhalten des Generalstabes 1882 bis 1890* (Berlin, 1980).
[77] L. Raschdau, "Das Ende des deutsch-russischen Geheimvertrages von 1887," *Berliner Monatshefte*, vol. 17, 1939, pp. 361–366.
[78] A. J. P. Taylor, *The Struggle for Mastery in Europe, 1848–1918* (Oxford, 1954), p. 278.
[79] A. J. P. Taylor, *Europe: Grandeur and Decline* (Harmondsworth, 1967), p. 96.

One has to reckon with a series of probabilities and improbabilities and base one's plans upon this reckoning ... As long as he lives the statesman is always unprepared. In the attainment of that for which he strives he is too dependent on the participation of others, a fluctuating and incalculable factor ... Even after the greatest success he cannot say with certainty, "Now it is achieved; I am done with it," and look back with complacency at what has been accomplished ... To be sure, one can bring individual matters to a conclusion, but even then there is no way of knowing what the consequences will be. He came to the conclusion that in politics there are no such things as complete certainty and definitive results ... Everything goes continually uphill, downhill.[80]

As much as contemporary sensibilities may be gratified by the humbling of eminence, Bismarck was too reserved in his assessment. No statesman bore greater responsibility for the comparative stability and peace of Europe after 1871. He learned from the War-in-Sight crisis how different the constellation of interests across Europe had become since German unification, and resolved to work within them to preserve a delicate balance that secured the new Reich. By 1883, he had woven a complex web of alliances covering half of Europe. Some have criticized Bismarck for the contradictions inherent in that web, particularly the secret pledge of neutrality with Russia in 1887, and have argued that the presence of contradictions would seem to undercut the power and discretion that Bismarck commanded in international politics.

But such criticism misses the mark. The purpose of his strategy for safeguarding the German Empire was not to accrue and retain power, but to disperse and nullify it. In striking contrast to the strategic lights of the following generation, Bismarck's identity as a statesman and strategic actor was rooted in his *Kleindeutsche* sensibility, an awareness of how weak, exposed, and vulnerable Germany was in the center of Europe. As a result, his preoccupations were far more with the limitations of German power than with its potential, and he operated in the semi-paranoid manner of a man convinced that his nation's strategic sovereignty could dissolve as quickly as it had been gained. If Germany could not hope to become powerful enough to command the continent unilaterally, especially given its major inherent liabilities as a strategic entity, then Bismarck would labor to insure that no other nation or constellation of nations accrued enough power to dominate it, either. All, save France, found themselves bound in some fashion to Berlin, and none could build a hostile coalition or launch a war without violating those ties.

Among Bismarck's most striking characteristics as a strategist was an almost complete lack of faith in the permanence of any international accommodation. To the extent that one can apply such an anachronistic concept to him, grand strategy was an ongoing process of adaptation to shifting circumstances

---

[80] *GW*, vol. IX, pp. 397ff.; from Pflanze, "Bismarck's 'Realpolitik," pp. 497–498; the full text is reproduced in Eberhard Kolb, "Strategie und Politik in den deutschen Einigungskriegen: Ein unbekanntes Bismarck-Gespräch aus dem Jahr 1895 [Dokumentation]," *Militärgeschichtliche Mitteilungen*, vol. 48, 1990, pp. 123–142.

instead of a formula or handful of trite maxims. Understood in these terms, no successor could hope to equal his subtlety and insight, and none could consequently safeguard German security in the circumstances he created. Bismarck's diplomacy achieved its objectives while he remained in office, but ultimately its price for the future security of the Reich in Europe was high. By working through a series of formal, binding alliances during peacetime, Bismarck contributed to a growing climate of mistrust and insecurity on the continent, in part because the content of the treaties was often suspected rather than known.

Moreover, one method by which the chancellor bound the different powers to Berlin was by promising them territory at the expense of the increasingly fragile Ottoman Empire, even while he promoted Germany's relations with that dying regime. Bismarck lured Austria, Russia, Britain, Italy, and even, on occasion, France with the prospect of German support for their territorial ambitions in Europe and overseas. The logic behind his tortuous and often contradictory diplomacy appeared arcane to some of his subordinates, who never understood its wisdom, and their bafflement only grew as Bismarck's term of office neared its end. In 1890 shortly after Bismarck's dismissal, his successors decided not to renew the Reinsurance Treaty, believing it incompatible with Germany's other commitments. Their action led to a Franco-Russian entente, cemented into a formal alliance in 1894. German grand strategy had thereafter to contend with a far less favorable international environment.

This is not to suggest that Bismarck's strategic initiatives were hollow, but rather that one cannot appraise their historical ramifications and significance, if one is overawed by his putative genius. During his chancellorship the new German Empire was elevated to a dominant position in European international relations. Germany enjoyed what amounted to a soft hegemony, provided that it exercised that hegemony with restraint. The Reich's chancellor was Europe's preeminent statesman, whose abundant skills were satirized in the famous cartoon depicting the chancellor as a juggler able to keep five balls in the air simultaneously. At the same time, the empire's economic dynamism in the decades after unification and the reputation of its army commanded international attention and respect. Nevertheless, by the end of Bismarck's tenure in office, the strains on his strategic policy were already in evidence, and it was becoming increasingly unlikely that his system of improvised checks and balances could endure.

9   Dowding and the British strategy of air defense 1936–1940

Colin Gray

There was a distinct difference between the objectives of the opposing sides. The Germans were aimed to facilitate an amphibious landing across the Channel, to invade this country, and so to finish the war. Now, I wasn't trying with Fighter Command to win the war. I was trying desperately to prevent the Germans from succeeding in their preparations for an invasion. Mine was the purely defensive role of trying to stop the possibility of an invasion, and thus give this country a breathing spell. We might win or we might lose the war, or we might agree on a truce – anything might happen in the future. But it was Germany's objective to win the war by invasion, and it was my job to prevent an invasion from taking place. I had to do that by denying them control of the air   Hugh Dowding[1]

From its inception with an Observer Corps in 1915 to its culminating trial in 1940, the air defense of Britain offers one of history's most enthralling examples of successful strategy. The Royal Air Force's (RAF) Fighter Command applied its strategy at what today is known as the operational level of war, but its success literally under fire in 1940 was a critically essential enabler for much else that followed. A leading scholar of Britain's air defense in the years 1915 to 1940, John Ferris, has woven a compelling tale positing that the RFC/RAF enjoyed a systematic superiority in its approach to, and performance in, home air defense. In his studies of Fighter Command and its predecessor organizations, Ferris neither suggests explicitly nor implies that Fighter Command of 1936–1940 represented a force that performed beyond reasonable expectations.

Nonetheless, his argument that the RAF's victory in 1940 was a "walkover" and his judgment that Fighter Command's success was "one of the most one-sided victories in military history," reaches too far. On balance, his claim is plausible, but there is more than a suspicion of triumphalism and even determinism in such claims.[2] Paradoxically, perhaps, the thesis of an inevitable

---

[1] Air Chief Marshal Sir Hugh Dowding, quoted in Robert Wright, *Dowding and the Battle of Britain* (London, 1969), p. 146.
[2] In addition to John Ferris, "Achieving Air Ascendancy: Challenge and Response in British Strategic Air Defense, 1915–40," in Sebastian Cox and Peter Gray, eds., *Air Power History:*

victory shortchanges the RAF's strategic achievement.[3] In August–September 1940, Air Chief Marshal Sir Hugh "Stuffy" Dowding, and his battlefield air "general," Air Vice Marshal Sir Keith Park, Air Officer Commanding 11 Group, were rightly confident. Nevertheless, they never believed their campaign would be a "walkover."[4] By way of contrast, overconfidence was one among the lethal weaknesses in the German approach to air war in 1940.

This discussion does not seek to challenge the view that the RAF won the Battle of Britain not by a "narrow margin" but rather by a substantial one. Indeed, the book with that title, written by Derek Wood and Derek Dempster, first-rate for its time of publication in 1961, all but contradicted the claim in its title.[5] In his recent biography of Dowding, Vincent Orange is on more solid ground when he asserts:

There was indeed a "narrow margin" between survival and defeat in summer 1940. Despite the skillful, devoted efforts of Dowding and every member of Fighter Command, on the ground or in the air, Britain's survival depended ultimately on the "narrow margin" by which the dynamic, patriotic Churchill came to power and the vapid appeaser Halifax did not.[6]

Over the past 30 years, scholarship on the *Luftwaffe* and the RAF has yielded an unarguable understanding of why the RAF was likely to win in 1940. Inevitably, given the iconic and legendary status of "the few" in the Battle of Britain, the revisionist judgment on summer 1940 has yet to achieve much traction in

Turning Points from Kitty Hawk to Kosovo (London, 2002), the Ferris canon on air defense includes the following items: "The Theory of a 'French Air Menace,' Anglo-French Relations and the British Home Defence Air Force Programmes of 1921–25," *The Journal of Strategic Studies*, March 1987; "Airbandit: C^3I and Strategic Air Defence during the First Battle of Britain," in Michael Dockrill and David French, eds., *Strategy and Intelligence: British Policy during the First World* War (London, 1996); "'The Air Force Brats' View of History: Recent Writing and the Royal Air Force," *The International History Review*, March 1998; and "Fighter Defence before Fighter Command: The Rise of Strategic Air Defence in Great Britain," *The Journal of Military History*, October 1999.

[3] Other scholars such as Williamson Murray and Paul Kennedy, though making assessments of British strategic performance compatible with that of Ferris, prudently and with some humility acknowledge the benefit of hindsight. Murray notes that, "In retrospect, the task facing the Germans in the summer of 1940 was beyond their capabilities." Also, he advises, "In retrospect, the Luftwaffe faced insurmountable problems in coming to grips with Fighter Command." Williamson Murray, *Luftwaffe* (Baltimore, MD, 1985), p. 47; Murray, "Net Assessment in Nazi Germany in the 1930s," in Murray and Allan R. Millett, eds., *Calculations: Net Assessment and the Coming of World War II* (New York, 1992), p. 84. Dowding's achievement at Fighter Command is particularly impressive when considered in the context of Britain's less than stellar intelligence assessments in the late 1930s. See Paul Kennedy, "British 'Net Assessment' and the coming of the Second World War," in Murray and Millett, eds., *Calculations*, pp. 19–59.

[4] Two biographies by Vincent Orange are excellent: *Dowding of Fighter Command: Victor of the Battle of Britain* (London, 2008); and *Park: The Biography of Air Chief Marshal Sir Keith Park* (London, 2001).

[5] Derek Wood and Derek Dempster, *The Narrow Margin: The Battle of Britain and the Rise of Air Power, 1930–40* (London, 1967).

[6] Orange, *Dowding of Fighter Command*, p. 135.

the popular understanding in Britain. In sum, the revisionist view, amounting to a claim of an inevitable victory, overreaches. Admittedly, there is little room for doubt as to why Fighter Command won the air battle of 1940, or that the margin of victory was wide and not narrow. However, the apparently satisfactory state of scholarship has the potential to misinform. As this chapter explains, the Battle of Britain was the result of an air defense system that represented the cumulative product of nearly 25 years of careful, professional nurturing.

That said, it would also represent a serious error to conclude that the generally healthy history of British air defense preparation from 1915 to 1940 was the inevitable result of systemic genius. Individuals mattered greatly. Dowding's Fighter Command was a team project and effort. But, one needs to be careful lest the endeavor to show how robust the system of air defense was, and how much it depended on its systemic qualities, understates the strategic difference made by Dowding's personal performance over a decade. Single-handedly, he did not see off the *Luftwaffe* in 1940, but it would be difficult to exaggerate his contribution. He was the individual most responsible over a ten-year period for forging the integrated air defense system of 1940, for deciding on and overseeing execution of a unifying concept of operations, and for adaptively providing strategic direction. The air defense system was not organic and self-adjusting as if on operational and strategic autopilot: it needed leadership with strategic sense.

Understanding British air defense strategy, 1915–1940

Unfortunately, British air defense preparation and combat performance have rarely attracted a strategic assessment worthy of the subject. This should come as no surprise, because scholarship on strategy is generally thin or misleading.[7] In company with his critics in 1940, most current commentators fail to understand Dowding's strategy. The complexities of Fighter Command's strategy tend to be preempted by the easier accessibility of technical, tactical, and human issues. Strategy rarely figures significantly in historical narratives of the battle. Scholars rarely consider British air defense in sufficient historical breadth. Little more than a passing reference to prewar preparations accompanies their focus on the dramatic denouement of 1940. Moreover, such summary treatment rarely avoids being captured by the changes in form and substance that occurred in 1935 and 1936. Notwithstanding a record for competence in peacetime, the contribution of RAF air defense planning from 1918 to 1936 to the battle in 1940 receives insufficient attention. British air defense was neither invented nor recreated by Dowding when he assumed command at Bentley Priory in July 1936.[8]

---

[7] For a modest effort to improve understanding, see my book, *The Strategy Bridge: Theory for Practice* (Oxford, 2010).
[8] Orange, *Dowding of Fighter Command*, p. 82.

On the one hand, it is an error to imply that British air defense in the early 1930s required radar to perform well enough against the threats of its time. On the other, the technical invention of radar, though essential for effective air defense in the future, itself revolutionized nothing.[9] Dowding's crowning achievement was that he played the leading part in enabling a new, untried, and untested technology to play the critical role in 1940. Nazi Germany too had radar, but because of a shortage of strategic talent as well as structural restrictions on its military decision making, it lacked insights of Dowding's caliber. Arguably, British strategy for home air defense comprised a single narrative from 1917 to 1940. If there were a hiatus, it occurred immediately following the Great War and had ended by 1923. British air defense is a study in continuity, not discontinuity. Dowding's achievement was to adapt the air defense system successfully to meet extraordinary demands, technical and strategic, including audit by battle.

Both scholarly and popular treatments of the air defense story betray the familiar problems of hindsight. Although the consequences of the Battle of Britain were profound, one can portray the campaign in unduly simple terms. Indeed, there is an almost compelling clarity to its moral, operational, tactical, and strategic issues. Looking back to the late 1930s and 1940, in hindsight, one can identify heroes and villains and right and wrong answers. It was not so easy then; there was no foreseeable future – and there never is. While the contrasting strategic performances of the RAF and *Luftwaffe* in the Battle of Britain are not unduly difficult to explain, hindsight can seduce the unwary scholar. Events tend to flatter some actors at the expense of others. However, one of the necessary audits of a strategy is whether or not it coped well enough with the demands that flowed from the course of events, which no one can ever predict with confidence.

It is important that one does not anachronistically back-fit an intellectual conception on air warfare that is substantially inappropriate to the 1930s. The RAF regarded its new Bomber Command, created in 1936, as the senior of its two commands. Dowding did not dispute this. The most accurate way to characterize the bomber–fighter relationship is that RAF leaders viewed the bomber as fundamental to its strategic mission, while they accepted the air defense fighter as essential. The RAF in the 1920s and 1930s may have regarded the fighter as a regrettable necessity, but in practice it was steady in its belief in, and preparation for, homeland air defense, notwithstanding the faith in offensive air power for which Marshal of the Royal Air Force Sir Hugh Trenchard was the principal prophet.

---

[9] See Alan Beyerchen, "From Radio to Radar: Interwar Military Adaptation to Technological Change in Germany, the United Kingdom, and the United States," in Williamson Murray and Allan R. Millett, eds., *Military Innovation in the Interwar Period* (Cambridge, 1996), pp. 265–299.

Studies of strategy inherently bias toward structural explanations of events, much as students of strategic ideas and doctrine tend to privilege the intellectual component of fighting power over the moral and material. In the case of Fighter Command, the period 1936 to 1940 lends itself to the thesis that the RAF won the Battle of Britain before it made an interception. Frustratingly for analytical tidiness, the plausibility of the evidence and argument in support of such a proposition compels the application of the caveat against an assumption of predestination. As a general rule, historians underprivilege the role of strategy. On the other hand, when one focuses on strategy, there is the danger that one will underrepresent tactics in its implementation.

Several excellent historical analyses of British air defense in the interwar years leave the impression that the authors regard the Battle of Britain as an inevitable confirmation of events foreordained by previous decisions. This judgment may rest on a solid basis; nevertheless, one is uneasy with scholarship which so heavily privileges preparation for battle that confirmation in combat appears as an afterthought. The strategist's product is strategic effect, and military forces achieve such (net) effect through the agency of tactical performance.[10] So strong was the prewar performance of the RAF in preparing for home air defense, that it is not only easy but also necessary and appropriate for the historian to assign considerable weight to the forging of the air defense weapon. The cause (i.e., Fighter Command and its leadership from 1936 to 1940) and its most serious effect (i.e., victory in the Battle of Britain) form an equation that is both sound and yet can undervalue the roles of chance and contingency. Those who discuss strategy, as well as those who write strategy as plans, should never forget that military forces must execute strategy, if they are to secure its effect.

It is surprising how often scholars neglect the implications of the fact that war is a "duel" in Clausewitzian terms.[11] War is never analogous to solitaire; it is a collective, collaborative project between two or more opponents. The course and outcome of war are the dynamic products of the net strategic effects achieved as a result of competing, interacting strategic and tactical performances. As one commentator has noted: "War is a power struggle, a deadly interactive dance."[12] Not only will strategy adapt by wartime necessity, but driven by the enemy's strategy, it will alter in a continuous process of tacit, and sometimes explicit, negotiation among domestic stakeholders. "[Strategy] is a process ... that involves internal political influences

---

[10] See Gray, *The Strategy Bridge*, chp. 5 (I note the error in attaching talismanic significance to strategy per se on p. 255).

[11] Carl von Clausewitz, *On War*, ed. and trans. by Michael Howard and Peter Paret (Princeton, NJ, 1976), p. 75.

[12] Patrick Porter, *Military Orientalism: Eastern War Through Western Eyes* (London, 2009), p. 193.

and idiosyncrasies of individual behavior as well as the pressure of external events and threats."[13]

It is a truism that the enemy has a vote, both as an influence on our choices and even more significantly as judge of the effectiveness of our strategic performance. A state's multiple interests inevitably affect its strategic direction. Not until 1940 did an enemy possess the capabilities to test the competitive merit of Fighter Command's strategy. The Command did not enjoy the initiative in 1940; it had to respond to the threat posed by the *Luftwaffe* to the evacuation of the British troops from Dunkirk, and later to Britain itself.[14] Although decades of prewar preparation enabled Fighter Command's performance in 1940, there was, nevertheless, significant room for strategic choice, and hence for possible strategic error.

In contrast to scholars of war, scholars of strategy need to be vigilant lest they tell a unilateral, one-sided tale. Did Fighter Command win the Battle of Britain more than the *Luftwaffe* lost it? Given the inherently relational nature of strategy, the quality of Britain's air defense strategy set the bar high indeed for the *Luftwaffe*'s strategy in 1940. Because strategic history tends not to award the prize to the belligerent who fights well, but loses, it has to be the case that the enemy will inevitably audit the quality of a strategy, including his tactical performance in its battle space. In the end, the enemy's vote is apt to be conclusive. None of the criticisms leveled at Dowding weigh seriously against the dominant contemporary reality that what his command achieved was what Britain strictly needed strategically in 1940.[15]

Assessments of strategists and their strategies have to accommodate the contributions of friction and chance to the course of events.[16] Many of the factors for Fighter Command's success in 1940 rested on the competence of its leaders in making strategic and operational choices in the prewar period.

---

[13] Williamson Murray and Mark Grimsley, "Introduction: On Strategy," in Williamson Murray, MacGregor Knox, and Alvin Bernstein, eds., *The Making of Strategy: Rulers, States, and War* (Cambridge, 1994), p. 20.

[14] With some slight difficulty, I am resisting the orthodox but erroneous use of the adjective strategic to characterize both the German air campaign against Britain in 1940 and, by logical necessity, Fighter Command's defensive effort. What the *Luftwaffe* attempted assuredly had momentous strategic meaning, as did Fighter Command's effort and achievement. In that sense, the air warfare over Britain in 1940 was indeed profoundly strategic. However, everything that Germany and Britain did in the air in 1940 had strategic meaning. The fact that the *Luftwaffe* had to operate overseas, at long range, and for extraordinarily high military and strategic stakes in the Battle of Britain, did not define its performance as inherently strategic. For brief explanation of my point, see Clausewitz, *On War*, pp. 128, 177; and Gray, *The Strategy Bridge*, pp. 18–20.

[15] This discussion is not interested in debating the tactical and operational issues Dowding's critics have raised, save insofar as they might have strategic importance. Three books capture the less than edifying nature of public and private controversy over Dowding's command performance. Wright, *Dowding and the Battle of Britain*; Peter Brown, *Honour Restored: The Battle of Britain, Dowding, and the Fight for Freedom* (Staplehurst, 2005); and John Ray, *The Battle of Britain: Dowding and the First Victory, 1940* (London, 2000).

[16] Clausewitz, *On War*, pp. 119–121, 583.

Nevertheless, the context of 1940 underlines that effective military institutions, their strategies, and the grand strategies and policies they serve never appear overnight. Dowding and his associates made sufficiently correct choices to enable their command's victory in 1940. British strategy capitalized on German weaknesses and mistakes just as it derived advantage in home air defense out of the continental defeat of May–June 1940. It is also unwise, certainly ahistorical, to dismiss friction and chance from consideration. If one is to understand the British and German command performances in 1940, one requires empathy for the men and institutions who did not know how the iron dice would fall. After all, the friction distinguishes "real war from war on paper."[17]

Strategic analysis

This strategic analysis of Fighter Command navigates through the use of nine concepts that cluster in three trinities: width, depth, and context; ends, ways, and means; and structure, contingency, and performance.[18] Applied to Fighter Command, the first trinity advises "width" in the study of its strategy up to 1940. One can argue that a study of air defense should focus on how and why Fighter Command was sufficiently ready in 1940. Nevertheless, such an approach constitutes an unjustifiably truncated approach to strategy. For the case here, Fighter Command not only had a strategy, but it also followed that strategy tactically under fire in 1940. No strategy is fairly assayable, if one does not consider its (strategic) effect in action.[19]

"Depth," the second concept in Michael Howard's triptych, requires examination in as much relevant and diverse granularity as necessary, although not so much that one drowns the strategic plot in detail. Air war lends itself to numerical analysis, not invariably to the advantage of understanding. Unfortunately for strategic comprehension, the important numbers in air warfare are not always self-evident. What mattered strategically in 1940 was not so much the actual numbers, especially of operationally available pilots, planes, and combat losses, but rather what each side believed the numbers to be in the context of their assumptions. Strategic net assessment always requires an answer to the question, "so what?"

Howard's third concept, "context," is so high in content as to produce confusion rather than enlightenment. Despite that caveat, there is everything to be said in praise of the examination of British air defense in the contexts – plural – that enabled, propelled, and provided it with strategic meaning. For example, if one chooses to hazard a bold, but not implausible, causality, it is not inappropriate to venture that "It was in summer 1940, however, that

---

[17] Clausewitz, *On War*, p. 119.
[18] Michael Howard, *The Causes of Wars and Other Essays* (London, 1984), pp. 215–217.
[19] See Gray, *The Strategy Bridge*, chp. 6.

the Germans lost the war."[20] Nevertheless, in 1940 Dowding was attempting neither to win the whole war, nor even to defeat the *Luftwaffe* comprehensively. He calibrated strategy quite exactly to the limited, but essential, goal of effective homeland air defense. Thus, it is appropriate only to claim that Dowding and Fighter Command enabled a chain of strategic causation and effect that allowed the Allies to win the Second World War.[21]

The second trinity necessary to appreciate Dowding's performance in command lies in the familiar triptych of ends, ways, and means. Analyses that focus only on one, or even two, of the three components, usually privileging heavily the battle in 1940, fail to grasp the nature and quality of Dowding's achievement. His success was strategic in every sense. Dowding played the major role in shaping the means that comprised Fighter Command in 1940, but he was thoroughly innocent of responsibility for the strategic circumstances in which his command had to fight. He had played a key role in forging the maturing weapon that Fighter Command became in 1940. Moreover, he was principally responsible for the choice of strategy his command was to follow.[22]

Fighter Command could only achieve its strategic effect if its ends, chosen operational methods, and its human and material means were mutually compatible and supportive. Dowding's challenge was strategic, and he could only meet it strategically. Policy, driven by Churchill in May 1940, clashed with Dowding's strategic sense over the issue of reinforcing the French with additional Hurricane squadrons. No strategic performance is entirely immune from the influence or infection of imprudent demands triggered by the pressures of perceived political necessity. Fighter Command could have failed in 1940, had policy insisted that it attempt the impossible or imprudent; had Dowding (and Park) fought the battle unwisely; or had the flying sword itself and its vital non-flying enabling systems not been combat competitive.

It follows from that judgment that a sound assay of Dowding's performance as strategist must assess his choices and actions in a manner connecting political ends with the strategic ways he selected for operational guidance, to the fighting power that was his to command. One cannot consider these three elements in isolation. Fighter Command between 1936 and 1939 existed only to deter, if possible, and fight, if necessary. One can weigh no single element alone, nor sub-element, save in relation to the other elements. To assess the

---

[20] Murray, "Net Assessment in Nazi Germany in the 1930."

[21] Stephen Bungay, *The Most Dangerous Enemy: A History of the Battle of Britain* (London, 2001), chp. 31, is exceptionally plausible in explaining the strategic importance of Dowding's victory for what followed in the course and outcome of the war.

[22] Dowding's biographer, Vincent Orange, recognizes the debt that his subject owed to his functional predecessors when he characterized Dowding as the "principal builder rather than the architect," of victory in the Battle of Britain. Quoted in Henry Probert and Sebastian Cox, ed., *The Battle Re-Thought: A Symposium on the Battle of Britain* (Shrewsbury, 1991), p. 56.

potency of an air defense system, one must specify the quality of threat with which it had to cope.

The third trinity is that of embracing the factors of structure, contingency, and performance. This trio is akin to a skeleton key that provides perspectives on the subject. Dowding's Fighter Command constituted an evolving structure, a "system of systems." As with all organizations, Fighter Command was at the mercy of contingency: in other words, the impact of events to which it had not contributed.[23]

The growing reality of the Chain Home radar system and of the Spitfire and Hurricane did impact on the policy "ends" of British domestic politics in 1939, though they had no traceable influence on German policy. In the vital case of radar, this is scarcely surprising, since German intelligence failed to uncover that the British possessed a functioning radar system or, once recognized, how Fighter Command employed it. Science, though not all technology, is apt to frustrate efforts to insure secrecy. As science, radar was not and could not be secret by 1938.[24]

As with all leaders of defense planning and preparation in peace, Dowding could only hope the future would present strategic demands that would fall within the scope of Fighter Command's ability to deliver. The true test of defense planning is not to "get it right," but rather to "get it right enough," so that near- and literally real-time adaptation is possible to compensate for inevitable errors.[25] Although explanation of the structural reasons for Fighter Command's success in 1940 is important, readers should not believe that the *Luftwaffe*'s defeat was preordained. Fighter Command still had to achieve victory against a confident and tough opponent. Conduct of the Battle of Britain demanded competent British behavior. Dowding's sword needed to demonstrate conclusively its superiority to an enemy who did not know in July 1940 what it would learn painfully by mid September.

Master narrative: the argument

The principal thesis of this chapter is that Dowding and Keith Park remained steadfast in their commitment to a strategic concept that effectively guided Fighter Command's operations and tactics. Dowding's

---

[23] Although Dowding's Fighter Command was a true system of systems long before this term of art entered common usage, his conceptualization and strategic achievement bears only a slight resemblance to the astrategic theory advanced in the 1990s and beyond by Admiral Bill Owens.

[24] See Beyerchen, "From Radio to Radar"; and for the full technical and organizational story of relevance to Dowding's Fighter Command, David Zimmerman, *Britain's Shield: Radar and the Defeat of the Luftwaffe* (Phoenix Mill, 2001). A complete history of radar is attempted in Robert Buderi, *The Invention that Changed the World: The Story of Radar from War to Peace* (London, 1998).

[25] I explain this vital principle in my "Strategic Thoughts for Defence Planners," *Survival*, vol. 52, June–July 2010.

understanding of what would constitute victory was prudent, feasible, and compatible with Britain's grand strategy. That expression of grand strategy entertained no goal beyond national survival in 1940. This translated as a denial of victory to the *Luftwaffe* through the summer and, if need be, the early fall, when it became too late for invasion to be practicable. Due to the soundness of Fighter Command's strategy, Dowding made the right enough decisions as particular challenges emerged. The denial of victory to the *Luftwaffe* required only that Fighter Command remain a formidable adversary over the Channel, the invasion beaches, and their inland approaches. Fighter Command's actual combat power would be essential only if the Germans attempted an invasion. In summer 1940 it was the German analysis about the course of the air campaign that mattered most.

Dowding's achievement in 1940 was genuinely strategic and personal, but it did rest on the excellence of a British air defense that was nearly 25 years old in its basic architecture. Recent scholarship suggests that in 1936 Dowding inherited success, not failure. British air defense was not broken; so he did not have to rescue it from ruin. Dowding's contribution to the victory was indeed decisive, but one needs to understand that that victory required team effort over many years. A significant element in his contribution lay in his ability to select the military objective that best suited Britain's political objectives. Dowding's definition of victory was limited, but also conclusive in what it might enable.

Much of the criticism of Dowding's command performance, including his and Park's air generalship, is either wrong or, when reasonable is strategically relatively unimportant. To argue that Fighter Command did not achieve a perfect tactical, or strategic, performance in 1940, is simply to describe the universal and eternal human condition. The vital questions pertain to the scale of the errors committed and the ability to learn, adapt, and improve. The Command proved it was more than merely good enough to meet Britain's security requirements. As always, contingency was present throughout 1940. Ironically, the   unfolding of the *Luftwaffe*'s air campaign in 1940 was radically different from the "knock-out blow" anticipated in London. Moreover, as a result of France's disastrous collapse, the *Luftwaffe* no longer had to launch its assault across the North Sea from Germany, unescorted by single-seat fighters.

In 1940, Fighter Command had to defeat the *Luftwaffe* in a battle against the world's premier, and to that point all-conquering, air force. Sound system and prudent strategic concepts might have compensated for poor air battle generalship or inadequate fighting power by those at the sharp end. Happily, there was no great need for much compensation. Fighter Command's enemy provided no clear strategic direction to its forces. That said, the *Luftwaffe* was truly formidable tactically, albeit less so over southern England than over the continent. However, the German strengths in air warfare in 1940 proved grossly, not marginally, incapable of offsetting the *Luftwaffe*'s systemic weaknesses.[26]

Dowding and Fighter Command could not have delivered a victory conclusively predetermined by decades of careful preparation. Nothing was preordained in 1940. That long period of preparation, resting on the experience of defensive air warfare over Britain in the First World War, yielded decisive advantages. Yet, preparations, no matter how well thought through, cannot guarantee success in war. Those in command have to exploit the advantages gained from prudent effort in peacetime. The quality of British air defense planning and provision over many years, as well as the performance of individuals, not abstract ideas, organizations, and technologies, were what mattered. All were essential to the ability to adapt to the unexpected (e.g., the fact that Bf 109s were based in the Pas de Calais, six minutes from Dover). Fighter Command could not have improvised a "good enough" air defense of Britain in 1940. Dowding's victory represented a double achievement: he both directed and guided the many activities in the 1930s that created a competitive and effective air defense system that he then directed. These represented outstanding achievements.

The strategy of British air defense is a story of preparation and practice. The "bookends" of the defensive air battles of 1915–1918 and 1940 are really of one piece. The British created and matured the system in the First World War and then episodically modernized it in peace. Thus, the air defense system was ready enough to fight again in 1940. This is a story of continuity more than discontinuity, and teamwork as well as leadership.[27] One historian's judgment reads more persuasively than it should. On the evidence, he claims that

The *Luftwaffe* did not fail because it was wrongly equipped. It failed because it did not use its equipment properly. The failure came from the top, from a leadership

---

[26] The Luftwaffe became market leader in fighter combat tactics when Lt. Werner Mölders with Germany's Condor Legion in Spain rewrote the manual on air fighting. He recommended abandonment of the traditional "vic" formation and adoption of the *Schwarm* instead, the relaxed "finger-four" formation comprising two loose pairs (*Rotten*) staggered in height. The new tactics advised a separation of some 600 feet between aircraft. RAF Fighter Command remained wedded to the "vic" formation that it inherited from the biplane era and, of course, from the lesson-set of the Great War. See Wood and Dempster, *The Narrow Margin*, p. 52; and James Corum, *The Luftwaffe: Creating the Operational Air War, 1918–1940* (Lawrence, KS, 1997), p. 207.

[27] Stephen Bungay is particularly effective with his argument that the Battle of Britain was won by a "few" key men, ten to be exact, who designed, built, commanded and politically enabled the Fighter Command of 1940. His ten were: soldier Maj.-General E. B. Ashmore (creator of Britain's air defense system in 1917); scientists Henry Tizard (science administrator) and Robert Watson-Watts (radar); engineers Sydney Camm (the Hurricane), Reginald Mitchell (the Spitfire), and Ernest Hives (the Merlin engine for the Hurricane and Spitfire, inter alia); Ralph Sorley (eight-gun requirement for fighters); Hugh Dowding (air strategist); Keith Park (air general); and Winston Churchill (political and policy enabler). *The Most Dangerous Enemy*, pp. 380–381.

which asked its men to do the wrong things the wrong way. The plan they produced meant that they entered the Battle with the odds of success stacked heavily against them.[28]

So far so good, and persuasive; but he then risks straying from the easily defensible path of credible explanation when he adds: "However, nothing in history is inevitable. Alternative plans could have been produced which could have shifted the odds significantly in [the *Luftwaffe*'s] favour."[29] This is logically correct, but also misleading because, just as with Fighter Command, the principal reasons why the *Luftwaffe* performed as it did in summer of 1940 were shaped by its pre-1940 provenance. Moreover, it is essential to remind oneself that Dowding's knowledge of his enemy in 1940 was not formed by hindsight.

From Ashmore to Dowding: forging the air defense weapon, 1915–1936

Although neither the RAF nor the *Luftwaffe* could predict in the mid 1930s that they would face a tough and strategically crucial examination in summer 1940, Fighter Command's leaders and past had designed it precisely to fight the battle of 1940, while the *Luftwaffe* leaders had not.[30] For reasons of consistent organizational responsibility as well as efficient political and financial support, by 1940 Britain's home air defenses were prepared to meet the tactical and strategic challenges. Those forces had benefitted from continuity of endeavor in pursuit of a dominant aim – Fighter Command's protection of the British homeland from air attack.

From time to time the Command found its ability to perform the core of its mission endangered by pressing demands to perform other duties. With great determination, Dowding controlled, indeed stemmed and arrested, the danger of his force hemorrhaging from commitments that would have affected its basic mission to defend the British Isles. In particular, during the third week of May 1940, when the pressure was extraordinary to send additional Hurricane squadrons to aid the French, Dowding's steadfast refusal was strategically critical to Britain's survival.

It is beyond disputation that Dowding's strategic victory in 1940 rested on Britain's prewar preparations for air defense. The depth and multifaceted breadth of his personal contribution to 1940 undervalues the arguments of those who remain skeptical of that fact. Preceding his appointment to lead Fighter Command in 1936, Dowding had been a member of the air council for supply and research from 1930 until January 1935, and then for a year

---

[28] Ibid., p. 377.   [29] Ibid.
[30] See Air Historical Branch, Air Staff (RAF), *The Rise and Fall of the German Air Force, 1933–1945* (London, 1948), chs. 1–2; Murray, *Luftwaffe*, chp. 1; and *German Military Effectiveness* (Baltimore, 1992), chs. 2–3; and Corum, *The Luftwaffe*.

until July 1936 he served as the first air council member for research and development. These experiences were not the least among the many continuities that explain why Fighter Command acquitted itself in an effective fashion when the test came. His role was vital in the decisions to proceed speedily in reequipping Britain's air defense with Hurricanes and Spitfires, while his support was crucial in the rapid development and deployment of radar as a key enabler of a modern systemic approach to air defense.

In common with the Duke of Wellington, Dowding was respected and trusted, but not greatly loved. His was not a charismatic style of leadership. It was not Dowding, but rather Park, commander of 11 Group covering London and southeast England, who had the role of keeping morale intact in the face of the *Luftwaffe*'s assault. Nevertheless, Dowding had the rare talent of being able to see the big picture and the long-term "plot," while somehow remaining a meticulously detailed individual. We know that outside of uniform, he was warm, convivial, and witty, but he revealed those attractive traits only to a select few intimates on private or social occasions. Dowding was the consummate cold, calculating professional – a master of his subject – who convinced others by force of logic and the strength of the facts rather than the dazzle of personality. Although always open to other points of view, he rarely tolerated dissent from within Fighter Command once he had come to a decision. And he certainly did not appreciate contrary views expressed by his near peers, including his political and nominal military superiors. He did not suffer fools. He dedicated himself to fulfilling his command's primary mission in the face of pressing demands to direct resources to other tasks. Dowding won most of his major arguments with fellow air professionals and politicians simply because he had demonstrated that he was unanswerably in the right.

Although correct and courteous, Dowding did not win debates with smiles. He acquired the somewhat unaffectionate nickname "Stuffy" while a student in 1912–1913 at Camberley. He was not self-consciously a crowd-pleaser, and he never varnished disagreeable facts.[31] He won many minds, some reluctantly, but few hearts. Luckily for Britain he did not need lofty rhetoric or diplomatic cunning to succeed as a strategist. In that most vital of respects, his performance at Fighter Command from July 1936 to November 1940 was akin to walking through an open door. When he was truly challenged by unwelcome events – most especially the crisis in France in May 1940, and the crisis over night air defense in October and November – the facts were with him. On the important issues of equipment, personnel management, and strategy, it is hard to be generous to his critics. His was a command performance that has glittered ever brighter with passing years.

---

[31] See Orange, *Dowding of Fighter Command*, chp. 1. For a less sympathetic appraisal than that by Orange, see Peter W. Gray, "Dowding as Commander, Leader and Manager," in Gray and Sebastian Cox, eds., *Air Power Leadership: Theory and Practice* (London, 2002). In my view Peter Gray is overly critical.

A careful scholar of British air defense, John Ferris, claims that "Its [the RAF's] air defence system of 1940 stemmed directly from that of 1918."[32] That author explains:

During the First World War, in response to raids by German airships and aircraft, Britain developed a sophisticated air-defense system. It had an effective means of early warning, signals intelligence, while ground-based observers provided decent tactical information. Ground commanders could not communicate with aeroplanes in the air, which precluded effective and economical operations or guided interceptions. Instead, aircraft constantly flew along patrol lines, staggered at different altitudes, hoping that by chance one would sight an intruder.[33]

Plainly, Rome could not be built in a day. However, by 1918, the London Air Defense Area (LADA) represented:

a cybernetic structure, featuring what its commander [Major General E. B. Ashmore] called "a highly centralized intelligence and command system." Within one minute LADA could receive and process reports from thousands of observers over a 10,000 square mile area, place them before commanders, let them dispatch orders to aircraft standing ready on the runway, which were in the air within two-and-a-half to five minutes. Some 286 guns and 200 aircraft could act within two minutes of the report of one observer 50 miles away. At a moment's notice, each unit could switch from independent operations to fighting under LADA's orders and back again. By the end of the war, with R/T [radio/telephone] provided to some squadrons, this system was on the technical verge of being able to conduct ground directed interceptions of enemy bombers at 20,000 feet.[34]

This represented an impressive performance for 1918, with its effectiveness amply verified by the fact that, following an understandably stuttering beginning, it defeated the German Navy's, then the German Army's, Zeppelin onslaught in 1916, while "in 1917, it smashed daylight Gotha [long-range bomber] attacks, and in 1918, it broke German night raids."[35] Ferris then observes that "air defence demonstrated a remarkable ability to recalibrate in response to new challenges and to develop advanced information process, and command, control, communication and intelligence (C^3I) systems."[36]

Ferris has thus underlined how great the continuities were between the LADA in 1917–1918, and Fighter Command in 1940. The historical detail is interesting in its own right, but that detail yields a clear strategic narrative for British air defense that has an arc connecting 1918 and 1940. The barest of bare bones of the story are as follows: (1) That Britain created an effective integrated air defense system that defeated distinctive enemy campaigns between 1916 and 1918. (2) It resurrected and modernized the 1918 LADA in 1924 with the creation of a new organization, Air Defence Great Britain (ADGB), which encompassed a Fighting Area Headquarters (AAHQ). And

---

[32] Ferris, "Airbandit," p. 23.   [33] Ferris, "Achieving Air Ascendancy."   [34] Ibid.
[35] Ibid.   [36] Ibid.

(3) ADGB was redesigned and rebranded as Fighter Command in July 1936.[37] The "means" in the air defense strategy triptych were always evolving, as the threat posed new challenges, while science and technology proffered solutions. Necessarily, the "ways" of strategic air defense had to alter operationally and tactically. The "ends" of air defense, however, did not change – indeed, they could not. Nevertheless, the "ends" of Fighter Command regarded operationally and tactically – with profound possible strategic implications – were contested in practice, though not in principle in May 1940.

The narrative of British air defense in 1940 is so well known, so fascinating, and so much the stuff of legend that it is easy to miss or shortchange its strategic meaning. When one stands back from the details of "wizard boffins," exploiting discoveries on the frontier of electromagnetic spectrum research, it is clear that the military and civilian bureaucrats generally made prudent choices, the politicians frequently took sufficiently sound advice, and RAF personnel performed well enough in preparation and then in combat.[38] To summarize, the British air defense system: (1) defeated the enemy of the day repeatedly, in 1916, 1917, 1918, and 1940; (2) was always up with, or ahead of, the threat curve from 1923 until 1940;[39] (3) made either unarguably correct, or at the least, "right enough" decisions on most major matters of material, organizational, and procedural discretion, over a 20-year period; (4) suffered considerable punishment in 1940 as a consequence of its material and tactical mistakes, without that damage proving strategically fatal; (5) turned in a quintessentially holistic record of strategic success that resulted from professional competence, including clear strategic focus over a 25-year period.

Dowding and Park were the brightest stars at the sharp end of a team project that had lasted for decades. The father of British air defense was Ashmore in 1917–1919, as Dowding recognized. To the student of strategy, what is remarkable about the British experience in air defense is the sheer quantity, quality, and persistent record of competent choices. Those choices occurred in the face of a future that was profoundly uncertain. Moreover, effectiveness under fire depends on individuals capable of decisiveness in action. One should not forget the nature of the challenge to a force with a necessarily defensive function, air defense, posed by an evolving and largely unknowable, enemy. To be proven "right enough" by historical analysis, considering the political, technological, and military uncertainties of the 1920s and 1930s, represents an impressive achievement.

---

[37] The official in-house history is essential reading. See T. C. G. James, *The Growth of Fighter Command, 1936–1940* (London, 1942–43), chp. 1.

[38] Ferris, "Fighter Defence before Fighter Command."

[39] See Williamson Murray, *The Change in the European Balance of Power, 1938–1939: The Path to Ruin* (Princeton, 1984); and Paul Kennedy, "British 'Net Assessment' and the Coming of the Second World War," in Murray and Millett, eds., *Calculations*.

Beyond the familiar triptych of ends, ways, and means, a second – comprising structure (and network procedures in the process in the structure), contingency, and performance – is also necessary to explain the success of British thinking and strategy between 1918 and the Battle of Britain. While the settled structure was essential for mission accomplishment, the reduction of uncertainty was critical for performance in battle. The second and third items in the second triptych, contingency and performance, were unknowable in detail ahead of contact with the enemy. No matter how convincing a victory Fighter Command won in 1940, one must not underestimate the importance of contingency in Fighter Command's performance operationally and tactically. The generation of strategic effect flows solely from performance, which by definition lies in the realm of tactics.[40] Aerial combat itself is tactical; its meaning is strategic.

Dowding, the Air Ministry, and the government could not know how well or how poorly Fighter Command would perform on *the day*. A key source of that unknowable uncertainty was the lack of reliable knowledge of the *Luftwaffe*'s capabilities, or indeed what its forces would attempt and in what circumstances. The strategic aspects of air warfare lay beyond the frontier of historical precedent in the 1930s despite the harbingers of 1916–1918, the lessons of which are easier to identify today than in the 1930s.

The continuities in British air defense from 1918 to 1940 are startling, while most of the discontinuities are more apparent than real. The fundamental operating concept for Fighter Command did not differ significantly from Ashmore's in 1918. The strategic contexts were indeed vastly different, and the salient technologies and procedures were also distinctive. But Britain's air defense narrative is one of evolution, not revolution. Ferris has a plausible argument in claiming that "Hugh Dowding and Keith Park simply picked up from where Ashmore had left off. LADA's greatest victory occurred not in 1918, but 1940." Nevertheless, his choice of words does invite underappreciation of the performance of commanders in 1940.[41]

For an assertion that risks oversimplification, one can claim that for the RAF 1940 was 1918, albeit 1918 with radar and R/T. Moreover, R/T, as an enabler of Ground Controlled Interception (GCI), was as significant in intercepting *Luftwaffe* formations as radar. In 1918, air defense fighters were deaf, and as a consequence, somewhat blind once airborne. They had the benefit of intelligence from signal intercepts and a network of ground observers on German raids, but, once aloft, they were on their own. In 1940, air defense fighters enjoyed intelligence derived from radar, as well as from radio intercepts and the Observer Corps, and they benefitted from all sources of information in real-time, duly "filtered" from visual sightings and aerial interception.

---

[40] See Gray, *The Strategy Bridge*, chp. 5.   [41] Ferris, "Airbandit."

Britain's air defense strategy from 1918 to 1939 was one of modernization and innovation in the ways and means to exploit what became technically possible. Admittedly, political perceptions of strategic menace influenced the episodic nature of the air defense effort in its preparation. In the end, the loosening of the public purse, driven by political anxiety, enabled the creation of an effective systemic air defense. This describes the normal condition for defense policy and preparation in democracies in peacetime. What is impressive about British air defense in the 1920s and 1930s is that the ebb and flow of defense mindedness in the political climate, in other words the security anxiety index, had only a modest impact on RAF behavior.

The nominal dominance of offensive air power (bombers) in official thinking never threatened to cripple plans for effective home air defense. The RAF always recognized that air defense was essential, just as it appreciated that future wars would require an air offense. In practice contextual factors, as well as financial and material realities, settled the relationship between offensive air capabilities and air defense. Air defense was never a neglected stepchild during the interwar period. RAF leaders regarded it as being of secondary importance to the offensive, because only the latter could realize the full fruits of the air revolution.

For the British, 1940 was to be 1918 in modern dress. To understand LADA in 1918 is to understand much of what commentators have labeled the "Dowding system."[42] The details were ever in flux because of technological and consequently tactical evolution, while the state of play for air defense competence at the level of detail mattered profoundly for how well it would perform in battle. Nevertheless, one can claim a persistent effectiveness in British air defense. The proper approach to strategic assay has to be that of net assessment in historical context.[43] One can sensibly conduct an examination of British air defense at any time between the Armistice of 1918 and 1940 only if one places it in the context of the threat that existed at *that particular time*. ADGB's Fighting Area Headquarters (FAHQ) did not confront any threat to Britain in the late 1920s, while the Fighter Command of 1937 and 1938 would have had to thwart the unprepared *Luftwaffe* of those years, but not the enemy that it had become by 1940.

A "system-of-systems"

The Ashmore–Dowding system of air defense was a system-of-systems that functioned through the working of what is now termed C^3I (Command, Control, Communication, and Intelligence). The system was cybernetic in that it aided communications and control, but it was not cybernetic, if one defines that concept as processes that are automatic and self-correcting.

---

[42] See Bungay, *The Most Dangerous Enemy*, pp. 60–69.
[43] Murray and Millett, eds., *Calculations*, provides essential perspective.

Command responsibility in Fighter Command was delineated among sub-systems and cascaded down a series of levels, but command performance at every level was anything but automatic. It required judgment at every level from Dowding down to squadron commanders, the latter in sighting enemy formations and having to decide when and how to engage. Although the structure and procedures of the meta-system proved sufficient to enable combat performance that generated the strategic effect required, such was not and could not be the guaranteed result of preparation, no matter how careful. Success demands that commanders employ appropriate military forces competently. That distinctly Clausewitzian consideration explains why Britain's preparations for home defense in the interwar decades could guarantee little strategically.[44] Fighter Command could fail to deter air attack, while its ability to influence the ability and willingness of the Germans to hazard an invasion depended on the skill with which their leaders employed the *Luftwaffe*.

So what was Dowding's system and how did it function? Its imperium was the dynamic product of, and derived its meaning from and for its contexts (political; socio-cultural; economic; technological; military-strategic; geographical; and the historical).[45] Fighter Command represented the compound product of these contexts. In the main, Dowding and his organization remained obligated to cope with strategic circumstances they had not created. With the political and grand strategic contexts largely given, Dowding had to select a strategic concept to guide the operations of his command that would fit Britain's political and military strategies as well as be militarily feasible. Following Ashmore's precedent in leading the London Air Defense Area in 1918, as well as the air defense system as revived and modernized in 1924–1925, Dowding was committed to the creation of a centralized and integrated system that would function as a true network. He recognized that Fighter Command could only contribute to the endeavor of air defense, if a single strategic brain and one nervous system of C^3I guided its actions. The Command had to be more than the sum of its parts. And each part was vital to the whole. British air defense was a tale of a system that modernized by innovating and adopting procedural and technical development, and by adapting changes to each sub-system as and when necessary. With a clear command philosophy and a structural design keyed to a functional delegation of decision making, the effort rested on a unitary strategic concept.

---

[44] The structure, procedures, and material assets of RAF Fighter Command in the 1930s can be fitted without distortion into the following two sentences by Clausewitz: "It [Fighter Command: CSG] stood in about the same relationship to combat as the craft of the swordsmith to the art of fencing [air warfare for defense: CSG]. It did not yet include the use of force under conditions of danger, subject to constant interaction with an adversary, nor the efforts of spirit and courage to achieve a desired end." *On War*, p. 133.

[45] See Gray, *The Strategy Bridge*, pp. 38–41.

Dowding could not know exactly when Fighter Command would confront combat, but he knew what he needed to do, and against whom. He succeeded in meeting the most fundamental test for the defense planner: he got the big, and certainly the biggest, decisions right, so that he and his command could cope with the unpredictable but not fatally unanticipated. Fighter Command required intelligence on the enemy; reliable warning in order to react in a timely fashion; technologically up-to-date equipment effective for its purpose; and the whole had to knit together in order to function as an integrated combat instrument. Fighter Command had to be resilient in the face of a first-rate opponent. The most pertinent question for Dowding from 1936 to 1940 was "how well would his command perform in the calculations of the Germans (both predicted performance as well as in the event)?"

Warning and response

In summer 1940 Fighter Command enjoyed access to multiple sources of intelligence on the enemy: strategic information, trickling episodically to Dowding, some from Ultra decryption of *Luftwaffe* Enigma traffic; photo reconnaissance showing airfield runway expansion in northern France, Belgium, and Holland; operational information flowing from 54 (1 July 1940) and 76 (by 30 September) Chain Home (CH) and Chain Home Low (CHL) radar stations that provided coverage reaching out across the Channel (CH only) to the French and Belgian coasts; and tactical information coming from the RAF Wireless Intelligence Service ("Y" Service) and approximately 30,000 volunteer members of the Royal Observer Corps, who served in 1,550 posts across Britain.[46] In 1917–1918, Ashmore did not have radar or Ultra, but he did have good radio signals interception intelligence, a capability from which Dowding in his turn benefitted. Ashmore had also created a corps of observers on the ground. The demonstration in Britain of aircraft reflectivity to radio waves in 1935 was a purposefully focused experiment waiting to happen. Radio had fast-moving scientific and technological industrial frontiers in the interwar decades. The discovery that aircraft reflected radio waves was inevitable and had occurred by accident in the 1920s in several countries nearly simultaneously.[47]

But, there was nothing inevitable about the creation of effective chains of radar stations respectively for medium and high, and then for low altitude detection, integrated as warning pickets enabling GCI for a comprehensive system of national air defense. German radar was technically superior in

[46] See Peter Calvocoressi, *Top Secret* ULTRA (Kidderminster, 2001), pp. 90–95; Steven Twigge, Edward Hampshire, and Graham Macklin, *British Intelligence Secrets, Spies and Sources* (Richmond, UK, 2008), pp. 176–179; and Bungay, *The Most Dangerous Enemy*, p. 68.

[47] Zimmerman, *Britain's Shield*, p. 30.

some, though not all respects, but for reasons of geostrategic demand, politics, culture, and successive generations of military decision makers of exceptional talent, Ashmore and then Dowding, Britain alone enjoyed the services of a systemic approach to air defense.[48] This systemic, though not scientific or even technological, lead had profound strategic consequences. *Luftwaffe* intelligence never comprehended how Fighter Command employed radar to enable a centrally directed and flexibly adaptable air defense system. It is especially hard to defeat an enemy whom one does not understand.[49] The Germans did not understand that the RAF's centralized filtering of all CH and CHL radar data at FCHQ enabled Park and his staff at 11 Group HQ to direct chosen sector stations to deploy their aircraft aloft for combat. This was campaign direction, not simply locally commanded GCI, alerted by radar warning. The Germans did not use radar in a networked fashion in order to empower a true air defense system: as a result they did not understand how Dowding was profiting from radar.

It is worth speculating that, had the *Luftwaffe* deployed its radar forward along the French coast in summer 1940, it might have learned much about how the RAF was responding to its raids. It is distinctly possible that such information would have provided clear clues as to the way Fighter Command was using its radar assets in a centralized systemic way to manage the air defense battle. Of course, for this chain of epiphanies to occur, there would first be the need for German intelligence to ask the right questions, something it rarely if ever did. Intelligence on the German air threat was passed to Dowding at FCHQ, where a filter room provided threat discrimination. The command function cascaded down from FCHQ to the operational level of what one could term air generalship: especially number 11 Group HQ at Uxbridge in Middlesex. Park commanded in the main air battle space. From July to September 1940, he maintained an operationally ready order of battle at 11 Group of 19 or 20 squadrons of Spitfires and Hurricanes distributed among the group's sector stations and satellite

---

[48] Beyerchen, "From Radio to Radar."

[49] British scientific intelligence, in the context of intelligence more generally, comprised a major source of British advantage throughout the war. For an important example, on 20 June 1940, a young British physicist, Dr. R. V Jones, surprised the War Cabinet and its senior advisors, with Churchill in the chair, by claiming that the Germans intended to employ intersecting radio beams to enable reasonably accurate bombing. Jones' argument, which initially was challenged as being contrary to the laws of physics, was tested empirically and discovered to be correct. The consequence was that British scientists were able to jam the German bombing navigation system (*Knickebein*) effectively. The point is that the British war effort was generally open to radical improvement as a result of scientific speculation and then investigation, whereas the German was not nearly so accommodating. Although there are many reasons why the *Luftwaffe* was at a disadvantage in the summer of 1940, a major one was the inability of its leaders to adapt intelligently to the unexpected, by asking themselves challenging technical questions. R. V. Jones, *Most Secret War: British Scientific Intelligence, 1939–1945* (London, 1979), esp. pp. 139–150, 177–185. Also see Murray, *Military Adaptation in War: With Fear of Change* (Cambridge, 2011), pp. 167–173.

airfields.[50] Then, 11 Group's controller passed to the sectors guidance on how each should commit its two or three squadrons to, or temporarily withhold them from, the battle. In turn, sector station controllers ordered the relevant squadrons airborne, or to be held at readiness on the ground.

Once the enemy was in sight, command authority devolved to the airborne squadron commanders. The Post Office telephone system tied the entire air defense system together by using secure, though not quite bomb-proof, landlines. Operations and control rooms at every level of the air defense system – FCHQ, Group, and Sector – possessed identical raid-plotting tables and functioned with standard procedures and language. Fighter Command revived and broadly reproduced Ashmore's model with modern improvements, most especially, of course, with the addition of radar.

Fighter Command was a brilliant system-of-systems, simple where and when it needed to be, but accommodating of complexity and able to receive, evaluate, and use purposefully vast data flows. In one historian's judgment, "it was a system for managing chaos."[51]

[Fighter Command's] organisational structure was simple and roles were very clear. Everyone knew what they had to do. It was not parsimonious with information: plot data was shared widely and passed simultaneously to several levels at once. Bentley Priory [FCHQ, i.e., Dowding (CSG)] gave out information simultaneously to groups and sectors and sectors could plug into local Observer groups once they knew something was up in their area. It was in effect an analog intranet. Whilst it was used to transmit orders down the chain of command, it was also designed to allow anybody in the system to find out what they wanted when they wanted from anybody else. It was a network organisation based on telephone lines rather than e-mail.[52]

Nevertheless, while robust, the system did possess vulnerabilities which, in practice, proved more theoretical than real. Specifically, the radar stations with their high masts and above ground facilities were obvious targets. However, steel masts and cables are resistant to blast damage and, more pertinent still, the *Luftwaffe* failed to understand how effectively the air defense system centralized the use of the filtered radar data. One might think that, as a matter of prudent insurance, the *Luftwaffe* might well have decided to persist in bombing the CH stations, notwithstanding their physical resilience. Moreover, the supporting buildings co-located with the masts typically were not seriously blast-proof. Persistent bombing of only a handful of the CH sites would have blinded Fighter Command in southeast England. Given their necessarily peripheral coastal location – since CH and CHL could not cope with ground clutter returns over land in 1940 – the radar stations represented a significant risk to German amphibious or airborne special operations.

One might suppose that a *Luftwaffe* capable of staging a spectacular capture of the Belgian fortress at Eban-Emael by landing glider-borne troops on its

---

[50] Bungay, *The Most Dangerous Enemy*, p. 146.   [51] Ibid., p. 64.   [52] Ibid.

roof on 10 May 1940 might at least have tried to disable several Chain Home sites by unconventional raids. But, the Germans failed to make such attack, even though less than a handful of successful commando raids could have blinded the system. Fighter Command would then have had to depend on the sources available to Ashmore in 1918, though against an enemy flying two to three times as fast. Happily, in summer 1940 German special forces and airborne formations had yet to recover from their heavy losses in May. Moreover, a conventional military culture dominated the German view of special operations.

As well as the theoretical vulnerability of the coastal radars, Fighter Command was at risk of severe disruption and worse if the *Luftwaffe* had understood the role and functioning of 11 Group's seven sector stations. The system would have been in danger of collapsing had German attacks damaged the operations rooms on the section station airfields or severed their power and telephone lines. Fighter Command was not as prudent as it should have been in protecting these vital sector control stations; they were not armored, dispersed, or hidden. However, fortune favored the British, in that the *Luftwaffe* failed to appreciate the role of the sector hubs; among other defects, German aircraft lacked an effective bombsight for level bombing, and because of their vulnerability, the Germans had to withdraw the Ju 87 dive bombers precipitately early in the battle.

Everything material and tactical in Fighter Command preparations in summer 1940 was adequate to generate a sufficient strategic effect vis à vis the *Luftwaffe*'s daylight bombing threat, despite British weaknesses and errors. Nothing about the Command either was, or could, approach perfection. But, the sum of its tactical behavior in support of the appropriate strategic concept for air defense provided a winning edge that was neither slim nor accidental. Admittedly, Dowding's victory was contingent on German errors. On balance, however, it is likely that even a better equipped and more intelligently directed Luftwaffe would have failed. To that speculation one can add the thought that the Royal Navy alone posed an unacceptable danger to the prospects of any German amphibious operation attempting to make a sustained lodgment on the English southeast coast. The *Luftwaffe* might have succeeded in driving Fighter Command's Spitfires and Hurricanes to seek airfield sanctuaries further inland, but the crossing of the Channel and then the sustainment and reinforcement of a beachhead represented an insoluble problem for the continental-minded Germans. A crossing of the Channel by Rhine River barges protected by a single heavy cruiser and a handful of destroyers represented a guaranteed recipe for a disastrous defeat, especially since the British had stationed 70 destroyers at Harwich and Plymouth.

One can understand Fighter Command's victory in 1940 only if one notes its imperfections. Error and friction are ubiquitous and universal in human affairs. They are especially apt to blight the activities collectively known as planning and, with greater force and movement, the violent competitive behaviors of which war is comprised. At times, Dowding's command performance was flawed, as were his material and intellectual agents. But he succeeded anyway, as all successful strategists must, in the face of the possible chaos and potential catastrophe which may harass and impede even those endeavors that are soundly conceived.[53] Fighter Command could only be a work in progress in 1940.

Several aspects of the Command certainly could have been more effective than they were in summer 1940. Dowding had recommended urgent development of a radar-equipped (necessarily two-seat) night fighter in 1938 and again in 1939, but the Chamberlain government had refused to supply the funding, while the Air Ministry proved to be less than enthusiastic. To be fair to the Air Ministry, it is not obvious that Britain could have developed such a technically challenging weapon system in 1939–1940, given the funding levels and priority that had to be given to the daytime threat. With respect to air defense at night, the Command was thoroughly ineffective, a failure that contributed unjustly to Dowding's unceremonious ouster on 25 November 1940, notwithstanding his success in the daylight battle. Overall, three facts are of significance for the strategic analysis. First, Fighter Command won in spite of its limitations. Second, it represented a learning institution that proved adaptable; early evidence of this was Dowding's enthusiasm for including scientific advisors and operations analysts at his headquarters.[54] Dowding was not tolerant of dissent from decisions, once made, but he was entirely in favor of constant self-assessment within the Command to improve its ability to adapt to the threat. Admittedly, nearly all belligerents learn from their experiences in war. Thus, both Fighter Command and the *Luftwaffe* adapted. However, educability varies widely, as organizations have an uneven willingness and ability to learn. Moreover, they possess different possibilities for near-term adaptation and movement. Third, the weaknesses that one can identify in Fighter Command's preparations for battle, as well as in its operational and tactical performance, are insignificant in comparison with the unchallengeable fact of strategic victory.

Any strategic assessment of Dowding and air defense must address the salience of that core strategist's question, "so what?" To venture the reply that the Command should have done better distorts the strategic plot. That plot insists, on the evidence, that Fighter Command did well enough in creating the strategic effect that Churchill needed: that is a strategic victory. Although tactics inevitably influence strategy, it is strategy, not tactics, that matter in the end. Many of Dowding's critics have failed to understand that simple fact. The tactical performance of Dowding's command throughout his tenure rested on the foundation of two decades of competence in air defense. Moreover, in a short period of time, the Command had needed to

[53] See Gray, *The Strategy Bridge*, chp. 4.
[54] Zimmerman, *Britain's Shield*, pp. 159, 178–184.

adopt and adapt to new equipment that differed radically in its major tactical characteristics from what had gone before. It did so most successfully.

In the case of radar, the technology was adapted from radio, albeit for a novel purpose, which meant that the ability to use it was also new. From 1936 to 1940, technological innovation demanded well-trained operators and interpreters (filterers). Radar was only of value to Fighter Command as a provider of adequate warning time for its fighters to react as well as other indicators that current equipment, expertly handled, could reveal. From the returns on their display screens, the operators at radar stations had to identify the distance (range), bearing (direction of travel), numbers (strength), and altitude of incoming aircraft.

The last of the five was the most difficult. In 1940 Chain Home stations could reach out 80 miles (in theory 200) while Chain Home Low perhaps 30. The former generally could detect aircraft in substantial numbers above 1,000 feet and below 25,000 feet.[55] The latter could detect aircraft below 2,000 feet altitude. In summer 1940 Chain Home and Chain Home Low were good, but far short of excellent, and the phenomena they registered demanded trained, experienced, intelligent, somewhat creative, and alert operators. Fighter Command had to grow such people, identify procedures to exploit their increasing competence, and improve the technology in the three years of sub-systems' building that chanced to be available from 1937 to 1940. To move from a zero base of potential capability in early 1937, to adequate performance under fire in 1940, represented an extraordinary human, technical, tactical, operational, and strategic journey.

Dowding and his command had until late spring 1940 to get radar operationally right enough. He lacked the foreknowledge in 1937 to know that he had a three-year period of grace. The Air Ministry approved a then full-scale Chain Home radar system of 20 stations on 21 June 1937, and the Treasury blessed the project financially on 12 August. In July 1940, 21 Chain Home stations were operational with the additional support of Chain Home Low stations.[56] Obligingly, the somewhat desultory and dilatory campaign conducted by the *Luftwaffe* against Channel shipping in July and early August (the *Kanalkampf*) proved invaluable in providing the experience in raid detection that Dowding's radar operators and interpreters badly needed. This experience was not paralleled by learning on the German side.

Dowding inherited from Ashmore's integrated effort not only a Royal Observer Corps and the RAF Wireless Intelligence Service, but also anti-aircraft (AA) and balloon commands.[57] At the outbreak of war in 1939, Fighter Command's domain of control included the 1,204 heavy and 1,860 light guns of the former, and the 1,500 barrage balloons of the latter.

---

[55] Ibid., p. 203.   [56] Wood and Dempster, *The Narrow Margin*, p. 151.
[57] See Neil Hanson, *First Blitz: The Secret German Plan to Raze London to the Ground in 1918* (London, 2009), pp. 326–327.

These numbers expanded rapidly during the "phony war," which ended on 10 May 1940. Although there was some merit in AA artillery and barrage balloons, there is no serious dispute over the proposition that their value in 1940 was largely psychological: for public reassurance rather than military effectiveness. But, given the understandable uncertainty about air warfare and the resilience of civilian morale under concentrated air attack before 1940, the investment in such defenses was prudent. In principle, at least, flak was important for point protection of high-value assets, such as airfields and aircraft factories. Heavy artillery could also play a useful role in breaking up massed bomber formations, rendering them more vulnerable to fighters and unsettling German pilots and bomb-aimers.

AA artillery and balloons were well-integrated components of Dowding's air defense empire, although, then as today, the system had to take care in resolving confliction issues. On this issue Dowding became ever more anxious through 1939 that the RAF's boffins had not developed reliable Identification Friend or Foe (IFF) technology. This important deficiency, meaning that radar operators could not distinguish RAF from *Luftwaffe* "blips" on their radar screens, was corrected in a rush, belatedly, during 1940. "By October 1940 virtually every RAF aircraft was fitted with IFF."[58] Thus, the RAF developed and produced reliable IFF just in time. Later the Command understandably remained concerned not only that radar operators should not identify RAF aircraft as hostile, but also that the Germans might capture British IFF radio technology and use it to deceive the defenders.

Aircraft

Last, but not least, the most obvious and necessary component of Dowding's system, his combat aircraft and pilots, requires attention. The more closely one examines British air defense in the 1930s, the more one recognizes that the victory had deep roots. Though not reliably predetermined, because of the menace of contingency and errors in high politics, policy, and grand strategic judgment, nevertheless the Battle of Britain represented a success waiting to happen. In their impressive edited collection of studies of air forces that failed, Robin Higham and Stephen J. Harris concluded with a claim that speaks volumes about the reasons for Dowding's success: "The fall of an air force is the result of long-term failings, not an immediate failure "on the day" by an air arm that is essentially ready for its allotted role."[59]

Fighter Command could win in 1940 because its means were good enough tactically to function, and indeed to adjust, so that the strategic ends were achievable and indeed achieved. The narrative explaining Fighter

[58] Zimmerman, *Britain's Shield*, p. 187. Eventually, 21,000 Mark II IFF sets were produced.
[59] Robin Higham and Stephen J. Harris, "Conclusion," in Higham and Harris, eds., *Why Air Forces Fail: The Anatomy of Defeat* (Lexington, KY, 2006), p. 355.

Command's victory in 1940 has two essential strands: system-wide strengths that were the product of a quarter-century of professionally competent effort and excellence in leadership command in the most vital periods, particularly from July 1936 until November 1940. Extraordinary tactical competence, as was the case with the *Wehrmacht* in the Second World War, is thoroughly compatible with strategic disaster. RAF Fighter Command was capable of delivering strategic success, but somebody had to use it with a highly developed strategic sense. Dowding was the principal source of that sense in the 1930s and in 1940. The continuity in his service to all major aspects of British air defense should not obscure the cumulative weight of his contribution.

The principal flying combat agent was Fighter Command's single-seat fighter force, which in July 1940 consisted of 754 (Hurricanes and Spitfires) against the *Luftwaffe*'s total of 1,107 single-seat fighters (all Bf 109s). The number of serviceable aircraft was always approximately 25 percent fewer than the number possessed: the RAF's real number of combat ready single-seat fighters on 11 May was 546 (72 percent), compared with the *Luftwaffe*'s percentage of 73 percent operational.[60] However, the RAF waged the battle with all of its assets. Indeed, Bomber Command's contribution was substantial, yet continues to be underrecognized.[61] Nonetheless, the protracted duel between the rival single-seat fighter forces decided the battle. The *Luftwaffe*'s impressive, if somewhat aging, medium bomber force would have been important, perhaps crucial, to the securing of victory on land, if the Germans had invaded. But, the reality of summer 1940 was that the courageous crews of the *Luftwaffe*'s bombers had the unenviable mission of serving as bait to entice RAF fighters into combat.

Dowding's strategy and Park's generalship won the battle in 1940, but they won with aircraft that the RAF's system of development and procurement had delivered in the years of peace. Dowding required an aerial sword that could deny air superiority over the south of England to the *Luftwaffe*. At his date of appointment on 14 July 1936, he did not know how many years he had until Britain's air defenses would face their critical examination in combat. Furthermore, through the third week of May 1940, Dowding did not know whether the geostrategic context for his command would be one of an ongoing continental war, as in the first Battle of Britain of 1915–1918, or would become bilateral between Britain and Germany with no active continental European land complications and diversions. While the latter context would be agreeably simple in focus and demand, it would be tactically challenging because the *Wehrmacht*'s military success over the French would place Bf 109s within six minutes of Dover from the Pas de Calais. As a result, Chain Home

<hr/>

[60] Bungay, *The Most Dangerous Enemy*, p. 107.
[61] James Holland, *The Battle of Britain: Five Months that Changed History, May–October 1940* (London, 2010), pp. 606–607.

radar might well provide only four minutes of warning for Fighter Command to react. To appreciate the scale of Dowding's strategic achievement in 1940, one has to recognize what he did not and could not know in advance about the geostrategic terms under which his command would fight.

Dowding himself was not a scientist, an inventor, or even a great innovator. To succeed in combat, his command required (1) good to excellent combat aircraft (single-seat fighters); (2) good to excellent combat pilots, not merely competent pilots, with good enough plane killing firepower on his fighters; (3) a large enough single-seat fighter force to protect southern England (including London), the industrial Midlands, and Fighter Command's own forward-base structure with its facilities, aircraft, and air engine factories; (4) a sufficient reserve of aircraft immediately available to replace losses in combat and accidents (which meant an industrial infrastructure capable of producing aircraft in numbers matching or exceeding losses);[62] (5) a training program adequate to sustain an order of battle of approximately 50 squadrons, with 16 operationally ready pilots in each (on 3 September 1939, Fighter Command's order of battle included only 22 squadrons equipped with Hurricanes and Spitfires; by 1 July 1940, the Command had 29 Hurricane squadrons with 347 operational aircraft, and 19 Spitfire squadrons with 199 operational aircraft);[63] and (6) air fighting tactics suitable to the technology, the evolving enemy challenge, and the strategic context; and (7) a networked system of airfields capable of sustaining the air defense of the whole of Britain, but optimized to provide maximally effective, but sustainable, combat power over the southeast.

Even this extensive and intensive listing is not comprehensive. Dowding's direction and management of Fighter Command required not only a mastery of detail, but a grasp of the larger strategic "big picture" as well. Everything he directed from Fighter Command's HQ, while Keith Park would command in battle, once he arrived in April 1940 to command 11 Group, from his position as Dowding's deputy at Bentley Priory. They could and in tandem did make a major positive difference in the Command's performance in the strategic and tactical examination set by events, but the precise dates, context, and wording of the test or tests could only be guesswork before summer 1940.

Dowding's military technical choices both as a member of the air council responsible for the RAF's supply, research, and development of equipment from 1930 to 1936, and subsequently as the first air officer in chief commanding Fighter Command, were not of a heroic kind, but they did not need to be. Dowding needed only to make "right enough" (i.e., correctable) decisions on the principal military and technical issues of his tenure. Although a professional airman and not an engineer, he was certainly technically adept. His was

---

[62] See the useful discussion of British and German "first-line," "serviceable," and "reserve" aircraft strengths in Bungay, *The Most Dangerous Enemy*, pp. 103–105.

[63] Ibid., p. 136.

the primary responsibility for the specification that resulted in the Hurricane (Air Ministry specification F.36/34) and Spitfire (Air Ministry specification F.37/34). A prototype of the former first flew on 6 November 1935, the latter on 5 March 1936, although the first production model Spitfire did not fly until 14 May 1938. The Air Ministry ordered 600 Hurricanes in June 1936 and a further 400 in November. The ministry moved with exemplary speed in ordering 310 Spitfires on 3 June 1936, which, in one historian's judgment represented a "snip at £4,500 each, one of the best investments British governments have ever made." (Eventually, British industry would build 22,789 Spitfires).[64] Unfortunately, to order this production of a new generation of fighters is not the same as having them operationally ready and piloted by well-trained aircrew capable of flying combat missions against the world's leading air force.

While the Hurricane was Sydney Camm's adaptation to the monoplane era of biplane fighter design (his Hawker Fury), Reginald Mitchell's Spitfire represented a clear break from the biplane lineage of first-line RAF fighters.[65] The Spitfire enjoyed substantial provenance in the succession of Supermarine's Schneider Trophy airspeed trial winners. Among a host of technical challenges, Mitchell's revolutionary elliptical wings required craftsmen's skills to construct. Those wings, though apparently perilously thin, needed to accommodate eight Browning.303 machine guns situated outside the plane's propeller arc and calculated as necessary to destroy bombers in the two to three seconds expected for each combat engagement. The new generation of fighters, monocoque single-piece all-metal design in the Spitfire's case, attained speeds approaching 350 mph at 15,000 to 20,000 feet, and could climb to intercept altitude against bombers (anticipated to be at 10,000 to 12,000 feet) in well under ten minutes. In company with the *Luftwaffe*'s Bf 109s (which first flew on 28 May 1935), the Hurricane and Spitfire represented the first generation of fighter aircraft designed to be significantly faster than bombers.

Dowding's technical choices on fighter aircraft design specifications were wise, even far seeing, and they were in keeping with the vision on the frontier of aeronautics in the early to mid 1930s. His was not a lone campaign for the kind of fighter aircraft needed for future air defense. Dowding recognized, accepted, and acted upon the best technical and military advice he could obtain, and his major judgments were first-class. Unfortunately, the British aircraft industry in the late 1930s was not entirely fit for the purpose of mass-producing a new generation of aircraft. While Hawker, producer of the industrially less demanding Hurricane, already was of sufficient size for quantity production, Supermarine's factory in Southampton was closer to a hobby shop than a major manufacturing center for first-line fighters. But, by summer

---

[64] Ibid., p. 79.   [65] Ibid., chp. 5, is an outstanding accessible analysis.

1940, courtesy of new civilian official and industrial leadership and the expansion of industrial facilities, British fighter production outpaced that of the Germans. In the context of the air battle of attrition, this meant that Dowding's command, unlike Albert Kessling's *Luftflotte* 2, was never short of replacement aircraft.[66]

However, the Hurricanes and especially the Spitfires were slow to arrive in the late 1930s on Fighter Command's airfields. Whereas the first squadron to be reequipped with Hurricanes took its initial aircraft delivery in November 1937, the Spitfire did not enter squadron service until 4 August 1938 (the first production model Spitfire was not completed until February 1938). The *Luftwaffe* had its own problems in this period, even though its Condor Legion was learning useful tactical lessons in Spain. But, it was a contemporary fact of some strategic weight that Fighter Command had lagged behind the *Luftwaffe* in the creation of a modern fighter force. Nevertheless, besides sound basic design decisions, the Air Ministry and Dowding enjoyed adequate financial backing after 1937, made good enough technological choices, and British industry proved just sufficiently capable of building the material combat means in time.

Examination under fire: the long summer, from Dunkirk to the night Blitz

It is not difficult to identify distinctive phases to Fighter Command's experience of combat between May and November 1940, but in doing so it is important not to lose the strategic narrative. Fighter Command was a classic learning institution, the experience of which against a first-class enemy took place under favorable conditions. In France in May and June, including the events of the Dunkirk perimeter (which as late as 30 May was approximately 30 miles long), the Command lost 477 fighters, with 284 pilots killed.[67] Spitfires had not deployed from Britain to France, but they were employed in protection of BEF (British Expeditionary Force) and French forces at Dunkirk. The Command suffered the loss of 155 of these aircraft, a figure that includes the 65 lost "in accidents as aircrew tried to master the new equipment."[68] Park's biographer claims that "when it [the Battle of France and the Dunkirk evacuation] ended, Dowding had only 331 Spitfires and Hurricanes available for operations and all his squadrons were

[66] Three essential studies are Sebastian Ritchie, *Industry and Air Power: The Expansion of British Aircraft Production, 1935–1941* (Abingdon, 2007); David Edgerton, *England and the Aeroplane: An Essay on a Militant and Technological Nation* (Basingstoke, 1991); and Colin Sinnoff, *The Royal Air Force and Aircraft Design, 1923–1939: Air Staff Operational Requirements* (London, 2001).

[67] Richard Overy, *The Battle of Britain: Myth and Reality* (London, 2010), p. 8.

[68] Ibid. Dilip Sarkar, ed., *The Spitfire Manual* (Stroud, UK, 2010) is highly recommended as a practical complement to the less material topics privileged in much of my text.

disorganized."[69] The air battles over Flanders, especially Dunkirk, in May and June 1940 were sobering to both sides. At least *Luftwaffe* aircrew, if not its intelligence analysts, learned to respect British single-seat fighters and their pilots, if not their tactics. But they chose to learn from Dunkirk only that victory in air warfare against the RAF would entail some hard fighting, most probably brief. The Germans failed to recognize that a Fighter Command competitive over Dunkirk, lacking the benefit of its radar support, might prove unbeatable when fighting at home.

Notwithstanding heavy losses, indeed to some degree because of them, Dowding and his command's performance in and over France represented an experience of great value. There were significant achievements. First, Fighter Command contributed vitally to the *Luftwaffe*'s failure to prevent the evacuation of 338,226 British and French soldiers (initial estimates were that only 45,000 could be evacuated). Second, Dowding preserved the tactical and thereby the strategic integrity of his command by effectively resisting the pressing demands of his government (including Churchill) and from RAF commanders in France, to commit more of his dwindling Hurricane force to a campaign that appeared lost, certainly a losing cause, after less than a week. Dowding spoke somberly to the War Cabinet on 15 May, following up with a two-page, now iconic, memorandum to Under Secretary of State for Air Harold Balfour. Characteristically, he pulled no punches. He concluded with the warning that "if the Home Defence Force is drained away in attempts to remedy the situation in France, defeat in France will involve the final, complete and irremediable defeat of this country."[70] Third, in the air combat over Dunkirk, where both sides were fighting at a disadvantage, Fighter Command performed tactically at least respectably, and was wiser for the experience. The records indicate that the *Luftwaffe*'s campaign over France in May–June 1940 cost it 1,428 aircraft written off, with an additional 488 damaged.[71] These numbers approximated half of the *Luftwaffe*'s operational strength. Coming on top of the 285 aircraft lost and 279 damaged over Poland

[69] Orange, *Park*, p. 89.
[70] Dowding's famous memorandum, FC/S19048 is reprinted in the official history, James, *Growth of Fighter Command, 1936–1940*, pp. 131–132. It is interesting and scarcely surprising that General Joseph Vuillemin, the commander-in-chief of the French air force in 1940, wrote letters to the British government, via the French chief of the general staff, predicting Anglo-French defeat on the continent unless additional RAF fighter units were committed to France "on a very large scale." Air Vice Marshal Arthur Barratt, the commander-in-chief of the British air forces in France (BAFF), strove to support his French ally as loyally as he was able in impossible circumstances. It needs to be said that air–land cooperation was not a high priority for the RAF in 1940. See Stuart W. Peach, "A Neglected Turning Point in Air Power History: Air Power and the Fall of France," in Cox and Gray, eds., *Air Power History*, pp. 142–172. A letter from General Vuillemin written on 3 June that more than marginally parallels the tone of Dowding's of 16 May is reproduced in http://airpowerstudies.wordpress.com/2010/03/11/1940-and-the-problem-of-coalition-air-power/ (accessed 12 January 2012).
[71] Bungay, *The Most Dangerous Enemy*, p. 105.

in September 1937 (20 percent of operational strength), and the 260 aircraft lost in Norway in April 1940, it is easy to understand why the *Luftwaffe* needed time and effort to recover after its victory in France.[72]

On balance, it is churlish to question the strategic significance of Dowding's resistance to the leakage and wastage of significant numbers of his precious single-seat modern fighters to a continental campaign he believed already lost. However, he did commit his force without argument to protect the evacuation of the BEF, and he allowed Park to provide additional fighter assets from 11 Group for the campaign on the continent. These efforts were staged both from temporary, indeed fleeting, austere forward-basing in France, and at long range from airfields in Kent (especially for coverage of the Dunkirk evacuation).

The campaign narrative that is the operational history of the Battle of Britain (10 July until 30 October, the official dates) is familiar; strategic interpretation is another matter.[73] The air war opened in early July with the *Luftwaffe* attacking British shipping in the Channel. Its principal purpose was to entice Dowding's fighters out over the water, where they would lack home field advantage. This unhurried campaign had some small success, but because of the nature of attritional warfare between adversaries of comparable military weight, it was uncomfortably erosive of the *Luftwaffe*, as well as the RAF. One historian argues,

Considering both air forces as a whole, they were wreaking destruction on each other at roughly similar rates. From 10 July to 11 August, the RAF lost 115 fighters and 64 bombers in combat, a total of 179. This is not far short of the *Luftwaffe*'s total combat losses of 216. But for the *Luftwaffe* to achieve its ends, its forces had to shoot down more than 115 fighters a month, which British factories could easily replace. The [Germans] also had to remain intact to cover the invasion, which meant that they could not afford to lose three aircraft themselves for every two they shot down. Nor could they tolerate the losses in personnel . . . Pilot losses were running at almost 2:1 in Fighter Command's favour.[74]

Tactically, the *Luftwaffe* was fighting well, but not well enough for its tactical performance to have significant operational or strategic traction.

While both sides benefitted from the learning experience of the *Kanalkampf* in July, the RAF learned more. Admittedly, it had more to learn about air combat than did the *Luftwaffe*. Nevertheless, the Germans ought to have

---

[72] Ibid., p. 201.
[73] Narrative histories of the battle are legion, while those that strive to analyze seriously, let alone with an alert strategic sense, are in rather shorter supply. This study owes much to: T. C. G. James, *The Battle of Britain* (London, 1944); Wood and Dempster, *The Narrow Margin*; Francis K. Mason, *Battle over Britain* (London, 1969), pt. 2; Bungay, *The Most Dangerous Enemy*; Holland, *The Battle of Britain*; Patrick Bishop, *The Battle of Britain: A Day-by-Day Chronicle, 10 July 1940 to 31 October 1940* (London, 2009); and Overy, *The Battle of Britain*.
[74] Bungay, *The Most Dangerous Enemy*, p. 201.

derived more of an understanding of Fighter Command than they did. The benefits of the radar alerted Ground Controlled Interception (GCI) that was the heart of Dowding's system were greatly at a discount, given the short warning time provided to its forward-based squadrons at airfields in Kent and Sussex. Dowding and Park had to meet the demand to protect coastal shipping, but they endeavored to limit the commitment to conserve barely adequate fighter assets and minimize German learning about Britain's air defense system.

That main event began with a stuttering start on its designated opening Eagle Day, or *Adler Tag*, on 13 August. From then until 7 September, the *Luftwaffe* sought to destroy Fighter Command, though in practice the assault lacked the most basic intelligence, clear and strong direction, persistence, precise targeting, and destructive weight. Aside from such non-trivial limitations, it was nonetheless a powerful effort. One historian correctly comments that "The core problem for Kesselring [Commander of *Luftflotte* 2, Brussels] and [Hugo] Sperrle [Commander of *Luftflotte* 3] was that they literally did not know what they were doing."[75] The *Luftwaffe* suffered significantly from the absence of unity of operational command. Kesselring and Sperrle were regional commanders of mixed forces of fighters and bombers who had to coordinate the efforts of their *Luftflotten* (air forces).

Beginning on 12 August, the Germans launched attacks against several radar stations with temporary success but failed to repeat those efforts with operational consequences of great importance. Another historian observes that "there were six main raids against the radar stations on the south coast, most of them on 12 August; they were not attacked repeatedly, and hardly at all toward the end of the second phase of battle."[76] Fighter Command's airfields were bombed, but as with the radar stations, neither heavily nor persistently. Certainly Park had good reason to fear 11 Group's ability to continue to defend the skies over southeastern England, but he was never on the brink of defeat, where he would have to withdraw from the airfields in Kent and Sussex.[77] He resisted the idea of abandoning his sector stations at Biggin Hill and Kenley, because the efficiency of a sector's operational control for GCI would have been greatly impaired if it had to direct more than two to four squadrons. Withdrawal from the more forward sector stations meant overloading their control and maintenance, refueling, and rearming at the fields to the west and north of London (North Weald, Debden, and Northolt).

The RAF's continued fierce resistance puzzled *Luftwaffe* aircrews as August turned into September. They had fought hard, and they believed, well, for more than three weeks against an enemy who should have been on the brink of collapse, were his numbers close to those estimated by the highly incompetent

[75] Ibid., p. 236.   [76] Overy, *The Battle of Britain*, p. 69.
[77] Bungay, *The Most Dangerous Enemy*, p. 290.

intelligence chief Colonel Joseph "Beppo" Schmidt.[78] On the basis of his assessment, Fighter Command would find itself eviscerated within four days of *Adler Tag*, while the RAF as a whole would be *hors de combat* within a month. The *Luftwaffe* was supposed to win the air battle while retaining the strength to shape the course of a successful invasion scheduled for September. Ironically, whereas the *Luftwaffe* persisted in significantly underestimating Fighter Command's size and regenerative capacity, the latter greatly overestimated the *Luftwaffe*'s strength. The consequence of these mutual misperceptions was substantial. On one side, Dowding and Park were less confident of survival than they should have been. On the other side, the *Luftwaffe* initially was overconfident and eventually fell victim to demoralization as a consequence of its underestimation of RAF strength.

While British estimates of *Luftwaffe* strength were at least as faulty as were Beppo Schmidt's judgments, the gross errors in RAF intelligence estimates did not undermine the value of Dowding's strategy of minimal adequate operational response.[79] Dowding sought to sustain a punishing of the German air offensive, not to achieve some climactically decisive result. Rather, for him victory was the recognition in German minds that they had not won, were not winning, and stood no plausible prospect of winning. This German mental state should, and indeed did, produce the decision, de facto, to abandon serious planning and preparation for the invasion. On 17 August, Schmidt informed his superiors that Fighter Command had only 300 serviceable fighters in its active force. The true figures for Fighter Command at that time were, "855 [serviceable: CSG] with operational squadrons, 289 at storage units, and another 84 at training units, a total of 1,438, twice as many as in the beginning of July."[80] Subsequent claims of RAF aircraft downed (all exaggerated), led *Luftwaffe* leaders to believe they had all but won by early September.

On 7 September, the *Luftwaffe*'s high command diverted its operational emphasis away from a prolonged assault on Fighter Command, the main objective for the three weeks following *Adler Tag*. On 7 September, the Germans surprised the RAF with a massive daylight assault on London. The attack aimed at enticing the British into a conclusively decisive air battle, wherein Fighter Command would suffer lethally irrecoverable losses, and striking a deadly blow at Britain's political will. Ironically, the result would represent a strategic defeat for the *Luftwaffe*, because it allowed Fighter Command a substantial period to recover. Slightly more than a week later, a

---

[78] See Horst Boog, "German Air Intelligence in the Second World War," in Michael I. Handel, ed., *Intelligence and Military Operations* (London, 1990), pp. 350–424; and Murray, *Luftwaffe*, pp. 48–49; and "Net Assessment in Nazi Germany in the 1930s."

[79] Cox, "Comparative Analysis of RAF and Luftwaffe Intelligence in the Battle of Britain, 1940," in Handel, ed., *Intelligence and Military Operations*, p. 430.

[80] Bungay, *The Most Dangerous Enemy*, p. 224. Also see Alfred Price, *The Hardest Day: The Battle of Britain, 18 August 1940* (London, 1990), pp. 225–226, for detailed analysis of the *Luftwaffe*'s faulty intelligence appreciation of RAF Fighter Command issued on 17 August.

second massive attack ran into a buzz saw of Fighter Command's squadrons that broke the morale of the *Luftwaffe* bomber crews.

There were many reasons why the *Luftwaffe* failed to succeed strategically between mid August and mid September 1940, whether it strove to defeat Fighter Command specifically, or to break British public morale by attacking London and other cities. But one of the more basic reasons for the *Luftwaffe*'s failure was the quantity as well as the improving quality of the fighting power available to Dowding. One can easily explain the *Luftwaffe*'s strategic problem when one compares British single-seat fighter production in summer 1940 with the RAF's fighter losses. Between 1 June and 1 November, Britain built 1,367 Hurricanes and 724 Spitfires. These figures average respectively at 8.9 and 4.7 per diem, with Spitfire production doubling in August as compared to June.[81] Taking the longer period from 10 May to 4 November, the number of Hurricanes and Spitfires operationally lost averaged respectively 4.4 and 2.7 per diem.[82] Thus, the major reason why the *Luftwaffe* lost the Battle of Britain was because it had too few of the relevant aircraft, Bf 109s, while Fighter Command's strength steadily grew.[83] In theory, the *Luftwaffe* might have found compensation in superior technology, tactics, or strategy, but in practice, its technology, where superior (e.g., the supercharger on the Bf 109E), failed to provide a decisive tactical edge.

Luftwaffe combat tactics were initially more effective than those of the RAF. But this advantage diminished markedly, both as a result of RAF pilots learning from experience, and when Göring limited the Bf 109s in their free-ranging role by ordering that they provide close escort to the bombers (and even to Bf 110s). As for strategy and operational concepts of employment, the *Luftwaffe*'s egregious errors in strategic purpose and military operations more than offset its areas of technological and tactical superiority. It is an abiding truth of strategic history that if a military force, or an apparently superior weapon, is seriously misused with regard to its ultimate political purpose or military mission, it will certainly fail.

RAF's overestimation of the *Luftwaffe*'s strength had few negative consequences. Dowding was waging an attritional, but calculated, campaign to defeat the enemy's military strategy and thwart his political objective. His master concept, applied by Park's conduct of operations and executed tactically principally by the combat power of, and rotated through, 11 Group, aimed simply at denying the enemy the air superiority it expected. Göring ordered his subordinates to disable Fighter Command, an objective they strove to achieve by aerial combat as well as sporadic assaults on the RAF's infrastructure and Britain's aircraft industry. Of course, Park's aircrew needed to be combat competitive at altitude, but Dowding's strategy defined victory only as

---

[81] Overy, *The Battle of Britain*, p. 145.   [82] Ibid., p. 147.
[83] A different view is expressed forcefully in Stephen Budiansky, *Air Power: The Men, Machines, and Ideas that Revolutionized War from Kitty Hawk to Iraq* (London, 2005), pp. 237–238.

not losing. It did not really matter whether the *Luftwaffe* suffered truly crippling, heavy, or only moderate losses. What mattered was that Fighter Command did not purchase those losses at a dangerously high cost. Dowding was fighting the menace of invasion in the tangible form of its air power enabler.

The narrative at the battle's height was dramatic in appearance, if not so much with the luxury of strategic hindsight. The *Luftwaffe*'s concentration of intensive attacks on 11 Group's major air stations (principally Biggin Hill, Kenley, and Tangmere) in the last week of August and first in September tested Fighter Command. Both Dowding and Park understandably gave expression to the strain they felt, including the pessimistic, albeit unwarranted, judgment by the former on 7 September "that we *are* going downhill."[84] In fact, the Germans were going downhill faster. Dowding was concerned because Fighter Command was losing operational pilots at the appalling rate of 120 a week. However, the loss rate did not continue. Because the RAF had armed and mobilized in depth, actual pilot supply was never genuinely critical. Unlike the *Luftwaffe*, Fighter Command was not a "shop-window" force. From 1939 on, it was never short of first-rate, single-seat fighters for home defense, and it could always put pilots in the cockpit, though admittedly their training was dramatically foreshortened with predictable results. But, in attritional air warfare the enemy also suffers losses. Dowding's German foe had to survive the absence of radar (or other) enabled ground control assistance, flight over water, and combat with an enemy of comparable fighting power over that enemy's own territory. As if those disadvantages were not sufficient, the enemy's single-seat fighter force was becoming ever more combat competitive in skill and was rendered technically more potent by its use of 100-octane aviation fuel for emergency boost, whereas the Bf 109s were limited to 87-octane.

Hoping that strategic victory was only a climactic aerial clash or two away from achievement, the *Luftwaffe* had shifted focus on 7 September and turned its attention on London. Yet again, this proved to be mission impossible, not merely improbable. The daylight Blitz on London began on the 7th, climaxed on the 15th, and stuttered onward until the end of September. The attacks inflicted serious damage on the city, and did succeed in attracting Fighter Command into large-scale combat. However, the German medium bomber force lacked the weight in payload to achieve strategically significant damage, while, as an attack on public and political morale, the Blitz was a non-starter, as some *Luftwaffe* generals anticipated. London lay at the limit of the Bf 109s escort range, while the further inland German aircraft roamed, the easier it was for Fighter Command to harass and attack them. On 17 September Hitler indefinitely postponed the "planned" invasion of Britain – Operation SEALION.

---

[84] Dowding quoted in Orange, *Park*, p. 105.

In September the nighttime Blitz overlapped temporally the day offensive. The former then took over in October and through the winter of 1940/1 carried on the *Luftwaffe*'s offensive against Britain. It proved painful for Britain's population, but strategically pointless and therefore futile. In 1940 Fighter Command had no answer to the night Blitz, a fact that seemed to reflect badly on Dowding and Park. The principal culprit was, however, a deficiency of administrative grip over the radar research program, as illustrated by its ill-judged and panicky decamping from Suffolk to Aberdeen. In addition, the highest priority attached to Chain Home and Chain Home Low radar systems impacted negatively on the level of talent and effort available to the development of radar for night fighters.

Explaining Dowding's strategic victory

Why did "Stuffy" Dowding and his Fighter Command win in 1940? First, Dowding functioned persistently and consistently at the strategic level; he understood that, as the air officer commanding in chief, his responsibility was for the strategy of air defense. He committed himself to insuring that each of the classic constituents of strategy – ends, ways, and means, and their underpinning assumptions – had integrity both in and of themselves and, no less important, as vital enablers of the others. This chapter has also introduced the adjunct triptych of structure, contingency, and performance. The purpose was to explain that Dowding needed to modernize the system of air defense and its supporting infrastructure to insure that the ways and means were sufficiently adaptable to cope with unpredicted, even unanticipated, circumstances. Moreover, Dowding had to insure that the fighting power of his command – with its physical, moral, and conceptual components – could succeed in combat against the enemy on the day, whenever that day should dawn and for as long as it might last. Dowding's exercise of those responsibilities underlines that strategic sense.

Second, Dowding's major decisions over a ten-year period, including his long term on the air council from 1930 to 1936, proved "right enough." He passed what one can term the minimum regrets test. The successful strategist does not need to record flawless strategic performance, only one free of truly irrecoverably fatal mistakes. Wherever one looks at the ends, ways, and means of British air defense in the 1930s and into the 1940s, there is no serious room for doubt that Dowding was either right, or sufficiently correct, on the major decisions and in the ways in which they were to be implemented. His strategic sense enabled him to adapt to unanticipated circumstances, because he insured Fighter Command was sound in structure and functioning so that operational and tactical adjustments would not compromise its capabilities.

Third, British victory in 1940 was the result of a quarter-century of preparation that was nearly always paced well enough to be combat competitive with the extant or anticipated threat and its near future. Even in the short lifetime of air power, the Fighter Command of 1940 enjoyed a lengthy provenance. Dowding the strategist did not have to improvise on many significant aspects of his command's capability. Exceptions clearly included combat tactics, which in practice were adapted at the squadron level, and with respect to night fighting which Dowding insisted correctly could be improved only when airborne radar and suitable two-seat aircraft to carry and employ it were ready.

Fourth, Dowding succeeded in preparing an architecture of air defense that could cope with a German air menace that evolved rapidly and altered markedly in quality and quantity of tactical and operational menace as a result of unpredicted, certainly unpredictable, geostrategic changes. Fighter Command was not created, developed, and then fine-tuned to deal with a *Luftwaffe* based in northern France. In the 1930s RAF leaders had envisaged the German air threat primarily as a menace based in Germany, possibly the Low Countries, and taking the form of medium bombers without single-seat fighter protection. The Battle of Britain took place in a quite different and far more menacing context.

Fifth, although it is no great challenge to cite the errors, structural as well as discretionary, that blunted the *Luftwaffe*'s effectiveness in 1940, some might argue that Dowding's Fighter Command was always likely to win, almost regardless of German choices. With the *Luftwaffe* as it was in 1940, one can make a persuasive case that its campaign direction was not critically important. Given what the Germans did not know about Fighter Command, and what Clausewitz called the "grammar of war," one might argue that it did not much matter whether the Germans bombed airfields, cities, or both.[85] Fighter Command was resilient against the kind of performance that the *Luftwaffe* was capable of imposing – though one might add a judgment indicating that targeting choices shaped the Germans' performance. In principle, Britain's aircraft industry was vulnerable to attack, as also were the coastal facilities of the Chain Home radar architecture. But, principle and practice were far apart. And one should not be seduced either by imagination into believing that the *Luftwaffe* might have made different operational choices here and there, and as a consequence won the campaign.

There were deep systemic reasons why the *Luftwaffe* of 1940 performed as it did in the way it did. Dowding was certainly fortunate in his enemy's incompetence, but that is not to argue that he succeeded because he was lucky. It was true that Dowding was the fortunate command legatee of two decades of British competence in air defense. It is also true to say, however, that Dowding personally contributed significantly to the strength of that air defense by virtue of his enthusiastic endorsement of vital technical developments both before and after he assumed command in July 1936. Of course, a team of outstanding contributors to Fighter Command's combat potency was

---

[85] Clausewitz, *On War*, p. 605.

responsible for the successful defensive performance in 1940, but the overarching and most persuasive explanation for the victory was that superior strategic leadership provided Fighter Command decisive advantages over the *Luftwaffe*.

It was not luck that in 1940 Fighter Command had excellent equipment when it mattered; that a prudent and effective master operational concept guided its employment; that Park was Dowding's alter ego in his grasp and strategic sense; and that the Command consistently addressed the scientific and technical issues. Almost as much to the point, so much about Fighter Command and its commander was right that they could correct for the bad luck of some circumstances and their mistakes by timely adaptation. A Fighter Command headed by a man with little strategic sense might well have proven incapable of exploiting the *Luftwaffe*'s weaknesses. The principal, though far from sole, agent for the security of that benefit was Hugh Dowding.

Sixth, Dowding persisted with what history demonstrated to be the correct command philosophy and broad guiding concept of operations. As air officer commanding in chief of Fighter Command, he reserved for himself the role of strategist, though subject at times to harassment from the Air Ministry. He delegated operational command to his exceptionally capable subordinate, Park, at 11 Group, who played the role of Sherman to Dowding's Grant. Park, then, delegated tactical command to sector station controllers – up to the point of air-to-air contact, when squadron commanders aloft took charge. Because he adhered to a strategic standard of performance, Dowding selected a concept of operations that expressed the Command's strategic purpose.

Dowding never forgot that his goal was to deny the Germans a convincing narrative that would support the invasion option. He could not decide for Berlin how much damage his command needed to inflict on the *Luftwaffe*. What he could do, however, was insure that in no rational, if optimistic, briefing to the *Führer* could the *Luftwaffe* claim credibly to have defeated Fighter Command. Almost certainly, Hitler was not hard to dissuade from the hazards of amphibious warfare. Overy is plausible when he writes: "It is evident that not a lot was needed to deter Hitler from the idea of invading Britain. Fighter Command tipped the balance."[86] However, Dowding could not have known this at the time. He needed his forces to continue to hurt the *Luftwaffe*, all the while never ceasing to demonstrate that Fighter Command remained alive and well. He had to insure that nothing resembled in German perception a decisive victory over his command, lest Berlin believed it had achieved the green-light for invasion.

One can summarize Dowding's concept of operations as a minimum effective response, to deny the *Luftwaffe* even the possibility of a decisive victory in the air (or on airfields). Not surprisingly, many of Dowding's critics, both

[86] Overy, *The Battle of Britain*, p. 110.

in 1940 and afterwards, could not understand why Fighter Command committed only a fraction of its total force, most especially of its best fighter aircraft, the Spitfire, to combat at any one time. His was not the most exciting of operational concepts, but it was far and away the most prudent.

"Stuffy" Dowding won an uncommonly important victory. This claim is beyond reasonable dispute. One may argue that he won in spite of his mistakes and because of German errors. Both points have some merit, but generically regarded they are simply permanent features of the realities of history. This chapter has chosen not to dwell on Dowding's mistakes, both because they proved relatively minor in consequence, but also because they are simply evidence of the obvious truth that even successful strategists are human. One should not forget that an extremely powerful enemy tested Dowding's strategic performance in combat, and that the cost of his possible defeat could well have been defeat in the war as a whole. While Dowding might have fought a more perfect Battle of Britain, he might have also fought a far less perfect one. The probable strategic and political consequences of the latter compel respect.

10   US naval strategy and Japan

Williamson Murray

Innovation and surprise tested the plan's validity throughout the war. Certain changes had been anticipated by the planners, in outline if not in detail, and did not materially alter its relevance. Most of the unexpected developments were easily co-opted within the plan's framework, a tribute to its flexibility and broad aims. Only a few surprises compelled wartime leaders to depart from it. None compromised its fundamental principles.[1]

The US Navy during the period between 1919 and 1939 has received considerable attention from historians and political scientists, much of that interest driven by Andrew Marshall of the Office of Net Assessment. The author of this essay, in fact, was a willing and self-inflicted victim of one of those efforts in the early 1980s, when he and Allan Millett directed the "military effectiveness studies, recently reissued by Cambridge University Press."[2] At the time, the author, as with many other students of European military history, found himself intrigued with the German innovations in combined-arms tactics during the twenties and thirties.[3] Yet, nearly 30 years later, he finds himself far more impressed with the performance of America's military institutions in innovating during the interwar period than with the Germans.[4]

While the *Reichswehr* and the *Wehrmacht* addressed successfully the complex problems involved in developing combined-arms ground tactics during the interwar period, the German military also managed in the Second World War to repeat every strategic mistake that it had made 20 years

---

[1] Edward S. Miller, *War Plan Orange: The U.S. Strategy to Defeat Japan, 1897–1945* (Annapolis, MD, 1991), p. 347.

[2] Allan R. Millett and Williamson Murray, eds., *Military Effectiveness*, 3 vols., *World War I*, *The Interwar Period*, and *World War II* (Cambridge, 2011).

[3] See among others of the author's writings: Williamson Murray, "Armored Warfare, The British, French, and German Experiences," in Williamson Murray and Allan R. Millett, eds., *Military Innovation in the Interwar Period* (Cambridge, 1996).

[4] The author has attempted in the books that he has written and helped to edit to delineate innovation as a peacetime phenomenon and adaptation as a wartime phenomenon. For the former see Williamson Murray and Allan R. Millett, eds., *Military Innovation in the Interwar Period* (Cambridge, 1996); and Williamson Murray, *Military Adaptation in War: For Fear of Change* (Cambridge, 2011).

earlier.[5] It was not just a matter of repeating disastrous political and strategic mistakes of the First World War that made the German approach to war so flawed in the world war that followed 20 years later. It was also the fact that their understanding of the operational level of war lacked any grasp of the importance of logistics and intelligence.[6] In particular, the performance of the *Kriegsmarine* in two world wars displayed the same careless disregard for strategy, logistics, and intelligence that the army displayed, for example in the planning and execution of its invasion of the Soviet Union in 1941.[7] What this suggests is that there was a deep cultural bias in the German military that led to an overemphasis on tactics and a deep ignorance of strategic and political factors.[8]

In the case of the US Navy, however, innovation occurred at all the levels of war from grand strategy, to theater operational strategy, to the basic tactical framework within which the navy would fight the Pacific War from 1941 to 1945. Exacerbating the difficulties of innovation and the development of a coherent and effective theater strategy was the reality of the immense distances of the Pacific. Moreover, the increasing pace of technological change as well as an evolving political context challenged many of the deeply held traditions and strategic concepts of the navy's officers. Furthermore, this pace of technological change also introduced new uncertainties and ambiguities into the tactical and operational frameworks that guided strategic thinking. While the development of a military strategy for a potential war with Japan evolved over decades, the political framework of US grand strategy underwent a series of major changes, as political leaders confronted the difficult political and diplomatic problems in dealing with Japan.[9]

Thus, the performance of the US Navy in the interwar period demanded the ability to address a host of issues in a time of few resources, considerable shifts in the international environment, and rapid technological change. Inevitably, the conditions of the war proved quite different from what planners had expected. As Michael Howard has suggested about all military

---

[5] As this author and Allan Millett pointed out in 1989, effectiveness at the strategic level is of much greater importance than effectiveness at the operational and tactical levels of war. See Williamson Murray and Allan R. Millett, "Lessons of War," *The National Interest,* Winter 1988/9.

[6] Martin van Creveld underlined the abysmal performance of Germany's army in two world wars in logistics in his *Supplying War: Logistics from Wallenstein to Patton* (Cambridge, 2004). For a general critique of German military effectiveness, see Williamson Murray, *War, Strategy, and Military Effectiveness* (Cambridge, 2011), chp. 9.

[7] After all, the *Kriegsmarine* managed to get its codes compromised in both world wars with enormous consequences in the two conflicts.

[8] In this regard see particularly Isabel V. Hull, *Absolute Destruction: Military Culture and the Practices of War in Imperial Germany* (Ithaca, 2006).

[9] On grand strategy see Williamson Murray, Richard Hart Sinnreich, and James Lacey, eds., *The Shaping of Grand Strategy: Policy, Diplomacy, and War* (Cambridge, 2011).

organizations, the Americans initially got the next war wrong at its beginning.[10] But the thinking of the prewar period, the innovations in technology, and the intellectual preparation of the officer corps were such that the navy was able initially to improvise and then to adapt to *the actual conditions of the war that it confronted*. In the end, the navy's preparations proved "good enough," and, in the real world, "good enough" represents a major success, given the sorry performance of most military institutions at the strategic and operational levels.[11]

Thus, the conceptions and innovations that the navy developed during the interwar period allowed it to adapt its operational and tactical capabilities to solving the actual strategic realities it confronted in the war against Japan. What makes this case study so interesting in thinking about the future is the fact that the prewar navy's culture, within which the development of future military strategy of the Pacific War took place, underlines not only the pitfalls of the current approach to the future, but also the enormous importance that the values of honest, open debate, imagination, and serious, sustained study – all of which marked the interwar navy – have for the preparation of America's military forces for the next century.

The background

After the dust of the collapse of the Imperial Japanese Empire had settled, Fleet Admiral Chester Nimitz noted that the navy had foreseen everything that had happened in the Pacific War except for the damaging attacks the Kamikazes had launched in the last months of that conflict.[12] Nimitz was both right and wrong. He was wrong in the sense that, had the Japanese not sunk most of the US battle fleet, the Pacific Fleet's leaders might well have sallied forth with their ships in a vain effort to take the pressure off MacArthur's hard-pressed garrison in the Philippines as well as the deteriorating position of the Allies in Malaya and the Dutch East Indies. As is the case with all successful strategies, contingency played a major role in the navy's success in the Second World War. Thus, the shambles of 7 December 1941 may well have prevented a far worse disaster.

---

[10] Among others see Michael Howard, "The Use and Abuse of Military History," *Journal of the Royal United Services Institute*, vol. 107, February 1962, p. 6.
[11] I am indebted to Colin Gray for his use of the term "good enough," a term which underlines that in the real world "good enough" is more than sufficient, while the search for a perfect solution more often than not results in disaster. As for the performance of most at the political and strategic levels, Clausewitz notes with dripping irony that: "No one starts a war – or rather, no one in his senses ought to do so – without being clear in his mind what he intends to achieve by that war and how he intends to conduct it." Carl von Clausewitz, *On War*, ed. and trans. by Michael Howard and Peter Paret (Princeton, 1976).
[12] Chester Nimitz, Dennis A. Vincizi, *Human Factors in Simulation Training* (Boca Raton, FL, 2009), p. 17.

Although history is somewhat ambiguous on what Admiral Husband Kimmel, commander of the Pacific Fleet, might have done had the Japanese not sunk the battle fleet he commanded in Pearl Harbor, his record and reputation among his fellow officers suggests that he would have accepted the risks involved in challenging the Japanese to a great naval battle somewhere in the area between Wake and Guam. Kimmel's personality, as well as his preparation for war, predisposed him to launch an aggressive response on the outbreak of a war with Japan. His chief of plans, Captain "Soc" McMorris, suggested after the war that, had he known that Nagumo, his six fleet carriers, and two battleships were on a course headed for Pearl Harbor, he would have advised Kimmel that the American fleet should head west to meet them, even though the American battleships would have "suffered quite severely."[13] Gordon Prange noted that Kimmel's probable intention, had the Japanese not attacked, was "to sail forth to engage Yamamoto and waste no time about it."[14] At the time, such was the superiority of Japanese naval and air power, the latter both carrier- and island-based, that the slaughter of much of the American fleet would most probably have ensued. But even more disastrous than the loss of the ships would have been the loss of the officers, petty officers, and sailors, the personnel framework on which the navy's massive expansion would rest in the coming years.[15] The former, the immense productive capacity of American industry would have been able to replace. The latter could not have been replaced easily.

In the end, the success of strategy at any level depends on the personalities of those who conduct it. Thus, all the intellectual efforts in war gaming, concept development, and analysis of fleet exercises by American naval officers during the interwar period might have gone for naught had Admiral Yamamoto not decided to launch a surprise attack against Pearl Harbor – an attack that most of the Imperial Navy's senior officers opposed. The direct result of the Pearl Harbor disaster was that the president fired Kimmel and immediately appointed Nimitz to command the battered Pacific Fleet, an admiral far more in tune with the navy's culture than his predecessor.

Another factor underlies the potential of officers like Kimmel to undermine strategic approaches that have been developed through rigorous processes, and that lies in the failure to estimate the enemy's potential: in other words, the failure to understand the "other." On one hand, as we will see, the navy carried out its exercises at sea and its war games at Newport in the most rigorous fashion. In every war game and fleet exercise, the fleet units that represented the opposing sides possessed every opportunity to savage

---

[13] Quoted in Miller, *War Plan Orange*, p. 310.
[14] Gordon W. Prange with Donald M. Goldstein and Katherine V. Dillon, *Pearl Harbor: The Verdict of History* (New York, 1986), p. 475.
[15] This was, of course, why the saving of the British Army at Dunkirk was so important, because the rebuilding of the army in the aftermath of defeat would have been much more difficult without the officers and NCOs brought off the beaches.

their opponent's fleet. Yet, in his report on Fleet Exercise XV (1934), in which the opposing fleets had engaged in a running battle that inflicted heavy casualties on both sides, Admiral David Foote Sellers, CINCUS (Commander in Chief US Fleet) commented that, "it is by no means probable that an Asiatic power could wage such an efficient war of attrition as that waged by the GRAY fleet."[16] Given what was to happen, not only on 7 December 1941, but also at Savo Island eight months later, one can only conclude that too many naval officers in the interwar period agreed with Sellers that the capabilities and competence displayed by opposing fleets and their commanders in American fleet exercises were far superior to the actual effectiveness of the Imperial Japanese Navy. Events in the first year of the war would prove that assumption to be seriously flawed.

Kimmel never managed to sail the battle fleet west. Here chance, with the helping hand of the Admiral Yamamoto, determined there would be no great fleet engagement at the start of the war between the United States and Japan. Instead, that fleet engagement would take place six months later at Midway, when the navy was better prepared operationally and tactically to take on the Japanese in a major fleet engagement. From that point on, the navy's Pacific strategy crushed the power of Imperial Japan in three years by assembling the various intellectual, technological, and doctrinal pieces developed in the interwar period.

Thus, Nimitz was right in the sense that the theater strategic approach that American ground, sea, and air forces used to defeat the Japanese from summer 1943 on reflected the developments of the 1920s and 1930s, a period that typified the ambiguities that confront the creation of any successful strategy. In other words, the war games at Newport, fleet exercises of the twenties and the thirties, and education of officers in general provided the concepts, understanding, and particularly the culture necessary to adapt to the actual conditions of war and thus execute a successful strategy through to conclusion. In the end, the success or failure of a strategy depends on the context within which it is developed. "No theoretical construct, no set of abstract principles, no political science model can capture its essence ... Constant change and adaptation must be its companions if it is to succeed."[17]

The problem of a possible war with the Empire of Japan first appeared in the period immediately after the United States had crushed the Spanish Navy and colonial armies in the Spanish American War at the end of the nineteenth century. During most of the 40 years that followed, the US Navy focused on Imperial Japan and its navy as its most likely enemy.[18] To a considerable

---

[16] Quoted in Albert A. Nofi, *To Train the Fleet for War: The U.S. Navy Fleet Problems* (Newport, RI, 2010), p. 188.

[17] Murray et al., *The Shaping of Grand Strategy*, p. 11.

[18] Admittedly, there were other potential enemies. For many of the navy's officers, particularly King, who would lead the American naval effort in the Second World War, Britain was the enemy of choice.

extent, its plans and its conceptions of future war dealt with the problems associated with a war across the vastness of the Pacific.[19] That said, the period during which the navy examined the strategic problems raised by a war with Japan was one of constant change. At the level of American grand strategy, the outbreak of the First World War and America's eventual entrance into that conflict superseded thoughts of a war with Japan for all but a few from 1915 to 1919.

Similarly, throughout the 1920s and early 1930s, the idea that there might be a major war between the United States and Imperial Japan was inconceivable, not only to nearly all Americans, but to their political leaders as well. The Washington Naval Treaty of 1922 had apparently removed much of the tension between the triangle of naval powers – the United States, Japan, and Britain. Moreover, the return to "normalcy" of the 1920s, as well as the liberal, non-aggressive Japanese government of the period, further reduced those tensions. Even the Japanese seizure of Manchuria in 1931 hardly bothered an America sinking into the sloughs of the Depression. In one sense, the relative passivity and lack of tension through the mid thirties together with the demilitarization of the islands in the Central Pacific eased the military problems of an advance across the Pacific by making a war with Japan less likely. Nevertheless, while the political and strategic framework seemed to make a major conflict unlikely, the navy was forming an understanding of how to address the problems associated with such a conflict.

As the political landscape changed in the mid to late thirties, however, so did the tactical and operational problems, as it became apparent that the Japanese were fortifying and building airfields on the mandate islands in the Central Pacific, seized from the Germans at the outset of the First World War. At the same time, technological change as well as the increasing potential of weapons systems demanded that the fleet and its planners develop new and extend existing concepts of operations. Similarly, in serendipitous fashion, the navy's processes of change forced technologies in new and unexpected directions.[20] This chapter proposes to examine the development of

[19] Nimitz in his Naval War College thesis of 1923 posited that there were two potential naval wars the United States would face: the first against the Royal Navy; the second against the Imperial Japanese Navy. Nevertheless, his opening remarks make it clear that he believed the former case to be highly unlikely, while the latter was more likely. Chester V. Nimitz, "Naval Tactics," *Naval War College Review*, November–December 1982.

[20] Nowhere was this clearer than in the continuing development of radial engines. In the early 1920s the belief among aeronautical experts was that the in-line engine would provide a better means of developing engine power than the radial engine. But aircraft equipped with in-line engines proved to be a nightmare to maintain on board carriers, while radial engines were relatively easy to maintain. The result was that both the Japanese and US Navies pushed the development of radial engines in the late twenties into the thirties. That technology influenced the civilian airlines in the 1930s as well as the Army Air Corps. The result was that the only effective front-line American bomber or fighter in the Second World War to possess an in-line engine was the P-51.

American theater strategy in the Pacific through the lens of the influence of war gaming, fleet exercises, innovation in weapons systems, and technological change. Inherent in the processes of developing theater strategy, the reader must not forget the impact of individuals and their interplay, some of whom history has remembered, but most forgotten. Finally, it will examine how well that strategy actually worked out in the harsh laboratory of war.

The tyranny of distance and war planning

In thinking about a war with Japan, the greatest difficulty military leaders and planners faced lay in the enormous size of the Pacific theater. The distance from San Diego, whence US military operations would begin, to Oahu is 2,612 miles; from Honolulu to Tokyo is a further 3,862 miles; Honolulu to the Philippines, 5,305 miles; Pearl Harbor to Darwin, Australia, 5,388 miles; while the distance from Pearl Harbor to Micronesia is 3,088 miles. In the 1920s and 1930s, the distances of the Pacific presented problems of time, space, and logistics that no naval theater in history had ever before posed to military organizations proposing to mount a major campaign. Simply put, the great, vast emptiness that lay between Hawaii and the Home Islands of Japan offered no simple, easy, or direct solutions for naval planners in terms of the projection of military power against a major power. Thus, the development of the navy's theater strategy must begin with an understanding of the geography and distances of the Pacific.

Exacerbating the geostrategic problems of the Pacific was the fact that, in a fit of strategic absentmindedness, the United States had acquired the Philippines as one of the prizes of its victory in the Spanish–American War. In effect, those islands represented a hostage to fortune, easily accessible to attack from Japanese Home Islands much closer than the nearest American bases. Yet, initially, acquisition of the Philippines and Guam appeared advantageous to American naval strategy, since they offered the possibility of major naval bases on the far side of the Pacific. Certainly that was how naval planners viewed those possessions until the signing of the Washington Naval Treaty of 1922.

But that treaty, besides limiting the size of the Japanese battle fleet to only 60 percent of that of the United States, also forbade the United States from constructing major naval or military facilities in either the Philippines or Guam. Thus, the US Navy would have no such facilities in the Western Pacific from which to launch a campaign against the Japanese. This represented a major concession on the part of American negotiators in Washington, but one that was necessary to get to the Japanese to agree to a 60 percent limitation on the size of their battle fleet. In effect, it radically changed the options open to American strategic planners and made their world more difficult.

A recent history of the navy's General Board has posed the fundamental operational and strategic question with which the new treaty regime confronted strategic planners and thinkers in Washington and Newport: "How could the navy accomplish its strategic tasks with a doctrine and strategy based on the battleship and overseas bases when the Washington Treaty had severely limited both of these pillars of sea power?"[21] Ironically, the treaty also played a major role in expanding the capabilities the navy would need for such a campaign. Commander Chester Nimitz noted in his war college paper in 1923, "at no time in our history has the BLUE naval tactician been confronted with a problem as difficult of solution as that imposed by the restrictions of the Treaties."[22] Thus, American naval planners and strategists had to confront the tyranny of distance, which meant that any direct Mahanian approach to the Japanese Home Islands risked the problem that the Russians had confronted in the Russo-Japanese War: how a major fleet could cross the immense distances of the Pacific without suffering a crushing defeat similar to that which the Russians had suffered at Tsushima Straits.[23]

Nevertheless, through 1934, the "thrusters" – those who advocated an immediate move of American naval forces to the Western Pacific – remained a dominant voice in the councils of those responsible for designing War Plan Orange, the planning effort for a potential war with Japan. Nor did the "thrusters" entirely lose their voice in the councils of the navy over the period immediately before the war broke out, but they found themselves outnumbered by more cautious voices as the thirties wore on and as war with Japan became increasingly probable.

By the mid 1930s, more realistic voices among the navy's leaders came to dominate thinking about and planning for a war with Japan. Nevertheless, the conundrum naval planners faced was that a campaign to seize the island bases needed either to reinforce or to recapture Guam and the Philippines and eventually strike the Home Islands meant that the United States would have to wage a long war, a war which they believed the American people might not be willing to sustain. Quite simply, the capture of the island bases in the Western Pacific required for the projection of military power was going to require a lengthy campaign. In that respect, they agreed with Yamamoto's analysis in 1941 that the American people would not support a long war. At the time, they were undoubtedly being realistic, as the fact that the Congress of the United States renewed the draft by only a single vote in July 1941 underlined.[24]

---

[21] John T. Kuehn, *Agents of Innovation: The General Board and the Design of the Fleet that Defeated the Japanese Navy* (Annapolis, MD, 2008), p. 24.
[22] Commander Chester W. Nimitz, "Naval Tactics," *Naval War College Review*, Fall 1983; an abridged reprint of Nimitz's 1923 Naval War College thesis.
[23] See among others: Denis Warner and Peggy Warner, *The Tide at Sunrise: A History of the Russo-Japanese War* (New York, 1974), pp. 402–426 and 494–520.
[24] At the time Congress barely renewed the draft, German Panzer divisions were in the process of destroying a huge Soviet Army group on the Red Army's central front and capturing Smolensk, two-thirds of the way to Moscow. Senior American military experts gave the Soviet Union only several weeks before it collapsed.

The further the navy tested and evaluated its concepts and the possibilities of a war across the Central Pacific, the more difficult problems involving the capture of island bases, the supplying of naval forces at sea over great distances while underway, and the maintenance and repair of ships, aircraft, and island bases in the midst of ongoing naval operations appeared. Some of these, the navy could address immediately, but most had to be put on the back burner to solve later, if and when resources became available. But at least navy planners and strategists were aware of those issues. The most important impact that the Pacific's distances had on the navy's thinking was an increasing awareness among officers that logistical issues were going to prove crucial in the conduct of a war against Japan. The Washington Naval Treaty of 1922 obviously magnified that awareness, since there was now no hope of building major naval bases in either the Central or Western Pacific before a war actually erupted.

When the treaty regime finally collapsed in 1936, some within the navy pushed hard to build major naval bases in the Philippines and Guam, but Congress, as it does occasionally, saw matters in a more sensible light: such a program would have a disastrous impact on relations with the Japanese, which were increasingly difficult, but which had a considerable distance to go before the two nations were at war; would waste valuable taxpayer money; and made little strategic sense, at least for the foreseeable future. Not surprisingly, the distances in the Pacific and what those distances involved in the projecting of American power across that ocean with no bases available came to dominate the thinking of American planners in the late 1930s. As a result, the navy was intellectually prepared to wage a campaign that would depend on logistical capabilities as the starting point for war against Japan.

Yet, like a bad penny, in spite of any realistic analysis of the distances involved and the Japanese possession of the Mandate Islands, which lay across any route to the Western Pacific, the Philippines and Guam refused to go away. Here, army generals Leonard Wood and Douglas MacArthur, in particular, played a pernicious role. For the most part, the army as an institution and its planners cared little about saving the Philippines or fighting Japan. But in 1922, when navy planners drew the conclusion that the Philippines were indefensible given the distances, Wood, governor general of the islands – his consolation prize for not getting the Republican nomination for president in 1920 – squealed like a stuck pig to Washington. The uproar led navy planners to back down from their reasonable strategic position. Not until the 1930s were they in a position once again to revert to the more sensible strategic position that the Philippines were indefensible. Unfortunately, in 1940 Douglas MacArthur, now a field marshal in the Philippine Army and in charge of Philippine defense, again muddied the water by causing the diversion of substantial resources to the defense of his bailiwick, one that, given the correlation of forces at the time, was simply hopeless.

The treaty regime, unintended effects, and the navy

Beyond the normal cast of characters whom historians have singled out in apportioning blame for the unpreparedness of America's military in December 1941, many were to point to the influence of the treaty regime, beginning with the Washington Treaty of 1922, with its restraints on the size of the navies of the major powers, as a significant contributing factor in the disaster.[25] The United States did achieve battleship equality with the British and a ten-to-six ratio in its favor with the Japanese. Ironically, in spite of what many have argued, the actual settlement proved quite favorable in the long run to the development of the fleet during the interwar period as well as contributing to more realistic strategic concepts.

There are a number of reasons why the Washington Treaty proved strategically and militarily beneficial. First, the treaties prevented the United States from resourcing major naval bases and facilities in either Guam or the Philippines, which, as the events of 1942 would confirm, were basically indefensible. As Captain Frank Schofield indicated to an Army War College class in September 1923, the Washington Naval Treaties forced the navy to undergo a fundamental reassessment of its thinking about a future war with Japan: "Manifestly the provisions of the Treaty presented a naval problem of the first magnitude that demanded immediate solution. A new policy had to be formulated which would make the best possible use of the new conditions."[26] While it would take navy leaders almost a decade to give up the dream of fortified bases in the Western Pacific from which to launch the US fleet against the Home Islands, the writing was on the wall, at least for those willing to examine the strategic realities.[27]

The irony of the treaty regime is that, while it largely failed in its aim of limiting naval armaments, which had been the basis of the approach of the Harding and Hoover administrations, it proved beneficial in forcing the navy not only to alter the course of its strategic planning in more realistic directions, but also to develop a more capable and effective combat force. By restricting the navy to the 15 battleships already in the fleet, and with its moratorium on the building of new capital ships, the 1922 Washington Treaty forced the navy to focus on other areas of naval power. The treaty did allow the United States, Japan, and Britain to modernize their battleships as well as

---

[25] The political support for naval disarmament and limitations on new naval construction had to do with the belief that one of the major causes of the First World War had been the naval arms race of the decade immediately preceding the outbreak of war. In reality, the naval arms race among the powers had largely resulted from the increasing antagonism between the alliance systems. Thus, the arms race was a symptom rather than a cause.

[26] Quoted in Kuehn, *Agents of Innovation*, p. 38.

[27] For the difficulties navy leaders had in accepting the strategic realities or the implications of the demilitarization of the Western Pacific, see Edward S. Miller, *War Plan Orange, The U.S. Strategy to Defeat Japan, 1897–1945* (Annapolis, MD, 1994).

to add a further 3,000 tons to the displacement of those ships for increased protection against submarine and air attack, which did have the advantage of making them more difficult to sink.

Not surprisingly, the navy made a major effort to do precisely that, but the treaty also had a number of second and third order effects.[28] First, without the prohibition on new battleship construction, the navy might well have spent its money on new dreadnoughts instead of refurbishing and improving what it actually possessed. The modernization program for the battleships significantly improved their power plants, range, and the effectiveness of their armament. Moreover, the combination of thinking about the possibilities of a future war with Japan with the possibility that such a war might require the seizure of advance bases also forced the navy to think about other uses the battle fleet might serve. As the historian of the General Board has noted, "in this specific case the treaty system encouraged innovative operational thinking for using battleships in support of amphibious warfare."[29] The result of such thinking and initial testing were to have considerable consequences in the Pacific War.

But the larger impact of the treaty regime lay in its unintended effect on the rest of the fleet. In effect, the money that would have gone to the construction of new battleships flowed into the construction of other platforms. The most obvious benefit was the fact that the Washington Treaty allowed the conversion of the half-finished battle cruisers *Saratoga* and *Lexington* into aircraft carriers. Here again, the General Board was a major player in pushing for the navy to complete the conversion of these ships, originally laid down as battle cruisers, into the kind of platform required to test out the possibilities inherent in taking large numbers of aircraft to sea with the fleet. The navy's first carrier, the converted collier *Langley*, was both too small and too slow to provide the kinds of insights needed to understand how naval commanders might best utilize carriers and their attendant air power. The *Saratoga* and *Lexington*, on the other hand, were considerably faster than the battle fleet; and so, as soon as they joined the fleet, the new carriers offered the possibility of independent operations with ships the weapons systems of which possessed unmatched lethality and striking power. But beyond the need to let the carriers act independently, the two big ships indicated that large carriers would provide greater flexibility in employment than small carriers.[30]

---

[28] There is an excellent discussion of the General Board's influence over the modernization as well as the impact of that program on the navy as a whole in Kuehn, *Agents of Innovation*, chp. 5.

[29] Ibid., p. 85.

[30] The Japanese gained the same insight with the two battle cruiser hulls that they converted into the carriers *Kaga* and *Akagi*. The British, however, had no large battle cruisers under construction and so their carriers were of limited size and speed in comparison to the large carriers the Americans and Japanese possessed. For a careful discussion of the flawed nature of British carrier development, see the discussion in Thomas Hone, Mark David Mandeles,

Even before the two great carriers joined the fleet, a number of senior officers, supported by the General Board, were pushing for more carriers, since the navy still remained substantially under the carrier tonnage allowed by the Washington Treaty. However, the political and economic climate that lasted through to 1934 made executing such suggestions impossible. Additional carrier construction was out of the question, no matter how supportive of the idea the General Board and navy leaders might be. Instead, for a period in the early thirties, the General Board considered the possibility of flying-deck cruisers, which would marry the need for more cruisers with the need to supply additional air power for the fleet. Nothing came of the idea, because in 1934 the Roosevelt administration provided funding for naval construction.[31] What is particularly interesting about the General Board's discussion of the flying-deck heavy cruiser was that its design thinking included an angled-deck, a concept that the Royal Navy first incorporated into carrier design only after the Second World War.

The Japanese seizure of Manchuria in 1931 had been the cause of some alarm among Americans, but not enough to persuade the Hoover or Roosevelt administrations, mired as they were in the midst of the Depression, to begin a gradual program of rearmament.[32] But by 1934, it was clear that the Japanese were not going to renew the Washington Treaty. By using the argument of creating jobs, Roosevelt then authorized a modest program of naval construction. However, the outright refusal of the Japanese government to renew the naval limitation treaty and their initiation of a massive ship-building program led Roosevelt to reply in 1938 with a major American program that dwarfed the Japanese efforts and underlined how much the Washington Treaty of 1922 had been to Japan's advantage. The arrival of the 1938 major fleet units and those of the 1940 Two Ocean Naval Act, especially carriers, was to tip the correlation of forces in the Pacific decisively in favor of the United States beginning in July 1943.

The treaty regime, unintended effects, and the creation of amphibious warfare

Perhaps the most important unintended impact of the "treaty regime" was its impact on the development of the concepts as well as the understanding necessary for the conduct of amphibious warfare. With the prohibition of Guam

and Norman Friedman, *American and British Aircraft Carrier Development, 1919–1941* (Annapolis, MD, 1999).

[31] The funding for new ships by the administration seems largely to have been motivated by a desire to provide jobs and stimulate the economy rather than to address the navy's need for new ships.

[32] The Hoover administration had deeply absorbed the prevailing belief that limitation of armaments was by itself a good thing and the navy should not build the ships, such as cruisers and carriers, which the Washington Treaty authorized.

and the Philippines as major potential bases, as well as the fact that they were much closer to Japanese than to US naval power, the question was how the navy would acquire the bases that it needed to resupply the fleet, repair damaged ships, and project naval power against the Home Islands in the Central and Western Pacific. Simply put, the navy would have to capture those bases. And once the Japanese refused to renew the treaty regime, it was clear they would fortify their islands throughout Micronesia. Thus, a major part of the strategic problem would be how to capture those bases in successful amphibious landings against strong, prepared military forces. Nevertheless, until rather late in the game, amphibious warfare only occasionally held the navy's interest, while most army generals could have cared less about the possibilities that their soldiers might participate in such operations in time of war.[33]

The results of various amphibious operations in the First World War had been somewhat ambiguous. The Germans had launched a successful amphibious operation against the Baltic Islands in 1917, but by that point in the war, Russia's military forces were already in a state of dissolution in a nation wracked by revolution. The British experience in their landings at Gallipoli in April 1915 had been most disappointing. In effect, the tactical and technological performance of both the navy and army had been so dismal as to call into question the possibility of ever mounting a successful amphibious operation against a first-class enemy who held the shore line in strength and who possessed interior lines of communications that could rapidly reinforce the battlefront. That, anyway, was the conclusion that the British drew from their experiences at Gallipoli, which served to reinforce the attitudes of most other military organizations.[34]

The exception to such thinking was, of course, the United States Marine Corps. In search of a mission that would justify its continued existence, marine leaders had become interested in amphibious war as early as 1920 in their review of War Plan Orange. The Commandant, Major General John A. Lejeune, turned the problem over to Major Earl H. Ellis, a brilliant and iconoclastic marine, who produced a deeply insightful paper in 1921: "Advanced Base Operations in Micronesia," which Lejeune endorsed in July 1921.[35] Ellis' paper represented no more than a start to sketching out the nature of the problem.

---

[33] There is an explanation for the navy's attitude, namely that it had so many other issues with which it had to deal and was so short of resources that amphibious war ranked relatively low on its priorities.
[34] The British thinking about such operations was suggested in 1938 by the Deputy Chief of Naval Staff, Andrew Cunningham, who reported that "at the present time [the Navy staff] could not visualize any particular [joint] operation taking place and they were, therefore, not prepared to devote any considerable sum of money to equipment for [joint] training." PRO CAB 54/2, DCOS /30th Meeting, 15.11.38, DCOS (Deputy Chiefs of Staff) Sub-Committee, p. 4.
[35] For the development of amphibious warfare, see Allan R. Millett, "Assault from the Sea," in Williamson Murray and Allan R. Millett, eds., *Military Innovation in the Interwar Period* (Cambridge, 1996), pp. 70–78.

The challenge now was to put flesh on the bare bones of a skeleton. Adding to the difficulties the marines confronted in making headway with their preparations for amphibious war was the fact that an increasing share of their limited troop strength remained committed to what today would be called peace-keeping missions in Central America and the Caribbean.

Providing impetus to such efforts in the early thirties were the cost-cutting efforts of the Hoover administration, which was slicing funding for the services in the face of the Depression. For a period, these cuts even threatened to eliminate the marine corps.[36] But of greater importance was the change of foreign policy focus with the arrival of the Roosevelt administration in office in March 1933, with its emphasis on a "good neighbor policy" toward South America and the Caribbean. By the early 1930s, the corps was able to focus increasingly on the problems involved in amphibious warfare. That shift in policy ended American interventions in the hemisphere and provided the marine corps with the troop strength to participate in more extensive tests of amphibious doctrine and capabilities. In addition, the fact that the president was a longtime friend of the corps, dating back to the seven years that he had served as an assistant secretary of the navy under Wilson's administration, undoubtedly helped secure the corps' survival.

The Marine Corps Schools at Quantico became the center of efforts to develop an effective doctrinal framework for amphibious warfare. Helping the marines in their efforts was the fact that they populated the various schools at Quantico with their best officers, a reflection undoubtedly of their efforts to mold a professional culture that mirrored the strengths of those of the navy and army.[37] The study of amphibious warfare at the schools increased from 1925 through 1935 from 20 percent of the curriculum to 60 percent, with a heavy emphasis on learning the actual lessons of British mistakes at Gallipoli, rather than attempting to prove that such operations were impossible.[38] In 1931, institutional paranoia about being absorbed into the army reached the point that, for a considerable period of time, the schools shut down, while the faculty and students devoted themselves entirely to the writing of a detailed manual on how to conduct amphibious operations in the face of significant enemy operations. By 1934, the marines had produced the seminal doctrinal study, "Tentative Manual for Landing Operations," which provided the basic framework for amphibious warfare in Europe as well as in the Pacific.

Again, as with all the innovations that contributed to conduct of American strategy by maritime forces across the Pacific, the devil of amphibious war was in the details. Not until the late 1930s, as more funding became available with

---

[36] Such a fate befell the French marines who had found themselves transferred from the navy to the army in 1900.

[37] For the development of military professionalism in the marine corps see Allan R. Millett, *In Many a Strife: General Gerald C. Thomas and the U.S. Marine Corps, 1917–1956* (Annapolis, MD, 1993).

[38] Millett, "Assault from the Sea," p. 74.

a worsening international situation, did the pace of navy and marine corps amphibious exercises involving significant numbers and realistic scenarios accelerate. Even with increased resources, it was not until February 1940 that the marine corps' 1st Brigade possessed something equivalent to its wartime TO&E (table of organization and equipment), and the navy still had no attack transports; instead, it had to substitute old battleships and converted destroyers to transport the amphibious force in efforts to work out TTPs (tactics, techniques, and procedures). Nevertheless, whatever the difficulties the marines confronted as a result of lacking resources, America's concept of amphibious warfare was far in advance of what was occurring elsewhere. As Allan Millett has pointed out:

> The debate over amphibious warfare in the United States did not have the same closed character that it had in Britain and Japan. Articles on the subject appeared with regularity in service journals and even occasionally in civilian journals. More importantly, Congress followed the discussions in the annual reports of the service secretaries and in Congressional hearings. Whenever someone in or out of office, military or civilian, criticized the marine corps, it opened the issue of readiness for amphibious warfare.[39]

Nevertheless, as one of the historians of the fleet exercises during the interwar period has pointed out, amphibious warfare remained a "strategic afterthought" to most of the navy's leadership.[40] There is considerable justification for his criticism. Yet, there is also some justification for the navy's placement of amphibious warfare toward the bottom of its priorities. Perhaps, the most important explanation has to do with the complexity of the tactical and technological problems that the navy had to solve just in projecting naval forces across the distances of the Pacific. Thus, the time, funding, and resources were simply not available to do the experimentation required for building effective amphibious forces. But also important was the fact that the full complexity of amphibious operations could not emerge until US forces began storming positions held by the Japanese. Nevertheless, what the navy and marine corps managed to do with scarce resources in the interwar period proved sufficient to establish a solid doctrinal base from which the US could launch not only the great island hopping campaigns of the Second World War in the Pacific, but also the great invasions of North Africa, Sicily, Southern Italy, and Normandy in the Mediterranean and European theaters of operation.

War gaming, innovation, and the navy's culture

War gaming entered the picture as a particularly important factor in terms of the navy's development during the 1920s, to a degree which had not been the

---

[39] Ibid., p. 78.
[40] Craig C. Felker, *Testing American Sea Power: U.S. Navy Strategic Exercises, 1923–1940* (College Station, TX, 2007), p. 109.

case before the First World War. One of the seminal events in that development, as well as the navy's overall innovation in the interwar period, occurred
when Admiral William Sims returned from Europe, where he had served as
the commanding officer of America's naval forces against Germany. As his
last assignment in the navy before retirement, he chose to return to the
presidency of the Naval War College, which he had left in 1916. Sims was a
particularly strong advocate of the importance of professional military education for the navy. In a conversation with the secretary of the navy, he
commented,

when you go back to Washington at least put the [war college] on the plane of a
battleship [in terms of funding]; establish a complement for the War College, and
then write an order to the Chief of the Bureau of Navigation, and tell him to keep the
War College filled, even if he has to diminish some unimportant ship's complement.[41]

While Sims' decision to return to the war college seems somewhat strange
in terms of how today's navy views Newport, the Naval War College enjoyed
an extraordinarily high reputation throughout the interwar period. Future
Admiral Raymond Spruance not only was a student at the war college, but
also served two tours on the faculty of that institution without damaging his
reputation in the rest of the navy or his career prospects.[42] Significantly,
Spruance was not an exception. Future Admirals Joseph Reeves, Richard
L. Connolly, and Richmond Kelly Turner, among others, all served tours
on the faculty.[43] Service on the faculty not only furthered officers' understanding of the tactical, operational, and strategic problems the navy was
facing, but it also appears to have enhanced promotion possibilities. Indeed,
as a four-star admiral, Spruance, like Sims, chose to return from the Pacific to
take up the presidency of the Naval War College at the end of his career
commanding Fifth Fleet in the last years of the war. Nimitz himself indicated
in a postwar address to the students of the Naval War College in 1960 that the
war plans he had inherited at the start of the Second World War had included
the shutting down of educational activities at Newport. Instead he had made
considerable efforts not only to keep the war college open, but also to increase
its intake of officers.[44]

Sims' term as the president of the war college (1919–1922) was crucial
for both the college and the navy in developing new concepts and understanding of the potential impact of new technologies such as aircraft and

---

[41] Quoted in John H. Mauer, "The Giants of the Naval War College," *Naval War College
Review*, September–October 1984.
[42] In the late 1990s the author checked the bios of the navy's admirals to discover that nearly
half of that group of officers had attended neither a staff nor war college.
[43] Interestingly, unlike the Army War College and the Command and Staff College, the Navy
War College remained open throughout the war under one of the most distinguished prewar
admirals: Admiral Edward C. Kalbfus.
[44] Chester Nimitz, "An Address," Naval War College, 10 October 1960, Naval War College
Library.

submarines. Sims had been a maverick in the navy's officer corps before the First World War. As a lieutenant commander, unhappy with the navy's unwillingness to reform its inadequate gunnery system, he had written directly to President Theodore Roosevelt about the need to change his service's gunnery practices. The resulting pressure from the top had then forced the navy to alter those practices. Nevertheless, Sims' career did not suffer for his temerity, largely, one suspects, because he was right and his innovations substantially improved the fleet's accuracy. The protection of friends in high places undoubtedly helped.

Almost immediately upon arriving at his new assignment, Sims made clear his feelings on the future of the battleship. He argued that the navy should "arrest the building of great battleships and put money into the development of new devices and not wait to see what other countries were doing." Moreover, he argued "that an airplane carrier of thirty-five knots and carrying one hundred planes … is in reality a capital ship of much greater offensive power than any battleship."[45] As president, Sims encouraged the development of a series of strategic and tactical war games that examined the implications of technological change on future conflicts involving naval forces. The insights provided by the war games played a major role in the naval developments. Sims himself pushed students to examine a wide variety of tactical and technical possibilities in a realistic fashion. His intellectual approach was of crucial importance both to the incorporation of new technologies as well as in its impact on the navy's culture.

In 1965, Nimitz best caught the contribution that the war games and his study at the war college had made to the victory over the Japanese in a comment he made shortly before his death.

The enemy of our war games was always – Japan – and the courses were so thorough that after the start of World War II – nothing that happened in the Pacific was strange or unexpected. Each student was required to plan logistic support for an advance across the Pacific – and we were well prepared for the fantastic logistic efforts required to support the operations of war. The need for mobile replenishment at sea was foreseen – and [then] practiced by me in 1937...[46]

During the three years that Sims was at the college, he oversaw the creation of two important kinds of games: strategic games that examined the complexities of a war over the huge distances of the Pacific, and tactical board games that examined the potential interplay of fleets in combat. The latter, of course, could not fully explore the "mayhem of the close-in clashes of the Solomons where forces rapidly approached each other at point blank ranges, and ships combat lives were measured in minutes."[47] Nevertheless, the tactical war

---

[45] Quoted in Mauer, "The Giants of the Naval War College."
[46] Quoted in Kuehn, *Agents of Innovation*, p. 162.
[47] Peter P. Perla, *The Art of Wargaming: A Guide for Professionals and Hobbyists* (Annapolis, MD, 1990), p. 76.

games did suggest to the participants that fundamental reality of war that American forces have once again discovered in Iraq and Afghanistan: "the enemy gets a vote."

As one commentator on war gaming notes, Sims and the war games at Newport "contributed substantially to the development of ideas about how to employ the aircraft carrier."[48] What the games indicated was that the tactical framework of carrier operations needed to differ fundamentally from the dynamics of fleet gunfire engagements. Simply stated, the attrition equations developed by Frederick Lanchester best represented the relationship in gunnery duels between red and blue surface fleets. But the tactical games at Newport indicated that what mattered in terms of aircraft launched from carriers would be pulses of air power. Thus, the true measure of effectiveness would be how many aircraft carriers could launch how quickly in a single pulse from their decks, and then, after the completion of their strike, recover and rearm those aircraft successfully in preparation for another strike.

Long after Sims had left the presidency of the war college, the navy continued to feel the influence of his emphasis on war gaming. In 1931's war gaming, Newport's students and faculty tested out a concept for a light carrier/cruiser combination that the Navy's General Board was examining in its deliberations. Its report on the war games suggested that "The CLV is a decided menace to any battle cruiser (or even battleship) that might be deployed in connection with enemy scouting forces."[49] Not surprisingly, not all elements of the navy were happy with the war college's report, but it added to a general consensus, even among the battleship admirals, that air power was going to prove a crucial enabler, if not for attacking the enemy fleet, at least for reconnaissance as to the enemy's location.

What is particularly interesting about both the fleet exercises and war games at Newport was the rigor and honesty with which the participants carried them out. There was no school solution, no expected answer toward which the participants and the effort moved.[50] Here one is clearly dealing with the influence of the navy's culture as well as the success of individuals. Over the past three decades, while historians have become increasingly interested in the processes and problems associated with the effectiveness of military institutions, the various aspects of military culture have remained largely unexamined.[51] As this author and Barry Watts stated in another essay written for Andrew Marshall, "military organizations which have trouble being scrupulous about empirical data in peacetime may have the same

[48] Ibid., p. 70.   [49] Quoted in Kuehn, *Agents of Innovation*, p. 117.
[50] The naval officers of the interwar period would have been appalled by the MILLENNIUM CHALLENGE exercise of 1999, run by Joint Forces Command, where the disastrous results for Blue were immediately overturned, because the results carried with them uncomfortable implications for the current force structure of the United States.
[51] Millett and Murray, eds., *Military Effectiveness*, 3 vols.

trouble in time of war."[52] That ability to evaluate honestly the internal and external environment lies at the heart of all successful military cultures.

In this case, the navy's culture during the interwar period appears to have been open to clear, honest evaluations of its war games, its fleet exercises, and the training and education of its officers. Along these lines, the fleet exercises present a particularly useful example of the willingness to grapple with what the evidence actually indicated, rather than what senior officers hoped it would show. As Admiral James Richardson, CINCUS 1940–1941, commented after the war,[53] "The battles of the Fleet Problems were vigorously refought from the speaker's platform."[54] For example, in his critique of the 1924 fleet exercises, Vice Admiral Newton McCully not only criticized his own performance in not preparing for mine warfare, but also introduced the possibility that the enemy might utilize special operations as something to which the navy had to pay much closer attention.[55]

What is particularly interesting is that the navy's leaders did not limit these post-exercise critiques to a few of the more senior officers but, more often than not, included a wide selection of those officers who had been involved in the exercise, including junior officers. For example, the critique of Fleet Problem IX in 1929 took place before 700 officers, while the audience of Fleet Problem XIV totaled more than 1,000 officers.[56] The size of the audience with large numbers of mid-level and junior officers in attendance provided even junior officers with a sense that the navy's senior leadership not only encouraged, but also expected free and vigorous exchange of ideas and concepts among officers of different ranks. The impact was both direct and indirect on the overall culture of the officer corps and significantly influenced the willingness of the navy to incorporate new concepts and technologies into its approach both during the interwar period and after the war had broken out.

With such a large number of officers participating in these critiques, it was difficult, if not impossible, to obfuscate or distort the results to give a slanted picture of what had occurred. One historian of the fleet exercises has recently noted:

The conclusions [of the critiques], which were often quite frank, the lessons learned, and the recommendations usually incorporated excerpts of the individual reports, and at time entire individual reports, of the principal subordinate commanders. This was done even when the reports of subordinate commanders did not agree with the conclusions and recommendations made by CINCUS or the two fleet

---

[52] Watts and Murray, "Military Innovation in Peacetime," in Murray and Millett, eds., *Military Innovation in the Interwar Period*, p. 414.

[53] For obvious reasons King eliminated the title, when he took command of the navy, given the pronunciation of the acronym – "sinkus."

[54] Quoted in Alfred F. Nolfi, *To Train the Fleet for War: The U.S. Navy Fleet Problems* (Newport, RI, 2010), p. 40.

[55] Ibid., p. 64.   [56] Ibid., p. 40.

commanders. The comprehensive fleet problem report was published and widely circulated for study, evaluation, and comment.[57]

Moreover, such was the navy's culture of honesty that senior officers, whose performance in the fleet exercises was sometimes less than optimal, could find themselves the target of scathing criticism not only in front of their peers, but in front of large numbers of junior officers as well. At the end of Fleet Problem VIII (1928), CINCUS, Admiral Henry A. Wiley "devoted ten of the 21 paragraphs of his general comments to often severe criticism of [the] Orange [fleet commander]," Rear Admiral George Day. In contrast, at the same time he praised Blue's "thorough preparation and forceful execution."[58] Unhappy with the critique of how his force had performed, Day attempted to challenge the exercise's fundamental framework. Wiley ended Day's efforts at equivocation with the sharp comment: "Commander, ORANGE is fighting the problem."[59] All of this took place not only before a large audience of naval officers in Hawaii, but also before Major General Fox Connor, one of the most outstanding army officers during the interwar period, and the mentor and tutor of Dwight Eisenhower early in that officer's career.

Significantly, a weak performance in a command position during a major fleet exercise could have immediate effect on an officer's career. Rear Admiral Louis Nolton, commander of the Blue Fleet in Fleet Exercise X, mishandled his force so badly in the opening fleet engagement that he found himself removed from command of the fleet and relegated to serving as an umpire in the second portion of the exercise. Not surprisingly, CINCUS, Admiral William Pratt, severely criticized Nolton for his disposition of his fleet and his tying of his aircraft to protecting the battle line. The chief umpire further criticized Nolton for his failure to use his aircraft to scout ahead for the enemy fleet.[60]

On a number of occasions, the insights of these critiques fed directly back into the lessons and war games at the Naval War College. In fact, the final critique of Fleet Exercise VII in 1927 occurred at Newport before the students and faculty. The insights the critique highlighted were of considerable significance in pushing the navy toward a more realistic understanding of what it needed to emphasize. In spite of the fact that the navy possessed only the slow and inadequate *Langley* before 1929 to represent a carrier force, Admiral Joseph Reeves was already arguing that fleet commanders should receive "complete freedom in employing carrier aircraft."[61] But that was only one of a number of prescient insights highlighted in this single exercise. Among other points that the exercise's critique highlighted were the conclusions that the navy needed more fleet problems and additional light cruisers, while the capabilities of the fleet's submarines needed significant upgrading.

---

[57] Ibid., p. 41.   [58] Ibid., p. 102.   [59] Ibid., p. 309.
[60] Felker, *Testing American Sea Power*, pp. 53–55.   [61] Nofi, *To Train the Fleet*, p. 95.

Significantly, performance in these maneuvers often played a role in the prospects of senior officers for further advancement. In Fleet Exercise XIV, February 1933, Vice Admiral Frank Clark, widely seen as the next CNO (chief of naval operations), did not perform well as the commander of the Black Fleet. The post instead went to Reeves, the most senior aviator in the fleet and perhaps the navy's most innovative officer, who was to render superb service in that post. These exercises, for the most part, suggested which officers would shine under the pressures of war, because all were under considerable pressure. They knew that their performance was being rigorously evaluated by their peers as well as their superiors.

Nevertheless, one should not believe that all of those who ran the navy in the interwar period were brilliant tacticians who understood where the future was going. Even in a navy that valued rigor and intellectual discourse, there were those who took their stance firmly in the past and who displayed no willingness to learn or adapt. In Fleet Exercise XVIII, April–May 1937, the commander of the Black Fleet was Admiral Claude C. Bloch, COMBATFOR (commander battle force). Paying no attention to the air-minded officers on his staff, he kept the carriers tied closely to his battleships, because he believed that the role of aircraft was to provide aerial cover and spot for his battleships. Thus, he had no interest in striking the enemy fleet with his carrier aircraft. Bloch had clearly learned nothing from Nolton's failure seven years earlier. Not surprisingly, Bloch's fleet paid for its admiral's obtuseness. In the judgment of the umpires, the White Fleet mauled Bloch's force, sinking one of his carriers, a light cruiser, and seven destroyers; of the remainder of his fleet, he had two of his battleships, his two other carriers, a heavy and a light cruiser, and a destroyer all considered damaged.

None of this made the slightest impression on the admiral, who argued in the critique that "it is obvious that the decision to retain the carriers with the Main Body was sound."[62] There are also indications that, after the exercise, Bloch forced Vice Admiral Frederick J. Horne to recall a paper he had written urging that the navy emphasize an independent role for carriers. Since the carriers had already served in such a role in previous exercises, Bloch's action was particularly obtuse. But the evidence of the exercises and the follow-on critiques suggest that Bloch's unwillingness to learn from earlier fleet exercises or adapt to changing circumstances were the exception, even among battleship admirals.

Yet, whatever the difficulties that some admirals might have had in adapting to the notion that the free exchange of ideas was an essential part of improving the future capabilities, the navy as a whole encouraged a culture that would prove adaptive and imaginative in facing the problems raised by the war in the Pacific. As one of the navy's premier thinkers

---

[62] His other comments were equally obtuse. See Nofi, *To Train the Fleet*, pp. 223–225.

over the past several decades recently noted about Spruance and his staff under the pressures of war:

As operational commander of hundreds of ships and aircraft, Admiral Raymond A. Spruance had the capacity to distill what he observed – and sometimes felt – into its essence and to focus on the important details by a mental synthesis. He would then charge his staff with comprehensive planning to achieve his purpose. Often the plan would be rent asunder, but it would maintain its "tyranny of purpose" – roughly the mission – as Spruance's staff and commanders adapted to the circumstances.[63]

Spruance's year as a student at the Naval War College and two tours on the faculty were instrumental in honing his native abilities to distill his peacetime experiences into a coherent frame of reference. Once at war, he was then able to form a picture that reflected reality rather than to attempt to force reality to fit his preconceptions.[64]

The imperatives of innovation: Newport and fleet exercises

Inevitably, the implementation of naval strategy depends on the tactical and operational capabilities that the forces executing it have developed in peacetime. This involves the processes of concept development and the methods through which the organization incorporates new technologies into the actual employment of ships and aircraft at sea. More often than not, such efforts represent a complex process. As is true with so much of history, the devil is again in the details. War gaming in the early 1920s at the Naval War College had indicated that pulses of air power off carrier decks would prove to be the determining factor in the carrier battles of the future. But it was one thing to talk about "pulses of air power"; it was another to maximize the number of aircraft in each pulse. Thus, the navy needed to put that insight into practice. In the process of turning insight into real capabilities, the college had a direct role in the development of carrier-deck procedures that would turn aircraft carriers into such effective weapons of war.

The key position in early innovation with the *Langley*, the navy's first carrier, was that of commander, aircraft squadrons, battle force. The officer who held that position would determine the developmental processes on the *Langley*, a collier that the navy had converted to an experimental carrier with limited capabilities. That individual might have lacked the imagination and drive for this crucial task, had the navy's leadership made the wrong appointment. But the position went to Reeves. Interestingly, he had little aviation background other than the fact that he had attended the aviation observer course at Pensacola. But he had been both a student and faculty member at Newport;

---

[63] Captain Wayne P. Hughes, "Clear Purpose, Comprehensive Execution: Raymond Ames Spruance," *Naval War College Review*, Fall 2009.

[64] And served to make him one of the three great naval commanders the US Navy possessed during the Second World War – the other two being King and Nimitz.

in the latter capacity, he had headed the tactics department, where he had become thoroughly familiar with the most advanced thinking, developed in the war games, about the possibilities that air power offered.

With that background, Reeves set about in late 1925 developing deck procedures to increase the *Langley*'s striking power. This involved shortening the takeoff and recovery times for aircraft, creating an effective crash barrier, so that aircraft could land in a continuous stream without the deck crew of the Langley having to move each aircraft separately after landing down to the hanger deck below, and designing trip wires to bring aircraft to a halt as they landed. Within a year, the *Langley* was able to launch an aircraft every 15 seconds and recover an aircraft every 90 seconds. Thus, Reeves was able to increase the usable complement of aircraft the *Langley* carried from one squadron of 14 aircraft to four squadrons of 48 aircraft. The fact that the Royal Navy failed to develop similar deck procedures throughout the entire interwar period suggests how crucial individuals as well as service cultures can prove in pushing forward as well as retarding the processes of innovation. It was Reeves' experiences with the war games at the Naval War College that led him to push so hard to improve the *Langley*'s capabilities to handle greater numbers of aircraft.[65]

The initial problem with understanding how the navy might use carriers had to do with the fact that the *Langley*, as a former collier, was hardly the speediest ship in the fleet. In fact, it was barely able to keep up with the battle line. Nevertheless, in spite of its lack of speed, in its initial exercises it was given the putative capabilities of the aircraft carriers then under construction. The Washington Treaty had allowed the navy to take the hulls of two battle cruisers under construction, the *Lexington* and the *Saratoga*, and convert them into aircraft carriers, which would provide it not only with two very large carriers, but also with ships that were faster than any of the battleships. But they would not be ready until the late 1920s, so the *Langley* had to serve as a test bed. Completion of the carriers in the late 1920s entirely altered the complexion and framework of fleet exercises. In the first fleet exercise in which they operated in January 1929, the *Saratoga*, escorted only by a light cruiser, detached from the main Black Feet and launched a strike that caught the Panama Canal's defenders completely by surprise.[66] In that exercise, the use of the deck park concept along with crash barriers allowed the *Saratoga* to embark an air wing of 110 aircraft and 100 pilots.[67] That capability was the direct result of Reeves' experiments with the *Langley*. Its unintended effect was

---

[65] For the best comparison of the US Navy's and the Royal Navy's considerable differences in the development of carriers and carrier aviation, see Hone et al., *American and British Aircraft Carrier Development*.

[66] The exercise in which the carriers participated was Fleet Problem IX, 23–27 January 1929. Nofi, *To Train the Fleet for War*, pp. 111–112.

[67] Watts and Murray, "Military Innovation in Peacetime," in Murray and Millett, eds., *Military Innovation in the Interwar Period*, p. 402.

that with the large number of aircraft on board carriers, William Moffet, head of the navy's Bureau of Aeronautics, pushed successfully for substantial increases in the training and combat establishment of naval air forces.

Thus, the appearance of the *Lexington* and *Saratoga* represented a major upgrade in naval air power capability. Their employment in fleet exercises helped senior leaders understand the potential of seaborne air power. This was the case among a number of the so-called battleship admirals as well as among aviators. The fleet exercises in the period between 1929 and 1934 were particularly useful in pointing to the possibilities inherent in the independent employment of carriers or carrier task forces. This was useful because tying the carriers to the battle fleet only served to minimize their greater speed, as well as exposing them to chance encounters with enemy surface forces. The exercises also displayed a level of imagination that those in the Pacific in late 1941 could have used. Above all, the fleet exercises reinforced the lessons of the early war games at Newport regarding the importance of getting the first blow in against the enemy's carrier force. The importance of that lesson would appear early in the war, particularly in the Battle of Midway, when attacking dive bombers wrecked three Japanese carriers, the heart of the enemy fleet, as the first pulse of air power off US carriers struck.[68]

The impact of these exercises was particularly clear in the results of Fleet Problem X in 1930, when the Black Fleet's attacking aircraft caught the Blue Fleet's carriers and battleships by surprise. The Blue Fleet commander had tied the *Saratoga* and *Langley* closely to his battle fleet. Dive bombers from the Black Fleet's *Lexington* rendered both carriers *hors de combat*, leaving Black's aircraft free to attack Blue's surface forces with impunity. An early postwar examination of aviation in fleet exercises noted that "the suddenness with which an engagement could be completely reversed by the use of aerial power was brought home to the fleet in no uncertain terms."[69]

A joint army–navy exercise in January 1932 involved a surprise attack by a carrier task force on Oahu that caught the pursuit aircraft of the army air corps napping on the various airfields on the island. Similarly, Fleet Problem XIV in February 1933 began with the Black Fleet, representing Japan, launching carrier raids on the Hawaiian Islands in preparation for a Japanese move against Southeast Asia.[70] This would not be the only occasion on which carrier aircraft would strike bases in the Hawaiian Islands during fleet exercises. In the 1938 Fleet Exercise, a future CNO, Ernest King, would take the carrier *Saratoga* to the northwest of Oahu and launch a surprise attack on the army's Hickam and Wheeler fields, putatively destroying most of their aircraft.

---

[68] US aircraft would sink the fourth Japanese carrier, *Hiryu*, that afternoon.
[69] James M. Grimes, "Aviation in Fleet Exercises, 1911–1939," vol. XVI, *U.S. Naval Administrative Histories of World War II* (Washington, D.C., nd), p. 62.
[70] A number of the fleet exercises gave what happened on 7 December 1941 a distinct air of déjà vu all over again.

A recent history of the navy's fleet exercises points to Fleet Problem IX, January 1929, as the most significant of those conducted during the interwar period.[71] The opposing sides in the exercise were the Blue Fleet, largely consisting of the Atlantic fleet and the *Lexington*, and the Black Fleet, the Pacific Fleet with the *Saratoga*. It was in this exercise that the *Saratoga*, acting independently, snuck within Blue's defenses and launched a surprise attack on the Panama Canal. Subsequent operations in bad weather created a rather bizarre situation in which the two carriers approached closely enough to be able to exchange fire with their 8-inch guns.[72] Nevertheless, so impressed with the carriers were those who wrote up the final report that they devoted half of its pages to discussions about the implications of air power. The CNO, Admiral Charles F. Hughes, even testified to Congress later that year that, on the basis of the exercise, the *Lexington* and *Saratoga* were the "last ships he would remove from the active list."[73]

In the long term, Fleet Problem IX underlined that independent carrier task forces were going to play a significant role in any future conflict. The exercise the following year further confirmed that insight. The Black Fleet commander, with the *Lexington* under his command, followed the path that its sister ship had blazed the year previously. With a longer leash, its dive bombers attacked the Blue Fleet, which possessed both the *Langley* and the *Saratoga*, and caught both carriers by surprise. The umpires ruled that the strike had disabled both carriers and their air power. The fact that Black's battle wagons were then able to use the air superiority the *Lexington*'s dive bombers had achieved to gain an advantage over Blue's battle line drove home the implications of air superiority to virtually everyone. Black had achieved a decisive victory in the exercise. The bottom line was that the carrier force that launched the first blow was going to have a decisive advantage. From this point forward, this was to be a fundamental principle of American carrier doctrine.[74]

But learning from these exercises was not merely a matter of grand tactical experiments during fleet exercises. Often, relatively mundane matters provided important insights into what the fleet was going to need, should it come to a war with Japan. The exercises influenced deeply the navy's logistical structure that would prove so necessary to the sustained effort applied against

---

[71] Nofi, *To Train the Fleet for War*, p. 119.

[72] Underlying the uncertainties involved in the construction of the *Lexington* and the *Saratoga* was the equipping of them with 8-inch guns, apparently in the belief that after their aircraft had completed their scouting duties, the two carriers would join the battle line. That idea disappeared upon their arrival in the fleet. Nevertheless, it was not until 1940 that their 8-inch guns were removed and more appropriate anti-aircraft weaponry added. Affecting the judgment of the ship designers at the time was a belief, quite correct, that the range and capability of the aircraft were still quite limited.

[73] Nofi, *To Train the Fleet for War*, pp. 109–117.

[74] Hone et al., *American and British Aircraft Carrier Development*, p. 50.

the Japanese during the last year-and-a-half of the war. The war games in the last decade of the interwar period steadily lengthened, particularly those of the last five years. The increased length and activity of the exercises in turn underlined the logistical requirements that a fleet in heavy action during an extended campaign would encounter. As early as 1929, the exercises were suggesting that the refueling of ships at sea represented a major problem that the navy was going to have to solve. In Fleet Exercise XVI in 1935, the *Lexington*, executing high-speed operations over a period of five days, had found itself critically short of fuel. During intensive air operations over the course of a day, the *Saratoga* burned up 10 percent of the fuel in its bunkers. By this point, the message was clear: the navy was going to have to figure out how to carry out extensive refueling of carriers at sea, even while they were involved in major fleet operations.[75]

The lengthening of the fleet exercises during the late thirties also raised a number of other important issues. The problem of refueling the remainder of the fleet at sea reached a critical point during this period. Fleet Problem XVII saw the *Lexington* and *Ranger* experimenting with refueling their destroyers, while two of the battleships and a number of their cruisers also refueled their destroyers.[76] These efforts also made clear that the carriers particularly were going to need the capability to refuel at sea from oilers, not only for their own movement, but also to feed the voracious appetite of their aircraft.

The corollary to that insight was that the navy needed to develop the ability to replenish ammunition and sustenance for the crews while on extended operations. Nevertheless, it was not until Fleet Exercise XX that Admiral William Leahy, the CNO, over the objections of Admiral Bloch, ordered that extensive efforts be made to refuel the battleships and carriers while they were underway. Not surprisingly, Nimitz, who had been involved during the First World War in refueling destroyers crossing the Atlantic from an oiler, played the key role in developing the technology and conducting the test program to develop such capabilities.

The General Board: organizing for war

Much of the history written immediately after the Second World War tended to characterize the interwar navy as an organization dominated by the "big gun club," supposedly a hidebound group of battleship admirals, typified by the General Board. Given the costs of the war as well as what appeared to be the lack of readiness of much of the navy for the conflict, such a slant on history is not surprising, but it was unfair nevertheless. It reflected, of course, Monday-morning quarterbacking at its worst. The historians of the immediate postwar period missed the fact that, for those leading and developing the

---

[75] Nofi. *To Train the Fleet for War*, p. 203.   [76] Ibid., p. 214.

navy of the interwar period, the future remained uncertain, while the political and resource constraints on their decision making were considerable.

A recent and compelling history of the General Board has painted a quite different picture of that organization, which suggests that it served as a crucial enabler, transmitting and encouraging the dissemination of new developments, strategic issues, and the design of the fleet. The board was certainly not a collection of troglodytic retired admirals. Rather, its members discussed major issues confronting the navy in a collegial, but forthright fashion. More often than not, it foresaw the fundamental drift of where technology was taking naval power. In this regard, its members understood early on that air power was going to play an important role in the future. How exactly to define that role as well as to understand its future possibilities was a difficult task, *particularly given what was known at the time.*

A further indication of the importance of the General Board was the fact that the navy's personnel system saw service on the board as career enhancing. Thus, a number of major figures in the navy's conduct of operations in the Second World War served as members of the board in the 1930s. King, Turner, and Thomas Kinkaid were all members during this period as mid-level officers. All were aggressive, ambitious officers, who aimed at achieving higher rank. Moreover, the General Board's efforts to wring the maximum out of the paucity of funds various administrations made available to the navy until 1938 resulted in pulling a number of officers from the fleet into its deliberations.

In the case of discussions about the flying-deck cruiser, which attempted to expand the air resources available to the fleet and at the same time increase the number of cruisers in the fleet, the board sought out a wide variety of opinions.[77] The board's deliberations pulled King, Turner, Kinkaid, Mark Mitscher, John Towers, and Leahy in to participate in its discussions.[78] The cruiser design itself underlined the innovative characteristics of the navy's culture, because it included a slightly angled deck in the final design, a concept that the Royal Navy would not introduce until the 1950s and that the US Navy would copy thereafter.[79]

Putting the bits and pieces together: the making of military strategy in the Pacific

The disaster of Pearl Harbor confronted the United States and its navy with the harsh reality that it was going to have to pay a heavy price for the years of easygoing, placatory appeasement that its government had

---

[77] The thinking about light deck carrier/cruisers did not necessarily go for naught. When the navy realized that it was going to receive a sufficient number of light cruisers, it converted a number of the excess hulls into light attack carriers.

[78] Kuehn, *Agents of Innovation*, p. 123.   [79] Ibid., p. 118.

pursued.[80] Nevertheless, the Japanese attack brought in its wake two important advantages. First, it brought the American people wholeheartedly into the war, no matter how long it might take. Thus, the prewar qualms among many navy leaders about whether Americans would support a war long enough to allow the United States to mobilize its industrial strength disappeared in the oil-stained waters of Pearl Harbor. The American people were now in the war to the bitter end, united in a fashion only equaled in the North and the South during the American Civil War.

Secondly, the failure of leadership at Pearl Harbor allowed the president to make two crucial appointments. First, it opened the way for the appointment of a relatively junior admiral, Chester Nimitz, to the top naval position in the Pacific. In every respect, the navy and its educational system had combined with his own native ability to prepare Nimitz for the extraordinary challenges of the Pacific War. The other crucial appointment that Roosevelt made in December 1941 was that of Ernest King, whose appalling personal life as well as his obnoxious personality made him suitable for the highest positions only in the most desperate of times, which was precisely what the period after 7 December represented.[81]

In effect, the Japanese attack and the sinking of much of the battle fleet confronted the navy with no other choice other than the pursuit of a strategy of carefully husbanding its resources and conducting constrained defensive operations, combined with a strategy of attrition against the Japanese. For the next year-and-a-half, until the arrival of the fleet that the Two Ocean Navy Act of 1940 was creating, the navy had to fight a war of improvisation. Thus, for the moment the dream of a great drive through the Central Pacific had to disappear, as it had to defend Midway, Hawaii, and the sea route to Australia. Moreover, the Navy had to defend those crucial strategic areas against an enemy who possessed greater naval forces and, for the time being, considerable superiority in technology and tactics. Thus, until summer 1943, the navy was compelled to fight a defensive war, one which for the most part represented a conflict in which it reacted rather than acted.

The Imperial Japanese Navy, having made the major mistake of attacking Pearl Harbor, then proceeded to ignore US forces except in Guam and the Philippines. Meanwhile, the *Kidō Butai*, the great Japanese carrier force, sailed away into the seas off Southeast Asia and then on into the Indian Ocean for the next six months. That period allowed the Americans the time needed to adapt to the fact they were up against a tenacious and effective opponent. The results showed first in the Battle of the Coral Sea and subsequently at Midway, although the disaster off Savo Island in early August 1942 suggested

---

[80] Churchill accurately described these years in Britain as the "locust years."
[81] For a discussion of King's personality, see Williamson Murray and Allan R. Millett, *Fighting the Second World War* (Cambridge, MA, 2000), pp. 336–337.

that the processes of adaptation had only begun.[82] In terms of its historical impact, Midway was certainly decisive in reversing the tide of the war in the Pacific, but it was not the decisive battle that Mahan and his adherents had predicted in either its finality or tactical form. The opposing fleets never saw each other. Moreover, the Battle of Midway took place over possession of an island, but unlike prewar planning, the Americans found themselves defending rather than attacking.

Success at Midway allowed King and Nimitz to throw the unprepared 1st Marine Division ashore at Guadalcanal.[83] On that island, with the support of marine, navy, and army aircraft flying off Henderson Field, an airstrip largely constructed by the Japanese, the 1st Marine Division was able to put up a stubborn and effective defense.[84] That success rested to a considerable extent on Japanese overconfidence and their contempt for the fighting power of the Americans at sea, in the air, and on land. Midway should have provided a wakeup call for the Japanese, but unlike the publicity that Pearl Harbor received throughout the United States due to the efforts of the US government, in the secretive governmental culture of Imperial Japan, the Imperial Navy not only failed to inform the Japanese Army and society of the disaster, but much of the Japanese Navy itself remained in the dark.

If the Imperial Navy had made serious strategic mistakes in the Midway campaign in understanding its opponent, it proceeded to make even more serious ones in the Guadalcanal–Solomons campaign that followed. Instead of challenging the Americans with the full force of its battle fleet and what was left of the *Kidō Butai*, the Japanese committed their air, naval, and ground forces in dribs and drabs, forces sufficient to push the Americans up against the wall, but never enough to finish them off. The Naval Battle of Guadalcanal, which lasted from 12 through 15 November 1942, saw the Americans commit 24 warships to the fight, of which they lost two anti-aircraft cruisers and nine destroyers sunk, along with one battleship, three cruisers, and two destroyers damaged. In much the same way, as we have seen above, the Gray and Blue Fleets had slugged it out from 10 to 15 May 1934 in Fleet Exercise XV with lessons that prepared the navy to think about the complex problems of logistics, damage control, and battle damage repair.

By the time the battle for the Solomons was over, both sides had exhausted much of their prewar air and naval strength. By early 1943, the US Navy was

---

[82] On the problems involved in adaptation in war see Murray, *Military Adaptation in War*, chs. 1, 2, and 8.

[83] For the best study of the Guadalcanal campaign see the outstanding work by Richard Frank, *Guadalcanal: The Definitive Account* (London/New York, 1995).

[84] Here it is worth noting that the performance of the marines on Guadalcanal was as much about improvisation as about adaptation. Marine amphibious doctrine as developed in the 1930s had focused on seizing islands, not about defending them, and certainly not about defending an airstrip, which in the early fighting on the island was what the marines confronted.

down to a single undamaged carrier, the *Enterprise*. However, while the Japanese were in equally serious straits, the full weight of American industry was about to tip the scales. Beginning in July 1943, an Essex-class carrier with its fully trained air group reached the Pacific every month. By fall 1944, the main battle fleet in the Pacific – either Third or Fifth Fleet depending on whether Admiral Bill Halsey or Spruance was commanding it – was larger than all the rest of the world's navies combined.[85] Interestingly, in spite of the fact that he was not an aviator, Spruance proved to be the most perceptive and effective fleet commander in the war.[86]

During the Marianas campaign, Spruance understood that his primary *strategic* responsibility was to protect the landings, and that he should not take the *operational* risk of pursuing the Japanese carriers. Thus, he kept his fleet and the supporting carriers in position to protect the amphibious forces landing on Kwajalein. While Spruance's aircrews savaged the attacking Japanese aircraft in what became known as the "Marianas turkey shoot," most of the Japanese carriers escaped. However, they were largely useless, having lost virtually all of their aircraft and aircrews. In contrast, at Leyte Gulf, Halsey took the risk of chasing north after the Japanese carriers, leaving San Bernardino Strait open for the main force of Japanese battleships and heavy cruisers to steam through. Only the incompetence of Japanese Admiral Takeo Kurita, who turned away in the face of American escort carriers and destroyers, prevented a disaster from happening to the landing force.

Admittedly, tactical and operational problems still had to be solved, especially in attacking Japanese garrisons, once the navy's high command had decided on launching the Central Pacific drive.[87] Tarawa underlined that assumptions about the effectiveness of naval bombardment before amphibious forces landed were considerably off the mark. The Japanese defenses on Betio were formidable and the four-hour bombardment hardly neutralized the defenders. There were too few amtracs (amphibious tractors), while the analysis of the barrier reef proved inadequate at best. The resulting slaughter of the marines came as a nasty shock to everyone concerned.[88]

---

[85] Here the size of the increased fleet that had begun with the massive wave of construction initiated with the Two Ocean Navy of 1940 allowed the Americans to overwhelm the Japanese with sheer numbers. In comparison to the navy's size in 1940, American industry produced 50 percent additional battleships, 75 percent heavy cruisers, and 400 percent fast carriers. In addition, it produced a number of support vessels that almost beggars imagination and a huge fleet of merchant vessels. Miller, *War Plan Orange*, p. 353.

[86] Aficionados of the Royal Navy might argue that Admiral of the Fleet Andrew Cunningham was as competent as Spruance as a naval commander, given his performance as commander of the Mediterranean fleet against an Italian fleet that was superior at least in numbers in 1940.

[87] King had picked up on the possibilities of a drive across the Central Pacific as early as his experiences at the war college in 1931. Miller, *War Plan Orange*, p. 337.

[88] It should have impacted on the thinking of those planning to execute the landing on the Normandy coast. Despite the efforts of George Marshall, who sent one of his best division commanders from the Pacific theater, Major General Charles "Pete" Corlett, who had led

Thereafter, adaptation quickly took place at the tactical level, but the Americans soon confronted the fact that the Japanese were also adapting.[89] By Okinawa, they were no longer defending the beaches, but instead held much of their force back to defend the southern half of the island, where they inflicted terrible casualties on the attacking marines and soldiers. But it was Nimitz who showed the greatest grasp of what the superiority in military power offered the Americans at the operational level. Thus, over the opposition of his staff and operational commanders, he ordered the jump from Tarawa and the Gilberts to Kwajalein at the far end of the Marshalls. By so doing, Nimitz caught the Japanese by surprise with their defenses largely unprepared. Still, it is worth noting that, as early as 1937, navy planners were already considering the possibility of bypassing Japanese garrisons that were too heavily defended.[90] Meanwhile, the Japanese garrisons, given their logistical isolation, were incapable of supporting ground-based air power, most of which no longer existed. Thus, Japanese forces to the southeast of Kwajalein remained useless drains on manpower, isolated and incapable of affecting the war's course. With the immense superiority of its carrier-based air power, the US Navy was able to leapfrog its amphibious operations with increasing speed toward the Japanese Home Islands.

The landing and campaign in the Philippines did bring about the final defeat of the Imperial Japanese Navy and placed Japan in an absolutely hopeless strategic position. Yet, there is an irony in how the war ended. In spite of the ravaging of its cities, an almost total blockade of its ports and inland water transportation, and the obvious superiority of America's military forces, the Japanese were resolutely prepared to mount a fanatical and murderous defense of the Home Islands. Accordingly, the Americans were prepared to launch a massive landing on Kyushu on 1 November 1945. Only the dropping of the atomic bombs on Hiroshima and Nagasaki prevented the holocaust that would have ensued.[91]

---

the 7th Division in the amphibious landings on Attu and Kwajalein, to Europe to inform the planners about combat experiences in the Pacific, those in Europe had little interest in examining the lessons of that theater. As Bradley commented when briefed on the need for a longer naval bombardment before the landing, "anything that happened in the Pacific was strictly bush league stuff." The near disaster on Omaha Beach was the direct result. Murray and Millett, *A War To Be Won*, p. 419.

[89] For the problems involved in adaptation in war, see: Murray, *Military Adaptation*.
[90] Miller, *War Plan Orange*, p. 351.
[91] Far and away the best study on the ending of the war is Richard Frank's *Downfall* (New York, 1995), which examines the documents, especially the Magic military documents with great care. The result is a compelling argument that without the dropping of the bombs, the Japanese would not have surrendered and whatever the cost to the Americans would have suffered a self-inflicted genocide. For an extension of Frank's arguments in that the dropping of the atomic bombs saved huge numbers of Chinese, Australian, and Southeast Asian lives, see Max Hastings, *Retribution: The Battle for Japan, 1944–1945* (New York, 2009).

Conclusion

In the largest sense, Nimitz was right: the navy did foresee virtually every aspect of the Pacific War that it fought from 1943 through summer 1945. But that war followed a pattern as if the ironic gods of history had taken the kaleidoscope of prewar thinking, planning, concept development, and innovation, given the whole a huge shaking, and then allowed the pieces to play out over the three-and-a-half years of conflict in a fashion quite different from what the leaders and planning staffs of the prewar navy had expected.

Helmut von Moltke, the great Prussian general of the nineteenth century, is reputed to have said that "no plan survives contact with the enemy." If that is true in a tactical sense, it is equally true in a strategic sense. But that does not mean that strategic planning and thinking in interwar periods represents a useless exercise. In fact, such efforts, if done intelligently and honestly, prepare military organizations to think through the actual problems that war brings in its wake. At the very least, it alerts them to the important questions they must address. And unless one asks the pertinent questions, there are no right answers. Above all, for the US Navy, prewar planning suggested how to think about the problems involved in the conduct of military strategy in the vast distances of the Pacific Ocean. But there is a caveat. While prewar planning, thinking, and perceptive innovation may guide, inform, and determine the strategic adaptations that must take place in wartime, there is a negative as well as a positive aspect to this. If a military force and its leaders have failed to prepare themselves and their forces with honesty, imagination, and a willingness to challenge fundamental concepts, then they will pay a dark price in the blood of their sailors, soldiers, marines, and airmen.[92] This is largely because such military organizations will attempt to force reality to fit the assumptions about war they have developed in peacetime, rather than adapt their preconceived notions to the reality they confront.

War is also an activity where individuals play an enormous role in the outcome. One might note the correlation between performance in the last fleet exercises before the United States entered the war and performance of some of its leading officers during the war. Officers like Ernest King, Chester Nimitz, and Richmond Kelly Turner displayed the highest level of competence on staffs or in command, when given the chance in the various fleet

---

[92] For the performance of military services that underlines how disastrous military incompetence can be, the Italians in the Second World War offer a particularly graphic example. Well over 300,000 Italian soldiers, sailors, and airmen died in combat, so the Italian defeats had nothing to do with a lack of courage on the part of those on the sharp end. For the causes of Italian military ineffectiveness see MacGregor Knox, *Mussolini Unleashed, 1939–1941: Politics and Strategy in Fascist Italy's Last War* (Cambridge, 1986); and *Hitler's Italian Allies: Royal Armed Forces: Fascist Regime, and the War of 1940–1943* (Cambridge, 2000).

exercises of the interwar period. Their performance identified them as highly competent to their superiors as well as their contemporaries, while the demanding nature of the exercises prepared them for command in war. Thus, their performance during the war should not have been a surprise to their fellow officers.

However, there is another side to the coin. In Fleet Problem XX in February 1939, Vice Admiral Adolphus Andrews commanded the Black Fleet with the assigned strategic mission of preventing a European Fascist coalition's naval forces from landing a major expeditionary force in the Western Hemisphere against a nation described as Green (most probably Brazil). Should they succeed in doing so, the game's scenario indicated that a coup would take place which would overthrow the pro-American government and replace it with a pro-Fascist dictatorship. Thus, it was clear that the crucially important strategic target had to be the convoy of troopships bringing an invading army, which, if it got through, would have major strategic implications for the security of the United States. However, in what was almost a fanatical adherence to Mahan, Andrews went after the enemy fleet, and both the fleet and the convoy evaded his forces.[93]

Andrews lived up to that less than satisfactory performance in his first and last assignment in the war, as commander of Eastern Sea Frontier, which was supposed to protect the east coast of the United States from U-boat attack. Admittedly, the resources at his disposal were minimal, but Andrews made not the slightest effort to learn from the experiences of the First World War, not to mention the experiences of the Royal Navy during the previous two years of war. Instead, he plaintively recommended to King that "no attempt be made to protect coastwise shipping by a convoy system until an adequate number of suitable vessels are available."[94]

In fact, Andrews' recommendation flew in the face of everything that wartime experience had thus far indicated; and it resulted in a disastrous six-month period of sinkings along the east coast, until King finally replaced Andrews and assumed the task himself along with his other duties. King's presence brought effective leadership to the task. The larger point here is that an effective military organization will eventually bring about the adaptations required in war and usually prevent individuals like Andrews from reaching the highest positions. The Andrewses and

---

[93] The scenario had been designed by the president himself and undoubtedly drew on his extensive knowledge of history. In 1794 Admiral Lord Howe had the strategic mission of intercepting a major French grain convoy protected by what was left of the French Navy. Without that grain, the revolution in Paris might well have collapsed. Howe smashed the French fleet guarding the convoy, but nearly all the merchant ships got through, and the grain saved the revolution and its successor Napoleon to bedevil Europe for the next two decades.

[94] Quoted in Felker, *Testing American Sea Power*, p. 77.

Kimmels were the exception among the officers who led the navy into the cauldron of the war in the Pacific. Nevertheless, every military force will possess such unimaginative officers at the highest levels. The crucial point is that to be militarily effective in a future war, the organizational culture must keep the number of such officers to a minimum. To a considerable extent, the prewar US Navy met that standard in preparing its officer corps for war.

11 US grand strategy in the Second World War

Peter R. Mansoor

The history of American strategic decision making before and during the Second World War is a clear example of first-rate strategy transforming the great power status of a state. In 1935, with United States in the throes of the Depression, the nation's rise to superpower status seemed unlikely. Congress reflected the public's deeply isolationist mood, enacting the first of a series of Neutrality Acts intended to keep the nation out of another European conflict. The US military, other than its navy, did not reflect the nation's latent power. Most Americans neither expected nor desired world power. Yet in the space of just a single decade, this situation had completely altered. By 1945, the United States was one of the world's two acknowledged superpowers. Its powerful armed forces had played a major role in the defeat of the Axis in battles spanning the globe. Its economy was by far and away the most powerful in the world. And American diplomacy in large measure shaped the postwar world – a world the United States would dominate in nearly every major category of power and influence.

These developments did not happen accidentally. They were, rather, the result of foresight and the creation of a successful strategy that guided American actions, from the neutrality of the interwar period to final victory in 1945. The architect was Franklin D. Roosevelt, a skillful politician who understood both domestic constraints and international realities in crafting American strategy. Roosevelt, ably advised by army chief of staff, General George C. Marshall and the other members of the joint chiefs of staff (JCS), skillfully guarded America's neutrality, carefully managed its entry into the Second World War, and deftly shaped the contours of the postwar world – and did so without the massive national security bureaucracy that guides current administrations in their handling of foreign policy and military affairs.

America's isolationism and the relative weakness of other great powers conditioned strategic planning in the United States during the interwar period. Germany lay prostrate after the First World War, internal difficulties consumed the Soviet Union, and Britain and France were unlikely adversaries. Only Japan seemed a potential enemy, but during the 1920s, the Washington Naval Treaties, the first real triumph of arms control in the modern world, significantly reduced the potential of war in the Pacific.

314

Nevertheless, from the panoply of colored plans that US military officers prepared in the interwar period, War Plan Orange emerged as the most convincing, in large part because it focused on a realistic enemy and a known strategic problem. Japanese acquisition of German territories in the Central and Western Pacific after the First World War threatened the American line of communication to the Philippines in the event of war. War Plan Orange, approved in 1924, called for the army to hold Manila Bay, while the navy gathered its strength for a decisive battle in the Western Pacific. The United States would then defeat Japan by destroying its air and naval forces, interdicting its economic lifelines, and blockading the Home Islands.[1]

As Germany again became a serious threat to peace in Europe in the 1930s, US strategic planners faced a period of great uncertainty. The possibility of European intervention in the Western Hemisphere made its defense an important priority and undercut a key assumption underpinning War Plan Orange: that the United States and Japan would fight a war against each other without allies. The Munich crisis of September 1938 spurred the Joint Army–Navy Board to reassess the basis of its strategic plans. It tasked the joint planning committee to revisit the war plans in the event that German and Italian aggression in Europe and Japanese aggression in the Pacific were simultaneously to threaten American national security interests. The planners completed their work in April 1939. Were the United States to face simultaneous threats, they emphasized that US forces should assume the strategic defensive in the Pacific while securing vital positions in the Western Hemisphere, particularly the Panama Canal and the Caribbean. For the first time, the planners highlighted the importance of securing the South Atlantic and the need to coordinate defensive measures with Latin American states. Defense of the Western Hemisphere made practical sense to protect America's critical strategic possessions while mobilizing its armed forces for total war. The planners also recommended the creation of a new series of war plans, in part based on the possibility that the United States would fight the next war with allies. The Joint Board approved the report and in June 1939 ordered the preparation of the Rainbow series of war plans to explore the possibilities inherent in a coalition war.[2]

During the interwar years, continuous planning exercises at the Army War College greatly eased planning for coalition warfare. These developed the basic structure of US strategy between 1934 and 1940: defense of the Western Hemisphere to allow for mobilization of the nation's military power; a coalition war with Britain; defeat of Germany by bombardment and

---

[1] Louis Morton, "Germany First: The Basic Concept of Allied Strategy in World War II," in Kent Roberts Greenfield, ed., *Command Decisions* (Washington, 1960), pp. 14–15. For a complete analysis of the development of War Plan Orange, see Edward S. Miller, *War Plan Orange: The U.S. Strategy to Defeat Japan, 1897–1945* (Annapolis, MD, 2007).

[2] Morton, "Germany First," pp. 21–23.

blockade, followed by massive ground operations in Europe; and destruction of Japanese naval and air power followed by bombardment and blockade and, if necessary, invasion. These were not new concepts developed ad hoc once war began. Many of the participants in these exercises later went on to serve in the War Plans Division or in high-level staff and command positions during the Second World War.[3]

The president was not content to allow the services to plan strategy in a vacuum. On 5 July 1939, Roosevelt transferred the Joint Army–Navy Board and the Joint Army–Navy Munitions Board into the recently established Executive Office of the President, which put the president in a position directly to affect strategic planning. In turn, this enabled the joint board to concern itself with questions of grand strategy, rather than minor issues of inter-service cooperation. The move also placed the president directly in the position of refereeing strategic disputes between the services.[4] Even with this addition to the president's executive office, only a comparative handful of people advised the president on mobilization and war strategy.[5]

As war in Europe approached, the joint planning committee developed five Rainbow Plans to guide American strategy:

(1) Rainbow 1 assumed that the United States would fight alone and initially assume the strategic defensive to protect the Western Hemisphere north of 10 degrees south latitude (the bulge in Brazil). After US forces secured the Atlantic approaches, the navy would concentrate in the Pacific for offensive operations against Japan.

(2) Rainbow 2 assumed that the United States would be allied with Britain and France, but would assume the strategic offensive in the Pacific and limit commitments in Europe.

(3) Rainbow 3 assumed that the United States would fight alone. Upon the outbreak of war, US forces would immediately implement offensive operations in the Pacific against Japan. This plan mirrored War Plan Orange.

(4) Rainbow 4 mirrored Rainbow 1, except that the United States would defend the entire Western Hemisphere due to the collapse of Britain and France.

(5) Rainbow 5 assumed that the United States would be allied with Britain and France. After insuring hemispheric defense, US forces would project into the eastern Atlantic and conduct combined operations on the African

---

[3] Henry G. Gole, *The Road to Rainbow: Army Planning for Global War, 1934–1940* (Annapolis, MD, 2003).

[4] William Emerson, "Franklin Roosevelt as Commander-in-Chief in World War II," *Military Affairs*, Winter, 1958–1959.

[5] For an examination of the formation and growth of the Executive Office of the President from 1939 to 2008, see Harold C. Relyea, "The Executive Office of the President: An Historical Overview," Congressional Research Service, 26 November 2008, http://www.fas.org/sgp/crs/misc/98-606.pdf.

and European continents to defeat Germany and Italy. The United States would assume the strategic defensive in the Pacific until the situation in Europe allowed the transfer of substantial US forces to engage in a strategic offensive against Japan. Rainbow 5 came the closest to mirroring the eventual US strategy in the Second World War.[6]

Given the rapidly changing international situation in the late 1930s, good planning was essential to maintaining strategic flexibility. In the mid 1930s, the most likely scenario envisaged a war between the United States and Japan (Rainbow 3, or War Plan Orange). As Germany rearmed, remilitarized the Rhineland (1936), and occupied Austria (1938), the Sudetenland (1938), and Czechoslovakia (1939), increased caution dictated a more conservative plan (Rainbow 1, which the joint planning committee fleshed out prior to the outbreak of the Second World War). After the outbreak of the Second World War in Europe, Rainbow 2 seemed the most likely possibility. Just ten months later, the collapse of France dictated extreme caution (Rainbow 4). Finally, Britain's survival and Germany's invasion of the Soviet Union eventually led the Western Allies to choose "Germany first" (Rainbow 5) as their strategy.

Roosevelt's policy was to deter threats to vital US national interests while mobilizing American industry to support the Western democracies. Upon the outbreak of war in Europe on 1 September 1939, the president declared US neutrality and established an American security zone in the western Atlantic. He implicitly understood the vital importance of the Atlantic lifeline to the United States, both in terms of securing American trade and in denying a hostile power the ability to threaten the east coast of the United States with air and sea power.[7] The stated purpose of the navy's "neutrality patrol" was to report and track belligerent aircraft, surface ships, and submarines. In practice, the patrol broadcast the locations of German submarines it encountered and thus gave the Royal Navy a hand in defending Atlantic shipping.[8]

Americans broadly supported the administration's use of the navy to protect US neutral rights. Overcoming isolationist sentiment in an effort to support the Western Allies was more difficult. In response to the president's abortive attempt in 1937 to enact a policy calling for the "quarantine" of aggressors, isolationist senators threatened impeachment. Roosevelt lamented to an aide, "It's a terrible thing to look over your shoulder when you are trying to lead – and find no one there."[9] Now that Europe was once again at war, the president found the going somewhat easier. On 21 September 1939, Congress

---

[6] Maurice Matloff and Edwin M. Snell, *Strategic Planning for Coalition Warfare, 1941–1942* (Washington, 1953), pp. 7–8.

[7] Roosevelt had served as assistant secretary of the navy from 1913 to 1920 and was therefore well attuned to the importance of sea power to US security.

[8] B. Mitchell Simpson, III, *Admiral Harold R. Stark: Architect of Victory, 1939–1945* (Columbia, SC, 1989), p. 9.

[9] Doris Kearns Goodwin, *No Ordinary Time: Franklin & Eleanor Roosevelt: The Home Front in World War II* (New York, 1994), p. 22.

approved an adjustment to the Neutrality Acts allowing belligerents to purchase war materiel provided they financed the purchases with cash and transported the goods on their own vessels. In practice, only Britain and France had the foreign exchange reserves to buy war materiel. The Royal Navy's control of the Atlantic sea-lanes also prevented Germany from benefitting from the new policy. "Cash and Carry" was the beginning of a process that would, in time, turn the United States into the "arsenal of democracy."

Deterring Japanese aggression in the Pacific required a careful balancing act, one that ultimately failed. Japan had seized Manchuria in 1931 and since 1937 had been at war with China. With Britain, France, and the Netherlands committed to the war against Germany, their colonial empires in Asia appeared vulnerable. The US Fleet and economic sanctions were Roosevelt's primary tools in moderating Japanese aggression in the Pacific. In April 1940, the fleet sailed to Hawaii for its annual exercises.[10] While the fleet was to return to the West Coast on 9 May, Roosevelt ordered it to remain in Hawaii until further notice to deter Japanese aggression against Western colonial possessions. The fleet commander, Admiral James O. Richardson, complained often and loudly that stationing the fleet at Pearl Harbor would hurt its readiness and do little to deter Japanese aggression. The president was neither convinced nor appreciative of the advice; he relieved Richardson on 1 February 1941 and replaced him with Admiral Husband E. Kimmel.[11]

Roosevelt's relief of Richardson is instructive, for in most cases the president was a good judge of talent. During a meeting on 14 November 1938 in the White House, Roosevelt opined that his goal for American aviation production was 10,000 aircraft per year. The president's unstated objective was not merely to augment the army air corps, but also to produce aircraft with which to arm the British and French.[12] He canvassed the room seeking concurrence. When he came to Marshall, the president said, "Don't you think so, George?"[13] Marshall thought the idea unbalanced and vocally opposed the decision on the basis of its adverse impact on the rest of the rearmament program. As Marshall exited the room, the other attendees wished him well in retirement. But Roosevelt did not sack Marshall; rather, he promoted him to army chief of staff. Marshall accepted the position on the condition that he could speak his mind to the president, regardless of the unpleasant nature

---

[10] On 1 February 1941 the Navy Department abolished the United States Fleet and replaced it with a Pacific Fleet, commanded by Admiral Husband E. Kimmel; an Asiatic Fleet, commanded by Admiral Thomas C. Hart; and an Atlantic Fleet, commanded by Admiral Ernest J. King.

[11] Samuel Eliot Morison, *The Rising Sun in the Pacific, 1931–April 1942* (Boston, MA, 1948), pp. 43–47.

[12] Emerson, "Franklin Roosevelt as Commander-in-Chief," p. 185.

[13] Mark A. Stoler, *George C. Marshall: Soldier-Statesman of the American Century* (Boston, MA, 1989), p. 65.

of the news.[14] Roosevelt concurred; he welcomed candid advice that contradicted his thinking, provided that the advice was sound and that once the president made a decision, he knew the recipient would carry out his orders. In the case of stationing the US Pacific Fleet at Pearl Harbor, Roosevelt made his decision based on the deterrence effect such basing would have on Japanese leaders. Once the president made his decision, he expected Richardson to obey his orders. Richardson's subsequent objections fell on deaf ears; Roosevelt likely sensed that the admiral's argument rested on the basis of peacetime efficiency rather than on the strategic merit of stationing the fleet at Pearl Harbor.[15]

In 1940, the US Fleet enjoyed rough parity with the Imperial Japanese Navy, but this situation would radically change within a few years. Carl Vinson, a congressman from Georgia, was the prime mover of naval expansion. In 1938, after the Washington Treaties limiting naval armaments expired, Vinson sponsored a bill authorizing a 20 percent increase in naval tonnage. When completed, the program navy would possess 227 ships displacing 1,557,480 tons: 18 battleships, 8 aircraft carriers, 46 cruisers, 147 destroyers, and 58 submarines.[16] After the outbreak of war in Europe, Vinson and Chief of Naval Operations Admiral Harold R. Stark collaborated on another bill that would raise the tonnage by a further 25 percent. This increase would insure naval superiority against any single nation, but not against a coalition of powers.[17] A parsimonious Congress trimmed the expansion to 11 percent, but with US shipyards already near capacity, the cut was more apparent than real. On 15 June 1940 Roosevelt signed the bill.

The collapse of France dramatically changed the political equation in Congress. The United States now had to contend with the possibility that Germany would gain control of the French Fleet, and that the Royal Navy would no longer provide a barrier to Nazi expansion into the Western Hemisphere, should Britain sue for peace. On 17 June just two days after Roosevelt had signed the latest naval expansion bill, Vinson introduced a Two-Ocean Navy Act in the House. The bill called for a 70 percent increase in the navy's tonnage, a stunning 1,325,000 tons of new warships: 7 Iowa-class battleships, 7 Essex-class aircraft carriers, 29 cruisers, 115 destroyers, 43 submarines, and 20 auxiliary vessels. Vinson's committee was more than generous. Used to congressional parsimony, Stark then recommended $50 million to expand naval shipyards; the committee tripled this amount. Furthermore, it authorized the navy 4,500 aircraft on 14 June; a day later an aviation expansion bill upped this number to 10,000. Vinson then increased that figure further to 15,000 on the floor of the House as the Two-Ocean Navy

---

[14] Forrest C. Pogue, *George C. Marshall: Education of a General, 1880–1939* (New York, 1963), p. 330. The president was suitably impressed and as a mark of respect never called Marshall by his first name again.
[15] Simpson, *Admiral Harold R. Stark*, p. 60.   [16] Ibid., p. 25.   [17] Ibid., pp. 29–30.

Act underwent debate. The House approved the bill on 22 June, one week after its introduction; Senate passage was nearly as rapid. On 19 July 1940 Roosevelt signed the measure into law.[18]

The Japanese could read congressional legislation as well as the Navy Department. The Two-Ocean Navy Act pressured them to act quickly in the Pacific before the strategic balance tipped hopelessly against the Imperial Navy. By peacetime standards, the additional ships authorized would require six years to build, but the ship-building industry went on a wartime footing after France's fall.[19] By 1943 the strategic naval balance in the Pacific would tip irrevocably in the favor of the United States, a fact known to both American and Japanese naval leaders. In other words, the ships that would win the Pacific War were already on the slips before the Imperial Japanese Fleet dropped the first bomb on Pearl Harbor on 7 December 1941.

The fall of France also sparked the mobilization of American industry and US ground and air forces. In an effort to expand the nation's land forces to 1.4 million men by July 1941, Congress expanded the regular army to 375,000 soldiers and passed legislation activating the organized reserves and national guard for use in defense of the Western Hemisphere. An expanded munitions program aimed at equipping 2 million soldiers by the end of 1941, while the aircraft industry would expand to produce 18,000 planes a year by spring 1942.[20] When Congress passed the Selective Service Act on 16 September, for the first time in American history a peacetime draft would fill the expanded ranks of the army. American leaders did not know it at the time, but they had roughly 18 months in which to mobilize the nation for war. The manifest threat of Nazi expansionism accelerated other changes in US policy as well. Roosevelt used his executive authority to support Britain short of committing the United States as an active belligerent, and he did so against the counsel of his military advisors. On 15 May 1940, Winston Churchill sent his first message as prime minister to Roosevelt. "As you are no doubt aware," Churchill began, "the scene has darkened swiftly." Although the results of the battle for France remained uncertain, he was ready to continue the war alone if necessary. Churchill then pleaded with the president for all manner of aid short of war: the loan of 40–50 older destroyers; the sale of several hundred modern aircraft, anti-aircraft guns, and ammunition; the ability to purchase materiel on credit once Britain had exhausted her foreign exchange reserves; and a US naval presence in Iceland and Singapore to deter German and Japanese adventurism.[21] In the next few months, Roosevelt would act on a number of these proposals.

---

[18] Ibid., pp. 40–42.
[19] Samuel Eliot Morison, *The Battle of the Atlantic, September 1939–May 1943* (Boston, MA, 1947), p. 28.
[20] Richard M. Leighton and Robert W. Coakley, *Global Logistics and Strategy, 1940–1943* (Washington, 1955), p. 29.
[21] Winston S. Churchill, *Their Finest Hour* (Boston, MA, 1949), pp. 24–25.

Roosevelt was intent on supporting Britain as a primary pillar of his defense policy, while trying to convince a reluctant, isolationist public to support further measures short of war. This policy was more than mere Anglophilia; Roosevelt understood that the longer Britain remained in the fight, the more time the United States would have to rearm. Britain had just evacuated most of its army from Dunkirk, but had abandoned nearly all of its arms, ammunition, and equipment. If British forces were to repel a German invasion, they would need war materiel, and fast. Roosevelt determined to give the British at least part of what they needed.

While Roosevelt made his calculations, military planners reevaluated the strategic position of the United States, particularly in the event of the capture of the French and British fleets by the Axis powers. This possibility worried them enough that Marshall and Stark recommended in a memo to the president on 27 June that US forces should assume the strategic defensive in the Pacific, that the nation mobilize its resources to insure hemispheric defense, and that the United States cease material aid to the Allies.[22]

The president, however, rejected his advisors' call for suspending arms shipments to Britain. He believed American industry could meet British needs without jeopardizing rearmament, and that supporting the British in their war against the Axis was in US strategic interests. In early June, the president overruled his secretary of war to declare as "surplus," arms and ammunition the government would sell to a private corporation, which in turn would sell them to Britain to get around the Neutrality Acts. On 11 June 1940, the US government sold 500,000 Enfield rifles with 129 million rounds of ammunition (22 percent of US stockpiles), 80,000 machine guns, 25,000 Browning automatic rifles, 20,000 pistols, 895 75-mm guns with a million rounds of ammunition, and 316 mortars to the US Steel Corporation, which in turn sold the items to the British on the same day for the same price. This bit of subterfuge succeeded in providing crucial equipment to rearm the British in their great time of need. As he signed off on the transfer, Marshall "somewhat righteously observed that he could only define these weapons as surplus after going to church to pray for forgiveness."[23] The grumbling undoubtedly reached the ears of Congress, for, on 28 June, it passed legislation that required the army chief of staff to certify future transfers. Marshall limited shipments the next year on the principle that all equipment was needed to fulfill the army's mobilization plans.[24]

Roosevelt's decision to supply arms to Britain in June 1940 went against the advice of nearly all his advisors. "There was no time in his Presidential career," notes Robert Sherwood, "when he met with so much opposition in his own official family or when his position in the country was less secure."[25]

---

[22] Morton, "Germany First," pp. 29–30.   [23] Kearns Goodwin, *No Ordinary Time*, p. 66.
[24] Leighton and Coakley, *Global Logistics and Strategy, 1940–1943*, pp. 30–34.
[25] Robert E. Sherwood, *Roosevelt and Hopkins: An Intimate History* (New York, 1948), p. 150.

The decision was his alone, but he made it in the belief that Britain's survival would buy time for the United States to rearm. What is even more astonishing is that the president made his decision in an election year with his own job at stake. In a commencement address at the University of Virginia on 10 June, he publicly committed the United States to supplying material aid to the Allies fighting Germany and Italy. The media and the American people reacted favorably to his address.[26] Roosevelt then fired his secretary of war on 20 June and replaced him with Henry Stimson, an internationalist Republican. For navy secretary, Roosevelt chose Frank Knox, Alf Landon's running mate on the Republican ticket in 1936. A master of domestic politics, Roosevelt chose them to counter Republican isolationism in a bipartisan fashion.[27]

The ink was hardly dry on the contract to sell surplus arms when Roosevelt looked for the next opportunity to aid Britain. On 2 September 1940, the president authorized the trade of 50 over-age, but serviceable destroyers in return for 99-year leases on British air and naval bases in the Western Hemisphere. Roosevelt bypassed an isolationist Congress by presenting the destroyer deal, not as a sale (which would have required congressional approval), but as a trade (which did not). Americans approved of the destroyer-for-bases deal as being in the interests of national security.[28] Indeed, the trade was not merely a subterfuge to give more escort vessels to Britain; the United States badly needed bases to protect the Atlantic seaboard and Caribbean approaches to North America. In 1939, the navy was so desperate for airstrips that it leased Pan American Airways' facilities at Trinidad, Bermuda, and St. Lucia.[29]

The activity surrounding the presidential election consumed the administration in fall 1940. After Roosevelt's election for a third term, strategic decision making accelerated. In early November, Stark reengaged Knox and Roosevelt on America's strategic options. Known as the "Plan Dog" memorandum, Stark's study represented the most comprehensive and clear statement of America's strategic options since the beginning of the war. In the view of one of the army's official historians, "perhaps the most important single document in the development of World War II strategy."[30] Plan Dog represented anything but routine staff work. The chief of naval operations was its primary author, although a study at the Naval War College by Captain Richmond Kelly Turner influenced his thinking.[31]

---

[26] Kearns Goodwin, *No Ordinary Time*, pp. 67–69.   [27] Ibid., p. 71.   [28] Ibid., p. 149.
[29] Simpson, *Admiral Harold R. Stark*, p. 10.
[30] Morton, "Germany First," p. 35. Stark's analysis contained four strategic options, labeled A through D. Stark recommended option D, or "Dog" according to the military phonetic alphabet. Since the memo did not contain a subject line, it became known as "Plan Dog."
[31] Frederick D. Parker, "Introducing Purple," in *Pearl Harbor Revisited: United States Navy Communications Intelligence, 1924–1941* (Washington, 1994), p. 29, www.history.navy.mil/books/comint/ComInt-3.html#ComInt-13.

Stark completed the rough draft at home in a long day spent in his study. He then shared the paper with a group of naval planners, engaged in debate, and sharpened its conclusions. After a week, Stark sent the memo to Marshall for review and concurrence to make it a joint army–navy document. The personal involvement of the nation's top two military officers in drafting Plan Dog gave it an authority that would have been lacking in a more routine staff memo. On 13 November, Knox sent the memo to Roosevelt, who read it without comment. Given Roosevelt's recent pledge in the election to keep America out of the war, his silence on the strategic options for a war with the Axis powers was not unusual. But neither did he dismiss the memo outright. His silence gave the services tacit consent to make plans based on its conclusions.[32]

Stark was upfront with his assessment. "If Britain wins decisively against Germany we could win everywhere," Stark concluded, but "if she loses the problem confronting us would be very great; and, while we might not *lose everywhere*, we might, possibly, not *win anywhere*."[33] Stark began the memo by outlining how the United States might find itself at war with one or more members of the Axis coalition, either alone or in alliance with Britain. He then enumerated America's vital national interests: the preservation of the territorial, economic, and ideological integrity of the United States and the Western Hemisphere, the continued existence of the British Empire, and a balance of power in Asia that would protect America's economic and political interests in that area.[34] He warned that the United States could not discount the danger of a British collapse or Axis penetration of Latin America. In Asia, Japan had committed the bulk of its army to the war in China and defense of its border with the Soviet Union, but Japanese aggression against the Netherlands East Indies represented a significant threat. Stark then went on to outline the structure of War Plan Orange and the challenges involved in an offensive across the Central Pacific. Implementing War Plan Orange, in Stark's view, would jeopardize US security interests in the Atlantic and limit the ability to support Britain with arms and materiel.[35]

Stark continued to outline US strategic options were it to fight a war with allies. He understood that if the United States found itself drawn into war with Japan, public opinion might push US forces toward the Pacific anyway: "Thus, what we might originally plan as a limited war with Japan might well become an unlimited war; our entire strength would then be required in the Far East, and little force would remain for eventualities in the Atlantic and for the support of the British Isles."[36] Nevertheless, the United States needed to examine its strategic options in the Atlantic. Stark concluded that a land

[32] Simpson, *Admiral Harold R. Stark*, p. 66.
[33] Harold R. Stark, Memorandum to the Secretary of the Navy, 12 November 1940, Roosevelt Library, http://docs.fdrlibrary.marist.edu/psf/box4/a48b01.html.
[34] Ibid., http://docs.fdrlibrary.marist.edu/psf/box4/a48b03.html.
[35] Ibid., http://docs.fdrlibrary.marist.edu/psf/box4/a48b14.html.
[36] Ibid., http://docs.fdrlibrary.marist.edu/psf/box4/a48b16.html.

offensive would be required to defeat Germany and for this, British manpower was insufficient. The United States would therefore have to send large land and air forces to fight in Europe.[37]

Stark appealed for a comprehensive and rational policy to guide US actions in any future conflict. "With war in prospect," Stark wrote, "I believe our every effort should be directed toward the prosecution of a national policy with mutually supporting diplomatic and military aspects, and having as its guiding feature a determination that any intervention we may undertake shall be such as will ultimately best promote our own national interests."[38] Stark offered four possible courses of action: (a) Defense of the Western Hemisphere coupled with material aid to allies; (b) a major offensive against Japan coupled with a defensive effort in the Atlantic; (c) balanced support of Allied forces in both Europe and in Asia; and (d) a major offensive in conjunction with British forces in the Atlantic coupled with a defensive effort in the Pacific. This option could include a major land offensive on the European continent.

Stark concluded that until war appeared imminent, the United States should follow the course outlined in option a, but if the United States were to enter into the conflict, option d was the "most fruitful" for US interests.[39] In conclusion, Stark recommended that US planners engage in secret staff talks with their British, Canadian, and Dutch counterparts to craft plans and insure unity of effort in a future war involving the United States.[40]

It would be difficult to overstate the impact of the Plan Dog memorandum on US strategy in the Second World War. The Plan Dog memo was the only piece of written strategic guidance that Roosevelt kept in his office during the war.[41] It also crystallized the minds of the joint planning committee on the necessity of defeating Germany first in the event of war. On 21 December, the joint board approved the committee's recommendation to focus US military resources on hemispheric defense, but if the United States entered the war, to remain on the defensive in the Pacific, while focusing its effort in conjunction with the British against Germany and Italy. The guidance went as far as to state that, even if the United States were forced into war against Japan, it should immediately enter the war against Germany and Italy as well.[42]

Roosevelt agreed to convene secret staff talks between American and British planners. In discussions prior to the staff conversations, the president concurred that the United States should limit its commitments in the Pacific. Roosevelt prohibited any naval reinforcement of the Philippines; he even gave the commander of the Asiatic Fleet based in Manila discretionary

---

[37] Ibid., http://docs.fdrlibrary.marist.edu/psf/box4/a48b17.html.
[38] Ibid., http://docs.fdrlibrary.marist.edu/psf/box4/a48b18.html.
[39] Ibid., http://docs.fdrlibrary.marist.edu/psf/box4/a48b24.html.
[40] Ibid., http://docs.fdrlibrary.marist.edu/psf/box4/a48b26.html.
[41] Jim Lacey, *Keep from all Thoughtful Men: How U.S. Economists Won World War II* (Annapolis, MD, 2011), p. 19.
[42] Morton, "Germany First," p. 39.

authority to withdraw in the event of a Japanese attack. The president did not commit to a definitive strategy in the event of war, but he reemphasized his commitment to supporting Britain to the greatest extent possible.[43]

The first Anglo-American staff conversations took place in Washington from 29 January to 29 March 1941. During this period, US and British military planners hammered out the broad contours of Allied strategy for victory in a war that the United States had not yet entered. The resulting agreement, known as ABC-1, established the basic guidelines for Allied strategy in the Second World War. The British and American delegates agreed that, in the event the United States entered the war, defeating Germany would be the primary objective; and that their nations would accomplish this by military action in the Atlantic and European theaters. The future allies had different visions of the proper strategy for the Pacific, however. While they concurred on the strategic defensive against Japan, the British emphasized the importance of Singapore in the defense of India, Australia, and New Zealand, while the Americans had already for all practical purposes ceded the Philippines, Wake Island, and Guam as indefensible.[44]

The future allies agreed to sustain an economic blockade against the Axis powers, subject Germany to aerial attacks, to knock Italy out of the war as early as possible, subject Axis-held areas to raids, and support resistance movements. After securing bases in the Mediterranean and gathering the requisite military forces there and in Britain, the Allies would defeat the *Wehrmacht* in a climactic battle on the European mainland.[45]

Although not a binding agreement, ABC-1 formed the basis for further strategic planning under Rainbow 5. Work on Rainbow 5 had originally begun in May 1940, but had been put on the back burner after the fall of France seemed to invalidate the conditions under which the plan would be implemented. The survival of Britain, the Plan Dog memo, and the Anglo-American staff conversations resurrected Rainbow 5 as the centerpiece of US planning. Work proceeded rapidly, and by 30 April 1941, the army and navy had created a joint document that mirrored the ABC-1 agreement. A supplement to Rainbow 5, AWPD-1, provided the framework for a strategic bombing campaign against Germany. As usual, the president deferred approval of the document, but on the basis that he had not disapproved it, the services began to create specific plans to give substance to the strategy underpinning Rainbow 5.[46]

Plan Dog, ABC-1, and Rainbow 5 resulted in a policy–strategy match that provided direction to US planning and mobilization for war. An official Army historian concludes, "Made before American entry into World War II, in the context of a world threatened by Axis aggression in Europe and Asia, the judgment that Germany must be defeated first stands as the most important single strategic concept of the war."[47]

---

[43] Ibid., p. 40.   [44] Ibid., pp. 42–43.   [45] Ibid., p. 44.   [46] Ibid., pp. 45–47.
[47] Ibid., p. 11.

The best strategy for coalition warfare would do the future allies no good unless Britain could survive in the interim. Despite the measures of the Roosevelt administration to aid Churchill's government, by the end of 1940 Britain had nearly exhausted its foreign exchange assets to pay for war materiel. To solve this dilemma, in December 1940 Roosevelt proposed a system of lend-lease whereby the United States would provide (without payment) arms, ammunition, and materiel to belligerent nations when the president deemed the transfers vital to US defense. He bolstered his case for the legislation with a fireside chat to the American people on 29 December in which for the first time he invoked the image of the United States as the "arsenal of democracy" in support of Allied governments in their fight against Axis tyranny.

Despite the lofty rhetoric, the lend-lease legislation ran into a buzz saw of isolationist opposition in Congress.[48] Even with the manifest threat from Europe becoming clearer, Roosevelt rowed against a strong tide of isolationism in American society. In September 1940 a group of notable figures in American life formed the "America First" Committee, dedicated to keeping the United States out of foreign wars. Roosevelt took his case directly to the American people to educate them against the threat. By the time Congress passed the lend-lease bill on 11 March 1941, support for it among Americans had risen from 50 to 61 percent.[49] That effort represented a major part of the administration's policy throughout the war. During the next four years, the United States would supply a total of $50 billion ($720 billion in 2009 dollars) of war materiel, munitions, trucks, and raw materials to its allies, more than half to Britain.[50]

Roosevelt understood that, in a democracy, it was necessary to shape public opinion, while at the same time understanding just how far ahead of the people a leader could get and still maintain their support. In spring 1941, however, American public opinion was all over the map. A majority supported convoys into war zones to support the British, but four out of five Americans wanted the nation to remain out of the war. Seventy percent felt the United States was already doing enough to support Britain.

Roosevelt recognized that with education he could command a national majority on convoys and even on direct involvement in the war, but he feared that this consensus would quickly vanish if a substantial portion of the people felt that he, rather than a recognized threat to national security, had compelled involvement.[51]

---

[48] Sherwood, *Roosevelt and Hopkins*, pp. 228–229. The first witness before the House Committee on Foreign Affairs to testify against the lend-lease bill was Joseph Kennedy, who had recently resigned as US Ambassador to the United Kingdom over an indiscreet interview with a reporter from the *Boston Globe*.

[49] Kearns Goodwin, *No Ordinary Time*, p. 215.

[50] Leo T. Crowley, "Lend-Lease," in Walter Yust, ed., *10 Eventful Years, 1937–1946* (Chicago, 1947), vol. II, pp. 858–860.

[51] Kearns Goodwin, *No Ordinary Time*, p. 236.

To establish the political basis for a potential war with Nazi Germany, Roosevelt and Churchill met on 9 August 1941 in Newfoundland. After five days of meetings and discussion, they issued a joint statement known to history as the Atlantic Charter. The charter was Wilsonian in conception, a vision of a postwar world in keeping with American's penchant for moralistic foreign policy goals. The eight principles in the statement included a renunciation of territorial gains, the resolution of territorial disputes based on the wishes of those affected, the people's right to choose their government and the restoration of sovereignty to those deprived of it, freedom of trade and equal access to raw materials, economic collaboration with the goal of improving labor standards and advancing social security, a peaceful postwar world that would establish "freedom from fear and want," freedom of navigation on the high seas, and general disarmament of aggressor nations "pending the establishment of a wider and permanent system of general security."[52]

Roosevelt clearly aimed the Atlantic Charter at his domestic constituency. In a speech to Congress on 21 August, the president declared:

Finally, the declaration of principles at this time presents a goal which is worthwhile for our type of civilization to seek. It is so clear cut that it is difficult to oppose in any major particular without automatically admitting a willingness to accept compromise with Nazism; or to agree to a world peace which would give to Nazism domination over large numbers of conquered nations.[53]

One way to view the Atlantic Charter is as part of Roosevelt's continuing assault on American isolationists. Roosevelt likened opposition to the charter to the tacit support of Nazi domination of much of Europe. The president was also intent on influencing the American people and their attitudes toward the support of the Allies fighting Nazi Germany. If America ended up as a combatant, the Allies' legitimate war aims were now in the open for all to see. It was a theme to which the president would return after the United States entered the war in his fireside chat to the American people on Washington's Birthday, 23 February 1942.[54]

The president needed all the domestic political support he could muster. Selective Service was unpopular with the American public, and became more so as its expiration date neared. Draftees did not understand why they served, as the war in Europe seemed remote and unlikely to touch American shores. Roosevelt was loath to risk defeat in Congress by asking for the extension of the draft beyond one year, but Marshall was adamant that the risk to national

---

[52] "Joint Statement by President Roosevelt and Prime Minister Churchill," 14 August 1941, http://avalon.law.yale.edu/wwii/at10.asp.

[53] "President Roosevelt's Message to Congress on the Atlantic Charter," 21 August 1941, http://avalon.law.yale.edu/wwii/atcmess.asp.

[54] Franklin Delano Roosevelt, "Broadcast over a Nationwide and Worldwide Radio Hookup on the Occasion of the 210th Anniversary of George Washington's Birthday," 23 February 1942, www.mhric.org/fdr/chat20.html.

security was too great. The departure of the draftees would tear apart the army. On the final day of the Atlantic conference in August 1941, the House extended the draft by a margin of one vote. Nevertheless, Roosevelt had chalked up yet another victory in preparing America for war.[55]

As hostilities in Europe continued, the Roosevelt administration established policies, often against the advice of American military leaders, which put the United States on a path to war. Roosevelt's strategy aimed at aiding those fighting Germany, while building up US power in the Western Hemisphere, extending America's security zone further east into the Atlantic, and deterring Japanese aggression in the Pacific through sanctions and the forward positioning of the fleet. As the year progressed, Roosevelt ordered the navy to wage an undeclared war against the *Kriegsmarine* in order to protect merchant shipping in the Atlantic Ocean. Lend-lease would do little good if U-boats sank the materiel shipped across the Atlantic. Roosevelt understood the need for the newly created Atlantic Fleet to convoy lend-lease goods to Britain, but refused to move too far ahead of public opinion. The president instead ordered the US security zone pushed further east, while ordering Stark and the commander of the Atlantic Fleet, Admiral Ernest J. King, to begin planning for convoy operations.[56] On 24 April, the navy began observation patrols in a security zone that encompassed Greenland and extended to Iceland and the Azores. The president followed up this action a month later by declaring an "unlimited national emergency."[57] The president had some grounds for concern. On 21 May, a U-boat sank the American freighter *Robin Moor* in the South Atlantic, while the German battleship *Bismarck* and the heavy cruiser *Prinz Eugen* sortied into the North Atlantic. Ironically, the British sank the *Bismarck* on 27 May, the same day Roosevelt made his declaration.

The next step was to include Iceland in America's expanding defensive perimeter. British forces had occupied Iceland in May 1940; in April 1941 the Royal Navy began basing escort vessels at Hvalfjorour to protect convoys transiting the North Atlantic, the same month that US forces occupied Greenland. The British wanted US forces to take over the defense of Iceland to release their forces for use elsewhere. The government of Iceland invited US troops onto the island on 1 July 1941. Roosevelt immediately directed marines to land, followed shortly thereafter by army forces numbering 5,000 troops. Both Stark and Marshall opposed Roosevelt's order to station US forces in Iceland on the grounds of operational efficiency. Neither officer wanted to deploy scarce marine and regular army troops in such a remote location.[58]

[55] Sherwood, *Roosevelt and Hopkins*, pp. 366–367.
[56] Simpson, *Admiral Harold R. Stark*, p. 85.
[57] The nation had been in a "limited national emergency" since September 1939.
[58] Simpson, *Admiral Harold R. Stark*, p. 87. Congressional legislation prohibited the army from deploying draftees outside the Western Hemisphere, so the War Department had to deploy scarce regular army troops to Iceland.

The expansion of the security zone was not a practical solution to protecting lend-lease convoys; for that, naval escorts for convoys were required. Isolationist senators were wary of US ships escorting convoys, which would potentially result in a clash with the *Kriegsmarine* in the Atlantic. Despite the political risk, in a meeting on 9 July 1941, Roosevelt directed Stark and King to arrange for the protection of US convoys plying the waters between North America and Iceland. US planners did not formally schedule other nation's shipping in these convoys, but they could join if they wished. The navy made the convoy schedules known to the British and Canadians; thus, King's forces ended up providing much-needed convoy escort services to the British at a moment when U-boats were heavily taxing the Royal Navy. The arrangement went into effect on 26 July, putting the United States and Germany on a collision course.[59]

Between September and December 1941, the navy fought an undeclared war against the *Kriegsmarine*, while Roosevelt marshaled the American people toward supporting greater security measures short of war. On 4 September 1941, the *USS Greer* made contact with a U-boat, which fired two torpedoes at the destroyer. The *Greer* responded with depth charges. Although the torpedoes missed, the Germans had fired first and without warning. In a radio address on 11 September, Roosevelt labeled the attack an act of piracy and declared that from then on, US vessels would attack Axis warships without warning, if they ventured into the American security zone.[60] Roosevelt's "shoot on sight" order had the practical effect of removing any remaining combat restrictions on the American vessels escorting convoys in the Atlantic.

Another confrontation was not long in coming. On 17 October, a U-boat torpedoed the *USS Kearny* as it escorted convoy SC-48 through the waters of the Atlantic. The crippled destroyer made it back to Iceland for repairs, escorted by the *USS Greer*. Two weeks later, a German attack sank the *USS Reuben James* as it escorted convoy HX-156, resulting in the loss of 115 American sailors. Public attitudes now shifted to support increased action against the U-boats. Roosevelt, not content with merely reading polls and swaying with the wind of public opinion, had successfully turned Americans away from isolationism and toward increased support of the Allies. On 7 November 1941 Congress passed an amendment to the Neutrality Acts that allowed the arming of merchant ships, and on 13 November passed another

---

[59] Ibid., pp. 88–92. The US and Royal Navies developed more precise arrangements at the Atlantic Conference in August. The US Navy coordinated convoys with the Canadian and Royal Navies, which would pick up responsibility for escort south of Argentia (in the case of the Canadian Navy) and at a previously coordinated mid-ocean meeting point, or MOMP (in the case of the Royal Navy). See Ernest J. King, *Fleet Admiral King* (New York, 1952), pp. 343–344.

[60] Morison, *The Battle of the Atlantic*, p. 80. As Morison notes, "Thus ended the embarrassing position for the United States Navy of carrying the responsibility for protecting wide expanses of the North Atlantic, without authority to shoot."

that allowed them to enter war zones. American ships could now convoy lend-lease aid directly to Britain, and do so for much of the journey under navy protection. The question now was how and when the United States would become a formal belligerent.

By late fall 1941, worldwide developments had significantly altered the strategic landscape. Hitler's decision to invade the Soviet Union in June 1941 brought the Soviets into the conflict against Germany. In late summer, following a visit by presidential advisor Harry Hopkins to Moscow, Roosevelt ordered the War Department to develop a plan to aid the Soviet Union. After coordination with the British and the Russians, Roosevelt formally extended lend-lease aid to the Soviet Union on 7 November 1941 by declaring its survival as vital to the defense of the United States.[61]

By late fall 1941, events in Asia had also come to a head. More than a year earlier, on 2 July 1940, in retaliation for the Japanese seizure of northern Indochina, Congress passed (at Roosevelt's urging) legislation that embargoed exports to Japan of machine tools, aviation gasoline, and iron and steel scrap. The embargo had little effect on Japanese behavior. A year later, on 25 July 1941, Japanese forces entered southern Indochina. Roosevelt responded by freezing Japanese assets and extending export restrictions to cover all commodities (including oil); the president again acted against the advice of Marshall and Stark, who understood the decision likely meant war.[62]

To avert hostilities, either the United States would have had to alter its foreign policy or Japan would have had to moderate its expansionist aims in Asia. Neither prospect was "humanly possible."[63] Japan had stockpiled sufficient oil for approximately a year of military operations.[64] The army and navy chiefs knew that their forces were not yet fully prepared for a major war, and that forward-based forces in the Philippines, Guam, and Wake Island were vulnerable to concerted Japanese assaults.[65] The inability of the United States to defend the Philippines was "largely a matter of distance; one could demonstrate the proposition with a map of the Pacific and a pair of dividers."[66] The program to strengthen these forces was far from complete when the Japanese attacked Pearl Harbor on 7 December 1941. The long period of prewar planning and preparations had finally come to an end with a military crisis of the first order.

However, the situation was far from bleak. The Japanese had sunk a number of battleships, but had failed to touch the navy's carriers; the excellent US submarine force was ready for action; and the fleet repair and oil storage facilities on Oahu were untouched. Furthermore, in a year-and-a-half, the

[61] Leighton and Coakley, *Global Logistics and Strategy, 1940–1943*, pp. 99–102.
[62] Matloff and Snell, *Strategic Planning for Coalition Warfare, 1941–1942*, p. 64.
[63] Morison, *The Rising Sun in the Pacific*, p. 63.   [64] Ibid., pp. 63–64.
[65] Matloff and Snell, *Strategic Planning for Coalition Warfare, 1941–1942*, p. 78.
[66] Morison, *The Rising Sun in the Pacific*, p. 149.

fleet carriers and fast battleships authorized by Congress in 1938 and 1940 would begin appearing in force, irrevocably altering the naval balance.[67] In the weeks that followed the Japanese strike, Roosevelt committed the United States to the defense of the Southwest Pacific. The United States would reinforce the Philippines as far as practicable, but War Department planners understood the islands would most likely fall in a matter of months. Nevertheless, the US military put in motion steps to secure the line of communication to Australia and build a base of operations there to support future operations.[68] Finally, the Japanese "sneak attack" filled the American people with a deep resolve for revenge. Overnight, isolationism in the United States disappeared as a political force. Hitler's declaration of war four days later brought America into the war in Europe as an active belligerent and thereby solved the problem of implementing the "Germany first" strategy.

In the weeks after the Japanese attack on Pearl Harbor, the US government was in considerable disarray. Roosevelt relieved Kimmel and Lieutenant General Walter C. Short, the navy and army commanders in Hawaii responsible for the disaster at Pearl Harbor. In March 1942, the president reassigned Stark as commander of US naval forces in Europe. In December 1941, Roosevelt brought in the team that would command US forces in the great conflict to come: Admiral Chester W. Nimitz assumed duties as commander-in-chief, US Pacific Fleet, while the capable but irascible King became commander-in-chief, United States Fleet and, after Stark's reassignment, chief of naval operations. Interestingly, the president kept Marshall and General Henry H. "Hap" Arnold, the chief of the army air forces, in their positions despite some evidence that at least Marshall had not adequately supervised Short's preparations for defending of Hawaii.[69]

In mid December 1941, Churchill and his military commanders crossed the Atlantic for the Arcadia conference with their American counterparts. The Allies confirmed the conclusions of ABC-1 as the initial basis for their strategy.[70] Beyond that basic agreement, Arcadia did little to operationalize the strategy to defeat Germany. The British, haunted by memories of the Great War and desirous to retain their empire, argued for a strategy of "tightening the ring" around Germany through peripheral operations, particularly in the Mediterranean. American military leaders doubted such operations could defeat the *Wehrmacht*, but given the lack of planning for an alternative approach, agreed in principle for the moment to a strategy of limited operations. In the near term, the Americans agreed with British proposals to secure the Atlantic sea-lanes, prosecute operations in Egypt and

---

[67] On 7 December 1941 the US Navy possessed seven fleet carriers and one escort carrier; by the end of 1943 it would possess 50 carriers of both types, to include fleet carriers of the new Essex class.
[68] Matloff and Snell, *Strategic Planning for Coalition Warfare, 1941–1942*, pp. 87–88.
[69] Ray S. Cline, *Washington Command Post: The Operations Division* (Washington, 1951), p. 78.
[70] Matloff and Snell, *Strategic Planning for Coalition Warfare, 1941–1942*, p. 99.

332 *Peter R. Mansoor*

Libya, support the Soviet Union with arms and supplies, conduct a strategic bombing campaign against the German homeland, and encourage resistance movements throughout occupied Europe.[71]

What exactly the Allies would do after marshaling their military strength was an issue of much contention. The American people (not to mention their navy) clamored for revenge against Japan, and Roosevelt struggled to contain this emotional response to the attack on Pearl Harbor. The British raised the possibility of an invasion of North Africa, but US military leaders objected to the operation as a diversion motivated by British political goals that would do little to defeat Germany. Domestic political concerns were on Roosevelt's mind; he stated that it was "very important to morale, to give this country a feeling that they are in the war ... to have American troops somewhere in active fighting across the Atlantic."[72] The conference ended without a decision on invading North Africa, although the British supported the operation, which also clearly intrigued the president.

At Arcadia, American and British leaders also established the combined chiefs of staff as a coordinating mechanism to distribute military resources and map Allied strategy. The base of the combined chiefs of staff would be in Washington, unless the principals traveled to one of the eight wartime conferences held among the Allies outside of Washington after the US entry into the war. The formation of the combined chiefs of staff required US military leaders to meet to coordinate American policy and strategy. For this purpose, the old coordinating mechanism of the joint board was clearly insufficient. The first meeting of the US joint chiefs of staff was held on 9 February 1942. The group consisted of Marshall, Arnold, and Stark (until his departure to London, after which King took his place). In July 1942, Roosevelt appointed Admiral William D. Leahy as chief of staff to the president, and he became the group's de facto chairman. The US joint chiefs of staff operated without formal congressional charter, which allowed Roosevelt flexibility in assigning their duties.[73] The joint chiefs of staff formed a joint planning staff to correspond with the British joint planners; together, they constituted the combined staff planners, responsible to the combined chiefs of staff. The system did not mature until 1943; until then, most American planning occurred in the War and Navy Departments and was coordinated outside of official joint channels.[74]

The crisis brought on by the Japanese offensives in the Pacific resulted in the bulk of US Army troops and aircraft being sent to Hawaii, Australia, New Caledonia, and other islands in the South Pacific early in 1942. Failure

[71] Allan R. Millett and Peter Maslowski, *For the Common Defense: A Military History of the United States of America* (New York, 1994), pp. 424–425.
[72] Matloff and Snell, *Strategic Planning for Coalition Warfare, 1941–1942*, pp. 104–105.
[73] King, *Fleet Admiral King*, pp. 366–367.
[74] Gordon A. Harrison, *Cross-Channel Attack* (Washington, 1951), p. 5.

to defend the line of communication from Hawaii to Australia and the bases that protected them could result in the expansion of the zone of Japanese control. Throughout most of 1942, therefore, "Germany first" was a strategy in name only. Brigadier General Dwight Eisenhower, serving on the War Department's operations staff, summed up the army's frustration in his diary entry of 22 January 1942,

We've got to go to Europe and fight – and we've got to quit wasting resources all over the world – and still worse – wasting time. If we're to keep Russia in, save the Middle East, India and Burma; we've got to begin slugging with air at West Europe; to be followed by a land attack as soon as possible.[75]

The primary obstacle in this regard, according to Eisenhower, was not the British but the US Navy. "One thing that might help win this war is to get someone to shoot King," Eisenhower opined to his diary.[76]

The primary obstacle was not King's strategic concepts, but the paucity of American military resources. On 5 March 1942, King wrote a memo to Roosevelt in which he outlined his ideas for American strategy in the Pacific. Race played a part in his thinking. Australia and New Zealand were "white man's countries" that the United States could not allow to fall to the Japanese "because of the repercussions among the non-white races of the world." The United States had to hold Hawaii, Australia, New Zealand, and the line of communication linking them together across the South Pacific (Samoa, Fiji, New Caledonia, Tonga, New Hebrides, and the Ellice Islands). Once these key points were secure, US forces could begin to drive into the Solomons and the Bismarck Archipelago. These offensives would draw Japanese forces in from elsewhere, and in due course shift the strategic momentum in the Pacific War.[77] The strategy was sound – if the United States could afford the resources to execute it.

Marshall and his advisors were more concerned about coming to grips with the *Wehrmacht*. After the Arcadia conference, Marshall ordered Eisenhower and his staff to prepare a strategic plan to operationalize Rainbow 5. On 1 April, Eisenhower presented his concept, which included a build-up of forces in England (BOLERO) and an invasion of Northwest Europe in 1943 (ROUNDUP). A branch plan, SLEDGEHAMMER, would commit Allied forces to an invasion in 1942 should either a German or Soviet collapse appear imminent. BOLERO was designed to position 1 million men in 48 ground divisions and 5,800 combat aircraft in Britain for a major invasion of Northwest Europe in 1943.[78] The plan in this form lasted just two months. It was first scaled down, and then superseded by other strategic priorities that were a matter of great contention between British and American military leaders.

[75] Matloff and Snell, *Strategic Planning for Coalition Warfare, 1941–1942*, p. 156.
[76] Gole, *The Road to Rainbow*, p. 30.   [77] King, *Fleet Admiral King*, p. 385.
[78] Harrison, *Cross-Channel Attack*, pp. 16–19.

The army's faith in the direct approach, at least for the near term, was misplaced. The key question in 1942 was whether the Soviet Union could survive the next German onslaught once the ground dried in late spring and the *Wehrmacht* resumed offensive operations against the Red Army. Provided the Soviet Union survived, an Allied invasion could wait; if it could not survive, then the limited numbers of forces available to invade the continent of Europe in 1942 would not make a difference anyway. "BOLERO-ROUNDUP was an aberration, a one-front strategy in a multi-front war, a resort to force without finesse, when finesse was most needed to make up for lack of force," notes one historian. "For all the potency of the legend it left behind, its real impact on Allied strategy was slight."[79]

Roosevelt was cognizant of the need to support the Soviets via lend-lease aid and by engaging German forces. "It must be constantly reiterated," the president stated, "that Russian armies are killing more Germans and destroying more Axis materiel than all the twenty-five united nations put together."[80] In June 1942, the president and his advisors were thinking in terms of establishing air superiority over France, followed by an invasion with the limited forces available. The British objected to any operation that would likely end in another withdrawal, such as had already occurred at Dunkirk, Norway, Greece, and Crete. SLEDGEHAMMER would be so limited, they argued, that the 25 German divisions then in France could contain the invasion force without affecting the war on the eastern front. Furthermore, the execution of a limited invasion in 1942 would put at risk the larger operation (ROUNDUP) in 1943. Churchill and the British chiefs of staff offered other alternatives, such as an invasion of Norway to open up the northern route of supply to the Soviet Union or an invasion of North Africa.[81]

As British objections to SLEDGEHAMMER grew, Roosevelt revisited the idea of invading North Africa. The joint chiefs remained cool toward the plan, but they fought a losing battle. On 21 June 1942, in the midst of strategy discussions at the White House, Churchill received word of the fall of Tobruk to Rommel's forces. The British defeat in Libya in summer 1942 put the Suez Canal and the British position in the Middle East at risk. BOLERO was not dead, but it was on life support. Roosevelt and Churchill agreed to plan for operations in Northwest Europe, but stated that offensive action was essential in 1942. If SLEDGEHAMMER was not practical, then the best alternative was GYMNAST, an invasion of North Africa.[82]

Churchill and the British chiefs of staff soon took SLEDGEHAMMER off the table. On 8 July 1942, Churchill wrote to Roosevelt, "No responsible British general, admiral, or air marshal is prepared to recommend

[79] Richard M. Leighton, "OVERLORD Revisited: An Interpretation of American Strategy in the European War, 1942–1944," *American Historical Review*, July 1963, p. 937.

[80] Matloff and Snell, *Strategic Planning for Coalition Warfare, 1941–1942*, p. 221.

[81] Ibid., pp. 234–235.   [82] Harrison, *Cross-Channel Attack*, p. 26.

'Sledgehammer' as a practicable operation in 1942."[83] Churchill made it clear that, for the British, the options were an invasion of either North Africa or Norway, or continued inaction in the Atlantic theater.[84] Marshall and King continued to press for SLEDGEHAMMER, but more as a means of salvaging ROUNDUP for 1943 than because they thought that a cross-Channel attack in 1942 was viable. They and their planners thought in terms of a single, massive offensive into Northwest Europe; they had not yet considered a multi-front war against Germany in both Northwest Europe and the Mediterranean. If the British failed to support BOLERO-ROUNDUP, they argued in a 10 July memo to the president, the United States should shift its main effort to face Japan in the Pacific.[85] For the joint chiefs, the options in Europe were BOLERO and either SLEDGEHAMMER or ROUNDUP, or nothing at all.

Roosevelt was the only person who could overcome the impasse between the British and American strategic conceptions. Roosevelt flatly rejected his military advisors' call to shift the main effort against Japan. A focus on the war in the Pacific would clearly jeopardize "Germany first" – the primary pillar of American strategy. The president instead sent Hopkins, Marshall, and King to London to broker an agreement with the British that would result in American troops engaging in combat somewhere across the Atlantic by the end of 1942. His guidance specifically ruled out a diversion of the American effort to the Pacific, since defeating Japan would not defeat Germany and would make German domination of Europe more likely. To make his point even more clear, the president signed the guidance memo as "Commander-in-Chief," a rarity in his communications. Roosevelt had a clearer view of the strategic imperative driving Allied strategy than his military leaders. He insisted US forces engage in combat against Germany before year's end to forestall public pressure to turn American attention to the Pacific.[86]

With the Americans in disarray, the British position prevailed. The British chiefs of staff argued, reasonably enough, that the Germans had sufficient strength in France to contain an Allied invasion force without drawing strength away from other theaters, while the Allies would have difficulties in sustaining an expeditionary force in France given shortages of logistical units, shipping, and landing craft.[87] Furthermore, the possibility of defeat and another Dunkirk were real. Due to Roosevelt's insistence on action in 1942 and British solidarity, the Americans in the end reluctantly agreed to an invasion of North Africa, now christened Operation TORCH.

Marshall and King held out hope for reconsideration of TORCH and pushed to defer a final decision on the operation until 15 September.

---

[83] Winston Churchill, *The Hinge of Fate* (Boston, MA, 1950), p. 434.   [84] Ibid., p. 435.
[85] Leo J. Meyer, "The Decision to Invade North Africa (TORCH)," in Kent Roberts Greenfield, ed., *Command Decisions*, p. 183.
[86] Sherwood, *Roosevelt and Hopkins*, pp. 603–605.
[87] Meyer, "The Decision to Invade North Africa (TORCH)," p. 182.

To forestall delaying tactics in both Whitehall and the War and Navy Departments, Hopkins urged the president to set a firm date for the execution of the operation, preferably no later than 30 October 1942. Roosevelt concurred and told Hopkins to relay the message to Churchill.[88] Marshall and King feared that TORCH would preclude launching ROUNDUP in 1943. They attempted one last-ditch effort to forestall the North African invasion. They wanted the president to admit that by choosing to undertake TORCH, he was abandoning ROUNDUP. Roosevelt would not be deterred. On 30 July he announced that he had decided "that TORCH would be undertaken at the earliest possible date" and that "he considered that this operation was now our principal objective."[89] BOLERO and ROUNDUP were now on the back burner. Stimson, Marshall, and the War Department planners only grudgingly accepted this reality. Marshall openly believed that TORCH contributed to a defensive strategy of encirclement, but would do little to defeat Germany.[90]

Marshall and his planners were wrong in their assessment of TORCH. The invasion ultimately secured North Africa and opened the shipping lanes in the Mediterranean, thus freeing up nearly 3 million tons of Allied shipping and providing bases from which to execute future operations against the southern European littoral. Although the initial invasion engaged French forces, Hitler's decision to hold onto Tunisia consigned more than a quarter-million German and Italian soldiers to Allied prisoner-of-war camps by the time that the campaign concluded in early May 1943. This was a haul of Axis prisoners that rivaled the Red Army's triumph at Stalingrad, not to mention the Axis aircraft and shipping sacrificed to maintain a toehold in Africa.

British intransigence and Roosevelt's sagacity in forcing TORCH on the US joint chiefs of staff undoubtedly saved the Allies from a disastrous defeat in France. One need look no further than the ill-fated Dieppe raid in August 1942, the US failure at the Battle of Kasserine Pass in February 1943, and the disastrous air battles over Germany in fall 1943 to see that an early invasion would have been a bloody and likely catastrophic affair. Operation TORCH was a godsend to the US Army, which went through difficult but much-needed growing pains in North Africa.[91] Moreover, the Allied command apparatus was much more smoothly functioning and its senior commanders seasoned in the crucible of battle by mid 1944.

The problem for the Allies in 1942 was not the attraction of the Mediterranean, but the pull of the Pacific on US resources. In 1942, the Allies were

[88] Sherwood, *Roosevelt and Hopkins*, pp. 611–612.
[89] Matloff and Snell, *Strategic Planning for Coalition Warfare, 1941–1942*, p. 283.
[90] Ibid., p. 297.
[91] See Peter R. Mansoor, *The GI Offensive in Europe: The Triumph of American Infantry Divisions* (Lawrence, KS, 1999), chp. 4; and Rick Atkinson, *An Army at Dawn: The War in North Africa, 1942–1943* (New York, 2002).

unable to adhere to their commitment to resource the "Germany first" strategy. By the end of the year, nine of the 17 army divisions overseas were in the Pacific, along with nearly a third of the air combat groups. The requirement for service forces to maintain extended lines of communication resulted in the deployment of 346,000 army troops to the Pacific, a total that nearly equaled the 347,000 deployed to the United Kingdom and North Africa.[92]

The navy's victory at Midway in June 1942 created strategic equilibrium in the Pacific and relieved pressure on Roosevelt to accede to the wishes of the American people to place additional emphasis on the war against Japan. To take advantage of the opportunities created by Midway, on 25 June King proposed to Marshall that the 1st Marine Division, then en route to New Zealand, launch an offensive in the Solomons. After debates over a competing army plan and additional haggling over who would command the forces involved, the joint chiefs of staff issued on 2 July a directive for the operation, envisioned as the first stage in a three-phase campaign to seize Rabaul.[93] On 5 July, reconnaissance aircraft located a new Japanese air base on Guadalcanal, which made the pending operation even more critical, as Japanese bombers based there could potentially interdict US lines of communication to Australia. King pressed for the operation to begin on 1 August over the objections of MacArthur and Vice Admiral Robert L. Ghormley, commander of the South Pacific area, who thought the operation premature.

King won the argument, although he agreed to delay the operation by six days to allow for more preparation, as the 1st Marine Division was just arriving in Wellington, New Zealand, and needed time to sort itself out prior to loading on invasion transports.[94] The gamble paid off, as the marines quickly seized Guadalcanal and its vital airstrip from a completely unprepared Japanese garrison, and then grimly held on for several months against ferocious Japanese counterattacks.

Meanwhile, the Japanese seizure of Buna and Gona on the northeast coast of New Guinea convinced General Douglas MacArthur to send Australian troops and the US 32nd Infantry Division across the Owen Stanley Mountains to seize the outposts. The Guadalcanal and New Guinea operations occasioned a five-month battle of attrition in the South and Southwest Pacific, operations that altered the strategic momentum of the war against Japan. The pressing needs of this theater, however, led to ad hoc reinforcement of the effort without a "careful calculation of strategic goals in relation to logistical capabilities."[95] In short, the Pacific war soaked up service troops at a prodigious rate.

---

[92] Matloff and Snell, *Strategic Planning for Coalition Warfare, 1941–1942*, p. 359.

[93] John Miller, Jr., *Guadalcanal: The First Offensive* (Washington, 1949), pp. 11–18.

[94] Ibid., p. 31. The 1st Marine Division's leaders had believed they would receive several months in New Zealand in which to train for future operations. In fact, the unit was immediately committed to combat upon arrival, which makes its victory at Guadalcanal all the more remarkable.

[95] Leighton and Coakley, *Global Logistics and Strategy, 1940–1943*, p. 390.

Part of the problem in the Pacific was the lack of a unified command structure. Although the principle of unity of command is widely recognized, the United States found it difficult to implement in the war against Japan. Naval matters were of primary importance in the Pacific, but the towering figure of MacArthur in Australia made the appointment of a navy admiral as supreme commander problematical. The joint chiefs of staff instead assigned MacArthur as commander of the Southwest Pacific theater and Nimitz as commander of the Pacific Ocean Areas. The army and navy would conduct campaigns in their respective areas and would coordinate on matters of mutual interest, particularly concerning the allocation of air power and naval resources.[96]

Despite the convoluted command arrangements, the limited offensives in the Pacific now played into the hands of War Department planners. They saw three possibilities for continued operations after TORCH: an air offensive against Germany, a cross-Channel assault, or continued operations in the Mediterranean region. Since army planners understood, based on logistical shortfalls, that a large-scale invasion of Northwest Europe would be delayed into 1944, they viewed continued operations in the Mediterranean to clear the shipping lanes to Suez and knock Italy out of the war as a logical follow-on to TORCH. But they also believed these operations to be secondary to the main effort (in the future) of a cross-Channel attack. In the meantime, then, they argued that diversion of forces to the Mediterranean could be matched by similar diversion of forces to fight the Japanese in the Pacific. This logic served as a check on British aspirations for increased support for operations in the Mediterranean, since the US joint chiefs of staff could always respond by sending forces to the Pacific instead.[97] Indeed, King made the most of this leverage in inter-Allied conferences. "King is said to have had his eye on the Pacific. That is his Eastern policy," lamented British Rear Admiral C. E. Lambe. "Occasionally he throws a rock over his shoulder. That is his Western policy."[98]

British and American military leaders debated their strategic concepts again at the Casablanca conference in January 1943. By this point, the Allies understood that a lack of resources limited strategic options, particularly regarding a cross-Channel invasion in 1943. The chief of the British Imperial General Staff, Field Marshal Sir Alan Brooke, noted at Casablanca, "The shortage of shipping was a stranglehold on all offensive operations and unless we could effectively combat the U-boat menace we might not be able to win the war."[99] Use of shipping for lend-lease to the Soviet Union, along with shipping for operations in the Mediterranean and the Pacific, competed

---

[96] Forrest C. Pogue, *George C. Marshall: Organizer of Victory* (New York, 1973), pp. 161–162.
[97] Leighton and Coakley, *Global Logistics and Strategy, 1940–1943*, p. 367.
[98] Pogue, *George C. Marshall: Organizer of Victory*, p. 7.
[99] Harrison, *Cross-Channel Attack*, pp. 39–40.

with Marshall's desire to hoard it for BOLERO-ROUNDUP. Until the Allies won the Battle of the Atlantic, the planners could not answer with precision one of the most basic questions of strategy: what means would be available to execute planned operations? According to the official army history of the logistical effort in the Second World War, through mid 1943 shipping "remained perhaps the most baffling single question mark in the whole logistical equation."[100] Indeed, Marshall's estimate of 48 divisions in England for ROUNDUP in 1943 was a mirage; at Casablanca, Allied leaders understood the potential number to be only half of that figure.[101] Even had enough divisions been amassed for the full execution of BOLERO, lack of landing craft and cargo shipping would have made an invasion in 1943 problematic at best.[102]

Moreover, even were shipping and landing craft available in larger numbers, the munitions and other war materiel necessary to conduct extensive operations in Northwest Europe would not be available until spring 1944. As early as December 1941, War Production Board statistician Stacy May warned that the United States could realize only three-fourths of the Victory Program by September 1943.[103] This stark assessment ruled out an invasion of Northwest Europe in 1943, something that Marshall knew going into the Casablanca conference. In November 1942, JCS planners informed Marshall that the army's supply program would have to be cut by 20 percent due to insufficient industrial capacity.[104] As a result, the army would not possess a sufficient troop basis for an invasion of Northwest Europe until spring 1944.

Simply put, the conditions were not ripe for a cross-Channel attack in 1943. The Battle of the Atlantic had yet to be won and the Allied air forces had yet to achieve air supremacy over the skies of Western Europe. Allied navies achieved the former goal in May 1943, while the latter was not attained until May 1944 when the *Luftwaffe* fighter force finally cracked. The Allies launched the cross-Channel invasion at the right time, despite the protestations of the members of the War Department's operations division, who felt that the United States had made a serious strategic error in not launching ROUNDUP in 1943.[105] Indeed, despite the complaints of Brigadier General Albert C. Wedemeyer that the British got their way at Casablanca because of superior staff work, a cross-Channel invasion in 1943 under any realistic scenario was unlikely to succeed. "In early 1943 it was all too easy to forget how flimsy had been the logistical basis of the original BOLERO-ROUNDUP plans of March and April 1942," note the official historians of the logistical

[100] Leighton and Coakley, *Global Logistics and Strategy, 1940–1943*, p. 712.
[101] Harrison, *Cross-Channel Attack*, p. 37.
[102] Matloff and Snell, *Strategic Planning for Coalition Warfare, 1941–1942*, p. 186.
[103] Lacey, *Keep from all Thoughtful Men*, p. 90.   [104] Ibid., p. 135.
[105] Leighton, "OVERLORD Revisited," pp. 925–927.

effort. "The logistical estimates of the Casablanca planners, it almost immediately appeared, were just as flimsy."[106]

The question at Casablanca, then, was how to best capitalize on the
successful Allied invasion of North Africa. The British argued, with some
justification, that further Mediterranean operations would force the Germans
to disperse their strength to defend a number of strategically important points
such as Sardinia, Sicily, Corsica, Greece, and Italy. By knocking Italy out of
the war, the Allies would also force the Germans to move forces into the
Italian Peninsula. Opening shipping lanes through the Mediterranean to Suez
would economize approximately 225 ships that would otherwise have to
be used on the extended journey around Africa. Arnold saw the advantage
in seizing air bases in southern Italy for use in the strategic bombing offensive
against Germany. Marshall conceded that using troops already in the
Mediterranean for operations there would save on shipping that would otherwise be needed to bring them back to England.[107]

The combined chiefs of staff agreed that, after the Allies cleared the
Germans and Italians out of North Africa, Sicily would be the next objective.
Operation HUSKY would free the Mediterranean shipping lanes, divert
German strength from the eastern front, and pressure Italy to surrender.
The Allies also agreed to execute Operation POINTBLANK, a combined
bomber offensive against Germany, with the aim of achieving "the progressive
destruction and dislocation of the German military, industrial, and economic
system and the undermining of the morale of the German people to a point
where their capacity for armed resistance is fatally weakened."[108] Arnold
and his planners saw the advantages in having one more year of bombing
before the execution of a cross-Channel attack, but only to blast the German
economy to ruin.[109] Allied air leaders did not see the link between strategic
bombing and the attainment of air superiority over Europe at this time.
To begin planning for a cross-Channel invasion, the Allies agreed to establish
a planning staff, led by Lieutenant General Frederick E. Morgan.[110]

At the beginning of the war, US planners, conditioned by the experiences
of the American Expeditionary Forces in the First World War, thought
in terms of a single land campaign against Germany. Only after Casablanca
did they realize that the Mediterranean would remain an active theater of war
until the Allies had defeated Germany and Italy, and that a cross-Channel
invasion would be in addition to, not a replacement for, ongoing operations
elsewhere.[111]

---

[106] Leighton and Coakley, *Global Logistics and Strategy, 1940–1943*, p. 686.
[107] Maurice Matloff, *Strategic Planning for Coalition Warfare, 1943–1944* (Washington, 1959),
pp. 23–25.
[108] Harrison, *Cross-Channel Attack*, p. 45.
[109] Matloff, *Strategic Planning for Coalition Warfare, 1943–1944*, p. 28.
[110] Harrison, *Cross-Channel Attack*, p. 44.
[111] Matloff, *Strategic Planning for Coalition Warfare, 1943–1944*, p. 30.

Once the Allies committed forces to North Africa, subsequent operations to maintain the strategic initiative in the Mediterranean, clear the sea lines of communication to the Suez Canal, crush Italy and its military forces, and pressure German forces in the region followed a logical sequence that in retrospect is still valid. Perhaps the most significant shift in US strategy was the increased effort put into the Pacific in 1943. King wanted to maintain the initiative in the Pacific to insure that the Japanese would not be able to turn their defensive perimeter into an impregnable bastion.[112] Marshall supported King, and in return King supported Marshall in his insistence that a cross-Channel attack should be the top Allied priority. Ironically, the postponement of the invasion of France into 1944 enabled more resources to be put into the Pacific war against Japan. Although the United States was still formally wedded to the "Germany First" strategy, it implemented strategic offensives against both Germany and Japan that were powerful enough to defeat both nations by the end of summer 1945.

The most significant policy decision at Casablanca was Roosevelt's call for unconditional surrender of the Axis powers. Despite the president's later protestation that he announced the policy at a news conference on the spur of the moment, the written record says otherwise. Roosevelt held carefully prepared notes as he spoke, and these notes included a paragraph calling for the unconditional surrender of Germany, Italy, and Japan. Despite his look of surprise at the announcement, Churchill also knew of the policy before Casablanca.[113] The purpose of the policy was clear: to hold the Allies together until the end of the war and insure that German and Japanese leaders could not in the future claim to their people that their armed forces remained undefeated on the battlefield. There would be no *Dolchstosslegende* in this war.[114] For US military planners, unconditional surrender meant a singular focus on the military task of destroying the Axis armed forces. After Casablanca, many of the objectives of forthcoming campaigns fell to US military leaders to resolve in Allied councils.

The US joint chiefs of staff were adamant that limited offensives in the Pacific were necessary to keep the Japanese from consolidating their defensive perimeter. The campaigns in Guadalcanal and New Guinea had caused enormous attrition of Japanese combat power. On 21 March 1943, the joint chiefs approved the isolation of the main Japanese base at Rabaul (Operation CARTWHEEL) and the beginning of a complementary offensive in the Central Pacific, which would begin at Tarawa Atoll in November 1943.[115] These dual offensives would seize advanced bases from which to prosecute

---

[112] Leighton, "OVERLORD Revisited," p. 928.
[113] Gerhard L. Weinberg, *A World at Arms: A Global History of World War II* (New York, 1994), pp. 438–439.
[114] Sherwood, *Roosevelt and Hopkins*, pp. 696–697.
[115] Matloff, *Strategic Planning for Coalition Warfare, 1943–1944*, pp. 31–33; King, *Fleet Admiral King*, p. 434.

the air and naval war against Japan, liberate the Philippines, and position US forces within striking distance of the Japanese homeland.

The Allies met in conference again at the Trident conference in Washington, D.C. (12–25 May 1943) as the North African campaign wound down. They agreed to mount a cross-Channel invasion with a tentative date of 1 May 1944. This agreement masked substantial strategic differences in the British and American conceptions for the campaign in Northwest Europe. The British believed the Allies should undertake such an operation to administer the final blow to a fundamentally weakened *Wehrmacht*. US military leaders, on the other hand, viewed the invasion of Northwest Europe as the primary means of destroying the German armed forces. The British sought a Waterloo rather than a Passchendaele; the Americans looked forward to a campaign along the lines of Grant's 1864–1865 Overland Campaign in Virginia or Pershing's offensive in the Meuse-Argonne region during the First World War.

In the meantime, the Allies would continue to wage the anti-submarine war, prosecute the combined bomber offensive (supplemented by attacks from the Mediterranean once the Allies seized airfields within range of Ploesti and southern Germany), and support lend-lease aid to the Soviet Union. In the Pacific, American forces would mount twin drives across the Central and Southwest Pacific, retake the Aleutian islands of Attu and Kiska, and intensify submarine warfare and carrier raids against Japanese shipping and bases. In the China–Burma–India theater, the Allies would bolster the capacity of General Claire Chennault's Fourteenth Air Force, continue operations to open a land route to China, and prepare plans for an amphibious invasion along the west coast of Burma. In the Mediterranean, they agreed to plan for future operations to eliminate Italy from the war, although only with the forces then in theater, minus four American and three British divisions that the Allies would withdraw and redeploy to England in preparation for a cross-Channel attack.[116]

The successful invasion of Sicily achieved the strategic objectives set forth by the Allies for the campaign: it opened the Mediterranean shipping lanes, forced Germany to divert forces from the eastern front to Italy, and caused Italian resolve to waver.[117] Mussolini's government soon collapsed, an event that opened up further possibilities. At the Quadrant conference in Quebec in August 1943, the combined chiefs of staff authorized Eisenhower to invade the Italian mainland (Operation AVALANCHE), but only with the forces currently in the Mediterranean. These forces would be sufficient to establish air bases in Italy as far north as Rome, seize Sardinia and Corsica, and invade southern France in support of the cross-Channel attack. The Allies would rearm up to 11 French divisions for the campaign, while supporting

---

[116] Matloff, *Strategic Planning for Coalition Warfare, 1943–1944*, pp. 126–145.
[117] After the invasion of Sicily, Hitler called off Operation ZITADELLE, the offensive against the Kursk salient, in order to provide reinforcements for the Mediterranean.

guerilla forces in the Balkans and France. Beyond these objectives, the joint chiefs remained firm that the Allies should apply no more effort in the Mediterranean region. Indeed, they argued that the farther north the Allies advanced in Italy, the easier the German defensive problem would become, as shortened lines of communication and a shorter coastline would require fewer forces for defense. In the view of the joint chiefs, the primary achievement of the conference was the Allied confirmation of the date for the cross-Channel invasion (1 May 1944) and their approval of the tentative plan, now code-named Operation OVERLORD.[118]

At Quebec, the combined chiefs of staff approved the Central Pacific drive from the Gilberts to the Marianas, along with MacArthur's drive up the New Guinea coast and into the Admiralties and Bismarck Archipelago. US forces would neutralize Rabaul and let Japanese forces there wither on the vine. Allied discussions over the Pacific War revolved around access to landing craft more than the availability of ground forces. Brooke and the British chiefs of staff on the whole supported these operations, since they would leave the mass of American ground forces available for employment in Europe.[119]

In fall 1943, further operations in the Mediterranean competed directly with a spring 1944 cross-Channel invasion as alternative priorities for Allied forces. By then, operations in the Mediterranean had largely achieved the stated goals of the campaign. The Allies had cleared North Africa of Axis forces, secured the shipping lanes to Suez, established air bases from which Allied bombers could reach Ploesti and southern Germany, and knocked Italy out of the war. German forces were tied down in the defense of Italy, southern France, and the Balkans. Further offensive operations in Italy would not change these conditions. The question then became, what would be the purpose of continued operations in the Mediterranean in late 1943? As US planners saw the situation, further operations in the Mediterranean at that point would compete directly with preparations for a cross-Channel invasion in 1944.

After summer 1943, Allied strategy in the Mediterranean was anchored to operations in the Italian Peninsula. The US joint chiefs of staff resisted further reinforcement of the Mediterranean theater, which meant that Allied commanders would have to make do with the forces on hand in the region. Aside from the Italian campaign, there were enough divisions to support, at most, one more major operation in the region. From January to May 1944, this was the Anzio beachhead. At Eisenhower's insistence, after the seizure of Rome, the invasion of southern France took priority over other possibilities.

At the Cairo conference (Sextant, 22–26 November 1943), British political and military leaders pressed their American counterparts for continued

[118] Pogue, *George C. Marshall: Organizer of Victory*, pp. 243–248; Matloff, *Strategic Planning for Coalition Warfare, 1943–1944*, pp. 227–229.
[119] Ibid., pp. 255–256.

operations in the Mediterranean theater. Churchill argued (incorrectly
and unsuccessfully) that the Allies could materially assist the Soviets
by continued operations in Italy, giving support to resistance movements
in the Balkans, and through new ventures in the eastern Mediterranean,
beginning with the seizure of the island of Rhodes. The operations in the
eastern Mediterranean would require the retention of landing craft that
would cause a delay in OVERLORD until July 1944.[120] Roosevelt saw
clearly that the Rhodes operation, if executed, would inevitably lead to
British calls for the liberation of Greece.[121] The Americans refused to
commit to a course of action in Cairo but privately remained steadfast;
in their view, OVERLORD was the overwhelming priority for the Allies
in 1944, and they were not about to be talked into postponing it for what
they viewed as the sake of British imperial interests in the Mediterranean
and the Balkans.[122]

The presence of Chiang Kai-shek at Cairo brought into focus Allied strategy on the mainland of Asia. The British wanted to recapture Burma, but
largely on its own to atone for the defeat suffered by its forces in 1942. The
Americans put great stock in opening up a land route to China to turn its vast
manpower reserves into actual combat power to destroy the bulk of the
Imperial Japanese Army on the Asian mainland. However, Chiang Kai-shek
sought to preserve his forces for the coming postwar struggle against the
communists. The Allies could never reconcile these disparate objectives. "In
Eisenhower's command," notes Robert Sherwood, "harmonious and whole-
hearted co-operation was possible because British and American objectives
could be summed up in one word – 'Berlin.' In Southeast Asia, on the other
hand, the British and Americans were fighting two different wars for different
purposes, and the Kuomintang Government of China was fighting a third war
for purposes largely its own."[123]

Marshall emphasized the need to train and equip the Chinese Nationalist
armies for use against Japan and operations in Burma (with Commonwealth,
Chinese, and a few American troops) to open the Burma Road.[124] The joint
chiefs of staff pushed for an invasion of the west coast of Burma (BUCCANEER)
to drive out the Japanese. It was essential, in their view, to keep the Chinese
in the war. Chinese manpower would tie down the bulk of the Imperial
Japanese Army, while China's proximity to Japan provided US bombers
airfields from which to launch attacks against the Japanese Home Islands.[125]

---

[120] Richard M. Leighton, "OVERLORD versus the Mediterranean at the Cairo–Tehran
Conferences," in Kent Roberts Greenfield, ed., *Command Decisions*, pp. 264–265.
[121] Pogue, *George C. Marshall: Organizer of Victory*, p. 310.
[122] Mark A. Stoler, *Allies and Adversaries: The Joint Chiefs of Staff, the Grand Alliance, and U.S. Strategy in World War II* (Chapel Hill, NC, 2000), p. 166.
[123] Sherwood, *Roosevelt and Hopkins*, p. 773.
[124] Matloff, *Strategic Planning for Coalition Warfare, 1943–1944*, pp. 349–350.
[125] William D. Leahy, *I Was There* (New York, 1950), p. 202; King, *Fleet Admiral King*, p. 420.

The British felt (correctly) that the Americans overestimated the China's war effort and potential as a base.[126]

The British chiefs of staff instead proposed diverting landing craft allocated to BUCCANEER to support operations in the Aegean Sea. The US joint chiefs of staff, tired of continued British efforts to expand operations in the Mediterranean, exploded. "Before we finished," the affable Arnold recalled, "it became quite an open talk with everybody throwing his cards on the table, face up." Lieutenant General "Vinegar Joe" Stilwell, the US commander in the China–Burma–India theater, reported the exchange in starker terms: "King almost climbed over the table at Brooke. God, he was mad. I wished he had socked him."[127] American strategists, notes one historian, regarded the Balkans "with something akin to the superstitious dread with which medieval mariners once contemplated the unknown monster-infested reach of the Western Ocean."[128] On 24 November, when Churchill again attempted to convince the chiefs of the desirability of the proposed operation to seize the island of Rhodes, Marshall exclaimed, "Not one American soldier is going to die on [that] goddamned beach."[129]

Less than a week later in Tehran, it was Stalin's turn to weigh in on Allied strategy. The Soviet leader offered to enter the war against Japan after Germany was defeated and then came down decidedly on the side of launching OVERLORD in the spring, supported by a subsidiary invasion through southern France (ANVIL). He also pledged a contemporaneous Soviet offensive in the east to support the cross-Channel invasion.[130] Stalin's views aligned with Roosevelt's, and together they prevailed over Churchill's preference for new ventures in the eastern Mediterranean.[131] The president understood full well that Churchill's designs to enter Europe via the Balkans would antagonize Stalin, who viewed Eastern Europe as within the Soviet sphere of influence. Roosevelt was a realist in this regard; he was willing to cede Soviet influence in Eastern Europe for more important objectives elsewhere.

The Tehran conference was a significant watershed in American military policy during the war. Stalin's insistence on a cross-Channel invasion in May 1944 resulted in the Allied designation of OVERLORD and its subsidiary operation, ANVIL, as the supreme operations for 1944 – not just in Europe,

[126] Matloff, *Strategic Planning for Coalition Warfare, 1943–1944*, p. 356.
[127] Pogue, *George C. Marshall: Organizer of Victory*, p. 305. Known to his colleagues less than affectionately as "Blowtorch," King had a well-deserved reputation for his vicious temper. He hardly cared. Ibid., p. 7.
[128] Leighton, "OVERLORD Revisited," p. 932.   [129] Ibid., p. 307.
[130] Herbert Feis, *Churchill–Roosevelt–Stalin: The War They Waged and the Peace They Sought* (Princeton, NJ, 1957), p. 263.
[131] The British left Tehran still convinced that an operation against the island of Rhodes was possible, but Turkish demands for excessive military aid soon convinced Churchill to abandon his plans in the Aegean.

but worldwide.[132] For two years, the Pacific war had drawn nearly as many resources as the war in Europe. The Allies would finally support the "Germany first" strategy with ample resources. The British peripheral strategy was all but dead, replaced by operations designed to engage and destroy the *Wehrmacht* in the heart of Northwest Europe. OVERLORD would take priority, with ANVIL as a supporting operation. Operations in Italy and elsewhere in the Mediterranean would continue, but only with the resources already allocated to the theater.[133] The American strategy of defeating the *Wehrmacht* in a direct approach in Northwest Europe would be put to the test.[134]

The limiting factor in the strategy of the Western Allies in 1944 was the shortage of landing craft, particularly Landing Ship, Tanks (LSTs). In November 1943, during the Tehran conference, there were fewer than 300 LSTs to service the requirements of the Mediterranean theater, the Pacific theaters, and a cross-Channel invasion of Northwest Europe.[135] Early in January 1944, Field Marshal Bernard L. Montgomery and Eisenhower revised the OVERLORD plan to put five divisions ashore by sea on D-Day, along with three divisions to be dropped by parachute and glider. This decision required additional landing craft to support the operation. Something had to give. In the end, Roosevelt resolved the issue (again overruling the joint chiefs) by canceling BUCCANEER. King agreed to divert some landing craft production from the Pacific to the European theater, while Eisenhower eventually decided to make OVERLORD and ANVIL sequential rather than simultaneous operations.[136]

The successful execution of OVERLORD put in place the endgame for US strategy in Europe. The final decision was whether or not to proceed

[132] Matloff, *Strategic Planning for Coalition Warfare, 1943–1944*, p. 378.

[133] Shortly before Christmas 1943, Churchill revived a proposal for an amphibious turning movement around German lines in southern Italy at Anzio (Operation SHINGLE). He appealed to Roosevelt to allow a three-week delay in the movement of landing craft from the Mediterranean to England to support the operation. Roosevelt concurred, but in light of promises made to Stalin at Tehran, made it clear that operations in the Mediterranean could not be allowed to delay OVERLORD or ANVIL. Pogue, *George C. Marshall: Organizer of Victory*, p. 330.

[134] Five days after the conclusion of the Tehran conference, Roosevelt named Eisenhower to lead the allied forces in OVERLORD. Knowing that Marshall expected to lead the invasion force, Roosevelt told him, "I feel I could not sleep at night with you out of the country." Sherwood, *Roosevelt and Hopkins*, p. 803.

[135] Leighton, "OVERLORD Versus the Mediterranean at the Cairo–Tehran Conferences," p. 259. At Tehran Marshall told Soviet Marshal Kliment Voroshilov:

My military education and experience in the First World War has all been based on roads, rivers, and railroads. During the last two years, however, I have been acquiring an education based on oceans and I've had to learn all over again. Prior to the present war I never heard of any landing-craft except a rubber boat. Now I think about little else.

Sherwood, *Roosevelt and Hopkins*, p. 784.

[136] Harrison, *Cross-Channel Attack*, pp. 165–173.

with the invasion of southern France. Churchill and the British chiefs of staff opposed an American–French invasion, preferring instead a continued offensive in Italy and operations in the Balkans. The US joint chiefs of staff left the decision largely in Eisenhower's hands. Eisenhower remained firm. He valued ANVIL as a means to secure another port through which to pour men and materiel, to open up another avenue of advance to Germany, and as a conduit for support to the Maquis.[137] Eisenhower was correct on all three counts.[138] Moreover, ANVIL's opening up of the Rhone River Valley to Allied logistics proved crucial to supporting the western front on the German frontier until the Canadians finally opened up the Scheldt and Antwerp in late fall.

The final two wartime conferences at Yalta (4–11 February 1945) and Potsdam (17 July–2 August 1945) established the political contours of the postwar world. At Yalta, Roosevelt (with a *proforma* nod in a "Declaration of Liberated Europe" to the principles of the Atlantic Charter) continued to bend to Stalin's demands for what amounted to a free hand for the Soviets to dominate Eastern Europe in return for cooperation in the war against Japan, an orderly occupation of Germany, and Soviet participation in the United Nations.[139] Churchill's postwar criticism that the United States and Britain should have opposed Soviet aggrandizement in the region ignores the fact that, when the leaders met in the Crimea, the Red Army was poised on the Oder River, only 43 miles from Berlin, while Allied forces had just finished defeating the *Wehrmacht* in the Ardennes. The Western leaders were in no position to make demands on Stalin. At Potsdam, President Harry S. Truman and Prime Minister Clement Attlee saw more clearly the extent of Stalin's duplicity in honoring the Yalta agreements, but there was little they could do to budge the Soviet leader given the strength of the Red Army in Europe. The outlines of the Cold War were beginning to take shape.

The final strategic decisions in the Pacific were not so clear. Belatedly, Marshall and his planners came to the conclusion that their desire to use Chinese troops and bases as a major prong in the campaign to defeat Japan was little more than wishful thinking. At the second Cairo conference (4–6 December 1943), American military leaders reluctantly acquiesced to the cancellation of major amphibious operations in Burma.[140] The United States would henceforth defeat Japan via the Pacific route.

---

[137] Maurice Matloff, "The ANVIL Decision: Crossroads of Strategy," in Kent Roberts Greenfield, ed., *Command Decisions*, pp. 392–394.

[138] Eisenhower's decision to proceed with ANVIL proved critical to relieving the logistical burden on Allied troops in France caused by the British failure to open the Scheldt Estuary in September 1944, after the British XXX Corps had seized intact the port of Antwerp.

[139] "Protocol of Proceedings of Crimea Conference," 24 March 1945, www.fordham.edu/halsall/mod/1945YALTA.html.

[140] This decision had the beneficial effect of releasing more landing craft for the upcoming Normandy invasion.

King viewed the Marianas as "the key to the western Pacific."[141] Seizure of those islands would provide bases from which to interdict the Japanese lines of communication, provide air bases from which to bomb Japan, and perhaps bring about a decisive battle with the Imperial Japanese Navy. The joint chiefs agreed. In February 1944 planners concluded that 12 groups of B-29 bombers could be based in the Marianas, making an air offensive from China unnecessary. The China–Burma–India theater soaked up enormous numbers of service troops due to the primitive nature of the lines of communication. All supplies had to be flown over the "Hump" to China, which made operations based there incredibly inefficient.[142] To make matters worse, in spring 1944, the Japanese Army in China overran the only airfields from which B-29s could attack Japan. The China–Burma–India theater from this point forward became a backwater of American strategy, important only for tying down much of the Imperial Japanese Army.

On 11–12 March 1944, the joint chiefs decided that the Southwest and Central Pacific drives would converge in the Philippines, but gave priority to the Central Pacific approach in order to seize the key air bases in the Marianas for the commencement of a strategic bombing campaign against Japan.[143] Whether US forces would seize Mindanao or Leyte and then bypass Luzon to seize Formosa was still an open question. Carrier raids on Mindanao from 9 to 14 September 1944 showed the weakness of the Japanese position in the southern Philippines. Admiral William "Bull" Halsey recommended to Nimitz that the initial landings be made on Leyte in the central part of the islands instead. For two days, messages buzzed back and forth across the Pacific to Quebec, where the joint chiefs were attending the Octagon conference. On 14 September, the joint chiefs, MacArthur, and Nimitz agreed to advance the invasion timetable by two months and to invade Leyte on 20 October 1944.[144] King advocated bypassing Luzon in favor of an invasion of Formosa, but the shortage of service forces in the Pacific, the vulnerability of Formosa to Japanese forces across the straits in China, and the Japanese summer offensive in China decided the issue in favor of an invasion of Luzon.[145] MacArthur felt the liberation of Luzon was necessary in any case due to the moral obligation of the United States

---

[141] King, *Fleet Admiral King*, p. 444.
[142] Matloff, *Strategic Planning for Coalition Warfare, 1943–1944*, p. 445. The Ledo Road was not completed until January 1945, much too late to affect the course of the war.
[143] Ibid., pp. 455–459.
[144] King, *Fleet Admiral King*, pp. 571–572.
[145] One of King's reasons for taking Formosa was to open a port on the Chinese coast through which the allies could send war materiel to the Chinese. The Japanese summer offensive, which pushed the Nationalist lines back several hundred miles to the west, made such an arrangement impractical. See Robert Ross Smith, "Luzon Versus Formosa," in *Command Decisions*, Kent Roberts Greenfield, ed., *Command Decisions*, pp. 470–475.

to liberate the Philippine people.[146] US forces in the Central Pacific would instead invade Iwo Jima and Okinawa.[147]

The annihilation of the *Wehrmacht* and the forces of Imperial Japan in the campaigns of 1944–1945 was the result of a carefully crafted grand strategy that established the conditions for total victory over the Axis. The two atomic bombs dropped on Japan – a decision made by Roosevelt's successor, Truman – merely added exclamation marks to an outcome that was already all but certain. The United States and the Soviet Union, reluctant belligerents and unlikely allies, had emerged as the arbiters of global destiny.

Fleet Admiral William Leahy put an appropriate postscript on the conflict when he noted that, on V-J Day, "What the people of the United States, and of the entire world, were celebrating was the definite end of a war which started in 1914, had a temporary adjournment for further preparations from 1918 to 1939, and which had been fought to this successful conclusion for the past six years."[148] By just about any measure, American strategy in the Second World War was astonishingly successful. The United States suffered fewer per capita losses than any other major power that fought the war, and it exited the conflict in better shape than other nations in just about every measure of power and influence.[149] How were America's political and military leaders able to engineer this outcome?

Americans commonly view the Second World War as a conflict in which US political leaders gave the military a great deal of leeway in designing the strategy that defeated the Axis. Nothing could be further from the truth; indeed, political direction was absolutely essential to the successful crafting of strategy before and during the war. Initially, Roosevelt subordinated the readiness of US forces to his program of aid to active belligerents in the war against Germany. If he had agreed to the advice from his military advisors, the United States would have severely curtailed programs such as cash-and-carry and lend-lease, with a detrimental impact on the ability of Britain to remain in the war. After Pearl Harbor, had Roosevelt put the strategic direction of the war in the hands of his generals and admirals, either the United States would have suffered an enormous setback in a premature cross-Channel invasion, or the US main effort would have shifted to the Pacific, with dire ramifications later in the war.[150] The myth that Roosevelt turned over the strategic direction of the war to the joint chiefs is a reflection of the increasing

---

[146] Douglas MacArthur, *Reminiscences* (New York, 1964), pp. 197–198.

[147] Matloff, *Strategic Planning for Coalition Warfare, 1943–1944*, p. 531.

[148] Leahy, *I Was There*, p. 437.

[149] Only the Soviet Union had a larger army, but its air force, navy, and economy were substantially weaker than those of the United States.

[150] Had the United States put its main effort in the Pacific, the war in Europe would have extended into 1946, and may very well have ended with an atomic bomb being dropped on Berlin. The extension of the Holocaust would most likely have resulted in the deaths of millions more Jews, Slavs, Gypsies, and other undesirables of Hitler's new order.

convergence of their views in 1944 and 1945, as opposed to the earlier period in which the president's views were often at odds with those of his generals and admirals.[151]

Roosevelt's quest for options in strategic planning clashed with the desire of military leaders to determine a single course of action that they could then resource and organize in finite detail. The president may have exasperated the joint chiefs with his hesitancy to make decisions, but this seeming indecisiveness masked a deeper need to retain strategic (and political) flexibility. When required, Roosevelt could make quick and decisive decisions – witness his orders in July 1942 that resulted in the adoption of the invasion of North Africa as Allied strategy.

Roosevelt initiated or approved all major American strategic decisions in the war, to include the priority of defeating Germany first, the undeclared war against U-boats in the Atlantic in 1941, lend-lease, the invasion of North Africa, and the unconditional surrender policy. After Pearl Harbor, the president overruled his military advisors on a number of strategic decisions.[152] He guided American strategy by allowing the joint chiefs to direct US forces, but intervened as necessary when they strayed from his desired course. Roosevelt held firm to his support of Britain, never wavered from the priority of defeating Germany first, and eventually supported an invasion of Northwest Europe, but only after Allied forces took advantage of more immediate and promising opportunities in the Mediterranean region. In assessing Roosevelt's role in the Second World War, one must agree with the official army historian who concludes, "Every President has possessed the constitutional authority which that title indicates, but few Presidents have shared Mr. Roosevelt's readiness to exercise it in fact and in detail and with such determination."[153]

To accomplish his objectives, Roosevelt carefully managed relations among the Allies and his own military advisors. His aim was to win the war against the powers as quickly as possible, while maintaining alliance harmony in order to insure cooperation in the postwar world. These goals worked against Churchill's desire to play balance-of-power politics, a game for which the American people had little stomach. Having educated the American people on the need to destroy Hitler's Germany, it is unlikely that Roosevelt could have persuaded them to fight the conflict for anything less than total victory. Roosevelt's decision to announce unconditional surrender at Casablanca was an attempt to keep the coalition intact and the American people in the fight to the end. Roosevelt understood the fragile nature of the Allied coalition, and most likely believed that only a demand for unconditional surrender

---

[151] Emerson, "Franklin Roosevelt as Commander-in-Chief," p. 193.
[152] Leighton, "OVERLORD Revisited," p. 929.
[153] Mark S. Watson, *The War Department: Chief of Staff: Prewar Plans and Preparations* (Washington, 1950), p. 5.

could keep the three major powers together. It was an inspired policy, albeit one that proved problematic in execution during the endgame in the Pacific.

Through the mists of history, the Anglo-American alliance during the Second World War is popularly seen as close and cordial. Yet, the veneer of cooperation hides real and significant disagreements on strategy that played out in the nine inter-Allied strategic conferences held during the war. Although the Allies on the whole reached consensus, they only achieved such outcomes after intense and often bitter discussion. The more debate and conflict over the strategy, the better it turned out. Intense debates forced the various sides to present the logic behind their strategic concepts and to defend their assumptions against sharp questioning. Criticism often emanated from inter-service rivalry as much as from inter-Allied discord. "The history of Allied conferences would be simpler if one could speak of an American case and a British case," notes Marshall's biographer. "In actuality one finds the Americans against the British, the Army and Air Forces against the Navy, and the Navy against MacArthur, with Marshall attempting to find a solution somewhere between."[154] These forceful debates prevented an outbreak of groupthink and allowed the best strategic concepts to flourish. In the end, the United States and its allies won a multi-front war – a rarity in military history.

American strategy was opportunistic. Once Roosevelt made the decision to invade North Africa, the joint chiefs of staff saw the logic in continuing operations in the Mediterranean to seize Sicily, knock Italy out of the war, and then to launch a subsidiary invasion of southern France. War production would not support a major 1943 invasion of the European continent in any case. Likewise, as the war progressed the joint chiefs supported an advanced timetable of operations in the Pacific to take advantage of Japanese weakness. America's aim was not to become globally dominant, but a series of incremental decisions made over time resulted in that outcome. US military leaders focused their strategic thinking on the expeditious defeat of the Axis. When political and military objectives collided, they invariably focused on the military goal of the destruction of the enemy's armed forces. As the end of the war in Europe neared on 28 April 1945, Marshall wrote to Eisenhower, "Personally and aside from all logistic, tactical or strategical implications, I would be loath to hazard American lives for purely political purposes."[155] Roosevelt's untimely death just prior to the end of the war resulted in the military view prevailing as the Allies closed in on Berlin and Tokyo.

One final note on US strategic decision making in the Second World War is in order. The United States was capably served by the officers who worked in the service and joint planning divisions. In retrospect, it is astonishing how a relative handful of officers performed the tasks required to craft strategic

---

[154] Pogue, *George C. Marshall: Organizer of Victory*, p. 206.
[155] Matloff, *Strategic Planning for Coalition Warfare, 1943–1944*, pp. 532–534.

plans and policy in the greatest war in history. During the interwar period, no more than a dozen officers were assigned to the War Plans Division of the US Army General Staff, most of them majors and lieutenant colonels. Yet these officers fulfilled the duties inherent in joint and service strategic planning, mobilization, and exercises.[156] The key to their performance was solid and thorough professional military education. Officers assigned to the Army War College participated in planning exercises that mirrored studies conducted by the War Plans Division. The habit of thinking about war at the national strategic level "explains in part how American officers, whose command experience of skeletal units was typically at lower levels, were capable of stepping into key positions near the apex of political power and into high command with a great degree of confidence and competence."[157] Military education also explains how the small interwar military produced such excellent strategists. It is a lesson the US military would do well to emulate today.

[156] Gole, *The Road to Rainbow*, p. 29.   [157] Ibid., p. 158.

12 American grand strategy and the unfolding of the Cold War 1945–1961

Bradford A. Lee

In early 1947, Secretary of State George Marshall told an audience at Princeton University that "I doubt seriously whether a man can think with full wisdom and deep convictions regarding some of the basic international issues of today who has not at least reviewed in his mind the period of the Peloponnesian War and the Fall of Athens."[1] Marshall was drawing an analogy between the emerging Cold War of his time and the "war like no other" that had been of pivotal importance in the Greek world 2,400 years earlier.[2] Such analogies from a previous war can provide a useful intellectual point of departure for assessment of the nature of a war upon which one is embarking, especially if that war seems peculiar at first sight.

Without due regard to differences as well as similarities, however, simple analogies can be a treacherous guide to action. Even when the similarities seem compelling, one ought to bear in mind the jibe of social-science methodologists that "anyone can draw a straight line between two dots." We can gain greater analytical power by connecting a greater number of dots in patterns that are more complex but that still exhibit key factors to guide assessment of the dynamics of a conflict as it unfolds and selection of courses of action for winning that conflict. The premise of this essay is that one can insightfully evaluate American grand strategy in the Cold War in terms of generic factors of success gleaned from previous big wars – not just the Peloponnesian War, but also such wars as those between Rome and Carthage in the ancient world and Britain and France in the eighteenth and early nineteenth centuries as well as the two world wars of the twentieth century. As that sample suggests, "major wars" are those violent conflicts between great powers that occur for high political stakes, that have both sides seeking to put together and sustain coalitions, that spread across multiple theaters, and that involve the use of many instruments of power and influence.

The thesis of this chapter is that there are four recurring keys to success in big wars: (1) the winning side does a better job of building and maintaining

---

[1] As quoted in Walter Robert Connor, *Thucydides* (Princeton, NJ, 1987), p. 3.
[2] Victor Davis Hanson, *A War Like No Other: How The Athenians and Spartans Fought the Peloponnesian War* (New York, 2005).

a cohesive coalition; (2) the winning side does a better job of developing and integrating different instruments of military power and non-military influence; (3) the losing side engages in egregiously self-defeating behavior, usually in strategic overextension; and (4) the winning side does a better job of cultivating, exploiting, and sustaining economic superiority (at least in modern big wars). These are *generic* keys to success that typically weigh heavily in the outcome of major wars.

Along with the common features of big wars, each big war has its myriad of distinctive features. Thus, there may also be *idiosyncratic* elements of success in each war that deserve to be added to the list of generic keys for success for that particular case. We should expect the balance of generic keys and idiosyncratic elements to vary from case to case. Even in cases where generic keys to success are quite important, as in this essay's interpretation of the Cold War, the distinctive features of the case manifest themselves in the particular ways in which the four generic keys play themselves out. That was especially true of the Cold War, the most distinctive feature of which was that the two principal belligerents never *openly* engaged in conventional military operations against each other. Non-military elements of success were more important in the Cold War than in the other major wars under consideration in this volume.

Such a patterned approach to grand strategy is by no means deterministic. As Clausewitz stressed, in thinking about war, the most to which one can intellectually aspire is a sense of probabilities, never certainty.[3] Not only should one bear in mind that generic keys to success may fall short of accounting for 100 percent of the outcome, but one should also never lose sight of the role of contingency and choice. The outcome of a major war – indeed, any war – is hard to predict and never foreordained. What counts for most in the outcome of such conflicts are the strategic choices the belligerents made. Thinking in terms of generic keys to success directs our attention to the kinds of choices that will have the most important strategic consequences.

In applying a patterned approach to the unfolding of the Cold War from the mid 1940s to the early 1960s, this essay will examine three underlying questions: (1) To what extent did American leaders focus on the factors that I posit as keys to success in big wars? (2) To what extent were they guided by broad strategic assessments and general strategic concepts in making decisions related to these factors? And (3) to what extent did their decisions play out with increasing strategic effectiveness over time? The overall answer to these three questions appears to be: "to a considerable extent, but. ..." That "but" is especially pertinent with regard to the third question. American leaders were remarkably focused on and did a reasonably good job with the four keys to success, but they seem to have lost sight of a "theory of victory"

---

[3] Carl von Clausewitz, *On War*, ed. and trans. by Michael Howard and Peter Paret (Princeton, NJ, 1989), p. 167.

that might ultimately bring the Cold War to an end on political terms highly favorable to the United States. Their most important strategic concept, "containment," which in its earliest form had considerable promise as a strategy, as a way of bringing about the "mellowing" or the "break-up" of the Soviet Union, had become a policy, an end in itself, by the early 1960s. Not until the early 1980s did a focus on winning the Cold War reemerge at the senior levels.

Strategic concepts and strategic assessments

From 1940, when American leaders began seriously thinking about projecting power on a truly global scale, to the end of the Cold War a half-century later, the most idiosyncratic feature of US grand strategy was the importance placed on general strategic concepts as a potential guide to the selection of particular courses of action. Eliot Cohen has extolled this feature with regard to US strategy in the Second World War.[4] John Gaddis has done the same for US strategy in the Cold War.[5] In the Second World War, the key concept was the Europe first strategic priority adumbrated by Admiral Harold Stark, chief of naval operations, in his Plan Dog memorandum of November 1940.[6] An important subsidiary concept was attrition of adversary capabilities, while the long process of mobilizing overwhelming military power from American economic potential was coming to fruition. President Franklin Roosevelt articulated the notion of attrition to the public, military commanders, and the Allies, and it rested on his assessment of the foreshortened peak of German and Japanese mobilization.[7]

Both concepts had a part to play in the subsequent story of the Cold War. The attrition of Soviet economic capabilities became prominent toward the end of that story. The Europe first concept carried over into the Cold War

---

[4] Eliot Cohen, "The Strategy of Innocence? The United States, 1920–1945," in Williamson Murray, MacGregor Knox, and Alvin Bernstein, eds., *The Making of Strategy: Rulers, States, and War* (Cambridge, 1994), pp. 463–464.

[5] See especially John Lewis Gaddis, *Strategies of Containment: A Critical Appraisal of American National Security Policy during the Cold War*, 2nd edn. (Oxford, 2005).

[6] Memorandum of 12 November 1940, by Chief of Naval Operations Admiral Harold Stark, addressed to Secretary of the Navy Frank Knox and passed on to President Franklin Roosevelt, Box 4, President's Safe Files, Franklin D. Roosevelt Presidential Library, Hyde, Park, NY.

[7] Bradford A. Lee, "A Pivotal Campaign in a Peripheral Theater: Guadalcanal and World War II in the Pacific," in Bruce Elleman and S. C. M. Paine, eds., *Naval Power and Expeditionary Wars: Peripheral Campaigns and New Theaters of Naval Warfare* (London, 2011), pp. 84–98; "Address of the President Delivered by Radio from the White House," 23 February 1942, at http://docs.fdrlibrary.marist.edu/022342.html; Roosevelt to General Douglas MacArthur, May 6, 1942, RG 4, Box 15, MacArthur Papers, MacArthur Memorial, Norfolk, VA; and Roosevelt's remarks at the first plenary meeting of the Tehran conference on 28 November 1943, in US Department of State, *Foreign Relations of the United States: Diplomatic Papers: The Conferences at Cairo and Tehran 1943* (Washington, D.C., 1961), p. 488.

from the beginning, not least because of the policy-making roles played in 1947–1961 by two American military leaders of the Second World War, George Marshall and Dwight Eisenhower. But that strategic priority became subsumed in a larger concept of containment. And that overall concept came to have another important subsidiary concept, nuclear deterrence. These concepts connected to strategic assessments of adversaries, environments, and situations.

Indeed, one of the most remarkable features of American strategy in the early Cold War was a series of assessments and reassessments of the Soviet Union and the United States: (1) George Kennan's "Long Telegram" of February 1946; (2) Kennan's "X" article in *Foreign Affairs* July 1947; (3) Paul Nitze's NSC 68, circulated in April 1950; and (4) Eisenhower's Solarium exercise, initiated in May 1953 and culminating in NSC 162/2 of October 1953. All four have been the subject of much discussion by diplomatic historians, who have interpreted these documents in terms of the development and intensification of a cold war that, many of them judge, might have been avoided, or at least attenuated. From a strategic perspective, however, it makes sense to assume that a formidable array of factors made a cold war highly likely after the defeat of the Axis powers in the Second World War.[8] If so, rather than try to prevent the conflict after the fact, students and practitioners of grand strategy may well find it more intellectually rewarding to look in these documents for the emergence of American concepts for prevailing in the conflict without fighting a hot war. Ultimately, the point of strategy is to win in some sense, not simply to coexist with an implacable adversary.

What lay behind Kennan's famous Long Telegram from the US Embassy in Moscow in early 1946 was his contempt for the futile attempts at negotiating diplomatic compromises with the Soviets, most recently by Secretary of State James Byrnes, at the Moscow conference of foreign ministers in December 1945.[9] The telegram provided an assessment of the deep, intertwined cultural and ideological roots of efforts by the Soviet Union's elite to expand its power outward and to undermine the cohesion of the United States and other Western nations. Kennan gave general reasons to believe that America could successfully deal with the Soviet problem, but he failed to offer specific strategic concepts for so doing.[10]

An assessment oriented toward "knowing the enemy" is an important step toward a strategy for dealing with the enemy.[11] Kennan's X article of 1947 stretched that step beyond his telegram of 1946 in a way that should

---

[8] Colin Gray, "Mission Improbable: Fear, Culture, and Interest: Peace Making, 1943–1949," in Williamson Murray and Jim Lacey, eds., *The Making of Peace: Rulers, States, and the Aftermath of War* (Cambridge, 2009), pp. 265–291.

[9] George F. Kennan, *Memoirs 1925–1950* (Boston, 1967), pp. 283–295.

[10] Kennan's Long Telegram of 22 February 1946 is in Department of State, *Foreign Relations … 1946*, vol. VI, pp. 695–709.

[11] Sun Tzu, *The Art of War*, trans. Samuel B. Griffith (Oxford, 1963), p. 129.

command the attention of those interested in grand strategy.[12] To his assessment of the traditional strategic culture of the Russian elite and the foreign policy implications of Marxist-Leninist ideology, he added an even more important assessment of the Stalinist political system, which was a practical guide to action. To "attack the enemy's political system" is ultimately the most important strategic concept for winning a war or prevailing in a long-term competition.[13] To engage in such an "attack" with a reasonable hope of success, one needs to identify the vulnerabilities of the "system." Kennan did that through the clever intellectual maneuver of turning the tools of Marxist analysis against the Stalinist regime: "Soviet power, like the capitalist world of its conception, bears within it the seeds of its own decay."[14] Those "seeds" – what Marxists would call "contradictions" and strategists would call "critical vulnerabilities" – Kennan found aplenty, in the Soviet regime's messianic outlook, its "uneven development" of heavy industry to the neglect of agriculture and consumer goods, the severe strains in the relationship between the regime and the mass of the people, and the enormous potential for instability when it came time for the transfer of power after Stalin's death, in the absence of any settled mechanism for succession.[15]

The external behavior of the regime masked its internal vulnerabilities. To describe its outward expansion, Kennan used the vivid metaphors of "a persistent toy automobile wound up and headed in a given direction, stopping only when it meets with some unanswerable force," and of "a fluid stream" that "filled every nook and cranny available to it in the basin of world power."[16] There was no point in foreign diplomats trying to reason with their Soviet counterparts, and any negotiated arrangement in the near term would only represent a temporary "tactical maneuver" on the part of Moscow. But, equally, the United States need not contemplate a spasm of military violence to prevent further Soviet expansion, for Stalin was not reckless, as Hitler had been.[17] If, over the long run, the adversaries of the Soviet Union could counter its external expansion with a purpose as steady and sustained as that which motivated it, the internal vulnerabilities of the Soviet system would inevitably appear.

Here emerged the strategic concept of "containment" that, in due course, gave an unusual degree of coherence to the American side of the Cold War. Kennan defined it as "the adroit and vigilant application of counter-force at

---

[12] X (George Kennan), "The Sources of Soviet Conduct," *Foreign Affairs*, vol. 25, July 1947, pp. 566–582.
[13] Bradford A. Lee, "Strategic Interaction: Theory and History for Practitioners," in Thomas G. Mahnken, ed., *Developing Competitive Strategies for the 21st Century* (Stanford, CA, 2012), pp. 41–43.
[14] X, "Sources," p. 580.   [15] Ibid., pp. 576–580, 582.   [16] Ibid., pp. 574–575.
[17] The Soviets were "more sensitive to contrary force, more ready to yield on individual sectors of the diplomatic front when that force is felt to be strong, and thus more rational in the logic and rhetoric of power." Ibid., p. 575.

a series of constantly shifting geographical and political points, corresponding to the shifts and maneuvers of Soviet policy."[18] In his article, he did not go on to enumerate specific courses of action. Later he complained that those who played up the role of the military instrument in supporting containment misconstrued his words "contrary force" and "counter-force." There is no doubt that Kennan was professionally and temperamentally inclined to play up the importance of non-military instruments. But during the gestation of his article, when he was a faculty member at the National War College, he was more attuned to military instruments than he was to be later. Indeed, at the war college, he worked on concepts for the rapid deployment of joint military task forces "capable of delivering at short notice effective blows on limited theaters of operation far from our own shores."[19] What is more, the X article grew out of a memorandum he prepared for Secretary of the Navy James Forrestal, to whom Kennan was indebted for advancing his career, first by circulating the Long Telegram around the highest levels, then by involving himself in Kennan's assignment to the war college, and finally in helping him become the first head of the new policy planning staff at the State Department.[20] Kennan had good reason in 1947 to give due regard to the role of the military in conjunction with non-military instruments.

Kennan was by no means content to outline a strategy – as containment was in its original formulation – without attaching it to a policy. As the political objectives of the intense 10–15-year contest with the Soviet Union that he contemplated, he held out the prospect of "the break-up or the gradual mellowing of Soviet power."[21] In Clausewitzian parlance, the former represents an unlimited political objective; the latter, a limited one. When the mellowing of the Soviet political system came to pass in the late 1980s, and the break-up followed in the early 1990s, Kennan complained yet again. In wanting no part of the credit for the outcome, he was not being modest. Alienated from what he saw as the heavy-handed applications of containment from the time of NSC 68 in 1950 to the Reagan administration in the 1980s, he was being disingenuous. The political outcome was truly what he had anticipated in 1947, albeit delayed by a generation. It was a remarkable achievement to lay out a strategy and a policy for the emerging Cold War in the way that Kennan did in his X article.

As a "theory of victory" – a realistic set of assumptions by which envisioned courses of action would translate into the desired political endgame – the

[18] Ibid., p. 576.   [19] Kennan, *Memoirs*, p. 311.
[20] For the Kennan–Forrestal relationship, see David Mayers, "Containment and the Primacy of Diplomacy: George Kennan's Views, 1947–1948," *International Security*, vol. 11, no. 1, Summer 1986, pp. 129–133; Wilson D. Miscamble, *George Kennan and the Making of American Foreign Policy, 1947–1950* (Princeton, NJ, 1992), pp. 10, 27–28, 109–114; and John Lewis Gaddis, *George F. Kennan: An American Life* (New York, 2011), pp. 218–219, 232, 239, 252, 258–262, 271.
[21] X, "Sources," p. 582.

article had shortcomings. How would the effects of containment play out in the Soviet political system? What would ultimately cause the mellowing or break-up of that system? How exactly would the systemic vulnerabilities manifest themselves in a chain reaction of cause and effect? Kennan's answers to those questions were not altogether clear. One can interpret containment as a strategy of denial.[22] Containing Soviet expansion would deny the Soviet leaders "incremental dividends" – periodic successes that would lend credence to their ideological conceit that time was on the side of communism and that would accumulate political capital for their political system among the people over whom they ruled. Denied such successes, Kennan suggested, Soviet leaders would become frustrated, and "no mystical, Messianic movement – and particularly not that of the Kremlin – can face frustration indefinitely without eventually adjusting itself in one way or another to the logic of that state of affairs."[23] In the end he failed to spell out the mechanisms by which that psychological effect would play out in the Soviet political system.

Instead of going on after July 1947 to develop further his embryonic theory of victory, Kennan proceeded to pull back from its logic after being confronted with powerful counterarguments laid out by the journalist Walter Lippmann, "US journalism's best-known pundit" of the era.[24] Kennan respected him for his formidable intellect and perhaps also because the two men saw similar strategic pathologies in the mass democratic culture of the American political system.[25] Emotionally insecure in the face of any criticism, Kennan was all the more stung by the pointed critique of a kindred spirit. Put in terms used by strategists later, Lippmann's basic point was that Kennan had not done a good *net assessment*, which must involve an analysis of the two sides' strengths and weaknesses in relation to each other.[26] On the one hand, according to Lippmann, Kennan's assumption about the psychological susceptibility of the Soviets to frustration was dubious, and his lack of explicit focus on the political impact of the Red Army in the middle of Europe represented a policy–strategy match.

On the other hand, Lippmann suggested that Kennan's assessment of the American side amounted to little more than wishful thinking. Lippmann

---

[22] Lee, "Strategic Interaction," p. 33.   [23] X, "Sources," p. 582.

[24] *Time Magazine*, 22 September 1947. Lippmann's critique appeared in a long series of *New York Herald Tribune* columns that were collected in Walter Lippmann, *The Cold War: A Study in U.S. Foreign Policy* (New York, 1947).

[25] For Lippmann's views on American political culture, see Patrick Porter, "Beyond the American Century: Walter Lippmann and American Grand Strategy, 1943–1950," *Diplomacy & Statecraft*, vol. 22, no. 4, December 2011, pp. 557–577. Kennan's similar views are brought out nicely in Gaddis, *George F. Kennan*.

[26] Though net assessment has achieved strategic prominence as a result of Andrew Marshall's work at the Pentagon since the 1970s, its *locus classicus* is in speeches by the Athenian leader Pericles and the Spartan leader Archidamnus at the onset of the Peloponnesian War. Thucydides, *The Landmark Thucydides: A Comprehensive Guide to the Peloponnesian War*, ed. Robert B. Strassler (New York, 1996), pp. 45–47, 80–85.

emphasized that the nature of the American political, economic, and military systems would badly constrain the agility necessary to execute a strategy of applying "counter-force at a series of constantly shifting geographical and political points." Trying to do so in response to "the shifts and maneuvers of Soviet policy" would, moreover, give the initiative to the adversary. In the parlance of Sun Tzu, the Soviets would be able to attack their enemy's strategy and alliances better than the Americans could do to them, by applying pressure in places where containment was most vulnerable.[27] There would be many such places because, as Lippmann pointed out, containment would require the United States to form coalitions in different, far-flung theaters with countries that lacked effective political systems. The upshot would likely be mounting frustration, and mounting costs, on the American side, more so than on the Soviet side. Rather than dissipate energy on implementing containment, Lippmann proposed a focus on getting the Red Army, along with the American and British armies, out of the heart of Europe by negotiating a diplomatic settlement that would center on the reunification of Germany.

Kennan never published, nor even sent to Lippmann, a rebuttal that he wrote in 1948.[28] Tellingly, during that year, Kennan's proposed courses of action gravitated in Lippmann's direction. He focused on restricting containment only to areas of vital interest to the United States, even though doing so cut against the "denial" logic of the X article's theory of victory. More curious still, he fell for Lippmann's fantasy of an early, grand diplomatic settlement, even though the Long Telegram and the X article had highlighted the futility of high-stakes negotiations with the Soviets, at least until they underwent long-term "mellowing." Kennan lost the confidence that Marshall's successor Dean Acheson initially had in his judgment.[29] After two good years, 1946 and 1947, it turned out that Kennan's mercurial brilliance was better suited to scholarly contemplation than strategic practice.

The next path-breaking assessment of the Cold War by American grand strategists was the NSC 68 document put together in April 1950 by Paul Nitze, Kennan's successor as head of the policy planning staff. Kennan looked askance at this assessment, and so have many diplomatic historians since the document was declassified and published in the *Naval War College Review* in 1975.[30] They saw in it much inflation of the Soviet threat, militarization

[27] Sun Tzu, *The Art of War*, pp. 77–78. For different ways of attacking the enemy's strategy, see Lee, "Strategic Interaction," pp. 37–41.
[28] The letter, dated 6 April 1948, is in the Kennan papers at Princeton University. There is a good summary of it in David Mayers, *George Kennan and the Dilemmas of US Foreign Policy* (Oxford, 1988), pp. 116–119.
[29] Gaddis, *George F. Kennan*, pp. 327–336, 341–343, 347–351; and Miscamble, *Kennan*, pp. 145–154.
[30] "NSC 68: A Report to the National Security Council," 14 April 1950, *Naval War College Review*, vol. 27, no. 6, May/June 1975, pp. 51–108. The NSC 68 report was then reprinted in Department of State, *Foreign Relations of the United States 1950*, vol. I (Washington, D.C., 1977), pp. 235–312. My page citations will be to this *Foreign Relations* volume. For an early

of containment, and hyper-ideological salesmanship. Nevertheless, from the perspective of strategic practitioners and strategic theorists alike, NSC 68 deserves a new and more empathetic look.

As Clausewitz averred: "The first, the supreme, the most far-reaching act of judgment that the statesman and commander have to make is to establish ... the kind of war on which they are embarking."[31] The Cold War was still in its infancy in early 1950, but Nitze and his collaborators, most of whom he had inherited from Kennan's staff, had a strong sense of its nature. As one can see from their report, they recognized that it involved high political and ideological stakes, expanding coalitions, multiple theaters, a multiplicity of instruments of power, and a contest of economic production. They also knew that it differed from previous big wars in its degree of ideological intensity and in the implications of what they called "weapons of mass destruction," now possessed by both superpowers. It was indeed the Soviet test of a nuclear device in 1949, followed by Truman's directive in early 1950 to develop thermonuclear weapons, which had led to the establishment of Nitze's State-Defense Committee to produce the NSC 68 report. That document explicitly referred to "the strategy of the cold war." The point of such a strategy was to win without fighting a disastrous hot war.

Winning in this context, as in all wars, meant achieving the nexus of political purposes and political objectives that falls under the label "policy." NSC 68 did not represent a major departure from Kennanesque precedent in the realm of policy.[32] Historians often confuse policy and strategy, and that is especially easy to do with containment. In NSC 68, as in the X article, containment was still a strategy – ways and means to achieve a political end – not a policy – that is to say, not an end in itself (as it was subsequently to become). In NSC 68, the political end remained what it had been in the X article: a major change in the Soviet political system that would wind down the Cold War.

Containment in the defensive or reactive sense, so conspicuous in the X article, was a way of bringing about that change. But, as Kennan subtly indicated in public in 1947 and then more vigorously propounded inside the government in 1948, there ought to be "political warfare" (his preferred term) that would challenge in non-military ways Soviet control over its emerging imperium.[33] Such proactive political warfare was part and parcel of a strategy

example of reactions by diplomatic historians, see Samuel F. Wells, Jr., "Sounding the Tocsin: NSC 68 and the Soviet Threat," *International Security*, vol. 4, no. 2, Autumn 1979, pp. 116–158.

[31] Clausewitz, *On War*, p. 88.
[32] My conclusions on this issue have more in common with Melvyn P. Leffler, *A Preponderance of Power: National Security, the Truman Administration, and the Cold War* (Stanford, CA, 1992), pp. 355ff., than with Gaddis, *Strategies of Containment*, chp. 4.
[33] Sarah-Jane Corke, *US Covert Operations and Cold War Strategy: Truman, Secret Warfare and the CIA, 1945–53* (London, 2008), chp. 3.

(in the words of the X article) "to increase enormously the strains under which Soviet policy must operate" and "thus promote the tendencies which must eventually find their outlet in either the break-up or the mellowing of Soviet power."[34] Likewise, Nitze and his collaborators in NSC 68 wanted to "induce a retraction of the Kremlin's control and influence" in a way that, in conjunction with blocking "further expansion of Soviet power," would "so foster the seeds of destruction within the Soviet system that the Kremlin is brought at least to the point of modifying its behavior to conform to generally accepted international standards."[35] Though it might seem at first sight that alternative policies – "containment" and "rollback" or "liberation" – were at odds with each other, a more penetrating insight suggests that Kennan and Nitze were trying to combine reactive and proactive elements in an augmented *strategy* of containment.[36]

It is in the realm of strategic means, rather than strategic ways or political ends, that NSC 68 represented a major departure from the Kennan of the X article and the pre-1950 posture of the Truman administration more generally. NSC 68 addressed non-military means for waging a cold war, but stood out for its new thinking about military means. One can best understand its contribution here in the context of another major element of sound strategic thinking derived from Clausewitz: the importance of strategy being in line with policy.[37] Nitze and his collaborators perceived that an alarming gap was opening up between American policy and American strategy, even if one regarded containment as a policy of "holding the line" against Soviet expansion. In their view, once the Soviet Union developed nuclear weaponry, the United States could no longer count on nuclear deterrence to maintain the status quo.

What would it take to close the gap between policy and strategy? To answer that question, a forward-looking net assessment was necessary. NSC 68 presented the first noteworthy high-level net assessment by the US government in the Cold War. Kennan's assessments had focused on Soviet intentions. Military planners were wont to focus on capabilities. Nitze and his collaborators broadened the scope to include both capabilities and intentions on both sides. As Nitze later said, "There is always an inter-relationship between capabilities and intentions."[38] In 1950, he did not like what he saw as he looked forward. Drawing on CIA estimates, he envisaged a Soviet

---

[34] X, "Sources," p. 582.   [35] NSC 68, *Foreign Relations ... 1950*, vol. I, p. 252.
[36] The words "roll back" appear on p. 284 of NSC 68, *Foreign Relations ... 1950*, vol. I. The use of military force to roll back North Korea in the fall of 1950, discussed later in this essay, was a significant departure from a strategy of containment. Both Kennan and Nitze opposed that adventure in military rollback. See Nicholas Thompson, *The Hawk and the Dove: Paul Nitze, George Kennan, and the History of the Cold War* (New York, 2009), p. 119.
[37] Clausewitz, *On War*, books 1 and 8.
[38] Paul Nitze, "The Development of NSC 68," *International Security*, vol. 4, no. 4, Spring 1980, p. 175.

"fission bomb stockpile" of 200 by mid 1954. He also noted evidence of Soviet activities directed toward producing thermonuclear weapons. And he assessed a Soviet bomber capability sufficient to put 80–120 bombs on targets in the United States four years from the time of the NSC 68 report.[39] All this projected nuclear potential would come on top of existing Soviet conventional military forces that, according to estimates of the joint chiefs of staff summarized in NSC 68, were already sufficient, even in the event of an American nuclear response, "[t]o overrun Western Europe, with the possible exception of the Iberian and Scandinavian Peninsulas; to drive toward the oil-bearing areas of the Near and Middle East; and to consolidate Communist gains in the Far East."[40]

Given that the NSC 68 report imputed far-reaching intentions to the Soviet Union, and given that the projected increase in the latter's nuclear capabilities would put "new power behind its design," the risk was that Soviet strategy by the mid 1950s would go beyond current efforts at "infiltration" and "intimidation." In worst case, the Soviets might launch a nuclear surprise attack on the United States. At the least, they would be better positioned for "piecemeal aggression against others" or more effective coercion of American allies. In such cases, the United States would face "the risk of having no better choice than to capitulate or precipitate a global war."[41]

To ward off such a grim prospect, NSC 68 strenuously advocated a major build-up of American conventional and nuclear forces. In addition to bringing US capabilities in line with commitments, it argued for major assistance to allies, so that they, too, could increase their military capabilities.[42] NSC 68 did not hazard an estimate of the budgetary cost to the United States, but made clear the cost would be high. It did not justify the cost simply in terms of the growing threat from a deteriorating balance of power. It also highlighted the political stakes of the Cold War in such terms as "the fulfillment or destruction ... of this Republic" and "of civilization itself."[43] In a clear statement of strategic rationality, Clausewitz declared that carrying on a conflict only makes sense if the "value of the object" exceeded the cost in magnitude and duration of effort.[44] Nitze and his collaborators wanted to make sure that those officials in the government likely to oppose a military build-up understood the value of the object.[45]

From a strategic perspective, what seems most striking, or puzzling, about NSC 68 is not its impassioned rhetoric in the service of strategic rationality; after all, Clausewitz had stressed that passion and rationality were intermixed

[39] NSC 68, *Foreign Relations ... 1950*, vol. I, p. 251.   [40] Ibid., p. 249.
[41] Ibid., pp. 263–264.   [42] Ibid., pp. 282–284.   [43] Ibid., p. 238.
[44] Clausewitz, *On War*, p. 92.
[45] As Secretary of State Acheson later wrote: "The purpose of NSC-68 was to so bludgeon the mass mind of 'top government' that not only could the president make a decision but that the decision could be carried out." Dean Acheson, *Present at the Creation: My Years in the State Department* (New York, 1969), p. 374.

elements of war.[46] Rather, in hindsight, there seems to be much uncertainty, and perhaps some lack of imaginative forethought, in NSC 68 about what the burgeoning effects of "weapons of mass destruction" would mean for deterrence. Nitze and his cohort assumed that the interaction between a nuclear-armed United States and a nuclear-armed Soviet Union would be dangerously unstable. They thought possession of nuclear weapons would make Soviet leaders more reckless and perceived there would be an incentive to strike first in the new nuclear age (before there had emerged a concept and a capability for an assured second strike). The Soviets might find themselves tempted by the advantages of a surprise nuclear attack, and the Americans, despite their new Central Intelligence Agency and what was soon to become the National Security Agency, might be susceptible to surprise, as at Pearl Harbor.

But would not the prospect of catastrophic nuclear retaliation by the United States deter extreme Soviet risk taking? Nitze had been centrally involved in the decision to develop thermonuclear weapons and had some foreknowledge of how much more destructive a hydrogen bomb would be than an atomic bomb.[47] The key piece to the puzzle may lie in NSC 68's positing of 1954 as the year of maximum danger. Perhaps Nitze foresaw that by 1955 the United States would have a deployed capability to deliver thermonuclear bombs against the Soviet Union (as proved to be the case). The peak of danger would then be surmounted (at least until the Soviets had a thermonuclear capability). In any event, the engagement between deterrence and containment in NSC 68 was a troubled one. Later, on the verge of the so-called 1954 peak, strategies of nuclear deterrence and a policy of containment found themselves matched in a durable, if doleful, marriage. The next major reassessment of American grand strategy, the Eisenhower administration's NSC 162/2 document arising from the Solarium project of 1953, was a crucial matchmaker for that marriage.

The Solarium deliberations that Eisenhower initiated after becoming president in 1953 represented a major reassessment of grand strategy.[48] With vast experience and great confidence in his own judgment, the new president no doubt had a good idea of where he wanted the reassessment to end up – with an overall concept in which some calibrated degree of pressure on Soviet alliances would augment containment, wedded more openly to

---

[46] Clausewitz's key notion of a "trinity" (*On War*, p. 89) identified – as I would paraphrase its aspects – rational political purpose, creative talent in dealing with chance and the dynamics of interaction, and passions arising from violent enmity as the three fundamental elements of war.

[47] Paul Nitze, with Ann M. Smith and Steven L. Rearden, *From Hiroshima to Glasnost: At the Center of Decision – A Memoir* (New York, 1989), chp. 5.

[48] Written by one retired US Army general about another, Douglas Kinnard's book *President Eisenhower and Strategy Management* (Lexington, KY, 1977), chp. 1, provides a good overview of the circumstances in which Eisenhower led the reassessment of 1953.

extended nuclear deterrence (to prevent not only a Soviet attack in Europe but also a recurrence of Korea), and supported by a diminished level of military spending (bringing an end to the NSC 68 surge) that a free market American economy and an unregimented political system could sustain. But Eisenhower's self-confidence was by no means so overweening as to incline him toward slighting the thoughts of others. He had long valued the process of planning, which could elicit new concepts, examine alternative courses of action, and, if properly led, build teamwork and "buy-in" among key players. He established three Solarium task forces and gave different guidance to each one. He saw the groups as both competitive and complementary.[49]

Task Force A, headed (and dominated) by Kennan, the only civilian among the leaders of the three groups, was to make a case for carrying on with the augmented containment, even though Republican campaign rhetoric in 1952, some of it coming from the new secretary of state, John Foster Dulles, had derided that concept. Eisenhower no doubt hoped that Kennan's presentation of Task Force A's report in July 1953 to a gathering of high-level officials, with Dulles in a front-row seat, would be an educational experience for the secretary of state and other policy makers.[50] The president also hoped that the case made by Kennan's team would provide support for cuts in military expenditure that Eisenhower envisaged.[51] That hope did not materialize.

Task Force A imparted another twist that Eisenhower likely did not welcome. Still evidently bearing the imprint of Lippmann's critique of containment, Kennan made a vigorous case for an immediate diplomatic initiative to bring about a unified, independent, and rearmed Germany from which both NATO and Soviet military forces would withdraw, at least to coastal enclaves, if not altogether. Imaginative as always, Kennan made a clever exposition of how such an initiative would put the Soviets on the horns of a dilemma and, in the best case, might lead to their withdrawal from Austria and Poland, not just East Germany. Diplomacy could thus serve as a way of attacking the Soviet alliance. But what would Kennan's diplomatic twist mean for the American alliance in Europe? Task Force A emphasized, early in its report, the importance for the United States of alliance cohesion, especially since it detected numerous signs since 1951 of some trans-Atlantic divergence within NATO. Later, when Kennan pushed forward his German

---

[49] My commentary on the work of the three task forces is based on the reports that they produced in July 1953. Those reports, not yet published, are at the Eisenhower Presidential Library in Abilene, Kansas. I thank Colin Jackson for providing me with copies.

[50] Earlier in 1953, Dulles had informed Kennan that there would no longer be a place in the State Department for the father of containment. Kennan delivered his presentation in July 1953 with an eye on Dulles and with a degree of *Schadenfreude*. See Gaddis, *George F. Kennan*, p. 487, and Kennan's recollections in William B. Pickett, ed., *George F. Kennan and the Origins of Eisenhower's New Look: An Oral History of Project Solarium* (Princeton, NJ, 2004), p. 19.

[51] "A Report to the National Security Council by Task Force 'A' of Project Solarium," 16 July 1953, pp. 38–56.

hobby horse, Task Force A had to concede that France and Britain would object to the unification of a rearmed Germany outside the control of the Western alliance.[52] Eisenhower could not have contemplated such a diplomatic initiative in 1953 with equanimity. Already, after Stalin's death in March 1953, he had responded cautiously to suggestions about having a four-power conference on Germany, lest it impede progress toward German rearmament as part of the European Defense Community, which France had proposed in 1950.[53]

Task Force B, headed by Major General James McCormick, Jr., a leading air force authority on nuclear weapons, had for its assignment the completion of a line of containment around the Soviet bloc that the United States had so far established only in the NATO area and the Western Pacific. To deter communist military forces from advancing anywhere beyond that extended line, there was to be an explicit threat of "general war" – that is to say, of a nuclear response by the United States directly against the Soviet Union, even if it was one of the Soviets' allies that made the military advance. Members of this task force counted on nuclear deterrence to prevent, as they vividly put the point, "a series of costly peripheral wars, each one of which leads only to another."[54] Otherwise, the United States would become increasingly overextended, and in the end undermine itself by trying to maintain the "desirable levels of all types of forces that would be needed to fight the variety of possible wars the Soviet Union might choose to force upon us."[55] Recommending a public declaration of a continuous "line of no aggression," without any gaps around the existing perimeter of the Soviet bloc, they hoped to avoid a recurrence of Korea. Unlike Kennan in the X article, they did not hold out the prospect that containing communist aggression along the frontiers of Eurasia would lead to a major change in the Soviet political system. They merely did "not reject the possibility" that in the long term there might be a Soviet evolution away from aggressive tendencies.[56]

There were two questions that Task Force B maneuvered around gingerly, but that were bound to loom large for Eisenhower and America's allies. First, in the event of a breach of containment in a place of peripheral importance, would the United States follow through on its declaratory posture, especially since a "general war" would be "terribly destructive even to the victor," given

[52] Ibid., pp. 12–14, 69, 86–96.
[53] Saki Dockrill, *Eisenhower's New-Look National Security Policy* (New York, 1996), p. 28.
[54] "A Report to the National Security Council by Task Force 'B' of Project Solarium," 16 July 1953, p. 18.
[55] Ibid., p. 54.
[56] Ibid., p. 23. Even Kennan's Task Force A did not wax eloquently about the prospect of a major change in the Soviet political system. Rather, it simply noted the possibility of Soviet rulers "adjusting their objectives to those of peaceful co-existence with the Free World." Report of Task Force A, p. 18.

nuclear weapons?[57] Second, as the Soviets attained "atomic plenty" – the task force optimistically assessed a Soviet lag of five to ten years behind the United States in nuclear destructive power – would the reliance on extended deterrence lose credibility?[58]

That the United States needed to be well on its way to winning the Cold War before the Soviets attained "atomic plenty" was the basic thrust of Task Force C, led by Vice Admiral Richard Conolly, president of the Naval War College. Whereas Task Force A assumed time would remain on the side of the United States, and Task Force B assumed that growing Soviet nuclear capabilities would not negate a strategy of nuclear deterrence, Task Force C asserted (without discernible evidence beyond communist success in China) that the United States was losing the Cold War, and that its prospects would dim unless it increased its pressure on the Soviet bloc by all means short of "general war."[59] Successes in attacking the enemy alliance would divert the Soviets from expansion and toward preservation of their own bloc.[60] Though at first American allies "would draw back in terror at the thought of our adopting a policy that would risk war," American successes would "produce a climate of victory encouraging to the free world."[61] Kennan in 1947 had adumbrated the psychological effects on the Soviet political system, if American strategy denied it incremental dividends; Task Force C anticipated a psychological resurgence of the "free world," if American strategy generated incremental dividends. Criticizing Task Force A for offering "no end product of the present conflict" and Task Force B for providing "an objective only in a negative way," Task Force C trumpeted "a true American Crusade" to win the Cold War.[62]

In fact, the end state envisioned by Task Force C was more indistinct than that sketched by Kennan in his X article, but it seemed to include a "final breakdown" of the Soviet political system.[63] In its three-phase plan for victory presented in a report of nearly 300 pages, it emphasized more prominently the need to bring about a Soviet withdrawal from East Germany and either undermining the Chinese communist regime or separating it from the Soviets. Though the report said much about the potential importance of a combination of diplomacy, propaganda, economic measures, subversion,

---

[57] The "terribly destructive" quotation is on p. 12 of Task Force B's report.

[58] See ibid., p. 12, for the assessment of the Soviet lag. Note on p. 34 of the report, for example, how Task Force B did not come to grips with the issue of credibility.

[59] Task Force C defined the Cold War as "every form of military and political conflict *short of* a general war of global scope with our principal adversary, the U.S.S.R. itself." In such conflict, it asserted, "one is either winning or losing" – there could be no stable balance or stalemate. See "A Report to the National Security Council by Task Force 'C' of Project Solarium," 16 July 1953, pp. 9, 11.

[60] This notion foreshadowed the concept of "competitive strategies" developed two decades later in the Cold War by Andrew Marshall. For the role of diversionary effects in competitive strategies, see Lee, "Strategic Interaction."

[61] "Report ... by Task Force 'C,'" pp. 1, 19, 21.   [62] Ibid., pp. 70–72.   [63] Ibid., p. 69.

shows of force, and even military operations against the People's Republic of China (either by the United States, if a truce did not end the Korean War, or by the Nationalist Chinese), its courses of actions were not connected by a plausible theory of victory to the dissolution of the Soviet bloc and still less to the demise of the Soviet political system. A reader who made it through the analysis, buried deep in the report, of possible reactions by the Soviets and corresponding risks, might well have come away with the impression that Task Force C's courses of action would mean an intensified coalition struggle with an uncertain outcome.[64]

From Eisenhower's perspective, the threat to the Western alliance's cohesion was the first of three strikes against Task Force C's more extreme ideas; the other two were that they would raise the risk of general war and require a continued surge in military expenditure.[65] Still, the president had shown interest in doing more through covert operations inside the Soviet bloc. At the end of the presentation of the Solarium reports in July 1953, he directed that members of the National Security Council (NSC) staff, along with members of the task forces, put together a synthesis of the best ideas from the three reports. That proved no easy task. The process of synthesis was further complicated by the need to take account of two other sources of ideas. One source was the incoming joint chiefs of staff, whom Eisenhower had also asked for strategic concepts. Under the leadership of their new chairman, Admiral Arthur Radford, they played up the overextension of American military forces and called for the redeployment especially of ground forces back to the United States. That idea would raise the specter among allies of a relapse of the United States into Fortress America.[66] The other source of ideas was from budget-cutters, Treasury Secretary George Humphrey and Budget Director Joseph Dodge, who insisted that the economic strength to sustain the Cold War in the long run depended on the restoration of a balanced budget, which in turn required major reductions in military expenditure.[67]

The friction generated by these competing ideas dragged out the search for synthesis for more than three months. The upshot, NSC 162/2, emerged

---

[64] Ibid., pp. 232–243.

[65] Two staffers who worked for Eisenhower, General Andrew Goodpaster and Robert Bowie, later recollected that the president was not keen on "rollback." Goodpaster said that Eisenhower put him on Task Force C to have "somebody with some common sense" make sure that the group "didn't go completely off in their analysis." Pickett, ed., *Oral History*, pp. 22, 24, 30.

[66] See Robert J. Watson, *The Joint Chiefs of Staff and National Policy 1953–1954*, vol. V: *History of the Joint Chiefs of Staff* (Washington, D.C., 1986), pp. 14–21; and Admiral Arthur W. Radford, *From Pearl Harbor to Vietnam: The Memoirs of Admiral Arthur W. Radford*, ed. Stephen Jurika, Jr. (Stanford, CA, 1980), chp. 23.

[67] The budget-cutting campaign of Humphrey and Dodge can best be followed in Department of State, *Foreign Relations of the United States 1952–1954*, vol. II, pt. 1 (Washington, D.C., 1984); and Richard M. Leighton, *Strategy, Money, and the New Look 1953–1956*, vol. III: *History of the Office of the Secretary of Defense* (Washington, D.C., 2001), chs. 7–9.

in late October 1953.[68] Not surprisingly, it represented the lowest common denominator rather than high-quality strategic thought. It lacked the conceptual verve of what Kennan and Nitze had produced earlier in the Cold War. Nevertheless, it was less intellectually insipid than the so-called strategic documents that emanated from the ponderous national security bureaucracies after the Cold War was over.[69] Containment loomed large in NSC 162/2, much as it had in the Truman administration's strategic approach, but by October 1953 it was far along the path toward being an end in itself, moving ever more distant from its starting point as a strategy, a way to bring about the break-up or mellowing of the Soviet system. NSC 162/2 rejected the aim of trying "to dictate the internal political and economic organization of the USSR."[70] It held out some hope that, over time, the revolutionary zeal of the Soviet leadership might slacken. If the United States and its allies could maintain their strength and cohesion, the Soviet Union might become willing to negotiate "acceptable" agreements, "without necessarily abandoning its basic hostility to the non-Soviet world."[71] References to "the long pull" suggest that, whereas Kennan in 1947 anticipated that the Cold War might wind down in a decade or so, the Eisenhower administration was assuming a generation or more of strategic conflict. Accordingly, NSC 162/2 put nearly as high a priority on economic staying power as on military power. The trade-off between priorities heightened the emphasis on threatening "massive retaliatory damage" with nuclear weapons.

There was also conspicuous emphasis on the importance of allied help in meeting US defense needs.[72] Of course, the accumulation of security commitments to allies risked overextension. NSC 162/2 conceded what the JCS had claimed: "As presently deployed in support of our commitments, the armed forces of the United States are over-extended." But it did not accept the call for strategic redeployment: "any major withdrawal of US forces from Europe or the Far East would ... seriously undermine the strength and cohesion of the coalition."[73] What is more, NSC 162/2 envisioned an extension of the line of containment. A careful reader could infer that, soon, the only gaps in that line would be on the southern rimlands of the Soviet Union and Communist China: one would be Afghanistan; the other would be the area between Pakistan and Indochina. But after following the line-drawing of Task Force B that far, NSC 162/2 did not endorse the argument that the United States should issue a public declaration that Soviet aggression or that of its allies across the line would mean general war. In response to JCS urging, NSC 162/2 did note that "In the event of hostilities, the United States

---

[68] NSC 162/2, as approved by President Eisenhower on October 30, 1950, has been reprinted in *Foreign Relations ... 1952–1954*, vol. II, pt. 1, pp. 577–597.
[69] See Bradford A. Lee, "Teaching Strategy: A Scenic View from Newport," in Gabriel Marcella, ed., *Teaching Strategy: Challenge and Response* (Carlisle, PA, 2010), p. 115.
[70] *Foreign Relations ... 1952–1954*, vol. II, pt. 1, p. 595.   [71] Ibid., p. 581.
[72] Ibid., pp. 582–583.   [73] Ibid., p. 593.

will consider nuclear weapons to be available for use as other munitions."[74] That did not mean, however, that US military leaders could count on using nuclear weapons in any war. Eisenhower wanted to decide in each case. He refused to be the prisoner of prior pronouncements, especially since, over time, as NSC 162/2 pointed out, "increasing Soviet atomic capability may tend to diminish the deterrent effect of US atomic power against peripheral Soviet aggression."[75]

In the last section of the document, under the heading "Reduction of the Soviet Threat," NSC 162/2 circumspectly addressed the issues raised and the instruments brandished by Task Force C. It accepted that "the United States should take feasible political, economic, propaganda and covert measures ... to create and exploit troublesome problems for the USSR, impair Soviet relations with Communist China, complicate control in the satellites, and retard the growth of the military and economic potential of the Soviet bloc." But the point of imposing such "pressures" was to "induce the Soviet leadership to be more receptive to acceptable negotiated settlements."[76] In other words, its aim was not to implode the Soviet political system.

This excursion through these assessments reveals how self-conscious and highly conceptual the American approach to grand strategy was in the 1940s and 1950s. One would be hard pressed to find a comparable approach by belligerents in other eras. It also reveals how prominent in the strategic thinking of the two administrations were concerns about the four key success factors identified at the beginning of this essay. The main changes from Truman to Eisenhower took the form of heightened emphases. There was more explicit concern with the maintenance of American economic superiority from 1953 on, in part because there was a greater expectation of a more protracted conflict. There was a renewed concern about strategic overextension, given the experience of Korea. To sustain containment without overextension, there was heavier weight placed on integrating nuclear deterrence into the American military posture. To augment containment without incurring greater costs or risks, there was to be enhanced effort to combine more effectively covert operations, propaganda, and other non-military instruments of influence. Not least, there was a preoccupation with making sure American courses of action did not cut against the cohesion of the coalition that had emerged under Truman and was to be extended under Eisenhower.

Coalitions

The single most important key to success in a major conflict lies in the courses of actions that make for a cohesive coalition. Containment of the Soviets, or communism more generally, required for its effective implementation

---

[74] Ibid., p. 593.   [75] Ibid., p. 581.   [76] Ibid., p. 595.

anti-communist coalitions against the Soviet Union and its allies, or associated movements. For a cohesive coalition to emerge, not only the United States, but also its other major allies-to-be had to break with their historical traditions of policy and strategy.[77] Who could have predicted at the end of the Second World War that the following momentous changes would occur? Americans would lose their deep-rooted fear of entangling alliances and of a large peacetime military establishment. Rather than relapse into isolationism, American leaders would be willing to sustain a forward military presence on Eurasia's rimlands. The British would get over their past reluctance to accept a continental commitment in Europe, form military alliances with France and Germany, and, like the Americans, deploy troops on the ground to support their allies before a hot war actually occurred. The Germans would get over their *Sonderweg* (the special path) and their recurrent hegemonic impulses, tolerate the partition of the nation Bismarck had created, and accept a subordinate place in a multilateral Western alliance rather than maneuver between West and East for maximum advantage. The French would move toward a consensus that the Germans were no longer their primary enemy, accommodate a reindustrialized and rearmed West Germany, and trust the British and the Americans to be more reliable allies than in the past. The Japanese would descend from the mystical notion of *kōdō* (the imperial way) that had justified their wars in Asia, retreat from the quest for strategic autonomy, and accept an extended American military presence on their soil despite the thrust of Japan's history to keep foreigners at arm's length.

That all this happened in the first decade or so of the Cold War owed much to a looming and palpable Soviet threat. Steeped in ideological notions about "contradictions" among the capitalist powers, Stalin had supposed at the end of the Second World War that there would be violent conflicts among the imperialist powers. But Stalin's own imperialism soon created a cohesive alliance system on the other side.[78] Still, for coalitions truly to be cohesive, more than recognition of the same primary enemy is necessary. The members of a coalition must also possess a common political objective. The defensive aspect of containment served that purpose quite well. On the other side, the Soviets had to put war plans for offensive operations against Western Europe under a nominally defensive cover in order to make them palatable

---

[77] On this point, and on other points in my discussion of coalitions in the early Cold War, I elaborate here on the analysis in Bradford A. Lee, "The Cold War as a coalition struggle," in Bruce A. Elleman and S. C. M. Paine, eds., *Naval Coalition Warfare: From the Napoleonic War to Operation Iraqi Freedom* (London, 2008), pp. 146–157. For a major work by a historian of American foreign policy who gives due regard to the coalition issue, see John Gaddis, *We Now Know: Rethinking Cold War History* (New York, 1997), chp. 7.

[78] For brilliant insight into how Stalin ended up with a different outcome than he initially expected, see William Taubman, *Stalin's American Policy: From Entente to Détente to Cold War* (New York, 1982).

to their Warsaw Pact allies.[79] Shared political purpose facilitates strategic coordination, a further important element of coalition cohesion. The United States and its allies, especially in NATO, were able to agree on and periodically revise basic military concepts to deter and, if necessary, fight against an attack by the Soviets and their allies. NATO instituted elaborate mechanisms for coordination. The Soviets meanwhile were hesitant about turning the Warsaw Pact into a tight-knit multilateral institution. When Eisenhower left office in 1961, there was a massive gap between NATO and the Warsaw Pact in their functioning as cohesive military alliances.

The unique history of the formation of the early Cold War coalitions helps to explain differences in degrees of cohesion. Historians of American foreign policy have tended to overlook the crucially formative role played by British policy maker Ernest Bevin, foreign secretary in Clement Attlee's Labour government from 1945 to 1951. Consider the major milestones on the path to a Western alliance clustered around the notion of containment: (1) the American decision in early 1947 to aid Greece and Turkey, which the Truman Doctrine embellished in public; (2) the Marshall Plan that arose from the secretary of state's speech at Harvard in June 1947; (3) the establishment of a West German state in 1949 out of the British, American, and French occupation zones; and (4) the formation of NATO in 1949. The first, third, and fourth items arose primarily from initiatives by Bevin that served to nudge forward his American counterparts.[80] The British foreign secretary's role in the formation of NATO was especially prominent. Thus, the American leadership of the Western coalition was the result of invitation.[81] In contrast, the Soviets imposed the Warsaw Pact on their allies. The way in which the two coalitions formed had considerable ramifications for their different degrees of cohesion thereafter.

There were, of course, recurrent strains in the NATO alliance, as in all alliances. Notwithstanding the interest of Truman and Eisenhower in coalition cohesion, shifts in the American strategic posture generated the greatest strains on NATO. One major shift occurred after the surprise attack by North Korea on South Korea in June 1950, when there was widespread fear that further communist aggression might follow in Europe. Secretary of State Acheson presented the famous package deal whereby the United States would

---

[79] There is material on Soviet/Warsaw Pact war planning in Vojtech Mastny and Malcolm Byrne, *A Cardboard Castle? An Inside History of the Warsaw Pact, 1955–1991* (Budapest, 2005).

[80] For Bevin's approach to the United States about Greece and Turkey, see Alan Bullock, *Ernest Bevin: Foreign Secretary 1945–1951* (London, 1983), pp. 368–370; for Bevin and the merging of Western occupation zones in Germany, see Anne Deighton, *The Impossible Peace: Britain, the Division of Germany, and the Origins of the Cold War* (Oxford, 1993); and for Bevin and the origins of NATO, see John Baylis, *The Diplomacy of Pragmatism: Britain and the Formation of NATO, 1942–1949* (Kent, OH, 1993).

[81] Geir Lundestad, "'Empire' by Invitation? The United States and Western Europe, 1945–1952," *Journal of Peace Research*, vol. 23, no. 3, September 1986, pp. 263–277.

deploy four additional divisions to Europe and assign an American general to serve as SACEUR, if the Europeans would agree to West German rearmament and build up their own forces. The idea of rearming the former enemy so soon after the war caused consternation, especially in France.

But by spring 1952, the allies appeared to have surmounted this challenge to cohesion. They had agreed on ambitious conventional force levels for the defense of West Germany and had also agreed in principle to the European Defense Community (EDC), which the French had proposed as a politically clever (but militarily dubious) solution to the problem of West German rearmament. The prospect of restored cohesion proved ephemeral. The NATO allies stalled their rearmament efforts at approximately half the promised levels, while successive French governments failed to ratify the EDC treaty. By the end of 1954, the allies had surmounted this second challenge. The British and French had converged on a straightforward way to integrate a rearmed West Germany into NATO, and NATO had also accepted a new strategic concept embracing the emphasis the Eisenhower administration placed on massive retaliation.[82]

Once again, cohesion dissipated, year by year, until again restored. In 1955, a NATO exercise simulated the use of 335 tactical nuclear weapons with an estimated casualty toll of 1.7 million Germans dead, 3.5 million incapacitated, and countless more stricken with radioactivity. News of that estimate ignited controversy in West Germany and caused Chancellor Konrad Adenauer to think more deeply about what the actual execution of US nuclear strategy would mean for his country.[83] In 1956, a press leak of the so-called Radford Plan, according to which the JCS chairman advocated major cuts in US ground forces, caused Adenauer to question just how committed the United States was to defending West Germany.[84] In 1957, the Soviets' launch of the Sputnik satellite was an alarming indicator of an emerging ICBM

---

[82] For the NATO strategic concept, MC 48 of November 1954, see Gregory W. Pedlow, ed., *NATO Strategy Documents 1949–1969* (Brussels, 1996). The most thoroughly researched account of the development of this concept is Robert Allen Wampler, "Ambiguous Legacy: The United States, Great Britain and the foundations of NATO strategy, 1948–1957," Ph.D. dissertation, Harvard University, 1991. For the French and British roles in West German rearmament, see Saki Dockrill, *Britain's Policy for West German Rearmament* (Cambridge, 1991); Georges-Henri Soutou, "France and the German Rearmament Problem," in R. Ahmann, A. M. Burke, and M. Howard, eds., *The Quest for Stability: Problems of West European Security 1918–1957* (London, 1993), pp. 487–512; William I. Hitchcock, *France Restored: Cold War Diplomacy and the Quest for Leadership in Europe, 1944–1954* (Chapel Hill, NC, 1998), chs. 5–6; and Michael Creswell, *A Question of Balance: How France and the United States Created Cold War Europe* (Cambridge, MA, 2006).

[83] Hans Speier, *German Rearmament and Atomic War: The Views of German Military and Political Leaders* (Evanston, IL, 1957), chp. 10; and Annette Messemer, "Konrad Adenauer: Defence Diplomat on the Backstage," in John Gaddis et al., eds., *Cold War Statesmen Confront the Bomb: Nuclear Diplomacy since 1945* (Oxford, 1999), p. 242.

[84] Klaus Schwabe, "Adenauer and Nuclear Deterrence," in Wilfried Loth, ed., *Europe, Cold War and Coexistence 1953–1965* (London, 2004), pp. 38–39.

capability that, together with the H-bomb the USSR had already tested, diminished the credibility of US nuclear strategy. Adenauer was not sure which to fear more: the Americans' evident willingness to use nuclear weapons in response to a Soviet attack or their possible unwillingness to risk the destruction of their own cities on behalf of their ally. What Adenauer recognized was the need to shore up deterrence by getting some degree of West German control over nuclear weapons.

But pursuit of that ambition would put a strain on coalition cohesion, not least because it might provoke the Soviets. Indeed, in 1958, the Soviet leader, Nikita Khrushchev, instigated a Berlin crisis, in part because he feared the prospect of growing West German power and a possible German finger on the nuclear trigger.[85] The Berlin crisis was the greatest test of NATO cohesion during the Cold War. It came at a time and place calculated to put maximum pressure on that cohesion. But by 1960 NATO had emerged intact from that crisis. Khrushchev had backed off from the threat that had started it; he waited until John F. Kennedy became president to resume the pressure on Berlin.

Meanwhile, the alliance that the United States had made with Japan was holding up under the challenges that it faced. In terms of US coalitions embracing the Second World War's defeated powers, Stalin had proved to be the Soviet Union's worst enemy. It was his decision to support the North Korean invasion of South Korea that convinced the United States not only to turn NATO into a full-fledged military alliance, but also to make a military alliance with Japan. To be sure, even before the Korean War, as China fell to Mao Zedong's communists in the late 1940s, the Truman administration had begun to build up Japan as a bulwark of containment. To insure bipartisan support for American policy in spring 1950, Acheson had asked Dulles to take charge of working out a transition from the occupation of Japan to a subsequent United States–Japan security relationship. The Korean War provided impetus to that process.[86] The upshot in 1951–1952 was a soft peace treaty that ended the occupation and a hard security treaty that allowed the United States to maintain forces and bases on Japanese territory for an indefinite period with minimal restrictions.

Late in the Truman and early in the Eisenhower administrations, there was an expectation among US policy makers and military strategists that Japan would be willing to rearm on nearly the same scale as contemplated for West Germany.[87] Japanese Prime Minister Yoshida Shigeru pointed out

---

[85] For the issue of "nuclear sharing" in NATO, especially with regard to West Germany, see the provocative interpretation in Marc Trachtenberg, *A Constructed Peace: The Making of the European Settlement* (Princeton, NJ, 1999), chs. 5–7.

[86] Aaron Forsberg, *America and the Japanese Miracle: The Cold War Context of Japan's Postwar Economic Revival, 1950–1960* (Chapel Hill, NC, 2000), chp. 2.

[87] John Swenson-Wright, *Unequal Allies? United States Security and Alliance Policy Toward Japan, 1945–1960* (Stanford, CA, 2005), pp. 188ff. The United States envisioned a Japanese army of ten divisions, as compared to a West German army of 12 divisions.

that in 1946–1947 – before the Cold War had come to East Asia – the US occupation authority had imposed a constitution on Japan that forbade any resort to war or a restoration of military forces. Hoping to entice him to reconsider, the Americans bestowed military aid on Japan in 1954. Yoshida gladly took the money, but gave ground slowly. He seemed quite content for his nation to depend entirely on the United States for its security. Japan had risen as a modern power in the late nineteenth century under the mantra "rich nation, strong army." The latter had outpaced the former, with disastrous results. Yoshida wanted Japan to rise again by concentrating first, foremost, and perhaps forever on the goal of "rich nation."[88]

Not all Japanese leaders were ready to cast aside the "strong army" tradition. From 1957 to 1960, the Japanese prime minister, Kishi Nobusuke, wanted rearmament in tandem with a revision of the 1951 Security Treaty to make it less unequal. American policy makers were receptive.[89] Kishi had a decisive leadership style that projected well in Washington, but not so well in Tokyo. While the Americans were willing to overlook the fact that their occupation authority had imprisoned Kishi as a war criminal for serving as munitions minister in the war cabinet, his opponents in Japan were not so willing to forget his past. When Kishi rammed the new security treaty through the Diet in 1960 before a scheduled visit by Eisenhower, huge demonstrations brought his cabinet down. Americans were shocked by this tumultuous challenge to their alliance with Japan. But it turned out that the Japanese were shocked, too. Kishi's successor, Ikeda Hayato, calmed the storm and made amends with the Americans.[90]

Along with the difficulties in achieving a major rearmament of Japan, the United States fell short of its desire to see a multilateral Pacific alliance. Japan shunned any strategic role beyond its own territory, while the newly independent nations of East Asia shunned any strategic ties with the imperial power that had conquered and colonized them. The United States ended up serving as the hub from which several bilateral alliances (or trilateral, in the case of the ANZUS alliance) radiated across the Pacific. The Eisenhower administration added two spokes, one with South Korea (ROK) at the end of the Korean War in 1953 and one with the rump Republic of China (ROC) during the first Taiwan Strait crisis in 1954–1955. These alliances looked to contain China and also to restrain Syngman Rhee and Chiang Kai-shek from trying to reunify their countries through force. Both alliances served

[88] Richard J. Samuels, *Securing Japan: Tokyo's Grand Strategy and the Future of East Asia* (Ithaca, NY, 2007), pp. 14–15, 29–37.
[89] For a sympathetic treatment of Kishi, with much interesting analysis of Japanese party politics, see Tetsuya Kataoka, *The Price of a Constitution: The Origin of Japan's Postwar Politics* (New York, 1991), chs. 7–8.
[90] George R. Packard III, *Protest in Tokyo: The Security Treaty Crisis of 1960* (Princeton, NJ, 1966) remains the best English-language account of the demonstrations and their aftermath.

American purposes quite well, though not without some dramatic tensions between the Americans and their prickly Asian partners.[91]

In making these security treaties, Eisenhower and Dulles were turning what had developed as informal coalitions under Truman into formal alliances. A greater, but ill-fated, innovation of the Eisenhower administration took the form of multilateral treaty organizations in Southeast Asia and the Middle East, areas along the Eurasian rimland in which the Truman administration had not gotten so deeply involved. The Southeast Asian Treaty Organization (SEATO), established in 1954, and the Baghdad Pact, consummated in 1955 (without formal American adherence), represented exercises in drawing containment lines such as Task Force B of Project Solarium and NSC 162/2 had envisioned.

The need for a containment line in Southeast Asia became urgent with the French debacle in Indochina in 1954. The problem with SEATO as an underwriter of containment was that it did not embody the key elements of coalition cohesion. For the Americans, their primary enemy in Southeast Asia was China, and their political objective was to contain that enemy first and foremost. The other members of SEATO, however, were fearful of finding themselves dragged into a war with China by American impetuosity. Each of them was more wrapped up in its own specific problems than in the general American project of extended containment.

Moreover, the Americans were quite reluctant to commit ground forces to help their SEATO allies deal with local security problems. Their strategic concept for regional security was to deter Chinese expansion and, if deterrence failed, respond to Chinese aggression by waging nuclear war against the PRC, not by fighting on the ground wherever aggression took place. They counted on SEATO to provide political backing in such a contingency. They also hoped for SEATO support for efforts to establish and sustain a new state in South Vietnam. Given the lack of genuine cohesion in SEATO from the outset, it is no wonder that the alliance was of no help to the United States later, after 1959, when the Vietnamese communists renewed their insurgency to bring about the unification of their country.

While SEATO proved disappointingly ineffectual in Southeast Asia, the Baghdad Pact proved downright counterproductive in the Middle East. The idea was to have a "northern tier" containment line of Turkey, Iraq, Iran, and Pakistan. Britain backed up the line. The United States, though involved in the formation of the pact, did not join, because at a time when Arab

---

[91] Frustrated by Rhee's efforts to undermine an armistice in the Korean War, American political and military leaders in the summer of 1953 entertained a plan to replace him with a military government. Cooler heads prevailed, and the idea of a coup was superseded by the offer of a security treaty to gain his acquiescence in the agreement with the Chinese and North Koreans. See John Kotch, "The Origins of the American Security Commitment to Korea," in Bruce Cumings, ed., *Child of Conflict: The Korean–American Relationship, 1943–1953* (Seattle, WA, 1983), pp. 239–259.

nationalism was on the rise, American policy makers thought it impolitic to be so formally associated with the British. Indeed, the leading anti-British Arab nationalist, Gamal Abdel Nasser of Egypt, reacted negatively to the formation of the new coalition, which he saw as a threat to his transnational ambitions as well as a tool of British imperialism.[92] The Eisenhower administration found itself further rattled by Soviet efforts in 1955 to spread its influence in the area through arms sales and economic aid.[93] Eisenhower and Dulles were caught in a predicament: on the one hand, they wanted to support their British allies; on the other hand, they wanted to keep Nasser from aligning with the Soviets. The turning point came with the Suez crisis of 1956, when Eisenhower decided to stop the Anglo-French-Israeli invasion of Egypt by exerting economic pressure on the British and their allies. A curious zigzag followed this turning point. Having in effect saved Nasser's regime, the Eisenhower administration in 1957 pursued a policy aimed at containing the Egyptians.[94] It did not go well. In 1958, what Lippmann had warned in 1947 – the dangers of coalitions with unstable governments – came to pass. There were military coups in Iraq and Pakistan, and American relations with those states deteriorated. From an American perspective, the situation in the Middle East was in utter disarray.

With the benefit of hindsight, a story arc emerges. The Truman and Eisenhower administrations did a remarkably good job of forming a cohesive multilateral coalition in Europe, the Cold War's most important theater. They also did rather well in the second most important theater, East Asia, in making and sustaining bilateral coalitions with Japan, South Korea, and the Republic of China. But as the administration extended containment farther south on Eurasia's western and eastern rimlands the challenges became more difficult. In Southeast Asia and the Middle East, the Americans had appeared in the wake of British and French imperialism. They were dealing with newly independent countries, whose leaders stood out more for their nationalist passions than for their ability to build stable and effective states. Even when anti-communist, they were not necessarily good strategic partners for a policy of containment.

If by 1954 policy makers no longer shared the theory of victory embedded in the X article of 1947 – that denying incremental dividends to the Soviets wherever they (or their allies or associated movements) encroached would lead to the mellowing or break-up of the Soviet system – one has to ask: What might be the payoff for American grand strategy of extending containment to Southeast Asia or the Middle East? The answer by American strategists

---

[92] Burton I. Kaufman, *The Arab Middle East and the United States: Inter-Arab Rivalry and Superpower Diplomacy* (New York, 1996), pp. 19–21.

[93] Robert J. McMahon, "The Illusion of Vulnerability: American Reassessments of the Soviet Threat, 1955–1956," *International History Review*, vol. 18, no. 3, August 1996, pp. 603–606.

[94] Salim Yaqub, *Containing Arab Nationalism: The Eisenhower Doctrine and the Middle East* (Chapel Hill, NC, 2004).

would have pointed to a negative objective, avoiding the risk of dominos falling. But what if the dominos were being toppled by someone other than the Soviets? American policy makers by 1954 were already aware that what Mao did was not simply a function of Moscow's leadership, that what the Vietnamese communists gained was not simply an outgrowth of Chinese help, and that what Nasser aspired to achieve was not aligned with a communist agenda. They still felt they had to contain instability before it spun out of control. There was another conundrum. As the Eisenhower administration made the extension of containment a central strategic thrust, it created friction with core allies. Britain and Japan, for example, shuddered whenever the United States seemed to approach the brink of nuclear war with China. From an American perspective, the story revealed here is that of a trade-off between maintaining a cohesive coalition in the most important theaters of the Cold War and building a more extensive coalition in new theaters.

Instruments of power and influence

The second key to strategic success lies in developing and integrating different forms of military power and non-military influence. The early Cold War was especially notable for the creation of such instruments. In the military arena, American strategic leaders had to come to grips with the new and difficult issue of what role nuclear weapons should play in support of policy. In the non-military realm, they had to consider how to make use of diplomacy, political warfare, and economic instruments. As we evaluate their chosen courses of action, the challenge is to figure out the strategic effects of what they did. In a limited space, it makes sense to concentrate on the integration of military instruments – conventional and nuclear – and the one non-military realm – that of economic instruments – in which the strategic effects were arguably the most positive from the perspective of US grand strategy.

The quintessential non-military instrument, diplomacy was eventually to play a crucial role in bringing the Cold War to an end, but it was unable to prevent the intensification of the Cold War from the late 1940s to the early 1960s. A grand diplomatic settlement would have had to involve compromises over the divided countries – Germany, China, and Korea – but the ideological gap between the two sides made that difficult indeed. Even had diplomats had negotiated the composition of coalition governments or agreed on "third force" leaders for these divided countries, such formulas for reunification would likely have dissolved into conflict. When war broke out in Korea, it took two years of negotiations simply to agree on the terms of a truce, even though both sides were paying a high cost in lives and treasure. When crises erupted over Germany and China, diplomacy played a role in defusing them, but not in removing the underlying problems. Where, then, did the exercise of diplomatic influence matter most for the United States in early Cold War? The answer lies with friends, not foes. The diplomatic instrument linked up with the first key to success in a major war, coalitions, by bringing Germany and Japan from occupation into alliance and maintaining cohesion in NATO.[95]

What about political warfare? In Kennan's use of the term, it covered both covert operations, such as efforts to subvert a communist regime, and overt operations, such as propaganda. The Soviets by the late 1940s had much experience in political warfare, and American officials believed that the United States had to catch up with them. There ensued much American activity but not much coordination among different organizations.[96] There were some intriguing concepts for how to attack a communist political system by operations short of war, but no obvious success in doing so. In the uprisings in Hungary in 1956, Radio Free Europe's Hungarian broadcasts from Munich encouraged insurgents in a manner at odds with the Eisenhower administration's aversion to taking risks in support of the rebellion.[97] American words and deeds at some crucial junctures of the Cold War were better aligned on the Western side of the Iron Curtain. The flow of US aid to Europe under the Marshall Plan was well supported by a propaganda campaign about the American way of life, though one should not presume targeted audiences were as receptive to the messages as they were to the money.[98]

Because diplomacy was ineffective in dealing with the key political issues of the early Cold War, and because the specter of a nuclear conflagration made the risk of war seem so terrifying to American political leaders, one should not be surprised that American strategists explored unconventional ways of gaining competitive advantage. But the strategic effects of their efforts seem not to have been conspicuous. Rather, the effects were more evident in the formation and maintenance of the American coalition. It is not surprising to find that relationship between two keys to success in a major conflict.

[95] For the role of diplomacy in the transition of Germany and Japan, see Thomas Alan Schwartz, *America's Germany: John J. McCloy and the Federal Republic of Germany* (Cambridge, MA, 1991), and Richard B. Finn, *Winners in Peace: MacArthur, Yoshida, and Postwar Japan* (Berkeley, 1992).
[96] As primary sources have become available on these activities, a flood of historical descriptions of them has swelled. For recent examples, see Corke, *US Covert Operations*; Gregory Mitrovich, *Undermining the Kremlin: America's Strategy to Subvert the Soviet Bloc, 1947–1956* (Ithaca, NY, 2000); and Kenneth Osgood, *Total Cold War: Eisenhower's Secret Propaganda Battle at Home and Abroad* (Lawrence, KS, 2006).
[97] Charles Gati, *Failed Illusions: Moscow, Washington, Budapest, and the 1956 Hungarian Revolt* (Washington, D.C. and Stanford, CA, 2006), chs. 3 and 5. A survey by the United States Information Agency of 1,000 Hungarian refugees after the revolt found that more than half believed Radio Free Europe broadcasts "gave the impression" that United States would intervene militarily. Chris Tudda, "Reenacting the Story of Tantalus: Eisenhower, Dulles, and the Failed Rhetoric of Liberation," *Journal of Cold War Studies*, vol. 7, no. 4, Fall 2005, pp. 3–35.
[98] See Brian Angus McKenzie, *Remaking France: Americanization, Public Diplomacy, and the Marshall Plan* (New York, 2005).

After all, it is easier to have influence on those already inclined to agree with one's political purposes. But such affinities will not count for so much in the absence of a favorable balance of military power and favorable prospects for economic well-being. That justifies giving the closest attention to the military and economic instruments of power and influence and the ways in which they were integrated.

In the military realm, in most past big wars, it had been ground operations and naval operations whose integration had proven crucial for strategic success. In the Second World War it had proven of critical importance to add various types of air operations into the mix. In the larger Cold War, the most important aspect of integrating instruments for strategic purposes was to calculate the proper balance between nuclear weapons and conventional military forces. To accomplish that, strategic leaders had to think coherently about aligning ends, ways, and means. From a military perspective, the primary end was containment. The main pillar to support that end was deterrence. But if deterrence failed, American leaders needed ways to defeat the Soviets in what would likely be real war. The Truman administration and, even more, the Eisenhower administration displayed recurrent interest in compellence, ways of getting the Soviets or Chinese to back away from threatening courses of actions in a crisis. All the while, they had to engage in reassuring America's allies. The combination of nuclear and conventional means necessary to play out with a high probability of strategic success was already looming as expensive in the late 1940s. The pressure to spend more grew apace as the Soviets built up their nuclear arsenal in the 1950s. In this fiscal crunch, something had to give.

In May 1948 during the lead-up to the Berlin blockade, there was the first striking manifestation of that crunch. Early in the month, JCS planners briefed Truman on a war plan that featured the dropping of 50 atomic bombs on 20 Soviet cities in the event the Red Army invaded Western Europe.[99] The president was appalled. Having authorized the dropping of two atomic bombs on Japanese cities in 1945, he never again wanted to face another such decision.[100] He directed the JCS to develop an alternative plan based only on conventional forces. But in mid May, he put a low ceiling on the defense budget for Fiscal Year (FY) 1950, which effectively foreclosed a build-up of conventional forces sufficient to counter the Red Army without the use

---

[99] David Alan Rosenberg, "American Atomic Strategy and the Hydrogen Bomb Decision," *The Journal of American History*, vol. 66, no. 1, June 1979, p. 68. For a description of the war plan, see Steven T. Ross, *American War Plans 1945–1950* (New York, 1988), pp. 89–94. The plan did envision, along with a nuclear offensive, defensive operations by conventional forces in Western Europe.

[100] See the comments by Truman on several occasions to the chairman of the Atomic Energy Commission (which had custody of atomic weapons in the late 1940s), as recorded in the diaries of David Lilienthal, *The Atomic Energy Years 1945–1950* (New York, 1964), pp. 307, 342, 391, 474.

of atomic weapons.[101] Truman had determined to keep government expenditures in line with revenues and, if possible, generate a budgetary surplus
to pay down the high levels of debt incurred during the Second World War.
Moreover, the Republicans on Capitol Hill had passed a tax cut that reduced
the revenues available. Truman had his own domestic priorities that raised
expenditures, and the result severely squeezed the defense budget. After the
precipitous military demobilization of 1945–1947, the ceiling the president
imposed for FY 1950, and the even lower one that he set for FY 1951, left
room only for a strategy of nuclear deterrence. "The atomic bomb was
the mainstay and all he had ... the Russians would have probably taken over
Europe a long time ago if it were not for that."[102]

When the Soviets exploded their first atomic device in 1949, Truman
responded by approving a major step-up in the US nuclear program, but
before Korea he showed little intention of approving the parallel surge
of conventional forces that NSC 68 recommended. The North Korean attack
on South Korea and the Chinese intervention in the war brought about the
only major across-the-board increases in the US conventional forces in the
period. By the end of 1950, the president had directed the implementation
of much of NSC 68's program.[103] Yet, scarcely a year passed before the surge of
conventional rearmament began to subside for political and economic reasons,
even as the burgeoning of nuclear capabilities continued.[104] If Truman had
successfully run for reelection in 1952, the military posture (though
not the rhetoric surrounding it) of his next term might well have emphasized
nuclear weapons as much as did the Eisenhower administration in its first term.

Eisenhower, along with Dulles, devoted more thought to the role of nuclear
weapons than had Truman and his advisors. They also talked more about
them in public. Their rhetoric gave rise to a conceptual trident, with each of
the three prongs taking on a catchy label: massive retaliation, brinksmanship,
and the New Look. The broadcast of Dulles' speech at the Council of Foreign
Relations in January 1954 stimulated debate when he argued that to "contain
the mighty land power of the Communist world," the "local defense" of
forces of the American coalition "must be reinforced by the further deterrent

---

[101] Steven L. Rearden, *The Formative Years 1947–1950*, vol. I of *History of the Office of the Secretary of Defense*, ed. Alfred Goldberg (Washington, D.C., 1984), p. 327. Chapters 6–8 of this volume provide detailed accounts of the making of the military budget before the Korean War.

[102] The quotation is David Lilienthal's paraphrase of what Truman said to him on 9 February 1949. Lilienthal, *The Atomic Energy Years*, p. 464.

[103] For documents on the implementation of NSC 68, see Nelson Drew, ed., *NSC-68: Forging the Strategy of Containment* (Washington, D.C., 1994).

[104] On the leveling off of conventional rearmament, see Walter S. Poole, *History of the Joint Chiefs of Staff: The Joint Chiefs of Staff and National Policy*, vol. IV: *1950–1952* (Washington, D.C. 1998), chp. 4. For the continuing build-up of nuclear capability, see David Alan Rosenberg, "The Origins of Overkill: Nuclear Weapons and American Strategy, 1945–1960," *International Security*, vol. 7, no. 4, Spring 1983, pp. 22–24.

of massive retaliatory power." Using words suggested by Eisenhower, he added that the administration would "depend primarily upon a great capacity to retaliate instantly by means and at places of our choosing."[105] Political critics interpreted that to mean that any communist aggression across a containment line would automatically trigger an American nuclear blitz on the USSR or the PRC.

Actual nuclear strategy was more complex than the public debate indicated. Dulles by no means believed in the all-or-nothing approach toward which excessive reliance on massive nuclear retaliation might lead.[106] He appreciated the need for an array of means to support flexibility of potential responses. In an article in *Foreign Affairs* that followed his speech, he made clear that the United States "must not put itself in the position where the only response open to it is general war" and that the Eisenhower administration was not thinking of "turning every local war into a world war."[107] Placing the primary importance on coalitions, as he did, Dulles was sensitive to the risks posed to coalition cohesion by a reckless nuclear posture. In his view, a posture that left the enemy uncertain about how and where the United States would respond embodied a credible deterrent. He was interested in using nuclear weapons for compellence as well as for deterrence. In a crisis, brinksmanship – threats to use nuclear weapons in certain eventualities – might not only stop adversaries from taking further military steps, but also coerce them to retreat. He thought newly developed tactical nuclear weapons, which he played up as precise and relatively "clean" in the damage that they would inflict, were an appropriate instrument of brinkmanship.[108]

While Dulles did much of the talking about nuclear weapons, it was Eisenhower who decided on their role. Like the secretary of state, the president had great faith that nuclear deterrence would work, at least in the sense of preventing major military attacks on the United States or its allies. But the views of Eisenhower and Dulles about deterrence diverged significantly by 1956 as the Soviet nuclear capability to inflict damage on the American homeland loomed ever larger. Eisenhower had talked with great conviction

---

[105] *New York Times*, 12 January 1954; and Richard H. Immerman, *John Foster Dulles: Piety, Pragmatism, and Power in U.S. Foreign Policy* (Wilmington, DE, 1999), p. 83.

[106] For insight into Dulles' views about nuclear weapons, I have benefitted from John Lewis Gaddis, "The Unexpected John Foster Dulles: Nuclear Weapons, Communism, and the Russians," in Richard H. Immerman, ed., *John Foster Dulles and the Diplomacy of the Cold War* (Princeton, NJ, 1990), pp. 47–77; Immerman, *John Foster Dulles, passim*; and Neal Rosendorf, "John Foster Dulles' Nuclear Schizophrenia," in Gaddis et al., eds., *Cold War Statesmen Confront the Bomb*, pp. 62–86.

[107] John Foster Dulles, "Policy for Security and Peace," *Foreign Affairs*, vol. 32, no. 3, April 1954, pp. 353–364.

[108] In March 1955, at a particularly tense point in the first Taiwan Strait crisis, Gerard Smith (Dulles' advisor on atomic affairs) cautioned the secretary of state that tactical nuclear weapons were not in fact precise or clean. Matthew Jones, "Targeting China: U.S. Nuclear Planning and 'Massive Retaliation' in East Asia, 1953–1955," *Journal of Cold War Studies*, vol. 10, no. 4, Fall 2008, pp. 60–61.

about the extraordinary horror of nuclear warfare – at NSC meetings, to US allies, to the public, at the United Nations, and to the Soviets.[109] But before he received briefings in 1956 about the likely casualties resulting from a thermonuclear war in mid 1958, he had held the conviction that the United States could win such a war, in the narrow military sense that it could destroy the Soviet ability and will to carry on the fight without suffering utter destruction of the American homeland.

However, the briefings, while noting that an exchange of nuclear strikes in 1958 would damage the USSR more than the United States, estimated that between one-half and two-thirds of the American population would be killed or injured. Such carnage, Eisenhower now concluded, rendered any concept of victory meaningless.[110] Dulles, who from 1954 had already moved toward a more flexible posture of deterrence, now became enamored with the feasibility of limited war, even in Central Europe, as a way of bolstering deterrence.[111] Eisenhower, for his part, clung all the more tightly to the idea that, for deterrence to work, it had to be clear to everyone that the United States would respond instantly and massively to any major Soviet attack, especially in Central Europe. In his view, once the United States and USSR began fighting over a political object of high value, with passions erupting on both sides, it was absurd to suppose that they would limit their efforts to conventional forces and tactical nuclear weapons. The dynamics of inter-action would lead inexorably to maximum use of thermonuclear weapons.[112] Eisenhower's key assumptions were that the Soviet leadership had the same image of interaction and a sufficient degree of rationality to avoid the suicidal risks of war. He did not aim to keep the Soviets guessing about the US reaction; he wanted them to be certain.

Thus, from Eisenhower's perspective, investing in instruments of flexible response might erode, not enhance, deterrence. Such investments would also prove expensive. The main focus of the New Look had been to provide for national security at the lowest possible cost. The primary approach to

---

[109] Gaddis, *We Now Know*, pp. 226–230.
[110] Eisenhower diary entry, 23 January 1956, in *Foreign Relations ... 1955–1957*, vol. XIX, p. 187; Andrew P. N. Erdmann, "'War No Longer Has Any Logic Whatever': Dwight D. Eisenhower and the Thermonuclear Revolution," in Gaddis et al., eds., *Cold War Statesmen Confront the Bomb*, pp.106–107; and Campbell Craig, *Destroying the Village: Eisenhower and Thermonuclear War* (New York, 1998), pp. 62–63.
[111] Memorandum of Conversation, 7 April 1958, in National Security Archive, "The Nuclear Vault: Special Collection – Key Documents on Nuclear Policy Issues, 1945–1990," at http://www2.gwu.edu/~nsarchiv/nukevault/special/doc07.pdf. In the Clausewitzian tradition, "limited" refers to the scale of political aims; in the parlance of the 1950s, "limited war" denoted the scale of military effort. See, for example, Henry Kissinger, *Nuclear Weapons and Foreign Policy* (New York, 1957). Dulles' views on nuclear strategy were closer to those of Kissinger and other critics of the Eisenhower administration than was realized at the time.
[112] My interpretation of Eisenhower's views hews closely to that of Erdmann, "War No Longer Has Any Logic Whatever," and of Craig, *Destroying the Village*.

economizing on the military budget was to reduce ground forces. At first, that was not hard to do. The end of the Korean War led to the sort of "downsizing" of ground forces the United States has done after every war. The numbers in South Korea diminished from more than 300,000 in 1953 to fewer than 60,000 in 1955.[113] Meanwhile, Eisenhower hoped to make cuts in American troop strength in Europe.[114] Concerns about the reaction of NATO allies made that a harder task. From 1956 to 1960, the Eisenhower administration carried out a reduction of approximately 10 percent in Germany.[115] But it kept five-and-two-thirds US divisions in Europe despite the standing up of seven German divisions by 1960 (on the way to 12 by 1965).[116] The New Look's expectation that foresaw the waning of conventional forces thus scarcely materialized. But the expectation that foresaw nuclear forces waxing did materialize. Eisenhower presided over the development of a plethora of new platforms and the increase of the US nuclear stockpile from a little more than 1,000 weapons in early 1953 to more than 20,000 in late 1960.[117] From a budgetary perspective, the upshot was not what the New Look envisioned. Over an eight-year period, in which real GDP increased by one-fifth, defense outlays never fell below 9.25 percent of that increasing GDP. The annual ratio of defense outlays to economic output proved greater than under any other American president during the Cold War.[118]

Did all that spending pay off? What strategic effects did the increases of American military forces and instruments produce? The answer to those questions depends on an assessment of Soviet and Chinese policy aims. In Bolshevik strategic culture, there was a tendency to conceive of minimum and maximum aims. In the Cold War, the maximum aims arose from ideological visions of the long-term supersession of capitalism. The best recent historical overviews confirm that ideology was indeed important to Stalin, Mao, and Khrushchev.[119] They do not show an inclination on the part of

---

[113] William Stueck, "Reassessing U.S. Strategy in the Aftermath of the Korean War," *Orbis*, vol. 53, no. 4, Fall 2009, p. 585.

[114] Trachtenberg, *A Constructed Peace*, p. 148.

[115] There is a table of US troop numbers in Germany in Hubert Zimmerman, "The Improbable Permanence of a Commitment: America's Troop Presence in Europe during the Cold War," *Journal of Cold War Studies*, vol. 11, no. 1, Winter 2009, pp. 4–5.

[116] See the table on NATO force levels in John S. Duffield, *Power Rules: The Evolution of NATO's Conventional Force Posture* (Stanford, CA, 1995), p. 234.

[117] See the Natural Resource Defense Council's "Archive of Nuclear Data," at http://www.nrdc.org.

[118] My calculations use data on the websites of the Office of Management and the Budget in the White House and the Bureau of Economic Analysis in the Department of Commerce.

[119] Vladislav Zubok and Constantine Pleshakov, *Inside the Kremlin's Cold War: From Stalin to Khrushchev* (Cambridge, MA, 1996); Vladislav M. Zubok, *A Failed Empire: The Soviet Union in the Cold War from Stalin to Gorbachev* (Chapel Hill, NC, 2007); Jonathan Haslam, *Russia's Cold War: From the October Revolution to the Fall of the Wall* (New Haven, CT, 2011); Chen Jian, *Mao's China and the Cold War* (Chapel Hill, NC, 2001); and Lorenz M. Luthi, *The Sino-Soviet Split: Cold War in the Communist World* (Princeton, NJ, 2008).

those three leaders to risk nuclear war in the short term to accelerate the long-term global expansion of communism.

At the other end of the scale, the minimum aims remained anchored in national security interests and fears. The Soviets put a high value on defending their control of the territorial buffer the Red Army had delivered in the Second World War into Stalin's iron grip. Mao put a high value on consolidating his control of what the People's Liberation Army had delivered into his grasping hands. If this two-level sketch of aims captured the whole picture of Soviet and Chinese foreign policy, one might argue that all the United States needed was a minimal nuclear and conventional-force deterrent to discourage miscalculation or opportunism in Moscow and Beijing. But a simple distinction between minimum and maximum excludes the issue of divided countries, regarding which the danger of nuclear war was greatest during this period. The division of Germany left the Western sectors of Berlin isolated in the east, and gave rise to two Berlin crises. Stalin and Mao supported the reunification of Korea under the control of Kim Il-sung, thus fueling the Korean War. And Mao wanted to reunify China by taking over Taiwan, which provided the backdrop for two crises over the Taiwan straits, during which the United States came closer to nuclear warfare than at any other time in the 1950s. Control of key pieces of territory was not all that was at stake in these dramatic events of the Cold War. Stalin, Mao, and Khrushchev were also interested in attacking the American alliances in Europe and East Asia.[120]

While American nuclear superiority was not enough to keep Soviet and Chinese leaders from taking steps that produced a crisis, it did serve to make them calibrate their actions rather carefully. The deterrent effect of nuclear weapons is clear to this extent. It is less clear why the Soviets and Chinese ended up backing off in major crises. Were there compellent effects at work at the end of crises? If so, did they arise from Soviet or Chinese fear of "punishment" by American nuclear forces or from "denial" by American conventional forces?[121] Eisenhower and Dulles believed that threats to use nuclear weapons finally compelled the Chinese to agree to cease fighting in Korea in July 1953. The consensus of historians is that the threats were weak signals that did not get through clearly to the PRC leadership. In early spring 1953, when the Chinese decided to give way on the issue stalemating truce

---

[120] This aspect of Soviet and Chinese policy deserves more attention than it has received. Haslam, *Russia's Cold War*, throws some new light on the subject with regard to the USSR. As for the PRC, Mao from 1950 on perceived that the United States encircled China on three fronts – Korea, Taiwan, and Indochina – and wanted to break up that encirclement. See Hao Yufan and Zhai Zhihai, "China's Decision to Enter the Korean War: History Revisited," *The China Quarterly*, vol. 121, March 1990, pp. 106–108.

[121] For the distinction between deterrence and compellence, see Thomas Schelling, *Arms and Influence* (New Haven, CT), pp. 69–91. For "denial," see Glenn Snyder, *Deterrence by Punishment and Denial* (Princeton, NJ, 1959); Robert Pape, *Bombing to Win: Air Power and Coercion in War* (Ithaca, NY, 1996); and Lee, "Strategic Interaction."

negotiations – the American opposition to forced repatriation of enemy prisoners-of-war – the threat that weighed on their minds was a major US amphibious operation behind their lines.[122]

In two other cases, compellence through denial by conventional forces seems to have been even more decisive. The ability of American and British aviators to sustain a massive airlift of supplies into West Berlin led Stalin to end his blockade in spring 1949.[123] In the second Taiwan Straits crisis, by early fall 1958 a major deployment of US naval forces and their help in supplying Chiang Kai-shek's ground forces on the island outposts under attack created the conditions in which Mao relaxed military pressure and engaged in diplomatic talks.[124] The only case in which nuclear compellence may have played a key role was in the first Taiwan Strait crisis of 1954–1955. In March 1955, Dulles and Eisenhower made clear nuclear threats; the next month brought Chinese moderation.[125] In the Berlin crisis of 1958–1959, military instruments played no direct role. Khrushchev made a diplomatic threat and, in 1959, the United States parried that threat with diplomatic flexibility.[126]

A reasonable conclusion about the integration of American military instruments in the unfolding of the Cold War would be that nuclear deterrence kept threatening situations manageable for conventional forces. In turn, compellence through denial by conventional forces kept crises from escalating to nuclear warfare. Though the brinksmanship in crises was nerve-racking for America's allies, the resolution of a series of crises short of catastrophic war had the effect of re-assuring those allies. Without the combined effects of deterrence, compellence, and re-assurance that the integration of different forms of military power made possible, there might have been fighting without winning rather than winning without fighting.

---

[122] Shu Guang Zhang, *Deterence and Strategic Culture: Chinese and American Confrontations, 1949–1958* (Ithaca, NY, 1993), pp. 131–136.

[123] Haslam, *Russia's Cold War*, p. 107.

[124] On the scope of US conventional-force operations in the crisis, see Bruce A. Elleman, *High Sea Buffer: The Taiwan Patrol Force, 1950–1979* (Newport, RI, 2012), chp. 8; and Jacob Van Staaveren, "Air Operations in the Taiwan Crisis of 1958" (USAF Historical Division Liaison Office, November 1962), available in "The Nuclear Vault" of the National Security Archive at www.gwu.edu/~nsarchiv/nukevault/ebb249/index.htm. The United States, in addition to its own large deployment of forces, provided Chiang's air force with advanced air-to-air missiles that gave ROC pilots a major edge in the battle for air superiority. Marc S. Gallichio, "The Best Defense is a Good Offense: The Evolution of American Strategy in East Asia," in Warren I. Cohen and Akira Iriye, eds., *The Great Powers in East Asia 1953–1960* (New York, 1990), p. 78.

[125] Zhang, *Deterrence and Strategic Culture*, pp. 220–222. For a contrary view, see Gordon H. Chang and He Di, "The Absence of War in the U.S.–China Confrontation over Quemoy and Matsu in 1954–1955: Contingency, Luck, Deterrence?" *American Historical Review*, vol. 98, no. 5, December 1993, pp. 1500–1524.

[126] Marc Trachtenberg, *History and Strategy* (Princeton, NJ, 1991), chp. 5; and William Burr, "Avoiding the Slippery Slope: The Eisenhower Administration and the Berlin Crisis, November 1958–January 1959," *Diplomatic History*, vol. 18, no. 2, Spring 1994, pp. 177–205.

Among non-military means, the most significant American advantage lay with the economic instrument. The Truman and Eisenhower administrations saw in it ways to hurt foes, help friends, and sway those caught between the two sides. The primary way to use the economic instrument against enemies was to deny them access to something of material value. However, in the early Cold War, the impact of American restrictions on the Soviet economy was modest. One reason was the fact that the Soviets were not as vulnerable to economic pressure as they later became, because they did not yet need large amounts of hard currency to import food and because their government budget revenues and foreign exchange reserves did not yet depend critically on high energy prices.[127]

Another reason is that, early on, American strategic leaders did not think as carefully and creatively about the "negative" use of the economic instrument as their successors did much later.[128] The restrictions they imposed on economic intercourse with the Soviets prompted resistance from Allied governments, which wanted commercial considerations to weigh more heavily in the balance than security considerations. The basic restrictions focused on goods that would contribute to Soviet war-making potential. The American list of prohibited goods was longer than the Allied list. The Europeans were more dependent on trade to the east than Americans and were also more inclined to suppose that a mellow Soviet foreign policy might arise from expansion of trade rather than its restriction. To maintain coalition cohesion, Eisenhower ended up relaxing the American posture.[129]

Restrictions on trade with China were another matter. Because of China's intervention in the Korean War, the multilateral embargo on the PRC was much tighter than on the USSR, and the American embargo was absolute. But after the war's end, Britain (and Japan as well) sought to loosen restrictions. In 1957 the British unilaterally decided that their trade with China should be on the same basis as their trade with the Soviets. Other governments followed their lead. Maintaining coalition cohesion on this front was not so simple for Eisenhower, because a more relaxed American posture would

---

[127] Yegor Gaidar, *Collapse of an Empire: Lessons for Modern Russia*, trans. Antonina W. Bouis (Washington, D.C., 2007) is a pioneering study of Soviet economic vulnerabilities in the 1980s.

[128] For the distinction between "negative" and "positive" uses of the economic instrument, see Diane B. Kunz, "When Money Counts and Doesn't: Economic Power and Diplomatic Objectives," *Diplomatic History*, vol. 18, no. 4, Fall 1994, pp. 451–452. The sharpest negative use by the United States in the early Cold War was against allies, in the Suez Crisis of 1956. See Kunz, *The Economic Diplomacy of the Suez Crisis* (Chapel Hill, NC, 1991).

[129] There is a succinct analysis in Alan B. Dobson, "From Instrumental to Expressive: The Changing Goals of the U.S. Cold War Strategic Embargo," *Journal of Cold War Studies*, vol. 12, no. 1, Winter 2010, pp. 98–104. There is much more detail in Philip J. Funigello, *American–Soviet Trade in the Cold War* (Chapel Hill, NC, 1988), chs. 2–5.

arouse congressional criticism.[130] Nevertheless, the leading scholar of the embargo has argued that negative use of the economic instrument against China did have positive strategic effects for the United States.[131] Trade restrictions pushed the PRC into even closer economic dependence on the USSR. That did not sit well with Mao, who reacted by disentangling himself from his ally.

What about the positive use of the economic instrument? We need to consider two ways of making it work in relation to allies and the non-aligned. One is to provide direct economic aid to them. The more indirect approach is to construct an international economic order from which they can benefit. The United States did both as the Cold War unfolded, with more energy and creativity than with the negative use of the economic instrument. The Marshall Plan, proposed in 1947 and implemented in 1948–1951, has long stood as a success story for American grand strategy. Under what was officially known as the European Recovery Program (ERP), the United States provided the Western Europeans $13 billion (about $120 billion in 2012 prices), mostly in grants, not loans. That amounted to approximately 2 percent of the GDP of the United States and of the West European countries as a whole. During this period, the industrial production in the recipient countries increased by more than 50 percent.[132] There has been much debate in retrospect among economists and historians about the direct economic effects of ERP aid.[133] At the very least, in narrow economic terms, the Marshall Plan allowed the recipients of aid to maneuver around impediments to growth such as balance-of-payments crises, fiscal crunches, and shortages of raw materials.

But for students of grand strategy, it was the political effects of the Marshall Plan that demand closer attention. Those effects played out on two levels: the international balance of power in Europe and on the domestic balance of power in the countries receiving aid. Diplomatic historians see the Marshall Plan as consolidating the division of Europe in the Cold War.[134] The flow of US aid and surge of West European growth happened at the same time that the British, Americans, and French were engaged in the diplomacy that led to the creation of West Germany and the formation of NATO. Coalition

---

[130] Shu Guang Zhang, *Economic Cold War: America's Embargo against China and the Sino-Soviet Alliance, 1949–1963* (Washington, D.C. and Stanford, CA, 2001), chs. 5 and 7; and Dobson, "From Instrumental to Expressive," pp. 108–109.

[131] Zhang, *Economic Cold War*, pp. 218–236, 258, 274–276.

[132] Barry Eichengreen, "Lessons from the Marshall Plan," a "Background Case Note" prepared in April 2010 for the World Bank's *World Development Report* of 2011.

[133] The most substantial revisionist study is Alan S. Milward, *The Reconstruction of Western Europe 1945–1951* (Berkeley, CA, 1984). The best overall assessment of economic effects is J. Bradford DeLong and Barry Eichengreen, "The Marshall Plan: History's Most Succesful Structural Adjustment Program," in Rudiger Dornbusch et al., eds., *Postwar Economic Reconstruction and Its Lessons for the East Today* (Cambridge, MA, 1993), pp. 189–230.

[134] See the symposium on the Marshall Plan in the *Journal of Cold War Studies*, vol. 7, no. 1, Winter 2005.

cohesion increased with the integration of different instruments of power and influence. The flow of resources from the richer patron to the poorer partners served as an important lubricant of that cohesion. On the other side of Europe, one could see a stark contrast. While the United States injected $13 billion in aid into Western Europe in 1948–1951, the Soviet Union extracted an estimated $20 billion in reparations and seizures from Eastern Europe from 1945 to 1956.[135]

Not only was the European military balance more favorable to the West in 1951 than it had been in 1947, but the prospects for domestic political stability were brighter as well. Those two developments were connected. A coalition cohesive enough to contain the Soviet Union and its bloc required political leaders willing to remain aligned with the United States and able to maintain majority support in their democratic political systems. The Marshall Plan helped make Western European politics conducive to the tenure in office of such leaders. American material support and especially the Korean War boom had the same effect on Japanese politics. In Germany and Japan, where socialist parties desired a neutral stance, it was vital for the sake of coalition cohesion to forestall left-of-center electoral triumphs. With regard to France and Italy, where communist parties were powerful, international coalition cohesion depended on keeping those puppets of Soviet policy out of majority domestic coalitions.[136]

Truman, like many American leaders after him, wanted to replicate the payoff of the Marshall Plan elsewhere. In January 1949, point four of the president's inaugural address for his second term envisaged a proliferation of US foreign aid far beyond Europe. Theoretically, modernization would develop as injections of capital into developing economies stimulated growth. Economic growth in turn would facilitate nation building. Stable, democratic countries all over the world were the desired end state.[137] As usual, reality was more complex than theory. Friction abounded. It was hard to sustain support for foreign aid on Capitol Hill. Injections of foreign aid were not only less

---

[135] Zbigniew K. Brzezinski, *The Soviet Bloc: Unity and Conflict* (Cambridge, MA, 1969), pp. 124–126, 283–284. See also Austin Jersild, "The Soviet State as Imperial Scavenger: 'Catch Up and Surpass' in the Transnational Socialist Bloc, 1950–1960," *American Historical Review*, vol. 116, no. 1, February 2011, pp. 109–132.

[136] My thoughts on the political effects of the Marshall Plan have been carried along by a stream of Charles Maier's writings, which began with "The Politics of Productivity: Foundations of American International Economic Policy after World War II," *International Organization*, vol. 31, no. 4, Autumn 1977, pp. 607–633, and culminated in "The Making of 'Pax Americana': Formative Moments of United States Ascendancy," in R. Ahmann et al., eds., *The Quest for Stability*, pp. 389–434.

[137] For an attempt by a historian to trace the development of modernization theory in this period, see David Ekbladh, *The Great American Mission: Modernization and the Construction of an American World Order* (Princeton, NJ, 2010). See also Bevan Sewell, "Early Modernisation Theory? The Eisenhower Administration and the Foreign Policy of Development in Brazil," *English Historical Review*, vol. 125, no. 517, December 2010, pp. 1449–1480.

than envisioned, but also less stimulating to developing economies than expected. Newly independent countries lacked the institutional infrastructure of Western Europe and Japan that had enabled growth. Further complicating affairs, Khrushchev jumped into the arena in the mid 1950s with Soviet foreign aid initiatives targeting non-aligned states.[138] By the early 1960s, Khrushchev and Mao were competing to support "wars of national liberation" in the Third World.

Of the more than 30 newly independent countries in which the United States found itself involved, only two – South Korea and Taiwan – became both prosperous and democratic during the Cold War.[139] They did not attain that state of affairs until the 1980s, long after the Truman and Eisenhower administrations and the heyday of American aid. Indeed, their economic rise owed more to trade than aid. Following the path marked out by Japan, they plugged their economies into the new international economic order that the United States had constructed in the early Cold War.[140] In this construction project, the Americans not only served as the provider of security, but also as the lender and export market of first resort. Even more important ultimately, the United States was the pioneer of the technological frontier toward which it beckoned others to follow in the process of "convergence."

That is the long-term international success story of the American economic instrument. If its opening act featured the "golden age" that Western European economies enjoyed in the first half of the Cold War, its denouement in East Asia was the transformation of that area from a cockpit of conflict to a dynamo of economic growth. In 1961, however, no one in Washington had an inkling of what lay ahead. For the short-term story in East Asia during the 1950s was one of more limited and tenuous payoffs from the use of the economic instrument. It allowed the Eisenhower administration to maintain coalitions with its local partners. It provided the administration some measure of control over the military posture of those partners, but it failed to provide much leverage over the behavior of the French with regard to the people of Indochina or over the domestic policies of the new authoritarian mandarins of the old Confucian political culture – Chiang Kai-shek, Syngman Rhee, and

---

[138] Khrushchev's brandishing of the economic instrument in the Third World caused considerable alarm in the Eisenhower administration. Robert J. McMahon, "The Illusion of Vulnerability: American Reassessments of the Soviet Threat, 1955–1956," *International History Review*, vol. 18, no. 3, August 1996, pp. 591–619.

[139] Odd Arne Westad, *The Global Cold War: Third World Interventions and the Making of Our Times* (Cambridge, 2007), p. 404.

[140] G. John Ikenberry, *After Victory: Institutions, Strategic Restraint, and the Rebuilding of Order after Major Wars* (Princeton, NJ, 2001), chp. 6 sketches the big picture. The difficulties of construction are filled in by Jim Lacey, "The Economic Making of Peace," in Williamson Murray and Jim Lacey, eds., *The Making of Peace*, pp. 293–322; Milward, *The Reconstruction of Western Europe*; and Francine McKenzie, "GATT and the Cold War: Accession Debates, Institutional Development, and the Western Alliance, 1947–1959," *Journal of Cold War Studies*, vol. 10, no. 3, Summer 2008, pp. 78–109.

Ngo Dinh Diem. Those coalition relationships repeatedly brought the United States to the verge of strategic overextension, a major pitfall in the Cold War.

Strategic overextension

In a conflict, it is not sufficient to consider what one intends to do to one's enemies. One must also consider the options open to them. In major conflicts, new enemies may arise in new theaters. If one fails to contest what they do, the balance of power may turn unfavorably. But if one contests new theaters, one may strategically overextend one's capabilities. Marshall, in his reference to the Peloponnesian War in early 1947, may well have been thinking about the disastrous Athenian expedition to Sicily in 415–413 BC. In his personal experience, the opening of new theaters in the Second World War had had a crucial impact on the war's outcome. Indeed, Nazi Germany and Imperial Japan defeated themselves by overextending their military forces. One could make a similar argument for Germany in the First World War. In the Cold War, the Soviets were more prudent, at least at first. Beyond the primary theater of Europe, Soviet allies or associated movements opened almost all new secondary theaters, until the Soviets finally – and fatally – did so in Afghanistan. In each case, the US leaders had to consider how to react, with the fate of actual or potential allies at stake but with the possibility of strategic overextension on their minds.

In principle, the strategic concept of containment should have served as a powerful guide to American decisions about where and when to intervene in new theaters. In practice, policy makers could make reasonable arguments for extending containment everywhere major threats arose or for limiting containment to areas deemed vital to US security.[141] In retrospect, a more refined analytical framework, not a single concept open to differing interpretations, is necessary to evaluate American decisions with regard to new theaters: (1) Will one be fighting the principal enemy in a new place or (as with Athens in Sicily) a new enemy? (2) Can one be operationally effective in the new theater? (3) At the same time, one needs to ask: What is the strategic importance of the new theater to the overall war? What will be the broader payoff for operational success there, relative to the price one will have to pay? (4) Even if likely costs outweigh likely benefits, one needs to consider scenarios, if one refuses to engage. (5) Even if likely benefits seem to outweigh likely costs, one needs to consider "opportunity costs."

One can apply the most relevant parts of this framework to the following important American decisions in the early Cold War: the decision not to intervene militarily in the Chinese Civil War in 1947–1948; the decision to intervene militarily in the Korean War in late June 1950; the decision to

---

[141] Lee, "The Cold War as a Coalition Struggle," p. 153.

plunge deep into North Korea in the fall of 1950; the decision not to intervene militarily in the French Indochina War in 1954; and the decision to stand behind the Republic of China in the Taiwan Strait crises of 1954–1955 and 1958.[142] None of these decisions involved a foregone conclusion.

The risk of American overextension was most conspicuous in China, because Chiang Kai-shek had been an ally in the Second World War and because his country was so potentially important. Shortly before Marshall made the decision not to intervene militarily in the Chinese Civil War, the president had enunciated what became known as the Truman Doctrine, which was on its face a declaration of extended containment. "I believe that it must be the policy of the United States," Truman told Congress (and other audiences), "to assist free peoples who are resisting attempted subjugation by armed minorities or by outside pressures." He did not put geographical restrictions on this statement, though he did indicate that "our help should be primarily through economic and financial aid."[143] When extraordinary amounts of such aid proved insufficient to prevent a stunning reversal of military momentum from Chiang to Mao from 1947 on, one could make a case for involving American military forces in the fray, if only to serve as operational advisors or to salvage a partition of China at, say, the Yangtze River (rather than at the Taiwan Strait). Marshall nonetheless ruled out, with Truman's concurrence, any such American military intervention.[144]

With one exception, Marshall's reasoning aligned well with the above framework for thinking about new theaters. At a time when the Soviets were becoming more adversarial in Europe, he did not want to take on a new enemy in China, especially since it was not yet clear that Mao would closely align with Stalin. At a time when postwar demobilization and occupation duties in Germany, Austria, and Korea had drastically reduced US combat power, he doubted that the United States could be operationally effective in the vast theater of China, where indigenous forces numbered in the millions and where, once the Chinese communists had gained control of the Manchurian theater, it would be impossible to deny them access to Soviet support. Moreover, from recent personal experience, Marshall knew Chiang would be neither competent nor cooperative as a local partner. He thus feared that the costs of military intervention would far exceed any strategic payoff, and as a longtime advocate of the "Europe first" priority, he assumed that scarce resources deployed to China could bring a greater strategic payoff if

---

[142] In an essay forming part of a larger volume, available space does not permit coverage of all US decisions from 1945 to 1961 about opening or contesting new theaters. Notable omissions in this essay are China in 1950–1951, Lebanon in 1958, and Laos in 1959–1960.

[143] Truman's speech and archival documents relating to it are at www.trumanlibrary.org/whistlestop/study_collections/doctrine/large/index.php.

[144] The best analysis of decision making in this China case is Ernest R. May, *The Truman Administration and China, 1945–1949* (Philadelphia, PA, 1975), which includes primary source documents.

employed on the other side of the world. Marshall evidently did not consider future scenarios involving a Sino-Soviet alliance.

Through a multi-dimensional chain reaction, the American decision not to contest Mao's drive to power in China militarily soon generated another decision about a nearby theater: whether or not to intervene militarily against the North Korean invasion of South Korea in June 1950. If one considers assessments of South Korea's relative lack of strategic importance by the Pentagon in 1947 and MacArthur in 1949, as well as the withdrawal of American occupation troops from Korea in 1948–1949, and perhaps above all the exclusion of South Korea from an American offshore "defense perimeter" by Acheson in his famous speech of January 1950, it would seem that American military intervention in Korea was by no means a foregone conclusion.[145] Yet, in this case, there was no hesitation. Morally outraged by North Korea's attack, the president reacted impulsively. He does not seem to have thought much, if at all, about the elements of assessment highlighted in the above framework. He does not even seem to have thought in terms of containment.

Instead Truman fell back on notions of collective security and recollections of how its failure in the 1930s had led to the Second World War. Acheson, who had a strong influence on Truman's decisions, thought more about the relationship of Korea to the larger Cold War and to the concept of containing the Soviets. Assuming that Stalin was behind the attack (we now know that he did not come up with the idea, but supported it in crucial ways), the secretary of state had to assess whether it was a test or trap. If it was a test, and if the United States did not intervene decisively in Korea, there would be an elevated probability of a follow-on attack elsewhere, quite possibly in Europe. If it were a trap, and if the United States overextended in Korea, that, too, would raise the probability of aggression in another theater.[146]

Until September 1950, American policy and strategy in Korea were improvised. The decision to plunge into North Korea was not improvised. Nor did it simply represent the outbreak of "victory fever" after the success at Inchon. Rather, it was the outcome of an intense two-month debate that began in the State Department in July 1950 and soon drew in the new national security institutions, including the Department of Defense and the Central Intelligence Agency, none of which distinguished themselves by the quality of their assessments. The arguments for eliminating North Korea were that doing so would punish aggression, please the South Koreans, and preclude another invasion attempt by Kim Il-sung. There was no well-developed counterargument about how, even if the Soviets or Chinese did not counter

---

[145] See, for example, Ernest R. May, *"Lessons" of the Past: The Use and Misuse of History in American Foreign Policy* (Oxford, 1973), chp. 3.

[146] Robert L. Beisner, *Dean Acheson: A Life in the Cold War* (Oxford, 2006), pt. IV provides much useful information on how Acheson responded.

394 Bradford A. Lee

the advance to the north, the postwar security of a unified Korea might well require a large and protracted commitment of American troops along 500 miles of border with China and the Soviet Union. Such a commitment would cut against plans to bolster NATO in Europe, the primary theater of the larger Cold War. The final directive to MacArthur, patched together in the National Security Council, represented a messy bureaucratic compromise.[147] Its restraining verbiage – halt if and when there were signs of Soviet or Chinese intervention – the theater commander ignored. MacArthur assured Truman that air interdiction could slaughter the Chinese if they intervened. He also held out hope that American troops would be out of Korea by Christmas.[148] Instead, massive Chinese forces intervened, lured MacArthur into an operational trap, and inflicted a major military setback.

Eisenhower wanted to avoid any repetition of such overextension, but aimed at avoiding the loss of territory to communism. Those cross-cutting objectives made for an excruciating predicament whenever his administration confronted a decision about contesting a new theater with military forces. His first such decision came in 1954, when the French effort in Indochina was on its last legs. If the United States were to intervene militarily, it would have to deal with a new enemy, the Vietnamese communists, and if China also intervened, with an old enemy in a new place. Given the geography of Southeast Asia, there was little the United States could do to interdict Chinese access to the theater. Moreover, the terrain of the theater worried Eisenhower. He doubted American forces could operate effectively in Indochina's jungles.[149] As for local partners, the United States had already experienced trouble working with the French, who did not think much of American military advice and had long resisted American political pressure to grant independence to the nationalities of Indochina.

From Eisenhower's perspective, Indochina was not of great strategic value in and of itself. But he feared that, if it fell, there would be significant repercussions in Asia. Indeed it was at this juncture in spring 1954 that he first talked publicly about the "domino theory."[150] His options were to use force to prevent the first domino from falling or to set up what became SEATO to prevent the fall of further dominos. He conflated the two options for a time in seeking support from the British and Asian states for immediate military intervention to relieve the Viet Minh siege of Dien Bien Phu. When the British

---

[147] For the debate and the resulting compromise, see *Foreign Relations ... 1950*, vol. VII, pp. 393–782.

[148] Notes compiled by General Omar Bradley of a meeting at Wake Island, 15 October 1950, in ibid., pp. 949, 953.

[149] Richard H. Immerman, "Between the Unattainable and the Unacceptable: Eisenhower and Dienbienphu," *Reevaluating Eisenhower: American Foreign Policy in the 1950s*, ed. Richard A. Melanson and David Mayers (Urbana, IL, 1987), p. 123.

[150] Eisenhower press conference, 7 April 1954, in *Public Papers of the Presidents of the United States: Dwight D. Eisenhower, 1954* (Washington, D.C., 1960), pp. 381–390.

refused to go along, Eisenhower decided against the use of force, which left SEATO as the fallback position. Here as elsewhere, coalition considerations dominated Eisenhower's thinking.

Eisenhower's next Asian challenges arose along the China coast between Vietnam and Korea. The Taiwan Strait crises of 1954–1955 and 1958 were unlikely to produce overextension in the form of major intervention by US ground troops. The PRC bombardment of small ROC-held islands, Quemoy (Jinmen) and Matsu (Mazu), near the Chinese mainland, triggered the crises. If resolute Chinese amphibious assaults were to follow, it would likely take heavy American air strikes, probably delivering nuclear bombs, to compel Mao to cease and desist. The danger of overextension in such an eventuality would take the form of nuclear escalation that would draw in the Soviet Union and carry the risk of alienating Japan and Britain.

Because Quemoy and Matsu were hard to defend, Eisenhower in both crises hoped to persuade Chiang Kai-shek that it was in the ROC's interest to evacuate the islands or at least regard them as expendable.[151] But Chiang was not a cooperative partner. After the first crisis, he proceeded to deploy more troops on Quemoy and Matsu – one-third of the Nationalist Army's divisions by 1958. Eisenhower found himself on the horns of a dilemma. If he allowed Quemoy and Matsu to fall, the shock to the morale of the ROC military and the legitimacy of the regime might lead to the end of Chiang's rule in Taiwan, the loss of a key link in the "first island chain" (the maritime segment of the US containment line in the Western Pacific), and the fall of other "dominos" in Asia. If, however, a commitment on his part to defend Quemoy and Matsu led, either by provoking Mao or encouraging Chiang, to a hot war between the United States and China, the damage to American relations with more important allies might prove profound.

Eisenhower avoided impalement in both 1954–1955 and 1958. As he suspected, Mao did not want a war with the United States. The PRC's leader had multiple purposes in instigating the two Taiwan Strait crises. Both were useful for domestic political mobilization.[152] That was the only purpose

---

[151] The best detailed studies of American policy and diplomacy in the two Taiwan Strait crises are by Robert Accinelli: *Crisis and Commitment: United States Policy toward Taiwan, 1950–1955* (Chapel Hill, NC, 1996), chs. 8–10, and "A Thorn in the Side of Peace: The Eisenhower Administration and the 1958 Offshore Islands Crisis," in Robert S. Ross and Jiang Changbin, eds., *Re-examining the Cold War: U.S.–China Diplomacy, 1954–1973* (Cambridge, MA, 2001), chp. 4. For good glimpses into Eisenhower's thinking, see his letter to Winston Churchill, 29 March 1955, and his long memorandum for Dulles, 5 April 1955, both in *The Papers of Dwight David Eisenhower*, vol. XVI: *The Presidency: The Middle Way*, eds. Louis Galambos and Daun Van Ee (Baltimore, MD, 1996), pp. 1639–1642, 1654–1659.

[152] Chen Jian, *Mao's China*, pp. 169–175. For a more detailed analysis of Mao's domestic-political purposes in 1958, see Thomas J. Christensen, *Useful Adversaries: Grand Strategy, Domestic Mobilization, and Sino-American Conflict, 1947–1958* (Princeton, NJ, 1996), chp. 6.

actually fulfilled. Both crises were also ways to test Soviet willingness in the post-Stalin era to support the PRC in its quest to reunify Chinese territory. That purpose backfired. Soviet support was lukewarm. As Sino-American tensions rose in early 1955, Mao concluded China needed its own nuclear weapons. The Soviets agreed to help the Chinese develop those weapons. But in the 1958 crisis, Mao's cavalier utterances about nuclear war appalled Khrushchev, who then ended Soviet support for the Chinese nuclear program.[153]

Mao's Sun Tzuian hope that he could attack American alliances did not work out so well in 1954–1955. In his view, the first crisis was supposed to halt negotiations between Chiang's government and the Eisenhower administration for a security pact. Mao's belligerence actually had the effect of accelerating its completion. In 1958, Mao conceived of a further Sun Tzuian stratagem. He told his colleagues that Quemoy and Matsu made for an "iron noose" into which the Americans had overextended and by which he could cause them further strategic problems.[154] He also evidently told Soviet foreign minister Andrei Gromyko that if the United States responded with a nuclear attack on China, Chinese forces would lure American troops deep into the countryside.[155] Unlike MacArthur in 1950, Eisenhower did not fall into a trap.

Imprudent military plunges into new theaters are not the only form of strategic overextension. A cold war, after all, is a long-term competition only occasionally punctuated by hot wars in different theaters that pit "proxies" or partners of one side against partners and, in some cases, the principal power of the other. In such long-term competitions, another form of strategic overextension can materialize when the resources one of the principal powers devotes to military and non-military instruments outrun the economic base from which governments must extract those resources. Eisenhower, however, remained mindful of the need for a balance between strategic efforts and economic considerations. The issue that loomed large over time was whether economic expansion could keep pace with what the grand strategy required as a competitive US–USSR interaction evolved dynamically.[156]

---

[153] John Wilson Lewis and Xue Litai, *China Builds the Bomb* (Stanford, CA, 1988), pp. 22–42, 60–72; Nikita Khrushchev, *Khrushchev Remembers*, ed. Strobe Talbott (Boston, 1970), pp. 469–470; and Nikita Khrushchev, *Khrushchev Remembers: The Glasnost Tapes*, eds. Jerrold L. Schechter and Vyacheslav V. Luchkov (Boston, 1990), pp. 147–150.

[154] Mao's speeches to the Supreme State Council, 5 and 8 September 1958, in "New Evidence on Mao Zedong's Handling of the Taiwan Straits Crisis of 1958: Chinese Recollections and Documents," *Cold War International History Project Bulletin*, Issues 6–7, Winter 1995/1996), pp. 215, 217; Chen Jian, *Mao's China*, p. 187. For more on Mao in relation to Sun Tzu's concepts, see Lee, "Strategic Interaction," p. 38.

[155] Andrei A. Gromyko, *Memoirs* (New York, 1989), pp. 251–252.

[156] For an even broader perspective, see Aaron L. Friedberg, *In the Shadow of the Garrison State: America's Anti-Statism and Its Cold War Grand Strategy* (Princeton, NJ, 2000).

Economic superiority

In the world wars of the twentieth century, economic superiority rose in relative importance among the keys to success in a major war. In the Second World War, it was a trump card for the United States, which turned its vast economic potential into both military power projected across oceans and the supplies shipped to its allies on a scale that dwarfed what Britain had done in the First World War. Equally remarkable was the fact that the United States achieved something that no other great power had ever managed in a major war: at the end of the Second World War, its economy was twice as large as it had been at the beginning. In contrast, the economies of its future allies and future enemies were 50 percent less than they had been in 1939.[157] This essay has already considered what the United States did to help its old and new friends recover. It now needs to evaluate American economic performance in relation to its main enemy in a cold war that proved more than ten times longer than American belligerency in the Second World War. The former posed different economic challenges than the latter. A multi-year surge of production for military purposes, such as in the Second World War, might turn out to be necessary (on a smaller scale) at some junctures in the Cold War, as indeed in the early 1950s and early 1980s. But multi-decade sustained growth was more important. The key economic challenges were to avoid a recurrence of the Great Depression; to bring down the volume of public debt run up from 1941 to 1945; to manage a reasonably stable balance between levels of inflation and employment; and, above all, to achieve sufficient long-term growth to insure the Soviets could not catch up.

The relative economic outlook at the end of the Second World War did not discourage the Soviets. Their top expert on capitalist economies, Eugene Varga, predicted in good Marxist fashion that within a few years the United States would face a new "crisis of overproduction" that would result in another Great Depression.[158] Bourgeois pessimism among American economists, especially those influenced by Keynesian theory, mirrored his Marxist optimism. As the demobilization of military personnel and the decline of military spending proceeded apace, they anticipated massive unemployment arising from shrinking demand. Many thought long-term stagnation would follow a short-term economic downturn.[159] Economic reality, as is so often the case, confounded predictions based on theory. There was no depression, only a small dip in 1946 and 1947. Unemployment remained under 4 percent in both years. The national-income accounting that developed along with

---

[157] Charles S. Maier, "The Making of 'Pax Americana': Formative Moments of United States Ascendancy," in R. Ahmann et al., eds., *The Quest for Stability*, p. 406.

[158] See the summary of Varga's argument in Taubman, *Stalin's American Policy*, p. 84.

[159] Robert W. Fogel, "Reconsidering Expectations of Economic Growth After World War II from the Perspective of 2004," *IMF Staff Papers*, vol. 52, 2005, pp. 7–9.

Keynesian theory indicates that pent-up consumer demand and an unprecedented surge of net exports (the purchase of which foreign aid facilitated) came
close to making up for the sharp decline in government spending.[160]

Avoidance of a depression made it easier for Truman and Eisenhower
to decrease public debt. The story of how gross Federal debt fell from its
FY 1946 peak of 121.7 percent of GDP has yet to find its historian. Such an
inquiry ought to be stimulated by recent analysis of historical data that
suggests that "median growth rates for countries with public debt over 90 percent of GDP are roughly one percent lower than otherwise; average (mean)
growth rates are several percent lower."[161] Gross Federal debt did not fall
below 90 percent of GDP until 1951. At first sight, it may seem odd that the
crossover point came during the Korean War, when military spending put the
budget back into deficit after the surpluses of the late 1940s. The explanation
is that wartime price rises inflated nominal GDP and thus reduced the
proportionate burden of debt. After Korea, even though price levels stabilized,
Federal debt shrank steadily under Eisenhower to 55.2 percent of GDP in
FY 1961, not because of a fall in debt, but rather because of a rise of almost
30 percent in GDP from FY 1954 to FY 1961. Real GDP (i.e., adjusted
for inflation) rose over 20 percent in that period.[162]

In Keynesian perspective, the macroeconomic policy of the Truman and
Eisenhower administrations has long seemed stodgy and their macroeconomic performance far from spectacular, because the two presidents put a
high priority on balancing the budget and were not predisposed to embrace
new ideas for countercyclical management. Since most Keynesian economists
supported (and some served in) Democratic administrations, that judgment
was especially pronounced with regard to Eisenhower. It found expression
in the slogan of the Kennedy campaign in 1960 that it was time to get
the country moving again. But perspectives change with time. In the early
twenty-first century, a formidable pair of economists revisited the 1950s.[163]

---

[160] For the export story, see Jason E. Taylor, Bharati Basu, and Steven McLean, "Net Exports
and the Avoidance of High Unemployment During Reconversion, 1945–1947," *Journal of
Economic History* vol. 71, no. 2, June 2011, pp. 447–454.

[161] Carmen M. Reinhart and Kenneth S. Rogoff, "Growth in a Time of Debt," *American
Economic Review* vol. 100, no. 2, May 2010, pp. 573–578. The importance of the 90 percent
threshold has come under challenge in the wake of recalculations in Thomas Herndon,
Michael Ash, and Robert Pollin, "Does High Public Debt Consistently Stifle Economic
Growth? A Critique of Reinhart and Rogoff," April 2013, at www.peri.umass.edu/
fileadmin/pdf/working_papers/working_papers_301–350/WP322.pdf.

[162] My data are drawn from tables provided on the websites of the Office of Management and
the Budget in the White House and the Bureau of Economic Analysis in the Department of
Commerce.

[163] Christina D. Romer and David H. Romer, "A Rehabilitation of Monetary Policy in the
1950s," *NBER Working Paper 8800* (Cambridge, MA, 2002). Christina Romer, the top
economic historian of modern American business cycles, served as chair of the Council of
Economic Advisers in the Obama administration. Her husband David Romer is his
generation's leading theorist of long-term economic growth.

They discovered that macroeconomic policy under the Eisenhower administration did in fact bear the imprint of the new macroeconomic concepts pioneered by Keynes and other academic economists in the 1930s and 1940s; and notwithstanding three short recessions between 1953 and 1961, the performance of the American economy was, overall, reasonably good.[164]

What about the long-term outlook for the expansion of the productive capacity of the American economy in relation to the Soviet economy? Keynes famously quipped that "in the long run, we are all dead," as a way of trying to get economists and policy makers to focus on the short run. But long-run economic success mattered greatly in the Cold War because, as Eisenhower said in his famous Farewell Address, "unhappily the danger it poses promises to be of indefinite duration."[165]

All through the 1950s, there were attempts to assess the Soviet–American economic balance. Nitze's NSC 68 in 1950 highlighted the 4:1 disparity between the size of the two economies in making the case that the United States could afford a major surge of rearmament, and it held out a quasi-Keynesian hope that increased military spending would accelerate US growth. Kennan's Task Force A in Project Solarium in 1953 presented a number of graphs and tables assessing the current state of the economy and projecting estimates to the early 1960s. The most important of those projections was that American GNP would grow at an annual rate of 3.6 percent from 1952 to 1962, while Soviet GNP would achieve a 6.0 percent growth rate. Lest that comparison undercut the case that time was on the side of the United States, a graph in the report showed that because of the disparity in the size of the two economies, the gap between the aggregate output of the US economy and that of the Soviets would widen in spite of the superior Soviet growth rate.[166]

Outside official circles, by the end of the 1950s, there was increasingly pessimistic concern in the United States among economists that higher levels of economic growth would enable the Soviet Union to overcome American economic superiority in the next generation, as Khrushchev boasted. In fact over the next generation of the Cold War, both Soviet and American economic performance deteriorated. Then, in the final decade of the Cold War, the United States bounced back, while the Soviet economy, and with it the Soviet political system, collapsed.

---

[164] Christina Romer went on later to revisit the 1960s in a presentation to the Economic History Annual Meeting in September 2007 at the Lyndon Johnson Presidential Library. She concluded that the much more aggressive pursuit of expansionary macroeconomic policy in that decade was "a mistaken revolution."

[165] Dwight D. Eisenhower, "Farewell Address," 17 January 1961, at http://www.eisenhower. archives.gov/research/online_documents/farewell_address/1961_01_17_Press_Release.pdf.

[166] The economic section runs from p. 44 to p. 56 of Task Force A's report. Graph B1 comparing the American and Soviet economies follows p. 44.

So what?

This essay has examined both thought and action on the American side in the early Cold War from 1945 to 1961. The thought took the form of strategic assessments and strategic concepts. The action took the form of efforts to develop and sustain cohesive coalitions, develop and integrate the use of the instruments of military power and non-military influence, contest new theaters without over-extension, and exploit and sustain economic superiority. The thought represents the idiosyncratic aspect of US grand strategy in this period. The action replicates the generic keys to success that one can find by looking for strategic patterns in major conflicts from the Peloponnesian War to the Second World War.

The story that emerges is one of relative success. For all the Truman administration's floundering with the Chinese Communists in East Asia, the strategic position of the United States relative to the Soviet Union was more advantageous when Truman left office in January 1953 than at Potsdam in July 1945. Thanks in part to Stalin's self-defeating actions, the relative advantage stood out above all in terms of coalitions, the first and foremost key to success in a big war. For all of the Eisenhower administration's frustrations in integrating nuclear weapons and other instruments into its grand strategy and in trying to extend containment into the Third World, the strategic position of the United States relative to the Soviet Union was more advantageous when Eisenhower left office than when he had taken over eight years earlier. That story of relative American success was not to be sustained over the middle stage of the Cold War in the 1960s and 1970s. Rather than the incremental improvement of the period from 1945 to 1960, there was to be a decline from one administration to another over the following two decades. That sad story played out under both Democratic and Republican presidents.

This stark juxtaposition of relative success and failure invites one to ponder what makes for good grand strategy. One obvious place to look is in the nature of the strategists themselves. Good leadership is easy to invoke, but it is hard to determine its essence. Three of its elements worth exploring are temperament, intellect, and experience. Truman had the temperament to make difficult decisions when necessary, and he had an intellect improved by his interest in history. He lacked experience, but could count on the two best secretaries of state during the Cold War – Marshall and Acheson. Eisenhower was the only president during the Cold War to combine all three elements to a high degree. To those who question his intellect, it is worth noting that, according to Kennan, at the high-level Solarium gathering of July 1953, Eisenhower exhibited "a mastery of the subject matter and a thoughtfulness and a penetration that were quite remarkable ... President Eisenhower was a much more intelligent man than he was given credit for being."[167] His successors sorely lacked in one or more of those basic elements.

---

[167] Quoted verbatim in Pickett, ed., *Oral History*, p. 20.

Another obvious place to look for the underpinnings of good grand strategies lies in the institutional processes in which the strategists are embedded. The Truman administration was responsible for developing much of the new institutional infrastructure through which American grand strategy was conceived and executed. The new institutions failed badly in their first major test in Korea in the second half of 1950. Only after that did Truman involve himself more seriously in the workings of the infrastructure. By contrast, Eisenhower from the outset strengthened the institutional processes and played a central role in discussions with the major bureaucratic barons as they collectively wrestled with the most important strategic issues.[168]

Also standing out for consideration are the material resources that leaders and institutions take as inputs and convert through grand strategy into desired political outcomes; the more ineffable "strategic culture" that may permeate the minds of the leaders and the practices of the institutions; and the influence of foreign partners. But a less obvious place to search for good grand strategy has emerged in this essay: Clausewitz's illumination of the importance of understanding the nature of the war on which strategists are embarking. Achieving such understanding is often easier said than done, but American strategists in the early Cold War did it well. In this case, as in others, once one understood the nature of the war, the easier it became to assess its likely dynamics of interaction and grasp the probable keys to success.

This essay has run through a list of four such keys. But strategic practitioners should not delude themselves that winning a war is a straightforward matter of following a checklist. For, as this essay has shown, there were in the early Cold War, as in other major conflicts, conundrums to puzzle over within each item and trade-offs to work out across the different keys to success. Efforts to make coalitions more extensive often had the effect of making the relationship between the United States and its most important allies less cohesive. As more instruments of military power and non-military power came into play, the harder it became to integrate them conceptually and coordinate them institutionally. A general concept of containment was not easy to translate into specific choices about when, where, and how to open or contest new theaters of operations. Macroeconomic stability in the short term did not necessarily go hand in hand with economic dynamism in the long run. Efforts to economize on military spending by giving prominence to nuclear deterrence or to political warfare often strained alliance cohesion. Overextension in new theaters threatened macroeconomic stability in the short term, though it paid off in the long-term vitality of the international economic system the United States constructed.

To juggle adroitly different keys and handle wisely difficult trade-offs, practitioners need to be reasonably good thinkers themselves. There is also

---

[168] For a good comparison of Truman and Eisenhower in this regard, see Jeffrey G. Barlow, *From Hot War to Cold: The U.S. Navy and National Security Affairs, 1945–1955* (Stanford, CA, 2009), pp. 329ff.

a role in grand strategy for thinkers who are not temperamentally well suited to be practitioners, as in the case of Kennan. They should be able to provide deeper insight into what makes for a cohesive coalition. Strategic thinkers should be able to provide realistic theories of influence for new instruments in new domains, theories that go beyond the "arm-waving" that is much in evidence now about the information domain. Those with a grasp of military capabilities and concepts should be able to enhance operational and strategic understanding of when it makes sense to open or contest new theaters or a new arena of interaction in a long-term strategic competition. And, not least, those with a good grasp of economic history and theory should illuminate the complex, reciprocal relationship between long-term economic vitality and strategic success.

These intellectual tasks are challenging. It is hard to meet the challenges in the realm of pure abstraction. They need to be comprehended and confronted in relation to historical or anticipated conflicts against clearly acknowledged adversaries. Thinkers, like practitioners, have to understand, as Clausewitz emphasized, the conflict they confront, "neither mistaking it for, nor trying to turn it into, something that is alien to its nature."[169]

---

[169] Clausewitz, *On War*, p. 88.

13 The Reagan administration's strategy toward the Soviet Union

Thomas G. Mahnken

It has become fashionable in some quarters to argue that the US government is incapable of formulating and implementing a consistent strategy. In fact, it has done so on a number of occasions. During the Cold War, for example, the Eisenhower, Nixon, and Reagan administrations all consciously pursued coherent strategies for competing with the Soviet Union. It is the latter case that forms the subject of this essay. Ronald Reagan and a handful of his close advisors formulated a coherent strategy toward the Soviet Union between 1981 and 1983 and implemented that strategy consistently throughout the remainder of his eight years in office.

This strategic approach rested on a careful net assessment of relative Soviet and American strengths and weaknesses. Moreover, more than in previous administrations, it recognized enduring American strengths and Soviet weaknesses. Reagan's policy and strategy represented a sharp break from its predecessors, in that it sought, not to contain Soviet power, but rather to address the domestic sources of Soviet foreign behavior. His administration pursued this strategy consistently throughout its two terms in office. The shifts that occurred resulted from the inevitable adjustments needed to implement the strategy in the face of bureaucratic, congressional, and allied constraints, as well as responses to changes in the strategic environment, particularly the emergence of Mikhail Gorbachev as leader of the Soviet Union.[1]

This chapter begins by describing Reagan's assumptions about the US–Soviet competition and how they differed from the Cold War orthodoxy of containment. It then analyzes the Reagan administration's formulation of strategy, emphasizing the role of the National Security Council (NSC) staff during the administration's first two years in office. Specifically, the next section explores the drafting of two National Security Decision Directives (NSDDs) and three speeches between 1981 and 1983: NSDD 32, the classified national security strategy, and NSDD 75, the classified strategy for

---

[1] For another view, see James Mann, *The Rebellion of Ronald Reagan: A History of the End of the Cold War* (New York, 2009). Although Mann concedes the basic continuity of strategy throughout Reagan's eight years in office, he argues that Reagan made considerable changes between his early and later years in office.

competing with the Soviet Union, as well as Reagan's Notre Dame, West-minster, and "Evil Empire" speeches. The third section describes the imple-mentation of these strategies during the remainder of the administration. The chapter concludes with reflections on the experience and lessons for the future. What follows rests largely upon archival sources as well as memoirs of the participants. It is of necessity incomplete, as not all relevant documents have been declassified. However, the information now available is sufficient to describe in detail the formulation and implementation of the Reagan adminis-tration's strategy.

Understanding the nature of the competition

In the United States, grand strategy, which attempts to enlist all the instru-ments of national power in pursuit of a common set of objectives, is presiden-tial strategy; only presidents have the power and influence to unite the national security bureaucracy behind a common endeavor. This, in turn, requires a president who thinks strategically in terms of power and how he can wield it competitively and purposefully. It also requires what Peter Rodman termed "presidential command." It is insufficient for a president to declare or decree; to implement strategy, he must work actively to insure that his cabinet members and the bureaucracies they oversee faithfully execute his will.[2] Ronald Reagan entered office in 1981 with a clear electoral mandate to change the course of American foreign policy. He also possessed a view of the US–Soviet competition that was at odds with the Cold War consensus, and even with the beliefs of many members of his own party.

US national security policy throughout the Cold War rested upon four widely shared but implicit assumptions. Even though each would be proven false with the collapse of the Soviet Union, they had held sway over the US national security community in the decades that preceded it. The first was that the Soviet Union was a permanent feature of the international system. Indeed, beginning in the late 1970s, many, if not most, strategists saw the Soviet Union as getting stronger, as evidenced by its military build-up and increas-ingly adventurous activity in the Third World, culminating in the invasion of Afghanistan in 1979.[3]

The second assumption was that there was little the United States and its allies could do to change the nature of the Soviet regime. Some liberals pinned their hopes on the convergence of the Soviet Union and the West, a theory that rested both on the ability of the Soviet regime to become more demo-cratic and the West to become more socialist. Nonetheless, they saw the process of convergence as organic; its proponents believed there was little the

[2] Peter Rodman, *Presidential Command* (New York, 2009).
[3] For a taste of this literature, see Edward N. Luttwak, *The Grand Strategy of the Soviet Union* (New York, 1984).

United States could do to foster democracy in the Soviet Union. On the contrary, they believed that attempts to do so would lead to a backlash.

A third assumption was that efforts to confront the Soviets would lead to crisis and potentially a catastrophic conflict. To reduce friction, leaders needed to meet at summits and conclude diplomatic agreements. According to this logic, the arms control process played a large role in reducing super-power tension.

Fourth and finally, given the futility of efforts to change the Soviet regime and the dangers of confrontation, the wisest strategy was to contain Soviet expansion while seeking to accommodate the Soviet Union within the inter-national order.[4] Over time, many hoped, containment and conciliation would lead to the mellowing of Soviet behavior. However, the link between contain-ment and changes in Soviet actions was asserted more often than argued.[5]

Seen in this light, Reagan was a heretic who rejected the Cold War orthodoxy. He came to office with a different set of assumptions about the Soviet Union. He possessed an innate optimism about the United States and a commensurate pessimism about the Soviet Union. He thus weighed the balance between the two superpowers differently than most others, including many in his own party. First, he rejected the notion that the Soviet Union was a permanent feature of the international system. Whereas for decades Ameri-can policy makers had focused on how to live with communism and treat the Soviet Union as an equal, Reagan emphasized the transitory character of the communist regime. As early as 1975, he had termed communism "a tempor-ary aberration which will one day disappear from the earth because it is contrary to human nature."[6] Such statements, often dismissed as rhetoric, in fact reflected Reagan's deep convictions.

Second, Reagan believed that the United States had much greater leverage over the Soviets than many others credited it with. Indeed, he grasped that the Soviet Union was in the throes of a terminal illness.[7] He saw the powerful American economy as a weapon that the United States could wield against the Soviets. He also believed as early as 1977 that the United States could use the attraction of Western economic prosperity in effect to create de facto allies among Soviet citizens who wanted a better life for themselves and their children. Reagan became convinced that the Soviet economy "was a basket case, partly because of massive spending on armaments ... I wondered how we as a nation could use these cracks in the Soviet system to accelerate the process of collapse."[8] He also saw the Soviet regime as vulnerable in the realm

---

[4] Richard Pipes, *Vixi: Memoirs of a Non-Belonger* (New Haven, CT, 2003), pp. 162, 189.
[5] One prominent exception is X (George Kennan), "The Sources of Soviet Conduct," *Foreign Affairs*, vol. 25, no. 3, July 1947.
[6] Quoted in John Lewis Gaddis, *The Cold War: A New History* (New York, 2005), p. 217.
[7] Pipes, *Vixi*, p. 164.
[8] Quoted in John Lewis Gaddis, *Strategies of Containment* (Oxford, 2005), p. 351.

of ideas. In his view, détente had failed as a strategy precisely because it had not applied America's strengths against these weaknesses.[9]

Third, Reagan was willing to accept greater risk in standing up to the Soviets than the mainstream counseled. He did not shy away from confronting the Soviet leadership, either in word or in deed. As discussed at greater length below, the administration's confrontational rhetoric and actions alarmed the Soviet leaders even if they did not, as some have argued, bring the superpowers to the brink of war. Finally, and most fundamentally, he sought not to contain Soviet power but to transform the Soviet regime. Reagan sought to create a fundamental change in the character of the Soviet Union by pushing the communist regime to confront its weaknesses.[10] In so doing, he turned the United States away from the strategy of containment that it had followed in one form or another throughout the Cold War.

Developing political objectives

Although Reagan brought a set of ideas about the US–Soviet competition with him to Washington, he spent much of his first year in office formulating the policies that would guide his administration's strategy in the years that followed. The effort was fitful, however, hampered by divisions within the administration, a weak staff, and Reagan's style of collegial decision making. Reagan's advisors divided into two groups when it came to their assessment of the US–Soviet competition. Some, such as William P. Clark, Caspar Weinberger, William Casey, Jeane Kirkpatrick, and Ed Meese, believed that the United States could and should exert considerable leverage over the Soviet Union. Others echoed these views, including key members of the National Security Council staff, such as Richard Pipes, Thomas Reed, and Gus Weiss, defense officials such as Fred Iklé, Richard Perle, and Andrew Marshall, and members of the intelligence community, such as Henry Rowen and Herb Meyer. Other advisors, by contrast, believed that the Soviet Union was strong and that competition with the United States would endure, including George Shultz, Robert McFarlane, Michael Deaver, James Baker, George H. W. Bush, and Nancy Reagan.[11] In formulating policy, Reagan tended to play these groups off one another.[12]

Reagan's initial organization of his national security team further hindered policy formulation. He disliked the way Henry Kissinger had developed the National Security Council staff into a center of personal power, and he looked to Secretary of State Alexander Haig to take the lead in formulating foreign

[9] Ibid., p. 352.   [10] Ibid., p. 354.
[11] William E. Pemberton, *Exit with Honor: The Life and Presidency of Ronald Reagan* (Armonk, NY, 1997), p. 149.
[12] Gordon S. Barrass, *The Great Cold War: A Journey Through the Hall of Mirrors* (Palo Alto, CA, 2009), p. 264.

policy.[13] In contrast, Reagan's first national security advisor, Richard V. Allen, enjoyed limited access to and influence over the president. It soon became clear, however, that Haig did not share many of Reagan's convictions. Moreover, his prickly personality annoyed Reagan and alienated many close to him.

Reagan favored a relaxed, collegial form of decision making. What was most important to him was that decisions reflect his core beliefs; he left implementation to his subordinates. In the words of Richard Pipes, Reagan "was concerned with the 'what', not the 'how,'" a propensity that would hurt the president during his second administration.[14] The attempt on Reagan's life on 30 March 1981 and his long convalescence further slowed the process of formulating policy. From his early days in office, the new president gained a greater appreciation of the weakness of the Soviet economy. Director of Central Intelligence William Casey brought Reagan raw intelligence on the Soviet Union that portrayed economic stagnation.[15] Special National Intelligence Estimate 3/11–4–81, completed in November 1981, concluded that economic performance had deteriorated to a point that military expenditures left few resources for raising the living standards of Soviet citizens. It also highlighted the Soviet Union's dependence on Western technology and credits.[16] The chairman of the National Intelligence Council, Harry Rowen, further argued that the Soviet Empire was placing a considerable burden on the Soviet economy.[17]

Casey's special assistant, Herb Meyer, previously an editor of *Fortune* magazine, undertook a series of sensitive vulnerability assessments of the Soviet economy that revealed its susceptibility to outside pressure. As a result, Casey believed that the United States and its allies could compound Moscow's difficulties by restricting credit, tightening export controls, and imposing embargoes on critical materials that supported the Soviet oil and gas industry.[18] Such intelligence pointed the way to an approach to competing with the Soviets. As Reagan wrote in his diary on 26 March 1981, "Briefing on Soviet economy. They are in very bad shape, and if we can cut off their credit they'll have to yell 'uncle' or starve."[19]

Both in public and in private, Reagan began to articulate his vision of a different US–Soviet relationship. Speaking at the University of Notre Dame's commencement on 17 May, Reagan proclaimed, "The West won't contain

---

[13] Thomas C. Reed, *At the Abyss: An Insider's History of the Cold War* (New York, 2004), p. 229.

[14] Pipes, *Vixi*, p. 164.

[15] Peter Schweizer, *Victory: The Reagan Administration's Secret Strategy that Hastened the Collapse of the Soviet Union* (New York, 1994), p. 4.

[16] SNIE 3/11–4/81, "Dependence of Soviet Military Power on Economic Relations with the West," 17 November 1981, available at www.foia.cia.gov/Reagan.asp (accessed 28 May 2012).

[17] Reed, *At the Abyss*, p. 240.   [18] Pipes, *Vixi*, p. 157.

[19] Quoted in Schweizer, *Victory*, p. 6.

communism, it will transcend communism. It won't bother to ... denounce it, it will dismiss it as some bizarre chapter in human history whose last pages are even now being written."[20] Many at the time rejected the speech as pure rhetoric. In fact, it represented the president's opening public bid to reorient US national security policy.

Reagan also began formulating a different approach to the Soviet Union in private. At a July 1981 NSC meeting, he decided that "the overriding object-ive of US Policy toward the Soviet Union will be to blunt and contain Soviet imperialism. This goal involves raising the costs and risks of Soviet expansion and, to the extent feasible, encouraging democratic processes in the USSR."[21] Of note was Reagan's emphasis not only on confronting Soviet adventurism abroad, but also on attempting to address its domestic roots.

Matching strategy to policy: strategy formulation

Reagan's strategy for competing with the Soviet Union marked a break with the past. Rather than being constrained by the perceived limits of American power, it was defined by a sense of the weaknesses inherent in the Soviet regime. Carrying out such a change of course required that Reagan exercise "presidential command" to insure that both presidential appointees and career civil servants carried out his will.

In formulating strategy, Reagan had to contend with two groups that held views quite different from his. First, he faced opposition from so-called "realists," exemplified by Richard Nixon and Henry Kissinger. The realists argued that the Soviet Union was a state like any other, and that the United States should treat it as such. In particular, they believed that Washington should base relations with Moscow on the Kremlin's external actions rather than its internal behavior. Second, he had to contend with conservatives, many within his own party, who emphasized Soviet strength and American weakness. Particularly in Reagan's second term, many on the right attacked Reagan for allegedly going soft on communism.[22] He and his advisors also had to overcome resistance, both passive and active, from elements of the US national security bureaucracy, among the most fervent defenders of the Cold War orthodoxy.

Efforts to match policy to strategy got underway in earnest in 1982. The replacement of Richard Allen by William Clark as assistant to the president for national security affairs on 4 January 1982 spurred the new approach. Unlike

---

[20] Ronald W. Reagan, "Address at Commencement Exercises at the University of Notre Dame," 17 May 1981, in *Public Papers of the Presidents of the United States, Ronald Reagan, 1981* (Washington, D.C., 1982), p. 434.

[21] Richard Pipes, Memorandum for Richard V. Allen, "East–West Policy Study: Final Version," 16 July 1981, Box 5, Ronald Reagan Presidential Library (RRPL), National Archives and Records Administration (NARA), p. 1.

[22] Mann, *The Rebellion of Ronald Reagan*.

Allen, Clark was a longtime confidant of Reagan who had served as a justice of the California Supreme Court before being appointed deputy secretary of state at the outset of the administration. Clark agreed to take the job of national security advisor on the condition that he would enjoy unfettered access to the president and would be able to organize a new, more powerful NSC staff.[23] Clark saw his job as playing Joseph to Reagan's pharaoh. As he saw it, his role was "the conversion of [the president's] philosophy to policy."[24] In this task he was supported by a number of NSC staffers, including Thomas Reed, Roger Robinson, and Richard Pipes.

NSDD 32

Two documents – National Security Decision Directive (NSDD) 32, entitled "National Security Strategy," and NSDD 75, entitled "U.S. Relations with the USSR" – collectively served as the strategic blueprint of the Reagan administration. Other NSDDs played a supporting role, including NSDD 48, "International Economic Policy"; NSDD 54, "U.S. Policy toward Eastern Europe"; and NSDD 66, "East–West Relations and Poland Related Sanctions."

The Carter administration had produced a classified national security document, Presidential Directive (PD)/NSC-18, "U.S. National Strategy," on 24 August 1977. Despite its title, the directive had really only focused on the military dimension of the Soviet–American competition. The document argued, "In the foreseeable future, US–Soviet relations will continue to be characterized by both competition and cooperation, with the attendant risk of conflict as well as the opportunity for stabilizing US–Soviet relations." The Carter administration had sought Soviet assistance in resolving regional conflicts as well as involving "the Soviet Union constructively in global activities, such as economic and social developments and peaceful non-strategic trade."[25] The Reagan administration failed to formulate a similar statement of its national security policy and strategy during its first year in office. However, on 1 February 1982 Clark, his deputy Robert McFarlane, and NSC staffer Thomas C. Reed met with Reagan to discuss the need for a formal presidential directive on national security policy.[26] Four days later, Reagan signed National Security Study Memorandum 1, which directed a review of US national security objectives and the impact of Soviet power and behavior on them.[27]

---

[23] Reed, *At the Abyss*, p. 232.
[24] Ivo H. Daalder and I. M. Destler, *In the Shadow of the Oval Office* (New York, 2009), pp. 144–145.
[25] Presidential Directive/NSC 18, "U.S. National Strategy," 25 August 1977, pp. 1–2.
[26] Reed, *At the Abyss*, p. 235.
[27] William P. Clark, Memorandum, "National Security Study Directive (NSSD) 1–82, U.S. National Security Strategy," 5 February 1982, Executive Secretariat, NSC: National Security Study Directives (NSSDs), Box 1, RRPL, NARA.

Reagan chose Reed to lead the effort with the assistance of Colonel Allan Myer. Reagan had known Reed for a long time and trusted him to represent his views. Others involved in the process included Under Secretary of Defense for Policy Fred C. Iklé, Assistant Secretary of Defense for International Security Policy Richard Perle, Under Secretary of State for Political Affairs Laurence Eagleburger, and several other aides.[28]

Reed's interagency group (IG) met for the first time in the White House Situation Room on 18 February.[29] Over the course of several months, the IG drafted a nine-part study. Reagan received regular updates on the study's progress in the form of memoranda, read sections of the study as his team drafted them, discussed them with his advisors, and provided comments and recommendations. On 16 April, the National Security Council discussed and approved the first five sections of the study; it met again on 27 April to consider the final four.[30]

Reed later recalled that conducting the study was difficult, because the national security bureaucracy disliked the idea of presenting the president options. Instead, they sought to hand over a predigested consensus. Reed, however, knew the president's mind and sought to preserve his ability to make substantive decisions.[31] The resulting study, NSSD 1–82, "U.S. National Security Strategy," ran 87 pages, divided in three parts: national objectives and the international environment, implementing strategies, and the military component of national security strategy.

The document began with four broad and uncontroversial purposes for US national security strategy:

(1) To preserve the political identity, framework, and institutions of the United States as embodied in the Declaration of Independence and the Constitution. (2) To protect the United States – its national territory, citizenry, military forces, and assets abroad – from military, paramilitary, or terrorist attack. (3) To foster the economic well-being of the United States, in particular, by maintaining and strengthening nation's industrial, agricultural, and technological base and by ensuring access to foreign markets and resources. [And] (4) To foster an international order supportive of the vital interests of the United States by maintaining and strengthening constructive, cooperative relationships and alliances, and by encouraging and reinforcing wherever possible and practicable, freedom, rule of law, economic development and national independence throughout the world.[32]

---

[28] Peter Schweizer, *Reagan's War* (New York, 2002), p. 154.

[29] Reed, *At the Abyss*, p. 236.

[30] William P. Clark, Memorandum for the President, "U.S. National Security Strategy," 26 April 1982, Executive Secretariat, NSC: National Security Study Directives (NSSDs), Box 1, RRPL, NARA.

[31] Reed, *At the Abyss*, p. 236.

[32] NSSD 1–82, "U.S. National Security Strategy," April 1982, Executive Secretariat, NSC: National Security Decision Directives (NSDDs), Box 1, OA 91311, NSDD-32, RRPL, NARA, p. 1.

Where the document began to diverge from past studies was in its assessment of American and Soviet strengths and weaknesses. Its appraisal of the Soviet Union is notable for the emphasis it placed on Soviet vulnerabilities. These included the "serious structural weaknesses" of Soviet and Warsaw Pact economies as well as the fact that "the appeal of communist ideologies appears to be decreasing throughout much of the world, including the Soviet bloc itself."[33] Moreover, the Soviet invasion of Afghanistan had revealed the limits of Soviet power projection, while non-Russian nationalities in the Soviet Empire were becoming restive.[34]

The study envisioned pursuing US national objectives through "an interlocking set of strategies." As its authors noted, "The various instruments of US national power and the strategies for their use do not stand alone; rather, they are inextricably linked and, to be effective, must be mutually supportive."[35] The study also contained a balanced appraisal of Soviet military power. Although it acknowledged the Soviet military build-up of the 1970s, it also highlighted the fact that the Soviets possessed a number of military vulnerabilities, including the unreliability of non-Soviet Warsaw Pact allies, general-purpose forces that had difficulty dealing with unforeseen and quickly changing circumstances, and logistical vulnerabilities. The study pointed out that the Soviet bomber force was old, its ballistic missile submarines relatively noisy, and its anti-submarine warfare capability inadequate. Moreover, it assessed that Soviet strategic air defenses would perform poorly against low altitude penetrating aircraft.[36] Each of these vulnerabilities would subsequently serve as the target of competitive strategies to exploit them.[37]

The study also emphasized Soviet economic shortcomings, including low economic growth and stagnating standards of living "owing to the growing defense burden and inefficient investment practices."[38] It noted that the Soviet economy was consuming increasing amounts of energy at higher cost. Although oil exports represented a large source of hard currency for the Soviets, they were declining. As a result, the study concluded that it might be increasingly difficult for the Soviet Union to sustain growth in military spending.[39]

The study also highlighted the challenges the Soviet Union faced as a multinational empire. It noted that turmoil on the Soviet Union's borders had reinforced the regime's obsession with the need for order on its frontiers. Moreover, it emphasized internal unrest and insurgency among Soviet clients across the globe.[40] The document concluded with a warning but also the promise of a transformed relationship: "the decade of the eighties will pose the

[33] Ibid., p. 2.   [34] Ibid., p. 2.   [35] Ibid., p. 8.   [36] NSSD 1–82, p. 12.
[37] See, for example, Gordon S. Barrass, "U.S. Competitive Strategy During the Cold War" and John A. Battilega, "Soviet Military Thought and the U.S. Competitive Strategies Initiative" in Thomas G. Mahnken, ed., *Developing Competitive Strategies for the 21st Century: Theory, History, and Practice* (Palo Alto, CA, 2012).
[38] NSSD 1–82, p. 13.   [39] Ibid., p. 13.   [40] Ibid., p. 13.

greatest challenge to the survival and well-being of the U.S. since World War II. Our response to this challenge could result in a fundamentally different East–West relationship by the end of the decade."[41]

Reagan signed NSDD 32 on 20 May 1982. Although an unclassified version of the strategy was never released, the thinking behind it was outlined in two speeches: one by Clark at the Center for Strategic and International Studies in Washington, D.C. on 21 May and one by Reed to the Armed Forces Communications and Electronics Association (AFCEA) on 16 June.[42] In his speech, Clark made it clear that the United States should exploit Soviet economic weakness, noting, "We must also force our principal adversary, the Soviet Union, to bear the brunt of its economic shortcomings."[43] Although Clark's speech represented a clear signal of a change in strategy, it received little media coverage. Richard Halloran of the *New York Times* and Michael Getler of the *Washington Post* wrote stories about Clark's speech, but the NSC staff lamented that the media had missed its central point.[44]

NSDD 75

Whereas NSDD 32 provided an overall strategic framework for the Reagan administration, NSDD 75 applied that framework specifically to the Soviet Union. The document has received its share of accolades. Paul Kengor has called it "probably the most important foreign-policy document by the Reagan administration, institutionalizing the president's intention to undermine the Soviet communist empire."[45] NSC staffer Norman Bailey has dubbed it "the strategic plan that won the Cold War."[46] The primary author of NSDD 32, Tom Reed, called it "the blueprint for the endgame" and "a confidential declaration of economic and political war."[47]

The author of NSDD 75 was Richard Pipes with the assistance of Roger Robinson. Pipes, a Polish émigré, was a professor of history at Harvard who served as the NSC's director for Eastern European and Soviet affairs during the first two years of the Reagan administration; his office also included Paula Dobriansky, who would later serve as under secretary of state for global affairs in the George W. Bush administration, and Dennis Blair, who would rise to

---

[41] Ibid., p. 4.   [42] Reed, *At the Abyss*, p. 237.

[43] "National Security Strategy," speech to be delivered by Honorable William P. Clark, Assistant to the President for National Security Affairs, at the Center for Strategic and International Studies, Georgetown University, 21 May 1982, Executive Secretariat, NSC: National Security Decision Directives (NSDDs), Box 1, OA 91311, NSDD-32, Ronald Reagan Presidential Library, National Archives and Records Administration, p. 5.

[44] Paul Kengor and Patricia Clark Doerner, *The Judge: William P. Clark, Ronald Reagan's Top Hand* (New York, 2007), p. 167.

[45] Paul Kengor, "Crucial Cold War Secret," *The Washington Times*, 13 January 2008.

[46] Norman A. Bailey, *The Strategic Plan that Won the Cold War: National Security Decision Directive 75* (McLean, VA, 1998).

[47] Kengor, "Crucial Cold War Secret."

the rank of admiral and serve as commander of US Pacific Command and then director of national intelligence in the Barack Obama administration.[48] Like Reagan, Pipes had been arguing for years that the Soviet Union was in decline. As he later wrote, "Because Reagan knew what he wanted but could not articulate his feelings in terms that made sense to foreign policy professionals at home and aboard, I took it upon myself to do so on his behalf."[49]

Pipes painted a picture of a Soviet Empire stretched to its limits, vulnerable to ethnic strife, and lacking political legitimacy. Such a view, the accuracy of which became apparent within a decade, was nonetheless radical in the early 1980s, and it earned him ostracism among the foreign policy community. Indeed, the *Washington Post* declared, "for rank hysteria in scholarly garb, it's hard to top Harvard prof Richard Pipes."[50] Pipes was one of a relatively small group of people who shared the belief that the Soviet Union was structurally weak, that the Soviet elite had lost faith in the communist system, and that the US–Soviet competition was moving into areas where the Soviets could not compete.[51] Others who felt the same way included William Odom, Fritz Ermarth, and Wolfgang Leonhardt.[52]

The genesis of NSDD 75 predated NSDD 32's approval. Within days of joining the NSC staff, Pipes asked Allen for permission to draft a paper on US–Soviet relations. Although Allen agreed, the State Department opposed the idea of the NSC leading such an effort, and toward the end of February 1981, Haig commissioned Paul Wolfowitz to draft a strategy paper instead.[53] In early March, State convened the first Senior Inter-Agency Group (SIG) meeting to discuss the subject.

Later that month, Pipes received the first copy of the State paper. As he recalled, "It was predictable State Department boilerplate, the product, undoubtedly, of many hands. It spelled out how we were to react to Soviet aggression but avoided any suggestion of initiatives."[54] Pipes' NSC colleague, Carnes Lord, was even more blunt in his evaluation: "In general, I found the draft study banal, lacking in rigor and precision, too general to have any real policy utility, and substantively deficient in some important respects."[55] As Pipes wrote to Allen on 30 March,

None of this strikes me as bold, innovative, or likely to succeed. *We must put the Soviet Union on the defensive.* I cannot express the central idea of a Reagan Soviet policy more concisely. To do so, we must turn the tables on them and exploit their internal difficulties which are steadily worsening. State is not capable of thinking in

[48] Pipes, *Vixi*, pp. 149–150.   [49] Ibid., p. 194.
[50] Quoted in Schweizer, *Reagan's War*, p. 156.   [51] Barrass, *The Great Cold War*, p. 252.
[52] Richard Pipes, Memorandum for Richard V. Allen, "A Reagan Soviet Policy," 21 May 1981, Richard E. Pipes Files, Box 4, RRPL, NARA.
[53] Pipes, *Vixi*, p. 194.   [54] Ibid., p. 194.
[55] Carnes Lord, Memorandum for Richard Pipes, "Comments on East–West Policy Study," 9 April 1981, Richard E. Pipes Files, Box 4, RRPL, NARA, 1.

such terms. I propose that we duly comment on their paper and then shelve it in order to proceed with our own undertaking.[56]

Pipes offered to write a paper to "supplement" the State Department draft. As he later noted, "My intention was to articulate the theoretical rationale of his Soviet policy in the hope that it would serve as the foundation of an official document."[57] The resulting draft, written in May 1981, was entitled "A Reagan Soviet Policy."[58] It advanced four central propositions. The first was that communism was inherently expansionist. That would change only when the Soviet regime collapsed or at least was thoroughly reformed. Second, economic difficulties and imperial overstretch confronted the Stalinist model with a profound crisis. Third, the successors to Brezhnev were likely to be split into "conservative" and "reformist" factions.[59] Fourth, and finally, Pipes argued that "It is in the interest of the United States to promote the reformist tendencies in the USSR by a double-pronged strategy: *assisting pro-reform forces* inside the USSR and *raising for the Soviet Union the costs of its imperialism* elsewhere by a very determined strategy."[60]

In Pipes' view, there was an intimate relationship between the political and economic situation within the Soviet Union and its foreign policy. Moreover, he believed that it was impossible to cope with the external manifestations of Soviet power without coming to grips with their internal origins.[61] Such a view was controversial among academics and policy makers. As one commentator noted in 1982,

Pipes is wrong in assuming that there is a clear-cut division between two camps [in the Soviet Union]. Any U.S. policy designed to assure that some non-existent group of "moderates" will come to power is a chimera. It is conceivable that vigorous, sometimes bellicose anti-Soviet policies on the part of U.S. authorities could vindicate and strengthen their hard-line rivals. This is precisely what some Soviets hint might happen.[62]

Pipes argued for "frustrating" the Soviet leadership's strategy. As he later wrote, "it was a hopeless undertaking to try to prevent its [communism's] further spread at the periphery: one had to strike at the very heart of Soviet imperialism, its system."[63] This, in turn, required pairing external pressure on the Soviet Union with internal pressure on the regime itself. As he wrote, "It makes perfect strategic sense to exert maximum possible internal pressure

---

[56] Pipes, *Vixi*, pp. 194–195.   [57] Ibid., p. 194.

[58] Richard Pipes, "A Reagan Soviet Policy," May 1981, Richard E. Pipes Files, Box 4, RRPL, NARA.

[59] Indeed, three years before the emergence of Mikhail Gorbachev as General Secretary of the Communist Party of the Soviet Union, Pipes was focused on the prospect of generational change in the Soviet leadership. That having been said, Pipes may have overestimated the ability of outsiders to understand the dynamics of the Soviet leadership.

[60] Pipes, "A Reagan Soviet Policy," p. 1.   [61] Ibid., p. 5.

[62] Cited in Pipes, *Vixi*, p. 161.   [63] Ibid., p. 198.

on the Soviet regime, i.e., to supplement external deterrents with a major effort aimed at stimulating anti-expansionist, reformist forces inside the Communist bloc."[64]

Pipes submitted the manuscript to Allen in May 1981. However, it languished on Allen's desk for several months. It was not until September that he convened a small group to discuss the draft. Around Thanksgiving, Allen forwarded the draft to Reagan, who wrote on the cover of the manuscript that it was "very sound."[65] Clark's appointment as national security advisor in January 1982 breathed new life into the formulation of a strategy for competing with the Soviet Union. Clark shared Pipes' belief that it made little sense to resist Soviet aggression if US policy strengthened the regime internally by subsidizing the Soviet economy.[66] As a result, Clark asked Pipes to draft the terms of reference for a new NSDD on US–Soviet relations in the hope that Reagan would sign an NSDD in April. As it turned out, NSDD 75 was not approved until the following January.[67]

Pipes forwarded the draft terms of reference to Clark on 10 March 1982. He argued that the State Department's East–West policy study suffered from "two fundamental flaws." First, it was heavily centered on the military dimension of the US–Soviet competition and the problems of containment. In contrast, it provided no guidance as to the ultimate objectives of US policy. That is, it viewed containment as an end to itself rather than a means to achieve a greater end. Second, it was too long and unwieldy to serve as the basis of US strategy.[68] As a result, although Pipes included some of its points in the terms of reference, his draft represented an essentially fresh approach. Although the document assigned the chairmanship of the interagency group dealing with the study to the State Department, Pipes warned Clark that it would be an unworkable arrangement. In his view,

The differences between State and Defense on the subject of long-term policies toward the Soviet Union are profound and very hard to reconcile . . . It seems to me that if we are going to be serious about tackling the fundamental questions, rather than confining ourselves to issues where consensus is easy to obtain, then the NSC alone is capable of providing the needed arbitration.[69]

Pipes' concerns were warranted. The State Department argued that there was no need for an NSDD on US–Soviet relations. Rather, all that was needed was an update to the East–West Policy Study.[70]

---

[64] Pipes, "A Reagan Soviet Policy," p. 2.   [65] Pipes, *Vixi*, pp. 195, 197.
[66] Kengor and Doerner, *The Judge*, p. 170.   [67] Pipes, *Vixi*, p. 198.
[68] Richard Pipes, Memorandum for William P. Clark, "Terms of Reference of NSSD on Policy Toward the Soviet Union," 10 March 1982, Executive Secretariat, NSC: National Security Study Directives (NSSDs), Box 1, RRPL, NARA, p. 1.
[69] Pipes, "Terms of Reference of NSSD on Policy Toward the Soviet Union," pp. 1–2.
[70] L. Paul Bremer, III, Memorandum for Mr. William P. Clark, "Wheeler-Bremer Memorandum on this Topic of 26 March 1982," Executive Secretariat, NSC: National Security Study Directives (NSSDs), Box 1, RRPL, NARA.

As the formulation of strategy proceeded in secret, Reagan continued to articulate a new approach in public. The two tracks were, however, intertwined. Reagan's next major speech on US strategy toward the Soviet Union, delivered to members of the British parliament in Westminster on 8 June 1982, drew both on NSDD 32 and Pipes' policy paper.[71] The speech, drafted by presidential speechwriter Tony Dolan, was a rhetorical masterpiece. In it, Reagan used Marxist theory to portray a Soviet Union in crisis:

> In an ironic sense Karl Marx was right. We are witnessing today a great revolutionary crisis, a crisis where the demands of the economic order are conflicting directly with those of the political order. But the crisis is happening not in the free, non-Marxist West, but in the home of Marxist-Leninism, the Soviet Union. It is the Soviet Union that runs against the tide of history by denying human freedom and human dignity to its citizens. It is also in deep economic difficulty. The rate of growth in the national product has been steadily declining since the fifties and is less than half of what it was then ... What we see here is a political structure that no longer corresponds to its economic base, a society where productive forces are hampered by political ones.[72]

It was a public acknowledgment that Reagan understood the Soviet Union's perilous circumstances.

On 20 August 1982, Clark forwarded the terms of reference for NSSD 11–82, "U.S. Policy Toward the Soviet Union" to Reagan, emphasizing that

> The draft goes beyond previous policy formulations bearing on U.S.–Soviet relations in that it requires us to show concern not only for Soviet political and military *behavior*, but also for the *system* that makes behavior of this kind possible. This approach calls on us to adjust our policies toward Moscow in such a manner that instead of helping the further consolidation of the totalitarian and imperialist elements in the USSR, we promote the less aggressive, more domestically-oriented forces.[73]

The following day, Reagan approved the document and initiated a review of US policy toward the Soviet Union chaired by the NSC.

Several aspects of the terms of reference stand out. First, the review was to take a broad view of the US–Soviet competition, "with emphasis on its non-military aspects." Second, it was overtly strategic, in that it was meant to determine "the political, economic, military and ideological means at our disposal for achieving favorable changes in Soviet international behavior, including assessment of the costs and obstacles involved in using them." Third, it reflected Pipes' belief in the link between the internal composition of the Soviet regime and Soviet external behavior: "The review will proceed

---

[71] Reed, *At the Abyss*, p. 237; Pipes, *Vixi*, p. 197.
[72] Ronald W. Reagan, "Address to Members of the British Parliament," 8 June 1982, in *Public Papers of the Presidents of the United States, Ronald Reagan, 1982*, vol. I (Washington, D.C., 1983), p. 744.
[73] William P. Clark, Memorandum for the President, "Terms of Reference for NSSD on 'U.S. Policy Toward the Soviet Union,'" 20 August 1982, Box 5, RRPL, NARA.

on the premise that Soviet international behavior is determined not only by the external environment but also by political, economic, social, and ideological features of the Soviet system itself."[74]

The NSC staff convened an interagency group led by Deputy Secretary of State Walter Stoessel to conduct the review, with assistant-secretary level participation from the Department of Defense, joint chiefs of staff, CIA, Department of Treasury, Department of Commerce, International Communication Agency, Department of Agriculture, and NSC staff.[75] The study was meant to assess the likelihood of change in the Soviet system, Soviet internal and external vulnerabilities and strengths, the balance of internal forces making for continuity or change, meeting the Soviet challenge in the short and long term, measures to shape the Soviet environment, and recommended policies for the United States.

At the group's first meeting on 27 August, the State Department distributed an outline for review that differed considerably from what the president had approved. State also tried to restrict drafting of the NSDD to State and CIA. Paula Dobriansky, who attended the meeting for the NSC staff, suggested to Clark that the NSC should draft the introduction and objectives sections of the directive.[76]

Haig's resignation on 25 June 1982 allowed Clark to assert the NSC's authority. He authorized Pipes to take the lead in drafting the directive on US–Soviet relations.[77] At the working level of the government, there was considerable unease about the "offensive" rhetoric of the draft directive as well as the promotion of internal change in the Soviet Union as a US objective.[78] A number took their dissatisfaction to the press. As Strobe Talbott subsequently wrote,

Speaking privately, [some] Administration officials, especially professional diplomats and intelligence analysts with long experience in Soviet affairs, not only disavowed the notion that the United State could manipulate Soviet internal politics, but they expressed confidence that the Soviets recognized such theorizing for what it was: idiosyncratic, extremist, and much confined to the fringes of government.[79]

Nonetheless, by November 1982 the members of the interagency group had agreed on the substance of the strategy. State had agreed to concede on the crucial point that attacking the Soviet system should be a goal of US strategy.

---

[74] National Security Study Directive Number 11–82, "U.S. Policy Toward the Soviet Union," 21 August 1982, Box 5, RRPL, NARA, p. 1.

[75] William P. Clark, Memorandum, "National Security Study Directive on U.S. Policy Toward the Soviet Union," 21 August 1982, Box 5, RRPL, NARA.

[76] Paula Dobriansky, Memorandum for William P. Clark, "NSSD 11–82: U.S. Policy Toward the Soviet Union," 30 August 1982, Box 5, RRPL, NARA.

[77] Pipes, *Vixi*, p. 200.

[78] Thomas W. Simons, Memorandum for Richard Burt, "Your Participation in IG on NSSD 11–82, Tuesday November 2, 10:00am," nd, Richard E. Pipes Files, Box 5, RRPL, NARA.

[79] Strobe Talbott, *The Russians and Reagan* (New York, 1984), pp. 74–75.

In return, State got the NSC to concede that there were limits to the ability of the United States to promote change within the Soviet system.[80]

The response to NSSD 11–82 was completed on 7 December 1982. Its language represented a victory of Reagan's appointees over the bureaucracy. In line with Pipes' terms of reference, it argued that any strategy for dealing with the Soviet Union had to take account of the impact on the internal development of the Soviet Union. Based on that premise, it put forward the following long-term objectives for the United States: "(1) the decentralization and demilitarization of the Soviet economy; (2) the weakening of the power and privileged position of the ruling Communist elite (*nomenklatura*); (3) gradual democratization of the USSR."[81]

The report was not sanguine regarding the ability of the United States to effect changes in Soviet internal politics in the near to middle term. However, its authors argued, "it is also possible that carefully designed and implemented US policies could have an important, if marginal, beneficial impact on Soviet internal developments." As a result, the United States needed to compete effectively with the Soviet Union in the international arena and "undertake a coordinated, long-term effort to reduce the threat that the Soviet system poses to our interests."[82] The United States also needed to engage the Soviet Union in dialogue and negotiations in an effort to reach agreements based upon strict reciprocity and mutual interest. Moreover, all three tracks had to be implemented simultaneously and sustained over the long term.[83]

In line with previous assessments, the NSSD 11–82 study emphasized the Soviet Union's economic decline, noting that the Soviet Union was experiencing the lowest growth rate since the end of the Second World War. It also catalogued sources of popular discontent, including the perceived decline in the Soviet standard of living, restrictions on freedom of expression, and the growing self-consciousness of ethnic minorities. The authors portrayed a growing malaise in Soviet society that reflected an underlying loss of commitment to the Soviet system and government.[84] In the view of the report's authors, "An overriding issue is the extent to which Moscow's international posture will be affected by a growing preoccupation with the country's great, and growing, domestic problems." They argued that economic and social problems would provide the Soviet leadership with a strong impetus for systemic change over the decade of the 1980s.[85]

The report examined three alternative scenarios for the future of the Soviet Union. The study termed the first, a military coup, "highly unlikely" given the extent of communist party control. In contrast, the study's authors believed

[80] Pipes, *Vixi*, pp. 200–201.
[81] Response to NSSD 11–82, "U.S. Relations with the USSR," 6 December 1982, Executive Secretariat, NSC: National Security Decision Directives (NSDDs), Box 3, OA 91287, NSDD-75, RRPL, NARA, p. 1.
[82] Ibid., p. 2.   [83] Ibid., p. 2.   [84] Ibid., pp. 5–7.   [85] Ibid., pp. 12–13.

that the second scenario, a return to one-man rule, was "possible." The third scenario, liberalization of the Soviet system, was rated "a less likely prospect" because the authors felt that control mechanisms, economic leverage, and the patriotism and passivity of the population would allow the Soviet leadership to continue to rule. However, they conceded that the outlook was less predictable in the late 1980s, "as the gap between economic performance and leadership expectations widens, as the basis for optimism about future economic performance erodes, and as the generational change in the Soviet leadership takes hold."[86] In particular, the authors noted that the views of the younger generation of Soviet leaders (such as Mikhail Gorbachev, although neither he nor any of his cohort was singled out by name) were unknown. The authors concluded that, although the United States enjoyed limited leverage to effect change within the Soviet Union, "U.S. policies ... may be able to exacerbate weaknesses in Soviet foreign and domestic policy."[87] As a result, they argued that the implementation of US strategy should attempt to shape the environment in which Soviet decisions are made.[88]

The NSSD 11–82 study served as the basis of NSDD 75, a draft of which Clark transmitted to Reagan on 16 December 1982. In forwarding the study and draft directive, Clark highlighted the fact that the goal of exerting "internal pressure on the USSR" represented a new one. As he emphasized,

> It has always been the objective of U.S. policy toward the Soviet Union to combine containment with negotiations, but the attached document is the first in which the United States Government adds a third objective to its relations with the Soviet Union, namely encouraging antitotalitarian changes within the USSR and refraining from assisting the Soviet regime to consolidate further its hold on the country.[89]

Although the interagency study had forged a basic consensus on US strategy toward the Soviet Union, the use of economic instruments remained controversial. As a result, the draft directive contained two provisions that divided Reagan's advisors. The first was a statement that the United States should "induce the USSR to shift capital and resources from the defense sector to capital investment and consumer goods."[90] Whereas the Office of the Vice President, Office of the Secretary of Defense, and Department of Commerce supported this language, the State, Agriculture, and Treasury Departments objected. The second controversial statement was that the United States should "refrain from assisting the Soviet Union with developing natural resources with which to earn, at minimal cost to itself, hard currency."[91] Whereas the Office of the Secretary of Defense, NSC staff, and Office of the Vice President supported the language, the Commerce

---

[86] Ibid., pp. 18–19.   [87] Ibid., pp. 20–21.   [88] Ibid., p. 24.

[89] William P. Clark, Memorandum for the President, "NSSD 11–82: Draft NSDD and IG Study," 16 December, Executive Secretariat, NSC: National Security Decision Directives (NSDDs), Box 3, OA 91287, NSDD-75, RRPL, NARA.

[90] Ibid., p. 2.   [91] Ibid.

Department joined State, Treasury, and Agriculture in objecting to the language. Reagan decided to delete the two controversial points at an NSC meeting on 16 December 1982. His stated rationale was that they would leak and provide propaganda for the Soviet Union.[92] More likely, he was concerned over allied willingness to go along with such efforts.

Although Reagan somewhat weakened the use of economic instruments against the Soviets, he expanded the directive's use of technology transfer restrictions against the Soviet Union. The draft NSDD had contained language to prevent "the transfer of critical technology and equipment that would make a substantial contribution directly or indirectly to Soviet military power." At the meeting, United Nations Ambassador Jeane Kirkpatrick recommended omitting the word "critical," thus broadening the scope of the policy. The secretary of defense, chairman of the joint chiefs of staff and national security advisor concurred, whereas the secretaries of state, commerce, and treasury disagreed. In the end, Reagan sided with those who favored the broader wording.[93]

The president signed National Security Decision Directive 75, "U.S. Relations with the USSR," on 17 January 1983. The directive contained clauses that ran counter to the tenets of Cold War national security strategy. Rather than punishing unacceptable Soviet behavior, it sought to induce changes in the nature of the Soviet regime on the premise that it was the source of Soviet behavior. The directive stated that "U.S. policy toward the Soviet Union will consist of three elements: external resistance to Soviet imperialism; internal pressure on the USSR to weaken the sources of Soviet imperialism; and negotiations to eliminate, on the basis of strict reciprocity, outstanding disagreements."[94] As noted above, the second objective, internal pressure on the Soviet Union to weaken the Soviet regime, represented a major departure from containment.

The directive laid out three tasks to achieve these objectives: (1) "To contain and over time reverse Soviet expansionism by competing effectively on a sustained basis with the Soviet Union in all international arenas." (2) "To promote, within the narrow limits available to us, the process of change in the Soviet Union toward a more pluralistic political and economic system in which the power of the privileged ruling elite is gradually reduced." (3) "To engage the Soviet Union in negotiations to attempt to reach agreements which protect and enhance US interests and which are consistent with the principle of strict reciprocity and mutual interest."[95]

The second task represented a major change as well. For the first time, US strategy was aimed not merely at containing Soviet power, but also reforming

---

[92] Pipes, *Vixi*, p. 201.
[93] William P. Clark, Memorandum, "NSDD 75 on 'U.S. Relations with the USSR,'" 17 January 1983, Executive Secretariat, NSC: National Security Decision Directives (NSDDs), Box 3, OA 91287, NSDD-75, RRPL, NARA.
[94] NSDD 75, "U.S. Relations with the USSR," 17 January 1983, p. 1.   [95] Ibid.

its source. The directive went on to outline a multi-dimensional strategy with military, economic, and political components to put both external and internal pressure on Moscow. It put particular emphasis on: (1) "sustaining steady, long-term growth in US defense spending and capabilities"; (2) "creating a long-term Western consensus for dealing with the Soviet Union"; (3) "maintenance of a strategic relationship with China, and efforts to minimize opportunities for a Sino-Soviet rapprochement"; (4) "building and sustaining a major ideological/political offensive which, together with other efforts, will be designed to bring about evolutionary change of the Soviet system"; (5) "effective opposition to Moscow's efforts to consolidate its position in Afghanistan"; (6) "blocking the expansion of Soviet influence in the critical Middle East and Southwest Asia regions"; (7) "maintenance of international pressure on Moscow to permit a relaxation of the current repression in Poland and a longer-term increase in diversity and independence throughout Eastern Europe"; and 8) "neutralization and reduction of the threat to U.S. national security interests posed by the Soviet–Cuban relationship."[96]

Although NSDD 75 was a classified document,[97] its thrust appeared in Reagan's speech to the annual convention of the National Assembly of Evangelicals in Orlando, Florida on 8 March 1983, the so-called "Evil Empire" speech. In that speech, he termed the Cold War a "struggle between right and wrong and good and evil." He further said, "I believe that communism is another sad, bizarre chapter in human history whose last pages even now are being written."[98]

Implementing the strategy, 1983–1988

The Reagan administration implemented the strategy outlined in NSDD 32 and NSDD 75 throughout the remainder of its two terms. Indeed, there was much more continuity to the Reagan strategy than some historians admit. Formulating the strategy had involved forging a bureaucratic consensus behind a revised assessment of the US–Soviet balance and a more expansive set of political objectives. Implementing it required the Reagan administration to contend not only with bureaucratic opposition, but also congressional and allied constraints. Implementing the strategy thus led to tactical, though not strategic, adaptation.

One set of constraints involved congressional funding of the Reagan administration's initiatives. Although Congress funded a large-scale increase in

---

[96] Ibid., p. 8.
[97] Of note, the FBI determined that Soviet intelligence was trying to get a copy of the document. Message, From Director FBI, To NSC Staff Attn: Ken De Graffenreid, DTG 211908Z APR 83, RRPL, NARA.
[98] Ronald W. Reagan, "Remarks at the Annual Convention of the National Assembly of Evangelicals in Orlando, Florida," 8 March 1983, in *Public Papers of the Presidents of the United States, Ronald Reagan, 1983*, vol. I (Washington, D.C., 1984), p. 364.

defense expenditure, a number of programs, including the MX ICBM and the Strategic Defense Initiative, were controversial. So, too, was the administration's support of the Nicaraguan *contras* in Central America.

Another set of constraints derived from America's allies, particularly those in Europe. On the one hand, a number of key European leaders, including Margaret Thatcher and Helmut Kohl, were supportive of the Reagan administration's strategy. Moreover, the deployment of US *Pershing II* medium-range ballistic missiles and *Gryphon* ground-launched cruise missiles in Western Europe in the face of Soviet intimidation was a key demonstration of allied resolve. On the other hand, Europeans were reluctant to give up the fruits of détente with the Soviet Union, including expanded East–West trade. As a result, US efforts to exert economic leverage over the Soviet Union by, for example, blocking the construction of the trans-Siberian oil and gas pipeline, triggered an acrimonious debate within Europe.[99]

Military competition

The military competition with the Soviet Union was a central element of the Reagan strategy. NSDD 75 called for the United States to modernize its armed forces, with particular emphasis upon the development and acquisition of advanced technologies to provide it leverage against the Soviet Union and to impose costs on the Soviet economy. In so doing, the US government exploited Soviet fears, reported by the CIA, of being outpaced technologically by America's military forces.[100] Significantly, NSDD 75 emphasized Soviet perceptions of the military balance; US modernization was to be designed to insure that "Soviet calculations of possible war outcomes under any contingency must always result in outcomes so unfavorable to the USSR that there would be no incentive for Soviet leaders to initiate an attack."[101]

The Reagan administration witnessed the wholesale modernization of US conventional and nuclear forces.[102] During the presidential transition, the Reagan team had planned a 5 percent real increase in defense spending. However, the Carter administration had requested an increase of that magnitude during its last days in office. As a result, the incoming Reagan team pushed a 7 percent increase to emphasize that Reagan favored more defense than his predecessor.[103] In October 1981 Congress approved a defense expenditure of $1.5 trillion over five years, including the fielding of 100 MX (later

[99] Barrass, *The Great Cold War*, pp. 248, 283.
[100] CIA Directorate of Intelligence, "The Soviet Defense Industry: Coping with the Military Technological Challenge," SOV 87–10035DX, July 1987, p. iii.
[101] NSDD 75, p. 2.
[102] See Thomas G. Mahnken, *Technology and the American Way of War since 1945* (New York, 2008), chp. 4.
[103] Michael Kramer, "Electoral College: The Budget Crunch," *New York Magazine*, 15 November 1982, p. 31.

Peacekeeper) intercontinental ballistic missiles, 6 *Ohio*-class ballistic missile submarines armed with 96 *Trident* D5 submarine launched ballistic missiles, 3,000 air-launched cruise missiles, and 100 B-1 bombers.

The United States also adopted a more aggressive operational posture, including naval and air operations along the borders of the Soviet Union. US actions clearly alarmed the Soviet leadership. In May 1981, KGB Chairman Yuri Andropov became concerned that the United States was preparing for nuclear war with the Soviet Union. As a result, the Soviet leadership tasked the KGB and GRU to cooperate on Operation RYAN, an unprecedented effort to collect indicators of US preparations for nuclear war.[104]

In modernizing the US armed forces, the United States increasingly exploited its lead in the rapidly developing field of information technology. In 1975, the year that Microsoft was founded, the first personal computer (PC) hit the market; by 1981, annual PC sales in the United States topped one million.[105] The growth of information technology, in turn, spawned the development of new sensors and surveillance systems such as the Joint Surveillance Target Attack Radar System (JSTARS) aircraft, precision-guided munitions (PGMs) such as the Army Tactical Missile System (ATACMS) and the *Copperhead* artillery-launched PGM, and command and control networks to link them together.

The Soviet general staff was concerned about the development of advanced PGMs such as those being developed under the Defense Advanced Research Projects Agency's "Assault Breaker" program. The United States helped foster this perception by rigging advanced PGM tests to deceive the Soviets.[106] Soviet analysts saw PGMs as approaching nuclear weapons in effectiveness, while some saw the development of advanced conventional weaponry as presaging a revolution in warfare. In 1984 Marshal Nikolai Ogarkov, chief of the general staff, noted:

Rapid changes in the development of conventional means of destruction and the emergence in the developed countries of automated reconnaissance-and-strike complexes, long-range high-accuracy terminally guided combat systems, unmanned flying machines, and qualitatively new electronic control systems make many types of weapons global and make it possible to sharply increase (by at least an order of magnitude) the destructive potential of conventional weapons, bringing them closer, so to speak, to weapons of mass destruction in terms of effectiveness.[107]

American developments demanded a response – one that the Soviet economy was manifestly unable to provide. In 1985 there were perhaps 50,000 PCs in the Soviet Union, compared to 30 million more advanced ones in the United States.[108] As Ogarkov told an American visitor, "In America,

---

[104] Barrass, *The Great Cold War*, p. 278.   [105] Ibid., p. 249.   [106] Ibid., p. 275.
[107] Quoted in Barry D. Watts, *Long-Range Strike: Imperatives, Urgency and Options* (Washington, D.C.: Center for Strategic and Budgetary Assessments, 2005), p. 34.
[108] Barrass, *The Great Cold War*, p. 317.

small children play with computers ... For reasons you know well, we cannot make computers widely available in our society. We will never catch up with you in modern arms until we have an economic revolution. And the question is whether we can have an economic revolution without a political revolution."[109] In 1985, NATO mated emerging technologies with the doctrine of Follow-On Forces Attack (FOFA). FOFA envisioned using advanced sensors and strike systems to allow NATO forces to launch a counterattack deep into Poland. Two years later, to the consternation of the Soviets, NATO demonstrated this capability during an exercise dubbed *Certain Strike*.[110]

Reagan's announcement of the Strategic Defense Initiative on 23 March 1983 marked an even more explicit bid to use US technology to compete with the Soviet Union. As he put it:

Let us turn to the very strengths in technology that spawned our great industrial base and that have given us the quality of life we enjoy today.

What if free people could live secure in the knowledge that their security did not rest upon the threat of instant US retaliation to deter a Soviet attack, that we could intercept and destroy strategic ballistic missiles before they reached our own soil or that of our allies?

I call upon the scientific community in our country, those who gave us nuclear weapons, to turn their great talents now to the cause of mankind and world peace, to give us the means of rendering these nuclear weapons impotent and obsolete.[111]

The US National Intelligence Council assessed that the Soviet Union would encounter difficulties in developing and deploying countermeasures to SDI (Strategic Defense Initiative). As one September 1983 memorandum put it,

They are likely to encounter technical and manufacturing problems in developing and deploying more advanced systems. If they attempted to deploy new advanced systems not presently planned, while continuing their overall planned force modernization, significant additional levels of spending would be required. This would place substantial additional pressures on the Soviet economy and confront the leadership with difficult policy choices.[112]

In late 1983, in the midst of growing superpower tension, Soviet concern escalated further. NATO exercise Able Archer 83, which simulated a future war in Europe, including the use of nuclear weapons, heightened Soviet fears of a US nuclear attack.[113] The first report of the Soviet war scare reached the United States several months later, courtesy of Oleg Gordievsky, a

---

[109] Ibid., p. 293.   [110] Ibid., pp. 338–339.
[111] Ronald Reagan, "Announcement of Strategic Defense Initiative," 23 March 1983, at www. missilethreat.com/resources/speeches/reagansdi.html (accessed 16 August 2005).
[112] NIC M 83, 10017, "Possible Soviet Responses to the US Strategic Defense Initiative," 12 September 1983, viii, available at www.foia.cia.gov/Reagan.asp (accessed 28 May 2012).
[113] Barrass, *The Great Cold War*, p. 278.

Soviet KGB officer who was spying for the British Secret Intelligence Service.[114] The national intelligence officer for the Soviet Union and Eastern Europe, Fritz Ermarth, concluded that "We do not believe [Soviet activity] reflects authentic leadership fears of imminent conflict."[115] Subsequent information confirmed that the Soviets were concerned not that the United States was about to launch a war against the Soviet Union, but rather that the combination of Soviet economic and technological weakness and Reagan policies were turning the correlation of forces against Moscow.[116] The war scare nonetheless highlighted the dangers of superpower miscalculation and induced greater caution in Washington.

The challenge of US advanced technology appears to have had a marked impact on Soviet leaders. In the words of Soviet ambassador Anatoly Dobrynin, "Our leadership was convinced that the great technical potential of the United States had scored again." Soviet leaders "treated Reagan's statement as a real threat."[117] The memoirs and recollections of policy makers in Moscow confirm that they took Reagan seriously. An expensive competition in ballistic missile defenses appeared particularly unattractive to Soviet leaders, who were aware of the country's economic difficulties. SDI also highlighted the Soviet Union's lag in computers and microelectronics.[118]

Recent scholarship indicates that the announcement of SDI triggered a debate within the Soviet leadership over the wisdom of competing with the United States in space weaponry, as well as the form that competition should take. One historian suggests, for example, that the announcement of SDI ultimately set up a situation in which Soviet leaders who favored a high-technology competition with the United States in space arms initially carried the day, only to be discredited by their inability to field advanced weapons. That is, SDI put in motion a chain of events that ultimately made the Soviet leadership aware that it could not compete with the United States in high-technology weaponry.[119]

The resource implications of responding to SDI became particularly apparent after Mikhail Gorbachev assumed control of the Communist Party of the Soviet Union in 1985 and launched an effort to revive the lagging economy. As one 1987 CIA assessment put it,

---

[114] Ibid., p. 304.

[115] SNIE 11-10-84/JX, "Implications of Recent Soviet Military-Political Activities," 18 May 1984, available at www.foia.cia.gov/Reagan.asp (accessed 24 May 2012).

[116] Fritz W. Ermarth, "Observations on the 'War Scare' of 1983 from an Intelligence Perch," Parallel History Project on NATO and the Warsaw Pact, available at www.isn.ethz.ch/isn/Digital-Library/Publications/Detail/?id=108634&lng=en (accessed 6 June 2012). See also Dima Adamsky, "The 1983 Nuclear Crisis: Lessons for Deterrence Theory and Practice," *The Journal of Strategic Studies*, vol. 36, no. 1, February 2013, pp. 4–41.

[117] Quoted in Jeremi Suri, "Explaining the End of the Cold War: A New Historical Consensus?" *Journal of Cold War Studies*, vol. 4, no. 4, Fall 2002, p. 65.

[118] Ibid., p. 66.   [119] David E. Hoffman, *The Dead Hand* (New York, 2009).

the Soviets would find it difficult to mount a large response to SDI ... without curtailing other military programs. Significantly expanding procurement of weapon systems based on existing technologies would strain the Soviets' already taut component supply base. Reliance on more complex technologies would cause still greater strain because many Soviet weapons programs projected to reach initial operational capability in the late 1990s will compete for the same resources.

The assessment went on to note that the demand for advanced technology would hit the Soviet economy just as Gorbachev was trying to modernize Soviet industry through accelerated investment in advanced technology for manufacturing. Moreover, Gorbachev's "modernization plans call for many of the same scarce, high-technology resources – including microelectronics and flexible manufacturing systems – that would be required for advanced BMD systems and countermeasures."[120]

The United States also undertook several efforts to shape Soviet perceptions of the technological competition. One involved feeding deceptive information to the Soviets regarding the state of US military technology. In 1981 French intelligence recruited Colonel Vladimir I. Vetrov, a KGB officer, was assigned to collect intelligence on Western science and technology. Vetrov, dubbed "Farewell," gave the French more than 4,000 documents that demonstrated that Moscow relied on the theft of foreign science and technology to shore up the Soviet economy. The documents constituted a shopping list of the technologies the Soviets were seeking, information the French passed on to the Americans.[121] In early 1984, the CIA and Pentagon used their knowledge of Soviet collection requirements to begin feeding Moscow incomplete and misleading information. The disinformation campaign covered half a dozen sensitive military technologies that the Soviets were interested in, including stealth, ballistic missile defenses, and advanced tactical aircraft. The United States planted false information regarding development schedules, prototype performance, test results, production schedules, and operational performance.[122]

Economic competition

Military competition was not the sole, or perhaps even the most important, dimension of the US strategy toward the Soviet Union. The Reagan administration also adopted a strategic approach to economic policy, based upon its understanding of the dependence of the Soviet economy on Western technology and hard currency exports of oil and gas. NSDD 75 called for

---

[120] SOV 87–10063X, "Soviet SDI Response Options: The Resource Dilemma," November 1987. 19871101, vi, available at www.foia.cia.gov/Reagan.asp (accessed 28 May 2012).

[121] Gus W. Weiss, "The Farewell Dossier," *Studies in Intelligence* (1996) at www.cia.gov/csi/studies/96unclass/farewell.htm (accessed 14 October 2004).

[122] Schweizer, *Victory*, p. 189.

efforts to insure that technology transfer did not benefit the Soviet military and would avoid subsidizing the Soviet economy in a way that would dilute pressure to change. It also sought to minimize Soviet leverage on the West based upon trade, energy, and finance.[123] In the years that followed, the US government undertook a campaign to reduce dramatically Soviet hard currency earnings by working with the government of Saudi Arabia to drive down the price of oil, as well as to limit Soviet exports of natural gas to the West.

In order to implement the administration's economic policy, Clark and the NSC staff created the Senior Interdepartmental Group – International Economic Policy (ISG-IEP), a cabinet-level body chaired by the secretary of the treasury. The purpose of the group, which reported to the president through the national security advisor, was to insure that national security considerations would trump commercial interests in US international economic policy.[124]

The administration launched a global effort to reduce Soviet access to the Western high technology upon which the Soviet economy depended. In 1975, 32.7 percent of American goods sold to the Soviet Union involved high technology, amounting to $219 million in sales. By 1983, the volume had been reduced to 5.4 percent, amounting to only $39 million in sales.[125] Moreover, according to Peter Schweizer, the United States used US companies to provide the Soviet Union faulty information designed to disrupt the Soviet economy.[126]

A particular focus of US efforts was the Soviet oil and gas sector, which was Moscow's main source of hard currency. The spike in oil prices following the 1973 Arab oil embargo had been a boon to the Soviet Union, allowing it to boost revenues by 272 percent while only increasing oil and gas production by 22 percent. Indeed, for every dollar increase in a barrel of oil, the Soviet Union would earn $1 billion per year in hard currency. Conversely, every $10 drop in the price of a barrel of oil would cost Soviet Union $10 billion per year.[127] Thus, the United States sought to block technology transfer for the Soviet oil and gas industry, and particularly that bound for the trans-Siberian gas pipeline, which was to provide Moscow as much as $30 billion per year in hard currency. The embargo proved controversial with US allies, a number of whom had agreed to finance the purchase of equipment for the pipeline below market rates. Western European nations, suffering through the highest unemployment since the mid 1950s, looked to the project as a source of jobs. Although only partially successful, US sanctions cost the Soviets by their own reckoning two years and $2 billion.[128]

The administration also worked with Saudi Arabia to increase Riyadh's production of oil to drive down market prices and deny the Soviet Union hard

---

[123] NSDD 75, pp. 2–3.   [124] Kengor and Doerner, *The Judge*, p. 188.
[125] Schweizer, *Victory*, p. 139.   [126] Ibid., pp. 46, 187–188.
[127] Ibid., p. 105.   [128] Ibid., pp. 42, 216.

currency. The effort, spearheaded by Casey, culminated in the announcement by Sheikh Ahmed Zaki Yamani, the Saudi oil minister, on 13 September 1985 that Saudi Arabia had altered its oil policy by no longer protecting oil prices. During the next six months, Saudi Arabia regained its share in the world oil markets as its oil production increased fourfold, while global oil prices dropped significantly.

As a result of low oil prices, the Soviet Union lost approximately $20 billion in revenue per year. In May 1986, the CIA assessed that low energy prices, declining oil production, and the depreciation of the dollar would substantially cut into Moscow's ability to import Western equipment, agricultural goods, and industrial materials at the very time that Gorbachev was counting on increasing imports to revitalize the Soviet economy.[129] Four months later, a national intelligence estimate assessed that Soviet hard currency export earnings for the second half of the 1980s would be 30 percent below those of recent years, and that the Soviet Union would experience an even greater decline in its purchasing power because of the depreciation of the dollar, in which about two-thirds of Soviet exports were denominated.[130] In the view of Russian economist Yegor Gaidar, the drop in oil prices confronted the Soviet leadership with three options: cutting loose the communist regimes of Eastern Europe, drastically reducing imports of food to the Soviet Union, or dramatically cutting military expenditures. In the event, it chose none of these options, and the problems plaguing the Soviet economy grew progressively worse.[131]

Political action

More than any administration since that of Dwight D. Eisenhower, the Reagan administration used political action as an instrument of foreign policy. As the NSDD 11–82 study put it, "U.S. policy toward the Soviet Union must have an ideological thrust which clearly demonstrates the superiority of U.S. and Western values of individual dignity and freedom, a free press, free trade unions, free enterprise, and political democracy over the repressive character of Soviet communism."[132] Reagan's rhetoric was one aspect of the public face of this strategy, but it also had a covert aspect, including financial and logistical support to the Solidarity trade union in Poland.

---

[129] SOV 86–10027X, "USSR: Facing the Dilemma of Hard Currency Shortages," May 1986, p. iii, available at www.foia.cia.gov/Reagan.asp (accessed 28 May 2012).

[130] NIE 11–23–86, "Implications of the Decline in Soviet Hard Currency Earnings," September 1986, 3, available at www.foia.cia.gov/Reagan.asp (accessed 28 May 2012).

[131] Yegor Gaidar, "The Soviet Collapse: Grain and Oil," American Enterprise Institute, April 2007, pp. 4–5, available at www.aei.org/docLib/20070419_Gaidar.pdf (accessed 24 April 2012).

[132] Response to NSSD 11–82, p. 30.

The Reagan administration also implemented covert action to contest Soviet gains in the Third World. Indeed, Reagan inherited, but then considerably expanded, financial and military support to the Afghan resistance to Soviet occupation of Afghanistan and supplied the mujahidin to take the war to Soviet territory.[133] Similarly, the administration provided assistance to anti-Soviet resistance movements in Angola, Cambodia, Mozambique, and Nicaragua. As one commentator has noted, NSDD 75 "represented the codification of the strategy ... that two years later would receive the title 'Reagan Doctrine.'"[134]

The strategic framework constructed in the first years of the Reagan administration remained operative throughout Reagan's eight years in office. During the first four years of the Reagan administration, the United States emphasized the first two objectives outlined in NSDD 75: containing and reversing Soviet expansionism by competing with the Soviets and promoting change within the Soviet Union. The emergence of Mikhail Gorbachev as leader of the Soviet Union provided the occasion for Reagan to pursue the third objective: engaging the Soviets in negotiations to reach agreements to protect and enhance US interests. Both because of the pressure the United States had exerted on the Soviet Union and because of Gorbachev's recognition of the need to lessen tensions with the United States to implement needed domestic reforms, the Soviet leader agreed to the Intermediate-Range Nuclear Forces (INF) Treaty.

In June 1986, the NSC staff initiated a review of NSDD 32 in accordance with the recommendations of the Packard Commission. That review essentially endorsed the continued utility of the strategy. As the deputy secretary of defense, William H. Taft IV, wrote, "DoD basically agrees that NSDD 32 and its supporting study remain fundamentally sound."[135] The revisions that were recommended were minor and included a more explicit statement of the administration's policy of denying the Soviet Union military technology as well as an explicit statement of supporting, overtly and covertly, those combating communism.

President Reagan signed NSDD 238, "Basic National Security Policy," on 2 September 1986. The document recognized changes in the US–Soviet competition brought on by the United States' strengthened position as well as the emergence of Mikhail Gorbachev. The thrust of the document was nonetheless continuity rather than change. The objectives it contained were restatements or refinements of those that appeared in the former directive.[136]

---

[133] Steve Coll, *Ghost Wars* (New York, 2004).
[134] James M. Scott, *Deciding to Intervene: The Reagan Doctrine and American Foreign Policy* (Durham, NC, 1996), p. 21.
[135] William H. Taft, IV, Memorandum for the National Security Advisor to the President, "Review of NSDD 32," June 2, 1986, Executive Secretariat, NSC: National Security Decision Directives (NSDDs), Box 1, OA 91311, NSDD-32, RRPL, NARA.
[136] National Security Decision Directive 238, "Basic National Security Strategy," 2 September 1986, at www.fas.org/irp/offdocs/nsdd/nsdd-238.pdf (accessed 28 May 2012).

For its part, the NSC opted to retain NSDD 32 intact rather than adopting even these minor changes. NSDD 75 remained in force until the George H. W. Bush administration superseded it with NSD 23 on 14 May 1991.[137]

Conclusion

Scholars will debate the influence of US strategy on the outcome of the Cold War for decades to come. There should, however, be no debate over whether US actions influenced the outcome. Although one should always be wary of the fallacy of *post hoc ergo propter hoc*, it would indeed be strange if US actions had no effect whatsoever on the Soviet leadership.

A persuasive case can be made that the Cold War ended because US strategy forced the Soviet government to implement sweeping change in a bid to save the communist regime. The Soviets confronted a resurgent America at the very time the Soviet leadership had begun to comprehend the extent of the Soviet Union's economic and social malaise. In the economic realm, US efforts to depress oil prices and technology forced Soviet leaders to make hard choices between military and domestic spending. In the political arena, the Kremlin had to confront increasingly restive clients abroad as well as the population at home. In the military sphere, it appears as though Soviet military concerns about the widening gap between US and Soviet military technology helped to forge a confluence of interest between the Soviet political elite and elements of the defense industrial sector on the general need to reorient Soviet foreign policy.[138] Indeed, in February 1988 Gorbachev announced the need for defense cuts in order to restructure the domestic economy.[139]

This chapter demonstrates the challenges that a modern democracy faces in undertaking a shift in strategy. Formulating a new strategy required achieving a bureaucratic consensus through the exercise of presidential command. Implementation required the US government to deal with a different set of challenges from Congress and US allies, as well as interaction with the Soviet Union.

The strategic shift would not have occurred without the strategic leadership of Ronald Reagan. Primary source documents make it difficult to agree with Canadian Prime Minister Pierre E. Trudeau's judgment that "Reagan could be pleasant company for social conversation but was not a man for thoughtful

[137] National Security Directive 59, "Disposition of Reagan Administration Policy Papers," 14 May 1991, at http://bushlibrary.tamu.edu/research/pdfs/nsd/nsd59.pdf (accessed 28 May 2012).
[138] Stephen G. Brooks and William C. Wohlforth, "Power, Globalization, and the End of the Cold War," *International Security*, vol. 25, no. 3, Winter 2000/1.
[139] Schweizer, *Victory*, p. 343.

policy discussion."[140] As more and more of the archival record has become available, it is increasingly apparent that Reagan's detractors underestimate him. John Lewis Gaddis appears closer to the mark when he wrote, "Reagan was as skillful a politician as the nation had seen for many years, and one of its sharpest grand strategists ever."[141]

---

[140] Quoted in William E. Pemberton, *Exit with Honor: The Life and Presidency of Ronald Reagan* (Armonk, NY, 1997), p. 150.

[141] Gaddis, *The Cold War*, p. 217.

Afterword

Richard Hart Sinnreich

The thirteen essays in this volume originated in one explicit question and one implied belief. The question is how a national government, or an alliance, formulates and executes an effective military strategy. The belief is that doing so materially improves the likelihood of prosecuting war to a successful conclusion, or, better still, of averting it altogether. Both question and belief reflect widespread agreement among contemporary observers of US national security policy that, since the end of the Cold War, the US has been bereft of a coherent defense strategy, thereby incurring penalties ranging from the misallocation of defense resources to counterproductive military commitments. As the project's sponsor noted, "There is little attention paid to assessing the state of the competition, or evaluating strengths and weaknesses in ourselves or our potential opponents, and still less effort to develop genuine strategies that exploit the enduring strengths we bring to the competition."[1] In his Introduction, Williamson Murray points out that official declarations of strategic intention abound. But the conviction persists that, however useful they may be as wish lists, they have been much less useful in disciplining resource and commitment decisions. The cases examined here seek to illuminate how others – including we ourselves – previously have done better.

The term "strategy" is fraught with definitional difficulty, however. As Chapter 6 notes, it did not enter the English lexicon until borrowed at the beginning of the nineteenth century from the French, who themselves derived it from the Greek *strategos*, the leader of an army. In its original usage, therefore, strategy merely denoted the art of the general. It was in that narrow sense – as "the use of the engagement for the purpose of the war" – that Prussian theorist Carl von Clausewitz subsequently deployed it.[2] But while general and ruler were synonymous for much of military history, with the gradual bifurcation of military and political power and the state's growing reliance for military success on resources outside the military's purview,

---

[1] A. W. Marshall, "Memorandum for Participants: Strategy and History," Office of the Secretary of Defense, Director of Net Assessment, 9 June 2010.
[2] Carl von Clausewitz, *On War*, ed. and trans. by Michael Howard and Peter Paret (Princeton, NJ, 1976), p. 177.

the making of strategy became more complicated and applications of the term multiplied. Today, we find ourselves trying to reconcile grand strategy, defense strategy, economic strategy, information strategy, cyber strategy, and a welter of other such formulations.

One result of this terminological proliferation is definitional confusion, efforts to unravel which risk sterile, semantic debate. As Humpty Dumpty told Alice, "When I use a word ... it means just what I choose it to mean – neither more nor less."[3] However, if we are to generalize from history about strategy, there is some obligation to apply the term consistently. What follows, therefore, takes strategy to mean a scheme of behavior deliberately pursued to achieve a more or less explicit aim, reflecting a causal theory believed to connect them. It thus connotes a considered choice from among alternative courses of action. That formulation by no means excludes the possibility that non-conforming behavior might have impact recognizable after the fact as strategic. As Colin Gray suggests, Britain's crucial decision in the interwar period to build fighters rather than bombers resulted more from economic than strategic concerns. As that example indicates, however, impact alone is insufficient evidence of strategic intention.

That is the more true inasmuch as behavior having profound impact on the security of the state can differ vastly in duration; and the longer the duration, the greater the risk of misinterpreting impact as proof of intention. In fact, noted one distinguished historian elsewhere, "Once strategy moves beyond the near term, it struggles to define what exactly it intends to do."[4] Our own cases range in duration from Edward I's two-year conquest of Wales to half a millennium of Roman domination of the Mediterranean world. The first ended with Wales' submission to the English crown, the second, as all know, with the collapse of the Roman Empire. Conceding that both enterprises reflected definable strategies, should we thus consider the first to have been successful and the second a failure? Patently, that would be absurd. Acknowledging that absurdity, however, obliges us to decide when, in the fullness of time, a strategy arguably successful in achieving the aim to which it was directed should be absolved of responsibility for subsequent events that its very success may have set in motion.

Moreover, not all successes result from strategy, and strategy is not invariably responsible for every failure. The longer the period examined, the more true that is likely to be. As Murray notes, "Beyond several decades, it is almost impossible for statesmen and military leaders to plan, and those who believe that leaders can articulate strategies that will reach out far into the future are naïve and disregard the complexities that human interactions inevitably involve. The proof lies in the fact that successful strategies that last for a

---

[3] Lewis Carroll, *Through The Looking Glass*, www.gutenberg.org/files/12/12-h/12-h.htm.
[4] Hew Strachan, "Strategy and Contingency," *International Affairs*, vol. 86, no. 6, 2011, p. 1281.

decade or more are so extraordinarily rare." Consider, for example, Victor Davis Hanson's judgment that "while Themistoclean foresight helped defeat the Persians and found the Athenian Empire, it also led to a radicalization of the Athenian state that contributed to its eventual defeat and impoverishment by Sparta." Should Themistocles really be held to account for that belated consequence? Or what of Marcus Jones' acknowledgment that, while "for Bismarck, the essence of strategic policy, particularly when it involved the potential for war, consisted not in military success alone but in a stable and enduring settlement," in the end his policies "collapsed against the basic causes of European insecurity." How much, then, should Bismarck be blamed for the subsequent cataclysm of 1914–1918?

All these qualifications urge caution in claiming a linkage between behavior recognizable after the fact as having strategic impact and the presumed intentions and decisions that produced it; and even more care in generalizing from that assessment an answer to the question of how a state can with confidence formulate and execute a successful strategy. That is more true because, as our cases reveal, direct evidence that behavior was informed by deliberate strategic choice is not always easy to acquire. The terms of reference informing production of our cases cautioned that "What is most important is that there be real, concrete evidence of the thinking and analysis that led to a successful strategy ... instead of simply imputing a strategy to historical figures based on what we believe they might have been thinking."[5] Especially in historically remote cases, such guidance imposes an evidentiary burden that may be nearly impossible to satisfy. For that matter, even more recent cases rarely furnish evidence of strategic intention as unambiguous as Bismarck's candid declaration in July 1862 to future British Prime Minister Benjamin Disraeli:

I shall soon be compelled to undertake the conduct of the Prussian government. My first care will be to reorganize the army, with or without the help of the *Landtag* [the legislature] ... As soon as the army shall have been brought into such a condition to inspire respect, I shall seize the first best pretext to declare war against Austria, dissolve the German Diet, subdue the minor states, and give national unity to Germany under Prussian leadership. I have come here to say this to the Queen's ministers.[6]

But while some of our cases perforce rely more heavily on inference than on direct evidence, that need not devalue their contribution to understanding the strategic enterprise. As Umberto Eco once noted, "A child speaks his mother tongue properly, though he could never write out its grammar. But the grammarian is not the only one who knows the rules of the language; they are well known, albeit unconsciously, also to the child."[7] So too with strategy,

---

[5] A. W. Marshall, "Memorandum for Participants."
[6] Quoted in Jonathan Steinberg, *Bismarck: A Life* (Oxford, 2011), p. 174.
[7] Umberto Eco, "Reflections on *The Name of the Rose*," *Encounter*, April 1985, pp. 7–19.

which may be pursued implicitly even though not explicitly documented. Thus, James Lacey's contention that "a historian can glean sufficient information from various histories and the archeological record to demonstrate that Rome possessed and adhered to a grand strategy, even if never articulated as such."[8]

Accepting that view, it is nevertheless striking to realize how few of our cases reveal explicit discussion of strategic alternatives. That may help to explain why, on their evidence, the surest way to strategic success seems to be to acquire a great strategist or, at least, a strong decision maker perceptive enough to identify one and self-confident enough to listen to him. The great majority of our cases attribute success largely to the impact of such leaders – Themistocles, Edward I, Lincoln, Bismarck, Roosevelt, Truman, Reagan. Some of them had crucial help – Lincoln his Grant, Truman his Marshall and Kennan – but even then, strategic direction seems to have been the product of a relatively few like minds. Even Edward I's conquest of Wales fits that description, although in that case, the like mind in question was that of a long-dead cleric, and the principal evidence of its influence was the remarkable consistency of Edward's decisions with its injunctions.

The very prominence of individual genius in our cases suggests that, at least in the short run, strategy more reliably – or at least, more recognizably – governs behavior when authority over its formulation and execution resides in a single dominant decision maker. For one thing, such authority renders strategic choices less vulnerable to ancillary pressures. Commenting on the events precipitating Prussia's military reforms, Dennis Showalter notes that "the efflorescently collegial nature of the Prussian cabinet system was a major factor in the disaster of 1806 ... Frederick William III had not only consistently failed to impose his will on his advisors; he had ascribed his own indecision to the conflicting pressures of grayer, presumably wiser, heads." In contrast, while acknowledging that "Bismarck was extraordinarily sensitive to the inherent tension between domestic and foreign affairs," Jones rejects the suggestion that economic imperatives drove Bismarckian strategy, arguing that Bismarck "pointedly, perhaps self-servingly rejected the idea that a responsible statesman made decisions about the latter in light of the former." Similarly, Peter Mansoor convincingly demolishes suggestions that Franklin D. Roosevelt was merely the endorser of strategic choices reached by internal bargaining among his senior military and naval commanders.

Of course, even autocratic leaders are not wholly free to pursue strategies without reference to those needed to support their execution, and democratic

---

[8] As Lacey acknowledges, this view remains controversial. At very least, most scholars would agree that "Rome had objectives which transcended the whims of individual emperors, and broad principles toward which she consistently directed her impressive force." Emerson T. Brooking, "*Roma Surrecta*: Portrait of a Counterinsurgent Power, 216 BC–AD 72," *College Undergraduate Research Electronic Journal*, University of Pennsylvania, 2011, pp. 25–26.

leaders are even less so. As then Brigadier General Dwight D. Eisenhower commented early in the Second World War, "In a war such as this, when high command invariably involves a president, a prime minister, six chiefs of staff, and a horde of lesser planners, there has got to be patience – no one person can be a Napoleon or a Caesar."[9] Perhaps the most fascinating aspect of Wayne Hsieh's discussion of Abraham Lincoln's war strategy is how closely his dealings with the state governors on whom he depended for troops and resources resembled a coalition management process rather than the unilateral imposition of an idiosyncratic strategy. In that respect, there are striking parallels between the strategic challenge confronting Lincoln and that confronting FDR 80 years later. In such cases, strategy may be as much about creating and maintaining conditions allowing the strategic effort to be pursued as about achieving its ultimate aim.

Which raises the question, whether the strategy of an autocratic, or at least idiosyncratic, leader is as likely to survive the departure of its champion as one institutionalized in the decision-making culture of the state that it purports to guide. Where strategic success is proximate, of course, the answer may be immaterial. FDR's death left Truman to conclude the war against Germany and Japan, but there is no evidence that any significant change in military strategy resulted. Suggestions that FDR might have been less willing than his successor to use the atom bomb against Japan are purely speculative.[10] Similarly, Lincoln's assassination had virtually no impact on a war by then effectively won, although there is widespread agreement that it hugely influenced for the worse the peace that followed.

Where the strategic challenge is prolonged, on the other hand, a failure to institutionalize strategy may be more damaging. As Bradford Lee's essay makes clear, for example, containment in its original form did not survive the Truman administration.[11]

That story of relative American success was not to be sustained over the middle stage of the Cold War in the 1960s and 1970s. Rather than the incremental improvement of the period from 1945 to 1960, there was to be a decline from one administration to another over the following two decades.

Similarly, Lacey argues that, while Roman rulers hewed to the vital imperative to protect Rome's tax-producing provinces, the empire flourished. But as the combination of internal strife and external overreach eroded Rome's ability to secure its productive core, the empire began to fall apart.

---

[9] Quoted in Walter R. Borneman, *The Admirals: Nimitz, Halsey, Leahy, and King* (New York, 2012), p. 238.

[10] Herman S. Wolk and Richard P. Hallion, "FDR and Truman: Continuity And Context In The A-Bomb Decision," *Air Power Journal*, Fall 1995.

[11] Indeed, it did not even survive its author's retirement. In an interview with journalist James Strode years later, Paul Nitze, who replaced George Kennan in late 1949 as the director of policy planning, cheerfully acknowledged having "hijacked" containment. See Nicholas Thompson, *The Hawk and the Dove* (New York, 2009), p. 316.

For the purpose of drawing lessons for the future, of course, the problem is that great strategists do not grow on trees and are not easy to identify when they do come along. Few at the outset of the Civil War would have anticipated the strategic acumen of Lincoln and Grant, the one widely disparaged as a bumpkin lawyer, the other seen as a military and business failure. Ditto for Harry Truman, a small-town machine politician in whom even the president who chose him reposed little confidence. Truman of course had the assistance of two remarkable minds in the Georges, Marshall and Kennan. Even so, as Lee shows, the policies that guided the United States through the early years of the Cold War clearly bore the imprint of Truman's own instincts. Similarly, decades later, the policies that replaced a containment strategy that Thomas Mahnken argues had outlived its usefulness reflected Ronald Reagan's instincts, although he gave little more early evidence of strategic acumen.

In his Introduction, Murray regrets how few senior military and political leaders reach their strategically influential positions with a sound grounding in strategic history. Indeed, that was among the justifications for this volume and the project from which it emerged. And doubtless much could be done to improve senior leader education in strategy. But how significantly that would increase the statistical likelihood of producing or even of identifying great strategists is open to question. In Orson Scott Card's classic science-fiction novel *Ender's Game*, a future earth government confronting an existential alien threat selects and tests children to discover those with a native talent for war, then immerses them in progressively more difficult war games with a view to grooming those with a true genius for strategic direction.[12] It is a fascinating conceit, but more fiction than science. As Lee notes with respect to the declension in US Cold War strategy in the 1960s and 1970s, "that sad story played out under both Democratic and Republican presidents."

Instead, absent dominating leadership, strategy is more likely to emerge, to the extent that it emerges definably at all, from a more or less contentious political process. Of British operations in the War of the Spanish Succession, Jamel Ostwald writes

A heated debate occurred among English policy-makers over the nature of a future war effort. Whigs, who had been the continental strategy's strongest supporters in the previous war, naturally supported a rapid, vigorous response. But Tories and country Whigs hesitated to abandon diplomacy and cautioned restraint toward Louis' provocations. Behind this was a shared distrust of William and his foreign advisors, as well as the London financiers and court Whigs who profited from the land campaigns. This mistrust of their political foes combined with a deep cynicism towards their potential allies, whether Dutch or Imperial. As a result, war skeptics argued for a limited role with England serving as an "auxiliary."

Moreover, if strategy thus reflected politics, the reverse also applied. "By late 1711, the English public was exhausted with both the war and Whig policies.

[12] Orson Scott Card, *Ender's Game* (New York, 1985).

A backlash enabled a new Tory ministry to end the war, illustrating the limitations of a battle-seeking strategy."

Much the same dynamic influenced Britain's war against Napoleonic France. As government succeeded government, not only military choices but even war aims vacillated. The only persistent objective was preservation of Britain's safety from invasion and the maritime trade on which depended both her economic vitality and ability to sustain those willing to continue resisting Bonaparte. Hence, while Ostwald concludes his essay with the assertion that "[Great Britain's] real success in the War of the Spanish Succession was to create a formula of grand strategy that would allow it to win future wars of the eighteenth century even more decisively," it might be more accurate to say that Britain's real success was to create political and financial institutions sufficiently robust to weather repeated military disappointments until a successful strategic formula finally emerged.

Whether autocratically or politically driven, our cases suggest that no strategy is likely to survive for long in defiance of a nation's cultural predilections. As Mansoor confirms, for example, confronted with public rage over Pearl Harbor, Roosevelt's presumed "Europe first" strategy barely survived its nominal adoption. In a different context, rebutting suggestions that America's war against Japan was driven by racial prejudices, Showalter argues that it instead reflected an army–navy institutional equality deeply rooted in America's culture, "The Pacific campaign was in good part a strategic response to an institutional issue, not a racial one."[13]

Strategy is especially hostage to culture when the institutions through which it is effected must be transformed simply to marshal the resources needed to execute it. Thus, for Hanson, perhaps the most difficult challenge confronting Themistocles was overcoming Athens' attachment to hoplite warfare, reflecting both the memory of victory at Marathon and the resistance of the city's elites to a strategy that required empowering landless citizens. As he describes the prevailing attitude, "No walls or ships, or poor people, had been needed to save Athens from Persian hordes." Similarly, Showalter tells us, Prussian military reform required "nurturing a sense of [popular] commitment that would actualize the latent loyalty Prussians felt for state and crown."

Adapting strategy to cultural imperatives is the more essential because, as several of our cases demonstrate, successful strategy is as much about acquiring the means of defense as it is about employing them. Comments Hanson, "Most generals tried to best use the resources their societies put at their disposal; Themistocles, in contrast, insured that his society would have the wisdom and capability to put the right resources at his disposal." The same might be said, *inter alia*, of Lincoln, Dowding, and Reagan. In contrast,

---

[13] Dennis Showalter, "War to the Knife: The U.S. in the Pacific, 1941–1945," in *The Pacific War as Total War: Proceedings of the 2011 International Forum on War History* (Tokyo, 2012), pp. 91–92.

Lacey tells us, "Rome's inability, or unwillingness, to tax the accumulated wealth of its elites was a crucial handicap when the funds necessary to secure the empire ran short." Rogers scores a similar problem, arguing that "It would be fair to say that until 1276, the strategies the English had employed to attempt the conquest of Wales reflected too much concern with how best to use what they *had*, rather than how to get what they *needed*."

Britain's experience in the War of the Spanish Succession and the Napoleonic War demonstrates the problem with special force. In both cases, British military alternatives were circumscribed by a deep-seated cultural and political reluctance to enlarge the standing army, and thus an inescapable dependence on continental allies for military manpower. As Ostwald acknowledges, "England did not win the war by itself. Without the Grand Alliance, there would have been no victory for the English ... Even in the theaters most important to the English, their contributions were subsumed within larger allied efforts." The same applied to British land operations against Napoleon. As Chapter 6 notes with respect to Britain's ultimately successful campaign in Iberia, "With a volunteer army small to begin with compared with continental armies, more than half of it stationed in Ireland or deployed to secure Britain's expanding colonial seizures, British leaders could visualize no way of confronting the more than 200,000 French troops in Spain on their own with any hope of success." In both cases, Britain's success was hostage to the steadfastness of her continental allies, aided in Spain by Napoleon's overambition. At the same time, it was in part British leaders' acceptance of that constraint that helped them sustain public support for both wars despite their prolonged durations. The resonance with America's recent military experience needs no elaboration.

Military means having been acquired, whether from the state's own resources or through coalition, and barring outright battlefield defeat, strategic success hinges almost entirely on the conformity of strategic aims to available military means and the validity of the theory according to which the latter are committed. Concerning the first, while the term "strategy–force mismatch" is of relatively recent vintage, the problem that it tags is anything but new. Describing the military challenge confronting Rome, for example, Lacey reminds us that "the defense of the empire rested on 150,000 legionnaries along with a similar number of auxiliaries. In other words less than 0.5 percent of the empire's total population was responsible for the security of the remaining 99.5 percent." As long as Rome's soldiers kept their ambitions in check, those capabilities sufficed. Not so as those ambitions escalated.[14] Similarly, Jones writes, "After 1871, like a sorcerer's apprentice, [Bismarck] struggled with increasing futility to control the forces he had

---

[14] As one scholar argues, "By the turn of the second century AD, Rome's situation was much analogous to that of the British Empire at the turn of the nineteenth, in which Britain buckled under the weight of maintaining her 'formal' empire after being forced to absorb her 'informal' one." Brooking, *"Roma Surrecta,"* p. 23.

helped to release and to save the new German Empire from the strategic circumstances of its birth." Squeezed between a mercurial and ambitious young emperor and overaggressive military leaders, Bismarck proved unable to save Germany from a strategic overextension.

Most would agree that a similar problem currently confronts American leaders seeking to steer a sensible course between overextension and strategic passivity at a time of proliferating security challenges and diminishing resources. That no one yet has managed to articulate a course of action with which all or even most influential American politicians could agree is a measure of the current difficulty of reconciling strategic aims with available resources, the latter not excluding diminished public support for international engagement after a decade of frustratingly unrequited military effort. Elsewhere, the author has drawn a parallel with Britain's similar experience during the last years of the nineteenth century and the first decade of the twentieth, in which a global empire acquired during a century of British economic and naval supremacy found itself increasingly challenged in both arenas.[15] Britain's success in meeting those challenges reflected statesmanship of a high order indeed, but also required navigating repeated public and political controversies.

Not all strategic failures reflect overextension. They are equally likely – perhaps more likely – to reflect mistaken theories of success.[16] Often that misjudgment is a product of stubborn or unexamined adherence to outmoded military practices. Here history uncritically applied easily imprisons rather than enlightens. We have already noted Themistocles' need to overcome Athenian overconfidence in hoplite warfare resulting from their one-off victory at Marathon. Similar memories of Frederick the Great's victories impeded Prussian Army reform until Jena-Auerstädt forcibly revealed the need for change, while in the American Civil War, stubborn refusal to recognize how radically military technology had altered the battlefield since the Napoleonic era persisted on both sides nearly to the end of the conflict, as it later did even more expensively in the First World War. The US Navy's innovations between the world wars, and the Royal Air Force's parallel development of air defense doctrine, were remarkable in part because, from a historical perspective, such self-initiated reforms are so unusual absent a prompting defeat. Even then, as Murray and Gray reveal in their respective cases, both services had to overcome enormous resistance, not least from traditionalists within their own ranks.

More often, mistaken theories linking means to ends result from misreading the enemy, the context of the struggle, or both. Few of our strategists had the

---

[15] Richard Hart Sinnreich, "About Turn: British Strategic Transformation from Salisbury to Grey," in Williamson Murray and Richard Hart Sinnreich, eds., *The Shaping of Grand Strategy: Policy, Diplomacy, and War* (Cambridge, 2011), p. 113. The same theme has been picked up by others. See, e.g., Andrew F. Krepinevich et al., *Strategy in Austerity* (Washington, 2012), pp. 35–60.

[16] As that inimitable strategist Yogi Berra is reputed to have said, "In theory there is no difference between theory and practice. In practice there is."

benefit of an analysis as perceptive and complete as that produced by Gerald of Wales. As Rogers reveals, perhaps the most impressive feature of Gerald's proposal for subduing Wales was its thoughtful diagnosis of the strengths and weaknesses of both the land and people to be subdued and those seeking to do it – what we today would call a net assessment. In devising his plan, Rogers tells us, Gerald

expressly takes into account the lessons of history … He considers English strengths and weaknesses, Welsh advantages and disadvantages, and situational factors. Moreover, Gerald takes into account military, political, cultural, topographical, and economic considerations. Rather than taking force structure as a given, he reflects on the troops best suited to accomplish the mission, and implicitly recommends changes in recruitment, tactics, and equipment to reflect the task at hand.

Finally, and remarkably, Gerald goes so far as to conduct his own version of a "Red Team" analysis, imagining how the Welsh might frustrate such an enterprise.

Historically, such thoughtfully anchored strategic design, or at least, clear evidence of it, has been astonishingly rare. Indeed, for a modern appraisal as detailed as Gerald's, although perhaps less influential, one must travel forward all the way to 1907 and Sir Eyre Crowe's famous British Foreign Office "Memorandum on the Present State of British Relations with France and Germany," which, like Gerald's, called on history, geopolitics, and an appraisal of British and German strengths, weaknesses, and ambitions to urge the need for allied firmness in dealing with Kaiser Wilhelm II. Compare that with the conflicting and deceptive assessments about Vietnam revealed in the *Pentagon Papers*, which at one point led President Kennedy to ask two of his recently returned advisors whether they even had visited the same country.[17] Or, to cite a more recent example, recall General Scott Wallace's comment during the 2003 invasion of Iraq that "The enemy we're fighting is a bit different than the one we war gamed against,"[18] a frank appraisal that got the good general in trouble with his superiors, but that soon proved woefully understated. As a June 2012 joint staff analysis of military lessons learned during the previous decade admitted, "In operations in Iraq, Afghanistan, and elsewhere, a failure to recognize, acknowledge, and accurately define the operational environment led to a mismatch between forces, capabilities, missions, and goals."[19]

To be fair, in an era of accelerating change, even the soundest net assessment has its limits as a guide to strategic decision making. Any such appraisal

[17] Vietnam Taskforce, *United States–Vietnam Relations, 1945–1967*, part IV. B. 5., "Counterinsurgency: The Overthrow of Ngo Dinh Diem, May–Nov. 1963" (Washington, 1969), p. 26. Nor have matters apparently improved that much since, witness recent revelations of war-related decision making in both the G. W. Bush and Obama administrations.
[18] Quoted in Jim Dwyer, "A Nation at War: In The Field – V Corps Commander," *TNYT*, 28 March 2003.
[19] Joint and Coalition Operational Analysis Division, "Enduring Lessons from the Past Decade of Operations," *Decade of War*, vol. 1, Joint Staff J7, 15 June 2012, p. 3.

at best is a snapshot, after all, and the more transient the information on which it relies, the more quickly it risks invalidation. Today, among the preeminent challenges for strategists is distinguishing features of the strategic environment likely to endure from a welter of other compellingly immediate but also less reliably durable calls on a nation's attention and energies. For that reason if for no other, strategy is more likely to be successful the more modestly its objectives are defined and the more limited in scope and scale. Contrariwise, the more ambitious the stated goals and the longer the duration over which they must be pursued, the smaller the likelihood that any strategy based on a single net assessment however comprehensive will succeed.

Above all, strategic success is hostage to the willingness of political and military leaders to read and heed the evidence of the battlefield even at the price of jettisoning cherished assumptions. In the Civil War, as Hsieh points out, strategic success remained elusive until Lincoln and Grant, each independently, recognized that they were engaged in a war of societies, not merely of armies. "Like many other Northerners," Hsieh notes,

Lincoln began the war under the impression that a powerful current of widespread Unionism existed in the Confederacy, which could be exploited with a few military victories and moderate political measures. While Lincoln later embraced emancipation and other aggressive military measures directed at Confederate civilians, including confiscation of property, expulsions, and the use of martial law, he remained fixated on set-piece battles, as opposed to the sorts of operations Sherman made famous with his March to the Sea in 1864.

More than any moral impulse, it was that evolution in his understanding of the strategic problem he confronted that drove him to issue the Emancipation Proclamation (which, it will be recalled, affected only slaves in the rebellious states). Grant likewise began the war expecting it to be decided on the battlefield, not at the Southern people's homes and hearths. As he later wrote, "Up to the battle of Shiloh [I] believed that the rebellion against the Government would collapse suddenly and soon, if a decisive victory could be gained over any of its armies ... but [after Shiloh] I gave up all idea of saving the Union except by complete conquest."[20]

What was true in the mid-nineteenth century is even truer today, as American frustrations in Iraq and Afghanistan reveal only too clearly. In both conflicts, US and alliance leaders were slow to acknowledge that crucial contextual assumptions underwriting both military commitments were wrong, as the following passage from an army retrospective on Operation Iraqi Freedom confirms:

OIF began as a traditional, though very bold, conventional military offensive directed toward defeating Iraq's military forces and removing the Saddam regime from power. Following the accomplishment of this goal, most commanders and units expected to transition to a new phase of the conflict in which stability and

---

[20] Ulysses S. Grant, *Personal Memoirs* (New York, 1999), p. 198.

support operations would briefly dominate and would resemble recent experiences in Bosnia and Kosovo. This phase of the conflict would require only a limited commitment by the US military and would be relatively peaceful and short as Iraqis quickly assumed responsibility ... Few commanders foresaw that ... it would require US and Coalition military forces to take the lead in providing security, reconstruction, and governance for Iraq for years.[21]

In consequence, allied nations were compelled to adapt not only their means and methods, but also their strategic aims. In doing so, they at least were in good company. As Jones has written elsewhere about Bismarck, perhaps the preeminent strategist of his age, "what stands out in Bismarck's formulation is a conscious flexibility in achieving his ends, and quite possibly flexibility in framing the ends themselves."[22] For a more recent example of similar flexibility, consider Defense Secretary Leon Panetta's comment on evolving US strategy in June 2012:

In the past, the United States often assumed the primary role of defending others. We built permanent bases. We deployed large forces across the globe to fixed positions. We often assumed that others were not willing or capable of defending themselves. Our new strategy recognizes that this is not the world we live in anymore.[23]

In short, as the volatility of the operating environment increases, the need intensifies to balance long-term with opportunistic behavior. Each imposes different requirements and embodies different dangers. To be successful, long-term strategy requires both an accurate prompting diagnosis and the discipline to conform action to intention over time. Its greatest risk is target fixation – the failure to honor the evidence of the evolving environment when it begins to refute assumptions on which the strategy rested. An opportunistic strategy is more forgiving. But executing it effectively requires the freedom of action to engage and disengage at will and the political robustness to tolerate failure without fatally diminishing commitment to the aim. Its greatest risk is that so much energy will be dissipated on peripheral objectives that resources prove insufficient to seize the moment for decisive commitment when it finally arrives.

Finally, while strategy carefully devised and implemented can help an army or a nation make the most effective use of its resources, in the end, method alone is at best a temporary substitute for adequate means. As the Athenians rightly reminded the Melians, "The strong do what they can and the weak

---

[21] Dr. Donald P. Wright, Colonel Timothy R. Reese et al., *On Point II: Transition to the New Campaign: The United States Army in Operation IRAQI FREEDOM, May 2003–January 2005* (Fort Leavenworth, Kansas, 2008), pp. 3–4.

[22] Marcus Jones, "Strategy as Character: Bismarck and the Prusso-German Question, 1862–1878," in Murray and Sinnreich, eds., *The Shaping of Grand Strategy: Policy, Diplomacy, and War*, p. 86.

[23] Pentagon Press Conference, 28 June 2012.

suffer what they must."[24] Weak states, like weak armies, may prevail for a time over stronger but less clever adversaries. But unless cleverness can be translated into effective military power, a stronger contestant sooner or later will prevail absent a failure of political will. That does not argue for ignoring strategy; it does argue against expecting any strategy to compensate over the long haul for persistent failure adequately to resource military enterprises. As a familiar adage holds, at some point, quantity has a quality all its own.

Where organic military means are insufficient, states must seek additional resources through alliance or informal coalition. In several of our cases, coalitions provided the decisive ingredient of success. As those cases reveal, from a strategic perspective, coalitions are a two-edged sword. At best, reliance on allies to make up the difference between the means organic to the state and those required to achieve success typically will require adapting methods and sometimes the aims themselves to competing interests, predilections, and perceptions of risk. In both the War of the Spanish Succession and the Napoleonic War, for example, Britain found its strategic flexibility constrained by the need to accommodate continental allies whose exposure to the costs and risks of military operations were significantly greater. Similarly, Mansoor demonstrates, during the Second World War, sensitivity to the need to keep America's allies on board compelled Roosevelt repeatedly to overrule his own military commanders. Less obviously, to satisfy the political demands of the Northern governors on whom continued support for the defeat of the Confederacy depended, Lincoln and Grant were compelled to endure commanders such as Banks, Butler, and Sigel whose incompetence often proved strategically as well as tactically costly. For evidence that the problem persists today, one need look no further than recent NATO engagements from the Balkans to Afghanistan, in which the need to reconcile differing allied operational viewpoints and cost-tolerances has been a persistent strategic challenge, confirming Winston Churchill's notorious comment that "There is only one thing worse than fighting with allies, and that is fighting without them!"[25]

To square the resulting circle of strategic aim with coalition constraint, leaders in more than one of our cases have resorted to deliberate ambiguity of intention and occasionally to outright deception. Themistocles, Hanson tells us, not only blackmailed his Peloponnesian allies by threatening to abandon Greece altogether, but also negotiated with the enemy unbeknownst to them. Similarly, Ostwald describes the "betrayal" of Britain's Dutch allies at the Congress of Utrecht, the latter compelled to accept peace terms they opposed after being abandoned in the field by British troops.

[24] Robert B Strassler, ed., *The Landmark Thucydides* (New York, 1996), p. 352.
[25] Kay Halle (compiler), *The Irrepressible Churchill: Winston's World, Wars & Wit* (New York, 2011).

American leaders generally have proved less willing to indulge in such manipulations, or perhaps merely less adept in managing them, although not above resorting to euphemism and ambiguity to paper over politically inconvenient differences in allied perspective.[26] In any case, whatever its short-term advantages, playing fast and loose with one's allies is not calculated to sustain the relationship. As Hanson comments, "When a coalition leader must mislead his own allies, suspicion follows even in victory."

As the preceding remarks suggest, the ingredients of past strategic success vary with context, and thus offer no simple checklist to guide current and future political and military leaders. Notes Jones of Bismarck,

> Among [his] most striking characteristics as a strategist was an almost complete lack of faith in the permanence of any international accommodation. To the extent that one can apply such an anachronistic concept to him, grand strategy was an ongoing process of adaptation to shifting circumstances instead of a formula or handful of trite maxims.

Especially in an era of extreme strategic volatility and increasing information transparency, those charged with the security of their nations must more than ever be guided by the medical maxim, "First, do no harm." As Gray has argued elsewhere, "the key to quality in political and strategic leadership is not the avoidance of error, which is impossible. Instead, it is the ability to make small rather than large mistakes and to err generally in ways for which one can readily find adequate compensation."[27] To assert that is not to deprecate the need to devise and apply strategic priorities, but rather to insure that commitments do not so wed the nation to a single course of action that they become impossible to reconfigure when conditions change and/or evidence accumulates that the beliefs undergirding the chosen strategy were misconceived.

The last named requirement may be more important today than it ever has been before. While claims that today's strategic complexity is unprecedented probably overreach,[28] some novel challenges of the post-Cold War strategic environment are undeniable: the diffusion of economic power formerly concentrated in a relatively few industrialized nations; the latter's increased vulnerability to threats by groups not wedded to a definable geography and population and, having no intrinsic values of their own to protect, less susceptible to deterrence; the proliferation of military and militarily adaptable technologies once the virtual monopoly of developed nations; and global

---

[26] As the checkered history of NATO nuclear doctrine reveals. For one look at the problem, see David N. Schwartz, *Nato's Nuclear Dilemmas* (Washington, 1983).

[27] Colin Gray, "Harry S. Truman and the Forming of American grand strategy in the Cold War, 1945–1953," in Murray and Sinnreich, eds., *The Shaping of Grand Strategy: Policy, Diplomacy, and War*, p. 211.

[28] For a powerful argument debunking that claim and arguing that it leads to the opposite of strategic behavior, see Michael J. Gallagher et al., "The Complexity Trap," *Parameters*, Spring 2012, pp. 5–16.

information transparency that reveals and amplifies military behavior that previously would have remained below international and domestic political noise levels.

The question is whether these changes alter in any fundamental way the key ingredients of successful military strategy: achievable aims, adequate resources, and a theory of action linking the two that reasonably reflects both the strategic context and domestic constraints. Have we reached the end – or at least, an end – of history where military strategy is concerned, to the point where today's soldiers and statesmen must negotiate an entirely novel set of imperatives? Some argue that we have, and that future American defense strategy requires an entirely new lexicon.[29] In their view, deterrence and defense – indeed, the entire paradigm that limits military power to preserving security in a world in which conflict or its threat are endemic and ineradicable – are outmoded. Instead, for them, military power has become indistinguishable from national power, and its purpose is less to deter or win wars than to ameliorate the sources of conflict.

In a narrow sense, perhaps, they have a point. Today's strategic challenges, and those immediately foreseeable, in some respects resemble more closely those faced by Rome of the third century or Britain of the nineteenth than those that faced America of the twentieth. On the other hand, the United states is neither Imperial Rome nor Victorian Britain. Not just the threats that we confront, but also the cultural and political matrix within which we are obliged to deal with them is far more constricting. For better or worse, liberal democratic societies like our own have long since wedded themselves to precepts of behavior that foreclose resort to certain military solutions, while information transparency at once reveals transgressions more quickly and disseminates them more widely. So while unconventional security challenges may themselves not be novel, we lack the freedom of imperial predecessors to deal with even the most ruthless and unconventional enemies simply by making a desert and calling it peace.

Even so, that problem does not render irrelevant the lessons that can be gleaned from the essays in this book. There is no reason to believe that strategic success in the future will not depend on the same qualities that made strategy of the past successful: proactive rather than reactive choices, nimbleness rather than rigidity, and discipline rather than improvisation in pursuing chosen goals. Indeed, in a broader sense, the cases examined in our essays strongly suggest that the vital ingredients of successful strategy transcend the particular circumstances in which they must be applied.

Finally, it is worth reiterating Murray's reminder from Chapter 10 that "The success of strategy at any level depends on the personalities of those who conduct it." Whether the creation of a single strategic genius or the

---

[29] Mr. Y, "A National Strategic Narrative," Woodrow Wilson International Center for Scholars, 2011.

messier product of political sausage making, strategy is the product of a human process, not a computer program. In the end, because it must, it will reflect the culture, convictions, and prejudices of those whose energies and loyalties it seeks to marshal and apply. The strategist or leader who flies in the face of that reality invites resistance at best, repudiation at worst. Sun Tzu was right to admonish his readers that "The consummate leader cultivates the moral law ... [causing] the people to be in complete accord with their ruler, so that they will follow him regardless of their lives, undismayed by any danger."[30] In the end, sustaining the nation's determination to prevail is the crucial hallmark of any successful military strategy.

---

[30] Sun Tzu, *The Art of War*, trans. Lionel Giles, http://classics.mit.edu//Tzu/artwar.html.

Index

Made in the USA
Lexington, KY
02 August 2014